Bali &
Lombok

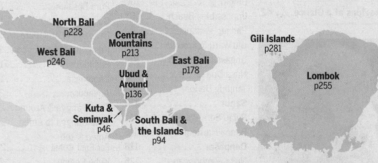

North Bali
p228

**Central
Mountains**
p213

West Bali
p246

East Bali
p178

**Ubud &
Around**
p136

**Kuta &
Seminyak**
p46

**South Bali &
the Islands**
p94

Gili Islands
p281

Lombok
p255

THIS EDITION WRITTEN AND RESEARCHED BY

Ryan Ver Berkmoes

Contents

PLAN YOUR TRIP

MACAQUES, UBUD P137

MATT MUNRO / LONELY PLANET ©

RICE FIELD, UBUD P137

PETE SEAWARD / LONELY PLANET ©

ON THE ROAD

Contents

SPECIAL FEATURES

Welcome to Bali & Lombok

The mere mention of Bali evokes thoughts of a paradise. It's more than a place; it's a mood, an aspiration, a tropical state of mind.

Island of the Gods

The rich and diverse culture of Bali plays out at all levels of life, from the exquisite flower-petal offerings placed everywhere, to the processions of joyfully garbed locals, shutting down major roads as they march to one of the myriad temple ceremonies, to the other-worldly traditional music and dance performed island-wide.

One Island, Many Destinations

On Bali you can lose yourself in the chaos of Kuta or the sybaritic pleasures of Seminyak and Kerobokan, surf wild beaches in the south or just hang out on Nusa Lembongan. You can go family-friendly in Sanur or savour a lavish getaway on the Bukit Peninsula. Ubud is the heart of Bali, a place where the spirit and culture of the island are most accessible. It shares the island's most beautiful rice fields and ancient monuments with east and west Bali. The middle of Bali is dominated by the dramatic volcanoes of the central mountains and hillside temples such as Pura Luhur Batukau (one of the island's estimated 10,000 temples). North and west Bali are thinly populated but have the kind of diving and surfing that make any journey worthwhile.

Bali's Essence

Yes, Bali has beaches, surfing, diving, and resorts great and small, but it's the essence of Bali – and the Balinese – that makes it so much more than just a fun-in-the-sun retreat. It is possible to take the cliché of the smiling Balinese too far but, in reality, the inhabitants of this small island are indeed a generous, genuinely warm people. There's also a fun, sly sense of humour behind the smiles. Upon seeing a bald tourist, many locals exclaim *'bung ujan'*, which means to-day's rain is cancelled – it's their way of saying that the hairless head is like a clear sky.

Lombok & the Gilis, Too

Almost as big as Bali, Lombok is the largely undiscovered island next door. From its volcanic centre to untrodden idyllic beaches such as Mawun, it rewards travellers who want to explore. Many are drawn to mighty Gunung Rinjani, Indonesia's second-highest volcano. Rivers and waterfalls gush down its fissured slopes, while its summit – complete with hot springs and a dazzling crater lake – is the ultimate trekker's prize. The fabled Gili Islands are three exquisite droplets of white sand sprinkled with coconut palms and surrounded by coral reefs teeming with marine life and, on Gili Trawangan, legendary nightlife.

Why I Love Bali & Lombok

By Ryan Ver Berkmoes, Author

In 1993 I visited Bali and Lombok for the first time. When I went through immigration, the officer glanced at my passport and said in the sweetest voice possible: 'Have a wonderful birthday on Bali'. Who wouldn't fall in love? I spent a lot of that trip slack-jawed with wonderment. I remember dancers and musicians materialising from across the rice fields to perform in Ubud; I remember Gili Trawangan with just a couple of cement huts and some amazing snorkelling. Since then, these places – like me – have changed greatly, but their essence still evokes love.

For more about our author, see page 400

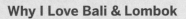

Above: Woman walking through rice terraces in Ubud (p137)

Bali & Lombok

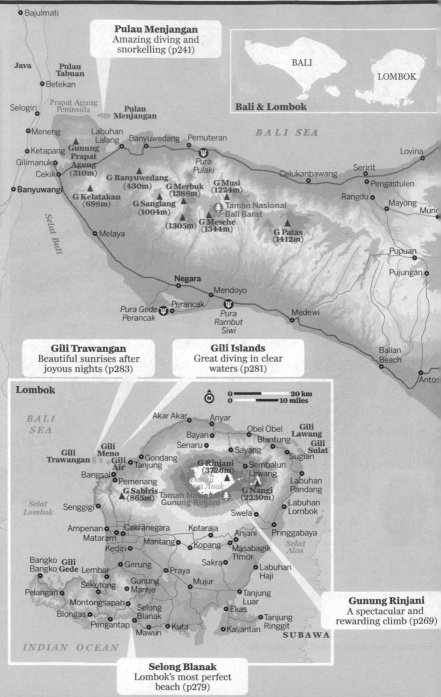

Pulau Menjangan
Amazing diving and
snorkelling (p241)

Bali & Lombok

BALI

LOMBOK

Bajulmati

Java

Pulau
Tabuan
Betekan

Selogiri

Prapat Agung
Peninsula

Pulau
Menjangan

BALI SEA

Meneng

Ketapang

Labuhan
Lalang

Banyuwedang

Pemuteran

Pura
Pulaki

Lovina

Gunung
Prapat
Agung
(310m)

Gilimanuk

Cekik

Banyuwangi

Celukanbawang

Seririt

Pengastulen

G Banyuwedang
(430m)

G Merbuk
(1388m)

G Musi
(1224m)

Rangdu

Mayong

Mund

G Kelatakan
(698m)

G Sanglang
(1004m)

Taman Nasional
Bali Barat

Melaya

(1305m)

G Mesehe
(1344m)

G Patas
(1412m)

Pupuan

Pujungan

Selat Bali

Negara

Mendoyo

Perancak

Pura Gede
Perancak

Pura
Rambut
Siwi

Medewi

Balian
Beach

Antos

Gili Trawangan
Beautiful sunrises after
joyous nights (p283)

Gili Islands
Great diving in clear
waters (p281)

Lombok

BALI
SEA

N

0   20 km
0   10 miles

Akar Akar

Anyar

Gili
Trawangan

Gili
Meno

Gili
Air

Gondang

Tanjung

Bayan

Senaru

Obel Obel

Blantung

Sayang

Gili
Lawang

Gili
Sulat

Sugian

Bangsal

Pemenang

G Sabiris
(865m)

G Rinjani
(3726m)

Danau
Segara Anak

Sembalun
Lawang

Labuhan
Pandang

Taman Nasional
Gunung Rinjani

G Nangi
(2230m)

Labuhan
Lombok

Selat
Lombok

Senggigi

Swela

Ampenan

Cakranegara

Kotaraja

Anjani

Pringgabaya

Mataram

Mantang

Kopang

Masabagik
Timor

Selat
Alas

Kediri

Bangko
Bangko

Gili
Gede

Lembar

Gerung

Praya

Sakra

Labuhan
Haji

Pelangan

Sekotong

Gunung
Mareje

Mujur

Tanjung
Luar

Montongsapah

Selong
Blanak

Ekas

Blongas

Pengantap

Kuta

Kaliantan

Tanjung
Ringgit

SUBAWA

Mawun

INDIAN OCEAN

Gunung Rinjani
A spectacular and
rewarding climb (p269)

Selong Blanak
Lombok's most perfect
beach (p279)

Jatiluwih Rice Fields
Green ribbons curving around hillsides (p225)

Ubud
Bali's cultural heart (p137)

ELEVATION

2000m
1500m
1000m
700m
500m
300m
200m
100m
0

0 — 20 km
0 — 10 miles

ⓝ N

ngsit
Kubutambahan
Pura Beji (Sangsit)
Yeh Sanih
Pacung
garaja
Pura Maduw Karang
Tejakula
asade
Sawan
Sambirenteng
Gitgit
G Catur (2096m)
Catur
Penulisan
G Penulisan (1745m)
Tembok
Tianyar
esong 60m)
Pura Ulun Danu Bratan (Candikunung)
Candikuning
Kintamani
Batur
G Batur (1717m)
Songan
Toya Bungkah
Kubu
phon 3m)
Pelaga
Penelokan
G Abang (2152m)
Tulamben
Batukau 2276m)
Pacung
Bedugul
G Agung (3142m)
Culik
Amed
ra nur kau
Jatiluwih
Kayuanbua
Besakih
Pura Sambu (Gunung Agung)
Aas
Penebel
Petang
Kayubihi
Pampatan
Pura Besakih
Tirta Gangga
G Seraya (1175m)
Marga
Pujung
Tampaksiring
Rendang
Muncan
Amlapura
Payangan
Bangli
Pura Kehen (Bangli)
Iseh
Ujung
Sangeh
Pejeng
Bukit Jambul
Sidemen
Tenganan
Candidasa
Selat Lombok
Tabanan
Ubud
Mas
Pura Pusering Jagat (Pejeng)
Sidan
Semarapura (Klungkung)
Padangbai
ediri
Mengwi
Batuan
Celuk
Gianyar
Lebih
Kusamba
Pura Goa Lawah
Sempidi
Sukawati
Seminyak
Bali's capital of glitz (p71)
Canggu
Batubulan
Ketewel
Denpasar
Selat Badung
Nusa Lembongan
Pura Dalem Penetaran Ped
obokan
Seminyak
Sanur
Jungutbatu
Lembongan
Toyapakeh
Sampalan
Legian
Kuta
Nusa Ceningan
Karangsari
Benoa Harbour
Benoa
(529m)
Semaya
Jimbaran
Tanjung Benoa
Kuta
All-night clubbing and partying (p67)
Nusa Penida
Bingen
Nusa Dua
Pecatu
Bukit Peninsula
INDIAN OCEAN
a Luhur Watu

Kuta Beach
Twelve kilometres of sand and surf (p48)

Bukit Peninsula Beaches
A string of sandy pearls (p96)

Bali & Lombok's
Top 17

1

Bali & Lombok's Festivals

1 There you are sipping a coffee at a cafe in, say, Seminyak or Ubud, when there's a crash of the gamelan and traffic screeches to a halt as a crowd of elegantly dressed people comes flying by bearing pyramids of fruit, tasselled parasols and a furred, masked Barong (mythical lion-dog creature) or two. It's a temple procession, disappearing as suddenly as it appeared, with no more than a fleeting sparkle of gold and white silk and hibiscus petals in its wake. Dozens occur daily across Bali. Below left: Celebration, Pura Samuan Tiga (p169), Ubud

Bukit Peninsula Beaches

2 A little plume of white sand rises out of the blue Indian Ocean and fills a cove below limestone cliffs clad in deep green tropical beauty. It sounds idyllic, and it is. The west coast of the Bukit Peninsula (p96) in south Bali is dotted with these very beaches, such as Balangan Beach, Bingin and Padang Padang. Families run surfer bars built on bamboo stilts over the tide, where the only views are the breaks, just metres away. Grab a lounger and be lulled by the waves. Below right: Balangan Beach (p99)

JONES/SHIMLOCK-SECRET SEA VISIONS / GETTY IMAGES ©

MICHELE FALZONE / GETTY IMAGES ©

Aaah, a Spa

3 Whether it's a total fix for the mind, body and spirit, or simply the desire for a bit of serenity, visitors to Bali spend many happy hours (sometimes days) being massaged, scrubbed, perfumed, pampered, bathed and blissed out. Sometimes all this attention to your well-being happens on the beach; other times it's in stylish, even lavish, surroundings. The Balinese massage techniques of stretching, long strokes, skin rolling and palm-and-thumb pressure result in an all-over feeling of calm; it's the perfect holiday prescription. Below: Spa, Ubud (p137)

Sybaritic Stays

4 On an island that honours art and serenity, is it any wonder you'll find some of the world's finest hotels and resorts here? From blissful retreats on south Bali's beautiful beach in Kerobokan (p84) or Seminyak (p75) to perches on cliffs above the dazzling white sands that dot the Bukit Peninsula (p96), these stylish hotels are as lovely outside as they are luxurious inside. Further resorts by vaunted architects can be found in the river valleys of Ubud (p152) and in remote idyllic coastal locations. Bottom: Resort, Jimbaran (p96)

TIBOR BOGNAR / GETTY IMAGES ©

PAUL KENNEDY / GETTY IMAGES ©

Diving

5 Legendary Pulau Menjangan (p241) thrills, one tank after another. It offers multiple types of diving around a protected island renowned for its coral walls. And that's just one of Bali's great dive sites. Under the waves at Nusa Penida (p133), you can feel small as a manta ray blocks out the sun's glow overhead, its fluid movement causing barely a disturbance in the surrounding waters as it glides past. And just when you think your dive can't get more dramatic, you turn to find a 2.5m sunfish motionlessly hovering, checking you out. Above: Diver exploring the *Liberty* shipwreck (p210), Tulamben

Ubud

6 Famous in books and movies, the artistic heart of Bali exudes a compelling spiritual appeal. The streets are lined with galleries where artists, both humble and great, create. Beautiful performances showcasing the island's rich culture grace a dozen stages nightly. Museums honour the works of those inspired here over the years, while people walk the rice fields to find the perfect spot to sit in lotus position and ponder life's endless possibilities. Ubud (p137) is a state of mind and a beautiful state of being. Top right: Kecak performance, Ubud (p164)

Never-Ending Kuta Nights

7 It starts with stylish cafes and bars in Seminyak (p80), open-air places where everything seems just that bit more beautiful amid the post-sunset glow and pulsing house beats. Later, the world-class clubs of Kuta (p68) draw you in, with international DJs spinning their legendary sets to packed dance floors. Some time before dawn, Kuta's harder, rawer clubs suck you in like black holes, spitting you out hours later into an unsteady daylight, shattered but happy. Above right: Bar, Kuta (p68)

ANDREY ARTYKOV / GETTY IMAGES ©

Surfing Bali

8 If it's a month containing the letter 'r', go east; during the other months, go west. Simplicity itself. On Bali you have dozens of great breaks in each direction. This was the first place in Asia where surfing took off and, like the perfect set, it shows no signs of calming down. Surfers buzz around the island on motorbikes with board racks, looking for the next great break. Waves blown out? Another spot is just five minutes away. Don't miss classic surfer hang-out Balian Beach (p250).

Underwater Gilis

9 Taking the plunge? There are few better places to dive than the Gilis (p287), encircled by coral reefs teeming with life and visited by pelagics such as cruising manta rays. Scuba diving is a huge draw – there are numerous professional schools and all kinds of courses taught (from absolute beginner to nitrox specialist). With easy access from beach to reef, snorkelling is also superb, and you're very likely to see turtles. Want to take snorkelling to the next level? Try freediving (p289), it's sweeping the Gilis. Top right: Clownfish, Gili Trawangan (p283)

Selong Blanak

10 Southern Lombok's coastline has a wild savage beauty and few visitors, generating lots of talk about the vast tourism potential of the region. When you set eyes on pristine Selong Blanak (p279) beach, you'll appreciate the hype. Cross a rickety bridge from the village to a perfect swathe of sand where the swimming in clear, turquoise-tinged water is superb. At the rear of the bay is a crescent of powdery white sand; a dream of a beach that is all but empty on most days.

Jatiluwih Rice Fields

11 Ribbons of green sinuously curve around hillsides crested by coconut palms: the ancient rice terraces of Jatiluwih (p225) are as artful as they are elegant, and are a timeless testimony to the Balinese rice farmers' love and respect for the land. You'll run out of words for green as you walk, bike or drive the little road that wanders through this fertile bowl of the island's sacred grain. The entire area is part of Bali's Unesco–recognised rice-growing traditions that are now on the World Heritage List.

Kuta Beach

12 Tourism on Bali began on Kuta Beach (p48) and is there any question why? A sweeping arc of sand curves from Kuta into the misty horizon northwest to Echo Beach. Surf that started far out in the Indian Ocean crashes to shore in long symmetrical breaks. You can stroll along the 12km of sand, enjoying a foot massage and cold beer with thousands of your new best friends in the south, or find a hip hang-out or even a plot of sand to call your own up north.

11

12

Seminyak

13 People wander around Seminyak (p71) and ask themselves if they are even in Bali. Of course! On an island that values creativity like few other places, the capital of glitz is where you'll find inventive boutiques run by local designers, the most eclectic and interesting collection of restaurants, and little boutique hotels that break with the island clichés. Expats, locals and visitors alike idle away the hours in its cafes, at ease with the world and secure in their enjoyment of life's pleasures.
Below: La Plancha (p80)

Sunrise over Trawangan

14 If you think Gili Trawangan (p283) is a stunner by daylight, you should see it at dawn after a night of partying. You won't find slick decor, flashy visuals, door staff and stiff entrance prices here, where the parties started as raves on the beach and still have a raw, unorganised spirit. Local DJs normally spin hypnotic tribal beats and superstar DJs have been known to turn up and play unannounced sets.

FELIX HUG / GETTY IMAGES ©

CREATIVITY IS BORDERLESS / GETTY IMAGES ©

Balinese Dance

15 The antithesis of Balinese mellow is Balinese dance. It's amazing how people who relish lounging in *bale* (open-sided pavilions) can also produce art that demands methodical precision. A performer of the Legong, the most beautiful dance, spends years learning minutely choreographed movements from her eyeballs to her toes. Each movement has a meaning and the language flows with a grace that is hypnotic. Clad in silk and ikat, the dancers tell stories rich with the very essence of Balinese Hindu beliefs and lore. Every night there are multiple shows in Ubud (p164).

Surfing Lombok

16 From the Antarctic to Lombok is virtually half the globe – that's some distance for the azure rollers of the Indian Ocean to build up speed and momentum, so it's no surprise that the island's coastline has some truly spectacular waves. Tanjung Desert (Desert Point, p32) is the most famous of them, an incredibly long ride that barrels over a sharp, shallow reef. If that sounds a little too hard core, head to the town of Kuta (p274), where you'll find dozens of challenging surf breaks a short distance away.

Hiking Rinjani

17 Glance at a map of Lombok and you'll see that virtually the entire northern half of the island is dominated by the brooding, magnificent presence of Gunung Rinjani (3726m), Indonesia's second-highest volcano. Hiking Rinjani (p269) is no picnic, and involves planning, hiring a guide and porters, stamina and sweat. The route winds up the sides of the great peak until you reach the rim of a vast caldera, where there's a magnificent view of Rinjani's sacred crater lake (an important pilgrim site) and the smoking, highly active mini-cone of Gunung Baru below.

Need to Know

For more information, see Survival Guide (p357)

Currency
Rupiah (Rp)

Language
Bahasa Indonesia and Balinese

Money
ATMs can be found in all but rural areas on Bali and tourist areas of Lombok. Credit cards accepted at midrange and top-end hotels and restaurants.

Visas
Usually a renewable 30 days granted on arrival.

Mobile Phones
Cheap local SIM cards work with any unlocked GSM phone.

Time
Indonesia Central Time (GMT/UTC plus eight hours)

When to Go

North Bali
GO year-round

Gili Islands
GO year-round

Ubud
● GO year-round

Lombok
GO year-round

South Bali
GO year-round

Tropical climate, wet & dry seasons
Tropical climate, rain year-round

High Season
(Jul & Aug)

➤ Rates increase by 50% or more.

➤ Many hotels are booked far ahead; the best restaurants need to be booked in advance.

➤ Christmas and New Year are equally expensive and crowded.

Shoulder Season (May, Jun & Sep)

➤ Coincides with the best weather (drier, less humid).

➤ You may find a room deal, and last-minute bookings are possible.

➤ Best time for many activities such as diving.

Low Season
(Jan–Apr, Oct & Nov)

➤ Deals everywhere, good airfares.

➤ Rainy season; however, rainfall is never excessive.

➤ Can do most activities except volcano treks.

Useful Websites

Bali Advertiser (www.bali advertiser.biz) Bali's expat journal with insider tips and good columnists.

Bali Discovery (www.bali discovery.com) Excellent weekly summary of news and features; hotel deals.

Bali Paradise (www.bali-paradise.com) Compendium site of info and links.

Lombok Guide (www.thelombok guide.com) Comprehensive site covering main areas of interest.

Travelfish (www.travelfish.org) Good features and reviews on Bali, Lombok and the Gilis.

Lonely Planet (www.lonely planet.com/indonesia) Destination information, hotel bookings, traveller forum and more.

Important Numbers

Numbers that begin with 08 are for mobiles. Drop the 0 in phone numbers when calling from abroad.

Indonesia country code	☑62
International call prefix	☑001/017
International operator	☑102
Directory assistance	☑108

Exchange Rates

Australia	A$1	10,577Rp
Canada	C$1	10,828Rp
Euro Zone	€1	14,778Rp
Japan	¥100	11,045Rp
New Zealand	NZ$1	9460Rp
UK	UK£1	19,633Rp
US	US$1	12,130Rp

For current exchange rates, see www.xe.com.

Daily Costs
Budget: Less than US$100

➡ Room at guesthouse/ homestay: less than US$50

➡ Cheap food and drink, meals under US$5

➡ Can survive on US$50 per day

Midrange: US$100–$220

➡ Room at midrange hotel: US$50–150

➡ Can eat and drink almost anywhere

➡ Spa treatments: US$7–30

Top end: Over US$220

➡ Room at top-end hotel/ resort: over US$150

➡ Major expenses will be luxe spas

➡ Car and driver per day: US$60

Opening Hours

Banks 8am–2pm Monday to Thursday, 8am–noon Friday, 8–11am Saturday

Convenience stores 24 hours (no time limit on beer sales)

Government offices 8am–3pm Monday to Thursday, 8am–noon Friday (although these are not standardised)

Post offices 8am–2pm Monday to Friday, longer in tourist centres

Restaurants and cafes 8am–10pm daily

Shops and services catering to visitors 9am–8pm daily

Arriving in Bali & Lombok

Ngurah Rai International Airport (p369) Taxi to Kuta is 50,000Rp, to Seminyak it's 85,000Rp and to Ubud it's 250,000Rp.

Lombok International Airport (p370) Taxi to Kuta is 84,000Rp, to Mataram it's 150,000Rp and to Senggigi it's 190,000Rp.

Getting Around

Bali and Lombok are both easy to get around.

Boat Small fast boats link the many islands but beware of rogue operators with dodgy safety standards.

Car Rent a small 4WD for under US$30 a day, get a car and driver for US$60 a day.

Motorbike Rent one for as little as US$5 a day.

Public Transit Bemos (small vans) provide very cheap transport on fixed routes but locals have switched to motorbikes.

Taxi Fairly cheap, but only use Bluebird Taxis on Bali and Lombok Taxis on Lombok, to avoid scams.

Walking The beach from Tuban through Seminyak and on is a great way to get around some of Bali's most popular areas.

Bali Is Easy

Forgot something at home? You can get it on Bali.

Don't speak the language? They probably speak yours.

Afraid of getting sick? Clean drinking water and healthy food are readily available.

Not sure how you'll get around? Friendly drivers will take care of that.

But aren't there touts and scammers? Easily avoided on 98% of the island.

Your biggest concern? Not wanting to leave.

For much more on **getting around**, see p371

PLAN YOUR TRIP NEED TO KNOW

What's New

Surfing Mania

Yes, Bali and Lombok have always had great surf and a lot of surfers enjoying it. But, recently, surf culture has managed to hit an even greater peak. From the Bukit Peninsula and Ulu Watu, to the Canggu area's Batu Bolong, to Keramas in the east and Tanjung Desert on Lombok, there are more surfers, surf-watchers, board-sellers, board-shapers, hip surf resorts and, well, more of everything to do with surfing.

Beachfront Resorts

From the Stones (p53) in Kuta to the ultra-luxe Alila Seminyak, a new crop of lavish resorts is lining the beach from Kuta north through to Kerobokan. Double-Six (p55), on its namesake beach, is the hippest of them all.

Sidewalks/Pavements

Call them what you will (depending on your national origins), some of Bali's most frequented streets in Seminyak and Kerobokan are finally getting sidewalks that let you stroll between shops, rather than run a hazard-filled gauntlet.

Canggu Area

This once quiet area (p88) is home to some of Bali's most creative new cafes. Batu Bolong beach has gone from sleepy to cool-kid hang-out.

Booming Bodong

This little village (p133) now has an outcrop of cheery cafes, a dive shop and places to stay for the growing number of people visiting Nusa Penida, the large island that's always been hiding in plain sight.

Ubud Nightlife

That old oxymoron has been laid to rest. Great new restaurants abound, not the least of which is celeb-chef Will Goldfarb's Room 4 Dessert (p163), a lounge centred on sweet fantasies.

Amed

Long known for its meandering strip of chilled guesthouses, Amed (p204) has a new vibrancy thanks to a slew of new budget homestays and a way-cool yoga-cum-freediving-cum-organic-joint called Apneista Cafe (p205).

Danaus Tamblingan & Buyan

Hikes around these beautiful twin mountain lakes (p222) just got easier thanks to two new groups of friendly guides waiting to show you ancient temples and natural wonders.

Mawun Beach

At one of south Lombok's best beaches (p279), the parking area and access road are paved, and the beach now has some simple but good cafes. People are discovering one of the region's secrets.

For more recommendations and reviews, see lonelyplanet.com/indonesia/bali

If You Like...

Beaches

Beaches ring the islands, but ones with white sand aren't as common as you'd think – most are a variation of tan or grey. Surf conditions range from limp to torrid.

Seminyak Beach This wide stretch of sand boasts great surf for both swimmers and surfers. Don't miss sunset. (p73)

Balangan Beach This curving white-sand beach is ramshackle in an endearing way and perfect for a snooze or booze. (p99)

Padang Padang Beach Great white sands and some of the best surfer-watching anywhere. (p102)

Nusa Lembongan Beaches Little coves of dreamy sand you can walk between, plus fab swimming. (p126)

Gili Island beaches Gorgeous beaches, with white sand, great snorkelling and a timeless traveller vibe. (p281)

Selong Blanak An idyllic Lombok bay and beach that astounds first-time visitors. (p279)

Temples

With more than 10,000 temples, Bali has such a variety that you can't even categorise them. The best evoke the unique form of Buddhism that's been shaped by priests for centuries.

Pura Luhur Batukau One of Bali's most important temples is a misty, remote place that's steeped in ancient spirituality. (p226)

Pura Taman Ayun A beautiful moated temple with a royal past; part of Unesco's recognition of Bali's rice traditions. (p248)

Pura Pusering Jagat One of the famous temples at Pejeng, which date to the 14th-century empire that once flourished here. (p170)

Pura Luhur Ulu Watu As important as it is popular, this temple has sweeping views, sunset dance performances and monkeys. (p103)

Nightlife

Nightclubs on Bali and the Gilis draw acolytes from across Southeast Asia. Large numbers of relatively well-heeled tourists combined with nonexistent licensing laws have spawned an ever-changing line-up of clubs.

Seminyak Beach clubs where the cocktails somehow taste better when you can hear the surf. (p80)

Kuta All raw energy and a mad mix of party-goers enjoying every aspect of Bali hedonism. (p67)

Legian Beach bars and beanbags on the sand where the glow of sunset segues into the twinkle of stars. (p68)

Gili Trawangan The place for pounding beats and party vibes just about every night (and day!) of the week. (p291)

Culture

The island's creative heritage is everywhere you look and there's nothing manufactured about it. Dance and musical performances are the result of an ever-evolving culture with a legacy that's centuries-long.

Dance Rigid choreography and discipline are hallmarks of beautiful Balinese dance, which no visitor should miss. (p332)

Gamelan The ensemble orchestra creates its unforgettable music with bamboo and bronze instruments at performances and celebrations. (p334)

Painting Balinese and Western styles merged in the 20th century and the results are often extraordinary. See some of the best in Ubud's museums. (p335)

Offerings Artful and ubiquitous, you'll discover them at your hotel room door and in huge stacks at temples. (p323)

Great Food

Balinese food is pungent and lively; it has evolved from years of cross-cultural cook-ups and trading with sea-faring pioneers. You can also enjoy superb international cuisines here.

Seminyak The spot with the greatest variety of top restaurants; on a 10-minute stroll you can wander the world. (p77)

Kerobokan The go-to area for the hottest restaurants, plus some great Balinese warungs. (p84)

Canggu area Bali's newest hot spot sees interesting cafes opening every week. (p88)

Denpasar Local cafes serve exceptional Balinese and Indonesian food in simple surrounds. (p121)

Ubud A profusion of creative restaurants and cafes, many organic, all delicious. (p159)

Shopping

Some consider Bali a great destination for shopping; for others it's their destiny. There's a plethora of shops and stalls across the island, selling cheap T-shirts, designer clothes, and items for all budgets in between.

Seminyak Sometimes it seems everyone in Seminyak is a designer; the reality is that many actually are. (p81)

Kerobokan A continuation of stores north of Seminyak offering everything from homewares to fashion. (p87)

Ubud Excellent for handicrafts, art, books, yoga-wear and more. (p165)

South of Ubud Artisan craft shops abound in towns like Mas; look for the don't-miss market in Sukawati. (p175)

Top: Women carrying offerings to a temple in Ubud (p137)
Bottom: Pura Taman Ayun (p248)

Month by Month

February

The rainy season pours on and the islands take a breather after the Christmas and New Year's high season.

✺ Nyale Festival

The ritual harvesting of *nyale* (wormlike sea fish) takes place on Seger Beach near Lombok's Kuta. The evening begins with poetry readings, continues with gamelan performances and carries on until the dawn, when the *nyale* start appearing. Can also be held in March.

March

The rainy season is ending and there is a lull in the crowds – this is low season for tourism.

✺ Nyepi (Day of Silence)

Bali's major Hindu festival, Nyepi celebrates the end of the old year and the start of the next. It's marked by inactivity – a strategy to convince evil spirits that Bali is uninhabited so they'll leave the island alone for another year. The night before Nyepi sees community celebrations with *ogoh-ogoh,* huge papier-mâché monsters that go up in flames. Can be held in early April.

April

The islands dry out after the rainy season, but things remain quiet on the visitor front.

✺ Bali Spirit Festival

A fast-growing yoga, dance and music festival from the people behind the Yoga Barn in Ubud. There are more than 100 workshops and concerts, plus a market and more. It's usually held in early April but may begin in late March. (p152)

◉ Malean Sampi

Yoked buffalo race over waterlogged earth in Narmada, near Mataram on Lombok, their jockeys clinging tight. It's as dangerous, muddy and fun as it sounds. Held early in the month.

May

A great month for visiting. It's not high season but trails are drying out for hiking yet the rivers are still high for rafting. The annual rains have stopped although you can still get downpours at any time.

✺ Bali Arts Festival, Singaraja

In this large, one-week, north Bali festival, dancers and musicians from some of the region's most renowned village troupes, such as those of Jagaraga, perform. It can happen anytime from May to July. (p231)

June

The airport is getting busier, but much of what makes May a good month also applies in June.

✺ Bali Arts Festival, Denpasar

The premier event on Bali's cultural calendar. Based at

the Taman Wedhi Budaya arts centre, the festival is a great way to see traditional Balinese dance and music, as village-based groups compete fiercely for local pride. Held mid-June to mid-July. (p119)

July

After August, July is the second busiest month for visitors on Bali and the Gilis (Lombok is always rather quiet). Don't expect to have your pick of places to stay, but do plan to enjoy the energy of big happy crowds.

✱✱ Bali Kite Festival

In south Bali scores of kites soar overhead much of the year. Often huge (10m-plus), they fly at altitudes that worry pilots. There's a spiritual connection: the kites urge the gods to provide abundant harvests. During this festival the skies fill with huge creations controlled by dozens of villagers. (p114)

August

The busiest time on Bali sees an ever-increasing number of visitors each year. Book your room and tables far in advance and expect crowds, even on the normally quiet nighttime streets of Ubud.

✱✱ Indonesia Independence Day

Celebrated across Indonesia, 17 August celebrates the day Indonesia's independence from the Dutch was declared in 1945. Legions

Top: Flying kites at the Bali Kite Festival (p114)
Bottom: Ceremony to prepare for Nyepi (Day of Silence; p318)

GALUNGAN & KUNINGAN

One of Bali's major festivals, Galungan celebrates the death of a legendary tyrant called Mayadenawa. During this 10-day period, all the gods come down to earth for the festivities. Barong prance from temple to temple and village to village, and locals rejoice with feasts and visits to families. The celebrations culminate with the Kuningan festival, when the Balinese say thanks and goodbye to the gods.

Every village in Bali celebrates Galungan and Kuningan in grand style, and visitors are welcome to join in.

The 210-day *wuku* (or Pawukon) calendar is used to determine festival dates. The calendar uses 10 types of weeks that are between one and 10 days long, which all run simultaneously, and the intersection of the various weeks determines auspicious days. Dates for future Galungan and Kuningan celebrations are as follows:

YEAR	GALUNGAN	KUNINGAN
2015	15 Jul	25 Jul
2016	7 Sep	17 Sep
2017	5 Apr & 1 Nov	15 Apr & 11 Nov

of school kids march with great enthusiasm on Bali's main roads. Traffic is snarled (as it is days before for rehearsals) and lots of fireworks are shot off.

October

The skies darken more often with seasonal rains, but mostly the weather is pleasant and the islands go about their normal business.

🎊 Ubud Writers & Readers Festival

This festival hosts scores of writers and readers from around the world in a celebration of writing – especially writing that touches on Bali. (p152)

🎊 Kuta Karnival

A big beach party on the big beach in Kuta, with games, art, competitions, surfing and much more on the first October weekend and the days right before. (p52)

November

It's getting wetter, but not really so wet that you can't enjoy the islands to the fullest. Usually a quiet month crowd-wise.

🎊 Perang Topat

This 'rice war' on Lombok is fun. It takes place at Pura Lingsar just outside Mataram and involves a costumed parade, and Hindus and Wektu Telu pelting

balls of *ketupat* (sticky rice) at each other. Can also be held in December.

December

Visitors rain on Bali and the Gilis ahead of the Christmas and New Year holidays. Hotels and restaurants are booked out and everybody is busy.

👁 Peresean

Martial arts, Lombok-style. Competitors, stripped to the waist, spar with sticks and cowhide shields. The winner is the first to draw blood. It's held annually in Mataram late in the month.

Itineraries

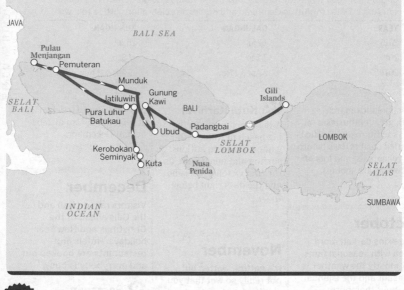

2 WEEKS Bali & the Gilis

See an incredible cross-section of Bali and enjoy the most popular parts of a Bali trip, including the Gili Islands.

Start your trip in **Seminyak**, which has the best places to go out for a meal, a drink or to buy a new frock. Allow at least three days to experience the refined charms of **Kerobokan** and the wild nights of **Kuta**. Once you're sated, head north, driving through the rice terraces of **Jatiluwih** and on to **Pura Luhur Batukau**, a holy temple up in the clouds. Head northwest to the crescent of mellow beach resorts at **Pemuteran**, from where you can snorkel or scuba Bali's best dive site at **Palau Menjangan**. Driving east, stop in **Munduk** for some hiking to remote waterfalls.

Carry on via Candikuning to **Ubud**, the cultural centre of Bali. Nights of dance and culture are offset by days of walking through the serene countryside. Do a day trip to the ancient monuments at **Gunung Kawi**. Then head down to the cute little beach and port town of **Padangbai** and catch a fast boat to the **Gili Islands**. Wander the islands, enjoy Gili T's pulsing nightlife and go snorkelling to spot a turtle.

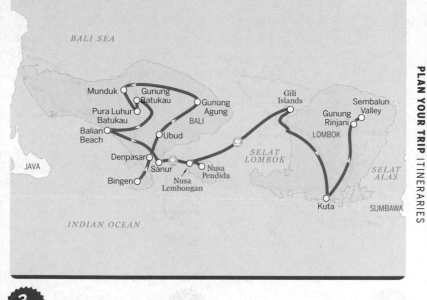

3 WEEKS Total Bali & Lombok

You'll visit six islands and countless beaches on a trip that takes you to the most interesting sites and places across Bali, Lombok and the Gilis.

Begin your trip at **Bingen**. Settle back in the sand and let the jet lag vanish. Then move to **Denpasar** for a purely Balinese lunch and head up the hill to **Ubud** to get a full taste of Balinese culture. Next, tackle **Gunung Agung**, the spiritual centre of the island. Start early to reach the top and take in the views before the daily onslaught of clouds and mist.

Having climbed Bali's most legendary peak, head west to the village of **Munduk**, which looks down to the north coast and the sea beyond. Go for a walk in the area and enjoy waterfalls, truly tiny villages, wild fruit trees and the sinuous ribbons of rice paddies lining the hills. Then head south to the wonderful temple of **Pura Luhur Batukau** and consider a trek up Bali's second-highest mountain, **Gunung Batukau**. Recover with some chillout time on popular **Balian Beach**, just west.

Next, bounce across the waves from **Sanur** to **Nusa Lembongan**, the island hiding in the shadow of **Nusa Penida**. The latter is visible from much of the south and east – it's almost unpopulated and makes a good day trip. Take in the amazing vistas from its cliffs and dive under the waves to check out the marine life.

Head to the **Gilis** via the direct boat from Nusa Lembongan for more tranquil time circumnavigating the three islands above and below the idyllic sapphire waters fringing them. Take a boat to Senggigi, but ignore the resorts and head south. Still off the beaten path, the south coast near Lombok's **Kuta** has stunning beaches and surfing to reward the intrepid. The seldom-driven back roads of the interior will thrill the adventurous and curious, with tiny villages where you can learn about the amazing local handicrafts. Many of these roads lead up the flanks of **Gunung Rinjani**, the volcanic peak that shelters the lush and remote **Sembalun Valley**. Trekking from one village to the next on the rim can take days but is one of Bali and Lombok's great walks.

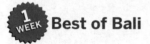 Best of Bali

Seven days will fly by on this trip which covers Bali's best.

Start at a beachside hotel in **Seminyak** or **Kerobokan**; shop the streets of both and spend time at the beach. Enjoy a seafood dinner at **Jimbaran** as part of a day trip to the monkey-filled temple at **Ulu Watu**.

In the east, take the coast road to wild beaches like the one near **Pura Masceti**, followed by the royal town of **Semarapura** with its ruins. Head north up the breathtaking **Sidemen Road**, which combines rice terraces with lush river valleys and cloud-shrouded mountains. Then go west to **Ubud**, the crowning stop on any itinerary.

To spoil yourself, stay in one of Ubud's many hotels with views across rice fields. Sample the offerings at a spa, then try one of the myriad of great restaurants. Bali's rich culture is most celebrated and most accessible in Ubud and you'll be captivated by nightly dance performances. Check out local craft studios, including the woodcarvers of **Mas**. Hike through the surrounding rice fields to river valleys, taking a break in museums full of paintings.

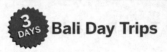 Bali Day Trips

This is for the traveller who wants to unpack only once, seeing what's possible on Bali during a series of easy day trips. Base yourself at a beachside hotel in **Sanur**, such as Hotel La Taverna or Tandjung Sari, both of which have a refined yet relaxed charm.

Day trip one starts with the short drive to the markets and museums of **Denpasar**, followed by a visit to the shops of **Seminyak** and **Kerobokan**. Finish up with a sunset seafood grill at **Jimbaran**.

Day trip two heads to **Ubud** for a halfday strolling the streets, looking at the shops, galleries and museums. Take different routes there and back so you can enjoy sights such as the temples of **Pejeng**, the carvers of **Mas** and the village market at **Sukawati**.

Day trip three follows the wave-tossed volcanic beaches along the east coast. Stop at **Lebih**, which has a temple and mica-infused glittering sand. Go inland to the temple ruins and market at **Semarapura**, then head north along the beautiful **Sidemen Road**. Next, loop west and head back down through **Gianyar**, where you can feast at the night market.

Above: Fetching water
from a river
in Ubud (p137)

Right: Woodcarvings.
Mas (p170)

JUERGEN RITTERBACH / GETTY IMAGES ©

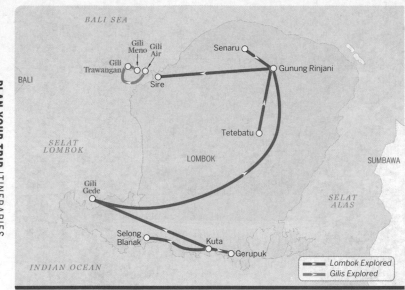

Lombok Explored

2 WEEKS

Lombok is all about the great outdoors, from its incredible beaches to its iconic volcano.

Kick off in gorgeous **Kuta** and spend a day or two finding the perfect beach. East or west of town there are a dozen or so bays to choose from: magnificent **Selong Blanak** is just one. While you're here, it would be rude not to sample the fabled south Lombok surf – tiny **Gerupuk** is an excellent place to either take a lesson or hitch a boat ride to an epic break. Not far away, tranquil southwest Lombok is ideal for more aqua action; swim in sheltered waters or explore the dozen or so islands by boat. Tiny **Gili Gede** makes a perfect base.

Sacred **Gunung Rinjani** is up next. You can explore its foothills from the rustic base of **Tetebatu**, or go the whole hog and trek from **Senaru** to the crater rim, the sublime crater lake or the summit itself (depending on your time, energy and commitment level). Just don't miss the beautiful Sembalun Valley. Finish off with a stay at one of the quietly luxurious resorts on the white beaches of **Sire**.

Gili Islands Explored

1 WEEK

These three little dots of white sand off Lombok can easily occupy your entire trip, with their top-class options for diving, partying and hanging out on the beaches.

The ideal place to get to grips with island life is **Gili Air**, where the main beachfront strip is perfect tropical lounging territory. You can while away a day or two doing nothing but chilling with a book, taking a cooling dip, snorkelling the offshore coral and feasting on inexpensive fresh seafood.

Next up is **Gili Trawangan**, where there's much more action. The perfect day here could start with a morning dive at a site such as Shark Point, followed by a healthy lunch and an afternoon snooze. Then take a gentle stroll round the sandy lanes of the island, slipping in a sunset cocktail on the west coast. After dinner, feel the beat at one of Trawangan's parties.

The final stop is **Gili Meno**, where, once you've secured the perfect place to stay, there's little to do except ponder the sheer desert-isle-ness of the place. If you can drag yourself away from the beach, you can go egret-spotting on the inland lake.

Plan Your Trip
Bali & Lombok Outdoors

Bali is an incredible place to get outside and play in. In its waters there's world-class diving and some of the world's best surfing. On land, hikes abound through rice fields, mountain lakes and up volcanoes. Lombok has fine diving, surfing (often in remote locations) and a famous volcano trek.

Surfing

Surfing kick-started Bali tourism in the 1960s and it's never looked back. Many Balinese have taken to surfing, and the grace of traditional dancing is said to influence their style.

Where to Surf: Bali

Swells come from the Indian Ocean, so the surf is on the southern side of the island and, strangely, on the northwest coast of Nusa Lembongan, where the swell funnels into the strait between there and the Bali coast.

In the dry season (around April to September), the west coast has the best breaks, with the trade winds coming in from the southeast; this is also when Nusa Lembongan is at its best. In the wet season, surf the eastern side of the island, from Nusa Dua around to Padangbai. If there's a north wind – or no wind at all – there are also a couple of breaks on the south coast of the Bukit Peninsula.

Note that the best breaks almost always have good beaches of the same name.

Balangan

Follow Jl Pantai Balangan and its new surfer crash pads until you reach the parking area overlooking the Balangan beach

Best Outdoor Adventures

Top Surfing

World famous Ulu Watu, which every serious surfer needs to tackle once; legendary and elusive Tanjung Desert (Desert Point) in Lombok; all-round great Batu Bolong.

Top Diving & Snorkelling

Spectacular Pulau Menjangan, whether you're just drifting or following a wall; Tulamben's sunken WWII freighter, and its snorkelling and diving from shore; all types of diving and snorkelling in the beautiful waters of the Gili Islands, where you may spot a sea turtle.

Top Hiking

Munduk's lush, spice-scented, waterfall-riven landscape; beautiful walks lasting from one hour to one day in Ubud and its rice-field surrounds; Tirta Gangg's emerald rice terraces, gorgeous views and temples.

Bali & Lombok Surf Breaks

cafes. Balangan is a fast left over a shallow reef, unsurfable at low tide, but good at mid-tide with anything over a 4ft swell; with an 8ft swell, it's magic.

Balian

There are a few peaks near the mouth of Sungai Balian (Balian River) in western Bali. The best break here is an enjoyable and consistent left-hander that works well at mid- to high tide if there's no wind. Choose from guesthouses simple to luxe.

Batu Bolong

North of Kerobokan, on the northern extremity of the bay, Batu Bolong (often called Canggu) has a nice beach with light-coloured sand, many surfers and a cool party scene. An optimum size for Batu Bolong is 5ft to 6ft. There's a good right-hander that you can really hook into, which works at high tide.

Bingin

Accessible down a cliff, this spot can get crowded. It's best at mid-tide with a 6ft swell, when it manufactures short but perfect left-hand barrels. The cliffs backing the beach are lined with plenty of accommodation options.

Impossibles

Just north of Padang Padang, this challenging outside reef break has three shifting peaks with fast left-hand tube sections that can join up if the conditions are perfect.

Keramas & Ketewel

These two beaches are northeast of Sanur. They're both right-hand beach breaks, which are dodgy at low tide and close out over 6ft. The surf is fairly consistent year-round and you can night surf at the new Komune Bali surf resort.

Kuta Area

For your first plunge into the warm Indian Ocean, try the breaks at Kuta's beach. At full tide, go out near the life-saving club at the southern end of the beach road. At low tide, try the tubes around **Halfway Kuta**, probably the best place in Bali for beginners to practise. Start at the beach breaks if you are a bit rusty, but treat even these breaks with respect.

Further north, the breaks at **Legian Beach** can be pretty powerful, with lefts and rights on the sandbars off Jl Melasti and Jl Padma.

For more serious stuff, go to the reefs south of the beach breaks, about a kilometre out to sea. **Kuta Reef**, a vast stretch of coral, provides a variety of waves. You can paddle out in around 20 minutes, but the easiest way to get there is by boat. The main break is a classic left-hander, best at mid- to high tide, with a 5ft to 6ft swell, when it peels across the reef and has a beautiful inside tube section.

Medewi

Further along the south coast of western Bali is a soft left called Medewi. It's a point break that can give a long ride right into the river mouth. This wave has a big drop, which fills up then runs into a workable inside section. There's accommodation here.

Nusa Dua

During the wet season, there are some fine reef breaks on the east side of the island. The reef off Nusa Dua has very consistent swells. The main break is 1km off the beach to the south of Nusa Dua – go past the golf course and look for the remaining shred of Gegar Beach up against the huge Mulia resort, where there will be some boats to take you out. There are lefts and rights that work well on a small swell at low to mid-tide. Further north, in front of the Club Med, there is a fast, barrelling right reef break called **Sri Lanka**, which works best at mid-tide.

Nusa Lembongan

In the Nusa Penida group, this island is separated from the southeast coast of Bali by Selat Badung (Badung Strait).

The strait is very deep and generates huge swells that break over the reefs off the northwest coast of Lembongan. **Shipwrecks**, clearly visible from the beach, is the most popular break, a longish right that gets a good barrel at mid-tide with a 5ft swell.

A bit to the south, **Lacerations** is a very fast, hollow right breaking over a very shallow reef – hence the name. Still further south is a smaller, more user-friendly left-hander called **Playgrounds**. Remember that Lembongan is best with an easterly wind, so it's dry-season surfing.

Padang Padang

Just Padang for short, this super-shallow, left-hand reef break is off a very popular beach and just below some rickety accommodation joints where you can crash *and* watch the breaks. Check this place carefully before venturing out. It's a very demanding break that only works over about 6ft from mid- to high tide.

If you can't surf tubes, backhand or forehand, don't go out. After a ledgy take-off, you power along the bottom before pulling up into the barrel. Not a wave for the faint-hearted and definitely not one to surf when there's a crowd.

Sanur

Sanur Reef has a hollow wave with excellent barrels. It's fickle and doesn't even start until there is a 6ft swell, but anything over 8ft will be world-class, and anything over 10ft will be brown-boardshorts material. There are other reefs further offshore and most of them are surfable.

Hyatt Reef, over 2km from shore, has a shifty right peak that can give a great ride at full tide. The classic right is off the Grand Bali Beach Hotel.

South Coast

The extreme south coast, around the end of the Bukit Peninsula, can be surfed any time of the year provided there is a northerly wind, or no wind at all – get there very early to avoid onshore winds. The peninsula is fringed with reefs, and big swells are produced, but access is a problem; the shoreline is all cliff (getting down to **Nyang-Nyang** requires traversing more than 500 steps).

Ulu Watu

When Kuta Reef is 5ft to 6ft, Ulu Watu, the most famous surfing break in Bali, will be 6ft to 8ft with bigger sets. It's way out on the southern extremity of the bay and consequently picks up more swell than Kuta.

Teluk Ulu Watu (Ulu Watu Bay) is a great set-up for surfers – local boys will wax your board, get drinks for you and carry the board down into the cave, which is the usual access to the waves. There are warungs (food stalls) and accommodation for every budget.

Ulu Watu has about seven different breaks. The **Corner** is straight in front of you to the right. It's a fast-breaking, hollow left that holds about 6ft. The reef shelf under this break is extremely shallow, so try to avoid falling head first. At high tide, the **Peak** starts to work. This is good from 5ft to 8ft, with bigger waves occasionally right on the Peak itself. You can take off from this inside part or further down the line. It's a great wave.

Another left runs off the cliff that forms the southern flank of the bay. It breaks outside this in bigger swells, and once it's 7ft, a left-hander pitches right out in front of a temple on the southern extremity. Out behind the Peak, when it's big, is a *bombora* (submerged reef) appropriately called the **Bommie**. This is another big left-hander and it doesn't start operating until the swell is about 10ft. On a normal 5ft to 8ft day, there are also breaks south of the Peak.

Observe where other surfers paddle out and follow them. If you are in doubt, ask someone. It is better having some knowledge than none at all. Climb down into the cave and paddle out from there. When the swell is bigger you will be swept to your right. Don't panic – it is an easy matter to paddle around the white water from down along the cliff. Coming back in you have to aim for the cave. When the swell is bigger, come from the southern side of the cave because the current runs to the north.

Where to Surf: Lombok

Lombok has some good surfing and the dearth of tourists means that breaks are generally uncrowded.

Gerupuk

This giant bay 6km east of Kuta boasts four surf breaks, so there's always some wave action no matter what the weather or tide. **Bumbang** is extremely dependable: best on an incoming tide, this right-hander over a flat reef is good for all levels and can be surfed year-round. **Gili Golong** excels at mid- to high tide between October and April. **Don-Don** needs a bigger swell to break but can be great at any time of year. Finally **Kid's Point** (or Pelawangan) only breaks with big swells, but when it does it's barrels all the way. You need to hitch a boat ride to each wave.

Gili Trawangan

Much better known as a diving mecca, Trawangan also boasts a surf spot off the island's southwestern tip, offshore from, yes, the Surf Bar. It's a quick right-hander

that breaks in two sections, one offering a steeper profile, over rounded coral. It can be surfed all year long and is best at high tide.

Mawi

About 18km west of Kuta, the stunning bay of Mawi has a fine barrelling left with a late take-off and a final tube. It's best in the dry season, from May to October, with easterly offshore winds and a southwest swell. As there are sharp rocks and coral underwater, and the riptide is very fierce, take great care.

Tanjung Desert

Located in an extremely remote part of Lombok, Tanjung Desert (Desert Point) is a legendary if elusive wave that was voted the 'best wave in the world' by *Tracks* magazine. Only suitable for very experienced surfers, it's a fickle beast, in a region known for long, flat spells.

On its day this left-handed tube can offer a 300m ride, growing in size from take-off to close-out (which is over razor-sharp coral). Tanjung Desert only really performs when there's a serious ground swell – May to September offers the best chance. Wear a helmet and boots at low tide.

Equipment: Pack or Rent?

A small board is usually adequate for the smaller breaks, but a few extra inches on your usual board length won't go astray. For the bigger waves – 8ft and upwards – you'll need a 'gun'. For a surfer of average height and build, a board around the 7ft mark is perfect.

If you try to bring more than two or three boards into the country, you may have problems with customs officials, who might think you're going to try to sell them.

There are surf shops in Kuta and elsewhere in south Bali. You can rent boards of varying quality (from 50,000Rp to 100,000Rp per day) and get supplies at most popular surf breaks. If you need repairs, ask around: there are lots of places that can help.

Other recommended equipment you might bring:

➡ Solid luggage for airline travel

➡ Board-strap for carrying

➡ Tough shoes for walking down rocky cliffs

A scuba diver with Purple Queen Anthias fish

➡ Your favourite wax if you're picky

➡ Wetsuit (a spring suit or shorty will be fine) and reef booties

➡ Wetsuit vest, rashvest or other protective cover from the sun, reefs and rocks

➡ Surfing helmet for rugged conditions (and riding a motorbike)

Surf Operators

Surf schools operate right off Kuta Beach in Kuta and Legian and north to Batu Bolong Beach. Kuta and the Bukit Peninsula have long been where surfers ride waves and crash; the Canggu area is also popular now.

South Bali has some renowned board shapers, including Kuta's Luke Studer (p69) and Canggu's Dylan Longbottom, who runs Dylan Board Store (p92).

Rip Curl School of Surf (p111) works out of Sanur, teaches windsurfing and also has stand-up paddle boards.

Surf Goddess (✆0858 997 0808; www.surfgoddessretreats.com) runs surf holidays for women that include lessons and lodging in a posh guesthouse in Seminyak.

Diving & Snorkelling

With its warm water, extensive coral reefs and abundant marine life, Bali offers excellent diving and snorkelling adventures. Reliable dive schools and operators all around Bali's coast can train complete beginners or arrange challenging trips that will satisfy the most experienced divers. The Gilis provide equally excellent opportunities, while Lombok is close behind with good sites, especially around its northwest coast.

Snorkelling gear is available near all the most accessible spots but it's definitely worth bringing your own and checking out some of the less-visited parts of the coasts. The Gilis have a professional freediving school if you want to take snorkelling to the next level. They also have Gili Islands Dive Association (GIDA), which sets professional and environmental standards.

Equipment: Pack or Rent?

If you are not picky, you'll find all the equipment you need in Bali, the Gilis and Lombok (the quality, size and age of the equipment can vary). If you bring your own, you can usually get a discount on your dive. Some small, easy-to-carry things to bring from home include protective gloves, spare straps, silicone lubricant and extra globes/bulbs for your torch/flashlight. Other equipment to consider bringing:

Mask, snorkel and fins Many people bring these as they are not too big to pack and you can be sure they will fit you. Snorkelling gear rents from about 30,000Rp per day and is often shabby.

Tanks and weight belt Usually included with the cost of a dive.

Thin, full-length wetsuit For protection against stinging animals and possible coral abrasions. Bring your own if you are worried about size. If diving off Nusa Penida, you'll need a wetsuit thicker than 3mm, as up-swells bring up 18°C water from the deep.

Regulators and BCVs Most dive shops have decent ones. (BCVs are also known as BCDs or buoyancy control devices.)

Dive Operators

Major dive operators in tourist areas can arrange trips to the main dive sites all around the islands. Distances can be long, so it's better to sleep relatively close to your diving destination.

For a local trip, count on US$60 to US$90 per person for two dives, which includes all equipment. Note that it is becoming common to price in euros.

Wherever there is decent local diving on Bali and Lombok there are dive shops. Usually you can count on some reefs in fair condition being reachable by boat. Recommended sites with shops include the following:

➡ Amed
➡ Candidasa
➡ Lovina
➡ Nusa Lembongan
➡ Padangbai
➡ Pemuteran
➡ Tulamben
➡ Sanur
➡ Gili Air
➡ Gili Meno
➡ Gili Trawangan
➡ Kuta (Lombok)
➡ Senggigi

In general, diving in Bali and Lombok is safe, with a good standard of staff training and equipment maintenance. There is one decompression chamber on the islands, in Sanur. Here are a few things to consider when selecting a well-set-up and safety-conscious dive shop.

➡ Are its staff fully trained and qualified? Ask to see certificates or certification cards – no reputable shop will be offended by this request. Guides must reach 'full instructor' level to teach. To guide certified divers on a reef dive, guides

---

BEST DIVING & SNORKELLING SITES

The following are Bali and Lombok's most spectacular diving and snorkelling locations, drawing people from near and far.

LOCATION	DETAILS	WHO SHOULD GO?
Nusa Penida	Serious diving that includes schools of manta rays and 2.5m sunfish	Skilled divers will enjoy the challenges, but novices and snorkellers will be in over their heads
Pulau Menjangan	Spectacular 30m wall off a small island, good for diving and snorkelling	Divers and snokellers of all skills and ages
Tulamben	Sunken WWII freighter; snorkelling and diving from shore	Divers and snorkellers with good swimming skills
Gili Islands	All types of diving and snorkelling in beautiful waters	Divers and snorkellers of all skills and ages, although some sites may require advanced skills
Southwest Lombok	Good reefs	Divers and snorkellers with good swimming skills

must hold at least 'rescue diver' or preferably 'dive master' qualifications.

➡ Do they have safety equipment on the boat? At a minimum, a dive boat should carry oxygen and a first-aid kit. A radio or mobile phone is also important.

➡ Is the boat's equipment OK and its air clean? This is often the hardest thing for a new diver to judge. To test this, smell the air: open a tank valve a small way and breathe in. Smelling dry or slightly rubbery air is OK. If it smells of oil or car exhaust, that tells you the operator doesn't filter the air correctly.

➡ When the equipment is put together, are there any big air leaks? All dive centres get some small leaks in equipment some time; however, if you get a *big* hiss of air coming out of any piece of equipment, ask to have it replaced.

➡ Is the organisation conservation-oriented? Good dive shops explain that you should not touch coral or take shells from the reef, and they work with local fishing people to ensure that certain areas are protected. Some even clean beaches.

Learning to Dive

If you're not a qualified diver and you want to try scuba diving in Bali, you have several options, including packages that include lessons and cheap accommodation in a pretty place.

COURSE	DETAILS	COST
Introductory/ orientation	Perfect for novices to see if diving is for them	US$60-100
Basic certification	Three- or four-day limited courses for the basics; popular at resorts	US$300
Open-water certification	The international PADI standard, recognised every-where	US$350-400

Responsible Diving

Bear in mind the following tips when diving and help preserve the ecology and beauty of reefs:

➡ Never use anchors on reefs, and take care not to run boats aground on coral.

➡ Avoid touching or standing on living marine organisms or dragging equipment across the reef.

➡ Be careful with your fins. Even without contact, the surge from fin strokes near the reef can damage delicate organisms. Don't kick up clouds of sand, which can smother organisms.

➡ Practise and maintain proper buoyancy control. Major damage can occur from reef collisions.

➡ Do not collect or buy coral or shells, or loot marine archaeological sites (mainly shipwrecks).

➡ Ensure that you take home all your rubbish and any other litter you may find as well. Plastics are a serious threat to marine life.

➡ Do not feed the fish.

➡ Minimise your involvement with marine animals. *Never* ride on the backs of turtles.

Hiking & Trekking

You could wander Bali and Lombok for a year and still not see all the islands have to offer, but their small size means that you can nibble off a bit at a time, especially as day hikes and treks are easily arranged. Guides can help you surmount volcanoes, while tour companies will take you to remote regions and emerald-green valleys of rice terraces. In terms of what to pack, you'll need good boots for mountain treks and solid hiking sandals for walks.

Where to Hike: Bali

Bali is very walkable. No matter where you're staying, ask for recommendations and set off for discoveries and adventures. Ubud, the Sidemen area and Munduk are obvious choices. The adjoining lakes of Danau Tamblingan and Danau Buyan are great places to explore now that two different groups of great local guides have set up shop. Even from busy Kuta or Seminyak, you can just head to the beach, turn right and walk north as far as you wish alongside the amazing surf while civilisation seems to evaporate.

For strenuous treks that verge on mountain climbing, consider Gunung Agung or Gunung Batur. There are varying routes, none of which take longer than a day. Bali does not offer remote wilderness treks beyond the volcano climbs and day trips within Taman Nasional Bali Barat. For the most part, you'll make day trips from the closest village, often leaving before dawn to avoid the clouds and mist that usually blanket the peaks by mid-morning. No treks require camping gear.

Where to Hike: Lombok

Gunung Rinjani draws trekkers from around the world. Besides being Indonesia's second-tallest volcano, it holds cultural and spiritual significance for the various people of the region. And then there's its stunning beauty: a 6km-wide cobalt blue lake some 600m below the rim of the vast caldera.

Expert advice is crucial on the mountain – people die on its slopes every year. You can organise explorations of Gunung Rinjani at Sembalun Valley, Senaru and Senggigi.

Equipment: Pack or Rent?

Any gear you'll need for your hike, you'll need to provide. Guides may have a few bits of gear but don't count on it. Depend-

ing on the hike, consider bringing the following:

➡ Torch (flashlight).

➡ Warm clothes for higher altitudes (it can get pretty chilly up there).

➡ Waterproof clothes because rain can happen at any time and most of the mountains are misty at the least.

➡ Good hiking sandals, shoes or boots – you definitely won't find these items locally.

Hiking Tour Operators

Guides and agencies are available in various areas such as Ubud, Gunung Agung and Tirta Gangga on Bali, and the Sembalun Valley on Lombok. In addition, there are Bali-wide agencies, including the following:

Bali Nature Walk (✆0817 973 5914; dade putra@hotmail.com) Walks in isolated areas in the Ubud region. Routes are customisable depending on your desires.

HIKING HIGHLIGHTS

One of Bali's great joys is hiking. You can have good experiences across the island, often starting right outside your hotel. Hikes can last from an hour to a day.

Bali

LOCATION	DETAILS
Danau Buyan & Danau Tamblingan	Natural mountain lakes, few people, great guides
Gunung Agung	Sunrises and isolated temples
Gunung Batukau	Misty climbs amid the clouds, with few people
Gunung Batur	Hassles but other-worldly scenery
Munduk	Lush, spice-scented waterfall-riven landscape
Sidemen Road area	Rice terraces, lush hills and lonely temples; comfy lodging for walkers
Taman Nasional Bali Barat	Remote, wild scenery, wildlife
Tirta Gangga	Rice terraces, gorgeous views, remote mountain temples
Ubud	Beautiful walks from one hour to one day; rice fields and terraces, river-valley jungles and ancient monuments

Lombok

Like the island itself, Lombok has walks and hikes that are often remote, challenging or both.

LOCATION	DETAILS
Air Terjun Sindang Gila	One of many waterfalls
Gilis	Beach-bum circumnavigations
Gunung Rinjani	Superb for trekking; climb the 3726m summit then drop into a crater with a sacred lake and hot springs
Sembalun Valley	Garlic-scented hikes on the slopes of Rinjani

Bali Sunrise Trekking & Tours (☑0818 552 669; www.balisunrisetours.com) Leads treks throughout the central mountains.

Safety Guidelines for Trekking

Before embarking on a trekking trip, consider the following points to ensure a safe and enjoyable experience:

➡ Pay any fees and carry any permits required by local authorities; often these fees will be rolled into the guide's fee, meaning that it's all negotiable.

➡ Be sure you are healthy and feel comfortable walking for a sustained period.

➡ Obtain reliable information about environmental conditions along your intended route – the weather can get quite wet and cold in the upper reaches of the volcanoes.

➡ Confirm with your guide that you will only go on walks/treks within your realm of experience.

➡ Carry the proper equipment. Depending on the trek and time of year this can mean rain gear or extra water. Carry a torch; don't assume the guide will have one.

Cycling

Cyclists are becoming common on Bali's busy roads. The main advantage of touring Bali by bike is the quality of the experience; you can be totally immersed in the environment, hearing the wind rustling in the rice paddies or the sound of a gamelan (traditional orchestra) while catching the scent of flowers. The island's back roads more than make up for the traffic-clogged streets of the south.

Lombok is also good for touring by bicycle. In the populated areas the roads are flat, and the traffic across the island is less chaotic than on Bali.

Some people are put off cycling in a tropical location, but when you're riding on level ground or downhill, the breeze really moderates the heat.

Where to Cycle: Bali

It's much easier to tell you where *not* to ride in Bali: Denpasar south through Sanur in the east, and Kerobokan to Kuta in the west, suffer from lots of traffic and narrow roads. Across the rest of the island you can find many rides that reward with lush tropical beauty. For something different, try the still-lonely lanes of Nusa Penida.

PLAN YOUR TRIP BALI & LOMBOK OUTDOORS

CYCLING SUGGESTIONS

You can't get too lost on an island as small as Bali. The following areas are good for exploring on two wheels:

LOCATION	DETAILS
Bukit Peninsula	Explore cliffs, coves and beaches along the west and south coasts; beach promenade at Nusa Dua; avoid the congested area by the airport
Central mountains	Ambitious routes; explore Danau Bratan, Danau Buyan and Danau Tamblingan; ride downhill to the north coast via Munduk and to the south via small roads from Candikuning
East Bali	Coast road lined with beaches; north of the coast is uncrowded with serene rice terraces; Sidemen Road has lodges good for cyclists
North Bali	Lovina is a good base for day trips to remote waterfalls and temples; the northeast coast has resorts popular with cyclists circumnavigating Bali
Nusa Lembongan	Small, with beaches that make good goals for each ride; cross the cool narrow suspension bridge and explore Nusa Ceningan
Nusa Penida	For serious cyclists who bring bikes; nearly traffic-free, with remote vistas of the sea, sheer cliffs, white beaches and lush jungle
Ubud	Many tour companies are based here; narrow mountain roads lead to ancient monuments and jaw-dropping rice-terrace views
West Bali	Rice fields and dense jungle rides in and around Tabanan, Kerambitan and Bajera; further west, small roads off the main road lead to mountain streams, deserted beaches and hidden temples

Where to Cycle: Lombok & Gilis

East of Mataram are several attractions that would make a good day trip: south to Banyumulek via Gunung Pengsong and then back to Mataram, for example. Some coastal roads have hills and curves like a roller coaster. Try going north from Senggigi to Pemenang along the spectacular, paved road, and then (if you feel energetic) return via the steep climb over the Pusuk Pass. The Gilis are good for riding only as a means to get around.

Equipment: Pack or Rent?

Serious cyclists will want to pack personal gear they consider essential. For top-end gear, there's **Planet Bike Bali** (☑0361-746 2858; Jl Gunung Agung 148, Denpasar; ☺9am-6.30pm Mon-Sat, 9am-3pm Sun), which stocks Giant, Trek, Shimano and other brands. Casual riders can rent bikes and helmets in many locations.

Cycling Tour Operators

Popular tours start high in the central mountains at places such as Kintamani or Bedugul. The tour company takes you to the top and then you ride down relatively quiet mountain roads, soaking up the lush scenery, village culture and tropical scents. The cost including bicycle, gear and lunch is US$40 to US$70. Transport to/from south Bali and Ubud hotels is usually included. A couple of considerations:

➡ Tours usually include hotel pickup, which can be as early as 6.30am in Kuta.

➡ The tours usually run 8.30am to 4pm and involve a lot of coasting and stopping.

➡ Not all companies provide helmets, which is outrageous. Be sure yours does.

The following are companies to consider:

Archipelago Adventure (☑0361-808 1769; www.archipelago-adventure.com; adult/child from US$55/45) Offers a huge and interesting range of tours, including ones on Java. In Bali, there are rides around Jatiluwih and Danau Buyan, and mountain biking on trails from Kintamani.

Bali Bike-Baik Tours (☑0361-978 052; www.balibike.com; tours from 450,000Rp) Tours run downhill from Kintamani. The emphasis is on cultural immersion and there are frequent stops in tiny villages and at rice farms.

Bali Eco Cycling (☑0361-975 557; www.baliecocycling.com; tours from 420,000Rp) Tours start at Kintamani and take small roads through lush scenery south to Ubud; other options focus on rural culture.

Banyan Tree Cycling Tours (☑0361-805 1620, 0813 3879 8516; www.banyantreebiketours.com; tours from 450,000Rp) Enjoy day-long tours of remote villages in the hills above Ubud. It's locally owned by Bagi and very popular. The tours emphasise interaction with villagers; there is also an extreme cycling tour.

C.Bali (☑0813 5342 0541; www.c-bali.com; tours from 430,000Rp) Offers excellent bike tours in and around Gunung Batur and the lake. The antidote to cookie-cutter bike tours.

Rafting

Rafting is popular, usually as a day trip from either south Bali or Ubud. Operators pick you up, take you to the put-in point, provide all the equipment and guides, and return you to your hotel at the end of the day. The best time is during the wet season (November to March) or just after. At other times, water levels can be too low.

Some operators use the Sungai Ayung (Ayung River), near Ubud, where there are between 25 and 33 Class II to III rapids (ie potentially exciting but not perilous). The Sungai Telagawaja (Telagawaja River) near Muncan in east Bali is also popular. It's more rugged than the Ayung and the scenery is more wild.

Discounts on published prices are common, so do ask. Consider the following operators:

Bio (☑0361-270 949; www.bioadventurer.com; adult/child from US$79/65) Get closer to the water on an individual river board or a tube. Tours go to west Bali.

Bali Adventure Tours (☑0361-721 480; www.baliadventuretours.com; rafting trips adult/child from $79/52) Sungai Ayung; also has kayak trips.

Mega Rafting (☑0361-246 724; www.megaraftingbali.com; adult/child from US$66/50) Sungai Ayung.

Sobek (☑0361-729 016; www.balisobek.com; adult/child US$79/52) Trips on both the Sungai Ayung and Sungai Telagawaja.

Plan Your Trip
Travel with Children

Travelling with *anak-anak* (children) in Bali is an enriching experience. Locals consider kids part of the community, and everyone has a responsibility towards them. Children of all ages will enjoy both the attention and the many diversions that will make their holiday as special as that of the adults.

Bali & Lombok for Kids

Children are a social asset when you travel in Bali, and people will display great interest in any Western child they meet. You will have to learn your child's age and sex in Bahasa Indonesia – *bulau* is month, *tahun* is year, *laki-laki* is boy and *perempuan* is girl. You should also make polite enquiries about the other person's children, present or absent.

Lombok is generally quieter than Bali and the traffic is less dangerous. People on Lombok are fond of kids but less demonstrative about them than the Balinese. The main difference on Lombok is that services for children are much less developed.

The obvious drawcards for kids are the loads of outdoor adventures available. But there are also many cultural treats that kids will love, including the following:

Dance A guaranteed snooze, right? Wrong. Check out an evening Barong dance at the Ubud Palace or Pura Dalem Ubud, two venues that look like sets from *Tomb Raider* right down to the flaming torches. Sure, the Legong style of Balinese might be tough going for fidgety types, but the Barong has monkeys, monsters, a witch and more.

Markets If young explorers are going to temples, they will need sarongs. Give them 100,000Rp at a

Highlights

Best Beaches

From surf schools at Kuta Beach to flying kites at Sanur Beach – kids of all ages will get their kicks.

Best Water Fun

Play in the ocean at Nusa Lembongan, or snorkel at Pulau Menjangan. For something different, walk across rice fields – who could resist the promise of muddy water filled with ducks, frogs and other fun critters?

Best Frolicking

Kids can make like monkeys at Bali Treetop Adventure Park in Candikuning or hit the aquatic playground of Waterbom Park in Tuban.

Best for Animals

Ubud's Sacred Monkey Forest Sanctuary; the Bali Bird Park south of Ubud; the Elephant Safari Park north of Ubud; and the Bali Safari & Marine Park, in east Bali.

Best Cool Old Things

Kids will love the Indiana Jones–like pools at Tirta Empul, the ancient water palace and park at Tirta Gangga northeast of Ubud; and Pura Luhur Ulu Watu, a beautiful temple with monkeys.

traditional market and let 'em loose. Vendors will be truly charmed as the kids try to bargain and assemble the most colourful combo (and nothing is too loud for a Balinese temple).

Temples Pick the fun ones. Goa Gajah (Elephant Cave) in Bedulu has a deep cavern where hermits lived and which you enter through the mouth of a monster. Pura Luhur Batukau is in dense jungle in the Gunung Batukau area with a cool lake and a rushing stream.

Planning

The critical decision is deciding where to base yourselves.

Where to Stay

There's a huge range of accommodation options for families.

➡ A hotel with a swimming pool, air-con and a beachfront location is fun for kids and very convenient, and still provides a good break for parents. Fortunately there are plenty of choices.

BEST REGIONS FOR KIDS

Although Bali and Lombok are generally quite kid-friendly, some areas are more accommodating than others.

LOCATION	PROS	CONS
Sanur	Beachside resorts, reef-protected beach with gentle waves, close to many kid-friendly activities, modest traffic	Can be dull, especially for teens
Nusa Dua	Huge beachside resorts, reef-protected beach with gentle waves, modest traffic, quiet	Can be dull for teens; insulated from the rest of Bali
Tanjung Benoa	Beachside resorts, reef-protected beach with gentle waves, close to many kid-friendly activities	Far from the rest of Bali; boring for teens
Lovina	Modest, quiet hotels near the beach, limited traffic, reef-protected beach with gentle waves	Far from the rest of Bali; boring for teens; limited diversions
Kuta	Teens will love it; kids will be able to buy all manner of cheap souvenirs and fake tattoos and get their hair braided; surf lessons	Teens will love it too much; busy road between beach and hotels; crowded, crazy, strong surf
Legian	Much the same as Kuta with beachfront resorts on the sand	Much the same as Kuta without the busy beach road (but there's traffic elsewhere); strong surf
Seminyak	Appealing mix for all ages; large hotels on beach	Traffic, strong surf
Kerobokan	Lots of family-friendly villa rentals	Adults love the shopping and nightlife but beach access can be too far for kids
Canggu Area	Family-friendly villas are fun; teens love Batu Bolong beach, a hotspot for local teens	Not much here for younger kids
Ubud	Quiet in parts; many things to see and do; walks, markets and shops	No beach; evenings may require greater creativity to keep kids amused; adults like it
Gili Air	Small island so kids won't get lost; gentle surf; many tourist amenities and activities such as snorkelling	Can feel cramped and maybe too close to Gili T debauchery
Senggigi	Modest, quiet hotels on the beach; limited traffic, reef-protected beach with gentle waves	Somewhat isolated; boring for teens; Lombok offers limited kid-specific diversions

➡ Many larger resorts from Tuban north through Legian and also at Nusa Dua have special programs for kids that include lots of activities during the day and evening. Better ones have special supervised pool areas and other fun kids' zones.

➡ Many hotels and guesthouses, at whatever price level, have a 'family plan', which means that children up to about 12 years old can share a room with their parents free of charge. The catch is that hotels may charge for extra beds, although many offer family rooms which can accommodate four or more.

➡ A family might enjoy a villa-style unit in Seminyak, Kerobokan or the Canggu area. Within your own small private compound you'll have your own pool and often more than one TV. Cooking facilities mean you can prepare familiar foods while the relative seclusion makes naps easy.

➡ Many hotels can arrange a babysitter during the day or evening. In Kuta, Cheeky Monkeys (p49) offers drop-off childcare during the day.

➡ Hotel staff are usually very willing to help and improvise, so always ask if you need something for your children.

➡ At family homestays and guesthouses, especially in Ubud, young travellers might just feel part of the family as they watch offerings being made and people their own age going about their daily business.

What to Pack

Huge supermarkets and stores in south Bali such as Carrefour stock almost everything you'd find at similar shops at home, including many Western foods. Nappies (diapers), Western baby food, packaged UHT milk, infant formula and other supplies are easily purchased. Suggested items to bring by age:

Babies & Toddlers

➡ A front or back sling or other baby carrier: Bali's barely walkable streets and paths are not suited to prams and pushchairs.

➡ A portable changing mat, hand-wash gel et al (baby changing facilities are a rarity).

➡ Kids' car seats: cars, whether rented or chartered with a driver, are unlikely to come with these.

Six to 12 Years

➡ Binoculars for young explorers to zoom in on wildlife, rice terraces, temples, dancers and so on.

➡ A camera or phone that shoots video to inject newfound fun into 'boring' grown-up sights and walks.

Eating with Kids

Eating out as a family is one of the joys of visiting Bali and Lombok. Kids are treated like deities by doting staff who will clamour to grab yours (especially young babies) while parents enjoy some quiet time together.

Bali especially is so relaxed that kids can just be kids. There are plenty of top-end eateries in Seminyak and elsewhere where kids romp nearby while their parents enjoy a fine meal.

If your children don't like spicy food, show caution in offering them the local cuisine. For older babies, bananas, eggs, peelable fruit and *bubur* (rice cooked to a mush in chicken stock) are all generally available. Many warungs will serve food without sauces upon request, such as plain white rice, fried tempeh or tofu, chicken, boiled vegetables and boiled egg. Otherwise, kid-pleasers like burgers, chicken fingers, pizza and pasta are widespread, as are fast-food chains in south Bali.

STAYING SAFE

The main danger to kids – and adults for that matter – is traffic and bad pavements and footpaths in busy areas.

The sorts of facilities, safeguards and services that Western parents regard as basic may not be present. Not many restaurants provide highchairs, places with great views might have nothing to stop your kids falling over the edge, and shops often have breakable things down low. Given the ongoing rabies crisis in Bali, be sure to keep children away from stray dogs.

It's also worth checking out conditions carefully for any activity. Just because that rafting company sells tickets to families doesn't mean they are well set up to cater to the safety needs of children.

Regions at a Glance

Kuta and Seminyak are the main towns in the most touristed part of Bali, the part of the south that follows the magnificent stretch of sand from the airport northwest to Echo Beach. The Bukit Peninsula combines remote surf breaks with vast resorts.

Ubud occupies the heart of Bali in many respects and shares some of the island's most beautiful rice fields with east Bali. The latter has no major centre but does have popular areas such as Padangbai and the Amed Coast.

Bali's centre is dominated by dramatic volcanoes. North and west Bali are thinly populated but have fine diving.

Lombok is largely mountainous, volcanic and rural, while the Gilis are tiny coral islands fringed with white sand.

Kuta & Seminyak

Beaches
Nightlife
Shopping

Kuta Beach

Kuta's famous sweep of wave-pounded sand extends for 12km past Legian, Seminyak, Kerobokan and Canggu, before ending up on the rocks near Echo Beach. At Kuta there are beach bars (eg chairs in the sand) and vendors where the atmosphere is always merry.

Party 'Til Dawn

Restaurants and cafes in Seminyak and Kerobokan are some of the best on Bali. Some have gorgeous sunset views, while the bars and clubs have a vaguely sophisticated air. Nightlife becomes manic in Kuta, where the party goes all night.

Seminyak's Shops

Shopping in Seminyak is reason enough to visit Bali; the choice is extraordinary.

p46

South Bali & the Islands

Beaches
Surfing
Diving

Balangan Beach

Beaches can be found right around south Bali: little coves of white sand like Balangan are idyllic and inspire one to just plop down on a beach chair and watch the gorgeous surf.

The Ulu Watu Breaks

You can't say enough about the surf breaks on the west coast of the Bukit Peninsula; Ulu Watu is famous the world over, and its multitude of breaks are world-renowned. Surfer guesthouses let you stay near the action.

Underwater Nusa Penida

The best diving is at the islands. Nusa Penida has challenging conditions and deep-water cliffs and you might even see large creatures, such as manta rays winging their way along.

p94

Ubud & Around

Culture
Indulgence
Walks

Dancers & Artists

Ubud is the nexus of Balinese culture. Each night there are performances of Balinese dance, music, puppets and more. It's also home to talented artists, including superb woodcarvers who make the masks for the shows.

Spas

Spas of every stripe, often with traditional medicine sessions and yoga classes, are the soul of Ubud indulgence. Services for mind and body abound, with options from bargain-priced massages to opulent all-day retreats.

Explore Nature

The rice fields surrounding Ubud are some of Bali's most picturesque. You can walk for an hour or a day, enjoying river valleys, small villages and natural beauty.

p136

East Bali

Beaches
Hikes
History

Pasir Putih

Beaches are found along much of the east Bali coast. While you'll come across many a dark volcanic sand strand along the coast road, the real star is remote Pasir Putih, with its swimmable surf, lovely sand and mellow vendors.

Wandering Sidemen

Some of Bali's most alluring rice fields and landscapes are found in the east. You're spoiled for choice along Sidemen Rd, which has walks aplenty through the verdant green hills and valleys. Or go all out, rise early and tackle Gunung Agung.

A Tragic Past

Taman Kertha Gosa has the moving remains of a palace lost when the royals committed ritual suicide rather than surrender to the Dutch in 1908.

p178

Central Mountains

Hikes
Culture
Solitude

Munduk Treks

The centre of the island offers hikes around volcanoes and lakes. Trails radiating from Munduk include these natural highlights along with misty walks through spice plantations and jungle to waterfalls.

A Top Temple

Pura Luhur Batukau never fails to touch the spirit of those who find this important temple on the slopes of Gunung Batukau. It is a mystical – and misty – place to contemplate Bali's beliefs and to commune with nature.

Remote Walks

Cooler than the rest of Bali, the mountains feel lonely. A visit to Pura Luhur Batukau can be followed by retreats to lodges, treks through the volcanic mountains and walks through the Jatiluwih rice fields.

p213

North Bali

Resorts
Chilling
Diving

Pemuteran's Resorts

The crescent of beach hotels at Pemuteran is the real star of north Bali. Beautifully built, the hotels form a fine human-scale resort area, and they're close to Pulau Menjangan.

Lovina's Quiet

Settle onto a mat on Lovina's tan and grey sand, pick up a book and let the day drift past at your low-cost, quiet getaway. Even the surf is mellow: much of the north coast is protected by reefs.

Pulau Menjangan

Pulau Menjangan lives up to its many superlatives. A 30m coral wall close to shore delights both divers and snorkellers with a cast of fish and creatures that varies from sardines to whales.

p228

West Bali

Surfing
Beaches
Rice Fields

Medewi

The breaks at Medewi have a following, and a small surfer community has sprung up with simple guesthouses and somewhat posher retreats. Hang out with locals who know the waters well and are ready to give lessons.

Balian Beach

Balian Beach is the main strand in the west and makes a good place to hang even if you're not surfing. Enjoy the range of accommodation from hip to simple.

Tabanan

Unesco has given Bali's system of growing rice World Heritage status. The area around Tabanan has some of the most beautiful rice fields plus a nice little museum and the nearby temple of Pura Taman Ayun.

p246

Lombok

Hiking
Coastline
Tropical Chic

Gunung Rinjani

A majestic volcano, Gunung Rinjani's very presence overshadows all of northern Lombok. Hiking trails sneak up Rinjani's astonishing caldera, where you'll find a shimmering crater lake, hot springs and a smoking mini-cone.

South Coast

Lombok's southern coastline is nature in the raw. There's absolutely nothing genteel about the magnificent shoreline, which is pounded by oceanic waves that make it a surfer's mecca. Empty beaches allow exceptional swimming in azure waters.

Sire

For total immersion in tropical-chic, the Sire area offers some gorgeous resorts that combine a bamboo and thatched motif with pampering.

p255

Gili Islands

Diving
Beaches
Chilling

Coral Reefs

Forming one of Indonesia's most species-rich environments, the Gilis' coral reefs teem with fascinating sea life. The islands are perfect for divers (including freedivers) and snorkellers, and you're almost guaranteed to see turtles.

Gili Air Beaches

Pack your sunscreen, mat, some water and a good book and head out in the morning to walk around Gili Air. Along the way stop at each and every beach that catches your fancy.

Gili Meno

We've all dreamed of finding the ultimate beach: a vision of palm trees, blinding white sands and a turquoise sea, plus a bamboo shack selling cool drinks and fresh fish. Yours might just be on Meno.

p281

On the Road

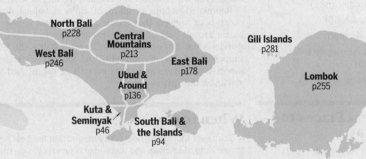

North Bali
p228

West Bali
p246

Central Mountains
p213

East Bali
p178

Ubud & Around
p136

Kuta & Seminyak
p46

South Bali & the Islands
p94

Gili Islands
p281

Lombok
p255

Kuta & Seminyak

Best Places to Eat

➡ Sardine (p85)

➡ Biku (p85)

➡ Take (p58)

➡ Gusto Gelato & Coffee (p86)

➡ Mama San (p77)

Best Places to Stay

➡ Hotel Tugu Bali (p91)

➡ Oberoi (p76)

➡ Double-Six (p55)

➡ Un's Hotel (p54)

➡ Samaya (p76)

Why Go?

Crowded and frenetic, the swathe of south Bali hugging the amazing wide ribbon of beach that runs north almost from the airport is the place many travellers begin and end their visit to the island.

In Seminyak and Kerobokan there is a bounty of cafes, restaurants, designer boutiques, spas and the like that rivals anywhere in the world, while Kuta and Legian are the choice for rollicking all-night clubbing, cheap singlets and hair-plaiting and carefree family holidays. North around Canggu are wild beaches and the new frontier of tourism.

Renowned shopping, all-night clubs, fabulous dining, cheap beer, sunsets that dazzle and relentless hustle and bustle are all part of the experience. But just when you wonder what any of this has to do with Bali – the island supposedly all about spirituality and serenity – a religious procession appears and shuts everything down. And then you know the answer.

When to Go

➡ Bali's ever-increasing popularity means that the best time to visit Kuta, Seminyak and their neighbours is outside the high season (July, August and the weeks around Christmas and New Year). Holidays during high season mean that visitor numbers spike and it can require actual effort to organise tables in the best restaurants, navigate trendy shops and get a room with a view.

➡ Many prefer April to June and September, when the weather is drier and slightly cooler, and the crowds manageable.

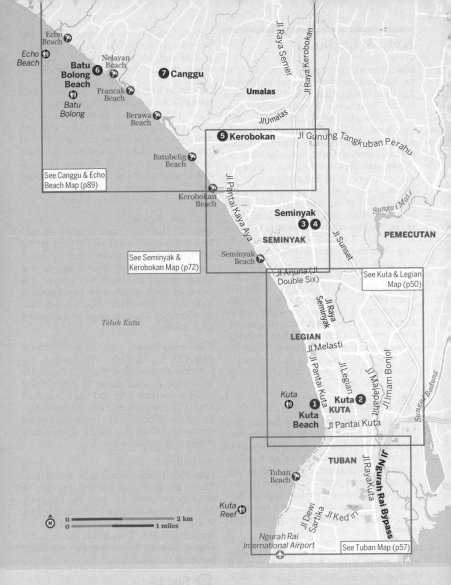

Kuta & Seminyak Highlights

① Lolling around on **Kuta Beach** (p48), Bali's original tourist magnet.

② Raving through the night in the manic clubs and legendary nightlife scene of **Kuta** (p67).

③ Ignoring your resolve while shopping in the myriad boutiques and designer outlets in **Seminyak** (p81).

④ Revelling in a technicolour sunset with a beer from a beach vendor or swanky bar in **Seminyak** (p81).

⑤ Savouring a meal at one of the many fabulous restaurants in **Kerobokan** (p84).

⑥ Joining the hip beach and surf scene at **Batu Bolong Beach** (p90).

⑦ Making a back-road discovery amid rice fields and villas on the twisting lanes of **Canggu** (p90).

Kuta & Legian

🎵 0361

Loud, frenetic and brash are just some of the adjectives commonly used to describe Kuta and Legian, the centre of mass tourism in Bali. Today's wall-to-wall cacophony has become notorious worldwide through often over-hyped media reports and the Australian TV show *What Really Happens in Bali*, with its focus on tourists behaving badly.

Although this is often the first place many visitors hit in Bali, the region is not for everyone. Kuta has ugly narrow lanes jammed with cheap cafes, surf shops, incessant motorbikes and an uncountable number of T-shirt vendors and bleating offerings of 'massage'. But flash new shopping malls and chain hotels show that Kuta's lure will only grow.

Kuta has Bali's most raucous clubs, and you can still find a simple room for US$15 in dozens of hotels. Legian appeals to a slightly older crowd (some say it's where fans of Kuta go after they're married) and is equally commercial and has a long row of family-friendly hotels close to the beach. Tuban differs little in feel from Kuta and Legian, but does have a higher percentage of visitors on package holidays.

🏊 Beaches

It's the beach that put Kuta on the map. The strand of sand stretching for over 12km from Tuban north to Kuta, Legian and beyond to Seminyak and Echo Beach is always a scene of surfing, massaging, games, chilling, imbibing and more. Sunsets are a time of gathering for just about everyone in south Bali. When conditions are right, you can enjoy an iridescent magenta spectacle better than fireworks.

★ Kuta Beach   BEACH
(Map p50) Tourism in Bali began here and is there any question why? Surf that started far out in the Indian Ocean crashes to shore in long symmetrical breaks. Low-key hawkers will sell you soft drinks and beer, snacks and other treats, and you can rent surfboards, lounge chairs and umbrellas (negotiable at 10,000Rp to 20,000Rp) or just crash on the sand.

You'll see everyone from bronzed international youths strutting their stuff to local families trying to figure out how to get wet and preserve their modesty. When the tide is out, the beach seems to stretch forever and you could be tempted to take a long stroll.

The best bit is south of the entrance where Jl Pantai Kuta reaches the beach.

★ Legian Beach   BEACH
(Map p50) An extension of Kuta Beach to the south, Legian Beach is quieter thanks to the lack of a raucous road next to the sand and fewer people. The section in front of the Sari Beach Hotel is far from any road, is backed by shady trees, is never crowded, has somnolent vendors and isn't crossed by a stream with dubious water. You'll even hear something rarely heard in Kuta: the surf.

Kuta Reef Beach   BEACH
(Map p57) This hidden gem of sand is reached by a tiny access road along the fence on the north side of the airport. There's shade, a couple of tiny warungs (food stalls), views of planes landing and rarely ever a crowd. You can head north on the lovely beach walk to Kuta Beach. Some still call this beach 'Pantai Jerman', a legacy of some long forgotten early tourist.

Double Six Beach   BEACH
(Map p50) Very popular, this beach is the northern continuation of Legian Beach. It's alive with pick-up games of football and volleyball all day long and has a perpetual buzz. There are scores of popular beach bars here. One off-note is the stream that crosses the beach, which is a source of unsavoury smells and dubious water.

Tuban Beach   BEACH
(Map p57) Tuban's beach is a mixed bag. There are wide and mellow stretches of sand to the south but near the Discovery Mall it disappears entirely. One bright spot is the very pleasant beach walk which extends south from Kuta Beach almost to the airport. Segara Beach (Map p57) is a sandy pocket at the south end.

👁 Sights

The real sights here are, of course, the beaches. Otherwise, you can immerse yourself in local life without even getting wet. Wanderers, browsers and gawkers will find much to fascinate, delight and irritate amid the streets, alleys and constant hubbub.

Memorial Wall   MONUMENT
(Map p50; Jl Legian; ⊙24hr) Reflecting the international scope of the 2002 bombings is this memorial wall, where people from

many countries pay their respects. Listing the names of the 202 known victims, including 88 Australians and 35 Indonesians, it is starting to look just a touch faded. Across the street, a parking lot (with the appalling name 'Ground Zero Legian') is all that is left of the **Sari Club site** (Map p50).

Vihara Dharmayana Temple BUDDHIST TEMPLE
(Chinese Temple; Map p50; Jl Blambangan; ⊙ 9am-8pm) Dating back nearly 200 years, this Buddhist temple is a colourful place of calm, slightly off the beaten path. Incense burns in the serene courtyard.

🏃 Activities

From Kuta you can easily go surfing, sailing, diving, fishing or rafting anywhere in the southern part of Bali and still be back for the start of happy hour at sunset.

Surfing
The beach break called **Halfway Kuta**, offshore near the Hotel Istana Rama, is popular with novices. More challenging breaks can be found on the shifting sandbars off Legian, around the end of Jl Padma, and at Kuta Reef, 1km out to sea off Tuban Beach.

Surf culture is huge in Kuta. Shops large and small sell mega-brand surf gear and boards. Stalls on the side streets hire out surfboards (for a negotiable 30,000Rp per day) and boogie boards, repair dings and sell new and used boards. Some can also arrange transport to nearby surfing spots. Used boards in good shape average US$200. See p69 for surfing shops.

Pro Surf School SURFING
(Map p50; www.prosurfschool.com; Jl Pantai Kuta; lessons from €45) Right along Kuta Beach, this well-regarded school has been getting beginners standing for years. It offers all levels of lessons.

Rip Curl School of Surf SURFING
(Map p50; ☑ 0361-735858; www.ripcurlschoolof surf.com; Jl Arjuna; lessons from 650,000Rp) Usually universities sell shirts with their logos; here it's the other way round: the beachwear company sponsors a school. Lessons at all levels are given across the south; there are special courses for kids. They have a location for wakeboarding and kitesurfing in Sanur.

Naruki Surf Shop SURFING
(Map p50; ☑ 0361-765772; Jl Lebak Bene; ⊙ 10am-8pm) One of dozens of surf shops lining the lanes of Kuta, the guys here will rent you a board, fix your ding, offer advice or give you lessons.

Massages & Spas
Spas have proliferated, especially in hotels. Check out a few before choosing.

Jamu Traditional Spa SPA
(Map p50; ☑ 0361-752520 ext 165; www.jamu traditionalspa.com; Jl Pantai Kuta, Alam Kul Kul; massage from 600,000Rp; ⊙ 9am-7pm) In serene surrounds at a resort hotel, you can enjoy indoor massage rooms that open onto a pretty garden courtyard. If you've ever wanted to be part of a fruit cocktail, here's your chance – treatments involve tropical nuts, coconuts, papayas and more, often in fragrant baths.

KUTA & SEMINYAK KUTA & LEGIAN

KUTA FOR KIDS

Besides cavorting on the beach all day, there are other activities in Kuta, Legian and Tuban that will delight kids, including special youth-oriented surf lessons at all the major surf shops. For more ideas, see the Travel with Children chapter, p39.

Waterbom Park (Map p57; ☑ 0361-755676; www.waterbom-bali.com; Jl Kartika Plaza; adult/child US$33/21; ⊙ 9am-6pm) This watery amusement park covers 3.5 hectares of landscaped tropical gardens. It has assorted water slides, swimming pools and play areas, a supervised park for children under five years old, and a 'lazy river' ride. Other indulgences include the 'pleasure pool', a food court and bar, and a spa.

Amazone (Map p57; Jl Kartika Plaza, Discovery Shopping Mall; ⊙ 10am-10pm) Has hundreds of screeching arcade games on the top floor of the mall.

Cheeky Monkeys (Map p50; ☑ 0361-846 5610; www.cheekymonkeysbali.com; Jl Pantai Kuta, Beachwalk, Level 3; half-day from 175,000Rp) Offers drop-in childcare for young children. There's a huge range of activities on offer; it's located in the back of the mall.

Kuta & Legian

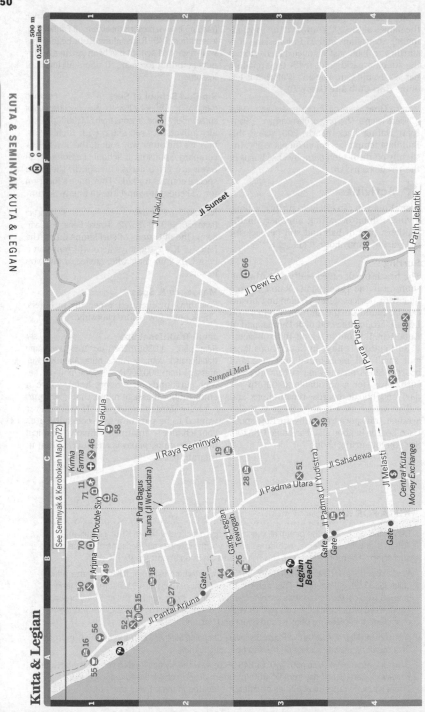

500 m
0.25 miles

See Seminyak & Kerobokan Map (p72)

Kimia Farma

Jl Nakula

Jl Sunset

Jl Dewi Sri

Jl Patih Jelantik

Jl Pura Puseh

Jl Raya Seminyak

Jl Nakula

Sungai Mati

Jl Pura Bagus Taruna (Jl Werkudara)

Jl Melasti

Jl Sahadewa

Jl Padma (Jl Yudistra)

Jl Padma Utara

Central Kuta Money Exchange

Gang Legian Tewogah

Jl Arjuna (Jl Double Six)

Jl Pantai Arjuna

Legian Beach

Gate

Gate

Gate

Gate

Gate

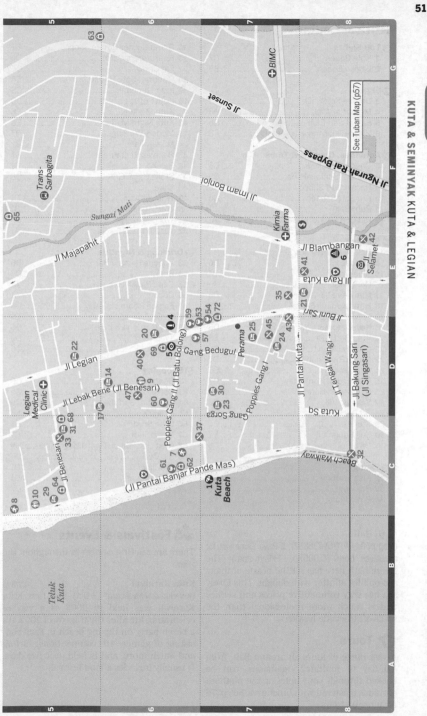

Kuta & Legian

◉ Top Sights
1	Kuta Beach	C7
2	Legian Beach	B3

◉ Sights
3	Double Six Beach	A1
4	Memorial Wall	D6
5	Site of Sari Club	D6
6	Vihara Dharmayana Temple	E8

⊕ Activities, Courses & Tours
7	Cheeky Monkeys	C6
8	Jamu Traditional Spa	C5
9	Naruki Surf Shop	D6
10	Pro Surf School	C5
11	Putri Bali	C1
12	Rip Curl School of Surf	A1

⊜ Sleeping
13	Bali Mandira Beach Resort	B4
14	Bendesa	D6
15	Blue Ocean	B1
16	Double-Six	A1
17	Hotel Ayu Lili Garden	D5
18	Hotel Kumala Pantai	B2
19	Island	C2
20	Kayun Hostel Downtown	D6
21	Kuta Bed & Breakfast	E8
22	Love Fashion Hotel	D5
23	Mimpi Bungalows	D7
24	Poppies Bali	D7
25	Puri Agung Homestay	D7
26	Sari Beach Hotel	B3
27	Seaside Villas	B2
28	Sri Beach Inn	C3
29	Stones	C5
30	Suji Bungalow	D7
31	Un's Hotel	C5

⊗ Eating
32	Ajeg Warung	C8
33	Balcony	C5
34	Balé Udang	F2
35	Bemo Corner Coffee Shop	E7
36	Boardriders Café	D4
37	Fat Chow	C6
38	Gourmet Sate House	E4
39	Indo-National	C3
40	Kopi Pot	D6
41	Kuta Market	E8
42	Kuta Night Market	E8
43	Made's Warung	D7
44	Mozarella	B2
45	Poppies Restaurant	D7
46	Saleko	C1
47	Stakz Bar & Grill	D6
48	Take	D4
49	Warung Asia	B1
50	Warung Murah	B1
51	Warung Yogya	C3
52	Zanzibar	A1

⊖ Drinking & Nightlife
53	Apache Reggae Bar	D6
54	Bounty	D7
55	Capil Beach Bar	A1
56	Cocoon	A1
57	Engine Room	D6
58	Jenja	C1
59	Sky Garden Lounge	D6
60	Twice Bar	D6
61	Velvet	C6

⊚ Shopping
62	Beachwalk	C6
63	Carrefour	G5
64	Freedom Surfshop	C5
65	Istana Kuta Galleria	F5
66	Luke Studer	E3
67	Mega Shop	C1
68	Next Generation Board Bags	C5
69	Rip Curl	D6
70	Sriwijaya	B1
71	Summervan	C1
72	Surfer Girl	D7

Putri Bali SPA
(Map p50; ☎ 0361-736852; Jl Raya Seminyak 13; massages from 60,000Rp; ☺ 9am-9pm) The cream bath here has set the hearts of many spa-ophiles aflutter with delight. This lovely spa has very competitive prices and service that is much more professional than the scads of streetside hawkers.

⌖ Tours

A vast range of tours all around Bali, from half-day to multiday excursions, can be booked through your hotel or the plethora of stands plastered with brochures. See p376 for more on tours.

✸ Festivals & Events

There are **surfing contests** throughout the year.

Kuta Karnival FESTIVAL
(www.kutakarnival.com; ☺ Oct) The first Kuta Karnival was held in 2003 as a way of celebrating life after the tragedy of 2002. It's a beach party on the big beach in Kuta consisting of games, art, competitions, surfing and much more, and is held over five days. It usually includes a food festival.

🛏 Sleeping

Kuta, Legian and Tuban have hundreds of places to stay. Tuban and Legian have mostly midrange and top-end hotels – the best places to find budget accommodation are Kuta and southern Legian. Almost every hotel in any price range has air-con and a pool. Dozens of new generic midrange chain hotels are appearing across the area. Many are very inconveniently located (see the boxed text, p359).

Any place west of Jl Legian won't be more than a 10-minute walk to the beach.

🛏 Tuban

There is a string of large hotels along the sometimes-non-existent Tuban Beach. These places are popular with groups; many have extensive activities geared to children.

Patra Jasa Bali Resort & Villas   RESORT $$
(Map p57; ☏ 0361-935 1161; www.thepatrabali. com; Jl Ir H Juanda; r US$80-200; ❋ 🛜 ❄) At the far south end of Tuban near Kuta Reef Beach, this low-key resort is very quiet yet close to all the action thanks to the beach walk. The spacious grounds have two pools and sprawling gardens. The 228 rooms have a standard charm; the villas have nice sea views from their terraces.

🛏 Kuta

Wandering the *gang* looking for a cheap room is a rite of passage for many. Small and family-run options are still numerous even as chains crowd in. Some of the hotels along Jl Legian are of the type that assume men booking a single actually aspire to a double.

ON THE BEACH

Note that hotels on Jl Pantai Kuta are separated from the beach by a busy main road south of Jl Melasti.

Stones   RESORT $$$
(Map p50; ☏ 0361-300 5888; www.stoneshotel bali.com; Jl Pantai Kuta; r from US$160; ❋ 🛜 ❄) Looming across the road from Kuta Beach, this vast new resort boasts a huge pool and nearly 300 rooms in five-storey blocks. The design is hip and contemporary and high-tech features such as huge HD TVs abound. It's one of the growing number of new mega-hotels along this strip; it's affiliated with Marriott.

CENTRAL KUTA

Good streets to shop for budget accommodation include: Gang Sorga, Gang Bedugul and Jl Lebak Bene.

★Hotel Ayu Lili Garden   HOTEL $
(Map p50; ☏ 0361-750557; ayuliligardenhotel@ yahoo.com; off Jl Lebak Bene; r with fan/air-con from 150,000/250,000Rp; ❋ ❄) In a *relatively* quiet area near the beach this vintage family-run hotel has 22 bungalow-style rooms. Standards are high and for more dosh you can add amenities such as a fridge.

Mimpi Bungalows   HOTEL $
(Map p50; ☏ 0361-751848; kumimpi@yahoo. com.sg; Gang Sorga; r 250,000-500,000Rp; ❋ 🛜 ❄) The cheapest of the 12 bungalow-style rooms here are the best value (and are fan only). Private gardens boast orchids and shade, and the pool is a good size.

Kuta Bed & Breakfast   GUESTHOUSE $
(Map p50; ☏ 0821 4538 9646; www.hanafi.net; Jl Pantai Kuta 77; r from 250,000Rp; ❋ 🛜) There are nine comfortable rooms in this spanking new guesthouse right across from Bemo Corner. It's got all the basics and is a 10-minute walk from the beach and a 10-minute ride from the airport.

Suji Bungalow   HOTEL $
(Map p50; ☏ 0361-765804; www.sujibglw. com; off Poppies Gang I; with fan/air-con from 250,000/380,000Rp; ❋ @ 🛜 ❄) This cheery place offers a choice of 47 bungalows and rooms in two-storey blocks set in a spacious, quiet garden around a pool (which has a slide into the kiddie area). The verandahs and terraces are good for relaxing. Not all rooms have wi-fi.

Bendesa   HOTEL $
(Map p50; ☏ 0361-754366; www.bendesa accommodation.com; off Poppies Gang II; r US$15-40; ❋ 🛜 ❄) The 42 rooms here are in a three-storey block overlooking a pleasant-enough pool area. The location somehow manages to be quiet amid the greater hubbub. The cheapest rooms – all clean – have cold water (some with bathtubs) and fan. Wi-fi is available in some rooms only.

Puri Agung Homestay   GUESTHOUSE $
(Map p50; ☏ 0361-750054; off Gang Bedugul; r with fan/air-con from 120,000/200,000Rp; ❋) Hungover travellers will appreciate the 12 dark, cold-water-only rooms at this attractive little

KUTA: WHERE BALI TOURISM BEGAN

Mads Lange, a Danish copra trader and 19th-century adventurer, set up a successful trading enterprise near modern-day Kuta in 1839. He mediated profitably between local rajahs (lords or princes) and the Dutch, who were encroaching from the north. His business soured in the 1850s and he died suddenly, just as he was about to return to Denmark. It's thought that his death may have been the result of poisoning by locals jealous of his wealth. His restored **tomb** (Map p57; Jl Tuan Langa) is at the site where he used to live in a quiet, tree-shaded area by the river. Lange bred Dalmatians and today locals assume that any dog with a hint of black and white has some of this blood.

Beach tourism got its start in Bali when Bob and Louise Koke – a globetrotting couple from the US – opened a small guesthouse on virtually deserted Kuta Beach in the 1930s. The guests, mostly from Europe and the US, were housed in thatched bungalows built in an idealised Balinese style. In a prescient move, Bob taught the locals to surf, something he'd learned in Hawaii.

Kuta really began to change in the late 1960s when it became a stop on the hippie trail between Australia and Europe. By the early 1970s it had relaxed losmen (small Balinese hotels) in pretty gardens, friendly places to eat, vendors peddling magic mushrooms and a delightfully laid-back atmosphere. Enterprising Balinese seized the opportunity to profit from the tourists and surfers, often in partnership with foreigners seeking a pretext to stay longer.

Legian, the village to the north, sprang up as an alternative to Kuta in the mid-1970s. At first it was a totally separate development, but these days you can't tell where one ends and the other begins.

place that features a tiny grotto-like garden. Nonvampires can find more light on the top floor.

Kayun Hostel Downtown　　HOSTEL $
(Map p50; ☑0361-758442; www.kayun-downtown.com; Jl Legian; dm from 190,000Rp; ❉✿❆) This new hostel has a real sense of style, which might go unnoticed due to its proximity to Kuta's most notorious clubs. Dorm rooms have from four to 20 beds. There's a small plunge pool and breakfast is included.

★**Un's Hotel**　　HOTEL $$
(Map p50; ☑0361-757409; www.unshotel.com; Jl Benesari; r US$33-80; ❉✿❆) A hidden entrance sets the tone for the secluded feel of Un's. It's a two-storey place with bougainvillea spilling over the pool-facing balconies. The 30 spacious rooms in a pair of blocks (the southern one is quieter) feature antiques, comfy cane loungers and open-air bathrooms. Cheaper rooms are fan only.

★**Poppies Bali**　　HOTEL $$
(Map p50; ☑0361-751059; www.poppiesbali.com; Poppies Gang I; r US$85-120; ❉@✿❆) This Kuta institution has a lush, green setting for its 20 thatch-roofed cottages with outdoor sunken baths. Bed choices include kings and twins. The pool is surrounded by stone sculptures and water fountains in a garden that almost makes you forget you are in the heart of Kuta.

Love Fashion Hotel　　HOTEL $$
(Map p50; ☑0361-849 6688; www.lovefhotels.com; Jl Legian 121; r from US$100; ❉✿❆) This gaudy new 202-room hotel in the heart of the Kuta strip (they claim Legian, but come on!) is an offshoot of the Fashiontv cable channel that's often shown in clubs. The design is suitably over-the-top, with mirrors, lighting effects designed to make you feel like a model and lurid sculptures everywhere. There's a rooftop spa bath and bar.

Legian

ON THE BEACH

North of Jl Melasti part of the beach road is protected by gates that exclude almost all vehicle traffic. Hotels here have what is in effect a quiet, paved beachfront promenade.

Sari Beach Hotel　　HOTEL $$
(Map p50; ☑0361-751635; www.saribeachinn.com; off Jl Padma Utara; r from US$60; ❉✿❆) Follow your ears down a long *gang* to the roar of the surf at this good-value beachside hotel that defines mellow. The 21 rooms have

patios and the best have big soaking tubs. Grassy grounds boast many little statues and water features. At times there is a three-night minimum.

Bali Mandira Beach Resort HOTEL $$$
(Map p50; ☑ 0361-751381; www.balimandira.com; Jl Padma 2; r from US$150; ❋ ⎙ ☎) Gardens filled with bird-of-paradise flowers set the tone at this 191-room, full-service resort. Cottages have newly-styled interiors, and the bathrooms are partly open air. A dramatic pool at the peak of a stone ziggurat (which houses a spa) offers sweeping ocean views, as does the cafe.

Seaside Villas VILLA $$$
(Map p50; ☑ 0361-737138; www.seasidebali.com; 18 Jl Pantai Arjuna; US$150-400; ❋ ⎙ ☎) Tucked into a popular stretch of sand just south of ever-so-happening Double Six Beach are these three villas set in lush gardens. There's a vague Santa Fe motif in the one- to three-bedroom units and the overall atmosphere is surprisingly intimate given the location. Pass through a double doorway, past a fountain and parked cars and you're on the beach.

CENTRAL LEGIAN
Island HOTEL $
(Map p50; ☑ 0361-762722; www.theislandhotelbali.com; Gang Abdi; dm from US$20, r from US$50; ❋ @ ⎙ ☎) A real find, literally. Hidden in the attractive maze of tiny lanes west of Jl Legian, this stylish hotel lies at the confluence of Gang 19, 21 and Abdi. It has a deluxe dorm room with eight beds.

Sri Beach Inn GUESTHOUSE $
(Map p50; ☑ 0361-755897; Gang Legian Tewngah; r with fan/air-con from 200,000/350,000Rp; ❋) Follow a series of paths into the heart of old Legian; when you hear the rustle of palms overhead, you're close to this guesthouse in a garden with five rooms. More money gets you hot water, air-con and a fridge. It offers cheap monthly rates.

DOUBLE SIX BEACH
Blue Ocean HOTEL $
(Map p50; ☑ 0361-730289; off Jl Pantai Arjuna; r with fan/air-con from 250,000/400,000Rp; ❋ ☎) Ideally located almost on the beach, the Blue Ocean is a basic place with hot water and pleasant outdoor bathrooms. Many of the 25 rooms have kitchens and there's action nearby day and night.

Hotel Kumala Pantai HOTEL $$
(Map p50; ☑ 0361-755500; www.kumalapantai.com; Jl Werkudara; r US$80-160; ❋ @ ⎙ ☎) The 173 rooms are large, with marble bathrooms featuring separate shower and tub. The three-storey blocks are set in very lush grounds across from popular Double Six Beach. Not all rooms have wi-fi.

Double-Six RESORT $$$
(Map p50; ☑ 0361-730466; www.double-six.com; 66 Double Six Beach; r from US$400; ❋ ⎙ ☎) Built on the site of the legendary club of the same name, this luxurious new high-tech resort features large rooms and suites, most with views of the eponymous beach. Amenities abound, including 24-hour butler service. The 120m pool is one of the largest in Bali. Planned amenities include a vast rooftop bar.

✖ Eating

There's a profusion of places to eat around Kuta and Legian. Tourist cafes with their cheap menus of Indonesian standards, sandwiches and pizza are ubiquitous. Look closely and you'll find genuine Balinese warung tucked in amid it all.

If you're looking for the laid-back scene of a classic travellers' cafe, wander the *gang* and look for the crowds. For quick snacks and 4am beers, Circle K convenience stores are everywhere and are open 24 hours.

Beware of the big-box restaurants out on Jl Sunset. Heavily promoted, they suffer from traffic noise and are aimed squarely at groups who go where the bus goes.

✖ Tuban

Tuban has oodles of chains and fast-food joints. The beachfront hotels all have restaurants or cafes, which are often good for nonguests to enjoy a snack or a sunset drink.

The south end of Jl Raya Kuta near the airport road is lined with good local warungs and cafes. Browse around and pick a favourite.

★ Pisgor SNACKS $
(Map p57; Jl Dewi Sartika; treats from 1000Rp; ☺ 10am-10pm) All sorts of goodness emerges from the ever-bubbling deep-fryers at this narrow storefront near the airport. The *piseng goreng* (fried bananas) are not to be missed and you can enjoy more esoteric fare such as *ote-ote* (vegetable cakes). Get a

mixed bag and munch away with raw chillies for accent.

Warung Nikmat
INDONESIAN $

(Map p57; ☎0361-764678; Jl Banjar Sari; meals 15,000-30,000Rp; ☺8am-9pm) This Javanese favourite is known for its array of authentic Indonesian dishes, including beef rendang, *perkedel* (fried corn cakes), prawn cakes, *sop buntut* (oxtail soup) and various curries and vegetable dishes. Get there before 2pm for the best selection.

Pantai
SEAFOOD $$

(Map p57; ☎0361-753196; Jl Wana Segara; meals 50,000-150,000Rp; ☺8am-10pm) It's location, location, location at this beachside bar and grill. The food is stock tourist (seafood, Indo classics, pasta etc) but the setting overlooking the ocean is idyllic. Each year it gets a bit more stylish and upscale but it still avoids pretence. Follow the beach path south past the big Ramada Bintang Bali resort.

Kafe Batan Waru
INDONESIAN $$

(Map p57; ☎0361-897 8074; Jl Kartika Plaza, Lippo Mall; meals 50,000-150,000Rp; ☺9am-11pm) The Tuban branch of the noted Ubud restaurant is a slicked-up version of a warung, albeit with excellent and creative Asian and local fare. There's also good coffee, baked goods and kid-friendly items. It's got a new high-profile spot in front of the glam new Lippo Mall.

B Couple Bar n' Grill
SEAFOOD $$

(Map p57; ☎0361-761414; Jl Kartika Plaza; meals 60,000-200,000Rp; ☺24hr) A vibrant mix of upscale local and international tourists tuck into Jimbaran-style grilled seafood at this slick operation. Pool tables, TV sports and live music add to the din while flames flare in the open kitchens.

✗ Kuta

Beach vendors are pretty much limited to drinks. Otherwise you'll find mostly surfer fare (pizzas, burgers, Indo classics) at myriad spots along the narrow streets.

CENTRAL KUTA

★ Ajeg Warung
BALINESE $

(Map p50; ☎0822 3777 6766; Kuta Beach; meals from 15,000Rp; ☺8am-8pm) This simple stall with shady tables is right on Kuta Beach. It dishes up some of the freshest local fare you'll find. Tops is a bowl of spicy *garang asem,* a tamarind-based soup with chicken or pork and many traditional seasonings. Enter the beach where Jl Pantai Kuta turns north and walk south 100m along the beach path.

Bemo Corner Coffee Shop
CAFE $

(Map p50; ☎0361-755305; Jl Pantai Kuta 10A; mains from 40,000Rp; ☺8am-10pm) An attractive oasis just off the madness of Jl Legian, this sweet little open-fronted cafe serves up excellent coffee drinks, smoothies and casual fare such as sandwiches and delicious baked goods.

Kuta Night Market
INDONESIAN $

(Map p50; Jl Blambangan; meals 15,000-25,000Rp; ☺6pm-midnight) This enclave of stalls and plastic chairs bustles with locals and tourism workers chowing down on hot-off-the-wok treats, grilled goods and other fresh foods.

Kuta Market
MARKET $

(Map p50; Jl Raya Kuta; ☺6am-4pm) Not big but its popularity ensures constant turnover. Look for some of Bali's unusual fruits here, such as the mangosteen.

GETTING AWAY FROM IT ALL

Dodging cars, motorcycles, touts, dogs and dodgy footpaths can make walking through Tuban, Kuta and Legian seem like anything but a holiday. It's intense and can be stressful. You may soon be longing for uncrowded places where you hear little more than the rustling of palm fronds and the call of birds.

Think you need to book a trip out of town? Well, think again. You can escape to the country without leaving the area. Swathes of undeveloped land and simple residential areas where locals live often hide behind the commercial strips.

In Legian, take any of the narrow *gang* (alleys) into the area bounded by Jl Legian, Jl Padma, Jl Padma Utara and Jl Pura Bagus Taruna and soon you'll be on narrow paths that go past local houses and the occasional simple warung or shop. Wander at random and enjoy the silence accented by, yes, the sound of palm fronds and birds.

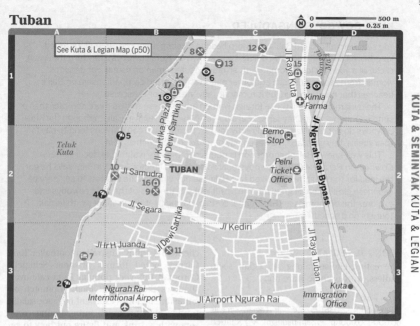

Tuban

Tuban

◎ Sights

1 Amazone	B1
2 Kuta Reef Beach	A3
3 Mads Lange Tomb	D1
4 Segara Beach	A2
5 Tuban Beach	B2
6 Waterbom Park	C1

⊜ Sleeping

7 Patra Jasa Bali Resort & Villas	A3

⊗ Eating

8 B Couple Bar n' Grill	B1
9 Kafe Batan Waru	B2
10 Pantai	B2
11 Pisgor	B3
12 Warung Nikmat	C1

⊖ Drinking & Nightlife

13 DeeJay Cafe	C1

⊜ Shopping

14 Discovery Mall	B1
15 Joger	C1
16 Lippo Mall Kuta	B2
17 Periplus Bookshop	B1

Poppies Restaurant INTERNATIONAL **$$**
(Map p50; ☎ 0361-751059; www.poppiesbali. com; Poppies Gang I; mains 65,000-120,000Rp; ⊙8am-11pm) Poppies was one of the first restaurants to be established in Kuta (Poppies Gang I is even named after it). It is popular for its lush garden setting which feels slightly mysterious in a romantic way. The menu is upmarket Western, Thai and Balinese. The *rijstaffel* (selection of Indonesian dishes served with rice) and seafood are popular.

Made's Warung INDONESIAN **$$**
(Map p50; ☎ 0361-755297; www.madeswarung. com; Jl Pantai Kuta; meals from 40,000Rp; ⊙8am-11pm) Made's was the original tourist warung in Kuta and its Westernised Indonesian menu has been much copied. Classic dishes such as *nasi campur* (rice served with a variety of side dishes) are served in an open-fronted setting that harks back to when Kuta's tourist hot spots were lit by gas lantern.

KUTA COWBOYS UNSADDLED

You see them all around Bali's southern beaches: young men who are buff, tattooed, long-haired and gregariously courtly. Long known as 'Kuta cowboys', they turn the Asian cliché of a younger local woman with an older Western man on its ear. For decades women from Japan, Australia and other nations have found companionship on Bali's beaches that meets a need, be it romantic, adventurous or otherwise.

The dynamic between these foreign women and Balinese men is more complex than a simple exchange of money for sexual services (which is illegal in Bali): although the Kuta cowboys do not receive money directly for sex, their female companions tend to pay for their meals, buy gifts, and may even pay other expenses such as rent.

This well-known Bali phenomenon is detailed in the very watchable documentary *Cowboys in Paradise* (www.cowboysinparadise.com). Director Amit Virmani says he got the idea for the film after he talked to a Balinese boy who said he wanted 'to sex-service Japanese girls' when he grew up. The result looks at the lives of the Kuta cowboys and explores the economics and emotional costs of having fleeting dalliances with female tourists on a schedule.

ALONG JL LEGIAN

The eating choices along Jl Legian seem endless; worthy choices are not.

Kopi Pot CAFE **$$**
(Map p50; ☑ 0361-752614; Jl Legian; meals 60,000-150,000Rp; ☺ 8am-midnight; ☏) Shaded by trees, Kopi Pot is a favourite, popular for its coffees, milkshakes and myriad desserts. The multilevel, open-air dining area sits back from noxious Jl Legian.

Boardriders Café CAFE **$$**
(Map p50; ☑ 0361-761838; Jl Legian 362; mains from 55,000Rp; ☺ 8am-10pm; ☏) Peruse surfer mags at this hip cafe that's part of a huge Rip Curl surf shop. Comfort food is the norm, look for shakes, burgers, fish and chips, a whole plethora of baked goods and plenty of juices and smoothies.

ON & AROUND POPPIES GANG II

★**Fat Chow** ASIAN **$$**
(Map p50; ☑ 0361-753516; www.fatchow bali.com; Poppies Gang II; mains from 45,000Rp; ☺ 10am-10pm) A stylish, modern take on the traditional open-fronted cafe, Fat Chow serves up Chinese and Asian-accented fare at long picnic tables, small tables and at loungers. The food is creative with lots of sharing-friendly options. Among the favourites: crunchy Asian salad, pork buns, Tokyo prawns and the Oriental burger.

Stakz Bar & Grill INTERNATIONAL **$$**
(Map p50; ☑ 0361-762129; www.stakzbarand grill.com; Jl Benesari; mains 40,000-80,000Rp; ☺ 8am-11pm) The notorious nature of the clientele (badboy Australian footballer Todd Carney, noted former prisoner Schapelle Corby) at this very popular Kuta cafe overshadows the excellent food. Top-notch organic fare includes excellent burgers, salads, sandwiches and much more. Lounge on a sofa with a drink and figure out how to get *your* name in the press.

Balcony INTERNATIONAL **$$**
(Map p50; ☑ 0361-757409; Jl Benesari 16; meals 50,000-150,000Rp; ☺ 6am-11pm) The Balcony has a breezy tropical design and sits above the din of Jl Benesari below. Get ready for the day with a long breakfast menu. At night it's pasta, grilled meats and a few Indo classics. It's all nicely done and the perfect place for an impromptu date-night.

EAST OF JL LEGIAN

★**Take** JAPANESE **$$**
(Map p50; ☑ 0361-759745; Jl Patih Jelantik; meals 70,000-300,000Rp; ☺ 11am-11pm) Flee Bali for a relaxed version of Tokyo just by ducking under the traditional fabric shield over the doorway at this ever-expanding restaurant. Hyper-fresh sushi, sashimi and more are prepared under the fanatical eyes of a team of chefs behind a long counter. The chef is a stalwart at the Jimbaran fish market in the early hours.

✖ Legian

Along the streets of Legian, the ho-hum greatly outnumber the good, so browse before choosing.

Bali & Lombok's Best Beaches

Bali and Lombok are ringed by beaches, with sand from white to black and surf from wild to tame. They draw visitors in droves for sunbathing, yoga, running, surfing, snorkelling, diving and good times aplenty. With so many to chose from, you'll find one – or several – for any mood.

➡ **Beaches**
➡ **Surfing**
➡ **Diving**
➡ **Marine Life**

Above: Sunset at Kuta Beach (p48), Bali

1. Kuta Beach (p274), Lombok **2.** Padang Padang Beach (p102)
3. Echo Beach (p92) **4.** Gili Trawangan (p283)

PAUL KENNEDY / GETTY IMAGES ©

Beaches

There are so many great beaches on Bali and Lombok that it's best to just categorise them by region. Within each of these five areas, you'll find many different patches of sand to enjoy.

Tuban to Echo Beach

Stretching some 12km from just north of the airport all the way northwest to Pererenan Beach (p93), this is the beach that made Bali famous. This multifaceted playground has multiple personalities, including surfer, hip, family, lonely, boozy and more.

Bukit Beaches

The cliffs on the west coast of the Bukit Peninsula (p96) often shelter little coves of beautiful white sand, like that found at Balangan, Bingin and Padang Padang. It can be hard to reach these sands (and their neighbours) but the rewards include incredible views of the surf breaks, nameless little bamboo warungs with Bintang and sublimely beautiful water.

East Coast Beaches

A vast crescent of black sand that started up the volcanic slopes of Gunung Agung sweeps from north of Sanur to the east side of the island (p179). Some beaches here are empty, others have surfers, while still more have temples and slices of local Bali life.

South Lombok Beaches

The best Kuta Beach isn't on Bali. Along Lombok's south coast (p273) running east and west from *that* Kuta, you'll discover a dozen gorgeous bays ringed with white sand and, often, not much else.

Gili Beaches

The Gili Islands (p281) – Trawangan, Meno and Air – are each ringed by beautiful sands. Walk the big loop, sample at the beach buffets, try some offshore snorkelling and just enjoy.

Surfing

Surfing is the top reason many come to Bali and surf culture is part of the island's fabric. On Lombok, the lifestyle is more low key but the breaks are not.

Kuta Beach

Kuta Beach (p48), Bali's original surf beach, is still a winner. You can't help but be drawn to this vast sweep of sand, where surfers of all stripes are drawn to the nonstop breaks right offshore. And you can easily learn to surf here. Schools abound and there are classes all day long.

Echo Beach

Echo Beach (p92) has wild waves and plenty of spectators. It's really an extension of equally popular Batu Bolong. Both have cafes that are always brimming with a good mix of locals and visitors.

Ulu Watu

Ulu Watu (p103) is where you'll find Bali's most legendary surfing. It's really the climax of a string of breaks that march down the west coast of the Bukit Peninsula. The conditions are challenging and you can spend days just sussing out the scene.

Nusa Lembongan

Nusa Lembongan (p126) off Bali is an excellent place for days of riding. Breaks – accessed by boat – are offshore, past the reefs. And there are cheap places to stay with good views of the action, so you can pick your moment to plunge in.

Tanjung Desert

Tanjung Desert (Desert Point; p261) on Lombok wins plaudits, and that's not just from surfers congratulating themselves for trekking out to this remote spot. Fickle (its season is a short one: May to September), this break is tough for even the most experienced and a reward for all.

1. Surfer, Ulu Watu (p103) **2.** Surfer, Bukit Peninsula (p96)
3. Carrying surfboards along Kuta Beach (48), Bali

Scuba diver, Nusa Penida (p133) **2.** Coral off Pulau Menjangan (p241) A diver examines the *Liberty* shipwreck at Tulamben (p210)

Diving

The islands have great diving and a whole bunch of great dive shops to support your explorations. From simple wall dives to challenging open-water observations of massive creatures, you'll find something here to fit your skills and desires.

Tulamben

Tulamben (p210) seems like a mere village along the coast road of east Bali – until you notice all the dive shops. The big attraction here lies right offshore: an old ship, the *Liberty*, sunk during WWII. You can dive and snorkel the wreck from right offshore.

Gili Trawangan

Gili Trawangan is a fabulous centre for diving and snorkelling (p284). Great places to explore the depths abound in the waters around all three Gilis. Freediving is popular here, you can snorkel right off the beaches and there are reefs in all directions.

Nusa Penida

Seldom-visited Nusa Penida (p133) is surrounded by what could be an underwater theme park. Conditions can be challenging – the services of an excellent dive shop are essential – but you might see huge, placid sunfish and manta rays.

Nusa Lembongan

Nusa Lembongan (p126) is a good base for exploring dozens of sites here, in the surrounding mangroves and at the two neighbouring islands. With the guidance of a good operator, you can drift dive between the latter and Lembongan.

Pulau Menjangan

Pulau Menjangan (p241) is Bali's best-known dive and snorkel area and has a dozen superb dive sites. The diving is excellent – iconic tropical fish, soft corals, great visibility (usually), caves and a spectacular drop-off. It's best visited as part of an overnight jaunt to Pemuteran.

Green sea turt

Marine Life

There is a rich variety of coral, seaweed, fish and other marine life in the coastal waters off the islands; in fact Indonesia's entire marine territory was declared a manta ray sanctuary in 2014. Much of the marine life can be appreciated by snorkellers, but you're only likely to see the larger marine animals while diving.

Dolphins

Dolphins can be found right around the islands and have been made into an attraction off Lovina (p233). But you're just as likely to see schools of dolphins if you take a fast boat between Bali and the Gilis.

Sharks

Sharks are always dramatic and there are very occasional reports of large ones, including great whites, throughout the region, although they are not considered a massive threat. In the Gilis, reef sharks are easily spotted at Shark Point (p287).

Sea Turtles

Sea turtles (p354) are common but greatly endangered. Long considered a delicacy by the Balinese, it is a constant struggle by environmentalists to protect them from poachers. Still, you can find them, especially in the Gilis.

Fish of All Kinds

Smaller fish and corals can be found at a plethora of spots around the islands. Everybody's favourite first stop is Bali's Menjangan (p241). Fish as large as whale sharks have been reported, but what thrills scores daily are the coloured beauty of an array of corals, sponges, lacy sea fans and much more. Starfish abound and you'll easily spot clownfish and other polychromatic characters.

Warung Murah   INDONESIAN $

(Map p50; Jl Arjuna; meals from 30,000Rp; ⊙9am-5pm) Lunch goes swimmingly at this authentic warung specialising in seafood. An array of grilled fish awaits; if you prefer fowl over fin, the *sate ayam* (chicken satay) is succulent *and* a bargain. Hugely popular at lunch; try to arrive right before noon.

Warung Asia   ASIAN $

(Map p50; ☑0361-742 0202; Jl Werkudara; meals from 35,000Rp; ⊙8am-10pm; 🤶) This very popular cafe serving Asian fare has a great new location on a large leafy courtyard. The food and coffee drinks are as good as ever and now you can enjoy fresh gelato and more.

Warung Yogya   INDONESIAN $

(Map p50; ☑0361-750835; Jl Padma Utara; mains from 20,000Rp; ⊙8am-10pm) Hidden in the heart of Legian, this simple warung is spotless and has a bit of mod style. It serves up hearty portions of local food for prices that would almost tempt a local. Try the *gado gado* (mixed vegetables with peanut sauce).

Saleko   INDONESIAN $

(Map p50; Jl Nakula 4; meals from 15,000Rp; ⊙8am-10pm) Just off the madness of Jl Legian, this modest open-front place draws the discerning for its simple Sumatran fare. Spicy grilled chicken and fish dare you to ladle on the volcanic sambal. Saleko is a perfect spot to start trying Indonesian fare that has not been de-spiced for timid tourist palates.

Gourmet Sate House   INDONESIAN $$

(Map p50; ☑0361-553 1380; Jl Dewi Sri 101; mains from 40,000Rp; ⊙11am-11pm) Heaven for sate fans or anyone else who likes barbecued meats and seafoods. All manner of cooked treats on a stick are on offer at this huge and popular place east of the centre. There's other Indonesian fare on the menu and some very good desserts.

Balé Udang   INDONESIAN $$

(Mang Engking; Map p50; ☑0361-882 2000; www.baleudang.com; Jl Nakula 88; mains 35,000-150,000Rp; ⊙11am-10pm) Serving the food of Indonesia, this large restaurant is a metaphor for the islands themselves, with various thatched dining pavilions set amid ponds and water features. The long menu focuses on fresh seafood. Service is snappy, but friendly.

Indo-National   SEAFOOD, INTERNATIONAL $$

(Map p50; ☑0361-759883; Jl Padma 17; mains 50,000-100,000Rp; ⊙8am-11pm) This popular restaurant is home away from home for legions of happy fans. Grab a cold one with the rest of the crew. Then order the heaped-up grilled seafood platter.

ON THE BEACH

Various restaurants and cafes face the water along Jl Pantai Arjuna, and there are more along Jl Padma Utara. All are good come sunset.

Mozarella   ITALIAN, SEAFOOD $$

(Map p50; www.mozzarella-resto.com; Maharta Bali Hotel, Jl Padma Utara; meals from 90,000Rp) The best of the beachfront restaurants on Legian's car-free strip, Mozarella serves Italian fare that's more authentic than most. Fresh fish also features; service is rather polished and there are various open-air areas for moonlit dining plus a more sheltered dining room.

Zanzibar   INTERNATIONAL $$

(Map p50; ☑0361-733529; Jl Arjuna; meals from 50,000Rp; ⊙8am-11pm) This popular patio fronts a busy strip at Double Six Beach. Sunset is prime time; the best views of the pink and orange hues are from the tables on the 2nd-floor terrace. Dishes include the nasi family and the burger bunch. If it's crowded, the many nearby competitors will also do just fine.

🍷 Drinking & Nightlife

Sunset on the beach around 6pm is the big attraction, perhaps while enjoying a drink at a cafe with a sea view or with a beer vendor on the beach. Later on, the legendary nightlife action heats up. Many ragers spend their early evening at one of the hipster joints in Seminyak before working their way south to oblivion.

It won't take you long to find out which places are the venues of the moment. The stylish clubs of Seminyak are popular with gay and straight crowds, but in general you'll find a mixed crowd anywhere in Kuta and Legian.

Check out the free mag *The Beat* (www.beatmag.com) for good club listings and other 'what's on' news.

Tuban

DeeJay Cafe
CLUB

(Map p57; ☑0361-758880; Jl Kartika Plaza 8X, Kuta Station Hotel; ☺midnight-9am) The choice for closing out the night (or starting out the day). House DJs play tribal, underground, progressive, trance, electro and more. Beware of posers who set their alarms for 5am and arrive all fresh.

Kuta

Jl Legian is lined with interchangeable bars with bar stools moulded to the butts of hard-drinking regulars. Expect come-ons from pimps, Viagra sellers and lots of cries of 'we got bloody cold beer, mate!'

Sky Garden Lounge
BAR, CLUB

(Map p50; www.skygardenbali.com; Jl Legian 61; ☺24hr) This multilevel palace of flash flirts with height restrictions from its rooftop bar where all of Kuta twinkles around you. Look for top DJs, a ground-level cafe and paparazzi-wannabes. Munchers can enjoy a long menu of bar snacks and meals, which most people pair with shots. Roam from floor to floor of this vertical playpen.

Apache Reggae Bar
BAR

(Map p50; Jl Legian 146; ☺11pm-4am) One of the rowdier spots, Apache jams in locals and visitors, many of whom are on the make. The music is loud, but that pounding you feel the next day is from the free-flowing *arak* (distilled palm and cane alcohol) served in huge plastic jugs.

DON'T MISS

SUNSET DRINKS IN KUTA & LEGIAN

Bali sunsets regularly explode in stunning displays of reds, oranges and purples. Sipping a cold one while watching this free show to the beat of the surf is the top activity at 6pm. Genial local guys offer plastic chairs on the sand and cheap, cold Bintang (20,000Rp).

In Kuta, head to the car-free south end of the beach; in Legian, the best place is the strip of beach that starts north of Jl Padma and runs to the south end of Jl Pantai Arjuna.

Twice Bar
BAR

(Map p50; Poppies Gang II; ☺7pm-2am) Kuta's best effort at an indie rock club, with all the grungy – and sweaty – feel you could hope for.

Bounty
CLUB

(Map p50; www.bountydiscotheque.com; Jl Legian; ☺8pm-4am) Set on a faux sailing boat amid a mini-mall of food and drink, the Bounty is a vast open-air disco that humps, thumps and pumps all night. Get down on the poop deck to hip-hop, techno, house and anything else the DJs come up with. Foam parties, go-go dancers, drag shows and cheap shots add to the rowdiness.

Velvet
BAR

(Map p50; ☑0361-2658 1405; www.vhbali.com; Jl Pantai Kuta, Beachwalk, Level 3; ☺11am-late) The sunset views can't be beat at this large terrace bar and cafe at the beach end of the Beachwalk mall. On many nights the venue morphs into a club after 10pm.

Engine Room
CLUB

(Map p50; Jl Legian; ☺8pm-late) Open to the street, this lurid club features go-go dancers in cages as a come-on. As the evening progresses almost everyone dances and clothing gets shed. It's a wild party and a favourite subject for Australian journalists decrying the downfall of the nation's youth.

Legian & Double Six Beach

Most of Legian's bars are smaller and appeal to a more sedate crowd than those in Kuta. The very notable exception is the area at the end of Jl Arjuna/Jl Double Six where there are cafes and clubs. A string of beach bars runs north from here on the Seminyak beachwalk.

Cocoon
CLUB

(Map p50; www.cocoon-beach.com; Jl Arjuna; ☺10am-late) A huge pool with a view of Double Six Beach anchors this sort of high-concept club (alcohol-branded singlets not allowed!), which has parties and events around the clock. Beds, loungers and VIP areas surround the pool; at night DJs spin theme nights.

Capil Beach Bar
CAFE

(Map p50; Double Six Beach; ☺9am-9pm) The non-glitzy alternative to the new Double-Six resort; this barely there beach bar has beanbags and loungers on the sand plus simple snacks and meals on offer. Cheap Bintang too (25,000Rp).

Jenja CLUB
(Map p50; ☎0361-882 7711; www.jenjabali.com; TS Suites, Jl Nakula 18; ⊙6pm-2am) A very slick, high-concept nightclub in the new TS Suites hotel. Spread over several levels, DJs rev it up with disco, R&B, funk, soul and more. The crowd is a mix of well-healed locals and expats. The restaurant serves upscale fare good for sharing.

🛍 Shopping

Kuta has a vast concentration of cheap, tawdry shops, as well as huge, flashy surf-gear emporiums. As you head north along Jl Legian, the quality of the shops improves and you start finding cute little boutiques, especially near Jl Arjuna (which has wholesale fabric, clothing and craft stores, giving it a bazaar feel). Continue into Seminyak for absolutely fabulous shopping.

Large malls are also making inroads. In Tuban, the Discovery Mall has a new rival in the flashy Lippo Mall. The Beachwalk complex is a huge bit of gloss on Jl Pantai Kuta. Kuta Sq stumbles along, in need of new energy.

Stalls with T-shirts, souvenirs, beachwear and gaudy junk are virtually everywhere. Bali's top-selling souvenirs for those left at home are penis-shaped bottle openers in a range of colours and sizes.

Beachwear & Surf Shops

A huge range of surf shops sells big-name surf gear – including Mambo, Rip Curl, Billabong and Quiksilver. Local names include Surfer Girl and Drifter. Most have numerous locations in south Bali.

You'll also find local surf shops with some renowned board shapers ready to make you a custom ride.

★Luke Studer SURFBOARDS
(Map p50; ☎0361-894 7425; www.studersurfboards.com; Jl Dewi Sri 7A; ⊙9am-7pm) The legendary board shaper works from this large and glossy shop. It offers shortboards, retro fishes, single fins and classic longboards that you can buy ready-made or custom-built.

Surfer Girl SURF GEAR
(Map p50; www.surfer-girl.com; Jl Legian 138; ⊙9am-10pm) A local legend, the winsome logo says it all about this vast store for girls of all ages. Clothes, gear, bikinis and plenty of other stuff in every shade of bubblegum ever made.

Rip Curl SURF GEAR
(Map p50; ☎0361-754238; www.ripcurl.com; Jl Legian 62; ⊙9am-10pm) Cast that mopey black stuff aside and make a bit of a splash! Bali's largest arm of the surfwear giant has a huge range of beach clothes, waterwear and surfboards.

Freedom Surfshop SURFBOARDS
(Map p50; ☎0361-767736; Jl Benesari 4A; ⊙10am-7pm) Jerry Jejor has been surfing Kuta Beach for over 25 years. His shop is lined with boards that are canvases for his creativity as a surfboard painter. His designs are highly personal and entirely dependent on his artistic temperament.

Next Generation Board Bags SURF GEAR
(Map p50; ☎0813 3700 0523; Jl Benesari; ⊙10am-7pm) Choose from myriad patterns and colours and then watch your bag (from 400,000Rp) get made on the shop floor in two days or less.

Bookshops

Small used-book exchanges can be found scattered along the *gang* and roads, especially the Poppies.

Periplus Bookshop BOOKS
(Map p57; ☎0361-769757; Jl Kartika Plaza, Discovery Mall) Large selection of new books.

Clothing & Fabric

Jl Arjuna makes for an interesting stroll if you're hunting for soft goods such as batik and silk.

Summervan
CLOTHING

(Map p50; ☑ 0361-738226; Jl Arjuna 26; ⊙ 10am-6pm) Groovy beach clothes and accessories with a summer of love bent.

Sriwijaya
TEXTILES

(Map p50; ☑ 0361-733581; Jl Arjuna; ⊙ 10am-6pm) Makes batik and other fabrics to order in many colours.

Mega Shop
CLOTHING

(Map p50; ☑ 0361-857 1456; Jl Arjuna; ⊙ 9am-7pm) An unadorned, old-fashioned shop that bursts with the colours of hundreds of saris. Buy one ready-made or place a custom order.

Malls & Department Stores

Beachwalk
MALL

(Map p50; www.beachwalkbali.com; Jl Pantai Kuta; ⊙ 10am-midnight) This vast open-air mall, hotel and condo development across from Kuta Beach is filled with international chains: from Gap to Starbucks. Water features course amid the generic retail glitz.

Discovery Mall
MALL

(Map p57; ☑ 0361-755522; www.discovery shoppingmall.com; Jl Kartika Plaza; ⊙ 9am-9pm) Swallowing up a significant section of the shoreline, this huge, hulking and popular enclosed Tuban mall is built on the water and filled with shops of every kind, including the large Centro and trendy Sogo department stores.

Istana Kuta Galleria
MALL

(Map p50; Jl Patih Jelantik) An enormous open-air mall that seems like a dud until you find an interesting shop amid the canyon of glass. There is a hardware store in the rear if your needs run towards rope and duct tape.

Carrefour
MALL

(Map p50; ☑ 0361-847 7222; Jl Sunset; ⊙ 9am-10pm) This large outlet of the French discount chain combines lots of small shops (books, computers, bikinis) with one huge hypermarket. It's the place to stock up on staples and there's a large ready-to-eat section and food court as well. The downside, however, is inescapable: it's a mall.

Lippo Mall Kuta
MALL

(Map p57; ☑ 0361-897 8000; www.lippomalls.com; Jl Kartika Plaza; ⊙ 10am-10pm) The latest large mall in south Bali only adds to the traffic chaos on Tuban's under-engineered streets. A huge Matahari department store is joined by scores of international chains, restaurants and a supermarket.

ℹ Information

DANGERS & ANNOYANCES

The streets and *gang* are usually safe but there are many annoyances. Touts offer prostitutes, Viagra and other tawdry diversions. You'll also grow weary of the cloying cries of 'massage?' and other dubious offers. But your biggest irritation will likely be the sclerotic traffic. See p364 for more on safety issues.

EMERGENCY

Police Station (Map p50; ☑ 0361-751598; Jl Raya Kuta; ⊙ 24hr) Ask to speak to the tourist police.

Tourist Police Post (Map p50; ☑ 0361-784 5988; Jl Pantai Kuta; ⊙ 24hr) This is a branch of the main police station in Denpasar. It's right across from the beach; the officers have a gig that is sort of like a Balinese *Baywatch*.

INTERNET ACCESS

The back lanes of Kuta and Legian have numerous internet spots, although speeds and hardware tend to be lethargic. Most hotels and many cafes now have wi-fi.

MEDICAL SERVICES

Kimia Farma (Map p50; ☑ 0361-755622; Jl Pantai Kuta; ⊙ 24hr) Part of a local chain of pharmacies, it's well stocked and carries hard-to-find items, like that antidote for irksome partiers in the morning: earplugs. Also has branches at Tuban (Map p57; ☑ 0361-757483;

KUTA'S FAVOURITE STORE

The mobs out the front look like they're making a run on a bank. Inside it's simply pandemonium. Welcome to **Joger** (Map p57; Jl Raya Kuta; ⊙ 11am-6pm), a Bali retail legend that is the most popular store in the south. No visitor from elsewhere in Indonesia would think of leaving the island without a doe-eyed plastic puppy (4000Rp) or one of the thousands of T-shirts bearing a wry, funny or simply inexplicable phrase (almost all are limited edition). Warning: conditions inside the cramped store are simply insane.

JI Raya Kuta 15; ☺24hr) and Legian (Map p50; JI Legian; ☺24hr).

Legian Medical Clinic (Map p50; ☑0361-758503; JI Benesari; ☺on call 24hr) Has an ambulance and dental service. It's 500,000Rp for a consultation with an English-speaking Balinese doctor. Hotel room visits can be arranged.

MONEY

ATMs can be found everywhere.

Central Kuta Money Exchange (Map p50; ☑0361-762970; JI Raya Kuta; ☺8am-6pm) Trustworthy; deals in numerous currencies. Has many locations, including a Legian branch (Map p50; JI Melasti; ☺8am-10pm) and counters inside some Circle K convenience stores.

POST

Postal agencies that can send mail are common.

Main Post Office (Map p50; JI Selamet; ☺7am-2pm Mon-Thu, 7-11am Fri, 7am-1pm Sat) On a little road east of JI Raya Kuta, this small and efficient post office is well practised in shipping large packages.

TOURIST INFORMATION

There's no useful official tourist office. Places that advertise themselves as 'tourist information centres' are usually commercial travel agents, or worse: time-share condo sales operations.

ⓘ Getting There & Away

BEMO

Bemos (minibuses) regularly travel between Kuta and the Tegal terminal in Denpasar – the fare should be 8000Rp. The route goes from JI Raya Kuta near JI Pantai Kuta, looping past the beach, then on JI Melasti and back past Bemo Corner for the trip back to Denpasar.

BUS

For public buses to anywhere in Bali, you'll have to go to the appropriate terminal in Denpasar first. Tourist shuttles are widely advertised on back streets.

Perama (Map p50; ☑0361-751551; www. peramatour.com; JI Legian 39; ☺7am-10pm) The main tourist shuttle-bus operation in town; may do hotel pick-ups and drop-offs for an extra 10,000Rp (confirm this with the staff when making arrangements). It usually has at least one bus a day to its destinations, which include Lovina (100,000Rp, 4½ hours), Padangbai (60,000Rp, three hours) and Ubud (50,000Rp, 1½ hours).

Trans-Sarbagita (Map p50; JI Imam Bonjol; fare 3500Rp; ☺5am-9pm) Bali's nascent public bus service has two routes that converge on the central parking area just south of Istana Kuta Galleria. Destinations include Denpasar, Sanur, Jimbaran and Nusa Dua.

ⓘ Getting Around

The hardest part about getting around south Bali is the traffic. Besides using taxis, you can rent a motorbike, often with a surfboard rack, or a bike – just ask at the place you're staying at. One of the nicest ways to get around the area is by foot along the beach.

TO/FROM THE AIRPORT

An official taxi from the airport costs 35,000Rp to Tuban, 50,000Rp to Kuta and 60,000Rp to Legian. When travelling *to* the airport, get a metered taxi for savings.

TAXI

In traffic, a ride into Seminyak can top 50,000Rp and take more than 30 minutes; walking the beach will be quicker.

Bluebird Taxi (☑0361-701111; www.bluebird group.com) Bluebird is the best option.

Seminyak

☑0361

Seminyak is flash, brash and arguably a bit phoney. It's also the centre of life for hordes of the island's expats (many of whom own boutiques, design clothes, surf, or do seemingly nothing at all). It may be immediately north of Kuta and Legian, but in many respects Seminyak feels almost like it's on another island.

It's also a very dynamic place, home to dozens of restaurants and clubs and a wealth of creative shops and galleries. World-class hotels line the beach, and what a beach it is – as wide and sandy as Kuta's but less crowded.

Seminyak seamlessly merges with Kerobokan, which is immediately north – in fact the exact border between the two is as fuzzy as most other geographic details in Bali. The many restaurants combine to give travellers the greatest choice of style and budget in Bali. Sure, there are exclusive boutiques, but there are also workshops where everything is wholesale.

🏄 Beaches

Kuta Beach morphs seamlessly into Legian, then Seminyak. Because of the limited road access, the sand in Seminyak tends to be less crowded than in Kuta. This also means that they're less patrolled and the water conditions are less monitored. The odds of encountering dangerous rip tides and other hazards are ever-present, especially as you head north.

Seminyak & Kerobokan

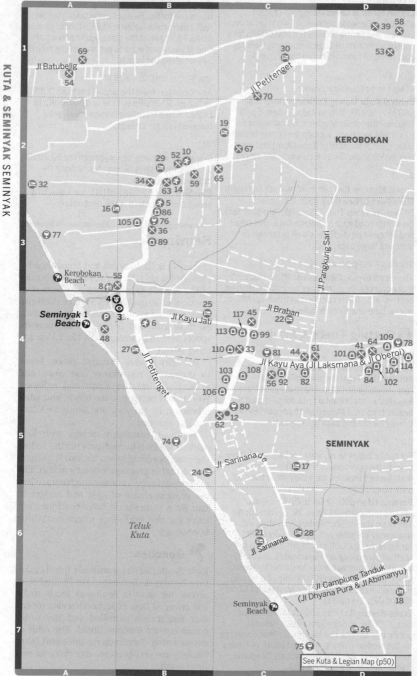

See Kuta & Legian Map (p50)

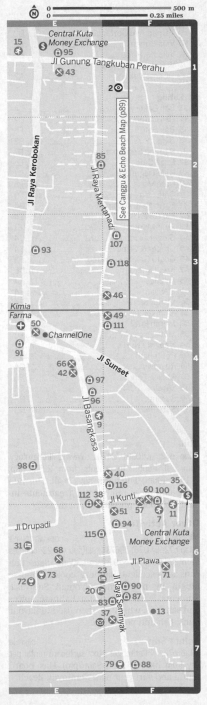

★ **Seminyak Beach** BEACH
(Map p72) A good stretch of Seminyak's beach is found near Pura Petitenget. It is usually uncrowded and has plenty of parking. It is often the scene of both religious ceremonies and surfing. Note that the stream to the north by Mano cafe is often unsavoury after rains.

Insiders favour the patch of sand just south of Ku De Ta. Vendors will sell you cold beers for less than half what the club charges yet you can still hear the throbbing soundtrack.

Enjoy sundowners on a fun strip of beach that runs south from the end of Jl Abimanyu to Jl Arjuna in Legian. The vendors here are mellow and a sunset lounger and ice-cold Bintang costs about 15,000Rp. A **beach walk** makes wandering this stretch a breeze and you can choose from various beach bars.

⊙ Sights

Pura Petitenget HINDU TEMPLE
(Map p72; Jl Pantai Kaya Aya) This is an important temple and the scene of many ceremonies. It is one of a string of sea temples that stretches from Pura Luhur Ulu Watu on the Bukit Peninsula north to Pura Tanah Lot in western Bali. Petitenget loosely translates as 'magic box', a treasured belonging of the legendary 16th-century priest Nirartha, who refined the Balinese religion and visited this site often.

The temple is renowned for its anniversary celebrations on the Balinese 210-day calendar. Upcoming dates include 2 September 2015 plus 30 March and 26 October in 2016.

Also in the compound, look for **Pura Masceti** (Map p72), an agricultural temple where farmers pray for relief from rat infestations, and savvy builders make offerings of forgiveness before planting yet another villa in the rice fields.

🏃 Activities

Massages & Spas
Seminyak's spas (and those of Kerobokan) are among the best in Bali and offer a huge range of treatments, therapies and pleasures.

★ **Jari Menari** SPA
(Map p72; ☎ 0361-736740; www.jarimenari.com; Jl Raya Basangkasa 47; sessions from 350,000Rp; ☺ 9am-9pm) Jari Menari is true to its name, which means 'dancing fingers': your body will be one happy dance floor. The all-male

Seminyak & Kerobokan

staff use massage techniques that emphasise rhythm.

Prana SPA

(Map p72; ☎0361-730840; www.pranaspabali.com; Jl Kunti 118X; massages from 450,000Rp; ⊗10am-10pm) A palatial Moorish fantasy that is easily the most lavishly decorated spa in Bali, Prana offers everything from basic hour-long massages to facials and all manner of beauty treatments. Feel internally cleansed after Ayurvedic treatments.

Bodyworks SPA

(Map p72; ☎0361-733317; www.bodyworksbali.com; Jl Kayu Jati 2; massages from 260,000Rp; ⊗9am-10pm) Get waxed, get your hair done, get the kinks rubbed out of your joints – all this and more is on the menu at this uber-popular spa in the heart of Seminyak.

Chill SPA

(Map p72; ☎0361-734701; www.chillreflexology.com; Jl Kunti; treatments from 225,000Rp; ⊗10am-10pm) The name says it all. This Zen place embraces reflexology; treatments include full body pressure-point massage.

Other Activities

★**Sate Bali** COOKING COURSE

(Map p72; ☎0361-736734; Jl Kayu Aya 22; courses from 375,000Rp; ⊗9.30am-1.30pm) Sate Bali runs an excellent Balinese cooking course taught by noted chef Nyoman Sudiyasa. Students learn to prepare Balinese spices and sambals, which are then used to flavour duck, fish and pork dishes.

Deluta Surf SURFING

(Map p72; Jl Petitenget 40x; surfboard rental per day from 100,000Rp; ⊗9am-7pm) Has board rental and surf gear near Seminyak Beach.

Sleeping

Seminyak has a wide range of places to stay, from world-class resorts to more humble hotels hidden away on backstreets. This is also the start of villa-land, which runs north from here through the vanishing rice fields. For many people, a private villa with its own pool is a holiday dream come true.

Note that oodles of midrange chain hotels have been popping up across south Bali that burnish their allure by adding Seminyak to their names even when they're as far away as Denpasar (see the boxed text, p359).

Jl Camplung Tanduk & Around

★ Ned's Hide-Away GUESTHOUSE $
(Map p72; ✆0361-731270; nedshide@dps.centrin.net.id; Gang Bima 3; r with fan/air-con from 150,000/200,000Rp; ❀🛜) The Ned's family

are real charmers. There are 16 good-value basic rooms here behind Bintang Supermarket. A newish expansion includes both extra-cheap and more plush rooms.

Green Room GUESTHOUSE $
(Map p72; ✆0361-738894; www.thegreenroombali.com; Gang Puri Kubu 63B; r US$40-80; ❀🛜🖥) The Green Room evokes *Robinson Crusoe*, from its hammocks to its banana-tree motif. You can lounge around the small, ink-blot-shaped pool or chill in the open *bale* (pavilion). Some of the rooms (the cheapest are fan only) in a two-storey block feature jungle themes. The beach is a 400m stroll away.

Inada Losmen GUESTHOUSE $
(Map p72; ✆0361-732269; putuinada@hotmail.com; Gang Bima 9; s/d from 130,000/150,000Rp) Buried in a *gang* behind Bintang Supermarket, this budget champ is a short walk

from clubs, beach and other Seminyak joy. The 12 rooms are small and somewhat dark.

Raja Gardens GUESTHOUSE **$$**
(Map p72; ☑ 0361-730494; jdw@eksadata.com; off Jl Camplung Tanduk; r fan/air-con from 400,000/600,000Rp; ❄❄🌐) Enjoy spacious, grassy grounds in this quiet inn located almost on the beach. The nine rooms are fairly barebones but there are open-air bathrooms and plenty of potted plants.

Villa Karisa HOTEL **$$**
(Map p72; ☑ 0361-739395; www.villakarisabali. com; Jl Drupadi 100X; r US$85-140; ❄🌐🌐) It's like visiting the gracious friends in Bali you wish you had. Ideally located on a little *gang* off busy Jl Drupadi, this large villa-style inn has a row of rooms filled with antiques and many comforts. Guests gather in the common room or around the 12m pool. Enjoy Javanese antique style in the Shiva room.

Sarinande Beach Inn HOTEL **$$**
(Map p72; ☑ 0361-730383; www.sarinande hotel.com; Jl Sarinande 15; r 450,000-650,000Rp; ❄@🌐🌐) Excellent value. The 26 rooms are in older two-storey blocks around a small pool; the decor is a bit dated but everything is well maintained. Amenities include fridges, satellite TV, DVD players and a cafe. The beach is three minutes by foot.

Luna2 Studiotel BOUTIQUE HOTEL **$$$**
(Map p72; ☑ 0361-730402; www.luna2.com; Jl Sarinande 20; r US$220-450; ❄🌐🌐) Is it Mondrian? Is it Roy Lichtenstein? We're not sure which modern artists are the inspiration for this eye-popping hotel but we can say the

---

ⓘ SEMINYAK'S CURVING SPINE

The thriving heart of Seminyak lines meandering Jl Kayu Aya (aka Jl Oberoi/Jl Laksmana). It heads towards the beach from bustling Jl Basangkasa and then turns north through a part of Seminyak along Jl Petitenget. The road is lined with a profusion of restaurants, upscale boutiques and hotels as it curves through Seminyak and into Kerobokan. The road has long been considered a pedestrian nightmare, but window-shopping and cafe-hopping have been eased by the installation of sidewalks. Now it's the drivers stuck in traffic who fume...

---

results astound. The 14 boldly decorated studio apartments feature kitchens, gadgetry, balconies and access to a rooftop bar, called Space. A 16-seat cinema shows movies, including Kubrick classics with sets that look like the hotel.

🍴 Jl Kayu Aya & Around

New resorts are appearing along the beach in Seminyak and Kerobokan. Among the most high-profile is the Alila Seminyak, which is near Pura Petitenget and is set for a 2015 opening.

Mutiara Bali HOTEL **$$**
(Map p72; ☑ 0361-734966; www.mutiarabali.com; Jl Braban 77; r US$70-140, villas from US$250; ❄@🌐🌐) Although hidden on a small road behind Jl Kayu Aya, the Mutiara is close to fine dining (200m) and the beach (800m). There are 29 good-sized and nicely furnished rooms in two-storey blocks around a frangipani-draped pool area, plus 17 private villas.

★Oberoi HOTEL **$$$**
(Map p72; ☑ 0361-730361; www.oberoihotels. com; Jl Kayu Aya; r from US$300, villas from US$550; ❄@🌐🌐) The beautifully understated Oberoi has been a refined Balinesestyle beachside retreat since 1971. All of the accommodation options have private verandahs, and as you move up the food chain, additional features include walled villas, ocean views and private pools. With a cafe overlooking the almost-private sweep of beach to the numerous luxuries, this is a place to spoil yourself.

★Samaya VILLA **$$$**
(Map p72; ☑ 0361-731149; www.thesamayabali. com; Jl Kayu Aya; villas from US$450; ❄@🌐🌐) Understated yet cultured, the Samaya is one of the best bets right on the beach in south Bali. It boasts 30 villas in a luxurious contemporary style, each featuring a private pool. The 'Royal Compound' across the road trades location for larger units. The food, from breakfast onwards, is superb.

Pradha Villas VILLA **$$$**
(Map p72; ☑ 0361-735446; www.pradhavillas. com; Jl Kayu Jati 5; villas US$250-500; ❄🌐🌐) Ground zero for Seminyak: the 11 villas are a short walk to some of the best restaurants and the beach. Units vary in size but each is a private walled compound with a swimming pool. Jacuzzis add an extra romantic

touch; wake up to a custom-prepared breakfast by the gracious staff.

Casa Artista   GUESTHOUSE $$$

(Map p72; ☎ 0361-736749; www.casaartistabali. com; Jl Sari Dewi; r US$135-200; ❖ 🐾 ❄) You can literally dance for joy at this cultured guesthouse where the owner, a professional tango dancer, offers lessons. The 10 compact rooms with names such as Passion and Inspiration are in an elegant two-storey house surrounding a pool. Some crystal chandeliers.

🍴 Eating

Jl Kayu Aya is the focus of Seminyak eating but there are great choices for every budget virtually everywhere. Note that some restaurants morph into clubs as the night wears on. Conversely, some bars and clubs also have good food.

Meanwhile, you're never far from top-notch coffee as Seminyak has a thriving cafe culture.

🍴 Jl Camplung Tanduk & Around

Warung Mimpi   INDONESIAN $

(Map p72; ☎ 0361-732738; Jl Camplung Tanduk; meals from 40,000Rp; ⏱ 8am-10pm) A sweet little open-air shopfront warung in the midst of cacophonous nightlife. A dear husband-and-wife team cook Indo classics simply and well. It's all fresh and tasty.

Kreol Kitchen   MODERN AUSTRALIAN $$

(Map p72; ☎ 0361-738514; www.kreolkitchen. com; Jl Drupadi 56; mains from 50,000Rp; ⏱ 8am-10pm Mon-Sat) You won't find pralines here but you will find modern Australian cuisine prepared with ingredients sourced in Bali. It's a fusion of Asian and Western flavours with daily and seasonal specials. The Melbourne-style dim sum is a hit as are the savoury pies and South Asian mains. The decor is lovingly sourced retro.

🍴 Jl Raya Seminyak & Jl Basangkasa

★ Buzz Cafe   CAFE $

(Map p72; ☎ 0818 350 444; Jl Raya Seminyak 99; mains from 30,000Rp; ⏱ 7am-10pm; 🌐) The name is eponymous at this busy cafe located behind some rare Seminyak trees right where Jl Kunti T-bones Jl Raya Seminyak. The open front lets you wave in fellow glit-terati as they saunter past. The fresh drink of choice is the Green Hornet – a combo of lemon, lime and mint.

Warung Taman Bambu   BALINESE $

(Map p72; ☎ 0361-888 1567; Jl Plawa 10; mains from 20,000Rp; ⏱ 9am-10pm; 🌐) You'll be diverted from reaching the pretty garden out back by the array of lovely food out front. This classic warung may look simple from the street but the comfy tables are – like the many fresh and spicy dishes on offer – a cut above the norm. There's a small stand for *babi guling* (suckling pig) right next door.

Warung Ibu Made   INDONESIAN $

(Map p72; Jl Basangkasa; meals from 12,000Rp; ⏱ 7am-7pm) The woks roar almost from dawn to dusk amid the constant hubbub on this busy corner of Jl Raya Seminyak, where several stalls cook food fresh under the shade of a huge banyan.

Café Moka   CAFE $

(Map p72; ☎ 0361-731424; www.cafemokabali. com; Jl Basangkasa; treats 15,000-30,000Rp; ⏱ 7am-10pm; ❖) Enjoy French-style baked goods (fresh baguettes!) at this popular bakery and cafe. Many escape the heat and linger here for hours over little French treats. The bulletin board spills over with notices for villa rentals.

Café Seminyak   CAFE $

(Map p72; ☎ 0361-736967; Jl Raya Seminyak 17; meals from 40,000Rp; ⏱ 7am-10pm) Right in front of the busy Bintang Supermarket, this cute and casual place has excellent smoothies and sandwiches made with freshly baked bread.

Bintang Supermarket   SELF-CATERING $

(Map p72; ☎ 0361-730552; Jl Raya Seminyak 17; ⏱ 8am-10pm) Always busy, this large supermarket is the grocery favourite among expats, who appreciate its broad range of food, including good fruit and veg. Affordable sunscreen, bug spray and other sundries as well.

★ Mama San   FUSION $$

(Map p72; ☎ 0361-730436; www.mamasan bali.com; Jl Raya Kerobokan 135; mains 80,000-200,000Rp; ⏱ noon-11pm) All the action is on the 2nd floor of this buzzy warehouse-sized restaurant. A long cocktail list provides liquid balm for the mojito set and has plenty of tropical-flavoured pours. The menu emphasises small dishes from across Southeast Asia.

Rolling Fork   ITALIAN $$
(Map p72; ☑ 0361-733 9633; Jl Kunti; mains from 60,000Rp; ☉ 8am-10pm) A gnocchi-sized little trattoria, Rolling Fork serves excellent Italian fare. Breakfast features gorgeous baked goods and excellent coffees. Lunch and dinner include authentic and tasty pastas, salads, seafood and more. The open-air dining room has an alluring retro charm; the Italian owners provide just the right accent.

Fat Gajah   ASIAN $$
(Map p72; ☑ 0361-868 8212; www.fatgajah. com; Jl Basangkasa 21; mains 50,000-80,000Rp; ☉ 8.30am-11pm) Noodles and dumplings rarely look this good. The open-front restaurant has a shaded terrace, while inside mirrors and dark wood give it a vintage colonial feel. Dishes are prepared with organic ingredients; dumplings come fried or steamed.

Mannekepis   BELGIAN $$
(Map p72; ☑ 0361-847 5784; www.mannekepis-bistro.com; Jl Raya Seminyak 2; mains 50,000-150,000Rp; ☉ noon-11pm; ☎) That little icon of Brussels is permanently peeing out front at this delicious Belgian bistro. Tear your eyes away from the fish swimming in the ceiling tank to peruse a selection of excellent steaks, all served with top-notch *frites*. Sit on the upper-floor terrace away from the bedlam of the street. There is live jazz and blues many nights.

Taco Beach   MEXICAN $$
(Map p72; ☑ 0361-854 6262; www.tacobeach grill.com; Jl Kunti 6; mains 40,000-60,000Rp; ☉ 9am-11pm; ☎) As sprightly as a chilli-accented salsa, this open-fronted casual cafe is known for its *babi guling* tacos. Obviously merging Bali's iconic suckling pig with Mexican flavours is a good thing. Expect the usual south-of-the-border standards plus good juices, smoothies and margaritas. They deliver.

Bali Deli   SELF-CATERING $$
(Map p72; ☑ 0361-738686; Jl Kunti 117X; ☉ 7am-10pm) The lavish deli counter at this market, located near Jl Sunset, is loaded with imported cheeses, meats and baked goods. This is the place to come for above-average wines for the villa or to prepare a picnic.

Jl Kayu Aya

Saddled by some with the unimaginative name 'Eat Street', this popular restaurant row rewards the indecisive as you can stroll the strip and see what sparks a craving.

PICK A NAME, ANY NAME

A small lane or alley is known as a *gang*, and most of them in Bali lack signs or even names. Some are referred to by the name of a connecting street, eg Jl Padma Utara is the *gang* going north of Jl Padma.

Meanwhile, some streets in Kuta, Legian and Seminyak have more than one name. Many streets were unofficially named after a well-known temple and/or business place. In recent years there has been an attempt to impose official – and usually more Balinese – names on the streets. But the old names are still common and some streets may have more than one.

Following are the old (unofficial) and new (official) names, from north to south:

OLD (UNOFFICIAL)	CURRENT (OFFICIAL)
Jl Oberoi/Jl Laksmana	Jl Kayu Aya
Jl Raya Seminyak	Northern stretch: Jl Basangkasa
Jl Dhyana Pura/Jl Abimanyu	Jl Camplung Tanduk
Jl Double Six	Jl Arjuna
Jl Pura Bagus Taruna	Jl Werkudara
Jl Padma	Jl Yudistra
Poppies Gang II	Jl Batu Bolong
Jl Pantai Kuta	Jl Pantai Banjar Pande Mas
Jl Kartika Plaza	Jl Dewi Sartika
Jl Segara	Jl Jenggala
Jl Satria	Jl Kediri

★ Revolver   CAFE $
(Map p72; off Jl Kayu Aya; snacks from 20,000Rp; ⊙7am-6pm; ✴ 🛜) Wander down a tiny *gang* and push through narrow wooden doors to reach this matchbox of a coffee bar which many claim has the best java, east of Java. There's just a few tables in the creatively retro room – nab one and enjoy tasty fresh bites for breakfast and lunch.

Warung Aneka Rasa   INDONESIAN $
(Map p72; Jl Kayu Aya; meals from 20,000Rp; ⊙8am-10pm) Decision time: you can get some bland, salty snack from the ubiquitous Circle K or you can dive into this local gem and try some Indonesian snacks. Suggestion: do the latter. Nutty, spicy and fiery treats are sold here as well as all manner of local classics in an inviting open-front cafe.

★ Petitenget   FRENCH, ASIAN $$
(Map p72; 🅙0361-473 3054; www.petitenget.net; Jl Petitenget 40; breakfast mains 30,000-70,000Rp, lunch & dinner mains 50,000-200,000Rp; ⊙7am-10.30pm; 🛜) If it wasn't so hot, you could be in Paris. Soft jazz classics play at this very appealing bistro that mixes a casual terrace, bar and a more formal dining area. The menu has seasonal specials and features flavours of Europe and Asia. Everything is artfully prepared; there's a fun little kids menu.

★ Earth Cafe & Market   CAFE $$
(Map p72; 🅙0361-732805; www.earthcafebali.com; Jl Kayu Aya; mains from 40,000Rp; ⊙7am-11pm; 🛜✏) ✒ The good vibes are organic at this newly expanded vegetarian cafe and store amid the upmarket retail ghetto of Seminyak. Choose from creative salads, sandwiches or wholegrain vegan goodies. The beverage menu includes fresh juice mixes with serious names such as 'bone builder', 'gas tonic' and 'party detox'.

Sate Bali   INDONESIAN $$
(Map p72; 🅙0361-736734; Jl Kayu Aya; meals from 100,000Rp; ⊙11am-10pm) Ignore the strip-mall location and enjoy traditional Balinese dishes at this small cafe run by chef Nyoman Sudiyasa (who also has a cooking school here). The multicourse *rijstaffel* is a symphony of tastes.

Ginger Moon   ASIAN $$
(Map p72; 🅙0361-734533; www.gingermoonbali.com; Jl Kayu Aya 7; mains 70,000-160,000Rp; ⊙11am-midnight; ✴🛜) Australian Dean Ked-

dell was one of scores of young chefs lured to Bali to set up restaurants. His creation is a very appealing, airy space with carved wood and palms. The menu features a sort of 'Best of' list of favourites served in portions designed for sharing and grazing.

Wacko Burger   BURGERS $$
(Map p72; 🅙0361-739178; www.wackoburger.com; Jl Kayu Aya; mains from 50,000Rp; ⊙noon-9.30pm) It's like you died and went to comfort-food heaven. The burgers here are beloved, as are the onion rings, fries, shakes and more. There are all manner of toppings and condiments to choose from. It's located back from the road in a cheesy art-filled strip mall.

Grocer & Grind   CAFE $$
(Map p72; 🅙0361-730418; www.grocerandgrind.com; Jl Kayu Jati 3X; mains from 40,000Rp; ⊙7am-10pm; ✴🛜) Keep your vistas limited and you might think you're just at a sleek Sydney cafe, but look around and you're unmistakably in Bali, albeit one of the trendiest bits. Classic sandwiches, salads and big breakfasts are popular at this fast-expanding local chain. Eat in the open air or choose air-con tables in the deli area.

Bali Bakery   CAFE $$
(Map p72; 🅙0361-738033; www.balibakery.com; Jl Kayu Aya; mains from 40,000Rp; ⊙7.30am-10.30pm; 🛜) The best features of the fashionable Seminyak Square open-air mall in the heart of Seminyak are this bakery's shady tables and long menu of baked goods, salads, sandwiches and other fine fare. A good place to linger before heading back out to shop.

Ultimo   ITALIAN $$
(Map p72; 🅙0361-738720; www.balinesia.co.id; Jl Kayu Aya 104; meals 60,000-220,000Rp; ⊙11am-11pm) This vast and always popular restaurant thrives in a part of Seminyak as thick as a good risotto with eateries. Choose a table overlooking the street action, out back in one of the gardens, or inside. Ponder the surprisingly authentic menu and then let the army of servers take charge.

La Lucciola   FUSION $$$
(Map p72; 🅙0361-730838; Jl Petitenget; mains 120,000-400,000Rp; ⊙9am-10pm) A sleek beachside restaurant with good views from the 2nd-floor tables across a lovely lawn and sand to the surf. The bar is popular with

sunset-watchers, although most then move onto dinner here. The menu is a creative melange of international fare with an Italian flair.

🍷 Drinking & Nightlife

Like your vision at 2am, the division between restaurant, bar and club blurs in Seminyak. Although it lacks any real hardcore clubs where you can greet the dawn (or vice versa), stalwarts can head south to the rough edges of Kuta and Legian in the wee hours. Mannekepis (p78) is noted for live jazz some nights.

Numerous bars popular with gay and straight crowds line Jl Camplung Tanduk, though noise-sensitive locals complain if things get too raucous.

🍷 Jl Camplung Tanduk & Around

★ La Plancha   BAR
(Map p72; ☑0361-730603; off Jl Camplung Tanduk; ⊗8am-midnight) The most substantial of the beach bars along the beach walk south of Jl Camplung Tanduk, La Plancha has its share of ubiquitous brightly coloured umbrellas and beanbags on the sand plus a menu of Spanish-accented bites. After sunset, expect DJs and special events such as beach parties, surfer movies and more.

★ Bali Jo   BAR
(Map p72; ☑0361-847 5771; www.balijoebar.com; Jl Camplung Tanduk; ⊗3pm-3am; ☜) Simply fun – albeit with falsies. Drag queens rock the house, the crowd lining the street and the entire neighbourhood, with songs amped to 11 nightly. Surprisingly intimate, it's a good place to lounge about sampling from the long cocktail list.

Ryoshi Seminyak House of Jazz   BAR
(Map p72; ☑0361-731152; Jl Raya Seminyak 17; ⊗music from 8pm Mon, Wed & Fri) The Sem-

inyak branch of the local chain of Japanese restaurants has live jazz three nights a week on an intimate stage under a traditionally thatched roof. Expect some of the best local and visiting talent.

Dix Club   GAY
(Map p72; ☑0878 6568 6615; Jl Camplung Tanduk; ⊗3pm-3am) Always hopping with a loyal mixed crowd, this smallish bar defines convivial. It also has regular live cabaret and floor shows. Beware of getting tickled by flying shrapnel off the feather boas.

🍷 Jl Kayu Aya

Red Carpet Champagne Bar   BAR
(Map p72; ☑0361-737889; www.redcarpetchampagnebar.com; Jl Kayu Aya 42; ⊗11am-late) Choose from over 200 types of champagne at this over-the-top glam bar on Seminyak's couture strip. Waltz the red carpet and toss back a few namesake flutes while contemplating a raw oyster and displays of frilly frocks. It's open to the street (but elevated, dahling) so you can gaze down on the masses.

Ku De Ta   CLUB
(Map p72; ☑0361-736969; www.kudeta.net; Jl Kayu Aya 9; ⊗8am-late) Ku De Ta teems with Bali's beautiful people (including those whose status is purely aspirational). Scenesters perfect their 'bored' look over drinks during the day, gazing at the fine stretch of beach. Sunset brings out crowds, who snatch a cigar at the bar or dine on eclectic fare at tables. The music throbs with increasing intensity through the night.

Townhouse   BAR
(Map p72; ☑0361-885 0577; www.thetownhousebali.com; Jl Kayu Aya; ⊗8am-midnight Sun & Mon, to 3am Tue-Sat) A one-stop shop of consumption, this hot spot combines a juice bar, stylish restaurant, swank cocktail lounge and a rooftop bar in one five-storey venue. Groove to the DJs, then head up to the roof for sweeping views of 'downtown' Seminyak and the Indian Ocean beyond.

Zappaz   BAR
(Map p72; ☑0361-742 5534; Jl Kayu Aya; ⊗11am-midnight) Brit Norman Findlay tickles the ivories nightly at this cheerful piano bar, where he's been not quite perfecting his enthusiastic playing for years and years. An enthusiastic cover band lures in gleeful crowds. Skip the food.

SEMINYAK SUNSETS

At the beach end of Jl Camplung Tanduk you have a choice: turn left for a beachy frolic at the string of beach bars, both simple and plush. Turn right for trendy beach clubs such as Ku De Ta or cheery vendors offering cheap Bintang, a plastic chair and maybe some bad guitar music.

🔒 Shopping

Seminyak shops could occupy days of your holiday. Designer boutiques (Bali has a thriving fashion industry), retro chic stores, slick galleries, wholesale emporiums and family-run workshops are just some of the choices.

The best shopping starts on Jl Raya Seminyak at about Bintang Supermarket and runs north through Jl Basangkasa. The retail strip branches off into the prime real estate of Jl Kayu Aya and Jl Kayu Jati while continuing north on Jl Raya Kerobokan into Kerobokan itself. Of course, this being Bali, try not to get too overwhelmed by the glitz or you'll step into one of the yawning pavement caverns that persist amid newly added sidewalks.

If you need help navigating this retail paradise, check out the 'Retail Therapy' feature in the *Bali Advertiser* (www.baliadvertiser. biz). It's written by the singularly named Marilyn (www.retailtherapybali.com), who brings a veteran retailer's keen eye to the local scene and offers custom shopping tours.

Accessories

★ Vivacqua   ACCESSORIES
(Map p72; 📞0361-736212; Jl Basangkasa 8; ⊘10am-6pm) There are bags of all shapes and sizes here, from stylish ones you'll take to a top Kerobokan restaurant so you can filch a breadstick to large ones ready to haul beach paraphernalia.

Sabbatha   ACCESSORIES
(Map p72; 📞0361-731756; Jl Raya Seminyak 97; ⊘10am-6pm) Mega-bling! The glitter, glam and gold here are almost blinding and that's just what customers want. Opulent handbags and other sun-reflecting accessories are displayed like so much king's ransom.

Beachwear & Surf Shops

Seminyak's surf shops rival those found in Kuta and you'll find branches of the big brands here as well.

★ Drifter   SURF GEAR
(Map p72; 📞0361-733274; www.driftersurf.com; Jl Kayu Aya 50; ⊘9am-9pm) High-end surf fashion, surfboards, gear, books and brands such as Obey and Wegener. Started by two savvy surfer dudes, the shop stocks goods noted for their individuality and high quality. There's also a small cafe and a patio.

Blue Glue   WOMEN'S CLOTHING
(Map p72; 📞0361-731130; www.blue-glue.com; Jl Raya Seminyak 16E; ⊘9am-9pm) 'The dream bikini of all women' is the motto of this brand that makes a big statement with its tiny wear. The swimwear is French-designed and made right in Bali. There's also an **outlet** (Map p72; Jl Basangkasa; ⊘9am-8pm) with prices as small as their bikinis.

O'Neill   SURF GEAR
(Map p72; 📞0361-733401; www.oneill.com; Jl Kayu Aya; ⊘9am-9pm) From one legendary surfing centre, Santa Cruz, California, to another: Bali. A famous line of casual wear, wetsuits and surfing gear.

Bookshops

Periplus Bookshop   BOOKS
(Map p72; 📞0361-736851; Jl Kayu Aya, Seminyak Sq; ⊘8am-10pm) A large outlet of the island-wide chain of lavishly fitted bookshops. Besides enough design books to have you fitting out even your garage with 'Bali Style', there's bestsellers, magazines and newspapers.

Clothing

Bali seems to have about as many talented designers as it has fabulous sunsets. Many produce their lines right on the island.

★ Lulu Yasmine   WOMEN'S CLOTHING
(Map p72; 📞0361-736763; www.luluyasmine. com; Jl Kayu Aya; ⊘9am-9pm) Designer Luiza Chang gets inspiration from her worldwide travels for her elegant line of clothes.

★ Paul Ropp   CLOTHING
(Map p72; 📞0361-735613; www.paulropp.com; Jl Kayu Aya; ⊘9am-9pm) The elegant main shop for one of Bali's premier high-end fashion designers for men and women. Most goods are made in the hills above Denpasar. And what goods they are – rich silks and cottons, vivid to the point of gaudy, with hints of Ropp's roots in the tie-dyed 1960s.

Biasa   CLOTHING
(Map p72; 📞0361-730308; www.biasabali.com; Jl Raya Seminyak 36; ⊘9am-9pm) Biasa is Bali-based designer Susanna Perini's premier shop. Her line of elegant tropicalwear for men and women combines cottons, silks and embroidery. Biasa's **outlet** store is at Jl Basangkasa 47.

Niconico CLOTHING
(Map p72; ☑0361-738875; Jl Kayu Aya; ☺9am-9pm) German designer Nico Genge has a line of intimate clothing, resort wear and swimwear that eschews glitz for a slightly more subtle look. Among his many Seminyak shops this one has both the full collection and an art gallery upstairs.

Milo's CLOTHING
(Map p72; ☑0361-822 2008; www.milos-bali.com; Jl Kayu Aya 992; ☺10am-8pm) The legendary local designer of silk finery has a lavish shop in the heart of designer row. Look for batik-bearing, eye-popping orchid patterns.

Divine Diva WOMEN'S CLOTHING
(Map p72; ☑0361-732393; www.divinedivabali.com; Jl Kayu Aya 1A; ☺9am-7pm) A simple shop filled with Bali-made breezy styles for larger figures. One customer told us: 'It's the essence of agelessness.' You can custom order from the onsite tailors.

Mist WOMEN'S CLOTHING
(Map p72; ☑0361-737959; www.mistasiapacific.com.au; Jl Kayu Aya 42; ☺9am-9pm) Australian designer Penny Pinkster is a master of comfortable understatement. Easy kaftans with style are her specialty.

Dinda Rella WOMEN'S CLOTHING
(Map p72; ☑0361-734228; www.dindarella.com; Jl Raya Seminyak; ☺10am-7pm) Upscale blingy frocks for women are designed and made on Bali by this much-honoured brand. The place to get that sexy little cocktail dress. There's another location on Jl Kayu Aya.

Le Toko CLOTHING
(Map p72; Jl Kunti; ☺9am-7pm) Offers stylish tropical-wear by a Bali-based French designer that will fill in for all the things you couldn't find at home before you came.

Animale CLOTHING
(Map p72; ☑0361-734223; www.animale.com; Jl Kayu Aya; ☺9am-9pm) One of Bali's top fashion brands, Animale has lines of both men's and women's wear in classic styles accented with colour and flair. Visit their **outlet** (Map p72; ☑0361-737 1544; Jl Raya Seminyak 31; ☺9am-8pm) for great deals on lines of casual wear.

Karma Koma WOMEN'S CLOTHING
(Map p72; ☑0361-741 7820; www.karmakoma.fr; Jl Basangkasa; ☺9am-8pm) Sensible cottony wear that's stylish and comfortable with a French flair.

Bamboo Blonde WOMEN'S CLOTHING
(Map p72; ☑0361-731864; www.bambooblonde.com; Jl Kayu Aya 61; ☺9am-9pm) Shop for frilly, sporty or sexy frocks and formal wear at this cheery designer boutique.

Lily Jean WOMEN'S CLOTHING
(Map p72; ☑0811 398 272; www.lily-jean.com; Jl Kayu Aya; ☺10am-8pm) Saucy knickers underpin sexy women's clothing; most is Bali-made. This popular shop has flash digs in fashion's ground zero. It has another plant-covered outlet for simple cottonwear nearby.

Galleries

★**Theater Art Gallery** PUPPETS
(Map p72; Jl Raya Seminyak; ☺9am-8pm) Newly expanded, this place specialises in vintage and reproduction puppets used in traditional Balinese theatre. Just looking at the animated faces peering back at you is a delight.

Kendra Gallery ART
(Map p72; ☑0361-736628; www.kendragallery.com; Jl Drupadi 88B; ☺10am-7pm) This high-end gallery regularly has shows that are thoughtfully and creatively curated. Has regular special events.

Biasa Art Space ART
(Map p72; ☑0361-847 5766; www.biasaart.com; Jl Raya Seminyak 34; ☺9am-8pm) This large, airy and chilly gallery is owned by Biasa designer Susanna Perini. Changing exhibits highlight bold works by local and international artists.

Kody & Ko ART
(Map p72; ☑0361-737359; Jl Kayu Cendana; ☺9am-9pm) The polychromatic Buddhas in the window set the tone for this vibrant shop that's full of art and decorator items. There's a large attached gallery with regular exhibitions.

Kemarin Hari Ini ART
(Map p72; ☑0361-735262; www.kemarinhariini.com; Jl Basangkasa; ☺9am-8pm) Glass objects created with laminated Japanese paper sparkle in the light at this airy gallery. Primitive works mix with the starkly modern.

Homewares

★**Ashitaba** HANDICRAFTS
(Map p72; Jl Raya Seminyak 6; ☺9am-8pm) Tenganan, the Aga village of east Bali, produces the intricate and beautiful rattan items sold here. Containers, bowls, purses and more (from 50,000Rp) display the very fine weaving.

White Peacock   HOMEWARES
(Map p72; ☑ 0361-733238; Jl Kayu Jati 1; ⊕ 9am-8pm) Styled like a country cottage, this is the place for cute cushions, throw rugs, table linens and more.

St Isador   TEXTILES
(Map p72; ☑ 0361-738836; Jl Kaya Aya 44; ⊕ 9am-8pm) The workshops upstairs spew forth lovely bed linens, pillows and other items made of fabrics imported from across Asia.

Indivie   HANDICRAFTS
(Map p72; ☑ 0361-730927; www.indivie.com; Jl Raya Seminyak, Made's Warung; ⊕ 9am-9pm) The works of young designers based in Bali are showcased at this intriguing and glossy boutique.

Samantha Robinson   HOMEWARES
(Map p72; ☑ 0361-737295; www.samantha robinson.com.au; Jl Kayu Jati 2; ⊕ 9am-8pm) The eponymous Sydney porcelain designer offers her full range of colourful and artful homewares at this small boutique.

ℹ Information

Seminyak shares many services with Kuta and Legian.

DANGERS & ANNOYANCES

Seminyak is generally more hassle-free than Kuta and Legian. But it's worth reading up on the warnings (see p364), especially those regarding surf and water pollution.

MEDICAL SERVICES

Kimia Farma (Map p72; ☑ 0361-916 6509; Jl Raya Kerobokan 140; ⊕ 24hr) At a major crossroads, this outlet of Bali's best chain of pharmacies has a full range of prescription medications.

MONEY

Central Kuta Money Exchange (Map p72; www.centralkutabali.com; Jl Kunti 117X, Bali Deli; ⊕ 7am-10pm) Reliable currency exchange.

POST

Postal Agency (Map p72; ☑ 0361-761592; Jl Raya Seminyak 17, Bintang Supermarket; ⊕ 8am-8pm) Convenient and friendly.

ℹ Getting There & Around

Metered taxis are easily hailed. A trip from the airport with the airport taxi cartel costs about 85,000Rp; to the airport, about 50,000Rp. You can beat the traffic, save the ozone and have a good stroll by walking along the beach; Legian is only about 15 minutes away.

Kerobokan
☑ 0361

Continuing seamlessly north from Seminyak, Kerobokan combines some of Bali's best restaurants, lavish lifestyles and still more beach. Glossy new resorts mix with villa developments. At times the mix of commerce and rice fields can be jarring.

🏖 Beaches

Kerobokan Beach   BEACH
(Map p89) Backed by flash resorts and trendy clubs, Kerobokan's beach is surprisingly quiet. A lack of access keeps away crowds because all the roads running west from Jl Petitenget dead end in developments. You can reach the sand from Seminyak Beach in the south or by walking down from Batubelig Beach.

The most direct access, however, is by waltzing through Potato Head (p86) or the W hotel (p84). The surf is more thunderous here than to the south, so be sure to take care when swimming.

Batubelig Beach   BEACH
(Map p89) The sand narrows here but there are some good places for a drink, both grand and simple. Easily reached via Jl Batubelig, this is a good place to start a walk along the curving sands northwest to the popular beaches as far as Echo Beach.

However, note that about 500m north a river and lagoon flow into the ocean, sometimes at a depth of 1m, other times not at all. After rains it may be much deeper. In this case, take the fun little footbridge over the lagoon to a low-key cafe where you can call a taxi (see also p90).

👁 Sights

Kerobokan is for eating, drinking, shopping, sleeping and going to the beach. One notable landmark is the notorious **Kerobokan jail** (Map p72; Jl Gunung Tangkuban Perahu), home to prisoners both infamous and unknown.

🏃 Activities

Sundari Day Spa   SPA
(Map p72; ☑ 0361-735073; www.sundari-dayspa. com; Jl Petitenget 7; massages from 230,000Rp; ⊕ 9am-8pm) This lovely spa strives to offer the services of a five-star resort without the high prices. The massage oils and other potions are organic and there's a full menu of therapies and treatments on offer.

Amo Beauty Spa SPA
(Map p72; ☑0361-275 3337; www.amospa.com; 100 Jl Petitenget; massages from 180,000Rp; ◎9am-9pm) With some of Asia's top models lounging about it feels like you've stepped into the studios of *Vogue*. Besides massages, other services range from hair care to pedicures and unisex waxing.

Jiwa Bikram Yoga YOGA
(Map p72; ☑0361-841 3689; www.jiwabikram yogabali.com; Jl Petitenget 78; classes from 175,000Rp; ◎9am-8pm) In a convenient location, this no-frills place offers several different types of yoga sessions including bikram, hot flow and yin.

Spa Bonita SPA
(Map p72; ☑0361-731918; www.bonitabali.com; Jl Petitenget 2000X; massages from 110,000Rp; ◎9am-9pm) Part of the Waroeng Bonita empire, this male-oriented spa has a range of services in a simple, elegant setting.

🛏 Sleeping

Bali's blight of poorly located midrange chain hotels has also infected Kerobokan (see p359). Otherwise you'll find some good-value choices amid sybaritic villa hotels and beach resorts.

Guess House Hostel HOSTEL $
(Map p72; ☑0361-473 0185; www.guesshouse hostel.com; Jl Petitenget; dm from 170,000Rp; ❈@⑃) Right in the heart of Kerobokan's action, this newish hostel has rooms with four, six and 10 beds. There's a kitchen, shared baths, included breakfast, luggage storage and more.

Grand Balisani Suites HOTEL $$
(Map p89; ☑0361-473 0550; www.balisani suites.com; Jl Batubelig; r US$80-200; ❈@⑃⛱) This elaborately carved complex is right on popular Batubelig Beach. The 96 rooms are large and have standard teak furniture plus terraces (some also have great views). Wi-fi is limited to public areas.

Villa Bunga HOTEL $$
(Map p72; ☑0361-473 1666; www.villabunga. com; Jl Petitenget 18X; r US$40-80; ❈⑃⛱) An excellent deal in the heart of Kerobokan, this small 13-room hotel has rooms set in two-storey blocks around a small pool. Rooms are also small but are modern, clean and have fridges.

Taman Ayu Cottage HOTEL $$
(Map p72; ☑0361-473 0111; www.tamanayu cottage.com; Jl Petitenget; r US$40-100; ❈@⑃⛱) This great-value hotel has a fabulous location. Despite the name, most of the 52 rooms are in two-storey blocks around a pool shaded by mature trees. Everything is a bit frayed around the edges, but all is forgotten when the bill comes.

⭐**Buah Bali Villas** VILLA $$$
(Map p72; ☑0361-854 9797; www.thebuahbali. com; Jl Petitenget, Gang Cempaka; villa from US$200; ❈⑃⛱) This small development has only seven villas, which range in size from one to two bedrooms. Like the many other nearby villa hotels, each unit has a private pool in a walled compound and a nice open-air living area. The location is superb: hotspots such as Biku and Potato Head are a five-minute walk.

W Retreat & Spa Bali – Seminyak RESORT $$$
(Map p72; ☑0361-473 8106; www.starwood hotels.com; Jl Petitenget; r from US$400; ❈@⑃⛱) Like many W hotels, the usual too-cute-for-comfort vibe is at work here (how about an Extreme Wow Suite?), but the location on a wave-tossed stretch of sand and the views are hard to quibble with. Stylish, hip bars and restaurants abound. The rooms all have balconies, but not all have ocean views.

🍴 Eating

Kerobokan boasts some of Bali's best restaurants, whether budget or top end.

🍴 Jl Petitenget

⭐**Warung Eny** INDONESIAN $
(Map p72; ☑0361-473 6892; Jl Petitenget; mains from 35,000Rp; ◎8am-10pm) The eponymous Eny cooks everything herself at this tiny open-front warung that's nearly hidden behind various potted plants. Look for the roadside sign that captures the vibe: 'The love cooking.' The seafood – such as large prawns smothered in garlic – is delicious and most ingredients are organic. Ask about her fun cooking classes.

Bali Catering Co BAKERY $
(Map p72; ☑0361-473 2115; www.balicatering company.com; Jl Petitenget 45; snacks from 30,000Rp; ◎8am-9pm; ❈) Like a gem store

KEROBOKAN'S WARUNGS

Although seemingly upscale, Kerobokan is blessed with many a fine place for a truly authentic local meal. Top choices include the following:

Warung Sulawesi (Map p72; Jl Petitenget; meals from 30,000Rp; ⊙10am-6pm) Here you'll find a table in a quiet family compound and enjoy fresh Balinese and Indonesian food served in classic warung style. Choose a rice, then pick from a captivating array of dishes that are always at their peak at noon. The long beans – yum!

Warung Kolega (Map p72; Jl Petitenget; meals 25,000Rp; ⊙11am-3pm) A Javanese halal classic. Choose your rice (we prefer the fragrant yellow), then pick from a delectable array that includes tempeh in sweet chilli sauce, *sambal terung* (spicy eggplant), *ikan sambal* (spicy grilled fish) and other daily specials. Most of the labels are in English.

Sari Kembar (☑0361-847 6021; Jl Teuku Umar Barat (Jl Marlboro 99); mains from 15,000Rp; ⊙8am-10pm) One of Bali's best places for *babi guling* (spit-roasted pig) is back off this busy street about 1.5km east of the junction with Jl Raya Kerobokan. Besides the succulent marinated pork, there's melt-in-your-mouth crackling, duck stuffed with cassava leaves, sausage and more. It's dead simple and amazingly good.

Blambangan Warung Syariah (Jl Gunung Salak; mains from 15,000Rp; ⊙24hr) The spicy foods of East Java are served around the clock at this simple roadside warung near some interesting shops. The chicken is all free range and stars in the *ayam gulai*, a sort of chicken curry. When in doubt, have the *nasi campur* and try a bit of everything.

of treats, this upscale deli-bakery serves an array of fanciful little delights. Many spend all day battling the temptation of the mango ice cream; others succumb to the croissants.

★**Biku** FUSION $$
(Map p72; ☑0361-857 0888; www.bikubali.com; Jl Petitenget; meals 40,000-120,000Rp; ⊙8am-11pm; 🛜) Housed in an old shop that used to sell antiques, hugely popular Biku retains the timeless vibe of its predecessor. The menu combines Indonesian and other Asian and Western influences; book for lunch or dinner. Dishes, from the exquisite breakfasts and the elegant local choices to Bali's best burger, are artful and delicious.

There's a long list of teas and myriad refreshing cocktails. You may swoon at the sight of the cake table.

★**Merah Putih** INDONESIAN $$
(Map p72; ☑0361-846 5950; www.merahputihbali. com; Jl Petitenget 100X; mains 60,000-150,000Rp; ⊙noon-3pm & 6-11pm) Merah Putih means 'red and white', which are the colours of the Indonesian flag. That's perfect for this excellent restaurant that celebrates food from across the archipelago. The short menu is divided between traditional and modern – the latter combining Indo flavours with diverse foods. The soaring dining room has a hip style and the service is excellent.

Cafe Degan ASIAN $$
(Map p72; ☑0361-744 8622; Jl Petitenget 9; meals 90,000-160,000Rp; ⊙noon-11pm) The menu at this upscale warung veers towards Indonesian but overall features dishes from the region you don't often find, such as *daging sambal hijau* (spicy beef with green chillies). A small air-con bakery has an array of delectables for dessert.

Waroeng Bonita INDONESIAN $$
(Map p72; ☑0361-473 1918; www.bonitabali.com; Jl Petitenget 2000X; mains 40,000-100,000Rp; ⊙11am-11pm) Balinese dishes such as *ikan rica-rica* (fresh fish in a spicy green-chilli sauce) and beef rendang (beef in a creamy, spicy sauce) are the specialities at this cute place with tables set out under the trees. On certain nights Bonita positively heaves because of the drag shows starring everyone from visiting queens to the busboy.

★**Sardine** SEAFOOD $$$
(Map p72; ☑0361-843 6111; www.sardinebali.com; Jl Petitenget 21; meals US$20-50; ⊙11.30am-11pm) Seafood fresh from the famous Jimbaran market is the star at this elegant yet intimate, casual yet stylish restaurant in a beautiful bamboo pavilion that is ably presided over by Pascal and Pika Chevillot. Open-air tables overlook a private rice field patrolled by Sardine's own flock of ducks.

The inventive bar is a must and open to 1am. The menu changes to reflect what's fresh. Booking is vital.

Sarong
FUSION $$$

(Map p72; ☑ 0361-473 7809; www.sarongbali.com; Jl Petitenget 19X; mains 150,000-350,000Rp; ⊙ 5-11pm) Largely open to the evening breezes, the dining room has plush furniture and gleaming place settings that twinkle in the candlelight. But opt for tables out the back where you can let the stars do the twinkling. The food spans the globe; small plates are popular with those wishing to pace an evening enjoying the commodious bar. No children allowed.

Métis
FUSION $$$

(Map p72; ☑ 0361-473 7888; www.metisbali.com; Jl Petitenget 6; mains US$15-35) Métis aims to be one of Bali's finest restaurants. It certainly has the provenance, with roots in the vaunted old Cafe Warisan (the current incarnation under that name bears no resemblance). Set ostentatiously in a surviving rice field, the restaurant works best when filled with buzzing crowds – think high season. Weekday lunch specials (from 90,000Rp) are good value.

Elsewhere in Kerobokan

★ Gusto Gelato & Coffee
ICE CREAM $

(Map p72; ☑ 0361-552 2190; www.gusto-gelateria. com; Jl Raya Mertanadi 46; treats from 15,000Rp; ⊙ 10am-9pm Mon-Sat; ❀ ☎) Bali's best gelato is made fresh through the day and served to throngs looking to lick something cool and fresh. The flavours pop; enjoy a coffee drink in the back garden.

Warung Sobat
SEAFOOD $$

(Map p72; ☑ 0361-473 8922; Jl Batubelig 11; mains 30,000-150,000Rp; ⊙ noon-11pm; ☎) Set in a sort of bungalow-style brick courtyard, this old-fashioned restaurant excels at fresh Balinese seafood with an Italian accent (lots of garlic!). First-time visitors feel like they've made a discovery, and if you have the sensational lobster platter (a bargain at 350,000Rp for two; order in advance), you will too. Book.

L'Assiette
FRENCH $$

(Map p72; ☑ 0361-735840; Jl Raya Mertanadi 29; meals 50,000-100,000Rp; ⊙ 10am-11pm; ☎) The huge quiet garden behind this airy cafe is the perfect place to enjoy a *salade niçoise* or any of the other fresh and tasty classic French-cafe fare here. Perhaps a *steak frites* or a terrine will strike your fancy. If not, there are Asian-accented dishes as well.

Naughty Nuri's
INDONESIAN $$

(Map p72; ☑ 0361-847 6722; Jl Batubelig 41; meals from 50,000Rp; ⊙ 11am-10.30pm) Inspired by the over-hyped Ubud original, this Nuri's is simply over-crowded. Remarkably, it has become a must-see stop for tourists from across Indonesia, who tuck into the American-style fare (such as ribs) with wonderment. The original's trademark kick-arse martinis remain on the menu. Queues often form for tables and watching the tourists watch each other is actually rather fun.

🍷 Drinking & Nightlife

Some of Kerobokan's trendier restaurants, such as Sardine and Tulip, have stylish bar areas that stay open late.

★ Potato Head
CLUB

(Map p72; ☑ 0361-473 7979; www.ptthead.com; Jl Petitenget; ⊙ 11am-2am; ☎) Bali's coolest beach club. Wander up off the sand or follow a long drive off Jl Petitenget and you'll discover a truly captivating creation on a grand scale. The clever design is striking and you'll find much to amuse, from an enticing pool to a swanky restaurant plus lots of loungers for chillin' the night away under the stars.

★ Mantra
LOUNGE

(Map p72; ☑ 0361-473 7681; www.mantrabali.com; Jl Petitenget 77X; ⊙ 3pm-late) Retro style meets tropical languor at this deservedly popular bar. There's a tree-shaded terrace out front that's the place to be late at night as dancing starts spontaneously. Inside the walls are lined with photos and art; there are regular special exhibits. Visiting DJs spin tunes and you can choose from creative drinks and snacks.

Pantai
BAR

(Map p89; Batubelig Beach; ⊙ 9am-9pm) The authorities regularly bulldoze away the impromptu drinking shacks that appear along this inviting stretch of beach just north of the W hotel. But Pantai has so far had more lives than a cat and stubbornly keeps offering up cheap drinks, mismatched tables and splendid surf and sunset views.

Mozaic Beach Club
CLUB

(Map p89; ☑ 0361-473 5796; www.mozaic-beach club.com; Jl Pantai Batubelig; meals from 150,000Rp; ⊙ 10am-1am) The original Mozaic restaurant in Ubud is renowned for its fanatical attention to detail and that tradition continues at this beautiful beachside club. You can lounge around the elegant pool or wander the elaborate multi-level restaurant and bar. It's never quite as crowded as you'd think it should be, and daily drink specials include free tapas.

🔒 Shopping

Look for boutiques interspersed with the trendy restaurants on Jl Petitenget. Jl Raya Kerobokan, extending north from Jl Sunset, has interesting shops primarily selling decorator items and homewares. Wander Jl Raya Mertanadi for an ever-changing line-up of homewares shops, many of them more factory than showroom.

⭐ **JJ Bali Button**   ARTS & CRAFTS
(Map p72; Jl Gunung Tangkuban Perahu; ⊙9am-7pm) Zillions of beads and buttons made from shells, plastic, metal and more are displayed in what at first looks like a candy store. Elaborately carved wooden buttons are 700Rp. Kids may have to be bribed to leave.

⭐ **Bathe**   BEAUTY, HOMEWARES
(Map p72; ☑0361-473 7580; www.bathestore. com; Jl Petitenget 100X; ⊙9am-8pm) Double-down on your villa's romance with the handmade candles and bath salts at this shop that evoke the feel of a 19th-century French dispensary. You can't help but smile at the tub filled with rubber ducks.

Namu   CLOTHING
(Map p72; ☑0361-279 7524; www.namustore.com; Jl Petitenget 23X; ⊙9am-8pm) Designer Paola Zancanaro creates comfortable and casual resortwear for men and women that doesn't take a holiday from style. The fabrics are lusciously tactile; many are hand-painted silk.

Ganesha Bookshop   BOOKS
(Map p72; Jl Petitenget; ⊙8am-11pm) In a corner of the fabulous Biku restaurant, this tiny branch of Bali's best bookstore up in Ubud has all manner of local and literary treats.

Hobo   HOMEWARES
(Map p72; ☑0361-733369; www.thehobostore.com; Jl Raya Kerobokan 105; ⊙9am-8pm) Elegance mixes with quirky at this enticing shop filled with gifts and homewares, most of which can slip right into your carry-on bag.

Carga   HOMEWARES
(Map p72; ☑0361-847 8180; Jl Petitenget 886; ⊙9am-9pm) This beautiful shop is set back from the cacophony of Jl Petitenget in a vintage house shaded by palm trees. The homewares are sourced across Indonesia and range from elegant to whimsical.

Pourquoi Pas   ANTIQUES
(Map p72; Jl Raya Mertanadi; ⊙9am-7pm) Owned by the French family behind L'Assiette, this adjoining antique store is filled with treasures from across the archipelago and Southeast Asia.

SHOPPING SAFARI

East of Seminyak and Kerobokan, a series of streets is lined with all manner of interesting shops selling and manufacturing homewares, baubles, fabric and other intriguing items. Head east of Kerobokan jail for about 2km on Jl Gunung Tangkuban Perahu and then turn south on – get this – a street with the same name (this is Bali, after all).

This particular Jl Gunung Tangkuban Perahu has been called 'the street of amazement' by a shopaholic friend. It meanders off to Jl Gunung Soputan, which has shops in both directions. South, it becomes Jl Gunung Athena, and then heads east as Jl Kunti II where it ends at the busy intersection with Jl Sunset and Jl Kunti.

IQI (☑0361-733181; Jl Gunung Tangkuban Perahu 274; ⊙9am-6pm) Placemats, runners and other woven items are made here; outfit your table for about US$5.

Wijaya Kusuma Brass (☑0813 3870 4597; Jl Gunung Soputan; ⊙9am-6pm) Brass accessories for furniture and your home. Who doesn't want to grab a frog pull to access their undies?

Yoga Batik (Jl Gunung Athena; ⊙9am-6pm) All manner of the iconic Indonesian fabric.

Rainbow Tulungagung (Jl Gunung Athena; ⊙9am-6pm) Handicrafts made from marble and stone. The soap dispensers are easily carried home.

Nôblis
HOMEWARES

(Map p72; ☑ 0815 5800 2815; Jl Raya Mertanadi 54; ⊙ 9am-7pm) Feel like royalty here with regal bits of decor from around the globe.

You Like Lamp
HOMEWARES

(Map p72; ☑ 0361-733755; Jl Raya Mertanadi; ⊙ 9am-7pm) Why yes, we do. All manner of endearing little paper lamps – many good for tea lights – are sold here cheap by the bag full. Don't see what you want? The staff working away on the floor will rustle it up immediately.

Bambooku
HOMEWARES

(Map p72; ☑ 0361-780 7836; www.bambooku.com; Jl Raya Mertanadi; ⊙ 9am-7pm) House linens made from bamboo are the specialty at this tidy shop. The fabric is amazingly soft and is much sought after by people with allergies. A set of sheets and pillowcases for a double bed costs 1,800,000Rp.

ℹ Information

Central Kuta Money Exchange (Map p72; www.centralkutabali.com; Jl Raya Kerobokan 51; ⊙ 8am-8pm) Reliable currency exchange.

ℹ Getting There & Around

Taxis from the airport will cost at least 100,000Rp. In either direction at rush hour the trip may verge on an hour. Note also that Jl Raya Kerobokan can come to a fume-filled stop for extended periods.

The plethora of villas can stymie even the savviest of cab drivers so it's helpful to have some sort of map or directions when you first arrive and for forays out and about during your stay. Taxis can be hailed along the main roads.

Although the beach may seem tantalisingly close, few roads or *gang* actually reach the sand from the east.

Canggu & Around
☑ 0361

The Canggu region, north and west from Kerobokan, is Bali's fastest growing area. Much of the growth is centred along the coast, anchored by the endless swathe of beach, which, despite rampant development, remains fairly uncrowded. Kerobokan morphs into Umalas inland and Canggu to the west, while neighbouring Echo Beach is a big construction site.

Cloistered villas lure expats who whisk past stooped rice farmers on motorbikes or in air-con comfort. Traffic may be the ulti-mate commoner's revenge: road building is a decade behind settlement. Amid this maze of too-narrow lanes you'll find offbeat cafes, tasty restaurants and unusual shops. Follow the sounds of the surf to great beaches including the one at Batu Bolong.

Umalas

Expat villas mix with rice fields north of Kerobokan. Look for surprises like a cute warung or an delightfully oddball shop on the back roads.

🏃 Activities

★ Bali Bike Hire
BICYCLE RENTAL

(Map p89; ☑ 0361-202 0054; www.balibikehire. com; Jl Raya Semer 61; rental per day from 60,000Rp) Run by people passionate about bikes, here you can choose from a variety of top-quality rides. They offer plenty of advice for navigating Bali's often tortuous roads, and have various guided tours by bike.

🍴 Eating

Go exploring the small roads east of Jl Raya Kerobokan and you'll discover lots of interesting warungs serving a variety of cuisines.

Nook
ASIAN $$

(Map p89; ☑ 0813 3806 0060; Jl Umalas I; mains from 40,000Rp; ⊙ 8am-10pm; 🛜) Almost as cute as the views of the rice fields out the back windows, this casual, open-air spot is popular for its creative takes on Asian fare. It's got a modern vibe mixed with tropical flavours. Good breakfasts and lunchtime sandwiches.

Bali Buda
CAFE $$

(Map p89; ☑ 0361-844 5936; www.balibuda.com; Jl Banjar Anyar 24; mains from 35,000Rp; ⊙ 8am-10pm; ✻🛜✐) This appealing outlet of the Ubud original has all the excellent baked goods and organic groceries you'd expect. The small cafe serves healthy juices and smoothies plus an array of mostly vegetarian fare. Stop in for breakfast on your way to visit Tanah Lot when sane people visit the temple: before noon.

🛍 Shopping

Reza Art 2
ANTIQUES

(☑ 0821 9797 4309; Jl Mertasari 99; ⊙ 10am-6pm) Oodles of lamps in many sizes mix with nautical antiques and junk (think old ship telegraphs and rudder wheels) in this shop that's more treasure hunt than retail establishment.

Canggu & Echo Beach

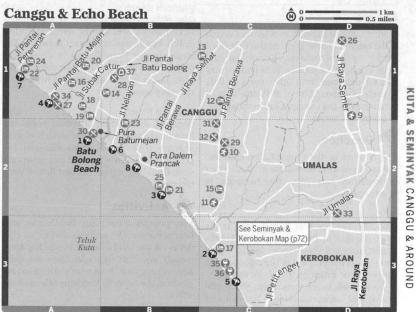

Canggu & Echo Beach

◎ Top Sights
1 Batu Bolong Beach	A2

◎ Sights
2 Batubelig Beach	C3
3 Berawa Beach	B2
4 Echo Beach	A1
5 Kerobokan Beach	C3
6 Nelayan Beach	B2
7 Pererenan Beach	A1
8 Prancak Beach	B2

✈ Activities, Courses & Tours
9 Bali Bike Hire	D1
10 Canggu Club	C2
11 Desa Seni	C2

⊟ Sleeping
12 Big Brother Surf Inn	C1
13 Canggu Bed & Breakfast	C1
14 Coconuts Guesthouse Canggu	B1
15 Desa Seni	C2
16 Echoland	A1
17 Grand Balisani Suites	C3
18 Green Room	A1
19 Hotel Tugu Bali	A1

20 Jepun Bali	A1
21 Legong Keraton	B2
22 Pondok Nyoman Bagus	A1
23 Serenity Eco Guesthouse & Yoga	B2
24 Surfers Paradise	A1
25 Widi Homestay	B2

✕ Eating
26 Bali Buda	D1
27 Beach House	A1
28 Betelnut Cafe	B1
29 Bungalow	C2
30 Dian Cafe	A2
31 Green Ginger	C2
32 Indotopia	C2
Monsieur Spoon	(see 37)
33 Nook	D2
Old Man's	(see 30)
34 Sate Bali	A1

🍸 Drinking & Nightlife
35 Mozaic Beach Club	C3
36 Pantai	C3

🛍 Shopping
37 Dylan Board Store	B1

Canggu

More a state of mind than a place, Canggu is the catch-all name given to the villa-filled stretch of land between Kerobokan and Echo Beach. It's a popular area both to stay and for day trips from other parts of Bali. A stretch of about 1km of Jl Pantai Berawa running near the Canggu Club is the de facto centre of Canggu.

🏖 Beaches

The beaches of the Canggu area continue the sweep of sand that starts in Kuta. Their personalities vary from hip hang-out to nearly empty.

⭐ Batu Bolong Beach   BEACH

(Map p89) The beach at Batu Bolong is the most popular in the Canggu area. There's almost always a good mix of locals, expats and visitors hanging out in the cafes, surfing the breaks or watching it all from the sand.

It's a classic beach scene, with rental umbrellas and loungers available. You can rent surfboards (100,000Rp per day) and take lessons. Overlooking it all is the centuries-old **Pura Batumejan** (Map p89) complex with a striking pagoda-like temple.

Taxis here can take you around the Canggu area (50,000Rp) or to more distant points such as Seminyak (100,000Rp).

Berawa Beach   BEACH

(Map p89) Greyish Berawa Beach has a couple of surfer cafes by the pounding sea; the grey volcanic sand here slopes steeply into foaming water. Overlooking it all is the vast estate of fashionista Paul Ropp.

BEACH WALK

You can usually walk the 4km of sand between Batubelig Beach and Echo Beach in about one to two hours. It's a fascinating stroll and you'll see temples, tiny fishing encampments, crashing surf, lots of surfers and outcrops of upscale beach culture. The only catch is that after heavy rains, some of the rivers may be too deep to cross, especially the one just northwest of Batubelig. In any case, put your gear in waterproof bags in case you have to do some fording.

It's easy to find taxis at any of the larger beaches if you don't want to retrace your steps.

Prancak Beach   BEACH

(Map p89) A couple of drink vendors and a large parking area are the major amenities at this beach, which is rarely crowded. The large temple, **Pura Dalem Prancak** (Map p89), is often the site of large ceremonies. Berawa Beach is an enjoyable 1km walk along the wave-tossed sands.

Nelayan Beach   BEACH

(Map p89) A collection of fishing boats and huts marks the very mellow stretch of sand at Nelayan Beach that fronts villa-land. Depending on the river levels, it can be an easy walk from here to Prancak and Batu Bolong beaches.

🏃 Activities

Very popular for surfing, the Canggu area beaches draw a lot of locals and expat residents on weekends. Access to parking areas usually costs 2000Rp and there are cafes and warungs for those who work up an appetite in the water or watching others in the water.

Desa Seni   YOGA

(Map p89; ☎ 0361-844 6392; www.desaseni.com; Jl Kayu Putih 13; classes from 140,000Rp; ⊙ varies) Desa Seni comprises classic wooden homes that have been transformed into a luxurious hotel. It is also renowned for its wide variety of yoga classes, which are offered daily and have a large following among local expats and nonguests.

Canggu Club   HEALTH & FITNESS

(Map p89; ☎ 0361-844 6385; www.cangguclub. com; Jl Pantai Berawa; day pass adult/child 240,000/120,000Rp; 🐾) Bali's expats shuttlecock themselves silly at the Canggu Club, a New Age version of something you'd expect to find during the Raj. The vast, perfectly virescent lawn is manicured for croquet. Get sweaty with tennis, squash, polo, cricket, the spa or the 25m pool. Many villa rentals include guest passes here. The garish new **Splash Waterpark** is hugely popular.

🛏 Sleeping

⭐ Widi Homestay   HOMESTAY $

(Map p89; ☎ 0819 3303 2322; widihomestay@ yahoo.co.id; Jl Pantai Berawa; r from 250,000Rp; ❄🐾) There's no faux hipster vibe here with fake nihilist bromides, just a spotless, friendly family-run homestay. The four rooms have hot water and air-con; the beach is barely 100m away.

Serenity Eco Guesthouse & Yoga
GUESTHOUSE $

(Map p89; ☑0361-747 4625; www.balivillaserenity. com; Jl Nelayan; s/d from 180,000/350,000Rp; ❄☎⊠) ⌀ This hotel is an oasis among the sterility of walled villas. Rooms range from shared-bath singles to quite nice doubles with bathrooms. The grounds are appealingly eccentric; Nelayan beach is a five-minute walk. There are yoga classes (from 75,000Rp) and you can rent surfboards, bikes, cars and more.

Canggu Bed & Breakfast
GUESTHOUSE $

(Map p89; ☑0818 568 364; www.hanafi.net; Jl Raya Semat, Gang Jalat X 1265; r 350,000-500,000Rp; ❄☎⊠) In a small village with good, cheap warungs, this new guesthouse is built in a U-shaped compound around a lovely pool. Rooms have all the comforts. It's about 2km from the beaches and just off Jl Raya Semat.

Big Brother Surf Inn
GUESTHOUSE $

(Map p89; ☑0819 9937 3914; www.bigbrother bali.com; Jl Pantai Berawa 20; r from US$33; ❄☎) This sleek take on a traditional Balinese guesthouse has clean lines and plenty of minimalist white. The six rooms are airy and have outdoor sitting areas overlooking a small garden. It's in a quiet location back off the road; despite the name your hijinks are unlikely to end up on a reality TV show.

★Coconuts Guesthouse Canggu
GUESTHOUSE $$

(Map p89; ☑0361-800 0608; www.coconutsguest house.com; Jl Pantai Batu Bolong; r from US$70; ❄☎) The five breezy rooms at this modern guesthouse are very comfortable. Some have lovely views of the (surviving) rice fields, and all have fridges and a relaxed motif. Enjoy sunsets from the rooftop lounge area or take a dip in the 10m pool. Batu Bolong beach is a 700m walk.

Green Room
HOTEL $$

(Map p89; ☑0361-846 9186; www.thegreen roombali.com; Jl Subak Catur; r US$60-150; ☎⊠) At ground zero for Canggu's surf scene, the Green Room exudes hippie chic. Lounge on the 2nd-floor verandah and check out the waves (and villa construction) in the distance. The 14 rooms are comfy and breezy.

Legong Keraton
HOTEL $$

(Map p89; ☑0361-473 0280; www.legongkeraton hotel.com; Jl Pantai Berawa; r US$80-250; ❄@☎⊠) Right on the quiet sands of Berawa Beach, the well-run 40-room Legong Keraton is the perfect place for a corporate retreat. The grounds are shaded by palms and the pool borders the beach. The best rooms are in bungalow units facing the surf.

★Hotel Tugu Bali
HOTEL $$$

(Map p89; ☑0361-473 1701; www.tuguhotels. com; Jl Pantai Batu Bolong; r from US$250; ❄@☎⊠) Right at Batu Bolong Beach, this exquisite hotel blurs the boundaries between a museum and a gallery, especially the Walter Spies and Le Mayeur Pavilions, where memorabilia from the artists' lives decorates the rooms. There's a spa and customised dining options.

The stunning collection of antiques and artwork begins in the lobby and extends throughout the hotel. Cooking classes (from US$100) are quite luxe.

Desa Seni
HOTEL $$$

(Map p89; ☑0361-844 6392; www.desaseni.com; Jl Kayu Putih 13; r US$135-400; ❄@☎⊠) ⌀ One person described this place as a hippie Four Seasons, and that's not far from the truth. The ten classic wooden homes up to two centuries old were brought to the site from across Indonesia and turned into luxurious quarters. Guests enjoy a menu of organic and healthy cuisine plus yoga courses.

✗ Eating

★Green Ginger
ASIAN $

(Map p89; ☑0878 6211 2729; Jl Pantai Berawa; meals from 30,000Rp; ⊗8am-9.30pm; ⌀) Art, a profusion of flowering plants and eccentric bits of furniture mark this cool little boho cafe on the fast-changing strip in Canggu. The menu has fresh and tasty vegetarian and noodle dishes from across Asia.

Monsieur Spoon
CAFE $

(Map p89; Jl Pantai Batu Bolong; snacks from 20,000Rp; ⊗6am-9pm; ❄) Beautiful French-style baked goods (the almond croissant, wow!) are the specialty at this small Bali chain of cafes. Enjoy pastries, sandwiches on picture-perfect bread and fine coffees at a table in the garden or inside.

Bungalow
CAFE $

(Map p89; ☑0361-844 6567; Jl Pantai Berawa; mains from 30,000Rp; ⊗8am-6pm; ❄) Set just far enough back from the road to avoid the fumes, this cafe reflects the retro-chic design sensibilities of its parent homeware emporium. Relax amid distressed wood surrounds on the verandah and choose from a vast range of coffee drinks, juices, smoothies, sandwiches, salads and desserts.

Indotopia
ASIAN $

(Map p89; ✍ 0822 3773 7760; Jl Pantai Berawa 34; mains from 30,000Rp; ⊘ 8am-10pm; 🛜) Otherwise known as 'Warung Vietnam', the bowls of *pho* (rice noodle soup) here are simply superb. Lots of rich beefy goodness contrasting with perfect noodles and fragrant greens. Prefer something sweeter? Go for the Saigon banana crêpes.

Dian Cafe
INDONESIAN $

(Map p89; ✍ 0813 3875 4305; Jl Pantai Batu Bolong; mains from 30,000Rp; ⊘ 8am-10pm) Old-school Indo and Western standards are served up cheap at this open-air pavilion just a few metres from the beach. They also have showers for surfers.

Betelnut Cafe
CAFE $$

(Map p89; ✍ 0821 4680 7233; Jl Pantai Batu Bolong; mains from 45,000Rp; ⊘ 7am-10pm; ❋🛜) There's a hippy-chic vibe at this thatched cafe with a mellow open-air dining room upstairs. The menu leans healthy but not too healthy – you can get fries. There are juices and lots of mains featuring vegies. Good baked goods, nice shakes.

Old Man's
BURGERS, INTERNATIONAL $$

(Map p89; ✍ 0361-846 9158; Jl Pantai Batu Bolong; mains from 50,000Rp; ⊘ 8am-midnight) You'll have a tough time deciding just where to sit down to enjoy your beer at this vast open-air joint back off Batu Bolong Beach. The menu is aimed at surfers and surfer-wannabes: burgers, pizza, fish and chips and for the New Age surfers: salads. On many nights there's live music (think classic rock).

🛍 Shopping

Dylan Board Store
SURFBOARDS

(Map p89; ✍ 0857 3853 7402; Jl Pantai Batu Bolong; ⊘ noon-6pm) Famed big-wave rider Dylan Longbottom runs this custom surfboard shop. A talented shaper, he creates boards for novices and pros alike. He also stocks plenty of his designs ready to go.

ℹ Information

ATMs, basic shops and markets can be found on Canggu's main strip, Jl Pantai Berawa.

ℹ Getting There & Around

You can reach the Canggu area by road from the south by taking Jl Batubelig west in Kerobokan

almost to the beach and then veering north past various huge villas and expat shops along a curved road. It's much longer to go up and around via the traffic-clogged Jl Raya Kerobokan.

Getting to the Canggu area can cost 80,000Rp or more by taxi from Kuta or Seminyak. Don't expect to find taxis cruising anywhere, although any business can call you one.

This is good motorbike country – many of the impromptu roads are barely wide enough for one car let alone two.

Echo Beach

One of Bali's most popular surf breaks, Echo Beach has reached critical mass in popularity; surf shops abound. Construction has not been kind to the area and there's an unsightly dormant resort complex just to the east. If it seems too crowded here, walk along the sands for 200m in either direction for quietude.

Sunsets draw crowds who enjoy drinks coloured by the rosy glow.

A local taxi cooperative will shuttle you back to Seminyak and the south for 100,000Rp or more.

Echo Beach
BEACH

(Pantai Batu Mejan; Map p89) Surfers and those who watch them flock here for the high-tide lefthander that regularly tops 2m. The greyish sand right in front of the developments can vanish at high tide, but you'll find wide strands both east and west. Batu Bolong Beach is 500m east.

🛏 Sleeping & Eating

Cafes from basic to vaunted front the surf break. Enjoy a beverage while critiquing the board-riders, or take the plunge yourself.

Echoland
GUESTHOUSE $

(Map p89; ✍ 0361-887 0628; www.echolandbali.com; Jl Pantai Batu Mejan; dm from 160,000Rp, r fan/air-con from 420,000/600,000Rp; ❋🛜🛁) There are 17 private rooms plus dorms in this compact two-storey compound about 300m from the beach. The rooftop lounge has a nice cover for shade and predictably good views. Yoga classes are offered from 80,000Rp per hour.

Jepun Bali
GUESTHOUSE $

(Map p89; ✍ 0361-361 0613; www.jepunbali homestay.com; Jl Pantai Batu Mejan; r from 250,000Rp; 🛜) There are nine modern rooms in a two-storey block about 600m back from

Echo Beach. Accommodation is spartan albeit clean, and you can enjoy outdoor movies on sprawling grounds.

Sate Bali
INDONESIAN $

(Map p89; ☑ 0361-853 3626; Echo Beach; mains 25,000-75,000Rp; ⊙ 8am-7pm) Better than usual surfer fare is served at this branch of the excellent Seminyak restaurant. From its corner location on the waterfront you can survey the surf while enjoy Indonesian standards prepared a cut above average.

★ Beach House
CAFE $$

(Map p89; ☑ 0361-747 4604; www.echobeach house.com; Jl Pura Batu Mejan; mains 40,000-110,000Rp; ⊙ 8am-10pm; ☎) Face the Echo Beach waves from stylish loungers or chill on a variety of couches and picnic tables. Enjoy the menu of breakfasts, salads, grilled fare and tasty dishes such as calamari with aioli. Evening barbecues are popular – especially on Sunday – and feature fresh seafood, steaks and live music.

Pererenan Beach

Yet to be found by the right developer, **Pererenan Beach** (Map p89) is for you if you want your sand windswept and your waves unridden. It's an easy 300m walk further on from Echo Beach across sand and rock formations (or about 1km by road). This also marks the end of the vast sweep of sand that begins near the airport.

🛏 Sleeping & Eating

There are a couple of simple cafes here that don't have the mobs of Echo Beach but still enjoy sweeping surf views.

Pondok Nyoman Bagus
GUESTHOUSE $

(Map p89; ☑ 0361-848 2925; www.pondok nyoman.com; Jl Pantai Pererenan; r 300,000-600,000Rp; ❄☎▨) Just behind the beach, there are 14 rooms with terraces and balconies in a newish two-storey building that boasts a rooftop infinity pool with some of the best views in Bali. The 2nd-floor cafe has average food and fine views.

Surfers Paradise
BUNGALOW $$

(Map p89; ☑ 0818 567 538; www.andysurfvilla. com; Jl Pantai Pererenan; r 500,000-700,000Rp; ❄☎▨) Five small bungalows surround a compact courtyard and are watched over by a charming Balinese family; 12 people can rent the entire complex and throw a nonstop party.

South Bali & the Islands

Best Places to Eat

→ Bumbu Bali (p109)

→ Char Ming (p115)

→ Warung Satria (p122)

→ Café Teduh (p122)

→ Minami (p114)

Best Places to Stay

→ Indiana Kenanga (p130)

→ Temple Lodge (p101)

→ Alila Villas Uluwatu (p104)

→ Belmond Jimbaran Puri (p97)

→ Tandjung Sari (p113)

Why Go?

You won't have seen Bali if you haven't fully explored south Bali. The island's capital, Denpasar, sprawls in all directions from the centre and is a vibrant place, offering traditional markets, glitzy malls, great eating and plenty of Balinese history and culture, even as it threatens to absorb the tourist hubs of Seminyak, Kuta and Sanur.

The Bukit Peninsula (the southern part of south Bali) has multiple personalities. In the east, Tanjung Benoa is a beach-fronted playground of modest resorts while Nusa Dua attempts to bring order out of chaos with an insulated pasture of five-star hotels. The west side, however, is where the real action is. Small coves and beaches are dotted with edgy little guesthouses and luxe eco-resorts. There's a cool, carefree vibe, derived from the fab surfing around Ulu Watu.

To the east, Nusa Penida dominates the horizon, but in its lee you'll find Nusa Lembongan, the ultimate island escape from the island of Bali.

When to Go

→ The best time to visit south Bali is outside the high season, which is July, August and the weeks around Christmas and New Year's Day. During the high season, visitor numbers spike and rooms from Bingin to Tanjung Benoa and Sanur to Nusa Lembongan may be filled. Many prefer April to June and September when the crowds are manageable.

→ Surfing is best at the world-class breaks along the west coast of the Bukit Peninsula from February to November, with May to August being especially good.

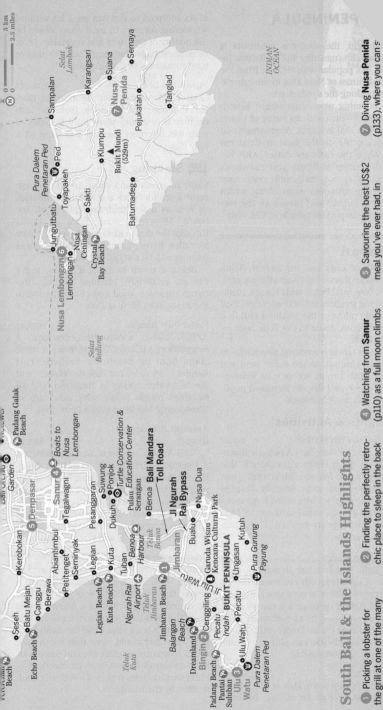

INDIAN
OCEAN

5 km
2.5 miles

South Bali & the Islands Highlights

1 Picking a lobster for the grill at one of the many beachfront seafood joints in **Jimbaran** (p97).

2 Finding the perfectly retro-chic place to sleep in the back lanes of **Bingin** (p100).

3 Surfing **Ulu Watu** (p103), Bali's ultimate swell magnet.

4 Watching from **Sanur** (p110) as a full moon climbs over Nusa Penida, casting a mysterious glow over land and sea.

5 Savouring the best US$2 meal you've ever had, in **Denpasar** (p121).

6 Escaping one island (Bali) for a more peaceful, smaller one: **Nusa Lembongan** (p126).

7 Diving **Nusa Penida** (p133), where you can see with manta rays and large fish.

southern peninsula is ... aning 'hill' in Bahasa Indonesia ... r with visitors, from the Nusa Dua to the sybaritic ... outh coast.

... west coast (often generically called Pecatu) with its string-of-pearls beaches is a real hot spot. Accommodation sits precariously on the sand at Balangan Beach while the cliffs are dotted with idiosyncratic lodges at Bingin and elsewhere. New places sprout daily and most have views of the turbulent waters here, which have world-famous surf breaks all the way south to the important temple of Ulu Watu.

Jimbaran

Just south of Kuta and the airport, Teluk Jimbaran (Jimbaran Bay) is an alluring crescent of white-sand beach and blue sea, fronted by a long string of seafood warungs (food stalls) and ending at the southern end in a bushy headland, home to the Four Seasons Jimbaran Bay.

Jimbaran remains a relaxed alternative to Kuta and Seminyak to the north (and you can't beat the airport access!). Its markets are fun to visit and despite increased popularity, it's still fairly laid-back.

⊙ Sights & Activities

★ Jimbaran Fish Market   MARKET
(Jimbaran Beach; ⊘6am-3pm) A popular morning stop on Bukit Peninsula ambles is this smelly, lively and frenetic fish market – just watch where you step. Brightly painted boats bob along the shore while huge cases of everything from small sardines to fearsome langoustines are hawked. The action is fast and furious.

★ Jimbaran Beach   BEACH
One of Bali's best beaches, Jimbaran's 4km-long arc of sand is mostly clean and there is no shortage of places to get a snack, a drink, a seafood dinner or to rent a sun lounger. The bay is protected by an unbroken coral reef, which keeps the surf more mellow than at Kuta, although you can still get breaks that are fun for bodysurfing.

Morning Market   MARKET
(Jl Ulu Watu; ⊘6am-noon) This is one of the best markets in Bali for a visit, because:

a) it's compact so you can see a lot without wandering forever; b) local chefs swear by the quality of the fruits and vegetables (ever seen a cabbage that big?); and c) they're used to tourists trudging about.

Pura Ulun Siwi   HINDU TEMPLE
(Jl Ulu Watu) Across from the morning market, this ebony-hued temple from the 18th century is a snoozy place until it explodes with life, offerings, incense and more on a holy day.

🛏 Sleeping

Some of south Bali's most luxurious large resorts are found in and around Jimbaran, as well as a few midrange places off the beach. Most offer some form of shuttle through the day to Kuta and beyond. A new Meridien Resort near the southern seafood warung will be a stylish addition.

Being a much more 'real' place (ie it's not an artificially planned resort), Jimbaran makes a good resort alternative to the monoliths of Nusa Dua.

Hotel Puri Bambu   HOTEL $$
(☑0361-701468; www.hotelpuribambu.com; Jl Pengeracikan; r US$50-120; 🖭@🛜🖭) A mere 200m from the beach, the flash-free Puri Bambu is an older but well-run place – and the best-value option in Jimbaran. The 48 standard rooms (some with tubs) are in three-storey blocks around a large pool.

Keraton Jimbaran
Resort   HOTEL $$
(☑0361-701961; www.keratonjimbaranresort.com; Jl Mrajapati; r US$110-200; 🖭@🛜🖭) Sharing the same idyllic Jimbaran beach as the neighbouring pricier resorts, the low-key Keraton is great value for a beachfront resort. Its 102 rooms are scattered about one- and two-storey bungalow-style units. The grounds are spacious and typically Bali-lush.

Udayana Kingfisher
Ecolodge   LODGE $$
(☑0361-747 4204; www.udayanaecolodge.com; Jl Kampus Bukit; r from US$80; 🖭@🛜🖭) 🍽 Feel like a butterfly perched in a green canopy from the 2nd-floor common areas of this lodge, which is an oasis amid the Bukit hubbub. There are grand views over south Bali; the 15 rooms are comfortable and there is an inviting common area, with an excellent library that includes copies of a butterfly book written by the managers.

Jimbaran

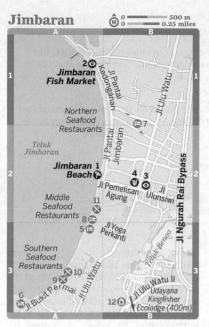

you can get a good table and enjoy the solar show over a couple beers before you dine.

Fixed prices for seafood platters in a plethora of varieties have become common and allow you to avoid the sport of choosing your fish and then paying for it by weight on scales that cause locals to break out in laughter. However, should you go this route, be sure to agree on costs first. Generally, you can enjoy a seafood feast, sides and a couple of beers for under US$20 per person. Lobster (from US$30) will bump that figure up considerably.

The best kitchens marinate the fish in garlic and lime, then douse it with chilli and oil while grilling over coconut husks. Thick clouds of smoke from the coals are part of the atmosphere, as are roaming bands, who perform cheery cover tunes (think the 'Macarena'). Almost all restaurants take credit cards.

★ **Belmond Jimbaran Puri**   RESORT **$$$**
(📞 0361-701605; www.belmond.com; off Jl Ulu Watu; cottages from US$350; ❄@🛜☒) This luxurious beachside retreat is set in nice grounds complete with a maze-like pool that looks onto open ocean. The 64 cottages and villas have private gardens, large terraces and a stylish room design with sunken tubs. It's a lavish yet low-key escape.

Four Seasons Jimbaran Bay   RESORT **$$$**
(📞 0361-701010; www.fourseasons.com; Jl Bukit Permai; villas from US$800; ❄@🛜☒) Each of the 147 villas here is designed in a traditional Balinese manner, complete with a carved entrance way, which opens onto an open-air living pavilion overlooking a plunge pool. The site is a hillside overlooking Jimbaran Beach, which is a short walk away; most villas have sweeping views across the bay.

✗ Eating & Drinking

Jimbaran's three groups of seafood restaurants cook fresh barbecued seafood every evening (and lunch at many), drawing tourists from across the south. The open-sided affairs are right by the beach and perfect for enjoying sea breezes and sunsets. Tables and chairs are set up on the sand almost to the water's edge. Arrive before sunset, so

✗ Northern Seafood Restaurants

The northern seafood restaurants run south from the fish market along Jl Kedonganan and Jl Pantai Jimbaran. This is the area you will likely be taken to by a taxi if you don't specify otherwise. Most of these places are restaurant-like, with tables inside and out on the raked sand. However the area lacks the fun atmosphere of the two areas to the south.

LOCAL KNOWLEDGE

PASCAL CHEVILLOT: SEAFOOD CHEF

Owner of the very popular Sardine (p85) restaurant in Kerobokan, Chevillot is a fixture at the Jimbaran fish market (p96) up to six mornings a week – so he knows what's been brought in fresh.

Best Reason to Visit
New seafood arrives constantly as boats pull up to the beach. You know you'll find certain things like excellent shellfish all the time, but it's also an adventure as you are constantly surprised.

Best Fish for Sale Here
Opaka-paka, king fish, grouper and barramundi.

Best Way to Visit
Get there as early as possible and then stay out of the way. Wander around the dark interior; it's like a warren and you'll be surprised at what Bali's waters yield. The vendors are actually happy to see you there, figuring you'll eat more seafood.

✖ Middle Seafood Restaurants

The middle seafood restaurants are in a compact and atmospheric group just south of Jl Pantai Jimbaran and Jl Pemelisan Agung. These are the simplest affairs, with old-fashioned thatched roofs and wide-open sides. The beach is a little less manicured, with the fishing boats resting up on the sand. Huge piles of coconut husks await their turn on the fires.

Warung Bamboo   SEAFOOD $$
(off Jl Pantai Jimbaran; meals 80,000-200,000Rp; ⊘noon-10pm) Warung Bamboo is slightly more appealing than its neighbours, all of which have a certain raffish charm. The menu is dead simple: choose your seafood and the sides and sauces are included.

✖ Southern Seafood Restaurants

The southern seafood restaurants (also called the Muaya group) are a compact and festive collection of about a dozen places at the south end of the beach. There's a parking area off Jl Bukit Permai, and the beach here is well groomed, with nice trees.

★ Lei Lei Seaside Barbeque   SEAFOOD $$
(☑0361-703296; off Jl Bukit Permai; meals 80,000-200,000Rp; ⊘noon-10pm) An especially cheery outpost, with sparkling tanks filled with future taste-treats. The furniture here is slightly nicer than elsewhere.

Made Bagus Cafe   SEAFOOD $$
(☑0361-701858; off Jl Bukit Permai; meals 80,000-200,000Rp; ⊘noon-10pm) Tucked away at the north end of the southern group; the staff serving their narrow patch of tables on the beach here radiate charm. Go for one of the mixed platters and ask for extra sauce, it's that good.

Rock Bar   BAR
(☑0361-702222; Jl Karang Mas Sejahtera, Ayana Resort; ⊘4pm-1am; ☎) Star of a thousand glossy articles about Bali, this bar perched 14m above the crashing Indian Ocean waves is very popular. In fact at sunset the wait to ride the lift down to the bar can top one hour. Still, it's a dramatic location and late at night you can take in the stars without the crowds.

🛍 Shopping

Jenggala Keramik Bali Ceramics   CERAMICS
(☑0361-703311; www.jenggala.com; Jl Ulu Watu II; ⊘8am-8pm) This modern warehouse showcases beautiful ceramic homewares that are a favourite Balinese purchase. There's a viewing area where you can watch production, as well as a cafe. Ceramic courses are available for adults and children.

ℹ Getting There & Away

Plenty of taxis wait around the beachfront warungs in the evening to take diners home (about 100,000Rp to Seminyak). Some of the seafood warungs provide free transport if you call first. Expect to pay upwards of 5000Rp per vehicle to use the beach access roads.

Around Jimbaran

Folding around limestone bluffs, sightly **Tegalwangi Beach**, 4.5km southwest of Jimbaran, is the first of cove after cove holding patches of alluring sand all down the west coast of the peninsula. A small parking area lies in front of **Pura Segara Tegalwangi** temple, a popular place for addressing the ocean gods. There's usually a lone drinks vendor offering refreshment before – or after – you make the short but challenging trip over the bad paths down to the beach. Immediately south, the vast Ayana resort sprawls over the cliffs.

From Jimbaran, take Jl Bukit Permai for 3km until the gates of the Ayana, where it veers west 1.5km to the temple.

Central Bukit

Jl Ulu Watu goes south of Jimbaran, climbing 200m up the peninsula's namesake hill, affording views over southern Bali. As the region has surged in popularity, traffic has become a major problem.

Garuda Wisnu Kencana Cultural Park (GWK; ☑ 0361-703603; www.gwk-culturalpark. com; Jl Raya Ulu Watu; admission 100,000Rp; ☉ 9am-10pm; ⊕) is the yet-to-be-completed, potentially huge cultural park intended to be home to a 66m-high statue of Garuda. This Brobdingnagian dream is supposed to be erected on top of a shopping and gallery complex, at a total height of 146m. So far the only completed part of the statue is the large bronze head. Despite the hype, there's not much to justify the entrance fee.

About 2km south of GWK is a vital crossroads with a useful landmark, the **Nirmala Supermarket** (Jl Ulu Watu; ☉ 8am-10pm). There are ATMs and cafes here, including a small branch of the Ubud-based **Bali Buda** (☑ 0361-701980; Jl Ulu Watu; snacks from 20,000Rp; ☉ 8am-8pm) bakeries. It has shady tables where you can enjoy its healthy foods and juices.

Balangan Beach

Balangan Beach is a long, low strand at the base of rocky cliffs. It's covered with palm trees and fronted by a ribbon of near-white sand, picturesquely dotted with sun umbrellas. Surfer bars, cafes in shacks and even slightly more permanent guesthouses precariously line the shore where buffed First World bods soak up rays amid Third World sanitation. Think of it as a bit of the Wild West not far from Bali's glitz.

At the northern end of the beach is a small temple, **Pura Dalem Balangan**. Bamboo beach shacks line the southern end; visitors laze away with one eye cast on the action at the fast left surf break here.

You can access the beach via rough tracks from two parking areas: the north end is near the uncrowded temple, the south end is near the beach bars.

🛏 Sleeping & Eating

Balangan Beach has some established guesthouses up on the bluff, five minutes from the surf. Down on the sand, things are much more ad hoc, with everything seeming to be one pass of a bulldozer from oblivion. At the latter option you can negotiate for small, windowless thatched rooms in bars next to cases of Bintang. Don't pay more than 150,000Rp.

Numerous guesthouses are appearing on the access road from Jl Ulu Watu, many are far from the beach.

Balangan Sea View Bungalows GUESTHOUSE $
(☑ 0812 376 1954; www.balanganseaviewbunga low.com; off Jl Pantai Balangan; r with fan/air-con from 375,000/450,000Rp; ❄ ☎ ⛱) A cluster of thatched bungalows with 25 rooms surrounds a small pool in an attractive compound. The small cafe has wi-fi. It is directly across from Flower Bud Bungalows on the knoll.

Nerni Warung GUESTHOUSE $
(☑ 0813 5381 4090; r from 200,000Rp; mains from 30,000Rp) Down on the sand at the south end of the beach, this simple place has great views from its cafe. Nerni keeps a close watch on things and the simple rooms are cleaner than the competition. She may seem dour but she's smiling on the inside. We think.

Flower Bud Bungalows GUESTHOUSE $$
(☑ 0828 367 2772; www.flowerbudbalangan.com; off Jl Pantai Balangan; r 500,000-1,200,000Rp; ☎ ⛱) On the knoll. Eight bamboo bungalows are set on spacious grounds near a classic kidney-shaped pool. There's a certain Crusoe-esque motif and a small spa.

Balangan Beach & Ulu Watu

0 / 2 km
0 / 1 mile

Teluk Kuta

34

8
29
27 16
22 7

Jimbaran
(2km)

Bukit
Peninsula

Jl Pantai Balangan

Cenggiling

9

17 11
12 5 3
6 24 18
31
14

13 28 32 26
25
21
33

Pecatu
Indah

Jl Pantai
Bingin

Jl Labuan
Sait

Jl Melasti

30

27

Jl Ulu Watu

Jl Nasula

Ungasan
(1.5km)

Ulu Watu

19

Jl Pantai
Suluban

Pecatu

Pura Luhur 1
Ulu Watu 35

INDIAN OCEAN

10

15 20

Nasa Café CAFE $

(meals from 30,000Rp; ☺8am-11pm) Inside the shady bamboo bar built on stilts above the sand, a vibrant azure ribbon of crashing surf is the wraparound view through the drooping thatched roof. Simple Indo meals set the tone for the four bare-bones rooms off the bar (about 150,000Rp), which are little more than a mattress on the floor. It's one of several similar choices.

ⓘ Getting There & Away

Balangan Beach is 6.2km off Jl Ulu Watu on Jl Pantai Balangan. Turn west at the crossroads at Nirmala Supermarket.

Taxis from the Kuta area cost at least 60,000Rp per hour for the round trip and waiting time.

Pecatu Indah

This 400-hectare resort complex rises between central Bukit Peninsula and the coast. The land is arid but that hasn't stopped developers from building a huge hotel, condos, houses and a water-hungry 18-hole golf course. Follow the grand boulevards and you can see a lot of tank trucks hauling water in from Bali's central mountains.

The centrepiece of the development is a privatised beach, a one-time surfer hang-out called Dreamland. It's now been saddled with the moniker 'New Kuta Beach', which to some is sort of like calling your boat the *New Titanic*. It is overlooked by a gaudy and pricey club.

Bingin

An ever-evolving scene, Bingin comprises scores of unconventionally stylish lodgings scattered across cliffs and on the strip of white-sand **Bingin Beach** below. Smooth Jl Pantai Bingin runs 1km off Jl Melasti (look for the thicket of accommodation signs) and then branches off into a tangle of lanes.

The scenery here is simply superb, with sylvan cliffs dropping down to surfer cafes and the foaming edge of the azure sea. The beach is a five-minute walk down fairly steep paths. The surf here is often savage but the boulder-strewn sands are serene and the sight and sound of the roaring breakers is mesmerising.

An elderly resident collects 5000Rp at a T-junction near parking for the trail down to the beach.

Balangan Beach & Ulu Watu

🛏 Sleeping & Eating

Numerous places to stay are scattered along and near the cliffs. All have at least simple cafes, although for nightlife you'll want to head towards Ulu Watu. You can get bare-bones accommodation down the cliff at a string of bamboo and thatch surfer crash pads near the water. Expect to pay about 100,000Rp.

★ **Adi's Home Stay** BUNGALOW $
(📞 0816 297 106, 0815 5838 8524; off Jl Pantai Bingin; r with fan/air-con from 250,000/400,000Rp; ❄🛜) The nine bungalow-style rooms facing a nice garden are new and comfy. It's down a very small lane, near the beach parking. It has a small cafe.

Bingin Garden GUESTHOUSE $
(📞 0816 472 2002; tommybarrell76@yahoo.com; off Jl Pantai Bingin; r from 250,000Rp; 🏊) Six bungalow-style rooms are set around tidy grounds with a large pool. It's back off the cliffs and about 300m from the path down to the beach.

★ **Temple Lodge** BOUTIQUE HOTEL $$
(📞 0857 3901 1572; www.thetemplelodge.com; off Jl Pantai Bingin; r US$70-250; 🛜🏊) 'Artsy' and 'beautiful' just begin to describe this collec-

tion of huts and cottages made from thatch, driftwood and other natural materials. It sits on a jutting shelf on the cliffs above the surf breaks and there are superb views from the infinity pool and some of the seven units. You can arrange for meals and there are morning yoga classes.

Mick's Place BOUTIQUE HOTEL $$
(📞 0812 391 3337; www.micksplacebali.com; off Jl Pantai Bingin; r from US$100, villa from US$300; ❄🛜🏊) The turquoise water in the postage-stamp-sized infinity pool matches the turquoise sea below. A hippie-chic playground where you rough it in style; there are never more than 16 guests. Five artful bungalows and one luxe villa are set in lush grounds. By day there's a 180-degree view of the world-famous surf breaks.

Mu GUESTHOUSE $$
(📞 0361-847 0976; www.mu-bali.com; off Jl Pantai Bingin; r $90-200; ❄🛜🏊) The 12 very individual bungalows with thatched roofs are scattered about a compound dominated by a cliffside infinity pool. All have open-air living spaces; some have air-con bedrooms and hot tubs with a view. Two units have multiple bedrooms.

Impossibles Beach

About 100m west of Jl Pantai Bingin on Jl Melasti you'll see another turn towards the ocean. Follow this paved road for 700m and look for a scrawled sign on a wall reading **Impossibles Beach**. Follow the treacherous path and you'll soon understand the name. It's a tortuous trek but you'll be rewarded with an empty cove with splotches of creamy sand between boulders.

Padang Padang

Small in size but not in perfection, **Padang Padang Beach** is a cute little cove. It is near Jl Labuan Sait where a small river flows into the sea. Parking is easy and it is a short walk through a temple and down a well-paved trail where you'll be hit up for bananas by monkeys. There are patches of shade near the sand plus a couple of simple warungs. You can rent surfboards to hit the breaks right offshore. It can get very crowded in high season.

If you're feeling adventurous, you can enjoy a much longer stretch of nearly deserted white sand that begins on the west side of the river. Ask locals how to get there or take the precipitous stairs by Thomas Homestay.

A metered taxi from Kuta will cost about 150,000Rp and take at least an hour, depending on traffic.

🍴 Sleeping & Eating

Padang Padang is getting dotted with good places to eat and sleep along Jl Labuan Sait. One strip is 200m up from the beach entrance and has ATMs.

To get really close to the waves, consider one of the cliffside guesthouses that are reached by a steep path down from the bluff. The trail starts at the end of a twisting lane that runs for 200m from Jl Labuan Sait just west of Om Burger. Simple meals are available and you can buy water, Bintang and other essentials.

On Saturday and full-moon nights there's a party on the beach, with grilled seafood and tunes until dawn.

Bali Rocks   GUESTHOUSE $
(📞 0817 344 788; www.bali-rocks.com; r 125,000-150-000Rp) Down the cliff face, this thatched bit of wonder has dead simple rooms with stunning views of the surf breaks and ocean. Showers and toilets are down a couple flights of stairs from the room. At high tide you can jump directly in the water.

Thomas Homestay   GUESTHOUSE $
(📞 0813 3803 4354; off Jl Labuan Sait; r from 250,000Rp) Enjoy stunning views up and down this spectacular coast. The 13 very simple rooms (some share bathrooms) lie at the end of a very rough 400m track off the main road. You can take a long walk down stairs to the uncrowded swathe of Padang Padang Beach west of the river. The cafe is a secret find for its views.

★ Le Sabot   BUNGALOW $$
(📞 0812 3768 0414; www.lesabotbali.com; r from US$60) Revel in this 1960s surfer fantasy on the Bukit cliffs; the four bungalow-style units here are almost plush. There's hot water, electricity, fridges, large beds and decks with some of Bali's finest views. It's also quite a slog down the cliff face.

PILLAGING BUKIT PENINSULA

Many environmentalists consider the always arid Bukit Peninsula a harbinger for the challenges that face the rest of Bali as land use far outpaces the water supply. The small guesthouses that once perched above and on the string of pearls that are the beaches on the west side are being supplanted by large water-sucking developments. Besides the vast Pecatu Indah complex, many more projects are carving away the beautiful limestone cliffs to make way for huge concrete structures housing resorts.

There are few controls to regulate the growth; many of the vehicles stuck with you in traffic jams on Jl Ulu Watu will be water trucks that service the area's thirst by the hundreds daily. Meanwhile, a road-building frenzy on the southern coast has sparked a villa building boom, most with private pools.

Grassroots efforts to control growth have been diverted to an effort to save the vast Benoa Bay mangroves at the base of Bukit from development.

Pink Coco Bali HOTEL $$
(☑0361-824 3366; www.pinkcocobali.com; Jl Labuan Sait; r US$60-150; ❄🐶🌊) One of the pools at this romantic hotel is suitably tiled pink. The 21 rooms have terraces and balconies plus artistic touches. There is a lush Mexican motif throughout. Surfers are catered to and you can rent bikes and other gear.

Om Burger BURGERS $$
(☑0812 391 3617; Jl Labuan Sait; mains from 50,000Rp; ⊗8am-10pm; 🐶) 'Superfood burgers' – that's the come-on at this joint with nice 2nd-floor views. The burgers are indeed super and are actually super-sized. There are intimations of health across the menu: baked sweet potato fries, vitamin-filled juices and more. It's very popular; expect to wait for a table at night.

Ulu Watu & Around

Ulu Watu has become the generic name for the southwestern tip of the Bukit Peninsula. It includes the much-revered temple and the fabled namesake surf breaks.

About 2km north of the temple there is a dramatic cliff which has steps that lead to the legendary Ulu Watu surf breaks. All manner of cafes and surf shops spill down the nearly sheer face to the water below. Views are stellar and it is quite the scene.

Sights & Activities

★ **Pura Luhur Ulu Watu** HINDU TEMPLE
(Jl Ulu Watu; admission incl sarong & sash rental adult/child 20,000/10,000Rp; ⊗8am-7pm) This important temple is perched precipitously on the southwestern tip of the peninsula, atop sheer cliffs that drop straight into the ceaseless surf. You enter through an unusual arched gateway flanked by statues of Ganesha. Inside, the walls of coral bricks are covered with intricate carvings of Bali's mythological menagerie.

Only Hindu worshippers can enter the small inner temple that is built onto the jutting tip of land. However, the views of the endless swells of the Indian Ocean from the cliffs are almost spiritual. At sunset, walk around the clifftop to the left (south) of the temple to lose some of the crowd.

Ulu Watu is one of several important temples to the spirits of the sea along the south coast of Bali. In the 11th century the Javanese priest Empu Kuturan first established

---

ⓘ DAMN MONKEYS

Pura Luhur Ulu Watu is home to scores of grey monkeys. Greedy little things, when they're not energetically fornicating, they snatch sunglasses, handbags, hats and anything else within reach.

If you want to start a riot, peel them a banana...

---

a temple here. The complex was added to by Nirartha, another Javanese priest who is known for the seafront temples at Pura Tanah Lot, Rambut Siwi and Pura Sakenan. Nirartha retreated to Ulu Watu for his final days when he attained *moksa* (freedom from earthly desires).

A popular Kecak dance is held in the temple grounds at sunset, when traffic jams form during high season.

Ulu Watu SURFING
Ulu Watu (Ulu's) is a storied surf break – the stuff of dreams and nightmares. Its legend is matched closely by nearby **Pantai Suluban**. Since the early 1970s these breaks have drawn surfers from around the world. The left breaks seem to go on forever.

The area boasts numerous small inns and warungs that sell and rent out surfboards, and provide food and drink, ding repairs or a massage – whatever you need most.

🛌 Sleeping & Eating

The cliffs above the main Ulu Watu breaks are lined with cafes and bars. There are also plenty of cheap and midrange places to stay; your best bet is to wander around and check out a few.

Gong GUESTHOUSE $
(☑0361-769976; www.thegonguluwatubali.com; Jl Pantai Suluban; r from 200,000Rp; @🌊) The 12 tidy rooms have good ventilation and hot water and face a small compound with a lovely pool; some 2nd-floor units have distant ocean views. It is about 1km south of the Ulu Watu cliffside cafes; the host family is lovely.

★ **Uluwatu Cottages** BUNGALOW $$
(☑0361-207 9547; www.uluwatucottage.com; Jl Labuan Sait; r from US$60; ❄🐶🌊) This newcomer is a very welcome addition to the Ulu Watu scene. Its 14 bungalows are spread across a large site right on the cliff, just 400m east of the Ulu Watu cafes (about

200m off Jl Labuan Sait). The units are comfortable and the views are superb.

Mamo Hotel   HOTEL **$$**
(☑0361-769882;   www.mamohoteluluwatu.com;
Jl Labuan Sait; r US$60-100; ✳🛜❄) Right at
the entrance to the area above the Ulu Watu
breaks, this modern 30-room hotel is a good
mainstream choice. The three-storey main
building surrounds a fine pool and there's a
popular and breezy cafe.

Delpi Rock Lounge   CAFE **$**
(meals from 50,000Rp; ⊘noon-9pm) At this
branch of the Delpi empire you can nab a
sunbed on a spectacular platform atop a
rock nearly surrounded by surf. Further up
the cliff there's a cafe which has three simple
rooms for rent (from 350,000Rp).

Yeye's Warung   CAFE **$**
(Jl Labuan Sait; meals from 30,000Rp; ⊘noon-
midnight) A gathering point away from the
cliffs at a spot between Padang Padang and
Ulu Watu, Yeye's has an easy-going ambi-
ence, cheapish beers, tasty Thai food and
good pizza.

Single Fin   CAFE **$$**
(☑0361-769941; meals from 60,000Rp; ⊘8am-
11pm) The views of the surf action from this
triple-level cafe are breathtaking. Watch the
never-ending swells march in across the
Indian from this cliffside perch and as the
waves form, try to guess which of the myriad
surfers will catch a ride. Drinks here aren't
cheap and the food is merely passable, but
especially at sunset, who cares?

☆ Entertainment

★Kecak Dance   DANCE
(Pura Luhur Ulu Watu, off Jl Ulu Watu; admission
100,000Rp; ⊘sunset) Although the performance obviously caters for tourists, the
gorgeous setting at Pura Luhur Ulu Watu in
a small amphitheatre in a leafy part of the
grounds makes it one of the more evocative
on the island. The views out to sea are as
inspiring as the dance. It's very popular in
high season.

❶ Getting There & Away

The best way to see the Ulu Watu region is with
your own wheels. Note that the cops often set
up checkpoints near Pecatu Indah for checks
on motorcycle-riding Westerners. Be aware you
may pay a fine for offences such as a 'loose' chin
strap.

Coming to the Ulu Watu cliffside cafes from the
east on Jl Labuan Sait you will first encounter an
access road to parking near the cliffs. Continuing over a bridge, there is a side road that leads
to another parking area, from where it is a pretty
200m walk north to the cliffside cafes.

A taxi ride out here will cost at least
200,000Rp from Seminyak and take more than
an hour in the coagulated traffic.

Ungasan & Around

If Ulu Watu is all about celebrating surf culture, Ungasan is all about celebrating yourself. From crossroads near this otherwise
nondescript village, roads radiate to the
south coast where some of Bali's most exclusive oceanside resorts can be found. With
the infinite turquoise waters of the Indian
Ocean rolling hypnotically in the distance
it's hard not to think you've reached the end
of the world, albeit a very comfortable one.

◉ Sights & Activities

Pura Mas Suka   HINDU TEMPLE
This diminutive temple is reached by a twisting narrow road through a mostly barren
red-rock landscape that changes dramatically when you reach Karma Kandara, which
surrounds the temple. A perfect example of
a Balinese seaside temple, although it is often closed so consider that before setting off
on the rough track to the temple.

Finns Beach Club   BEACH CLUB
(☑0361-848 2111; www.finnsbeachclub.com; off
Jl Masuka; daypass adult/child 250,000Rp/free;
⊘8am-8pm) Set on a pocket of powdery
white sand at the base of a cliff, this private
beach club offers a full day's worth of activities and pampering. Admission includes a
150,000Rp credit, which will go quickly in the
bars, beachside spa pavilions etc. There are
weekend afternoon DJs, sunset bonfires and,
crucially, an elevator up and down the cliff.

🛏 Sleeping & Eating

★Alila Villas Uluwatu   RESORT **$$$**
(☑0361-848 2166; www.alilahotels.com; Jl Be-
limbing Sari; r from US$760; ✳@🛜❄) Visually
stunning, this vast resort has an artful con-
temporary style that is light and airy while
still conveying a sense of luxury. The 85-unit
Alila offers gracious service in a setting where
the blue of the ocean contrasts with the green
of the surrounding (hotel-tended) rice fields.
It's 2km off Jl Ulu Watu.

PANDAWA BEACH

An old quarry on the remote southern coast of the Bukit Peninsula has been transformed into a Hindu-shrine-cum-beach-attraction. Pay a steep admission price (10,000Rp) to guards (who were swilling Bintang when we were there) and you descend on a road through dramatically cut limestone cliffs. Large statues of Hindu deities are carved into niches in the stone. At the base, you'll find a long swathe of sand known as Pandawa Beach, which is all but deserted weekdays except for a few village seaweed farmers. But come weekends this is a major daytrip for the Balinese.

Some warungs (food stalls) provide refreshments and sun-lounger rental and the reef-protected waters are good for swimming. Look for Pandawa Beach signs on the main road between Ungasan and Nusa Dua, Jl Dharmawangsa. It's 2km down to the village where you can park by the sand.

Karma Kandara RESORT $$$
(☑0361-848 2200; www.karmaresorts.com; Jl Villa Kandara Banjar; villas from US$600; ❋@🛜🏊) This beautiful resort clings to the side of hills that roll down to the sea. Stone paths lead between walled villas draped in bougainvillea and punctuated by painted doors, creating the mood of a tropical hill town. The restaurant, Di Mare (meals US$15 to $30), is linked to the bifurcated property by a little bridge; there's a beach elevator.

Nusa Dua

Nusa Dua translates literally as 'Two Islands', although they are actually small raised headlands, each with a small temple. But Nusa Dua is much better known as Bali's gated compound of resort hotels. It's a vast and manicured place where you leave the rest of the island behind as you pass the guards. Gone is the hustle, bustle and engaging chaos of the rest of the island.

Built in the 1970s, Nusa Dua was designed to compete with international beach resorts the world over. Balinese 'culture', in the form of attenuated dances and other performances, is literally trucked in for the masses nightly.

With nearly 20 large resorts and thousands of hotel rooms, Nusa Dua can live up to some of its promise when full, but during slack times it's rather desolate. Certainly, it is closer in atmosphere to a generic beach resort than to anything Balinese – although some of the hotels try to apply a patina of Bali style.

👁 Sights & Activities

Nusa Dua's beaches are clean and raked; offshore reefs catch the swells, so the surf is almost nil.

All the resort hotels have pricey spas that provide a broad range of therapies, treatments and just plain, simple relaxation. The most lauded of the spas are at the Amanusa, Westin and St Regis hotels. All are open to nonguests; expect fees for a massage to start at US$100.

★Pasifika Museum MUSEUM
(☑0361-774559; Bali Collection Shopping Centre, Block P; admission 70,000Rp; ⏰10am-6pm) When groups from the nearby resorts aren't around, you'll probably have this large museum to yourself. Art of Pacific Ocean cultures spans several centuries and includes over 600 paintings (don't miss the tikis). The influential wave of European artists who thrived in Bali in the early 20th century is well represented. Look for works by Arie Smit, Adrien Jean Le Mayeur de Merpres and Theo Meier.

Pura Gegar HINDU TEMPLE
Just south of Gegar Beach is a bluff with a good cafe and a path that leads up to Pura Gegar, a compact temple shaded by gnarled old trees. Views are great and you can spot swimmers who've come south in the shallow, placid waters around the bluff for a little frolic.

Beach Promenade WALKING
One of the nicest features of Nusa Dua is the 5km-long beach promenade that stretches the length of the resort and continues north along much of the beach in Tanjung Benoa.

Bali National Golf Resort GOLF
(☑0361-771791; www.balinationalgolf.com; Kawasan Wisata; course fees from US$185; ⏰6.30am-6.30pm) This 18-hole links meanders through Nusa Dua and boasts a grand new clubhouse. The course plays to over 6500 metres.

Nusa Dua

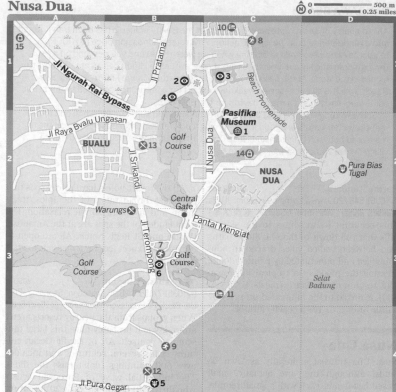

Gegar Beach   BEACH
(admission 5000Rp) The once gem-like Gegar Beach is now gem-sized with the addition of a 700-room Mulia resort. The public area has some cafes, rental loungers and water activities (kayak rental 30,000Rp per hour); it gets jammed on weekends. Boats out to the **Nusa Dua Surf Break** beyond the reef cost 150,000Rp. You can still use the immaculate public sands in front of the resorts.

🛏 Sleeping

The Nusa Dua resorts are similar in several ways: they are all big (some are huge) and almost every major international brand is represented. Most are right on the placid beach.

Note the major international brands such as Westin and Hyatt have invested heavily, adding loads of the amenities (such as elaborate pools and day camps for kids). Other hotels seem little changed from when they were built during the heyday of the Suharto era in the 1970s. Some properties, including the Courtyard by Marriott and the Novotel, are off the beach.

If you're considering a stay at Nusa Dua, search for deals. During the low season you can get excellent rates.

**Sofitel Bali Nusa Dua
Beach Resort**   RESORT $$$
(📞 0361-849 2888; www.sofitelbalinusadua.com; Jl Nusa Dua; r from US$200; ❅ @ 🛜 ☀) A huge new addition to the resort strip, the Sofitel has a vast pool that meanders past the 415 rooms, some of which have terraces with direct pool access. The room blocks are huge, many rooms have at least a glimpse of the water. Sofitel's Nikki Beach Bali is another outlet of the glossy international chain of hipster beach clubs.

The Sofitel's lavish Sunday brunch (11am to 3pm) is one of Bali's best; it costs from 400,000Rp.

Nusa Dua

St Regis Bali Resort RESORT $$$
(☎0361-847 8111; www.starwoodhotels.com; ste from US$500; ❄@🛜🏊) This lavish Nusa Dua resort leaves most of the others in the sand. Every conceivable luxury is provided, from the electronics to the furnishings and marble to a personal butler. Pools abound and units are huge. The golf course and beach adjoin.

✗ Eating

Restaurants charging resort prices can be found by the dozen in the huge resorts. For people not staying at the hotels, the best reason to venture in is if you want a bounteous Sunday brunch such as the Sofitel's.

Good **warungs** cluster at the corner of Jl Srikandi and Jl Pantai Mengiat. Also along the latter street, just outside the central gate, there is a string of open-air eateries offering an unpretentious alternative to Nusa Dua dining. None will win any culinary awards, but most will provide transport.

Nusa Dua Beach Grill INTERNATIONAL $
(☎0361-743 4779; Jl Pura Gegar; meals 50,000-150,000Rp; ⊙8am-10pm) A hidden gem, this warm-hued cafe is south of Gegar Beach and the huge Mulia resort on foot, but a circuitous 1.5km by car via the temple. The drinks menu is long, the seafood fresh and the at-

mosphere heavy with assignations. [...] your afternoon away in the laid-b[...] Call for local transport.

Warung Dobiel BALINESE
(Jl Srikandi; meals from 25,000Rp; ⊙10am-3pm) A bit of authentic food action amid the bland streets of Nusa, this is a good stop for *babi guling*. Pork soup is the perfect taste-bud awakener, while the jackfruit is redolent with spices. Diners perch on stools and share tables; service can be slow and tours may mob the place. Watch out for 'foreigner' pricing.

☆ Entertainment

Many of the hotels offer Balinese dances on one or more nights, usually as part of a buffet deal. Hotel lounges also often have live music, from crooners to mellow rock bands.

🛍 Shopping

Bali Collection MALL
(☎0361-771662; www.bali-collection.com; off Jl Nusa Dua; ⊙8am-10pm) Often empty except for the assistants in the glacially air-conditioned Sogo Department Store, this security-conscious mall gamely soldiers on. Chains such as Starbucks and Bali brands such as Animale mix with humdrum outlets offering souvenirs.

ⓘ Information

ATMs can be found at the Bali Collection mall, some hotel lobbies and at the huge Hardy's Department Store out on the Jl Ngurah Rai Bypass.

ⓘ Getting There & Around

The Bali Mandara Toll Road (10,000Rp) greatly speeds journeys between Nusa Dua and the airport and Sanur.

BUS
Bali's Trans-Sarbagita Bus System serves Nusa Dua on a route that follows the Jl Ngurah Rai Bypass up and around past Sanur to Batabulan.

SHUTTLE
Find out what shuttle-bus services your hotel provides before you start hailing taxis. A free **shuttle bus** (☎0361-771662; ⊙9am-10pm) connects all Nusa Dua and Tanjung Benoa resort hotels with the Bali Collection mall about every hour. Better still, walk the delightful beach promenade.

TAXI
The fixed taxi fare from the airport is 120,000Rp; a metered taxi to the airport will be much less. Taxis to/from Seminyak average 90,000Rp, although traffic can make this a 90-minute trip.

Tanjung Benoa

The peninsula of Tanjung Benoa extends about 4km north from Nusa Dua to Benoa village. It's flat and lined with family-friendly resort hotels, most of midrange calibre. By day the waters buzz with the roar of dozens of motorised water-sports craft. Group tours arrive by the busload for a day's aquatic excitement, straddling a banana boat among other thrills.

Overall, Tanjung Benoa is a fairly sedate place, although the Bali Mandara Toll Road speeds access to the nightlife diversions of Kuta and Seminyak.

◉ Sights

The village of Benoa is a fascinating little fishing settlement that makes for a good stroll. Amble the narrow lanes of the peninsula's tip for a multicultural feast. Within 100m of each other are a brightly coloured **Chinese Buddhist temple**, a domed **mosque** and a **Hindu temple** with a nicely carved triple entrance. Enjoy views of the busy channel to the port. On the dark side, Benoa's back streets hide Bali's illegal trade in turtles, although police raids are helping to limit it.

🏃 Activities

⭐ Bumbu Bali
Cooking School   COOKING COURSE
(☑ 0361-774502; www.balifoods.com; Jl Pratama; course US$90; ◷ 6am-3pm Mon, Wed & Fri) This much-lauded cooking school at the eponymous restaurant strives to get to the roots of Balinese cooking. Courses start with a 6am visit to Jimbaran's fish and morning markets, continues in the large kitchen and finishes with lunch.

ⓘ PRATAMA PERILS

Restaurants and hotels are strung out all along Jl Pratama, which runs the length of the peninsula. The southern end may be one of the most perilous streets in south Bali for a stroll. From Nusa Dua north to the Conrad Bali Resort, there are no footpaths and in many places nowhere to walk but on the narrow road, which also has blind curves. Fortunately, the **Beach Promenade** is a wonderful alternative. It continues from Nusa Dua north to the Bali Khama.

Jari Menari   SPA
(☑ 0361-778084; www.jarimenarinusadua.com; Jl Pratama; massage from 350,000Rp; ◷ 9am-9pm) This branch of the famed Seminyak original offers all the same exquisite massages by the expert all-male staff. Call for transport.

🛏 Sleeping

Tanjung Benoa's east shore is lined with midrange low-key resorts aimed at groups. They are family-friendly, offer kids' programs and enjoy repeat business by holiday-makers who are greeted with banners such as 'Welcome Back Underhills!' There's also a couple of simple guesthouses.

Pondok Agung   GUESTHOUSE $
(☑ 0361-771143; www.pondokagung.com; Jl Pratama 99; r 250,000-500,000Rp; ❇🌢) The nine airy rooms (most with tubs) in a large, house-like building are spotless. Higher-priced rooms come with small kitchens. The gardens are large, shady and attractive.

Pondok Hasan Inn   GUESTHOUSE $
(☑ 0361-772456; hasanhomestay@yahoo.com; Jl Pratama; r from 200,000Rp; ❇🌢) Back 20m off the main road, this family-run homestay has nine immaculate hot-water rooms that include breakfast. The tiles gleam on the outdoor verandah shared by the rooms, and there is a small garden.

Rumah Bali   GUESTHOUSE $$
(☑ 0361-771256; www.balifoods.com; off Jl Pratama; r US$85-110, villas from US$350; ❇@🌢🏊) Rumah Bali is a luxurious interpretation of a Balinese village by Heinz von Holzen of Bumbu Bali fame. Guests have large family rooms or individual villas (some with three bedrooms) with their own plunge pools. Besides a large communal pool, there's also a tennis court. The beach is a short walk away.

Bali Khama   RESORT $$$
(☑ 0361-774912; www.thebalikhama.com; Jl Pratama; villas US$140-250; ❇@🌢🏊) Located on its own crescent of sand at the northern end of the beach promenade. The mostly individual walled villas are large, tasteful and – obviously – private. More expensive ones have plunge pools; there are also honeymoon and multiroom villas.

🍴 Eating & Drinking

The usual batch of ho-hum tourist restaurants can be found along Jl Pratama, with their modestly priced pasta and seafood for the masses.

Tanjung Benoa

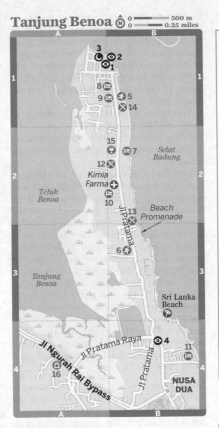

SOUTH BALI & THE ISLANDS TANJUNG BENOA

★ **Bumbu Bali**   BALINESE **$$**
(📞 0361-774502; www.balifoods.com; Jl Pratama; mains from 90,000Rp, set menus from 270,000Rp; ⊙ noon-9pm) Long-time resident and cookbook author Heinz von Holzen, his wife Puji and a well-trained and enthusiastic staff serve exquisitely flavoured dishes at this superb restaurant. Many diners opt for one of several lavish set menus.

The *rijstaffel* (rice table) shows the range of cooking in the kitchen, from sate served on their own little coconut husk grill to the tender *be celeng base manis* (pork in sweet soy sauce), with a dozen more courses in between.

Another highlight is the amazingly tasty and different *jaja batun bedil* (sticky dumpling rice in palm sugar). Tables are set under the stars and in small pavilions. The sound of frogs can be heard from the fish ponds. There's complimentary transport in the area. Book ahead.

There's a second location a short distance north; we prefer this, the original location. Note that some *rijstaffels* have a two-person minimum.

Bali Cardamon   ASIAN **$$**
(📞 0361-773745; www.balicardamon.com; Jl Pratama 97; mains from 60,000Rp; ⊙ 8am-10pm) A cut above most of the other restaurants on the Jl Pratama strip, this ambitious spot has a creative kitchen that takes influences from across Asia. It has some excellent dishes including pork belly seasoned with star anise. Sit under the frangipani trees or in the dining room.

Atlichnaya Bar   BAR
(📞 0813 3818 9675; www.atlichnaya.com; Jl Pratama 88; ⊙ 8am-late; 🛜) The lively and convivial alternative to the stiff hotel bars, this rollicking place serves up a long list of cheap mixed drinks and even offers massages (from 50,000Rp). There's cheap and cheery Indo and Western menu items as well.

ℹ Information

Kimia Farma (☑ 0361-916 6509; Jl Pratama; ⊗24hr) Reliable chain of pharmacies.

ℹ Getting There & Around

Taxis from the airport cost 135,000Rp. Bemos (minibuses) shuttle up and down Jl Pratama (5000Rp) – although after about 3pm they become scarce.

A free **shuttle bus** (☑ 0361-771662; ⊗9am-10pm) connects all Nusa Dua and Tanjung Benoa resort hotels with the Bali Collection shopping centre about every hour. Or stroll the Beach Promenade. Many restaurants will provide transport from Nusa Dua and Tanjung Benoa hotels.

SANUR

☑ 0361

Maybe Sanur is the Bali beachfront version of the youngest of the Three Bears, the one that's not too frantic (like Kuta) or too snoozy (like Nusa Dua). Many do indeed consider Sanur 'just right', as it lacks most of the hassles found to the west while maintaining a good mix of restaurants and bars that aren't all owned by resorts.

The beach, while thin, is protected by a reef and breakwaters, so families appreciate the limpid waves. Sanur has a good range of places to stay and it's well placed for day trips around the south, and north to Ubud. Really, it doesn't deserve its local moniker, 'Snore.'

Sanur stretches for about 5km along an east-facing coastline, with the lush and green landscaped grounds of resorts fronting right onto the sandy beach. West of the beachfront hotels is the busy main drag, Jl Danau Tamblingan, with hotel entrances and oodles of tourist shops, restaurants and cafes.

Noxious, traffic-choked Jl Ngurah Rai Bypass skirts the western side of the resort area, and is the main link to Kuta and the airport. Don't stay out here.

⊙ Sights

Sanur's sights – views to Nusa Penida and of local life amid the tourism – are all readily apparent from its lovely beachfront walk.

★ Museum Le Mayeur   MUSEUM
(☑ 0361-286201; adult/child 10,000/5000Rp; ⊗8am-4pm Sat-Thu, to 12.30pm Fri) Le Mayeur de Merpres (1880–1958) arrived in Bali in 1932. Three years later, he met and married the beautiful Legong dancer Ni Polok when she was just 15. They lived in this compound, which houses the museum, when Sanur was still a quiet fishing village. After the artist's death, Ni Polok lived in the house until she died in 1985.

The house is an interesting example of Balinese-style architecture – notice the beautifully carved window shutters that recount the story of Rama and Sita from the Ramayana.

Despite security (some of Le Mayeur's paintings have sold for US$150,000) and conservation problems, almost 90 of Le Mayeur's paintings are displayed inside the museum in a naturalistic Balinese interior of woven fibres. Some of Le Mayeur's early works are impressionist paintings from his travels in Africa, India, the Mediterranean and the South Pacific. Paintings from his early period in Bali are romantic depictions of daily life and beautiful Balinese women – often Ni Polok. The works from the 1950s are in much better condition, displaying the vibrant colours that later became popular with young Balinese artists. Look for the haunting black-and-white photos of Ni Polok.

Stone Pillar   MONUMENT
The pillar, down a narrow lane to the left as you face Pura Belangjong, is Bali's oldest dated artefact and has ancient inscriptions recounting military victories from more than a thousand years ago. These inscriptions are in Sanskrit and are evidence of Hindu influence 300 years before the arrival of the Majapahit court.

Bali Orchid Garden   GARDENS
(Map p176; ☑ 0361-466010; www.baliorchid gardens.com; Coast Rd; admission 100,000Rp; ⊗8am-6pm) Orchids thrive in Bali's warm weather and rich volcanic soil. At this garden you can see thousands of orchids in a variety of settings. It's 3km north of Sanur along Jl Ngurah Rai just past the major intersection with the coast road, and is an easy stop on the way to Ubud.

🏃 Activities

Watersports
Sanur's calm waters and steady breezes make it a natural centre for wind- and kite-surfing.

WATER SPORTS

Water sports centre along Jl Pratama in Tanjung Benoa and offer daytime diving, cruises, windsurfing and waterskiing. Each morning convoys of buses arrive from all over south Bali bringing day-trippers, and by 10am parasailers float over the water.

All feature unctuous salespeople whose job it is to sell you the banana boat ride of your dreams while you sit glassy eyed in a thatched-roof sales centre and cafe. Check equipment and credentials before you sign up, as a few tourists have died in accidents.

Among the established water-sports operators is **Benoa Marine Recreation** (☎ 0361-771757; www.bmrbali.com; Jl Pratama; ☉ 8am-4pm). As if by magic, all operators have similar prices. Note that 'official' price lists are just the starting point for bargaining. Activities here include the following (with average prices):

→ **Banana-boat rides** Wild rides for two as you try to maintain your grasp on the inflatable fruit moving over the waves (US$20 per 15 minutes).

→ **Glass-bottomed boat trips** The non-wet way to see the denizens of the shallows (US$50 per hour).

→ **Jet-skiing** Go fast and belch smoke (US$25 per 15 minutes).

→ **Parasailing** Iconic; you float above the water while being towed by a speedboat (US$20 per 15-minute trip).

→ **Snorkelling** Trips include equipment and a boat ride to a reef (US$35 per hour).

One nice way to use the beach here is at **Tao** (www.taobali.com; Jl Pratama 96; mains 60,000-100,000Rp; ☉ 8am-10pm) restaurant, where for the price of a drink, you can enjoy resort-quality loungers and a pool.

Sanur Beach
BEACH

Sanur Beach curves in a southwesterly direction and stretches for over 5km. It is mostly clean and overall quite serene – much like the town itself. Offshore reefs mean that the surf is reduced to tiny waves lapping the shore. With a couple of unfortunate exceptions, the resorts along the sand are low-key, leaving the beach uncrowded.

Surf Breaks
SURFING

Sanur's fickle breaks (tide conditions often don't produce waves) are offshore along the reef. The best area is called **Sanur Reef**, a right break in front of the Grand Bali Beach Hotel. Another good spot is known as the **Hyatt Reef**, in front of, you guessed it, the Bali Hyatt Regency.

You can get a boat out to the breaks from Surya Water Sports for US$10 (a fishing boat could cost as much as 400,000Rp).

Crystal Divers
DIVING

(☎ 0361-286737; www.crystal-divers.com; Jl Danau Tamblingan 168; intro dives from US$80) This slick diving operation has its own hotel (the Santai) and a large diving pool. Recommended for beginners, the shop offers a long list of courses, including PADI open-water for US$500.

Rip Curl School of Surf
WINDSURFING

(☎ 0361-287749; www.ripcurlschoolofsurf.com; Beachfront Walk, Sanur Beach Hotel; lessons from 1,100,000Rp, rental per hr from 100,000Rp; ☉ 8am-5pm) Sanur's reef-protected waters and regular offshore breezes make for good windsurfing.

M & M
KITESURFING

(☎ 0813 3745 2825; Beachfront Walk; lessons from US$90, rental per 90min 350,000Rp; ☉ 9am-6pm) Made Sambuk offers kitesurfing lessons right on the beach.

Surya Water Sports
WATER SPORTS

(☎ 0361-287956; Jl Duyung 10; ☉ 9am-5pm; ⊞) One of several water-sports operations along the beach, Surya is the largest. You can go parasailing (US$20 per ride), snorkelling by boat (US$40, two hours) or rent a kayak and paddle the smooth waters (US$10 per hour).

Other Activities

★ **Jamu Traditional Spa**
SPA

(☎ 0361-286595; www.jamutraditionalspa.com; Jl Danau Tamblingan 41, Tandjung Sari Hotel; massages from 600,000Rp; ☉ 8am-9pm) The beautifully carved teak and stone entry sets the mood at this gracious spa, which offers a range of treatments including a popular Earth & Flower Body Mask and a Kemiri Nut Scrub.

Power of Now Oasis
YOGA

(📞0813 3831 5032; www.powerofnowoasis.com; Beachfront Walk, Hotel Mercure; classes from 80,000Rp; ⏰varies) Enjoy a yoga class in this lovely bamboo pavilion on Sanur Beach. Several levels are offered.

Glo Day Spa & Salon
SPA

(📞0361-282826; www.glo-day-spa.com; Jl Danau Poso 57, Gopa Town Centre; sessions from 195,000Rp; ⏰8am-6pm) An insider pick by the many local Sanur expats, Glo eschews a fancy setting for a clean-lined storefront. Services and treatments span the gamut, from skin and nail care to massages and spa therapies.

🛏 Sleeping

Usually the best places to stay are right on the beach; however, beware of properties that have been coasting for decades. West of Jl Danau Tamblingan there are budget guesthouses, oodles of new midrange chains and villas.

🛏 Beachfront

Amid the larger resorts you'll find some smaller beachfront hotels that are surprisingly affordable.

Kesumasari
GUESTHOUSE $

(📞0361-287824; villa_kesumasari@yahoo.com; Jl Kesumasari 6; r with fan/air-con from 400,000/450,000Rp; ❄🛜🏊) The only thing between you and the beach is a small shrine. Beyond the lounging porches, the multihued carved Balinese doors don't prepare you for the riot of colour inside the 15 idiosyncratic rooms at this family-run homestay.

Pollok & Le Mayeur Inn
HOMESTAY $

(📞0361-289847; pollokinn@yahoo.com; Jl Hang Tuah, Museum Le Mayeur; r fan/air-con from 230,000/330,000Rp; ❄🛜) The grandchildren of Ni Polok and Le Mayeur de Merpres run this small homestay which you reach via a discreet path on the north side of the museum compound. The 17 rooms vary in size so ask to see a couple.

⭐ Hotel La Taverna
HOTEL $$

(📞0361-288497; www.latavernahotel.com; Jl Danau Tamblingan 29; r US$100-200, ste from US$150; ❄@🛜🏊) One of Sanur's first hotels, La Taverna has been thoughtfully

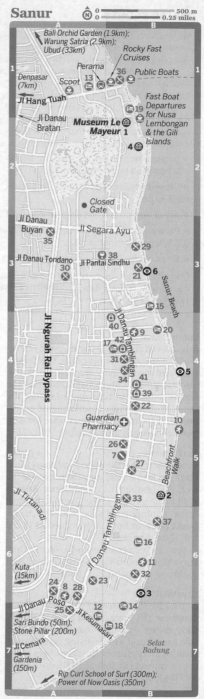

Sanur

Sanur

SOUTH BALI & THE ISLANDS SANUR

updated while retaining its artful, simple charms. The pretty grounds and paths linking buildings hum with a creative energy that infuses the 36 vintage bungalow-style units with an understated luxury. It all seems timeless yet with just a hint of sly youth. Art and antiques abound; views beckon.

★ **Tandjung Sari** HOTEL $$$
(☏ 0361-288441; www.tandjungsari.com; Jl Danau Tamblingan 29; bungalows from US$200; ❄ @ 🛜 ☀) One of Bali's first boutique hotels, it has flourished since its start in 1967 and continues to be lauded for its style. The 26 traditional-style bungalows are beautifully decorated with crafts and antiques. At night, lights in the trees above the pool are magical. The gracious staff are a delight. Balinese dance classes are taught by one of Bali's best dancers.

Fairmont Sanur Beach Bali RESORT $$$
(☏ 0361-301 1888; www.fairmont.com; Jl Kesumasari 8; r from US$300; ❄ @ 🛜 ☀ 🐾) This bold newcomer to the Sanur beachfront opened as the Regent Bali in 2013 but changed its allegiance to Fairmont in 2014. It has 120 suites and villas on a sprawling

site that includes a 50m infinity pool overlooking 200m of beachfront. The design is strikingly modern and high-tech pleasures abound. There are also lavish spas and restaurants. Kids get their own pool.

Hyatt Regency Bali RESORT $$$
(www.bali.resort.hyatt.com; Jl Danau Tamblingan) *The* landmark Sanur beachfront resort, the former Bali Hyatt is getting a slightly grander name and much grander makeover for a late 2015 reopening.

⊨ Off the Beach

The following are near Jl Danau Tamblingan and are short walks from the beach, cafes and shopping. Lacking sand as a feature, many try a bit harder than their beachfront brethren (as well as being more affordable).

Abian Boga Guesthouse HOTEL $
(☏ 0361-284174; www.abianboga.com; Jl Kesumasari 5; r from US$20; ❄ 🛜 ☀) This recently built small hotel is barely two minutes' walk from the beach. Its 24 rooms are incredible value and while basic, are modern and have DVD players.

Keke Homestay

GUESTHOUSE $

(📞 0361-287282; Jl Danau Tamblingan 100; r with fan/air-con from 150,000/250,000Rp; ❄) Set 150m down a *gang* (alley) from the noisy road, Keke welcomes backpackers into its genial family (who are often busy making offerings). The five quiet, clean rooms vary from fan-only to air-con cool.

Agung & Sue Watering Hole

GUESTHOUSE $

(📞 0361-288289; www.wateringholesanurbali.com; Jl Hang Tuah 35; r 275,000-350,000Rp; ❄🛜) Ideally located for an early fast boat to Nusa Lembongan or the Gili Islands, this long-running guesthouse has a veteran conviviality. Rooms are standard, but the beer is indeed cold and Sanur beach is a five minute walk. A good place if you have that early fast boat to catch.

Gardenia

GUESTHOUSE $$

(📞 0361-286301; www.gardeniaguesthousebali.com; Jl Mertasari 2; r from US$45; ❄🛜) Like its many-petalled namesake, the Gardenia has many facets. The seven rooms are visions in white and sit well back from the road. Nice verandahs face a plunge pool in a pretty courtyard. Up front there is a good cafe.

🍴 Eating & Drinking

Dine on the beach in a traditional open-air pavilion or in a genial bar – the choice is yours in Sanur. Although there are plenty of uninspired places on Jl Danau Tamblingan, there are also some gems.

For groceries and personal items, try the large **Hardy's Department Store** (📞 0361-285806; Jl Danau Tamblingan 136; ⏰ 8am-10pm). Nearby is the gourmet market of Cafe Batu Jimbar.

There's a weekly **organic market** (Jl Danau Tamblingan; ⏰ 10am-4pm Sun) held near Sand Restaurant.

The **Pasar Sindhu night market** (off Jl Danau Tamblingan; ⏰ 6am-midnight) sells fresh vegetables, dried fish, pungent spices and various household goods.

Many of Sanur's drinking establishments cater to retired expats and are, thankfully for them, air-conditioned. This is not a place where things go late.

🍴 Beachfront

The beach path offers restaurants, cafes and bars where you can catch a meal, a drink or a sea breeze. Sunset drink specials are common (though the beach faces east, so you'll need to enjoy the reflected glow off Nusa Penida).

⭐ Minami

JAPANESE $$

(📞 0812 8613 4471; Beachfront Walk, Segara Village Hotel; mains from 50,000Rp; ⏰ 11am-11pm) With its minimalist white decor, bright open-air atmosphere and vast range of ultra-fresh fish, this authentic Japanese place is a great find on Sanur beach. Yes, there's sushi, plus various tempura, gyoza, salads, noodle dishes and much more. Standards are very high.

Warung Pantai Indah

CAFE $$

(Beachfront Walk; mains 40,000-100,000Rp; ⏰ noon-11pm) Sit at battered tables and chairs on the sand under a tin roof at this timeless beach cafe. Just north of the Hotel Peneeda View and near some of Sanur's most expensive private beach villas, this outpost of good cheer has cheap beer and regular specials on fresh-grilled seafood. The views are splendid.

KITE-FLYING OVER SANUR

Travelling through south Bali you can't help but notice scores of kites overhead much of the year. These creations are often huge (10m wide or more, with tails stretching up to an astonishing 160m) and fly at altitudes that worry pilots. Many have noisemakers called *gaganguan* producing eerie humming and buzzing noises that are unique to each kite. Like much in Bali there are spiritual roots: the kites are meant to whisper figuratively into the ears of the gods suggestions that abundant harvests might be nice. But for many Balinese, these high-fliers are simply a really fun hobby (although it has its serious side as when one of these monsters crashes to earth it can kill and injure).

Each July, hundreds of Balinese and international teams descend – as it were – on open spaces north of Sanur for the **Bali Kite Festival**. They compete for an array of honours in categories such as original design and flight endurance. The action is centred around **Padang Galak Beach**, about 2km up the coast from Sanur. You can catch kite-flying Balinese-style here from May to September.

SANUR'S BEACHFRONT WALK

Sanur's **beachfront walk** has been delighting locals and visitors alike from day one. Over 4km long, it curves past resorts, beachfront cafes, wooden fishing boats under repair and quite a few elegant old villas built decades ago by the wealthy expats who fell under Bali's spell. While you stroll, look out across the water to Nusa Penida.

Even if you're not staying in Sanur, the beach walk makes a good day trip or stop on the way to someplace else. A few highlights north to south:

Grand Bali Beach Hotel (Jl Hang Tuah) Built in the Sukarno-era, this vast hotel is now slowly fading away. Local leaders, properly horrified at its outsized bulk, imposed the famous rule that no building could be higher than a coconut palm.

Turtle Tanks (Beachfront Walk) A nice display about Bali's endangered sea turtles that usually includes some young hatchlings.

Small Temple (Beachfront Walk) Amid the tourist bustle, this little shrine is shaded by huge trees.

Batu Jimbar (www.villabatujimbar.com; Beachfront Walk) Just north of the Bali Hyatt Regency, this villa compound has a colourful history: it was redesigned by the famous Sri Lankan architect Geoffrey Bawa in 1975, Mick Jagger and Jerry Hall were unofficially married here in 1990 and it's been lodgings for celebrities from Yoko Ono to Sting to Fergie. If your income approaches theirs, you too can stay here.

Fishing Boats (Beachfront Walk) Just south of the Hyatt is a long area where multihued fishing boats are pulled ashore and repaired under the trees.

Sanur Bay SEAFOOD **$$**
(✷0361-288153; Jl Duyung; meals 60,000-160,000Rp; ⊘8am-10pm) You can hear the surf and see the moonlight reflected on the water at this classic beachside seafood grill, set on the sand amid palm trees and fishing boats. Revenue goes to community groups.

Beach Café INTERNATIONAL **$$**
(✷0361-282875; Beachfront Walk; meals 50,000-100,000Rp; ⊘8am-10pm; 🛜) Brings a bit of flashy Med style to the Sanur beach cliché of palm fronds and plastic chairs. Zone out on wicker sofas or hang on a low cushion on the sand. Enjoy salads and seafood.

✖ Jl Danau Tamblingan

★Manik Organik ORGANIC **$**
(www.manikorganikbali.com; Jl Danau Tamblingan 85; meals from 50,000Rp; ⊘8am-10pm; ✎) 🍃 Actual trees shade the serene terrace at this creative and healthful cafe. Vegetarians are well-cared for but there are also meaty dishes made with free-range chicken and the like. Smoothies include the fortifying 'immune tonic'.

Porch Cafe CAFE **$**
(✷0361-281682; Jl Danau Tamblingan, Flashbacks; meals from 40,000Rp; ⊘7am-10pm; ❄🛜) Housed in a traditional wooden building, this cafe offers a tasty mix of comfort food including burgers and freshly baked goods such as ciabatta. Snuggle up to a table on the porch or shut it all out in the air-con inside. Popular for breakfast; there's a long list of fresh juices. A cute guesthouse, Flashbacks, is in the rear.

Warung Mak Beng BALINESE **$**
(✷0361-282633; Jl Hang Tuah 45; meals 35,000Rp; ⊘11am-9pm) You don't need a menu at this local favourite: all you can order is its legendary BBQ fish, which comes with various sides and some tasty soup. Service is quick, the air fragrant and diners of all stripes very happy.

Warung Babi Guling Sanur BALINESE **$**
(✷0361-287308; Jl Ngurah Rai Bypass; meals from 25,000Rp; ⊘11am-7pm) Unlike many of Bali's *babi guling* places, which buy their suckling pigs pre-cooked from large suppliers, this small outlet does all its cooking right out back. The meat is succulent and shows the benefits of personal attention.

★Char Ming ASIAN **$$**
(✷0361-288029; www.charming-bali.com; Jl Danau Tamblingan 97; meals 100,000-200,000Rp; ⊘6-11pm) Barbecue with a French accent. A daily menu board lists the fresh seafood available for grilling. Look for regional dishes, many with modern flair. The highly stylised location features lush plantings and

ROYALTY & EXPATS

Sanur was one of the places favoured by Westerners during their pre-WWII discovery of Bali. Artists Miguel Covarrubias, Adrien Jean Le Mayeur de Merpres and Walter Spies, anthropologist Jane Belo and choreographer Katharane Mershon all spent time here. The first tourist bungalows appeared in Sanur in the 1940s and '50s, and more artists, including Australian Donald Friend (whose antics earned him the nickname Lord Devil Donald), made their homes in Sanur.

During this period Sanur was ruled by insightful priests and scholars, who recognised both the opportunities and the threats presented by expanding tourism. They established village cooperatives that owned land and ran tourist businesses, ensuring that a good share of the economic benefits remained in the community.

The priestly influence remains strong, and Sanur is one of the few communities still ruled by members of the Brahmana caste. It is known as a home of sorcerers and healers, and a centre for both black and white magic. The black-and-white chequered cloth known as *kain poleng*, which symbolises the balance of good and evil, is emblematic of Sanur.

carved-wood details from vintage Javanese and Balinese structures.

Three Monkeys Cafe
ASIAN $$

(✆0361-286002; Jl Danau Tamblingan; meals 60,000-150,000Rp; ☉8am-11pm; 🛜) This branch of the splendid Ubud original is no mere knock-off. Spread over two floors, there's cool jazz playing in the background and live performances some nights. Set well back from the road, you can enjoy Sanur's best coffee drinks on sofas or chairs. The creative menu mixes Western fare with pan-Asian creations.

Pregina Warung
BALINESE $$

(✆0361-283353; Jl Danau Tamblingan 106; mains 40,000-80,000Rp; ☉11am-10pm) Classic Balinese duck dishes and crowd-pleasers such as sate are mainstays of the interesting menu at this restaurant that serves local foods several cuts above the all-too-common bland tourist versions. The dining room has spare, stylish wooden decor.

Café Smorgås
CAFE $$

(✆0361-289361; Jl Danau Tamblingan; meals 50,000-150,000Rp; ☉8am-10pm; ✲🛜✐) Set back from the traffic, this popular place has nice wicker chairs on a large terrace outside and cool air-con inside. The menu has a healthy bent of fresh Western fare from breakfasts to sandwiches to soups and salads.

Massimo
ITALIAN $$

(✆0361-288942; Jl Danau Tamblingan 206; meals 80,000-200,000Rp; ☉8am-10pm) The interior is like an open-air Milan cafe, the outside like a Balinese garden – a combo that goes together like spaghetti and meatballs. Pasta, pizza and more are prepared with authentic Italian flair. No time for a meal? Nab some gelato from the counter up front.

Kalimantan
BAR

(Borneo Bob's; ✆0361-289291; Jl Pantai Sindhu 11; mains from 40,000Rp; ☉11am-midnight) This veteran boozer has an old *South Pacific* thatched charm and is one of many casual bars on this street. Enjoy cheap drinks under the palms in the large, shady garden. The Mexican food features homegrown chilli peppers.

🍴 South Sanur

Sari Bundo
INDONESIAN $

(✆0361-281389; Jl Danau Poso; mains from 20,000Rp; ☉24hr) This spotless Padang-style shopfront is one of several at the south end of Sanur. Choose from an array of fresh and very spicy food. The curry chicken is a fiery treat that will have your tongue alternatively loving and hating you.

Denata Minang
INDONESIAN $

(Jl Danau Poso; meals from 15,000Rp; ☉8am-10pm) One of the better Padang-style warungs, it's located just west of Cafe Billiard, the rollicking expat bar. Like its brethren, it has fab *ayam* (chicken) in myriad spicy forms – only better.

Fire Station
INTERNATIONAL $$

(✆0361-285675; Jl Danau Poso 108; mains from 80,000Rp; ☉5pm-late) There's some old Hollywood style here at this open-fronted new hot spot. Vaguely 1960s Hollywood-esque portraits line walls; you expect to see a young Dennis Hopper lurking in the rear. Enjoy pitchers of sangria and other interesting drinks along with a varied menu that features many specials.

🛍 Shopping

Sanur is no Seminyak in the shopping department, although a few designers from there are opening branches here. You can kill an afternoon browsing the length of Jl Danau Tamblingan.

For cheap and tatty souvenirs, try one of the various markets along the beachfront walk.

A-Krea   CLOTHING
(☑ 0361-286101; Jl Danau Tamblingan 51; ☺ 9am-8pm) A range of items designed and made in Bali are available in this attractive store that takes the colours of the island and gives them a minimalist flair. Clothes, accessories, homewares and more are all handmade.

Ganesha Bookshop   BOOKS
(www.ganeshabooksbali.com; Jl Danau Tamblingan 42; ☺ 9am-8pm) Bali's best bookshop for serious readers has a branch in Sanur. Besides excellent choices in new and used fiction, Ganesha has superb selections on local culture and history. There's also a special reading area for kids.

Nogo   TEXTILES
(☑ 0361-288765; www.nogobali.com; Jl Danau Tamblingan 104; ☺ 9am-8pm) Look for the wooden loom out front of this classy store, which bills itself as the 'Bali Ikat Centre.' The goods are gorgeous and easy to enjoy in the air-con comfort.

Goddess on the Go   WOMEN'S CLOTHING
(☑ 0361-270174; Jl Danau Tamblingan; ☺ 9am-8pm) Super-comfortable clothes for women, who like the name says, travel a lot.

ℹ Information

Guardian Pharmacy (☑ 0361-284343; Jl Danau Tamblingan 134) The chain pharmacy has a doctor on call.

ℹ Getting There & Away

BEMO
Green bemo go along Jl Hang Tuah to the Kereneng bemo terminal in Denpasar (7000Rp).

BOAT
Fast boats The myriad fast boats to Nusa Lembongan, Nusa Penida, Lombok and the Gilis depart from a strip of beach south of Jl Hang Tuah. None of these services use a dock – be prepared to wade to the boat. Most companies have shady waiting areas facing the beach.

Public boats Regular boats to Nusa Lembongan and Nusa Penida depart from the beach at the end of Jl Hang Tuah.

Rocky Fast Cruises (☑ 0361-801 2324; www.rockyfastcruise.com; Jl Hang Tuah 41; ☺ 8am-8pm) Has an office for its services to Nusa Lembongan.

Scoot (☑ 0361-285522; www.scootcruise.com; Jl Hang Tuah; ☺ 8am-8pm) Has an office for its network of services to Nusa Lembongan, Lombok and the Gilis.

TOURIST SHUTTLE BUS
The **Perama office** (☑ 0361-285592; www.peramatour.com; Jl Hang Tuah 39; ☺ 7am-10pm) is at Warung Pojok at the northern end of town. Its destinations include Ubud (40,000Rp, one hour), Padangbai (60,000Rp, two hours) and Lovina (125,000Rp, four hours).

ℹ Getting Around

Taxis from the airport cartel cost 125,000Rp.

Bemos go up and down Jl Danau Tamblingan and Jl Danau Poso for 5000Rp, offering a greener way to shuttle about the strip than a taxi.

AROUND SANUR

Pulau Serangan

Otherwise known as Turtle Island, Pulau Serangan is an example of all that can go wrong with Bali's environment. Originally it was a small (100-hectare) island offshore of the mangroves to the south of Sanur. However, in the 1990s it was selected by Suharto's infamous son Tommy as a site for new development. More than half of the original island was obliterated while a new landfill area over 300 hectares in size was grafted on. The Asian economic crisis pulled the plug on the scheme. Since then regular development schemes have been reported.

Meanwhile, on the original part of the island, the two small and poor fishing villages, **Ponjok** and **Dukuh**, remain, as does one of Bali's holiest temples, **Pura Sakenan**, just east of the causeway. Architecturally it is insignificant, but major festivals attract huge crowds of devotees, especially during the Kuningan festival.

Benoa Harbour

Bali's main port is at the entrance of Teluk Benoa (Benoa Bay), the wide but shallow body east of the airport runway. Benoa Harbour is on the northern side of the bay – a square of docks and port buildings on reclaimed land. It is linked to mainland Bali by a 2km causeway which is now also part of the Bali Mandara Toll Road. It's referred to as Benoa port or Benoa Harbour to distinguish it from Benoa village, on the southern side of the bay.

Benoa Harbour is the port for some tourist day-trip boats to Nusa Lembongan and for Pelni ships to other parts of Indonesia; however, its shallow depth prevents large cruise ships from calling.

DENPASAR

☑ 0361

Sprawling, hectic and ever-growing, Bali's capital has been the focus of a lot of the island's growth and wealth over the last five decades. It can seem a daunting and chaotic place but spend a little time on its tree-lined streets in the relatively affluent government and business district of Renon and you'll discover a more genteel side.

Denpasar might not be a tropical paradise, but it's as much a part of 'the real Bali' as the rice paddies and clifftop temples. This is the hub of the island for 800,000 locals and here you will find their shopping malls and parks. Most enticing, however, is the growing range of authentic and tasty restaurants and cafes aimed at the burgeoning middle class. You'll also want to sample Denpasar's markets, its important museum and its purely modern Balinese vibe.

Most visitors stay in the tourist towns of the south and visit Denpasar as a day trip (if traffic is kind you can get here in 15 minutes from Sanur and 30 minutes from Seminyak).

History

Denpasar, which means 'next to the market,' was an important trading centre and the seat of local rajahs (lords or princes) before the colonial period. The Dutch gained control of northern Bali in the mid-19th century, but their takeover of the south didn't start until 1906. After the three Balinese princes destroyed their own palaces in Denpasar and made a suicidal last stand – a ritual *puputan* – the Dutch made Denpasar an important colonial centre. As Bali's tourism industry expanded in the 1930s, most visitors stayed at one or two government hotels in the city of Denpasar.

The northern town of Singaraja remained the Dutch administrative capital until after WWII when it was moved to Denpasar because of the new airport; in 1958, some years after Indonesian independence, the city became the official capital of the province of Bali. Recent immigrants have come from Java and all over Indonesia, attracted by opportunities in schools, business, construction and the enormous tourist economy. Denpasar's edges have merged with Sanur, Kuta, Seminyak and Kerobokan.

◉ Sights

Take time for the Museum Negeri Propinsi Bali, but the real appeal of Denpasar is simply exploring everyday Bali life. Roam the traditional markets and even the air-conditioned malls to see how people live today.

★**Museum Negeri Propinsi Bali**   MUSEUM
(☑0361-222680;   adult/child   10,000/5000Rp; ⊙8am-12.30pm Fri, to 4pm Sat-Thu) Think of this as the British Museum or the Smithsonian of Balinese culture. It's all here, but unlike those world-class institutions, you have to work at sorting it out. The museum could use a dose of curatorial energy; most displays are labelled in English.

Museum staff often play music on a bamboo gamelan to magical effect; visit in the afternoon when it's uncrowded. Ignore 'guides' who offer little except a chance to part with US$5 or US$10.

The museum comprises several buildings and pavilions, including many examples of Balinese architecture.

➡ **Main Building**

Has a collection of prehistoric pieces downstairs, including stone sarcophagi and stone and bronze implements. Upstairs are examples of traditional artefacts, including items still in everyday use. Look for the intricate wood-and-cane carrying cases for transporting fighting cocks, and tiny carrying cases for fighting crickets.

➡ **Northern Pavilion**

Built in the style of a Tabanan palace; houses dance costumes and masks, including a sinister *rangda* (widow-witch), a healthy-looking Barong (mythical lion-dog creature) and a towering Barong Landung (tall Barong) figure.

➡ **Central Pavilion**

The spacious verandah is inspired by the palace pavilions of the Karangasem kingdom (based in Amlapura), where rajahs held audiences. The exhibits are related to Balinese religion, and include ceremonial objects, calendars and priests' clothing.

➡ **Southern Pavilion**

Rich displays of textiles, including *endek* (a Balinese method of weaving with pre-dyed threads), double ikat (woven cloth), *songket* (silver- and gold-threaded cloth, hand-woven using a floating weft technique) and *prada* (the application of gold leaf or gold or silver thread in traditional Balinese clothes).

★ **Pura Jagatnatha** TEMPLE

(Jl Surapati) The state temple, built in 1953, is dedicated to the supreme god, Sanghyang Widi. Part of its significance is its statement of monotheism. Although the Balinese recognise many gods, the belief in one supreme god (who can have many manifestations) brings Balinese Hinduism into conformity with the first principle of Pancasila – the 'Belief in One God.'

The *padmasana* (temple shrine) is made of white coral, and consists of an empty throne (symbolic of heaven) on top of the cosmic turtle and two *naga* (mythical snakelike creatures), which symbolise the foundation of the world. The walls are decorated with carvings of scenes from the Ramayana and Mahabharata.

Two major festivals are held here every month, during the full moon and new moon, and feature *wayang kulit* (leather shadow puppet) performances.

Puputan Square PARK

(Jl Gajah Mada) This bit of urban open space commemorates the heroic but suicidal stand of the rajahs of Badung against the invading Dutch in 1906. A monument depicts a Balinese family in heroic pose, brandishing the weapons that were so ineffective against the Dutch guns. The woman also has jewels in her left hand, as the women of the Badung court reputedly flung their jewellery at the Dutch soldiers to taunt them.

The park is popular with locals at lunchtime and with families near sunset. Vendors sell chicken sate and other snacks plus drinks. On weekends the park can fill with kite-flyers of all ages.

Pura Maospahit TEMPLE

(off Jl Sutomo) Established in the 14th century, at the time the Majapahit arrived from Java, this temple was damaged in a 1917 earthquake and has been heavily restored since. The oldest structures are at the back of the temple, but the most interesting features are the large statues of Garuda and the giant Batara Bayu.

Bajra Sandhi Monument MONUMENT

(Monument to the Struggle of the People of Bali; ☑0361-264517; Jl Raya Puputan, Renon; adult/child 10,000/5000Rp; ⊙9am-4.30pm) This huge monument is as big as its name. Inside the vaguely Borobudur-like structure are dioramas tracing Bali's history. Taking the name as a cue, you won't be surprised that they have a certain jingoistic soap-opera quality. But they're a fun diversion. Note that in the portrayal of the 1906 battle with the Dutch, the King of Badung is literally a sitting target.

Taman Wedhi Budaya ARTS CENTRE

(☑0361-222776; off Jl Nusa Indah; ⊙8am-3pm Mon-Thu, to 1pm Fri-Sun) This arts centre is a sprawling complex in the eastern part of Denpasar. Its lavish architecture houses an art gallery with an interesting collection. From mid-June to mid-July, the centre comes alive for the Bali Arts Festival, with dances, music and craft displays from all over Bali. Book tickets at the centre for more popular events.

🏃 **Activities**

Kube Dharma Bakti MASSAGE

(☑0361-749 9440; Jl Serma Mendara 3; massage per hr 75,000Rp; ⊙9am-10pm) Many Balinese wouldn't think of having a massage from anyone but a blind person. Government-sponsored schools offer lengthy courses to certify blind people in reflexology, shiatsu massage, anatomy and more. In this airy building redolent with liniments you can choose from a range of therapies.

🎊 **Festivals & Events**

★ **Bali Arts Festival** PERFORMING ARTS

(www.baliartsfestival.com; Taman Wedhi Budaya; ⊙mid-Jun–mid-Jul) This annual festival, based at the Taman Wedhi Budaya arts centre, is an easy way to see a wide variety of traditional dance, music and crafts. The productions of

Denpasar

Ubung Bus & Bemo Terminal (1.5km)

Wangaya Bemo Terminal

Jl Pattimura

Jl Setiabudi

Jl Sutomo

Jl Kartini

Jl Nakula

Jl Kedondong

17

18

9

Jl Werkudara

Jl Sahedawa

Jl Karna

Jl Durian

Jl Belimbing

Jl Melati

Jl Kambola

Jl Piawa

5

Poltabes Denpasar (1km)

19

Jl Arjuna

8

Jl Gajah Mada

23

24 20

Jl Thamrin

Jl Sumatra

Jl Gajah Mada

2 Pura Jagatnatha

4

Kereneng Bemo Terminal

14

Jl Surapati

21

Jl Hasanudin

1

Museum Negeri Propinsi Bali

Jl Sugianyar

Jl Imam Bonjol

Tegal Bemo Terminal

Jl Udayana

Jl Kapten Agung

Jl Diponegoro

22

Jl Ki Hajar Dewantara

Jl Jayagiri

Jl Nusakambangan

12

RENON

Jl Udayana

State Railway Company

26

Kimia Farma

Jl Teuku Umar

Letda Tantular

25

SANGLAH

7

Australian Consulate

Nasi Uduk (1.2km)

15

Rumah Sakit Umum Propinsi Sanglah

Jl Nias

13

Jl Tukad Gangga

Jl Pulau Kanrata

Jl Diponegoro

Jepun Bali (750m); Benoa Harbour (6km)

the *Ramayana* and *Mahabharata* ballets are grand, and the opening ceremony and parade in Denpasar are spectacles. Tickets are usually available before performances, schedules are available online and at the Denpasar tourist office.

The festival is the main event of the year for scores of village dance and musical groups. Competition is fierce, with local pride on the line at each performance ('our Kecak is better than your stinkin' Kecak' etc). To do well here sets a village on a good course for the year. Some events are held in a 6000-seat amphitheatre, a venue that allows you to realise the mass appeal of traditional Balinese culture.

🛏 Sleeping

Denpasar has many new mid-priced chain hotels, but it's hard to think of a compelling reason to stay here unless you want to revel in the city's bright lights.

★ **Nakula Familiar Inn**   GUESTHOUSE $
(☑ 0361-226446;   www.nakulafamiliarinn.com; Jl Nakula 4;   r with fan/air-con from 155,000/ 200,000Rp; ❊ ☎) The eight rooms at this sprightly urban family compound, which has been a traveller favourite since before Seminyak existed, are clean and have small balconies. There is a nice courtyard and cafe in the middle. You can enjoy a classic slice of urban Balinese life at the street market around the corner. Tegal–Kereneng bemos go along Jl Nakula.

Inna Bali   HOTEL $$
(☑ 0361-225681; www.innabali.com; Jl Veteran 3; r from 350,000-700,000Rp; ❊ ☎ ☷) The Inna Bali has simple gardens, a huge banyan tree and a certain nostalgic charm; it dates from 1927 and was once the main tourist hotel on the island. Room interiors are standard, but many have deeply shaded verandahs. The ongoing renovations should freshen things up a bit. Get the veteran employees talking – they have many stories.

The hotel is a good base for the **Ngrupuk parades** that take place the day before the Nyepi festival, as they pass in front.

🍴 Eating & Drinking

Denpasar has the island's best range of Indonesian and Balinese food. Savvy locals and expats each have their own favourite warungs and restaurants.

New places open regularly on Jl Teuku Umar, while in Renon there is a phenomenal

Denpasar

strip of eating places on Jl Cok Agung Tresna between Jl Ramayana and Jl Dewi Madri and along Letda Tantular. See what you can discover.

★**Warung Satria** INDONESIAN $
(Jl Kedondong; dishes 10,000-20,000Rp; ⊘11am-5pm) On a quiet street; try the seafood sate served with a shallot sambal. Otherwise, choose from the immaculate displays, but don't wait too long after lunch or it will all be gone. There is a **second location** (Map p176; Jl WR Supratman; ⊘10am-5pm) near the junction where the main road to Ubud branches off from the bypass, east of the centre of Denpasar.

Warung Wardani INDONESIAN $
(☏0361-224398; Jl Yudistira 2; meals from 25,000Rp; ⊘8am-4pm) Don't be deceived by the small dining room at the entrance: there's another vastly larger one out back. A critical detail as the top-notch *nasi campur* (rice with a variety of side dishes) draws in the masses for lunch daily. The food is halal, the chicken tastefully tender, the sate succulent and the rice fragrant.

Nasi Uduk INDONESIAN $
(Jl Teuku Umar; meals 8000-15,000Rp; ⊘8am-10pm) Open to the street, this spotless little stall has a few chairs and serves up Javanese treats such as *nasi uduk* (sweetly scented coconut rice with fresh peanut sauce) and *lalapan* (a simple salad of fresh lemon basil leaves).

Pasar Malam Kereneng MARKET $
(Kereneng Night Market; Jl Kamboja; meals from 10,000Rp; ⊘6pm-5am) At this excellent night market dozens of vendors dish up food until dawn.

Bhineka Djaja COFFEE
(☏0361-224016; Jl Gajah Mada 80; coffee 5000Rp; ⊘9am-4pm Mon-Sat) Home to Bali's Coffee Co, this storefront sells locally grown beans and makes a mean espresso, which you can enjoy at the two tiny tables while watching the bustle of Denpasar's old main drag.

✗ Renon

Aromas of good cooking waft through the slightly gentrified air here.

★**Café Teduh** INDONESIAN $
(☏0361-221631; off Jl Diponegoro; mains 10,000-20,000Rp; ⊘10am-10pm; 🐾) Amid the big shopping malls, this little oasis is hidden down a tiny lane. Hanging orchids, trees, flowers and ponds with fountains are a good setting to enjoy food from Manado. Try *ayam dabu-dabu* (grilled chicken with chilli paste, tomatoes, shallots, lemongrass and spices) or *nasi bakar cumi hitam* (rice and marinated squid wrapped in banana leaf and grilled).

Cak Asmo INDONESIAN, CHINESE $
(Jl Tukad Gangga; meals from 25,000Rp; ⊘8am-10pm) Join the government workers and students from the nearby university for superb

dishes cooked to order in the bustling kitchen. Order the buttery and crispy *cumi cumi* (calamari) with *telor asin* sauce (a heavenly mixture of eggs and garlic). Fruity ice drinks are a cooling treat. An English-language menu makes ordering a breeze.

Ayam Goreng Kalasan   INDONESIAN $
(Jl Cok Agung Tresna 6; mains 10,000-20,000Rp; ⊙8am-10pm) The name here says it all: fried chicken *(ayam goreng)* named for a Javanese temple (Kalasan) in a region renowned for its fiery, crispy chicken. Note the hint of lemongrass imbued by a long marination before cooking.

Bakso Supra Dinasty   BALINESE $
(Jl Cok Agung Tresna; mains from 15,000Rp; ⊙8am-10pm) One taste of the soup assembled to order out of the steaming vats at this small stall and you'll agree that the name (translated: Meatball Super Dynasty) is fully deserved. The broth is rich and the meatballs filled with flavour.

Warung Lembongan   INDONESIAN $
(✆0361-236885; Jl Cok Agung Tresna 6C; meals 17,000-25,000Rp; ⊙8am-10pm) Silver folding chairs at long tables, shaded by a garish green awning out front. These are details you will quickly forget after you have the house speciality: chicken lightly fried yet delicately crispy like the top of a perfect crème brûlée. The other specialty is a spicy *soup kepala ikan* (fish soup).

Warung Bundaran Renon   BALINESE $
(✆0361-234208; Jl Raya Puputan 212; meals from 40,000Rp; ⊙9am-5pm) A slightly upscale *babi guling* (spit-roasted pig) place with excellent plate lunches of the same. It feels a bit like a suburban house and there's a shady patio.

Pondok Kuring   INDONESIAN $
(✆0361-234122; Jl Raya Puputan 56; meals from 20,000Rp; ⊙10am-10.30pm) The foods of the Sundanese people of west Java are the speciality here. Highly spiced vegetables, meat and seafood draw flavours from an array of herbs. This glossy restaurant has an arty dining room and a lovely and quiet garden out back.

🔒 Shopping

For a complete slice of local life, visit the traditional markets and the large air-con shopping malls.

Markets

Denpasar's largest traditional markets are in a fairly compact area that makes visiting them easy, even if navigating their crowded aisles across multiple floors is not. Like other aspects of Balinese life, the big markets are in flux. Large chain supermarkets are biting into their trade and the evolving middle class say they prefer the likes of Carrefour because it has more imported goods. But the public markets aren't down yet. This is where you come for purely Balinese goods, such as temple offerings, ceremonial clothes and a range of foodstuffs unique to the island, including numerous types of mangosteen.

★ Pasar Badung   MARKET
(Jl Gajah Mada; ⊙6am-8pm) Bali's largest food market is busy in the morning and evening (although dull and sleepy from 2pm to 4pm); it's a great place to browse and bargain. You'll find produce and food from all over the island, as well as easy-to-assemble temple offerings that are popular with working women.

Get lost here as it won't be permanent and revel in the range of fruits and spices on offer. Ignore the services of 'guides'.

Kampung Arab   MARKET
(Jl Hasanudin & Jl Sulawesi) Has jewellery and precious-metal stores run by scores of Middle Eastern and Indian merchants.

Pasar Kumbasari   MARKET
(Jl Gajah Mada; ⊙8am-6pm) Handicrafts, a plethora of vibrant fabrics and costumes decorated with gold are just some of the goods at this huge market across the river from Pasar Badung. Note that the malls have taken their toll and there are a lot of empty stalls.

Textiles

Follow Jl Sulawesi north and, just as the glitter of Kampung Arab fades, the street glows anew as you come upon a strip of fabric stores. The textiles here – batiks, cottons, silks – come in colours that make Barbie look like an old purse. It's immediately east of Pasar Badung. Many shops are closed Sunday.

★ Jepun Bali   TEXTILES
(✆0361-726526; Jl Raya Sesetan, Gang Ikan Mas 11; ⊙call for appointment) It's like your own private version of the Museum Negeri Propinsi Bali: Gusti Ayu Made Mardiani is locally

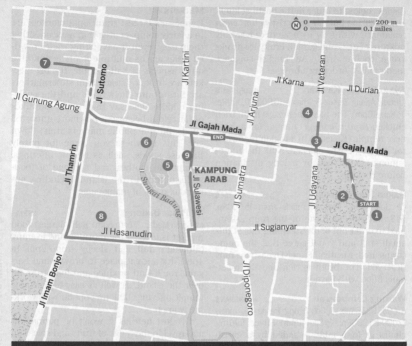

🏃 City Walk
Strolling Denpasar

START MUSEUM NEGERI PROPINSI BALI
END JL GAJAH MADA
LENGTH 2.5KM; TWO HOURS

While Denpasar can seem formidable and traffic choked, it rewards those who explore on foot. This walk includes most attractions in the historic centre of town and a few vestiges of when Denpasar – and Bali – moved at a much slower pace. Allow extra time for visiting the museum or for shopping.

Start the walk at ❶ **Museum Negeri Propinsi Bali** (p118). Opposite is large and green ❷ **Puputan Square** (p119).

Back on the corner of Jl Surapati and Jl Veteran is the towering ❸ **Catur Muka statue**, which represents Batara Guru, Lord of the Four Directions. The four-faced, eight-armed figure keeps an eye (or is it eight eyes?) on the traffic around him. Head 100m north on Jl Veteran to the ❹ **Inna Bali hotel** (p121), a favourite of longtime Indonesian dictator Sukarno.

Return to the Catur Muka statue and head west on Jl Gajah Mada (named after the

14th-century Majapahit prime minister). Go towards the bridge over the grubby Sungai Badung (Badung River). Just before the bridge, on the left, is the renovated ❺ **Pasar Badung** (p123), the main produce market. On the left, just after the bridge, is ❻ **Pasar Kumbasari** (p123), where you will find handicrafts, fabrics and costumes.

At the next main intersection, detour north up Jl Sutomo, and turn left along a small *gang* (alley) leading to the ❼ **Pura Maospahit temple** (p119).

Turn back, and go south along Jl Thamrin to the junction of Jl Hasanudin. On this corner is the ❽ **Puri Pemecutan**, a palace destroyed during the 1906 Dutch invasion. It's been rebuilt and you can look inside the compound, but don't expect anything palatial.

Go east on Jl Hasanudin, then north onto ❾ **Jl Sulawesi**, past its markets. Continue north past Pasar Badung market to return to Jl Gajah Mada. You could save your visit to the Museum Negeri Propinsi Bali for the end, when you'll just want to move slowly.

famous for her *endek* and *songket* clothes woven using traditional techniques. You can visit her gracious home and workshop and see the old machines in action, then ponder her beautiful polychromatic selections in silk and cotton. She's in south Denpasar.

Adil TEXTILES
(☎0361-234601; Jl Sulawesi 13; ⊘9am-6pm) Jammed into a string of fabric stores just east of Pasar Badung, this narrow shop stands out for its huge selection of genuine Balinese batik. The colours and patterns are bewildering, while the clearly marked reasonable prices are not.

Shopping Malls

Western-style shopping malls are jammed on Sundays with locals shopping and teens flirting; the brand-name goods are genuine.

Most malls have a food court with stalls serving fresh Asian fare, as well as fast-food joints (which have sated more than one homesick tourist tot).

Mal Bali MALL
(Jl Diponegoro; ⊘9am-10pm) This hive of consumerism has the Ramayana Department Store, Bali's largest. Also a big supermarket, food court and many clothing shops.

ℹ Information

Denpasar has many medical providers that serve the entire island. See p378 for details.
Denpasar Tourist Office (☎0361-234569; Jl Surapati 7; ⊘8am-3.30pm Mon-Thu, to 1pm Fri) Deals with tourism in the Denpasar municipality (including Sanur), but also has some information about the rest of Bali. It's not worth a special trip, but may have the useful *Calendar of Events* booklet. Has an official 'tourist toilet.'
Kimia Farma (☎0361-227811; Jl Diponegoro 125; ⊘24hr) The main outlet of the island-wide pharmacy chain has the largest selection of prescription medications in Bali.
Main Post Office (☎0361-223565; Jl Panjaitan; ⊘8am-9pm Mon-Fri, to 8pm Sat) Your best option for unusual postal needs. Has a photocopy centre and ATMs.
Tourist Police (☎0361-224111)

ℹ Getting There & Away

Denpasar is a hub of public transport in Bali – you'll find buses and minibuses bound for all corners of the island.

AIR

Sometimes called 'Denpasar' in airline schedules, Bali's Ngurah Rai International Airport is 12km south of Kuta.

BEMO & MINIBUS

The city has several bemo and bus terminals – if you're travelling independently around Bali you'll often have to go via Denpasar, and transfer from one terminal to another. The terminals for transport around Bali are Ubung, Batubulan and Tegal, while Kereneng serves destinations in and around Denpasar. Each terminal has regular bemo connections to the other terminals in Denpasar for 7000Rp.

Note that the bemo network is sputtering and that fares are approximate and at times completely subjective. Drivers often try to charge non-locals at least 25% more. See p371 for details.

Ubung

Well north of the town, on the road to Gilimanuk, the **Ubung Bus & Bemo Terminal** (Map p176) is the hub for northern and western Bali. It also has long-distance buses in addition to the ones serving the terminal 12km northwest in Mengwi (see the boxed text, p371).

DESTINATION	FARE
Gilimanuk (for the ferry to Java)	30,000Rp
Mengwi bus terminal	15,000Rp
Munduk	22,000Rp
Singaraja (via Pupuan or Bedugul)	25,000Rp

Batubulan

Located a very inconvenient 6km northeast of Denpasar on a road to Ubud, this terminal is for destinations in eastern and central Bali.

DESTINATION	FARE
Amlapura	25,000Rp
Padangbai (for the Lombok ferry)	18,000Rp
Sanur	7000Rp
Ubud	13,000Rp

Tegal

On the western side of town on Jl Iman Bonjol, **Tegal Bemo Terminal** is the terminal for Kuta and the Bukit Peninsula.

DESTINATION	FARE
Airport	15,000Rp
Jimbaran	17,000Rp
Kuta	13,000Rp

Kereneng

East of the town centre, **Kereneng Bemo Terminal** has bemos to Sanur (7000Rp).

Wangaya

Near the centre of town, this small **terminal** is the departure point for bemo services to northern Denpasar and the outlying Ubung bus terminal (8000Rp).

BUS

Long-distance bus services continue to use the Ubung Bus & Bemo Terminal. Most long-distance services also stop at the Mengwi terminal.

TRAIN

Bali doesn't have trains but the state railway company does have an **office** (☑ 0361-227131; Jl Diponegoro 150/B4; ⊙ 8am-3pm Mon-Fri, 9am-2pm Sat & Sun) in Denpasar. Buses leave from the nearby **Damri office** (Jl Diponegoro) and travel to eastern Java where they link with trains at Banyuwangi for Surabaya, Yogyakarta and Jakarta among others. Fares and times are comparable to the bus but the air-conditioned trains are more comfortable, even in economy class.

❶ Getting Around

BEMO

Bemos take various circuitous routes from and between Denpasar's many bus/bemo terminals. They line up for various destinations at each terminal, or you can try and hail them from anywhere along the main roads – look for the destination sign above the driver's window.

TAXI

As always, the cabs of **Bluebird Taxi** (☑ 0361-701111) are the most reliable choice.

NUSA LEMBONGAN & ISLANDS

Look towards the open ocean southeast of Bali and the hazy bulk of Nusa Penida dominates the view. But for many visitors the real focus is Nusa Lembongan, which lurks in the shadow of its vastly larger neighbour. Here, there's great surfing, amazing diving, languorous beaches and the kind of laid-back vibe travellers cherish.

Once ignored, Nusa Penida is now attracting visitors, but its dramatic vistas and unchanged village life are still yours to explore. Tiny Nusa Ceningan huddles between the larger islands. It's a quick and popular jaunt from Lembongan.

The islands have been a poor region for many years. Thin soils and a lack of fresh water do not permit the cultivation of rice, but other crops such as maize, cassava and beans are staples grown here. The main cash crop has been seaweed, although the big harvest now comes on two legs.

Nusa Lembongan

☑ 0366

Once the domain of shack-staying surfers, Nusa Lembongan has hit the big time. Yes, you can still get a simple room with a view of the surf breaks and the gorgeous sunsets but now you can also stay in a boutique hotel and have a fabulous meal.

But even as Nusa Lembongan grows in popularity, it remains a mellow place. The new-found wealth is bringing changes, though: you'll see boys riding motorcycles 300m to school, temples being expensively renovated, high-end luxuries being introduced, and time being marked by the arrival of tourist boats rather than the crow of a rooster or the fall of a coconut.

◉ Sights

◉ Jungutbatu

The village itself is mellow, although lanes buzz with motorcycles. **Pura Segara** and its enormous banyan tree are the site of frequent ceremonies.

The north end of town holds the metal-legged **lighthouse**. Follow the road around east for about 1km to **Pura Sakenan**.

Jungutbatu Beach   BEACH
The beach here, a mostly lovely arc of white sand with clear blue water, has views across to Gunung Agung in Bali. The pleasant **seawall walkway** is ideal for strolling, especially – as you'd guess – at sunset. Floating boats and seaweed being farmed and dried save the scene from being clichéd idyllic.

◉ Pantai Selegimpak

The long, straight **beach** is usually lapped by small waves at this remote-feeling spot with a couple of places to stay (one of which has unfortunately built its seawall *below* the low-tide line). About 200m east along the shoreline path where it goes up and over a

Nusa Lembongan

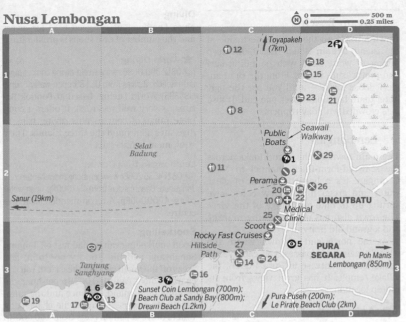

Nusa Lembongan

⊚ Sights

1 Jungutbatu Beach	C2
2 Lighthouse	D1
3 Pantai Selegimpak	B3
4 Pantai Tanjung Sanghyang	A3
5 Pura Segara	C3
6 Sacred Tree	A3

⊛ Activities, Courses & Tours

7 Bounty Pontoon	A3
8 Lacerations	C1
9 Lembongan Dive Center	C2
10 Monkey Surfing	C2
11 Playground	C2
12 Shipwreck	C1
World Diving	(see 20)

⊜ Sleeping

13 Alam Nusa Huts	A3

14 Batu Karang	C3
15 Indiana Kenanga	D1
16 Morin Lembongan	B3
17 Nusa Bay by WHM	A3
18 Pemedal Beach	D1
19 Point Resort Lembongan	A3
20 Pondok Baruna	C2
21 Pondok Baruna Frangipani	D1
22 Secret Garden Bungalows	C2
23 Star Two Thousand Cafe & Bungalows	C1
24 Ware-Ware	C3

⊗ Eating

25 99 Meals House	C2
26 Bali Eco Deli	D2
27 Deck Cafe & Bar	C3
28 Hai Bar & Grill	B3
29 Pondok Baruna Warung	D2

knoll is a minute **cove** with a nub of sand, good swimming and a tiny warung.

◉ Tanjung Sanghyang

This beautiful bay, unofficially named Mushroom Bay after the mushroom corals offshore, has a crescent of bright white **beach**. By day, the tranquillity can be disturbed by banana-boat rides or parasailing. At other hours, this is a beach of dreams. Look for the enormous **sacred tree** amid **Pura Segara.**

The most interesting way to get to Tanjung Sanghyang from Jungutbatu is to walk along the trail that starts from the southern end of the Jungutbatu beach and follows the coastline for a kilometre or so. Alternatively, get a boat from Jungutbatu for about 50,000Rp.

◎ Dream Beach

Down a track, on the southwestern side of the island, **Dream Beach** is a 150m deep pocket of white sand with pounding surf and pretty azure waters. From the right angle it looks lovely – until you see the ugly hotel that's been built over one end. It also gets crowded with day-trippers.

◎ Lembongan

The main town on the island looks across the seaweed-farm-filled channel to Nusa Ceningan. It's a beautiful scene of clear water and green hills. A few cafes have sprung up to take advantage of the view. The town also has an interesting **market** and a grand old **banyan tree**.

At the north end of town where the island's main road passes, you can ascend a long stone staircase to **Pura Puseh**, the village temple. It has great views from its hilltop location.

🏃 Activities

Most places rent out gear for aquatic fun.

Surfing

Surfing here is best in the dry season (April to September), when the winds come from the southeast. It's definitely not for beginners, and can be dangerous even for experts. There are three main breaks on the reef, all aptly named. From north to south are **Shipwreck**, **Lacerations** and **Playground**. Depending on where you're staying, you can paddle directly out to whichever of the three is closest (although at lowest tide you may have to do some walking so booties are essential); for others it's better to hire a boat. Prices are negotiable – from about 50,000Rp for a one-way trip. You tell the owner when to return. A fourth break – **Racecourses** – sometimes emerges south of Shipwreck.

The surf can be crowded here even when the island isn't – charter boats from Bali sometimes bring groups of surfers for day trips from the mainland for a minimum of 1,000,000Rp.

Monkey Surfing   SURFING
(☑ 0821 4614 7683; www.monkeysurfing.com; Jungutbatu Beach; surfboard rental per day 100,000Rp, lessons from 550,000Rp; ⊙ 8am-7pm) Rent surfboards and stand-up paddle boards from this shop on the beach.

Diving

Nusa Lembongan is a good base for divers and the number of dive shops is proliferating.

★ World Diving   DIVING
(☑ 0812 390 0686; www.world-diving.com; Jungutbatu Beach; 2 dives from US$85, open-water course US$395) World Diving, based at Pondok Baruna, is very well regarded. It offers a complete range of courses plus diving trips to dive sites all around the three islands. Their equipment is first-rate.

Lembongan Dive Center   DIVING
(☑ 0821 4535 2666; www.lembongandivecenter.com; Jungubatu Beach; s dive from 450,000Rp, open-water course 4,000,000Rp) A recommended local dive centre.

Snorkelling

Good snorkelling can be had just off Tanjung Sanghyang and the **Bounty pontoon**, and areas off the north coast of the island. You can charter a boat from 150,000Rp per hour, depending on demand, distance and the number of passengers. A trip to the challenging waters of Nusa Penida costs from 400,000Rp for three hours; to the nearby mangroves costs about 300,000Rp. Snorkelling gear can be rented for about 30,000Rp per day.

There's good drift snorkelling along the mangrove-filled channel west of Ceningan Point, between Lembongan and Ceningan.

Cruises

A number of cruise boats offer day trips to Nusa Lembongan from south Bali. Trips include hotel transfer from south Bali, basic water sports, snorkelling, banana-boat rides, island tours and a buffet lunch. Note that with the usually included hotel transfers the following trips can make for a long day.

Bounty Cruise   CRUISE
(☑ 0361-726666; www.balibountycruises.com; adult/child US$95/47.50) Boats dock at the garish yellow offshore Bounty pontoon with water slides and other amusements.

Island Explorer Cruise   CRUISE
(☑ 0361-728 088; www.bali-activities.com; adult/child from US$92/50) Affiliated with Coconuts Beach Resort; uses a large boat that doubles as the base for day-trip aquatic fun. Also has a sailing ship.

Hiking & Biking

You can circumnavigate the island in a day on foot, or less on a bike. It's a fascinating journey into the small island's surprisingly diverse

DIVING THE ISLANDS

There are great diving possibilities around the islands, from shallow and sheltered reefs, mainly on the northern side of Lembongan and Penida, to very demanding drift dives in the channel between Penida and the other two islands. Vigilant locals have protected their waters from dynamite bombing by renegade fishing boats, so the reefs are relatively intact. And a side benefit of tourism is that locals no longer rely so much on fishing. In 2012, the islands were designated the Nusa Penida Marine Protected Area, which encompasses over 20,000 hectares of the surrounding waters.

If you arrange a dive trip from Padangbai or south Bali, stick with the most reputable operators, as conditions here can be tricky and local knowledge is essential. Diving accidents regularly happen and people die diving in the waters around the islands every year.

Using one of the recommended operators on Nusa Lembongan puts you close to the action from the start. A particular attraction are the large marine animals, including turtles, sharks and manta rays. The large (3m fin-to-fin) and unusual *mola mola* (sunfish) is sometimes seen around the islands between mid-July and October, while manta rays are often seen south of Nusa Penida from June to October.

The best dive sites include **Blue Corner** and **Jackfish Point** off Nusa Lembongan and **Ceningan Point** at the tip of that island. The channel between Ceningan and Penida is renowned for drift diving, but it is essential you have a good operator who can judge fast-changing currents and other conditions. Upswells can bring cold water from the open ocean to sites such as **Ceningan Wall**. This is one of the world's deepest natural channels and attracts all manner and sizes of fish.

Sites close to Nusa Penida include **Crystal Bay**, **SD**, **Pura Ped**, **Manta Point** and **Batu Aba**. Of these, Crystal Bay, SD and Pura Ped are suitable for novice divers and are good for snorkelling. Note that the open waters around Penida are challenging, even for experienced divers.

scenery. Start along the hillside path from **Jungutbatu** and overcome whatever obstacles developers have put on the path to **Tanjung Sanghyang**; with a little Tarzan spirit you can stay with the faint trail (you can't do this segment by bike: use the roads inland).

Next head to **Lembongan** village where you can take the suspension bridge to **Nusa Ceningen**. Alternatively, from Lembongan village you take a gentle uphill walk along the sealed road to the killer hill that leads *down* to Jungutbatu, which cuts the circuit to about half a day.

To fully explore the island by foot, stick to the paved road that follows the channel between Nusa Lembongan and Nusa Ceningen. After a rugged uphill detour, curve back down and go north along the mangroves all the way to the **lighthouse**.

Bikes are easily rented for about 30,000Rp per day.

🛏 Sleeping & Eating

Rooms and amenities generally become increasingly posh as you head south and west along the water to Mushroom Bay. Almost every property has a cafe serving – unless noted – basic Indonesian and Western dishes for about 30,000Rp. At sunset, pick your favourite venue for a sundowner.

🛏 Jungutbatu

Many lodgings in Jungutbatu have shed the surfer shack cliché and are moving upmarket. But you can still find cheapies with cold water and fans.

Pemedal Beach GUESTHOUSE $
(☑ 0822 4441 4888; www.pemedalbeach.com; Jungutbatu Beach; r with fan/air-con from 400,000/500,000Rp; ❉ 🛜 ⓢ) Your posh budget option. Seaweed has been banished from the wide beach at this end of the island and the 11 bungalows are set back from a nice pool. Rooms have a rich wood interior.

Secret Garden Bungalows GUESTHOUSE $
(☑ 0813 5313 6861; www.bigfishdiving.com; Jungutbatu Beach; r from US$20; 🛜 ⓢ) ✿ Affiliated with Big Fish Diving, there are nine bungalow-style cold-water and fan rooms in this palm-shaded compound back off the beach. They have onsite yoga classes for 100,000Rp. Aquatic Alliance gives regular talks here about the amazing marine ecology around the islands.

AQUATIC ALLIANCE

The waters around Nusa Lembongan, Ceningan and Penida are filled with some truly spectacular creatures: huge manta rays, the ponderous *mola mola* (sunfish) and more. Yet while they are regularly spotted by flocks of divers who explore these rich waters, little is known about the actual ecology of the area – except that it's remarkable.

Since 2012, a group called **Aquatic Alliance** (www.aquaticalliance.org) has worked to change that. Through extensive field studies they are beginning to understand just what's swimming around out there. One early discovery: like whales, manta rays have markings that make it easy to identify individuals. The group's website is filled with fascinating information and you can learn more at their regular public talks at the Secret Garden Bungalows (p129).

Star Two Thousand Cafe & Bungalows GUESTHOUSE $
(☑ 0812 381 2775; Jungutbatu Beach; r 200,000-500,000Rp; ❄ 🛜 ☒) Grassy grounds surround 28 rooms in two-storey blocks; some have hot water and air-con. There's a fun cafe-bar right on the sand, with various sunset drink specials.

★ Pondok Baruna GUESTHOUSE $$
(☑ 0812 394 0992; www.pondokbaruna.com; Jungutbatu Beach; r 250,000-650,000Rp; ❄ 🛜 ☒) Associated with World Diving, this place offers four comfy rooms with terraces facing the ocean. The views make them an excellent option. Six plusher rooms surround a dive pool behind the beach. There are another eight rooms at **Pondok Baruna Frangipani** (❄ 🛜 ☒) back in the palm trees around a large pool. Staff, led by Putu, are charmers.

The dining end of the empire, **Pondok Baruna Warung** (meals from 40,000Rp; ☺ 8am-10pm), serves up excellent Indonesian cuisine.

★ Indiana Kenanga HOTEL $$$
(☑ 0828 9708 4367; www.indiana-kenanga-villas.com; Jungutbatu Beach; r US$150-600; ❄ 🛜 ☒) Two posh villas and 16 stylish suites shelter near a pool behind the beach at Lembongan's most upscale digs. The French designer-owner has decorated the place

with purple armchairs and other whimsical touches. The restaurant has an all-day menu (mains 70,000Rp to 200,000Rp) of seafood, sandwiches and various surprises cooked up by the skilled chef.

Bali Eco Deli CAFE $
(☑ 0812 3704 9234; www.baliecodeli.net; Jungutbatu; mains from 35,000Rp; ☺ 7am-10pm) 🍃 This irresistable cafe has great green cred and is noted for giving back to the community. But what it gives customers is also good: fresh and creative breakfasts, healthy snacks, delicious baked goods, good coffees and juices plus an array of salads.

99 Meals House INDONESIAN, CHINESE $
(Jungutbatu Beach; mains from 15,000Rp; ☺ 8am-10pm) An absolute bargain. Fried rice, omelettes, Chinese stir-fries and more prepared by a family at this great open-air spot overlooking the beach.

🛏 Hillside

The steep hillside just south of Jungutbatu offers great views and an ever-increasing number of luxurious rooms. The uppermost rooms at some places have gorgeous views across the water to Bali (on a clear day say hello to Gunung Agung), but such thrills come at a cost: upwards of 120 steep concrete steps. A motorcycle-friendly path runs along the top of the hill, good for leg-saving drop-offs.

★ Morin Lembongan GUESTHOUSE $
(☑ 0812 385 8396; wayman40@hotmail.com; r US$30-50; @) More lushly planted than many of the hillside places, Morin has woodsy rooms with views over the water from their verandahs. This is a good choice if you want to feel close yet removed from Jungutbatu. Wayan, the owner, is a great surf guide.

Ware-Ware GUESTHOUSE $$
(☑ 0812 397 0572; www.warewaresurfbungalows.com; r from US$60; ❄ 🛜 ☒) The nine units at this hillside place are a mix of square and circular numbers with thatched roofs. The large rooms (some with fan only) have rattan couches and big bathrooms. The cafe scores with a spectacular, breezy location on a cliffside wooden deck.

Batu Karang HOTEL $$$
(☑ 0366-559 6376; www.batukaranglembongan.com; r from US$250; ❄ @ 🛜 ☒) This upmarket

resort perched on a terraced hillside has a large infinity pool. Some of its 23 luxury units are villa-style and have multiple rooms and private plunge pools. All have open-air bathrooms and wooden terraces with sweeping views. Right on the hillside path, **Deck Cafe & Bar** (snacks from 20,000Rp; ☻7am-11pm; ☏) is a good pause for a gourmet snack or a drink.

Tanjung Sanghyang

It's your own treasure island. This shallow bay has a nice beach, plenty of overhanging trees and some of the most atmospheric lodging on Lembongan. Get here from Jungutbatu by foot or with a ride (15,000Rp) or boat (50,000Rp).

Alam Nusa Huts   GUESTHOUSE $
(☏0819 1662 6336; www.alamnusahuts.com; Tanjung Sanghyang; r from US$40; ❊☏) This small property is less than 100m from the beach. Four bungalows sit in a small, lush garden; each has an open-air bathroom and a secluded terrace. The interiors feature a lot of rich wood and bamboo. Staff are especially welcoming.

Nusa Bay by WHM   HOTEL $$$
(☏0361-484 085; www.wakahotelsandresorts.com; Tanjung Sanghyang; bungalows from US$180; ❊☏❊) A primitive motif blends with creature comforts at this low-key resort run by the Waka group. The 10 thatch-roofed bungalows are set on sandy grounds at the shore. The beachside restaurant and bar are shaded by coconut palms and you can dine on the sand.

Hai Bar & Grill   INTERNATIONAL $$
(☏0366-559 6415; Tanjung Sanghyang, Hai Tide Beach Resort; mains from 60,000Rp; ☻8am-11pm; ☏) This wide-open bar with wide-open views of the bay and sunsets is a stylish place for a drink, snack or meal. The menu mixes Asian and Western dishes and there are comforts such as fresh-baked muffins. Open-air movies are shown some nights; call for pick-up from Jungubatu.

Elsewhere on Lembongan

Poh Manis Lembongan   GUESTHOUSE $
(☏0819 9923 3913; www.pohmanislembongan.com; r from US$45; ❊☏❊) If Nusa Lembongan is a getaway, this is the getaway from Nusa Lembongan. Perched on a bluff on the southeast corner of the island, there are

sweeping views of the other two Nusas. The pool area is lovely and the seven rooms have a woodsy charm.

★**Sunset Coin Lembongan**   GUESTHOUSE $$
(☏0812 364 0799; www.sunsetcoinlembongan.com; Sunset Bay; r 600,000-750,000Rp; ❊☏❊) Run by an awesome family, this collection of cottages is everything an island escape should be. It's near the sweet little spot of sand called Sunset Bay and the six units have large terraces where you can relax or have a meal.

Point Resort Lembongan   INN $$$
(www.thepointlembongan.com; ste from US$150; ❊☏❊) About 500m west of Tanjung Sanghyang is this eponymously named property with four plush suites. The views are sweeping and should pirates sail in you can watch them get dashed on the rocks below the infinity pool. There's a two-night minimum here.

Beach Club at Sandy Bay   SEAFOOD $$
(☏0828 9700 5656; www.sandybaylembongan.com; Sunset Bay; mains from 50,000Rp; ☻8am-11pm; ☏) Pushing the distressed bleached wood look for all its worth, this appealing beach club has a fine position on a sweet pocket of sand most call Sunset Beach (unless you're this place and call it Sandy Bay...). The menu spans Asia and Europe, with a detour to Burgerville. The evening seafood BBQs are popular.

ℹ Information

Small markets can be found near the bank, but unless you're on a diet of bottled water and Ritz crackers, the selection is small.

It's vital that you bring sufficient cash in rupiah for your stay, as there is only one ATM and it won't accept most foriegn cards, even when it actually has cash to dispense.

Medical Clinic (consultation 200,000Rp; ☻8am-6pm) The medical clinic in the village has a new building and is well versed in minor surfing injuries and ear ailments.

> ## ℹ BOAT SAFETY
>
> There have been accidents involving boats between Bali and the surrounding islands. These services are unregulated and there is no safety authority should trouble arise. See the boxed text on p373 for more info on travelling safely by boat.

SOUTH BALI & THE ISLANDS NUSA LEMBONGAN

❶ Getting There & Away

Getting to/from Nusa Lembongan offers numerous choices, some quite fast. Note: anyone with money for a speedboat is getting into the fast-boat act; be wary of fly-by-night operators with fly-by-night safety.

Boats anchor offshore, so be prepared to get your feet wet. And travel light – wheeled bags are comically inappropriate in the water and on the beach and dirt tracks. Porters will shoulder your steamer trunk for 20,000Rp (and don't be like some low-lifes we've seen who have stiffed them for their service).

Perama (www.peramatour.com; Jungutbatu Beach) This tourist boat leaves Sanur at 10.30am (180,000Rp, 1¾ hours). The Lembongan office is near the Mandara Beach Bungalows.

Public Boats Regular public boats leave from the northern end of Sanur beach for Nusa Lembongan at 8am (60,000Rp, 1¾ to two hours). This is the boat used for supplies, so you may have to share space with a chicken. A public speedboat runs at 4pm (175,000Rp, 40 minutes).

Rocky Fast Cruises (☑0361-283624; www.rockyfastcruise.com; Jungubatu Beach) Fast boats several times daily (adult/child US$30/20, 30 to 40 minutes).

Scoot (☑0361-285522; www.scootcruise.com) Fast boats (adult/child 350,000/270,000Rp, 30 to 40 minutes) run several returns daily. It also serves the Gilis from Nusa Lembongan.

❶ Getting Around

The island is fairly small and you can walk to most places. There are no cars (although pick-up trucks are proliferating); bicycles (30,000Rp per day) and small motorcycles (50,000Rp per day) are widely available for hire. One-way rides on motorcycles or trucks cost 15,000Rp and up. One unwelcome development has been the arrival of SUV-sized golf carts that seem to be mostly rented by tourists who find a big cigar to be the perfect driving companion.

Nusa Ceningan

There is an atmospheric narrow **suspension bridge** crossing the lagoon between Nusa Lembongan and Nusa Ceningan, which makes it quite easy to explore. Besides the lagoon filled with frames for seaweed farming you'll see several small agricultural plots and a fishing village. The island is quite hilly and, if you're up for it, you can get glimpses of great scenery while wandering or cycling around.

To really savour Nusa Ceningan, take an overnight tour of the island with **JED** (Village Ecotourism Network; ☑0361-366 9951; www.jed.or.id; per person US$130), the cultural organisation that gives people an in-depth look at village and cultural life. Trips include family accommodation in a village, local meals, a fascinating tour with seaweed workers and transport to/from Bali.

There's a **surf break**, named for its location at Ceningan Point, in the southwest; it's an exposed left-hander.

🛏 Sleeping & Eating

Some cute cafes on both Nusa Lembongan and Nusa Ceningan overlook the lovely channel and bridge. Key roads have been paved, which is opening up the island, although it is still very rural.

FORSAKING SEAWEED

Few ice cream fans know this but they owe big thanks to the seaweed growers of Nusa Lembongan and Nusa Penida. Carrageenan, an emulsifying agent that is used to thicken ice cream as well as cheese and many other products, is derived from the seaweed grown here.

As you walk around the villages, you'll see – and smell – vast areas used for drying seaweed. Looking down into the water, you'll see the patchwork of cultivated seaweed plots. The islands are especially good for production, as the waters are shallow and rich in nutrients. The dried red and green seaweed is exported around the world for final processing.

But for how much longer is the real question. Farming seaweed is back-breaking work with tiny returns. Where just a decade ago 85% of Lembongan's people farmed seaweed, today that number is fast-diminishing as the population gets caught up in the tourist boom, with its comparatively better wages and much easier work.

And Nusa Penida is just a little way behind. We asked one former seaweed farmer who now works as a guide if he missed the work. His response was comically unprintable.

Secret Point GUESTHOUSE **$$**
(🖉 0819 9937 0826; www.secretpointhuts.com; r from 800,000Rp; ❄🛜❄) In the southwest corner of the island overlooking the Ceningan Point surf break, this cute little resort has a tiny beach and clifftop bar. From the latter you can dive into the surging waves for 50,000Rp.

Le Pirate Beach Club GUESTHOUSE **$$**
(🖉 0822 3767 0007; www.lepirate-beachclub.com; r from 700,000Rp; ❄) There's a handful of tiny cottages here with broad views of the channel. Everything is a sprightly white and blue; steps aren't friendly to those on peg legs. Two-night minimum.

Nusa Penida

📵 0366

Just beginning to appear on visitor itineraries, Nusa Penida still awaits discovery. It's an untrammelled place that answers the question: what would Bali be like if tourists never came? There are not a lot of formal activities or sights; rather, you go to Nusa Penida to explore and relax, to adapt to the slow rhythm of life here.

The island is a limestone plateau with a strip of sand on its north coast, and views over the water to the volcanoes in Bali. The south coast has 300m-high limestone cliffs dropping straight down to the sea and a row of offshore islets – it's rugged and spectacular scenery. The interior is hilly, with sparse-looking crops and old-fashioned villages. Rainfall is low and parts of the island are arid, although you can see traces of ancient rice terraces.

The population of around 60,000 is predominantly Hindu, although there is a Muslim community in Toyapakeh. The culture is distinct from that of Bali: the language is an old form of Balinese no longer heard on the mainland.

It's an unforgiving area: Nusa Penida was once used as a place of banishment for criminals and other undesirables from the kingdom of Klungkung (now Semarapura), and still has a somewhat sinister reputation. Yet it's also a centre of rebirth: the iconic Bali starling is being reintroduced here after being thought nearly extinct in the wild. And there's a burgeoning visitor scene near Ped.

PENIDA'S DEMON

Nusa Penida is the legendary home of Jero Gede Macaling, the demon who inspired the Barong Landung dance. Many Balinese believe the island is a place of enchantment and *angker* (evil power) – paradoxically, this is an attraction. Thousands of Balinese come every year for religious observances aimed at placating the evil spirits.

🏃 Activities

Nusa Penida has world-class **diving**. Most people make arrangements through a dive shop on Nusa Lembongan. Between Toyapakeh and Sampalan there is excellent **cycling** on the beautiful, flat coastal road. The roads elsewhere are good for mountain bikes. Ask around to rent a bike, which should cost about 25,000Rp per day.

Sampalan

Sampalan, the main town on Penida, is quiet and pleasant and strung out along the curving coast road. The interesting **market** is in the middle of town. It's a good place to absorb village life.

🛏 Sleeping & Eating

The following are good simple choices. For meals, try one of the small warungs in town; they're no more than 10 minutes by foot from any of the inns.

Made's Homestay HOMESTAY **$**
(🖉 0852 3764 3649; r from 150,000Rp) There are four small, clean rooms in a pleasant garden and a small breakfast is included. A little side road between the market and the harbour leads here.

Nusa Garden Bungalows GUESTHOUSE **$**
(🖉 0813 3812 0660; r from 150,000Rp; 🛜) Crushed-coral pathways running between animal statuary link the 10 rooms here. Rates include a small breakfast. Turn on Jl Nusa Indah just east of the centre.

Ped

Ped is home to a very important Balinese temple. Just 600m west, the tiny village of Bodong has a burgeoning traveller scene.

⊙ Sights & Activities

This entire area has a narrow strip of **beach** along the sea.

★ Pura Dalem Penetaran Ped   HINDU TEMPLE

The important temple of Pura Dalem Penetaran Ped is near the beach at Ped, 3.5km east of Toyapakeh. It houses a shrine for the demon Jero Gede Macaling that is a source of power for practitioners of black magic, and a place of pilgrimage for those seeking protection from sickness and evil. The temple structure is sprawling and you will see people making offerings for safe sea voyages from Nusa Penida; you may wish to join them.

Octopus Dive   DIVING

(☑0878 6246 3625; www.octopusdive-pelabuhanratu.com; Bodong; two-tank dives from 800,000Rp) A small and enthusiastic local operator.

🛏 Sleeping & Eating

Several establishments aimed at visitors have set up shop in Bodong.

Jero Rawa   HOMESTAY $

(☑0878 6246 3625; Bodong; r from 150,000Rp) There are seven nice new bungalow-style rooms in a tiny compound across the street from the beach.

Ring Sameton Inn   GUESTHOUSE $$

(☑0813 3798 5141; www.ringsameton-nusapenida.com; Bodong; r from US$50; ❉🌐❄) There are 12 comfortable rooms in this refined guesthouse. There's a pool, large cafe and quick beach access.

★ Gallery   CAFE $

(☑0819 9988 7205; Bodong; mains 25,000Rp; ⊙8am-8pm) A popular spot for volunteers at the NGOs, this small cafe and shop is run by the ever-charming Mike, who is a font of Penida knowledge. There's art on the walls, hand-roasted coffee and a Western menu of breakfast items and sandwiches.

Warung Pondok Nusa Penida   INDONESIAN $

(Bodong; mains from 20,000Rp; ⊙9am-9pm) A cute little breezy place right on the beach. Enjoy well-prepared Indo classics and seafood (plus the odd Western item) while taking in the views to Bali. Try the 'seaweed mocktail'.

Made's Warung   INDONESIAN $

(mains 8000-15,000Rp; ⊙8am-10pm) Right across from the temple, this very clean warung has tasty *nasi campur*.

Toyapakeh

If you come by boat from Nusa Lembongan, you'll probably be dropped at the beach at Toyapakeh, a pretty village with lots of shady trees. The beach has clean white sand, clear blue water, a neat line of boats, and Gunung Agung as a backdrop. There's a good warung overlooking the sand and usually people ready to help you sort transport.

Crystal Bay Beach

South of Toyapakeh, a paved 10km road through the village of Sakti leads to idyllic **Crystal Bay Beach**, which fronts the popular dive spot. The sand here is very white; palm trees add a *South Pacific* motif. The beach is popular with Bali day-trippers who arrive in boats (one operator is Bali Hai Cruises; www.balihaicruises.com). But mostly the beach remains blessedly rural. A couple of warungs sell drinks and snacks and rent snorkelling gear. The temple, **Segara Sakti**, adds the perfect touch.

NUSA PENIDA VOLUNTEERS

Various environmental and aid groups are active on Nusa Penida, with volunteers needed for a variety of projects. They normally pay a fee (about US$20 per day) that includes accommodation and contributes to the cause. Two organisations with programs you can join:

Friends of the National Parks Foundation (FNPF; ☑0361-977978; www.fnpf.org) This group has a centre near Ped on the island's north coast. Volunteer work includes aid in the restoration of the native Bali starling and teaching in local schools. Accommodation is in simple but comfortable rooms with fans and cold water.

Green Lion Bali (☑0812 4643 4964; www.greenlionbali.com) Has an award-winning program to breed and protect turtles along Penida's north shore. Volunteers sign on for at least two weeks and work in the turtle compound as well as teaching in local schools. There is a nearby guesthouse.

A very steep 1km back from the beach, on the road to Toyapakeh, French-owned **Namaste** (☎ 0819 1793 3418; www.namaste-bungalows.com; r with fan/air-con from 350,000/500,000Rp; ✳ 🛜 ⚊) is a high-concept guesthouse with 10 rustic-style bungalows set around a large pool. It has a good cafe.

Around the Island

A trip around the island, following the north and east coasts and crossing the hilly interior, can be completed in half a day by motorcycle or in a day by bicycle if you're in shape. You could spend much longer, lingering at the temples and the small villages, and walking to less accessible areas, but there's no accommodation outside the two main towns. The following description goes clockwise from Sampalan.

The coastal road from Sampalan curves and dips past bays with fishing boats and offshore seaweed gardens. After about 6km, just before the village of Karangsari, steps go up on the right side of the road to the narrow entrance of **Goa Karangsari** caves. There are usually people who can guide you through one of the caves for a negotiable fee of about 20,000Rp each. The limestone cave is over 15m tall in some sections. It extends more than 200m through the hill and emerges on the other side to overlook a verdant valley.

Continue south past a naval station and several temples to **Suana**. Here the main road swings inland and climbs up into the hills, while a very rough side track goes southeast, past more interesting temples to **Semaya**, a fishing village with a sheltered beach and one of Bali's best dive sites offshore, **Batu Aba**.

About 9km southwest of Suana, **Tanglad** is a very old-fashioned village and a centre for traditional weaving. Rough roads south and east lead to isolated parts of the coast.

A scenic ridge-top road goes northwest from Tanglad. At Batukandik, a rough road and 1.5km track leads to a spectacular **waterfall** *(air terjun)* that crashes onto a small beach. Get a guide (20,000Rp) in Tanglad.

Limestone cliffs drop hundreds of feet into the sea, surrounded by crashing surf. At their base, underground streams discharge fresh water into the sea – a pipeline was made to bring the water up to the top.

Back on the main road, continue to Batumadeg, past **Bukit Mundi** (the highest point on the island at 529m; on a clear day you can see Lombok), through Klumpu to **Sakti**, which has traditional stone buildings. Return to the north coast at Toyapakeh, about one hour after Bukit Mundi.

The road between Sampalan and Toyapakeh follows the craggy coast through Ped.

❶ Information

Sampalan has shops and a grocery store. The one ATM accepts few foreign cards, so bring cash.

Penida Tours (☎ 0852 0587 1291; www.penida tours.com; Bodong, Ped; ⊙ 9am-6pm) Great local operation with info on activities and sights on Penida, and also arranges tours.

❶ Getting There & Away

The strait between Nusa Penida and southern Bali is deep and subject to heavy swells – if there is a strong tide, boats often have to wait. Charter boats to/from Kusamba are not recommended due to their small size and the potential for heavy seas.

SANUR

Various speedboats leave from the same part of the beach as the fast boats to Nusa Lembongan, and make the run in under an hour.

Maruti Express (☎ 0852 6861 7972; www.balimarutiexpress.com; one-way adult/child 250,000/150,000Rp) One of several newish fast boats making the Penida run.

Semaya One (☎ 0361-877 8166; www.semaya cruise.com; one-way from adult/child 300,000/200,000Rp) Besides Sanur, has useful services from Nusa Penida to Nusa Lembongan, Padangbai and the Gilis.

PADANGBAI

Twin-engine fibreglass boats run across the strait from Padangbai to Buyuk, 1km west of Sampalan on Nusa Penida (75,000Rp, 45 minutes, four daily). The boats run between 7am and noon. A large car ferry also operates daily (passenger/motorcycle 27,300/39,000Rp, two hours).

NUSA LEMBONGAN

Nusa Penida public boats run between Jungutbatu and Toyapakeh (one hour) between 5.30am and 6am for 30,000Rp and there are also several trips a day between Lembongan village and Toyapekah on fast boats (50,000Rp). Otherwise, charter a boat for 400,000Rp return.

❶ Getting Around

Bemos are rare after 10am. There are often people who can set you up for transport where boats arrive. Options for getting around include:

Car & driver From 350,000Rp for a half-day.

Motorcycle Easily hired for 60,000Rp per day.

Ojek (Motorcycle that takes passengers) Not common, but when you find one, expect to pay about 40,000Rp per hour.

Ubud & Around

Best Places to Eat

➡ Locavore (p161)

➡ Pica (p161)

➡ Warung Sopa (p162)

➡ Mozaic (p163)

➡ Nasi Ayam
Kedewatan (p164)

Best Places to Stay

➡ Bambu Indah (p159)

➡ Amandari (p159)

➡ Swasti Eco Cottages (p157)

➡ Maya Ubud (p157)

➡ Warwick Ibah Luxury Villas & Spa (p157)

Why Go?

A dancer moves her hand just so and 200 pairs of entranced eyes follow the exact movement. A gamelan player hits a melodic riff and 200 pairs of feet tap along with it. The Legong goes into its second hour as the bumblebee dance unfolds with its sprightly flair and 200 backsides forget they're still stuck in rickety plastic chairs.

So another dance performance works its magic on a crowd in Ubud, the town amid a collection of villages where all that is magical about Bali comes together in one very popular package. From nightly cultural performances, to museums showing the works of artists whose creativity flowered here, to the unbelievably green rice fields that spill down lush hillsides to rushing rivers below, Ubud is a feast for the soul. Personal pleasures like fine dining, shopping, spas and more only add to the appeal.

When to Go

➡ The weather is slightly cooler but much wetter than in the south; expect it to rain at any time. At night, mountain breezes make air-con unnecessary and let you hear the symphony of frogs, bugs and distant gamelan practices echoing over the rice fields through your screened window.

➡ Temperatures during the day average 30°C and at night 20°C, although extremes are possible. Seasonal variation is muted, given the prevalence of precipitation.

➡ The real factor in deciding when to come is peak season: July, August and the Christmas holidays bring a huge influx of visitors.

UBUD

☏ 0361

Ubud is culture, yes. It's also home to good restaurants, cafes and streets of shops, many selling goods from the region's artisans. There's somewhere to stay for every budget, and no matter what the price you can enjoy lodgings that reflect the local Zeitgeist: artful, creative and serene.

Ubud's popularity continues to grow, adding on the hoopla created by the bestselling *Eat, Pray, Love*. Tour buses with day trippers can choke the main streets and cause traffic chaos. Fortunately Ubud adapts and a stroll away from the intersection of Jl Raya Ubud and Monkey Forest Rd, through the nearby verdant rice fields, can quickly make all right with the world.

Spend a few days in Ubud to appreciate it properly. It's one of those places where days can become weeks and weeks become months, as the noticeable expat community demonstrates.

History

Late in the 19th century, Cokorda Gede Agung Sukawati established a branch of the Sukawati royal family in Ubud and began a series of alliances and confrontations with neighbouring kingdoms. In 1900, with the kingdom of Gianyar, Ubud became (at its own request) a Dutch protectorate and was able to concentrate on its religious and cultural life.

The Cokorda descendants encouraged Western artists and intellectuals to visit the area in the 1930s, most notably Walter Spies, Colin McPhee and Rudolf Bonnet. They provided an enormous stimulus to local art, introduced new ideas and techniques, and began a process of displaying and promoting Balinese culture worldwide. As mass tourism arrived in Bali, Ubud became an attraction not for beaches or bars, but for the arts.

The royal family is still much a part of Ubud life, helping to fund huge cultural and religious displays such as memorable cremation ceremonies.

◉ Sights

Most sights in Ubud are easily reached on foot, all the better for exploring given the inherent interests and pleasures of the walks.

Ubud & Around Highlights

❶ Making like the ubiquitous ducks and wandering the rice fields in and around **Ubud** (p150).

❷ Feeling the rhythm of a traditional Balinese **dance performance** (p164), one of Ubud's great night-time pageants.

❸ Whiling away the hours among new friends at a breezy **Ubud cafe** (p159).

❹ Refining your batik technique and sambal recipes on a **course** (p148) with one of Ubud's talented locals.

❺ Exploring the green jungle and white water of the **Sungai Ayung Valley** (p148) around Sayan.

❻ Making like Indiana Jones at the towering ancient wonders of **Gunung Kawi** (p172).

❼ Exploring the myriad villages in the Ubud region, such as **Mas** (p170), for artworks, crafts, ceremonial objects and other treasures.

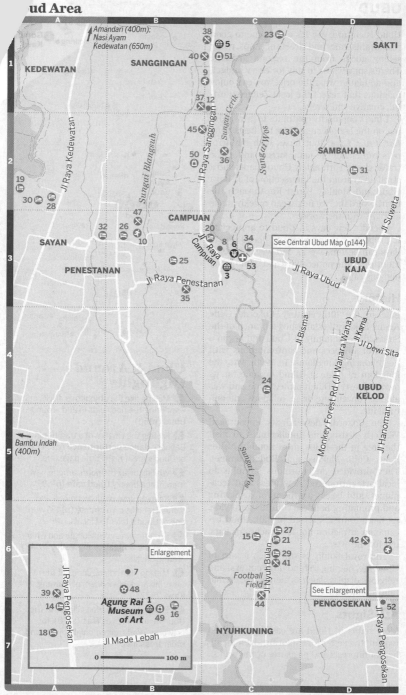

◎ Central Ubud

Temples, art galleries, museums and more dot the middle of Ubud. Some of the most important sit close to the main intersection at Jl Raya Ubud and Monkey Forest Rd.

★ Pura Taman Saraswati   HINDU TEMPLE

(Map p144; Jl Raya Ubud) Waters from the temple at the rear of this site feed the pond in the front, which overflows with pretty lotus blossoms. There are carvings that honour Dewi Saraswati, the goddess of wisdom and the arts, who has clearly given her blessing to Ubud. There are regular dance performances by night; by day painters set up easels.

Ubud Palace   PALACE

(Map p144; cnr Jl Raya Ubud & Jl Suweta; ⊙8am-7pm) The palace and **Puri Saren Agung** (Map p144; cnr Jl Raya Ubud & Jl Suweta) share space in the heart of Ubud. The compound was mostly built after the 1917 earthquake and the local royal family still live here. You can wander around most of the large compound exploring the many traditional, though not excessively ornate, buildings.

If you really like it, you can stay the night. Take time to appreciate the stone carvings, many by noted local artists such as I Gusti Nyoman Lempad. On many nights you can watch a dance performance here.

Just north, **Pura Marajan Agung** (Map p144; Jl Suweta) has one of the finest gates you'll find and is the private temple for the royal family.

Museum Puri Lukisan   MUSEUM

(Museum of Fine Arts; Map p144; ☎0361-975136; www.museumpurilukisan.com; off Jl Raya Ubud; adult/child 75,000Rp/free; ⊙9am-5pm) This museum displays fine examples of all schools of Balinese art. Just look at the lush composition of *Balinese Market* by Anak Agung Gde Sobrat to see the vibrancy of local painting.

The museum's collection is well curated and labelled in English. The museum has a good bookshop and a cafe. The lush, garden-like grounds alone are worth a visit.

It was in Ubud that the modern Balinese art movement started, when artists first began to abandon purely religious themes and court subjects for scenes of everyday life. Rudolf Bonnet was part of the Pita Maha artists' cooperative, and together with Cokorda Gede Agung Sukawati (a prince of Ubud's

Ubud Area

royal family) and Walter Spies, he helped to establish a permanent collection.

Building I, straight ahead as you enter, has a collection of early works from Ubud and the surrounding villages. These include examples of classical *wayang*-style paintings (art influenced by shadow puppetry), fine ink drawings by I Gusti Nyoman Lempad and paintings by Pita Maha artists. Notice the level of detail in Lempad's *The Dream of Dharmawangsa*. Classic works from the 1930s heyday of expats are also here.

Building II, on the left, has some colourful examples of the Young Artist style of painting and a good selection of 'modern traditional' works.

Building III, on the right, has classical and traditional paintings and is used for special exhibitions.

★ **Rio Helmi Gallery & Cafe** GALLERY
(Map p144; ✆ 0361-978773; www.riohelmi.com; Jl Suweta 06B; ⊙ 7am-7pm) Noted photographer and Ubud resident Rio Helmi has a small gallery where you can see examples of his journalistic and artistic work. Photos change often and offer beautiful insight into Helmi's travels worldwide and across Bali. His passionate pleas for the preservation of Bali in the face of massive change have appeared in the *Huffington Post* and elsewhere. Watch for special events.

Pura Desa Ubud HINDU TEMPLE
(Map p144; Jl Raya Ubud) The main temple for the Ubud community. It is often closed but comes alive for ceremonies.

Neka Gallery GALLERY
(Map p144; ✆ 0361-975034; Jl Raya Ubud; ⊙ 9am-5pm) Operated by Suteja Neka, the low-key Neka Gallery is a separate entity from the

Neka Art Museum. It has an extensive selection from all the schools of Balinese art, as well as works by European residents such as the renowned Arie Smit.

Threads of Life Indonesian
Textile Arts Center
GALLERY

(Map p144; ☑ 0361-972187; www.threadsoflife.com; Jl Kajeng 24; ⏱10am-7pm) This small, professional textile gallery and educational studio sponsors the production of naturally dyed, handmade ritual textiles, helping to recover skills in danger of being lost to modern dyeing and weaving methods. Commissioned pieces are displayed in the gallery, which has good explanatory material. It also runs regular textile-appreciation courses and has a good shop.

Komaneka Art Gallery
GALLERY

(Map p144; ☑0361-401 2217; Monkey Forest Rd; ⏱8am-9pm) Exhibiting works from established Balinese artists, this gallery is a good place to see high-profile art, in a large and lofty space.

◉ West Ubud

Strolling Jl Raya Campuan down to the bridge (note the older historic wooden bridge just south) over the Sungai Wos (Wos River) and then up the busy and interesting Jl Raya Sanggingan takes you past a range of interesting sights. Venture up the steep steps to Penestanan for walks among small guesthouses and rice fields coursing with water.

Pura Gunung Lebah
(Map p138; off Jl Raya Campuan) This which sits on a jutting rock at th of two tributaries of the Sungai River; *campuan* means 'two ri cently benefitted from a huge b paign. The setting is magical; listen to the rushing waters while admiring the impressive new multi-stepped *meru* (multi-tiered shrine) and a wealth of elaborate carvings.

Neka Art Museum
GALLERY

(Map p138; ☑0361-975074; www.museumneka. com; Jl Raya Sanggingan; adult/child 50,000Rp/ free; ⏱9am-5pm Mon-Sat, noon-5pm Sun) Quite distinct from Neka Gallery, the Neka Art Museum is the creation of Suteja Neka, a private collector and dealer in Balinese art. It has an excellent and diverse collection and is a good place to learn about the development of painting in Bali.

You can get an overview of the myriad local painting styles in the **Balinese Painting Hall**. Look for the *wayang* works.

The **Arie Smit Pavilion** features Smit's works on the upper level, and examples of the Young Artist school, which he inspired, on the lower level. Look for the Bruegel-like *The Wedding Ceremony* by I Nyoman Tjarka.

The **Lempad Pavilion** houses Bali's largest collection of works by I Gusti Nyoman Lempad.

The **Contemporary Indonesian Art Hall** has paintings by artists from other parts of Indonesia, many of whom have worked in

---

UBUD IN...

One Day
Stroll the streets of Ubud by starting with the classic loop of Monkey Forest Rd down to the namesake **park** and then coming back up along Jl Hanoman. You can spend hours browsing **shops** and **galleries** and stopping into characterful **cafes**. Wander side streets and *gang* (alleys), exploring Jl Dewi Sita and Jl Goutama, and venture a little further afield through the verdant **rice fields** for a great introduction to Ubud. Follow it up with an evening **dance performance**.

Three Days
During the mornings, take longer walks in the countryside, exploring the **Campuan Ridge** and **Sayan Valley**. Consider a guided walking tour. In the afternoons visit the **Museum Puri Lukisan**, **Neka Art Museum** and **Agung Rai Museum of Art**. By night, catch dramatic **dance performances** in Ubud and the nearby villages. Indulge at a local **spa**.

A Week or More
Do everything we've listed but take time to simply chill out. Get in tune with Ubud's rhythm: take naps, read books, wander about. Think about a **course** in Balinese culture. Compare and choose your favourite cafe, get out to craft villages and explore ancient sites.

The upper floor of the **East-West Art Annexe** is devoted to the work of foreign artists, such as Louise Koke, Miguel Covarrubias, Rudolf Bonnet, Han Snel, Donald Friend and Antonio Blanco.

The temporary exhibition hall has changing displays, while the **Photography Archive Centre** features black-and-white photography of Bali in the early 1930s and 1940s. Also look for the large collection of ceremonial kris (daggers).

The bookshop is noteworthy and there's a cafe.

Blanco Renaissance Museum MUSEUM
(Map p138; ☑ 0361-975502; www.blancomuseum.com; Jl Raya Campuan; admission 80,000Rp; ☉9am-5pm) The picture of Antonio Blanco mugging with Michael Jackson says it all. His former home and namesake museum captures the artist's theatrical spirit. Blanco came to Bali from Spain via the Philippines. He specialised in erotic art, illustrated poetry and playing the role of an eccentric artist à la Dalí. He died in 1999. More prosaically, enjoy the waterfall on the way in and good views over the river.

⊙ South Ubud

You can reach some of Ubud's best sights via walks along Jl Hanoman and Monkey Forest Rd, which are both lined with interesting shops and cafes.

★ **Sacred Monkey Forest Sanctuary** PARK
(Mandala Wisata Wanara Wana; Map p144; ☑ 0361-971304; www.monkeyforestubud.com; Monkey Forest Rd; adult/child 30,000/20,000Rp; ☉8.30am-6pm) This cool and dense swathe of jungle, officially called Mandala Wisata Wanara Wana, houses three holy temples. The sanctuary is inhabited by a band of grey-haired and greedy long-tailed Balinese macaques who are nothing like the innocent looking doe-eyed monkeys pictured on the brochures. Nestled in the forest, the interesting **Pura Dalem Agung** (Map p144) has a real *Indiana Jones* feel to it with the entrance to the inner temple featuring Rangda figures devouring children.

You can enter through one of the three gates: the main one at the southern end of Monkey Forest Rd; 100m further east, near the car park; or from the southern side, on the lane from Nyuhkuning. The forest has recently benefitted from an infusion of money. Useful brochures about the forest, macaques and temples are available. Note that the monkeys keep an eagle eye on passing tourists in hope of handouts (or an opportunity to help themselves). Don't feed these creatures.

Across from the main entrance, the forest's **office** (Map p144; ☑ 0361-971304; Monkey Forest Rd; ☉9am-4pm) accepts donations for a scheme to offset the carbon you created getting to Bali. Get a tree planted for 150,000Rp.

ARTISTS' HOMES

The **Spies house** (Map p138; Hotel Tjampuhan), home of German artist Walter Spies, is now part of Hotel Tjampuhan (p157); aficionados can stay if they book well in advance. Spies played an important part in promoting Bali's artistic culture in the 1930s.

Dutch-born artist **Han Snel** lived in Ubud from the 1950s until his death in 1999, and his family runs his namesake bungalows (p153) on Jl Kajeng.

Lempad's House (Map p144; Jl Raya Ubud; ☉daylight) FREE, the home of I Gusti Nyoman Lempad, is open to the public, caged birds and all, but it's mainly used as a gallery for a group of artists that includes Lempad's grandchildren. The Puri Lukisan and Neka museums have more extensive collections of Lempad's drawings.

Music scholar **Colin McPhee** is well known thanks to his evocative book about his time in Ubud, the perennial favourite *A House in Bali*. Although the actual 1930s house is long gone, you can visit the riverside site (which shows up in photographs in the book) at the Sayan Terrace (p159). The hotel's Wayan Ruma, whose mother was McPhee's cook, is good for a few stories.

Arie Smit (1916–) is the best-known and longest-surviving Western artist in Ubud. He worked in the Dutch colonial administration in the 1930s, was imprisoned during WWII, and came to Bali in 1956. In the 1960s his influence sparked the Young Artists school of painting in Penestanan, earning him an enduring place in the history of Balinese art. His home is not open to the public.

★ **Agung Rai Museum of Art** GALLERY
(ARMA; Map p138; ☑0361-976 659; www.arma bali.com; Jl Raya Pengosekan; admission 50,000Rp; ⊗9am-6pm, Balinese dancing 3-5pm Mon-Fri, classes 10am Sun) Founded by Agung Rai as a museum, gallery and cultural centre, the impressive ARMA is the only place in Bali to see haunting works by influential German artist Walter Spies, alongside many more masterpieces. The museum is housed in several traditional buildings set in gardens with water coursing through channels.

The collection is well labelled in English and features work by 19th-century Javanese artist Raden Saleh, including his enigmatic *Portrait of a Javanese Nobleman and His Wife*, which predates the similar *American Gothic* by decades. Exhibits also include classical Kamasan paintings, Batuan-style work from the 1930s and '40s, and works by Lempad, Affandi, Sadali, Hofker, Bonnet and Le Mayeur.

It's fun to visit ARMA when local children practise **Balinese dancing** and during **gamelan practice**. There are regular Legong and Kecak performances and myriad cultural courses offered here.

Enter the museum grounds from Kafe Arma on Jl Raya Pengosekan or around the corner at the ARMA Resort entrance.

Pranoto's Art Gallery GALLERY
(Map p176; ☑0361-970827; Jl Raya Goa Gajah, Teges; ⊗9am-5pm) Pranoto, a longtime Ubud artist, displays his works at this gallery/studio/home which backs up to beautiful rice fields southwest of Ubud. The scenes of Indonesian life are lovely. The studio is about 1km east of Jl Peliatan. Ask about a lovely walking path you can take back to central Ubud. There are figure-modelling sessions (30,000Rp) Wednesday and Saturday at 10am.

Museum Rudana GALLERY
(Map p138; ☑0361-975779; www.museum rudana.com; Jl Raya Mas; admission 100,000Rp; ⊗9am-5pm) This imposing museum is the creation of local politician and art-lover Nyoman Rudana and his wife Ni Wayan Olasthini. The three floors contain over 400 traditional paintings, including a calendar dated to the 1840s, some Lempad drawings, and more-modern pieces. The museum is beside the Rudana Gallery, which has a large selection of paintings for sale.

Ketut Rudi Gallery GALLERY
(Map p176; ☑0361-974122; Pengosekan; ⊗9am-7pm) These sprawling galleries showcase the works of more than 50 Ubud artists with techniques as varied as primitive and new realism. The gallery's namesake is on display as well; he favours an entertaining style best described as 'comical realism'. It's about 2km south of Ubud.

Agung Rai Gallery GALLERY
(Map p138; ☑0361-975449; Jl Peliatan; ⊗9am-6pm) This gallery is in a pretty compound and its collection covers the full range of Balinese styles. It functions as a cooperative, with the work priced by the artist and the gallery adding a percentage.

⊙ North Ubud

Wandering the many lanes running north from Jl Raya Ubud takes you past sweet little homestays. As the buildings thin out you are rewarded with beautiful views of rice fields and river valleys.

Petulu VILLAGE
Every evening at around 6pm, thousands of big **herons** fly in to Petulu, about 2.5km north of Jl Raya Ubud, squabbling over the prime perching places before settling into the trees beside the road and becoming a tourist attraction.

The herons, mainly the striped Java pond species, started their visits to Petulu in 1965 for no apparent reason. Villagers believe they bring good luck (as well as tourists), despite the smell and the mess. A few warung (food stalls) have been set up in the paddy fields, where you can have a drink while enjoying the spectacle. Walk quickly under the trees if the herons are already roosting.

Petulu is a pleasant walk or bicycle ride on any of several routes north of Ubud, but if you stay for the birds you'll be heading back in the dark.

🏃 Activities

Massage, Spas & Yoga

Ubud brims with salons and spas where you can heal, pamper, rejuvenate or otherwise focus on your personal needs, physical and mental. Visiting a spa is at the top of many a traveller's itinerary and the business of spas, yoga and other treatments grows each year. Expect the latest trends from any of many practitioners (the bulletin board outside Bali Buddha is bewildering) and prepare to

Central Ubud

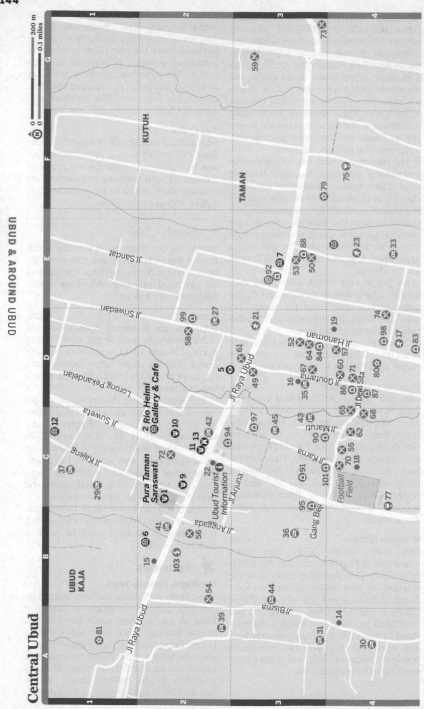

UBUD & AROUND UBUD

UBUD KAJA

KUTUH

TAMAN

2 Rio Helmi Gallery & Cafe

Pura Taman Saraswati

Ubud Tourist Information

Football Field

N

0   200 m
0   0.1 miles

Jl Raya Ubud
Jl Suweta
Jl Kajeng
Jl Bisma
Jl Arjuna
Jl Anggada
Gang Beji
Jl Kama
Jl Maruti
Jl Dewi Sita
Jl Goutama
Jl Hanoman
Jl Sriwedari
Jl Sandat
Lorong Pekandelan

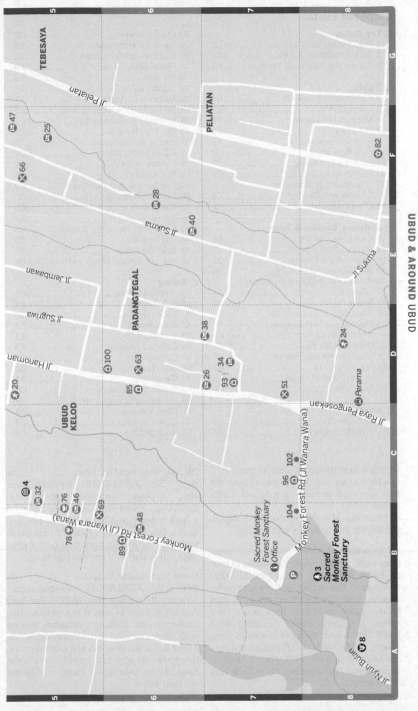

Central Ubud

try some new therapies, such as 'pawing'. If you have to ask you don't want to know. You may also wish to seek out a *balian* (traditional healer).

Many spas also offer courses in therapies, treatments and activities such as yoga.

★ Yoga Barn
YOGA

(Map p144; ☑ 0361-971236; www.balispirit.com; off Jl Raya Pengosekan; classes from 110,000Rp; ☺ 7am-8pm) The chakra for the yoga revolution in Ubud, the Yoga Barn sits in its own lotus position amid trees back near a river valley. The name exactly describes what you'll find: a huge range of classes in yoga, Pilates, dance and life-affirming offshoots are held through the week. Owner Meghan Pappenheim also organises the popular Bali Spirit Festival.

★ Bali Botanica Day Spa
SPA

(Map p138; ☑ 0361-976739; www.balibotanica. com; Jl Raya Sangginan; massage from 155,000Rp; ☺ 9am-9pm) Set beautifully on a lush hillside past little fields of rice and ducks, this spa offers a range of treatments including Ayurvedic ones. The herbal massage is popular. Will provide transport.

Ubud Sari Health Resort
SPA

(Map p138; ☑ 0361-974393; www.ubudsari.com; Jl Kajeng; 1hr massage from US$15; ☺ 9am-8pm) A spa and hotel in one. It is a serious place with extensive organic treatments bearing such names as 'total tissue cleansing'. Beside a long list of daytime spa and salon services, there are packages that include stays at the hotel. Many treatments focus on cleaning out your colon.

UBUD & AROUND UBUD

Ubud Wellness Spa SPA
(Map p138; ☑0361-970493; www.ubudwellness-balispa.com; off Jl Pengosekan; massage from 150,000Rp; ☺9am-10pm) A spa that concentrates on what counts, not the fru-fru. A favourite among Ubud's creative community.

Intuitive Flow YOGA
(Map p138; ☑0361-977824; www.intuitiveflow.com; Penestanan; yoga from 100,000Rp; ☺classes 9am daily, 4pm Mon-Fri) A lovely yoga studio up amid the rice fields – although just climbing the concrete stairs to get here from Campuan may leave you too spent for a round of asanas. Workshops in healing arts.

Taksu Spa SPA
(Map p144; ☑0361-971490; www.taksuspa.com; Jl Goutama; massage from 350,000Rp; ☺9am-9pm; ☎) Somewhat hidden yet still in the heart of Ubud, Taksu has a long and rather lavish menu of treatments as well as a strong focus on yoga. There are private rooms for couples massages, a healthy cafe and a range of classes.

Nur Salon SPA
(Map p144; ☑0361-975352; www.nursalonubud.com; Jl Hanoman 28; 1hr massage 155,000Rp; ☺9am-9pm) In a traditional Balinese compound filled with labelled medicinal plants, Nur offers a long menu of straightforward spa and salon services.

Cycling

Many shops and hotels in central Ubud display mountain bikes for hire. The price is usually a negotiable 35,000Rp per day. If in doubt where to rent, ask at your hotel and someone with a bike is soon likely to appear.

In general, the land is dissected by rivers running south, so any east–west route will involve a lot of ups and downs as you cross the river valleys. North–south routes run between the rivers, and are much easier going, but can have heavy traffic. Most of the sites in Ubud are reachable by bike.

Cycling is an excellent way to visit the many museums and cultural sites located around Ubud, although you'll need to consider your comfort level with traffic south of Ubud.

Ubud Bike Rental BICYCLE RENTAL
(Map p144; ☑0361-972170; www.ubudbikerental.com; Jl Raya Ubud; bike rental per day/per week 30,000/175,000Rp; ☺9am-5pm) A great shop with a huge range of bicycles for rent

at excellent prices. Also rents scooters and motorbikes.

Rafting

The **Sungai Ayung** (Ayung River) is the most popular river in Bali for white-water rafting. You start north of Ubud and end near the Amandari hotel in the west. Note that depending on rainfall the run can range from sedate to thrilling. A number of operators are based in Ubud (see p38).

🎓 Courses

Ubud is the perfect place to develop your artistic or language skills, or learn about Balinese culture and cuisine. The range of courses offered could keep you busy for a year. With most classes you must book in advance.

★ Museum Puri Lukisan   ART
(Map p144; www.museumpurilukisan.com; off Jl Raya Ubud; classes from 125,000Rp) One of Ubud's best museums teaches courses in puppet-making, gamelan, offering-making, Balinese dance, mask painting and much more. Classes are taught on demand; make arrangements at the museum ticket office.

Arma   CULTURAL
(Map p138; ✆0361-976659; www.armabali.com; Jl Raya Pengosekan; classes from US$44; ☺9am-6pm) A cultural powerhouse offering classes in painting, woodcarving and batik. Other courses include Balinese history, Hinduism and architecture.

Threads of Life Indonesian
Textile Arts Center   TEXTILE
(Map p144; ✆0361-972187; www.threadsoflife.com; Jl Kajeng 24; classes from 75,000Rp; ☺10am-7pm) Textile-appreciation courses in the gallery and educational studio last from one to

---

> **ℹ️ REFILL YOUR WATER BOTTLE**
>
> The number of plastic water bottles emptied in Bali's tropical heat daily and then tossed in the trash is colossal. In Ubud there are a few places where you can refill your water bottle (plastic or reusable) for a small fee, usually 3000Rp. The water is the same Aqua brand that is preferred locally and you'll be helping to preserve Bali's beauty, one plastic bottle at a time. A good central location is Pondok Pekak Library & Learning Centre.

---

eight days. Some classes involve extensive travel around Bali and should be considered graduate level.

Nirvana Batik Course   TEXTILE
(Map p144; ✆0361-975415; www.nirvanaku.com; Nirvana Pension & Gallery, Jl Goutama 10; classes from 485,000Rp; ☺classes 10am-2pm Mon-Sat) Nyoman Suradnya teaches the highly regarded batik courses. Classes cost about US$45 to US$50 per day depending on duration (one to five days).

Ida Bagus Anom Suryawan   ART
(Map p176; ✆0813 3844 8444; www.bali maskmaking.com; Jl Raya Mas, Mas; 2hr class 150,000Rp; ☺varies) Three generations of some of Bali's best mask-carvers will show you their secrets in a family compound right off the main road; in two weeks you might have something.

Wayan Karja Painting   ART
(Map p138; ✆0361-977810; Penestanan; classes from 250,000Rp) Intensive painting and drawing classes are run by abstract artist Karja, whose studio is on the site of his guesthouse, the Santra Putra.

Wayan Pasek Sucipta   MUSIC
(Map p144; ✆0361-970550; Eka's Homestay, Jl Sriwedari 8; classes from 100,000Rp) Learn the gamelan and bamboo drums from a master.

Pondok Pekak Library &
Learning Centre   LANGUAGE
(Map p144; ✆0361-976194; Monkey Forest Rd; classes per hour from 100,000Rp; ☺9am-5pm Mon-Sat, 1-5pm Sun) On the far side of the football field, this centre offers painting, dance, music, language and mask-carving classes; some are geared to kids.

Studio Perak   JEWELLERY
(Map p144; ✆0361-974244, 0812 365 1809; www.studioperak.com; Jl Hanoman; lessons per 3hr 350,000Rp) Specialises in Balinese-style silversmithing courses. In one three-hour lesson you'll make a finished piece. Classes can be geared to children.

Taman Harum Cottages   CULTURAL
(Map p176; ✆0361-975567; www.tamanharum cottages.com; Jl Raya Mas, Mas; lessons per hour from US$20) In the centre of Bali's wood-carving district, this hotel offers a palette of craft, culture, carving and painting courses. You can learn how to make the temple offerings found just about everywhere.

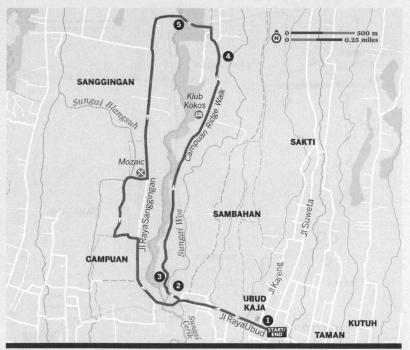

Walking Tour
Campuan Ridge

START UBUD PALACE
END UBUD PALACE
LENGTH 8.5KM; 3½ HOURS

This walk passes over the lush river valley of Sungai Wos (Wos River), offering views of Gunung Agung and glimpses of small village communities and rice fields.

Start at ❶ **Ubud Palace** (p139) and walk west on Jl Raya Ubud. At the confluence of Sungai Wos (Wos River) and Sungai Cerik (Cerik River) is Campuan, which means 'Where Two Rivers Meet'. This area was among the first to attract Western painters in the 1930s and you'll understand why from the still-lush foliage and the soothing roar of the rivers. The walk leaves Jl Raya Campuan here at the ❷ **Warwick Ibah Luxury Villas**. Enter the hotel driveway and take the path to the left, where a walkway crosses the river to the high-profile yet serene ❸ **Pura Gunung Lebah** (p141). From there follow the concrete path north, climbing up onto the ridge between the two rivers. Fields of elephant grass, traditionally used for thatched roofs, slope away on either side. You can see the rice fields above Ubud folding over the hills in all directions.

Continuing north along Campuan ridge past the Klub Kokos lodging, the road improves as it passes through paddy fields and the village of ❹ **Bangkiang Sidem**; from its outskirts, an unsigned road heads west, winding down to Sungai Cerik, then climbing steeply up to ❺ **Payogan**. From here you can walk south to the main road, and continue along Jl Raya Sanggingan, which seems to boast one or two more small boutiques and galleries every week. At Mozaic restaurant, veer to the west onto trails that stay level with the rice fields as the main road drops away. It's a fantasyland of coursing waterways and good views among the rice and villas. If you're entranced with Ubud and want to linger longer, many of the small bungalows are for rent by the month. When you come to the steep concrete steps, take them down to Campuan and back to Ubud.

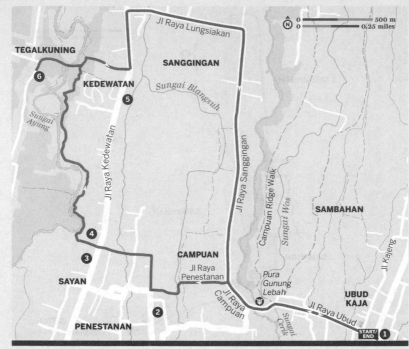

🏃 Walking Tour
Sungai Ayung Valley

START UBUD PALACE
END UBUD PALACE
LENGTH 6.5KM; FOUR HOURS

The wonders of Sungai Ayung (Ayung River) are the focus of this outing, where you will walk below the luxury hotels built to take advantage of the lush, tropical river valley.

From ❶ **Ubud Palace** (p139), head west on Jl Raya Ubud, over the Campuan bridge (noting the picturesque old bridge), past the beautifully expanded Pura Gunung Lebah below; here a steep uphill road, Jl Raya Penestanan, bends left and winds across the forested gully of Sungai Blangsuh (Blangsuh River) to the artists' village of ❷ **Penestanan**. West of Penestanan, head north on the small road (before the busy main road) that curves around to Sayan. The ❸ **Sayan Terrace** was Colin McPhee's home in the 1930s, as chronicled in his classic book *A House in Bali*. The views over the valley of the magnificent ❹ **Sungai Ayung** are superb. The best place to get to the riverside is just north of

the Sayan Terrace hotel – look for the downhill path before the gate to the rooms and follow the increasingly narrow tracks down (there are locals who'll show you for a tip of about 5000Rp.)

Following the rough trails north, along the eastern side of the Ayung, you traverse steep slopes, cross paddy fields and pass irrigation canals and tunnels. This is a highlight of the walk for many people, as we're talking about serious tropical jungle here. You don't need to follow any specific trail as you head slowly north along the river; instead just wander and see where your mood takes you. After about 1.5km you'll reach the finishing point for many white-water rafting trips – a good but steep trail goes from there up to the main road at ❺ **Kedewatan**, where you can walk back to Ubud. Alternatively, cross the river on the nearby bridge and take a steep, 1km loop through tropical forest to the very untouristy village of ❻ **Tegalkuning**. Return to Ubud on Jl Raya Sanggingan, with its shops and cafes offering respite.

Cooking

One of the most popular activities for visitors to Ubud. Cooking classes usually start at one of the local markets, where you can learn about the huge range of fruits, vegetables and other foods that are part of the Balinese diet.

★ **Casa Luna Cooking School**   COOKING
(Map p144; ☑ 0361-973282; www.casalunabali.com; Honeymoon Guesthouse, Jl Bisma; classes from 350,000Rp; ☺ 8am-1.30pm Mon-Sat) There are regular cooking courses at Honeymoon Guesthouse and/or Casa Luna. Half-day courses cover ingredients, cooking techniques and the cultural background of the Balinese kitchen (not all visit the market). Tours are also offered, including a good one to the Gianyar night market.

Mozaic Cooking Classes   COOKING
(Map p138; ☑ 0361-975768; www.mozaic-bali.com; Jl Raya Sanggingan; classes from 900,000Rp) Learn cooking techniques at one of Bali's best restaurants. A full menu of classes are taught, from casual to professional.

☞ Tours

Specialised tours in Ubud include thematic walks and cultural adventures. Spending a few hours exploring the area with a local expert is a highlight for many.

There are tours of the Ubud area by companies operating across Bali.

Bali Nature Herbal Walks   WALKING TOUR
(☑ 0812 381 6024; www.baliherbalwalk.com; walks US$18; ☺ 8.30am) Three-hour walks through lush Bali landscape; medicinal and cooking herbs and plants are identified and explained in their natural environment. Includes herbal drinks.

Bali Bird Walks   BIRDWATCHING
(Map p138; ☑ 0361-975009; www.balibirdwalk.com; tour US$37; ☺ 9am-12.30pm Tue, Fri, Sat & Sun) Started by Victor Mason more than three decades ago, this tour, ideal for keen birders, is still going strong. On a gentle morning's walk (from the long-closed Beggar's Bush Bar) you may see up to 30 of the 100-odd local species.

Dhyana Putri Adventures   CULTURAL TOUR
(☑ 0812 380 5623; www.balispirit.com/tours/bali_tour_dhyana.html) A bi-cultural, tri-lingual couple offer custom tours, with an emphasis on Balinese performing arts and in-depth cultural experiences.

Ubud Tourist Information   CULTURAL TOUR
(Yaysan Bina Wisata; Map p144; ☑ 0361-973285; Jl Raya Ubud; tours 150,000-240,000Rp; ☺ 8am-8pm) Runs interesting and affordable half- and full-day trips to a huge range of places, including Besakih and Kintamani.

---

❶ WALKING WISELY IN UBUD

Walking in and about the Ubud region with its endless beauty, myriad fascinations and delightful discoveries is a great pleasure and a superb reason to visit the area.

There are lots of interesting walks to surrounding villages and through the rice fields. You'll frequently see artists at work in open rooms and on verandahs, and the timeless tasks of rice cultivation continue alongside luxury villas.

A few points worth remembering to enjoy your walk:

Bring your own water In most places there are plenty of warung or small shops selling snack foods and drinks but don't risk dehydration between stops.

Gear up Bring a good hat, decent shoes and wet-weather gear for the afternoon showers; long trousers are better for walking through thick vegetation.

Start early Try to begin at daybreak, before it gets too hot. The air also feels crisper and you'll catch birds and other wildlife before they spend the day in shadows. It's also much quieter before the day's buzz begins.

Avoid tolls Some entrepreneurial rice farmers have erected little toll gates across their fields. You can a) simply detour around them, or b) pay a fee (never, ever accede to more than 10,000Rp).

Quit while ahead Should you tire don't worry about reaching some goal – the point is to enjoy your walk. Locals on motorbikes will invariably give you a ride home for around 20,000Rp.

BALI'S TRADITIONAL HEALERS

Bali's traditional healers, known as *balian* (*dukun* on Lombok), play an important part in Bali's culture by treating physical and mental illness, removing spells and channelling information from the ancestors. Numbering about 8000, *balian* are the ultimate in community medicine, making a commitment to serve their communities and turning no one away.

Lately, however, this system has come under stress in some areas due to the attention brought by *Eat, Pray, Love* and other media coverage of Bali's healers. Curious tourists are turning up in village compounds, taking *balians'* time and attention from the genuinely ill. However, that doesn't mean you shouldn't visit a *balian* if you're genuinely curious. Just do so in a manner that befits the experience: gently.

Consider the following before a visit:

➡ Make an appointment before visiting a *balian*.

➡ Know that English is rarely spoken.

➡ Dress respectfully (long trousers and a shirt, better yet a sarong and sash).

➡ Women should not be menstruating.

➡ Never point your feet at the healer.

➡ Bring an offering into which you have tucked the consulting fee, which will range from 100,000Rp to 250,000Rp per person.

➡ Understand what you're getting into: your treatment will be very public and probably painful. It may include deep-tissue massage, being poked with sharp sticks or having chewed herbs spat on you.

Finding a *balian* can take some work. Ask at your hotel, which can probably help with making an appointment and providing a suitable offering for stashing your fee. Or consider the following, who do see visitors to Bali: **Ketut Gading** (☑0361-970770); **Man Nyoman** (☑0813 3893 5369); **Sirkus** (☑0361-739538); and **Made Surya** (☑0361-788 0822; www.balihealers.com), who is an authority on Bali's traditional healers and offers one- and two-day intensive workshops on healing, magic, traditional systems and history, which include visits to authentic *balian*. His website is an excellent resource on visiting healers on Bali and he can also select an appropriate *balian* for you to visit and accompany you there as liaison and translator.

Some Western medical professionals question whether serious medical issues can be resolved by this type of healing, and patients should see a traditional healer in conjunction with a Western doctor if their ailment is serious.

⭐ Festivals & Events

One of the best places to see the many religious and cultural events celebrated in Bali each year is the Ubud area. The tourist office is unmatched for its comprehensive information on events each week.

Bali Spirit Festival   DANCE, MUSIC
(www.balispiritfestival.com; ⊙ early Apr) A popular yoga, dance and music festival from the people behind the Yoga Barn. There are over 100 workshops and concerts plus a market and more.

Ubud Writers & Readers Festival   LITERARY
(www.ubudwritersfestival.com; ⊙ Oct) Brings together scores of writers and readers from around the world in a celebration of writing –

especially writing that touches on Bali. A major event on the Ubud calendar.

🛏 Sleeping

Ubud has the best and most appealing range of places to stay on Bali, including fabled resorts, artful guesthouses and charming, simple homestays. Choices can be bewildering, so give some thought to where you want to stay, especially if you are renting private accommodation via the web.

Generally, Ubud offers good value for money at any price level. Simple accommodation within a family home compound is a cultural experience and costs around US$25. Ubud enjoys cool mountain air at night, so air-con isn't necessary, and with your windows open, you'll hear the symphony of sounds off the rice fields and river valleys.

Guesthouses may be a bit larger and have amenities like swimming pools but are still likely to be fairly intimate, often nestled amid rice fields and rivers. The best hotels are often perched on the edges of the deep river valleys, with superb views (although even some budget places have amazing views). Some provide shuttle service around the area.

Addresses in Ubud can be imprecise – but signage at the end of a road will often list the names of all the places to stay. Away from the main thoroughfares there are few streetlights and it can be challenging to find your way after dark. If walking, you'll want a torch (flashlight).

Due to its popularity and the lack (so far) of an invasion of chain hotels, Ubud is the one place on Bali where accommodation prices are rising sharply.

Central Ubud

JI Raya Ubud & Around

Sania's House GUESTHOUSE $
(Map p144; ☏0361-975535; sania_house@yahoo.com; Jl Karna 7; r 250,000-550,000Rp; @🛜🌊) Pets wander about this family-run place, where the large, clear pool, huge terrace and spacious rooms will have you howling at the moon. The 25 rooms are basic but clean; the market is nearly next door.

Raka House GUESTHOUSE $
(Map p144; ☏0361-976081; www.rakahouse.com; Jl Maruti; r 300,000-400,000Rp; 🌊🛜🌊) Six bungalow-style rooms cluster at the back of a compact family compound. You can soak your toes in a small trapezoidal plunge pool. More choices nearby.

★**Nirvana Pension & Gallery** GUESTHOUSE $$
(Map p144; ☏0361-975415; www.nirvanaku.com; Jl Goutama 10; r 450,000-600,000Rp; 🛜) There are *alang-alang* (thatched roofs), a plethora of paintings, ornate doorways and six rooms with modern bathrooms in a shady, secluded locale next to a large family temple. Batik courses are also held. It's a great location back off *über*-hot Goutama.

Puri Saren Agung GUESTHOUSE $$
(Map p144; ☏0361-975057; Jl Suweta 1; r from US$65; 🌊) Part of the Ubud royal family's historic palace. The three rooms are tucked behind the courtyard where the dance per-formances are held. Accommodation is in traditional Balinese pavilions, with big verandahs, four-poster beds, antique furnishings and hot water. Give a royal wave to wandering tourists from your patio.

Puri Saraswati Bungalows HOTEL $$
(Map p144; ☏0361-975164; www.purisaraswatiubud.com; Jl Raya Ubud; r US$60-80; 🌊🛜🌊) Very central and pleasant with lovely gardens that open onto the Ubud Water Palace. The 18 bungalow-style rooms are well back from Jl Raya Ubud, so it's quiet. Some rooms are fan-only; interiors are simply furnished but have richly carved details.

North of JI Raya Ubud

Padma Accommodation GUESTHOUSE $
(Map p144; ☏0361-977247; aswatama@hotmail.com; Jl Kajeng 13; r 300,000Rp; 🛜) There are four very private bungalows in a tropical garden here, with more on the way. Rooms are decorated with local crafts and the modern outdoor bathrooms have hot water. Nyoman Sudiarsa, a painter and family member, has a studio here and often shares his knowledge with guests.

Eka's Homestay HOMESTAY $
(Map p144; ☏0361-970550; Jl Sriwedari 8; r 350,000-450,000Rp; 🌊🛜) Follow your ears to this nice little family compound with seven basic rooms. Eka's is the home of Wayan Pasek Sucipta, a teacher of Balinese music. It's in a nice sunny spot on a quiet road (well, except during practice).

Han Snel Siti Bungalows GUESTHOUSE $
(Map p144; ☏0361-975699; www.sitibungalow.com; Jl Kajeng 3; bungalows US$25-40; 🌊🛜🌊) Owned by the family of the late Han Snel, a well-known Ubud painter, this quiet compound has eight bungalows with suitably artful stone designs. Some rooms are perched right on the edge of the river gorge and have excellent views; the small pool is part-way down.

Monkey Forest Road

Warsa's Garden Bungalows GUESTHOUSE $
(Map p144; ☏0361-971548; warsabungalow@gmail.com; Monkey Forest Rd; r 300,000-500,000Rp; 🌊🛜🌊) A good-sized pool with fountains enlivens this comfy but simple place in the heart of Monkey Forest action. The 23 rooms are reached through a traditional family-compound entrance. Some have tubs; some are fan-only.

WHERE TO STAY IN UBUD

Do you want to be in the centre or the quiet countryside? Have a rice-field view or enjoy a room with stylish design? Choices are myriad, especially on sites such as airbnb.com and homeaway.com where everything seems to be 'close to Ubud', even when the '10-minute drive' actually takes half an hour. The main areas of accommodation in Ubud are as follows.

Central Ubud

This original heart of Ubud has a vast range of places to rest your weary head and you'll enjoy a location that will cut down on the need for long walks or 'transport'. If you're near **Jl Raya Ubud**, don't settle for a room with noise from the main drag. Small and quiet streets to the east, including Jl Karna, Jl Maruti and Jl Goutama, have numerous family-style homestays. **North of Jalan Raya Ubud**, streets like Jl Kajeng and Jl Suweta offer a time-less tableau, with kids playing in the streets and many fine homestays. **Monkey Forest Road** has a high concentration of lodgings; go for one well off the traffic-choked road. **Jl Bisma** runs into a plateau of rice fields. New places are popping up all the time, especially down at the south end where a path links to Monkey Forest Rd.

Padangtegal & Tebesaya

East of central Ubud, but still conveniently located, Padangtegal has several budget lodg-ings along Jl Hanoman. A little further east, the quiet village of Tebesaya comprises little more than its main street, Jl Sukma, which runs between two streams. Cute homestays can be found down small footpaths.

Sambahan & Sakti

Going north from Jl Raya Ubud, you are soon in rolling terraces of rice fields. Tucked away here you'll find interesting and often luxurious hotels, yet you can have a beautiful walk to the centre in well under an hour.

★**Oka Wati Hotel**   HOTEL **$$**
(Map p144; ☑0361-973386; www.okawatihotel.com; off Monkey Forest Rd; r US$65-120; ❄❤✺) Owner Oka Wati is a lovely lady who grew up near the Ubud Palace. The 19 rooms have large verandahs where the delightful staff will deliver your choice of breakfast (do not miss the house-made yoghurt). The de-cor features vintage details like four-poster beds; some rooms view a small rice field and river valley. Follow narrow footpaths to get here.

Sri Bungalows   GUESTHOUSE **$$**
(Map p144; ☑0361-975394; www.sribungalows ubud.com; Monkey Forest Rd; r 700,000-1,200,000Rp; ❄@❤✺) Popular for its icon-ic views of rice fields (you think you hear it growing but really it's the sound of your soul decompressing). Be sure to get one of the comfy rooms (choose from 50) with relaxing loungers that command the views.

Lumbung Sari   GUESTHOUSE **$$**
(Map p144; ☑0361-976396; www.lumbungsari.com; Monkey Forest Rd; r 1,100,000-1,700,000Rp; ❄@❤✺) Artwork decorates the walls at the stylish Sari, which has a nice breakfast

bale (traditional pavilion) by the pool. The 14 rooms have tubs in elegant bathrooms finished with terrazzo.

Jl Bisma

Pondok Krishna   GUESTHOUSE **$**
(Map p144; ☑0361-977126; kriz_tie@yahoo.com; Jl Bisma; r 300,000Rp; ❄❤) This light and airy family compound has four rooms set among the frog-filled rice fields west of Jl Bisma. The open common area with its sunny loca-tion is good for nailing that tan.

Happy Mango Tree   HOSTEL **$**
(Map p144; ☑0812 3844 5498; www.thehappy mangotree.com; Jl Bisma 27; dm from 100,000Rp, d from 250,000Rp; ❤) This bright and bubbly hostel revels in its hippie vibe. Bright col-ours abound inside the rooms and out on the various terraces, some with rice-field views. Dorms have four beds, doubles come with names (and matching decor) like Love Shack and Ceiling Museum.

Ina Inn   GUESTHOUSE **$**
(Map p144; ☑0361-971093; Jl Bisma; r 300,000-350,000Rp; ❤✺) Stroll the thickly planted grounds and enjoy views across Ubud and

Nyuhkuning
A popular area just south of the Monkey Forest, Nyuhkuning has some creative guesthouses and hotels, yet is not a long walk to the centre.

Pengosekan
Immediately south of the centre, Pengosekan is good for shopping, dining and activities such as yoga.

Campuan & Sanggingan
The long sloping road that takes its names from these two communities west of the centre has a number of posh properties on its east side that overlook a lush river valley.

Penestanan
Just west of the Campuan bridge, steep Jl Raya Penestanan branches off to the left, and climbs up and around to Penestanan, a large plateau of rice fields and lodgings. Rooms and bungalows amid the rice are pitched at those seeking longer-term lodgings. Stroll the narrow paths and you'll find options at all prices. You can also get here via a steep climb up a set of concrete stairs off Jl Raya Campuan.

Sayan & Ayung Valley
Two kilometres west of Ubud, the fast-flowing Sungai Ayung (Ayung River) has carved out a deep valley, its sides sculpted into terraced paddy fields or draped in thick rainforest. Overlooking this verdant valley are some of Bali's best hotels.

the rice fields. The 10 fan-cooled rooms are basic but clean and comfy. The pool is ideal after a day of walking. If you want to take a plunge closer to your bed, the rooms have tubs.

Sama's Cottages   GUESTHOUSE $$
(Map p144; ☑ 0361-973481; www.samascottages ubud.com; Jl Bisma; r with fan/air-con from 580,000/650,000Rp; ❇ 🛜 ☷) Terraced down a hill, this lovely little hideaway has nine bungalow-style rooms with lashings of Balinese style layered on absolute simplicity. The oval pool feels like a jungle oasis. Ask for low-season discounts.

Komaneka at Bisma   BOUTIQUE HOTEL $$$
(Map p138; ☑ 0361-971933; www.komaneka.com; Jl Bisma; r from US$285; ❇ @ 🛜 ☷) Set well back in the rice fields near the river valley, this newish resort defines posh with a heavy overlay of Bali style. Accommodation ranges from suites to large three-bedroom villas. The compound exudes grace, along with thoughtful touches – ranging from Apple TVs loaded with movies to freshly baked cookies.

🛏 Padangtegal & Tebesaya

★ **Family Guest House**   HOMESTAY $
(Map p144; ☑ 0361-974054; www.familyubud.com; Jl Sukma; r 250,000-350,000Rp; 🛜) There's a bit of bustle from the busy family at this charming homestay. Healthy breakfasts are served. The six rooms have modern comforts in a traditional shell. Some have tubs. At the top is a balcony with a valley view.

Ni Nyoman Warini Bungalows   HOMESTAY $
(Map p144; ☑ 0361-978364; Jl Hanoman; r 200,000-350,000Rp; ❇ 🛜) There's a whole pod of simple family compounds with rooms for rent back on a little footpath off Jl Hanoman. It's quiet, and without even trying you'll find yourself enjoying the rhythms of family life. The eight rooms here have hot water and traditional bamboo furniture.

Suastika Lodge   GUESTHOUSE $
(Map p144; ☑ 0361-970215; suastika@hotmail.com; off Jl Sukma; r 150,000-250,000Rp; 🛜) On the little lane just east of Jl Sukma, you'll find four tidy rooms in a classic family compound. It's bungalow-style and you'll enjoy privacy and serenity.

ⓘ FINDING LONG-TERM ACCOMMODATION

There are many houses and flats you can rent or share in the Ubud area. For local information about options, check the noticeboards at Pondok Pekak Library (p148) and Bali Buda (p160). Also look in the free *Bali Advertiser* (www. baliadvertiser.biz) newspaper and the local website www.banjartamu.org. Prices start at about US$300 a month and climb as you add amenities.

Pande Home Stay GUESTHOUSE $
(Map p144; ☑ 0361-970421; pandehomestay@ gmail.com; Jl Sugriwa; r 150,000-250,000Rp; ☜) Yet another one of Ubud's great family-compound homestays, Pande is but one of many in a cluster here. It's close to the Yoga Barn and other highlights. The stone carvings are especially elaborate.

Puri Asri 2 GUESTHOUSE $
(Map p144; ☑ 0361-973210; Jl Sukma 59; r 200,000-300,000Rp; ✻☜▨) Work your way through a classic family compound and you'll find seven bungalow-style rooms with views of a ravine. It's a fabulous deal and rooms come with hot water. Cool off in the pool.

Aji Lodge HOMESTAY $
(Map p144; ☑ 0361-973255; ajilodge11@yahoo. com; off Jl Sukma; r 200,000-300,000Rp; ☜) A group of comfortable family compounds lines a footpath east of Jl Sukma. Enjoy one of six rooms here that are down the hill by the river for the full bedtime symphony of birds, bugs and critters.

Artini Cottages I HOMESTAY $
(Map p144; ☑ 0361-975348; www.artinicottage. com; Jl Hanoman; r from 250,000Rp; ☜) The Artini family runs a small empire of good-value guesthouses on Jl Hanoman. This, the original, is in an ornate family compound with many flowers. The three bungalows have hot water and large bathtubs. The more upscale Artini II, with rice-field views and a pool, is opposite.

★Matahari Cottages GUESTHOUSE $$
(Map p144; ☑ 0361-975459; www.matahari ubud.com; Jl Jembawan; r 400,000-800,000Rp; ✻☜▨) ✐ This delightful place has 15 flamboyant, themed rooms, including the 'Batavia Princess' and the 'Indian Pasha'. The library is a vision out of a 1920s fantasy. It also boasts a self-proclaimed 'jungle jacuzzi', an upscale way to replicate the old Bali tradition of river-bathing. There's a multicourse breakfast and high tea elaborately served on silver.

🛏 Sambahan & Sakti

Bali Asli Lodge HOMESTAY $
(Map p138; ☑ 0361-970537; www.baliaslilodge. com; Jl Suweta; r 250,000-300,000Rp) Escape the central Ubud hubbub here. The five rooms are in traditional Balinese stone-and-brick houses set on verdant gardens. There are terraces where you can let the hours pass; interiors are clean and comfy. Town is a 15-minute walk.

Ketut's Place GUESTHOUSE $$
(Map p138; ☑ 0361-975304; www.ketutsplace.com; Jl Suweta 40; r 550,000-850,000Rp; ✻@▨) The 10 rooms here range from basic with fans to deluxe versions with air-con and bathtub. All have artful accents and enjoy a dramatic pool shimmering down the hillside and river-valley views. On some nights, an impressive Balinese feast is served by Ketut, a local luminary and performer.

Ubud Sari Health Resort GUESTHOUSE $$
(Map p138; ☑ 0361-974393; www.ubudsari.com; Jl Kajeng; r with fan/air-con US$50/75; ✻☜▨) The name for the 19 rooms at this noted health spa says it all: Zen Village. The plants in the gardens are labelled for their medicinal qualities and the cafe serves organic, vegetarian fare. Guests can use the health facilities, including the sauna and whirlpool.

Klub Kokos GUESTHOUSE $$
(Map p138; ☑ 0361-849 3502; www.klubkokos.com; r US$70-100; ✻@☜▨) A beautiful 1.5km walk north along the Campuan ridge, Klub Kokos is a ridge-top hideaway with a big pool and seven appealing bungalow-style rooms. It's reachable by car from the north; call for directions. Rates include breakfast and snacks and there's a cafe.

Waka di Ume HOTEL $$$
(Map p138; ☑ 0361-973 178; www.wakadiume ubud.com; Jl Suweta; r from US$300, villas from US$500; ✻@☜▨) Located a gentle 1.5km uphill from the centre, this elegant compound enjoys engrossing verdant views across rice fields. New and old styles mix in the 33 large units; go for a villa with a view. Service is superb yet relaxed. Listening to

gamelan practice echoing across the fields at night is quite magical

Nyuhkuning

★ Swasti Eco Cottages
GUESTHOUSE $$

(Map p138; ☑ 0361-974079; www.baliswasti.com; Jl Nyuh Bulan; r 750,000-900,000Rp; @ 🛜 🛋) 🏊 Just five minutes' walk from the south entrance to the Monkey Forest, this guesthouse and bungalow compound has large grounds that feature an organic garden (produce is used in the excellent cafe). Some of the 16 rooms are in simple two-storey blocks; others are in vintage traditional houses brought here from across Bali.

Alam Indah
HOTEL $$

(Map p138; ☑ 0361-974629; www.alamindahbali.com; Jl Nyuh Bulan; r US$65-140; 🌹 🛜 🛋) Just south of the Monkey Forest in Nyuhkuning, this isolated and spacious resort has 16 rooms that are beautifully finished in natural materials and traditional designs. The Wos Valley views are entrancing, especially from the multilevel pool area. A companion property, Alam Jiwa, is a 10-minute walk further into the rice fields. Great cafe!

Kertiyasa Bungalows
GUESTHOUSE $$

(Map p138; ☑ 0361-971377; www.kertiyasabungalow.com; Jl Nyuh Bulan; r US$45-80; 🌹 🛜 🛋) Set in a quiet location, this attractive place has 13 rooms ranging from garden-view standards to private, very large rooms. The meandering pool is surrounded by beautiful plantings.

Saren Indah Hotel
HOTEL $$

(Map p138; ☑ 0361-971471; www.sarenhotel.com; Jl Nyuh Bulan; r US$55-80; 🌹 🛜 🛋) South of the Monkey Forest, this 15-room hotel sits in the middle of rice fields – be sure to get a 2nd-floor room to enjoy the views. Rooms have classic Balinese charm; better ones have fridges and stylish tubs.

Pengosekan

★ Agung Raka
BOUTIQUE HOTEL $$

(Map p138; ☑ 0361-975757; www.agungraka.com; Jl Raya Pengosekan; r from US$100, bungalow from US$150; 🌹 🛜 🛋) This 42-room hotel sprawls out across picture-perfect rice fields just south of the centre of Ubud. Rooms are large and suitably Balinese in motif but the real stars are the bungalows set back on a rice terrace amid palm trees. Fall asleep to the nighttime symphony of bugs and birds.

Casa Ganesha Hotel
HOTEL $$

(Map p138; ☑ 0361-971488; www.casaganesha.com; Jl Raya Pengosekan; r US$85; 🌹 🛜 🛋) A solid midrange choice in a great location just south of Ubud's centre, this 24-room hotel has two-storey blocks built around a pool. Rooms are straightforward and have terraces or balconies. There are pretty rice fields nearby.

Arma Resort
HOTEL $$$

(Map p138; ☑ 0361-976659; www.armabali.com; Jl Raya Pengosekan; r US$135-220, villas from US$300; 🌹 @ 🛜 🛋) Get full Balinese cultural immersion at the hotel enclave of the Arma compound. The expansive property has a large library and elegant gardens. The 10 villas come with private pools. The fabulous namesake museum is on the grounds.

Peliatan

★ Maya Ubud
LUXURY HOTEL $$$

(☑ 0361-977888; www.mayaubud.com; Jl Gunung Sari Peliatan; r from US$350; 🌹 @ 🛜 🛋) One of the most beautiful large hotels around Ubud, this sprawling property is well integrated into its surrounding river valley and rice fields. The 108 rooms and villas have the sort of open and light feeling combined with traditional materials that defines the concept of 'Bali style'.

Campuan & Sanggingan

Hotel Tjampuhan
HOTEL $$

(Map p138; ☑ 0361-975368; www.tjampuhan-bali.com; Jl Raya Campuan; r US$100-180; 🌹 @ 🛜 🛋) This venerable 69-room place overlooks the confluence of Sungai Wos and Campuan. The influential German artist Walter Spies lived here in the 1930s, and his former home, which sleeps four people (US$250), is part of the hotel. Bungalow-style units spill down the hill and enjoy mesmerising valley and temple views.

★ Warwick Ibah Luxury Villas & Spa
HOTEL $$$

(Map p138; ☑ 0361-974466; www.warwickibah.com; off Jl Raya Campuan; ste from US$250, villas US$450; 🌹 🛜 🛋) Overlooking the rushing waters and rice-clad hills of the Wos Valley, the Ibah offers refined luxury in 15 spacious, stylish individual suites and villas that combine ancient and modern details. Each could be a feature in an interior design magazine. The swimming pool is set into the hillside amid gardens and lavish stone carvings.

Uma by Como BOUTIQUE HOTEL **$$$**
([☎] 0361-972448; www.comohotels.com; Jl Raya
Sanggingan; r from US$270, villa from US$390;
[❄][☎][⊠]) One of Ubud's most attractive prop-
erties, the 46 rooms here come in a variety of
sizes but all have a relaxed naturalistic style
that goes well with the gorgeous views over
the gardens and the river valley beyond. Ser-
vice and amenities like the restaurant are
superb.

Penestanan

★ **Santra Putra** GUESTHOUSE **$**
(Map p138; [☎] 0361-977810; wayankarja@gmail.
com; off Jl Raya Campuan; r 300,000-350,000Rp;
[☎]) Run by internationally exhibited abstract
artist I Wayan Karja (whose studio/gallery
is also on site), this place has 11 big, open,
airy rooms with hot water. Enjoy paddy-field
views from all vantage points. Painting and
drawing classes are offered by the artist.

EAT, PRAY, LOVE & UBUD

'That damn book' is a common reaction by many Ubud residents, who fear the town's popularity is driven in part by *Eat, Pray, Love* fans. *Eat, Pray, Love* is the Elizabeth Gilbert book (and not-so-successful movie) that chronicles the American author's search for self-fulfilment (and fulfilment of a book contract) across Italy, India and, yes, Ubud.

Some criticise Gilbert for not offering a more complete picture of Ubud's locals, dance, art, expats and walks, warts and all. And they decry basic factual errors such as the evocative prose about surf spots on the north coast (there are none), which lead you to suspect things might have been embellished for the plot.

Then there are the genuine fans, those who found a message in *EPL* that resonated, validating and/or challenging aspects of their lives. For some an ultimately self-fulfilling journey to Ubud wouldn't have happened without *EPL*.

People in the Book

Two characters in the book are easily found in Ubud. Both receive large numbers of *EPL* fans and have lucrative livelihoods because of it:

Ketut Liyer (Map p138; [☎] 0361-974092; [⊙] hours vary, call) The genial and inspirational friend of Gilbert is easily found about a 10-minute walk south of Pengosekan (look for the bright signs). Any driver will happily bring you here. Hours vary and the ageing Ketut isn't always available, possibly due to the huge demand for an audience from Westerners. Expect to pay about US$25 for a short and public session, during which you will be told a variation on the theme that you're smart, beautiful, sexy and will live to 101. The actual Liyer compound is used in the movie, although Ketut is played by a schoolteacher from Java.

Wayan Nuriasih (Map p144; [☎] 0361-917 5991, 0361-884 3042; balihealer@hotmail.com; Jl Jembawan 5; [⊙] 9am-5pm) Another star of *Eat, Pray, Love*, Nuriasih is right in the heart of Ubud. Her open-fronted shop has a table where you can discuss your ailments with her and ponder a treatment. During this time, various buff male assistants will silently wander about and soon an elixir may appear at your elbow. The 'vitamin lunch' is a series of extracts and raw foods that is popular with many. Note that it is important to have a very clear understanding of what you're agreeing to, as it's easy to commit to therapies that can cost US$50 or more. For less, you can enjoy a cleansing, during which time several men whack at your body and might give you new pains that make you forget the old ones.

Locations in the Movie

Most of the Bali locations for *Eat Pray Love*, the movie, were filmed in and around Ubud. However, don't be surprised if on your walks in the area, you find beautiful rice fields that surpass those shown in the movie.

The beach scenes were shot at Padang Padang, on south Bali's Bukit Peninsula. Oddly, the real beach is more attractive than the sort of grey version seen in the film. But for those hoping to imbibe at the beach bar where Julia Roberts meets Javier Bardem, there's no point trying, as the bar was created for the movie.

Melati Cottages
HOTEL $$

(Map p138; ☑0361-974650; www.melati-cottages. com; Jl Raya Penestanan; r US$35-60; ☎) Set back among the rice fields, the deeply shaded Melati has 22 simple rooms in two-storey bungalow-style buildings. All have porches for listening to the sounds of the fields and taking the cool night air.

Villa Nirvana
BOUTIQUE HOTEL $$$

(Map p138; ☑0361-979419; www.villanirvana bali.com; Penestanan; r US$120-225; ❋🌐📶) You may find nirvana just for reaching Villa Nirvana: access is either along a 150m path through a small river valley from the west or along a rice-field path from the top of steep steps from the east. The eight-room compound, designed by local architect Awan Sukhro Edhi, is a serene retreat from daily life.

Sayan & Ayung Valley

Sayan Terrace
HOTEL $$

(Map p138; ☑0361-974384; www.sayanterrace resort.com; Jl Raya Sayan; r from US$100, villas from US$250; ❋@📶📶) Gaze into the Sayan Valley from this venerable hotel and you'll understand why this was the site of Colin McPhee's *A House in Bali*. Stay here while your neighbours housed in luxury resorts pay far more. Here the 12 rooms and villas are simply decorated but are large and have *that* view. Rates include afternoon tea.

★Bambu Indah
BOUTIQUE HOTEL $$$

(☑0361-975124; www.bambuindah.com; Banjar Baung; house US$135-370; 📶📶) ✐ Famed expat entrepreneur John Hardy sold his jewellery company in 2007 and became a hotelier. On a ridge near Sayan and his beloved Sungai Ayung, he's assembled a compound of 13 100-year-old royal Javanese houses, each furnished with style and flair. Several outbuildings create a timeless village with underpinnings of luxury.

★Amandari
HOTEL $$$

(☑0361-975333; www.amanresorts.com; Sayan; ste from US$950; ❋@📶📶) In Kedewatan village, the storied Amandari does everything with the charm and grace of a classical Balinese dancer. Superb views over the jungle and down to the river – the 30m green-tiled swimming pool seems to drop right over the edge – are just some of the inducements. The 30 private pavilions may prove inescapable.

Four Seasons Resort
HOTEL $$$

(Map p138; ☑0361-977577; www.fourseasons. com; Sayan; ste from US$760, villas from US$800; ❋@📶📶) Set below the valley rim, the curved open-air reception area looks like a Cinerama screen of Ubud beauty. Many villas have private pools and all share the same amazing views and striking modern design. At night you hear just the water rushing below from any of the 60 rooms.

Taman Bebek
HOTEL $$$

(Map p138; ☑0361-975385; www.tamanbebek bali.com; Jl Raya Sayan; r 1,200,000-1,600,000Rp; ❋📶📶) A spectacular, verdant location overlooking the Sayan Valley may keep you glued to your terrace throughout the day. Four suites and seven villas here wrap around the Sayan Terrace and enjoy a stylish common area. All have understated yet classic Balinese wood-and-thatch architecture as designed by the legendary Made Wijaya.

✗ Eating

Ubud's cafes and restaurants are some of the best in Bali. Local and expat chefs produce a bounty of authentic Balinese dishes, as well as inventive Asian and other international cuisines. Cafes with good coffee seem almost as common as frangipani blossoms. Be sure to be seated by 9pm or your options will narrow rapidly. Book dinner tables in high season.

Ubud Organic Market (www.ubudorganic market.com; ⊙9am-1pm) operates twice a week: Wednesday at Warung Sopa (p162) and Saturday at Pizza Bagus (p163). It attracts top vendors from around the region. Bali Buda's **BudaMart** (Map p144; www.bali buda.com; Jl Raya Ubud; ⊙8am-8pm) is a good source for organic produce and its baked goods are superb.

Delta Dewata Supermarket (Map p144; ☑0361-973049; Jl Raya Andong; ⊙8am-10pm) and **Bintang Supermarket** (Map p138; Jl Raya Sanggingan; ⊙8am-10pm) both have a large range of food and other essentials. The traditional **produce market** (Map p144; Jl Raya Ubud; ⊙6am-1pm) is a multilevel carnival of tropical foods and worth exploring despite the clamouring tourist hordes. Delta Mart convenience stores are common but, in our experience, so is the store's pricing variability. The ubiquitous Circle Ks are reliable and sell Bintang around the clock.

✕ Central Ubud

Jl Raya Ubud & Around

There are busy and tasty choices on Ubud's main street.

Bali Buda CAFE $
(Map p144; ☎0361-976324; www.balibuda.com; Jl Jembawan 1; meals from 30,000Rp; ⊗8am-10pm; ⬛) This breezy upper-floor place offers a full range of vegetarian *jamu* (health tonics), salads, sandwiches, savoury crepes, pizzas and gelato. It has a comfy lounging area and is candlelit at night. The bulletin board is packed with idiosyncratic Ubud notices.

Anomali Coffee CAFE $
(Map p144; Jl Raya Ubud; snacks from 20,000Rp; ⊗7am-11pm; ☏) Local hipsters get their Java from this place which is, well, from Java. Indonesia's answer to Starbucks takes its (excellent) coffee seriously and so does the young crowd that gathers here. A relaxed place filled with chatter.

Gelato Secrets ICE CREAM $
(Map p144; www.gelatosecrets.com; Jl Raya Ubud; treats from 15,000Rp; ⊗11am-11pm) Skip the Dairy Queen (yes, really!) on Ubud's main

---

WALKING FOR ORGANIC TREATS

Looking for a fun walk of an hour or so? Set in a beautiful location on a plateau overlooking rice terraces and river valleys, the small cafe **Warung Bodag Maliah** (Map p138; ☎0361-972087; www.sari-organik.com; Subak Sok Wayah; meals from 30,000Rp; ⊗8am-6pm) ⬛ sits in the middle of a big organic farm belonging to the locally popular Sari Organic brand.

Yes the food's healthy, but more importantly, given that half the fun is getting here, the drinks are cool and refreshing. Look for a little track heading north off Jl Raya Ubud that goes past Abangan Bungalows, then follow the signs along footpaths for another 800m.

Once you are walking through the lush rice fields, you can keep heading north as long as your interest or endurance lasts. Look for little offshoot trails to either side that lead to small rivers.

---

drag in favour of this temple to frozen goodness. Fresh flavours are made from local fruits and spices.

Lada Warung INDONESIAN $
(Map p144; Jl Hanoman; meals from 30,000Rp; ⊗8am-10pm; ☏) You can order off the menu at this neat-as-a-pin open-fronted warung or dine warung-style by choosing from an array of excellent dishes; come early for the best selection.

Casa Luna INDONESIAN $$
(Map p144; ☎0361-977409; www.casalunabali.com; Jl Raya Ubud; meals from 50,000Rp; ⊗8am-10pm) Enjoy creative Indonesian-focused dishes such as addictive bamboo skewers of minced seafood sate (try to pick out the dozen or so spices). Goods from its well-known bakery are also a must. The owner, Janet deNeefe, is the force behind the lauded Ubud Writers & Readers Festival (p152). There are regular literary events at night.

Clear FUSION $$
(Map p144; ☎0361-889 4437; www.clear-cafe-ubud.com; Jl Hanoman 8; meals US$4-15; ⊗8am-10pm; ⬛⬛) ⬤ This high-concept restaurant brings a bit of Hollywood glitz to Ubud. The dishes are relentlessly healthy but also creative – think soba noodles meets raw food meets curried tofu etc – done artfully and sourced locally. It has a deli counter for picnics and fresh snacks, plus a BYOB policy. There's also a kids' menu.

Black Beach ITALIAN $$
(Map p144; ☎0361-971353; www.blackbeach.asia; Jl Hanoman; mains 45,000-90,000Rp; ⊗11am-10pm) They beat their own dough and then let it slowly rise before turning it into good thin-crust pizza. If that doesn't sway you, the tasty pasta might. Views from the upstairs dining area are nice but what really draws in the intelligentsia is the regular showing of art-house movies on the terrace.

North of Jl Raya Ubud

Coffee Studio Seniman CAFE $
(Map p144; ☎0361-972085; www.senimancoffee.com; Jl Sriwedari; mains from 40,000Rp; ⊗8am-7pm; ☏) That 'coffee studio' moniker isn't for show: you see the roasters as you enter this temple of Joe. Take a seat on the large porch and choose from an array of Bali-grown brews. Foods are organic and creative.

Warung Ibu Oka BALINESE $
(Map p144; Jl Suweta; mains from 50,000Rp; ⊗10am-4pm) Opposite Ubud Palace, you'll

see lunchtime crowds waiting for one thing: the Balinese-style roast *babi guling* (suckling pig). Line up for a comparatively pricey version of the Balinese classic. Order a *spesial* to get the best cut. Get there early to avoid day-tripping bus tours.

Rio Helmi Gallery & Cafe CAFE $
(Map p144; Jl Suweta 5; mains from 40,000Rp; ⊙7am-7pm) As tasty as one of their famous cupcakes, this cafe in the eponymous gallery is the perfect place to pause for a coffee and/or an all-day breakfast and to soak up some Ubud vibe.

Monkey Forest Road

★Three Monkeys FUSION $$
(Map p144; Monkey Forest Rd; meals from 80,000Rp; ⊙8am-10pm) Have a passionfruit-crush cocktail and settle back amid the frog symphony of the rice fields. Add the glow of tiki torches for a magical effect. By day there are sandwiches, salads and gelato. At night there's a fusion menu of Asian classics.

Jl Dewi Sita & Jl Goutama

East of Monkey Forest Rd, a short stroll takes you into Ubud's best selection of restaurants.

Juice Ja Cafe CAFE $
(Map p144; 0361-971056; Jl Dewi Sita; mains from 30,000Rp; ⊙8am-10pm; 🛜) 🍴 Glass of spirulina? Dash of wheat grass with your papaya juice? Organic fruits and vegetables go into the food at this funky bakery-cafe. Little brochures explain the provenance of items such as the organic cashew nuts. Enjoy the patio.

Tutmak Cafe CAFE $
(Map p144; Jl Dewi Sita; mains 30,000-90,000Rp; ⊙8am-11pm; 🛜) The breezy multilevel location here, facing both Jl Dewi Sita and the football field, is a popular place for a refreshing drink or something to munch from the menu of Indo classics, sandwiches and salads. Local comers on the make huddle around their laptops plotting their next move.

Dewa Warung INDONESIAN $
(Map p144; Jl Goutama; meals 15,000-25,000Rp; ⊙8am-11pm) When it rains, the tin roof sounds like a tap-dance convention and the bare lightbulbs sway in the breeze. A little garden surrounds tables a few steps above the road where diners tuck into plates of sizzling fresh Indo fare. Cheap Bintang.

★Pica LATIN AMERICAN $$
(Map p144; 0361-971660; Jl Dewi Sita; mains 70,000-160,000Rp; ⊙11am-10pm Tue-Sun) Who knew? South American cuisine has travelled well to Ubud, thanks to the young couple behind this excellent restaurant. From the open kitchen, creative dishes making creative use of beef, pork, fish, potatoes and more issue forth in a diner-pleasing stream. The house sourdough bread is superb.

★Waroeng Bernadette INDONESIAN $$
(Map p144; 0821 4742 4779; Jl Goutama; mains from 60,000Rp; ⊙11am-11pm) It's not called the 'Home of Rendang' for nothing. The Javanese classic dish of long-marinated meats (beef is the true classic) is pulled off with colour and flair here. Other dishes such as gado-gado have a zesty zing that's missing from lacklustre tourist versions served elsewhere. The elevated dining room is a vision of kitsch.

Melting Wok ASIAN $$
(Map p144; 0361-929 9716; Jl Goutama; mains from 50,000Rp; ⊙10am-11pm Tue-Sun) Pan-Asian fare pleases the masses at this very popular open-air restaurant on the Goutama strip. Curries, noodle dishes, tempeh and a lot more fill a menu that makes decisions tough. Desserts take on a bit of colonial flavour: French accents abound. The service is relaxed but efficient. Bookings advised.

Cafe Havana LATIN AMERICAN $$
(Map p144; 0361-972973; Jl Dewi Sita; mains from 60,000Rp; ⊙8am-11pm) All that's missing is Fidel. Actually, the decrepitude of its namesake city is also missing from this smart and stylish cafe. Dishes exude Latin flair, such as the tasty pork numbers, but you can also expect surprises such as the fab crème brûlée oatmeal in the mornings. There's nightly salsa dancing and live music 7pm to 10pm.

★Locavore FUSION $$$
(Map p144; 0361-977733; www.restaurant locavore.com; Jl Dewi Sita; mains from US$30; ⊙noon-2.30pm, 6-10pm Mon-Sat; ✴) *The* foodie heaven in Ubud, this temple to locally sourced, ultra-creative foods is the town's toughest table. Book weeks in advance. Meals come as desgustations and can top out at nine courses (expect this cuisine nirvana to last upwards of three hours). Chefs Eelke Plasmeijer and Ray Adriansyah are magicians; enjoy the show.

Jl Bisma

Café des Artistes
EUROPEAN $$

(Map p144; ☑0361-972706; Jl Bisma 9X; meals from 120,000Rp; ⊙noon-11am) In a quiet and cultured perch up off Jl Raya Ubud, the popular Café des Artistes serves Belgian-accented food, although the menu strays into France and Indonesia as well. There's also some amazing steaks. Local art is on display and the bar is refreshingly cultured.

Padangtegal & Tebesaya

★Warung Sopa
VEGETARIAN $

(Map p144; ☑0361-276 5897; Jl Sugriwa 36; mains 30,000-60,000Rp; ⊙8am-10pm; ☎🍴) This popular, open-air place captures the Ubud vibe with creative and (more importantly) tasty vegetarian fare with a Balinese twist. Look for specials of the day on display; the ever-changing *nasi campur* (rice with side dishes) is a treat.

Warung Mangga Madu
INDONESIAN $

(Map p144; ☑0361-977334; Jl Gunung Sari; mains from 15,000Rp; ⊙8am-10pm) The slightly elevated dining terrace here is a fine place to enjoy excellent versions of Indo classics like *nasi campur*. That's your driver at the next table reading the *Bali Post* newspaper. Load up on road snacks to go.

Mama's Warung
INDONESIAN $

(Map p144; Jl Sukma; mains 20,000-40,000Rp; ⊙8am-10pm) A real budget find among the bargain homestays of Tebesaya. Mama and her retinue cook up Indo classics that are spicy and redolent with garlic (the avocado salad, yum!). The freshly made peanut sauce for the sate is silky smooth, the fried sambal superb.

Kafe
CAFE $

(Map p144; ☑0361-780 3802; Jl Hanoman 44; mains 15,000-40,000Rp; ⊙8am-11pm; 🍴) 🍲 Kafe has an organic menu great for veggie grazing or just having a coffee, juice or house-made natural soft drink. Breakfasts are healthy while lunch meals feature excellent salads and burritos, with many raw items. It's always busy.

Kebun
MEDITERRANEAN $$

(Map p144; ☑0361-780 3801; www.kebun bistro.com; Jl Hanoman 44; mains from 60,000Rp; ⊙11am-late) Napa meets Ubud at this cute little bistro and it's a good match. A long wine list (with specials) can be paired with French- and Italian-accented dishes large and small. There are daily specials including pastas and risottos. Dine inside or out on the appealing terrace.

Bebek Bengil
INDONESIAN $$

(Dirty Duck Diner; Map p144; ☑0361-975489; www.bebekbengil.com; Jl Hanoman; mains 70,000-200,000Rp; ⊙10am-11pm) This vast place is hugely popular for one reason: its crispy Balinese duck, which is marinated for 36 hours in spices and then fried. The ducks on one of the few surviving rice fields outside the open-air dining pavilions look worried.

Teges

Jl Raya Mas, which runs due south to the namesake village from Peliatan, has an excellent choice for Balinese food.

★Warung Teges
BALINESE $

(Map p138; Jl Cok Rai Pudak; mains from 20,000Rp; ⊙8am-10pm) The *nasi campur* is better here than almost anywhere else around Ubud. The restaurant gets just about everything right, from the pork sausage to the chicken, the *babi guling* (suckling pig) and even the tempeh. It's where Jl Raya Mas morphs into Jl Cok Rai Pudak.

Nyuhkuning

Warung Pojok
INDONESIAN $

(Map p138; ☑0361-749 4535; Jl Nyuh Bulan; mains 20,000-30,000Rp; ⊙8am-10pm; ☎) This quiet corner cafe has a serene spot overlooking Ubud's other football field. Besides plenty of rice and noodle dishes, there are lots of veggie options, lassies and juices.

Swasti
INTERNATIONAL $$

(Map p138; ☑0361-974079; www.baliswasti.com; Jl Nyuh Bulan; meals 40,000-80,000Rp; ⊙8am-10pm; ☎) 🍲 This cafe attached to the excellent guesthouse of the same name is reason enough to take a stroll through the Monkey Forest. Indonesian and Western dishes prepared from the large in-house organic garden are fresh and tasty. Have a glass of fresh juice with the beloved *fondant au chocolat* or mango mousse. Watch for children's evening dance performances.

Pengosekan

Many highly regarded restaurants are found along the curves of Jl Raya Pengosekan. It's always worth seeing what's new.

Pizza Bagus PIZZERIA **$$**
(Map p138; ☑0361-978520; www.pizza
bagus.com; Jl Raya Pengosekan; mains 40,000-
100,000Rp; ⊙9am-10pm; ✴️🛜) First-rate piz-
za with a crispy thin crust is baked here.
Besides the long list of pizza options, there's
pasta and sandwiches – all mostly organic.
Tables are in and out, there's a play area, and
it delivers.

Taco Casa MEXICAN **$$**
(Map p138; www.tacocasabali.com; Jl Raya Pen-
gosekan; mains from 50,000Rp; ⊙11am-10pm)
Sure, Mexico is almost exactly on the opposite side of the globe (get one and check!),
but the flavours have found their way to
Bali. Tasty versions of burritos, tacos and
more have just the right mix of heat and
spice. It delivers.

🍴 Campuan & Sanggingan

Warung Pulau Kelapa INDONESIAN **$**
(Map p138; ☑0361-821 5502; Jl Raya Sanggingan;
mains 20,000-40,000Rp; ⊙11am-11pm) Kelapa
has stylish takes on Indonesian classics plus
more unusual dishes from around the archipelago. The surrounds are stylish as well:
plenty of whitewash and antiques. Terrace
tables across the wide expanse of grass are
best.

Elephant VEGETARIAN **$$**
(Map p138; ☑0361-716 1907; Jl Raya Sanggin-
gan; mains 40,000-150,000Rp; ⊙8am-9.30pm)
High-concept vegetarian dining with gor-
geous views across the Cerik Valley. They do
pleasurable things with potatoes here – and
lots of other vegetables. Foods are well-sea-
soned, interesting and topped off with an
especially good dessert menu. It's well off
the road.

Naughty Nuri's BARBECUE **$$**
(Map p138; ☑0361-977547; Jl Raya Sanggingan;
meals from 80,000Rp; ⊙11am-11pm) This legendary expat hang-out now has lines of
people waiting for food through the day and
night. Proof that a little media hype helps,
the grilled steaks, ribs and burgers are popular, even if all the chewing needed gets in
the way of chatting. The original lures, potent martinis, are as large as ever.

★Mozaic FUSION **$$$**
(Map p138; ☑0361-975768; www.mozaic-bali.com;
Jl Raya Sanggingan; menus from 1,250,000Rp;
⊙6-10.30pm) Chef Chris Salans oversees
this much-lauded top-end restaurant. Fine
French fusion cuisine features on a con-
stantly changing seasonal menu that takes
its influences from tropical Asia. Dine in an
elegant garden or ornate pavilion. Choose
from four tasting menus, one of which is
simply a surprise.

Bridges FUSION **$$$**
(Map p138; ☑0361-970095; www.bridgesbali.
com; Jl Raya Campuan; mains US$15-35; ⊙11am-
11.30pm, happy hour 4-7pm) The namesake
bridges are right outside this multilevel restaurant with sweeping views of the gorgeous
river gorge. You'll hear the rush of the water
over rocks far below while you indulge in
a top-end cocktail over the rocks or choose
from the mix of Asian and European fusion
fare. Popular happy-hour drink specials.

🍴 Penestanan

Yellow Flower Cafe INDONESIAN **$**
(Map p138; ☑0361-889 9865; off Jl Raya Campuan;
mains from 30,000Rp; ⊙8am-9pm; 🛜) New Age
Indonesian right up in Penestanan along a
little path through the rice fields. Organic
mains such as *nasi campur* or rice pancakes
are good; snackers will delight in the decent
coffees, cakes and smoothies. Watch for excellent Balinese buffets.

Alchemy VEGAN **$$**
(Map p138; ☑0361-971981; Jl Raya Penestanan 75;
mains from 50,000Rp; ⊙7am-9pm) It could be
called 'Oxymorons' given that we're not sure
what 'Raw Vegan Ice Cream' is, although we
do know it's good. This proto-typical Ubud
restaurant has a vast customised salad
menu as well as cashew-milk drinks, durian

ROOM 4 DESSERT

In a sign of where Ubud is going, celeb-
rity chef Will Goldfarb, who gained fame
as *the* dessert chef in Manhattan, has
opened a place in Ubud that could be a
nightclub except that it just serves des-
sert. At **Room 4 Dessert** (Map p138;
www.room4dessert.asia; Jl Raya Sanging-
gan; treats from 100,000Rp; ⊙6pm-late),
Goldfarb brings his sweet science and
artistry to a line-up of nightly desserts
that are truly like nothing you've ever
had. Get some friends and order the
sampler. Pair everything with his classic
cocktails and wines and let the night
pass by in a sugary glow.

smoothies, fennel juice and a lot more. The raw-chocolate desserts are addictive.

✕ Kedewatan

★Nasi Ayam Kedewatan BALINESE $
(☏0361-742 7168; Jl Raya Kedewatan; meals 25,000Rp; ☺9am-6pm) Few locals making the trek up the hill through Sayan pass this simple place without stopping. The star is *sate lilit*: chicken is minced, combined with an array of spices including lemon grass, then moulded onto bamboo skewers and grilled. Stock up on traditional Balinese road snacks: fried chips combined with nuts and spices.

♉ Drinking & Nightlife

Ubud. Bacchanalia. Mutually exclusive. No one comes to Ubud for wild nightlife. A few bars get lively around sunset and later in the night, but the venues certainly don't aspire to the extremes of beer-swilling debauchery and club partying that's found in Kuta and Seminyak. Bars close early in Ubud, often by 11pm.

★Laughing Buddha CAFE
(Map p144; ☏0361-970928; Monkey Forest Rd; ☺9am-midnight; 🛜) People crowd the street at night in front of this small cafe with live music Monday through Saturday nights. Rock, blues, vocals and more. The kitchen is open late for Asian bites (meals 40,000Rp to 70,000Rp).

Jazz Café BAR
(Map p144; ☏0361-976594; www.jazzcafebali.com; Jl Sukma 2; ☺5-11.30pm Tue-Sun, to 12.30am Sat) Ubud's most popular nightspot (and that's not faint praise even though competition might be lacking), Jazz Café turns on a relaxed atmosphere amid a charming garden of coconut palms and ferns. The menu features Asian-fusion dishes; there is live music most nights.

Napi Orti BAR
(Map p144; Monkey Forest Rd; drinks from 12,000Rp; ☺noon-late) This upstairs place is your best bet for a late-night drink. Get boozy under the hazy gaze of Jim Morrison and Sid Vicious.

Lebong Cafe BAR
(Map p144; Monkey Forest Rd; ☺11am-midnight) Get up, stand up, stand up for your...reggae. This nightlife hub stays open at least until midnight, with live reggae and rock most nights. A few other places good for drinks are nearby.

☆ Entertainment

Few travel experiences can be more magical than attending a Balinese dance performance, especially in Ubud. Cultural entertainment keeps people returning and sets Bali apart from other tropical destinations. Ubud is a good base for the nightly array of performances and for accessing events in surrounding villages.

Dance
Dances performed for visitors are usually adapted and abbreviated to some extent to make them more enjoyable, but usually have appreciative locals in the audience (or peering around the screen!). It's also common to combine the features of more than one traditional dance in a single performance.

In a week in and around Ubud, you can see Kecak, Legong and Barong dances, Mahabharata and Ramayana ballets, *wayang kulit* puppets and gamelan orchestras. There are eight or more performances to choose from each night.

Ubud Tourist Information (p168) has performance information and sells tickets (usually 75,000Rp to 100,000Rp). For performances outside Ubud, transport is often included in the price. Tickets are also sold at many hotels, at the venues and by street vendors – all charge the same price.

Vendors often sell drinks at the performances, which typically last about 1½ hours. Before the show, you might notice the musicians checking out the size of the crowd – ticket sales fund the troupes.

One note about your phone: nobody wants to hear it; nor do the performers want camera flashes in their eyes. And don't be rude and walk out loudly in the middle.

Ubud Palace DANCE
(Map p144; Jl Raya Ubud) Performances are held here almost nightly against a beautiful backdrop.

Pura Dalem Ubud DANCE
(Map p144; Jl Raya Ubud) At the west end of Jl Raya Ubud, this open-air venue has a flamelit carved-stone backdrop and in many ways is the most evocative place to see a dance performance.

Pura Taman Saraswati   DANCE
(Ubud Water Palace; Map p144; Jl Raya Ubud) The beauty of the setting may distract you from the dancers, although at night you can't see the lily pads and lotus flowers that are such an attraction by day.

Arma Open Stage   DANCE
(Map p138; ☑ 0361-976659; Jl Raya Pengosekan) Has among the best troupes.

Padangtegal Kaja   DANCE
(Map p144; Jl Hanoman) A simple, open venue in a very convenient location. In many ways this location hints at what dance performances have looked like in Ubud for generations.

Puri Agung Peliatan   DANCE
(Map p144; Jl Peliatan) A simple setting backed by a large carved wall. Has some excellent performances.

Shadow Puppets

You can also find shadow-puppet shows – although these are greatly attenuated from traditional performances, which often last the entire night. Regular performances are held at **Oka Kartini** (Map p144; ☑ 0361-975193; Jl Raya Ubud; tickets 100,000Rp), which has bungalows and a gallery.

🛍 Shopping

Ubud has myriad art shops, boutiques and galleries. Many offer clever and unique items made in and around the area. Ubud is the ideal base for exploring the enormous number of craft galleries, studios and workshops in villages north and south.

The large market, **Pasar Seni** (Art Market; Map p144; Jl Raya Ubud; ⊙ 7am-8pm), is entirely devoted to souvenirs and kitsch.

With so much of central Ubud now devoted to visitors, the area's main shopping strip has moved over Jl Peliatan in Tebesaya and Peliatan. Here you'll find all the shops that supply locals with their daily needs.

What to Buy

You can spend days in and around Ubud shopping. The upper part of Jl Hanoman and Jl Dewi Sita have the most interesting local shops. Look for jewellery, homewares and clothing. Monkey Forest Rd is becoming the domain of upmarket chains. Arts and crafts are found everywhere and at every price point and quality. Yoga goods seem to be sold everywhere.

Ubud is the best place in Bali for books. Selections are wide and varied, especially for tomes on Balinese art and culture. Many sellers carry titles by small or obscure publishers.

DANCE TROUPES: GOOD & BAD

All dance groups on Ubud's stages are not created equal. You've got true artists with international reputations and then you've got some who really shouldn't quit their day jobs. If you're a Balinese dance novice, you shouldn't worry too much about this; just pick a venue and go.

But after a few performances, you'll start to appreciate the differences in talent, and that's part of the enjoyment. Clue: if the costumes are dirty, the orchestra seems particularly uninterested, performers break character to tell stale jokes (really!) and you find yourself watching a dancer and saying 'I could do that', then the group is B-level.

Excellent troupes who regularly perform in Ubud include the following:

Semara Ratih High-energy, creative Legong interpretations. The best local troupe musically.

Gunung Sari Legong dance; one of Bali's oldest and most respected troupes.

Semara Madya Kekac dance; especially good for the hypnotic chants. A mystical experience for some.

Tirta Sari Legong and Barong dance.

Cudamani One of Bali's best gamelan troupes. They rehearse in Pengosekan.

Finally, watch for temple ceremonies (which are frequent). Go around 8pm and you'll see Balinese dance and music in its full cultural context. You'll need to be appropriately dressed – your hotel or a local can tell you what to do.

The website **Ubud Now & Then** (www.ubudnowandthen.com) has schedules of special events and performances.

🔒 Central Ubud

Jl Raya Ubud & Around

★ Ganesha Bookshop · BOOKS

(Map p144; www.ganeshabooksbali.com; Jl Raya Ubud; ⊙10am-8pm) Ubud's best bookshop has an amazing amount of stock jammed into a small space: an excellent selection of titles on Indonesian studies, travel, arts, music, fiction (including used titles) and maps. Good staff recommendations.

Smile Shop · HANDICRAFTS

(Map p144; ✆0361-233758; www.senyumbali.org; Jl Sriwedari; ⊙10am-8pm) All manner of creative goods for sale in a shop to benefit the Smile Foundation of Bali.

Threads of Life Indonesian Textile Arts Center · TEXTILES

(Map p144; ✆0361-972187; www.threadsoflife.com; Jl Kajeng 24; ⊙10am-7pm) This small store is part of a foundation that works to preserve traditional textile creation in Balinese villages. There's a small but visually stunning collection of exquisite handmade fabrics in stock.

Moari · MUSICAL INSTRUMENTS

(Map p144; ✆0361-977367; Jl Raya Ubud; ⊙10am-8pm) New and restored Balinese musical instruments are sold here. Splurge on a cute little bamboo flute for 30,000Rp.

Neka Art Museum · BOOKS

(Map p138; ✆0361-975074; www.museumneka.com; Jl Raya Sanggingan; ⊙9am-5pm) This museum shop in Sanggingan has a good range of art books for sale.

Monkey Forest Road

Kou Cuisine · HOMEWARES

(Map p144; ✆0361-972319; Monkey Forest Rd; ⊙10am-8pm) A repository of small and exquisite gifts, including beautiful little jars of jam made with Balinese fruit or containers of sea salt harvested from along Bali's shores.

Goddess on the Go! · CLOTHING

(Map p144; ✆0361-976084; Monkey Forest Rd; ⊙10am-8pm) A large selection of women's clothes designed for adventure, made to be super-comfortable, easy-to-pack and eco-friendly.

Pondok Bamboo Music Shop · MUSICAL INSTRUMENTS

(Map p144; ✆0361-974807; Monkey Forest Rd; ⊙10am-8pm) Hear the music of a thousand bamboo wind chimes at this store owned by noted gamelan musician Nyoman Warsa, who offers music lessons and stages shadow-puppet shows.

Periplus · BOOKS

(Map p144; ✆0361-975178; Monkey Forest Rd; ⊙10am-10pm) A typically glossy outlet of the popular Bali chain.

SAVING BALI'S DOGS

Mangy curs. That's the only label you can apply to many of Bali's dogs. As you travel the island – especially by foot – you can't help but notice dogs that are sick, ill-tempered, uncared for and victims to a litany of other maladies.

How can such a seemingly gentle island have Asia's worst dog population (which now has a serious rabies problem)? The answers are complex, but benign neglect has a lot to do with it. Dogs are at the bottom of the social strata: few have owners and local interest in them is next to nil.

Some nonprofits in Ubud are hoping to change the fortunes of Bali's maligned best friends through rabies vaccinations, spaying and neutering, and public education. Donations are always greatly needed.

Bali Adoption Rehab Centre (BARC; Map p138; ✆0361-971208; www.balidogrefuge.com; Jl Raya Pengosekan) Cares for dogs, places strays with sponsors and operates a mobile clinic for sterilisation.

Bali Animal Welfare Association (BAWA; Map p144; ✆0811 389 004; www.bawabali.com) Runs lauded mobile rabies vaccination teams, organises adoption, promotes population control.

Yudisthira Swarga Foundation (✆0361-900 3043; www.yudisthiraswarga.org) Based in Denpasar, this foundation cares for thousands of Bali strays a year and has vaccination and population-control programs.

Jl Dewi Sita

★Kou
BEAUTY

(Map p144; ☑0361-971905; Jl Dewi Sita; ☺10am-8pm) Luxurious locally handmade organic soaps perfume your nose as you enter. Put one in your undies drawer and smell fine for weeks. The range is unlike that found in chain stores selling luxe soap.

★Tin Parrot
CLOTHING

(Map p144; www.tnparrot.com; Jl Dewi Sita; ☺10am-8pm) The trademark parrot of this T-shirt shop is a characterful bird and he (she?) appears in many guises on this shop's line of custom T-shirts. Designs range from cool to groovy to offbeat. Everything is made from high-quality cotton that's been pre-shrunk.

Confiture Michèle
FOOD

(Map p144; Jl Goutama; ☺10am-9pm) Preserves made from Bali's fruit bounty are the, er, preserve of this cute, sweet-smelling shop.

Eco Shop
ACCESSORIES

(Map p144; Jl Dewi Sita; ☺10am-8pm) 🖋 Household items, gifts, T-shirts, bags and much more made from recycled products are sold in this shop which draws a lot of its merchandise from industrious families in Balinese villages.

Padangtegal & Pengosekan

*Asterisk
JEWELLERY

(Map p144; ☑0361-749 1770; www.asterisk-shop.com; Jl Hanoman; ☺10am-8pm) Custom and artistically designed silver jewellery. The designs here are delicate and almost wistful.

Namaste
NEW AGE

(Map p144; ☑0361-796 9178; Jl Hanoman 64; ☺10am-8pm) Just the place to buy a crystal to get your spiritual house in order, Namaste is a gem of a little store with a top range of New Age supplies. Incense, yoga mats, moody instrumental music – it's all here.

Sama Sama
CLOTHING

(Pande; Map p144; ☑0361-976049; Jl Hanoman; ☺10am-8pm) T-shirts and other colourful wear featuring designs, some hand-painted, a lot more interesting than most.

Tegun Galeri
HOMEWARES

(Map p144; ☑0361-973361; Jl Hanoman 44; ☺10am-8pm) It's everything the souvenir stores are not, with beautiful handmade items from around the island plus ancient art.

Ashitaba
HOMEWARES

(Map p144; ☑0361-464922; Jl Hanoman; ☺10am-8pm) Tenganan, the Aga village of east Bali, is where the beautiful rattan items sold here (and in Seminyak) are produced. Containers, bowls, purses and more (from US$5) display the fine and intricate weaving.

Arma
BOOKS

(Map p138; ☑0361-976659; www.armabali.com; Jl Raya Pengosekan; ☺9am-6pm) Large selection of cultural titles.

Adi Musical
MUSICAL INSTRUMENTS

(Map p144; ☑0823 4100 3324; Jl Hanoman; ☺10am-7pm) A sweet little shop with everything from flutes to drums. If you have something special in mind, they might be able to make it.

❶ Information

Visitors will find every service they need and then some along Ubud's main roads. Bulletin boards at Bali Buda (p160) and Kafe (p162) have info on housing, jobs, classes and much more.

Ubud is home to many nonprofit and volunteer groups. See p367 for more information.

INTERNET ACCESS

@Highway (Map p144; ☑0361-972107; Jl Raya Ubud; per hour 30,000Rp; ☺24hr; 🛜) Full-service and very fast.

Hubud (Map p144; ☑0361-978073; www.hubud.org; Monkey Forest Rd; per month from US$20; ☺24hr) A complete shared workspace and digital hub. Ultrafast web connections, developer seminars and much more. Rice-field views as you create a billion-dollar app.

LIBRARIES

Pondok Pekak Library & Learning Centre (Map p144; ☑0361-976194; Monkey Forest Rd; ☺9am-5pm Mon-Sat, 1-5pm Sun) On the far side of the football field, this is a relaxed place. Charges membership fees for library use. Small cafe and a pleasant reading area.

MEDICAL SERVICES

Kimia Pharma (Map p138; Jl Peliatan; ☺7am-10pm) Large shop of the local and respected pharmacy chain.

Ubud Clinic (Map p138; ☑0361-974911; Jl Raya Campuan 36; consultations from 350,000Rp; ☺24hr)

MONEY

Ubud has numerous banks and ATMs.

Central Ubud Money Exchange (Map p144; www.centralkutabali.com; Jl Raya Ubud; ☺8am-9pm) A respected Bali-wide chain of currency exchanges.

POST

Main Post Office (Map p144; Jl Jembawan; ⏱ 8am-5pm) Also handles parcels.

TOURIST INFORMATION

Ubud Tourist Information (Yaysan Bina Wisata; Map p144; ☏ 0361-973285; Jl Raya Ubud; ⏱ 8am-8pm) The one really useful tourist office on Bali. It has a good range of information and a noticeboard listing current happenings and activities. The staff can answer most regional questions and has up-to-date information on ceremonies and traditional dances held in the area; dance tickets are sold here.

USEFUL WEBSITES

Bali Spirit (www.balispirit.com) The website of the group behind the annual Ubud festival has info on culture, classes, events, volunteer opportunities etc.

Ubud Now & Then (www.ubudnowandthen. com) Covers Ubud culture, food, art, activities and more. Content by notable Ubudians such as Rio Helmi, Janet DeNeefe and others.

ⓘ Getting There & Away

BEMO

Ubud is on two bemo routes. Bemos travel to Gianyar (10,000Rp) and Batubulan terminal in Denpasar (13,000Rp). Ubud doesn't have a bemo terminal; there are bemo stops on Jl Suweta near the market in the centre of town.

TOURIST SHUTTLE BUS

You'll see ads all around town for economical shared cars and buses to destinations across Bali.

Perama (Map p144; ☏ 0361-973316; www. peramatours.com; Jl Raya Pengosekan; ⏱ 9am-9pm) is the major tourist-shuttle operator, but its terminal is inconveniently located in Padangtegal; to get to/from your destination in Ubud will cost another 15,000Rp. Destinations include Sanur (40,000Rp, one hour), Padangbai (50,000Rp, two hours) and Kuta (50,000Rp, two hours).

ⓘ Getting Around

Many high-end spas, hotels and restaurants offer free local transport for guests and customers.

TO/FROM THE AIRPORT

Taxis with the cartel from the airport to Ubud cost 250,000Rp. A car with driver to the airport will cost about the same.

BEMO

Bemos don't directly link Ubud with nearby villages; you'll have to catch one going to Denpasar or Gianyar and get off where you need to. Bemos to Gianyar travel along eastern Jl Raya Ubud, down Jl Peliatan and east to Bedulu. The fare for a ride within the Ubud area shouldn't be more than 7000Rp.

CAR & MOTORCYCLE

With numerous nearby attractions, many of which are difficult to reach by bemo, renting a vehicle is sensible. Ask at your accommodation or hire a car and driver (see p375).

Ubud Bike Rental (p147) rents scooters and motorbikes and has a good selection. Daily rates are 30,000Rp.

TAXI

There are no metered taxis based in Ubud – those that honk their horns at you have usually dropped off passengers from southern Bali in Ubud and are hoping for a fare back. Instead, you'll use one of the ubiquitous drivers with private vehicles hanging around on the streets hectoring passersby (the better drivers politely hold up signs that say 'transport').

Most of the drivers are very fair; a few – often from out of the area – not so much. If you find a driver you like, get his number and call him for rides during your stay. From central Ubud to, say, Sanggingan should cost about 40,000Rp – rather steep actually. A ride from the palace to the end of Jl Hanoman should cost about 20,000Rp.

It's easy to get a ride on the back of a motorbike; rates are half those of cars.

AROUND UBUD

☏ 0361

The region around Ubud is thick with excursion possibilities. Close in there is the Elephant Cave and the craftsmakers in Mas. East and north are many of the most ancient monuments and relics in Bali. Some of them predate the Majapahit era and raise as-yet-unanswered questions about Bali's history. A prime example is Bali's own bit of Angkor at Gunung Kawi.

South of Ubud, there is another vast range of possibilities. These tend to be more commercial, however – from great market towns to villages filled with artists. Throw in some family-friendly attractions and you can spend days roaming about.

Bedulu

Bedulu was once the capital of a great kingdom. The legendary Dalem Bedaulu ruled the Pejeng dynasty from here, and was the last Balinese king to withstand the onslaught of the powerful Majapahit from

Java. He was defeated by Gajah Mada in 1343. The capital shifted several times after this, to Gelgel and then later to Semarapura (Klungkung). Today Bedulu is absorbed into the greater Ubud sprawl.

⊙ Sights

Goa Gajah CAVE

(Elephant Cave; Map p176; Jl Raya Goa Gajah; adult/child 10,000/5000Rp, parking 2000Rp; ⊙8am-6pm) There were never any elephants on Bali (until tourist attractions changed that); ancient Goa Gajah probably takes its name from the nearby Sungai Petanu, which at one time was known as Elephant River, or perhaps because the face over the cave entrance might resemble an elephant. It's located some 2km southeast of Ubud on the road to Bedulu.

The origins of the cave are uncertain – one tale relates that it was created by the fingernail of the legendary giant Kebo Iwa. It probably dates to the 11th century, and was certainly in existence during the Majapahit takeover of Bali. The cave was rediscovered by Dutch archaeologists in 1923, but the fountains and pool were not found until 1954.

The cave is carved into a rock face and you enter through the cavernous mouth of a demon. Inside the T-shaped cave you can see fragmentary remains of the lingam, the phallic symbol of the Hindu god Shiva, and its female counterpart the yoni, plus a statue of Shiva's son, the elephant-headed god Ganesha. In the courtyard in front of the cave are two square bathing pools with water trickling into them from waterspouts held by six female figures.

From Goa Gajah you can clamber down through the rice paddies to Sungai Petanu, where there are crumbling rock carvings of stupas (domes for housing Buddhist relics) on a cliff face, and a small cave.

Try to get here before 10am, when the big tourist buses begin lumbering into the large souvenir-stall-filled parking lot like, well, elephants. Sarong rental is 3000Rp.

Yeh Pulu HISTORIC SITE

(Map p176; adult/child 10,000/5000Rp) A man having his hand munched by a boar is one of the scenes on the 25m-long carved cliff face known as Yeh Pulu, believed to be a hermitage from the late 14th century. Apart from the figure of Ganesha, the elephant-headed

son of Shiva, most of the scenes deal with everyday life, although the position and movement of the figures suggests that it could be read from left to right as a story.

One theory is that they are events from the life of Krishna, the Hindu god.

You can walk between the sites, following small paths through the paddy fields, but you might need to pay a local to guide you. By car or bicycle, look for the signs to 'Relief Yeh Pulu' or 'Villa Yeh Pulu', east of Goa Gajah.

Even if your interest in carved Hindu art is minor, this site is quite lovely and rarely will you have much company. From the entrance, it's a 300m lush, tropical walk to Yeh Pulu.

Pura Samuan Tiga HINDU TEMPLE

(Map p176) The majestic Pura Samuan Tiga (Temple of the Meeting of the Three) is about 200m east of the Bedulu junction. The name is possibly a reference to the Hindu trinity, or it may refer to meetings held here in the early 11th century. Despite these early associations, all the temple buildings have been rebuilt since the 1917 earthquake.

❶ Getting There & Away

About 3km east of Teges, the road from Ubud reaches a junction where you can turn south to Gianyar or north to Pejeng, Tampaksiring and Penelokan. Ubud–Gianyar bemos will drop you off at this junction, from where you can walk to the sights. The road from Ubud is reasonably flat, so coming by bicycle is a good option.

THE LEGEND OF DALEM BEDAULU

A legend relates how Dalem Bedaulu possessed magical powers that allowed him to have his head chopped off and then replaced. Performing this unique party trick one day, the servant entrusted with lopping off the king's head and then replacing it unfortunately dropped it in a river and, to his horror, watched it float away. Looking around in panic for a replacement, he grabbed a pig, cut off its head and popped it upon the king's shoulders. Thereafter, the king was forced to sit on a high throne and forbade his subjects to look up at him; Bedaulu means 'he who changed heads'.

Pejeng

On the road towards Tampaksiring you come to Pejeng and its famous temples. Like Bedulu, this was once an important seat of power, as it was the capital of the Pejeng kingdom, which fell to the Majapahit invaders in 1343.

⊙ Sights

Museum Purbakala   MUSEUM
(Map p176; ✎ 0361-942354; I Raya Tampaksiring; admission by donation; ⊙ 8am-3pm Mon-Thu, 8am-12.30pm Fri) This archaeological museum has a reasonable collection of artefacts from all over Bali, and most displays are in English. The exhibits in several small buildings include some of Bali's first pottery from near Gilimanuk, and sarcophagi dating from as early as 300 BC – some originating from Bangli are carved in the shape of a turtle, which has important cosmic associations in Balinese mythology.

The museum is about 500m north of the Bedulu junction, and is easy to reach by bemo or by bicycle. It's a sleepy place and you'll get the most out of it if you come with a knowledgeable guide.

Pura Kebo Edan   HINDU TEMPLE
(Map p176; JI Raya Tampaksiring) Who can resist a sight called Crazy Buffalo Temple? Although not an imposing structure, it's famous for its 3m-high statue, known as the Giant of Pejeng, thought to be approximately 700 years old. Details are sketchy, but it may represent Bima, a hero of the Mahabharata, dancing on a dead body, as in a myth related to the Hindu Shiva cult.

There is some conjecture about the giant's giant genitalia – it has what appear to be pins on the side. Some claim this was to give the woman more pleasure.

Pura Pusering Jagat   HINDU TEMPLE
(Map p176; JI Raya Tampaksiring) So that's what it looks like? The large Pura Pusering Jagat is said to be the centre of the old Pejeng kingdom. Dating from 1329, this temple is visited by young couples who pray at the stone lingam and yoni.

Further back is a large stone urn, with elaborate but worn carvings of gods and demons searching for the elixir of life in a depiction of the Mahabharata tale 'Churning the Sea of Milk'. The temple is on a small track running west of the main road.

Pura Penataran Sasih   HINDU TEMPLE
(Map p176; JI Raya Tampaksiring) This was once the state temple of the Pejeng kingdom. In the inner courtyard, high up in a pavilion and difficult to see, is the huge bronze drum known as the Fallen Moon of Pejeng. The hourglass-shaped drum is 186cm long, the largest single-piece cast drum in the world. Estimates of its age vary from 1000 to 2000 years.

It is not certain whether the drum was made locally or imported – the intricate geometric decorations are said to resemble patterns from places as far apart as West Papua and Vietnam.

Balinese legend relates that the drum came to earth as a fallen moon, landing in a tree and shining so brightly that it prevented a band of thieves from going about their unlawful purpose. One of the thieves decided to put the light out by urinating on it, but the moon exploded and fell to earth as a drum, with a crack across its base as a result of the fall.

Although the big noise here is all about the drum, be sure to notice the statuary in the temple courtyard that dates from the 10th to the 12th century.

Mas

Just southeast of Ubud, Mas means 'gold' in Bahasa Indonesia, but woodcarving is the principal craft in this village. The great Majapahit priest Nirartha once lived here, and Pura Taman Pule is said to be built on the site of his home. During the three-day Kuningan festival, a performance of *wayang wong* (an older version of the Ramayana ballet) is held in the temple's courtyard.

Carving was a traditional art of the priestly Brahmana caste, and the skills are said to have been a gift of the gods. Historically, carving was limited to temple decorations, dance masks and musical instruments, but in the 1930s carvers began to depict people and animals in a naturalistic way. Today it's hard to resist the oodles of winsome creatures produced here.

This is the place to come if you want something custom-made in sandalwood – just be prepared to pay well (and check the wood's authenticity carefully). Mas is also part of Bali's booming furniture industry, producing chairs, tables and antiques ('made to order!'), mainly from teak imported from other Indonesian islands.

◎ Sights

★ Setia Darma House of Masks & Puppets
MUSEUM

(Map p176; ☑0361-977404; Jl Tegal Bingin; ⊙8am-4pm) FREE One of the best museums in the Ubud area, home to over 7000 ceremonial masks and puppets from Indonesia and across Asia, all beautifully displayed in a series of renovated historic buildings. Among the many treasures, look for the golden Jero Luh Mask as well as the faces of royalty, mythical monsters and even the common man. Puppets are unnervingly lifelike. The museum is about 2km northeast of the main Mas crossroads. It has a simple cafe with lovely views.

Tonyraka Art Gallery
GALLERY

(Map p176; ☑0361-781 6785; www.tonyrakaart gallery.com; Jl Raya Mas; ⊙hours vary) One of the premier galleries in the Ubud area, look for exhibitions here with some of Bali's best contemporary artists such as Made Djirna.

Ida Bagus Anom Suryawan
WORKSHOP

(Map p176; ☑0813 3844 8444; www.balimask making.com; Jl Raya Mas) Three generations of carvers produce some of Bali's most revered masks in this family compound, right off the main road in Mas. There is a small showroom with their works, but mostly the appeal is visiting with the family while they create something out of cedar; join them for lessons (p148) to create your very own masterpiece.

🛏 Sleeping & Eating

★ Taman Harum Cottages
HOTEL $

(Map p176; ☑0361-975567; www.tamanharum cottages.com; Jl Raya Mas; r from US$40, 2-bedroom villas from US$100; ❄@☂) Along the main road in Mas, this attractive hotel has 17 rooms and villas – some quite large. By all means get one overlooking the rice fields. They're behind a gallery, which is also a venue for a huge range of art and cultural courses. Ubud shuttles are free.

Suly Resort
HOTEL $$

(Map p176; ☑0361-976186; www.sulyresort.com; Jl Cok Rai Pudak; r from US$50; ❄☎) This excellent hotel has 50 rooms in a four-storey main building and another 17 in cottages with lovely rice-field views. Balinese architecture details abound; there are extensive yoga classes and spa treatments on offer. It's at the north end of Mas.

> ### BALI'S VILLAGE ARTISTS
>
> In small villages throughout the Ubud region, from Sebatu to Mas and beyond across Bali, you'll see small signs for artists and craftspeople, often near the local temple. As one local told us, 'we are only as rich of a village as our art,' so the people who create the ceremonial costumes, masks, kris, musical instruments and all the other beautiful aspects of Balinese life and religion are accorded great honour. It's a symbiotic relationship, with the artist never charging the village for the work and the village in turn seeing to the artist's welfare. Often there are many artists in residence because few events would bring more shame to a village than having to go to another village to procure a needed sacred object.

If the staff here seems both young and enthusiastic, it's because the Suly is run by a foundation that trains students from poor parts of Bali in the hospitality industry. Given the massive growth in tourism, graduates go on to great jobs across the island and beyond. Only a few applicants are accepted and tuition is free.

Semar Warung
BALINESE $$

(Map p176; ☑0878 8883 3348; Jl Raya Mas 165; mains from 50,000Rp; ⊙9am-10pm) It doesn't look all that promising from the front, but step through to the breezy dining area and you'll be wrapped up in a green vista of rice fields stretching off to palm trees. It's a beautiful view and the Balinese food lives up to it. This is a good lunch choice or a place for a drink at sunset.

It's 1km south of where Jl Raya Mas meets Jl Raya Pengosekan.

NORTH OF UBUD

North of Ubud, Bali becomes cooler and more lush. Ancient sites and natural beauty abound.

The usual road from Ubud north to Batur is through Tampaksiring with amazing Gunung Kawi, but there are other lesser roads up the gentle mountain slope. One of the most attractive goes north from Peliatan, past Petulu and its birds, and through the rice terraces between Tegallalang and

Ceking, to bring you out on the crater rim between Penelokan and Batur. It's a sealed road all the way and you also pass through **Sebatu**, which has all manner of artisans tucked away in tiny villages.

The one off-note will be Cekingan, where the rice terraces are beautiful but have attracted a strip of ugly tourist traps overlooking them.

Tegallalang

There are lots of shops and stalls in this busy market town you're likely to pass through on your visit to the area's temples. Stop for a stroll and you may be rewarded by hearing the practice of one of the local noted gamelan orchestras. Otherwise, plenty of carvers stand ready to sell you a carved fertility doll or the like.

You can pause at **Kampung Cafe & Cottages** (☑ 0361-901201; www.kampungtari.com; Ceking; r from US$70, mains 40,000-80,000Rp; ☺ 8am-9pm; ☜) in the village of Ceking, an attractive cafe (perfect for lunch) and upmarket guesthouse with jaw-dropping rice-terrace views. The design makes great use of natural rock. Nearby, scores of carvers produce works from albesia wood, which is easily turned into simplistic, cartoonish figures. The wood is also a favourite of wind-chime makers.

Go about 3km west of town on a small, very green road to **Keliki**, and you'll pass **Alam Sari** (☑ 0361-240308; www.alamsari.com;

> ### ⓘ BEST TIME TO VISIT GUNUNG KAWI
>
> Get to Gunung Kawi as early as possible for the best experience. If you start down the steps by 7.30am, you'll avoid all the vendors and you'll still see residents going about their morning business in the swift-flowing streams such as ablutions and cleaning ceremonial offerings. You can hear the birds, the flowing water and your own voice going 'ooh' and 'aah' without the distractions that come later when large groups arrive. In addition, you'll still have cool air when you start back up the endless steps. Be sure to have a sarong in case there is nobody yet offering them for use. If the ticket office is closed, you can pay on your way out.

Keliki; r from US$100; ❄ ☎ ☒) ☕, a small hotel in a wonderfully isolated location where the bamboo grows like grass. There are 12 luxurious yet rustic rooms, a pool and a great view. The hotel treats its own wastewater, among other environmental initiatives.

Tampaksiring

Tampaksiring is a small village about 18km northeast of Ubud with a large and important temple, Tirta Empul, and the most impressive ancient site on Bali, Gunung Kawi. It sits in the Pakerisan Valley, and the entire area has been nominated for Unesco recognition.

⊙ Sights

★ **Gunung Kawi**   MONUMENT
(adult/child 15,000/7500Rp, sarong 3000Rp, parking 2000Rp; ☺ 7am-5pm) At the bottom of a lush green river valley is one of Bali's oldest and largest ancient monuments. Gunung Kawi consists of 10 rock-cut *candi* (shrines) – memorials cut out of the rock face in imitation of actual statues. They stand in awe-inspiring 8m-high sheltered niches cut into the sheer cliff face. Be prepared for long climbs – it's over 270 steps.

The strenuous walk is broken up into sections and at times the views as you walk through ancient terraced rice fields are as fine as any on Bali. Each *candi* is believed to be a memorial to a member of the 11th-century Balinese royalty, but little is known for certain.

Legends relate that the whole group of memorials was carved out of the rock face in one hard-working night by the mighty fingernails of Kebo Iwa.

The five monuments on the eastern bank are probably dedicated to King Udayana, Queen Mahendradatta and their sons Airlangga, Anak Wungsu and Marakata. While Airlangga ruled eastern Java, Anak Wungsu ruled Bali. The four monuments on the western side are, by this theory, to Anak Wungsu's chief concubines. Another theory is that the whole complex is dedicated to Anak Wungsu, his wives, concubines and, in the case of the remote 10th *candi,* to a royal minister.

As you wander between monuments, temples, offerings, streams and fountains, you can't help but feel a certain ancient majesty here.

On the northern outskirts of town, a sign points east off the main road to Gunung Kawi and its ancient monuments. From the end of the access road, a steep, stone stair-

COFFEE LUWAK

Coffee luwak, also known locally as *kopi luwak*, has become as much a part of the tourist shopping experience on Bali as the ubiquitous penis-shaped bottle openers. Only it's much more costly.

The supposed allure of coffee luwak is that civets (small and winsome nocturnal critters that are distant relatives of cats) eat only the best coffee beans off coffee bushes. Then as the beans pass through the civet, various enzymes and digestive juices affect the chemistry of the bean. Once liberated from the civet turds, the beans are roasted and brewed, producing a somehow superior cup of coffee.

In the last few years the hype around coffee luwak has become shrill and as more and more tourists are willing to plop down cash for 'the world's most expensive cup of coffee' the number of people selling same has exploded. As you drive around Bali you will see come-ons everywhere for coffee luwak, especially along major roads in the hills. Besides the great opportunity for fraud, there are also real concerns about the treatment of the civets displayed as coffee luwak producers. Consider the following:

➡ There is no agreed upon flavour profile for coffee luwak, thus no one can say definitively what a cup should – or does – taste like.

➡ The only way you know you are drinking a cup of coffee luwak is because the person selling you this brewed beverage for US$10 or more says so.

➡ Despite the potential for outright fakery, huge factory farms for coffee luwak have sprung up. Here civets captured in the wild are kept caged and force-fed a diet of coffee beans, not unlike a foie gras goose. In the wild, civets roam widely and coffee is but a tiny part of their diet.

➡ You may well see a caged civet at a Bali coffee luwak attraction where the nocturnal creature is kept awake to amuse tourists. At one we listened while a guide explained that the sad-looking civet in the very small cage before us would only be on luwak duty for a few days. It would then spend its days and nights at a sort of civet fantasy farm where it would cavort with other civets.

For more on the controversies around coffee luwak, visit the website **Project Luwak Singapore** (projectluwaksg.wordpress.com). The BBC reported on the conditions of captive civets in 2013 (search for 'BBC coffee luwak') while journalist Cat Wheeler investigated the situation locally in the *Bali Advertiser* (www.baliadvertiser.biz/articles/greenspeak/2014/ethics.html).

UBUD & AROUND TAMPAKSIRING

way leads down to the river, at one point cutting through an embankment of solid rock.

Tirta Empul MONUMENT
(adult/child 15,000/7500Rp, parking 2000Rp; ☺8am-6pm) A well-signposted fork in the road north of Tampaksiring leads to the popular holy springs at Tirta Empul, discovered in AD 962 and believed to have magical powers. The springs bubble up into a large, crystal-clear pool within the temple and gush out through waterspouts into a bathing pool.

The waters are the main source of Sungai Pakerisan (Pakerisan River), the river that rushes by Gunung Kawi only 1km or so away. Next to the springs, Pura Tirta Empul is one of Bali's most important temples. Come in the early morning or late afternoon to avoid the tourist buses. You can also use the clean, segregated and free public baths here.

Other Sights

There are other groups of *candi* and monks' cells in the area once encompassed by the ancient Pejeng kingdom, notably **Pura Krobokan** and **Goa Garba**, but none so grand as Gunung Kawi. Between Gunung Kawi and Tirta Empul, **Pura Mengening** temple has a freestanding *candi,* similar in design to those at Gunung Kawi and much less visited.

The road running north to Penelokan is lined with dozens of **agritourism attractions**. In reality these are mostly gift shops selling coffee luwak and the usual carvings plus a few plants out back in labelled gardens. They give groups a reason to stop and shop.

Taro & Around

Abused and abandoned logging elephants from Sumatra have been given refuge on Bali at the **Elephant Safari Park** (☑0361-721480; www.baliadventuretours.com; Taro; tour incl transport adult/child US$65/44; ☉8am-6pm). Located in the cool, wet highlands of Taro (14km north of Ubud), the park is home to almost 30 elephants. Besides seeing a full complement of exhibits about elephants, you can ride an elephant for an extra fee, though animal welfare groups claim that elephant trekking is harmful for the animals. The park has received praise for its conservation efforts; however, be careful you don't end up at one of the rogue parks, designed to divert the unwary to unsanctioned displays of elephants.

The surrounding region produces ochre-coloured paint pigment. The gentle uphill drive from Ubud is a lush attraction in itself.

SOUTH OF UBUD

The roads between Ubud and south Bali are lined with little shops making and selling handicrafts. Many visitors shop along the route as they head to and from Ubud, sometimes by the busload, but much of the craftwork is actually done in small workshops and family compounds on quiet back roads.

For serious shopping and real flexibility in exploring these villages, it's worth arranging your own transport, so you can follow the back roads and carry your purchases without any hassles. Note that your driver may receive a commission from any place you spend your money – this can add 10% or more to the cost of purchases (think of it as his tip). Also, a driver may try to steer you to

workshops or artisans that he favours, rather than those of most interest to you.

The roads form a real patchwork and you'll be rewarded with surprises if you take some time to wander the lesser routes.

Blahbatuh & Around

The temple of **Pura Gaduh** (Map p176; Jl Kebo Iwa), 200m east of the Blahbatuh market, has a 1m-high stone head, believed to be a portrait of Kebo Iwa, the legendary strongman and minister to the last king of the Bedulu kingdom. Gajah Mada – the Majapahit strongman – realised that it wouldn't be possible to conquer Bedulu (Bali's strongest kingdom) while Kebo Iwa was there. So Gajah Mada lured him away to Java (with promises of women and song) and had him murdered. The stone head possibly predates the Javanese influence in Bali.

See looms busily making ikat and batik fabrics at **Putri Ayu** (Map p176; ☑0361-225 533; Jl Diponegoro 51; ☉8am-5pm). The workshops and showroom are a good complement to the textile shops in Gianyar and are just across from the temple.

West of here, there are sensational views of **rice terraces** off the main road near the village of Kemenuh.

Kutri

Heading north from Blahbatuh, Kutri has the interesting **Pura Kedarman** (Pura Bukit Dharma; Map p176). If you climb up Bukit Dharma behind the temple, there's a great panoramic view and a **hilltop shrine**, with a stone statue of the six-armed goddess of death and destruction, Durga, killing a demon-possessed water buffalo.

BALI'S CHOCOLATE FACTORY

You might think Swiss or Belgian when you think chocolate but soon you could be thinking Bali. **Big Tree Farms** (Map p176; ☑0361-846 3327; www.bigtreefarms.com; Sibang; tours from 40,000Rp; ☉tours 2pm), a local producer of quality foodstuffs that has made a big splash internationally, has built a chocolate factory about 10km southwest of Ubud in Sibang, a village on one of the roads linking Ubud to south Bali.

And this is not just any factory: rather it is a huge and architecturally stunning creation made sustainably from bamboo – an ethos that extends to the company's very philosophy. The chocolate made here comes from cocoa beans grown by over 13,000 farmers across Indonesia. The result is a high-quality chocolate that you can watch being made on tours.

Just seeing one of the world's largest bamboo structures is an attraction in itself; toss in fabulous chocolate and you've landed an all-round delectable experience.

TO UBUD VIA MAMBAL

There are various routes between Ubud and south Bali. But only one that can be considered 'new'. Thanks to the recent improvements of a road that links Mambal to the southwest part of Ubud, it's now possible to divert from the traditional store-lined routes and try something different. North of Mambal, the road crosses classic rice fields and plunges through dense river jungle. South of Mambal, the route follows a popular main road that goes due south into the heart of Denpasar. Along the way it passes every kind of farm and business that's part of modern Bali.

At Mambal you'll be close to some of the New Agey places that are spreading outwards from Ubud. Bamboo soars overhead at **Fivelements** (Map p176; ☎ 0361-469260; www.fivelements.org; Mambal; massage from 800,000Rp), an impressive and vast new retreat and healing centre about 10km southwest of Ubud. It's an intensive health retreat that draws on myriad therapies. It includes luxe guestrooms and a large public space that is the site of TEDx Ubud.

Just south of Mambal and west of the road you may get a glimpse of the **Green School** (Map p176; www.greenschool.org; Mambal), which has enjoyed a lot of hype as much for its unorthodox curriculum as its flamboyant bamboo architecture.

Bona & Belega

On the back road between Blahbatuh and Gianyar, Bona is a **basket-weaving centre** and features many articles made from *lontar* (specially prepared palm leaves). It is also known for fire dances. (Note: most road signs in the area read 'Bone' instead of Bona, so if you get lost, you'll have to ask: 'Do you know the way to Bone?') Nearby, the village of Belega is a centre for bamboo-furniture production.

Batuan

Batuan's recorded history goes back 1000 years, and in the 17th century its royal family controlled most of southern Bali. The decline of its power is attributed to a priest's curse, which scattered the royal family to different parts of the island.

Just west of the centre, the twin temples of **Pura Puseh** (Map p176) and **Pura Dasar** (donation 10,000Rp, includes sarong) are accessible studies in classic Balinese temple architecture. The carvings are elaborate and visitors are given the use of vermilion sarongs. There are regular daytime dance performances aimed at visitors.

Sukawati & Puaya

Once a royal capital, Sukawati is now known for its market and for its specialised artisans, who busily work in small shops along the roads.

🔒 Shopping

In Sukawati look for shops of the *tukang prada,* who make temple umbrellas, beautifully decorated with stencilled gold paint, which can be seen in their shops.

Puaya, about 1km northwest of Sukawati, specialises in high-quality leather shadow puppets and masks for Topeng and Barong dances.

★**Sukawati Market**   MARKET
(Map p176; Jl Raya Sukawati; ⊙ 6am-8pm) Sukawati Market is a highlight of any visit to the area. Always bustling, this large market is a major source of the flowers, baskets, fruits, knick-knacks and other items used in temple offerings. It's a riot of colour.

On the north side of the main building there's a lane where you can buy delicious sate from carts. Vendors with fruit you've likely never seen before are tucked into the corners of the typically grungy main food hall. Booths sell easy-to-assemble temple-offering kits to time-constrained Balinese faithful. On the surrounding streets you'll find some stalls with high-quality handicrafts mixed in with those peddling the Bintang singlet of your dreams. ATMs are at the ready.

Mask & Puppet Makers   ARTS & CRAFTS
(Map p176; Jl Raya Puaya; ⊙ 9am-5pm) On Puaya's main street, look for this row of workshops where they both make and sell ceremonial items for dance performances.

From the south: **Nyoman Ruka** has a slick shop with barong and masks; **Sari Yasa** is a family compound with a very busy workshop in which masks, costumes and

South of Ubud

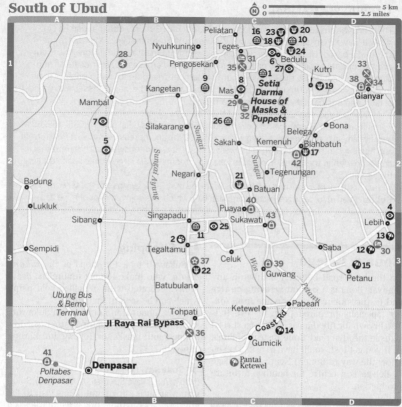

Map showing:
- Peliatan
- Nyuhkuning
- Teges
- 16 23 18 6 24 20 10 31 35 27 1
- Bedulu
- Kutri
- Pengosekan
- 28
- Kangetan
- Mas
- 9 8
- Setia Darma House of Masks & Puppets
- 33 38 34
- Gianyar
- Mambal
- 29
- 26 32
- 19
- 7
- Silakarang
- Belega
- Bona
- 5
- Sakah
- Kemenuh
- Blahbatuh
- 42 17
- Badung
- Negari
- 21
- Tegenungan
- Lukluk
- Batuan
- 40
- Sibang
- Singapadu
- Puaya
- Sukawati
- 43
- Lebih
- 4
- 2 11
- 25
- 13
- Sempidi
- Tegaltamu
- Celuk
- 12 30
- 15
- Saba
- Petanu
- 37 22
- Batubulan
- 39
- Guwang
- Ubung Bus & Bemo Terminal
- Tohpati
- Ketewel
- Pabean
- Jl Raya Rai Bypass
- 36
- Coast Rd
- 14
- 41
- Denpasar
- 3
- Gumicik
- Poltabes Denpasar
- Pantai Ketewel
- Sungai Ayung
- Sungai Wos
- Petanu

Scale: 0–5 km / 0–2.5 miles

puppets are being produced; **Mustika Collection** is another family compound with a workshop for masks and puppets; and just across the road, **Baruna Art Shop** has barong aplenty. All welcome visitors.

Guwang Pasar Seni   SOUVENIRS
(Craft Market; Map p176; Guwang; ⊙8am-6pm) About 2km south of Sukawati, this much-hyped and very touristy market has every type of knick-knack and trinket on sale.

Singapadu

The centre of Singapadu is dominated by a huge **banyan tree** (Map p176). In the past, these were community meeting places; even today the local meeting hall is just across the road. The surrounding village has a traditional appearance, with walled family compounds and shady trees.

⊙ Sights

Nyoman Suaka Home   HISTORIC BUILDING
(Map p176; Singapadu; requested donation 30,000Rp; ⊙9am-5pm) This home, 50m off the main road, is just south of the huge banyan tree. Pass through the carved entrance to the walled family compound and you'll see a classic Balinese home, which you can explore while the family goes about its daily business.

Bali Bird Park   ZOO
(Map p176; ☑0316-299352; www.bali-bird-park.com; Jl Serma Cok Ngurah Gambir; adult/child US$30/15; ⊙9am-5.30pm) More than 1000 birds from 250 species flit about here, including rare cendrawasih (birds of paradise) from West Papua and the all-but-vanished Bali starlings. Many are housed in special walk-through aviaries. A reptile section includes a Komodo dragon. The 2 hectares of landscaped gardens feature a fine collection of tropical plants. Popular with kids; allow at least two hours.

South of Ubud

UBUD & AROUND CELUK

Celuk

Celuk is the silver and gold centre of Bali. The flashier showrooms are on the main road, and have marked prices that are quite high, although you can always bargain.

Hundreds of **silversmiths** and **goldsmiths** work in their homes on the backstreets north and east of the main road. Most of these artisans are from *pande* families, members of a sub-caste of blacksmiths whose knowledge of fire and metal has traditionally put them outside the usual caste hierarchy. Their small workshops are interesting to visit, and have the lowest prices, but they don't keep a large stock of finished work. They will make something to order if you bring a sample or sketch.

Batubulan

The start of the road from south Bali is lined with outlets for stone sculptures – **stone carving** is the main craft of Batubulan (moonstone). Workshops are found right along the road to Tegaltamu, with another batch further north around Silakarang. Batubulan is the source of the stunning temple-gate guardians seen all over Bali. The stone used for these sculptures is a porous grey volcanic rock called *paras,* which resembles pumice; it's soft and surprisingly light. It also ages quickly, so that 'ancient' work may be years rather than centuries old.

The temples around Batubulan are, naturally, noted for their fine stonework. Just 200m to the east of the busy main road, **Pura Puseh Batubulan** (Map p176; admission by donation; ☉8am-6pm) is worth a visit for its moat filled with lotus flowers and perfectly balanced overall composition. Statues draw on ancient Hindu and Buddhist iconography and Balinese mythology; however, they are not old – many are copied from books on archaeology. An attenuated **Barong dance show** (Map p176; Pura Puseh Batubulan; admission 100,000Rp; ☉9.30am) about the iconic lion-dog creature is performed in an ugly hall; it's a tour-bus-friendly one-hour-long show. Note that Pura Puseh means 'central temple' – you'll find many around Bali. Some translations have 'Puseh' meaning 'navel', which is apt.

Batubulan is also a centre for making 'antiques', textiles and woodwork, and has numerous craft shops.

East Bali

Best Places to Eat

➡ Gianyar's Night Market (p183)

➡ Merta Sari (p191)

➡ Terrace (p196)

➡ Vincent's (p200)

➡ Warung Enak (p209)

Best Places to Stay

➡ Turtle Bay Hideaway (p201)

➡ Meditasi (p208)

➡ Alam Anda (p212)

➡ Samanvaya (p188)

➡ Santai (p207)

Why Go?

Wandering the roads of east Bali is one of the island's great pleasures. Rice terraces spill down hillsides under swaying palms, wild volcanic beaches are washed by pounding surf, and age-old villages soldier on with barely a trace of modernity. Watching over it all is Gunung Agung, the 3142m volcano known as the 'navel of the world' and 'Mother Mountain', which has a perfect conical shape you might glimpse on hikes from lovely Tirta Gangga.

You can find Bali's past amid evocative ruins in the former royal city of Semarapura. Follow the rivers coursing down the slopes on the Sidemen road to find vistas and valleys that could have inspired Shangri-La. Down at the coast is slow-paced Padangbai and relaxed Candidasa.

Resorts and hidden beaches dot the seashore and cluster on the Amed Coast. Just north of there, Tulamben is all about external exploration: the entire town is geared for diving.

When to Go

➡ The best time to visit east Bali is during the dry season – April to September – although recent weather patterns have made the dry season wetter and the wet season drier. Hiking in the lush hills from Gunung Agung over to Tirta Gangga is much easier when it isn't muddy.

➡ Along the coast there's little reason to pick one month over another; it's usually just tropical.

➡ Top-end resorts may book up in peak season (July, August and Christmas), but it's never jammed like south Bali.

Coast Road to Kusamba

☑ 0361

Bali's coast road running from just north of Sanur east to a junction past Kusamba should really be named Beach Road. It runs past a whole swathe of black-sand beaches and has made it easy to visit all sorts of sandy places you couldn't easily reach back when the road east meandered through towns far inland such as Gianyar and Semarapura.

Efforts to widen the two lanes to four are nearly complete and are sorely needed. The road is lined with scores of warungs and trucker cafes along its length. Tourism development has begun in earnest and you'll see plenty of new residential villas aimed at foreigners.

The coast road (formally the Prof Dr Ida Bagus Mantra Bypass – named for a popular 1980s Balinese governor who did much to promote culture) makes Padangbai, Candidasa and points east an easy day trip from south Bali, depending on traffic.

◎ Sights & Activities

Bali Safari & Marine Park AMUSEMENT PARK
(Map p176; ☑ 0361-950000; www.balisafari marinepark.com; Prof Dr Ida Bagus Mantra Bypass; adult/child from US$49/39; ⊙ 9am-5pm, Bali Agung show 2.30pm Tue-Sun) Kids love Bali Safari and Marine Park and their parents are happy they love someplace. This big-ticket animal-theme park is filled with critters whose species never set foot in Bali until their cage door opened. Displays are large and naturalistic. A huge menu of extra-cost options includes animal rides and a night safari. Visitors should note that the park stages animal shows which include elephants: animal welfare advocates claim that these are unnatural and harmful for the animals.

One of the major attractions is the glossy stage show **Bali Agung**. For the 60-minute show, Balinese culture is given the Vegas treatment with spectacular results. It's not traditional but it is eye-popping.

The park is north of Lebih Beach; free shuttles run to tourist centres across south Bali.

🏖 Beaches

As you head east on the coast road from Sanur, pretty much any road or lane heading south will end up at a beach. Some will take you to quiet beaches, others will lead you to beaches where development is underway and still others are already well-trod and lead to beaches where fun and frolic are established.

The shoreline is striking, with beaches in volcanic shades of grey pounded by waves. The entire coast has great religious significance and there are oodles of temples. At the many small coastal-village beaches, cremation formalities reach their conclusion when the ashes are consigned to the sea. Ritual purification ceremonies for temple artefacts are also held on these beaches.

Some key points:

➡ Ketewel and Keramas are top spots for surfing.

➡ Swimming in the often pounding surf is dangerous.

➡ Some beaches have no shade.

➡ Most beaches have a food or drinks vendor or two, at least.

➡ You'll need your own transport to reach these beaches.

➡ Locals will charge you an access fee – about 2000Rp to 5000Rp.

➡ Rubbish is a depressing fact at most of the beaches.

High-profile surf resort **Komune Bali** (Map p176; ☑ 0361-301 8888; www.komuneresorts.com; Jl Pantai Keramas; r from US$90; ❋ ⑦ ≋) 🏄 has erected light towers for night-surfing, which has proven hugely popular. Despite this, the hotel has actually done a good job of trying to blend into the existing landscape. It has a very attractive pool area and a cafe in the dune up from the high-tide line.

Unfortunately other new arrivals here have different attitudes. Wake Bali rents out all-terrain vehicles (ATVs) so people can screech around the beach. Worse, it has a pool with captive dolphins.

Pantai Ketewel BEACH
(Map p176) One of the first beaches you'll encounter off the coast road, Ketewel is known for its surfing, which demands advanced skills; it's a tricky reef-rocky right. Come here to surf – or watch.

Pantai Purnama BEACH
(Map p176) Small, but has the blackest sand, reflecting billions of sparkles in the sunlight. Religion is big here. The temple, **Pura Erjeruk**, is important for irrigation of rice fields, while some of Bali's most elaborate

East Bali Highlights

1 Counting the shades of green on one of the longest and best uphill treks of your life at **Pura Lempuyang** (p203).

2 Marvelling at the combination of the sacred and the sublime and lots of black sand at **Pantai Klotek** (p182).

3 Sensing Bali's violent past and proud traditions of sacrifice at Semarapura's **Kertha Gosa** (p184).

4 Trekking the picture-perfect valley at **Sidemen** (p187).

5 Chilling with new friends at the mellow cafes and laid-back beaches of **Padangbai** (p192).

6 Finding your perfect lotus position at an inn perched along the **Amed Coast** (p204).

7 Plunging into the blue waters at **Tulamben** (p210) to explore the famous shipwreck right off the beach.

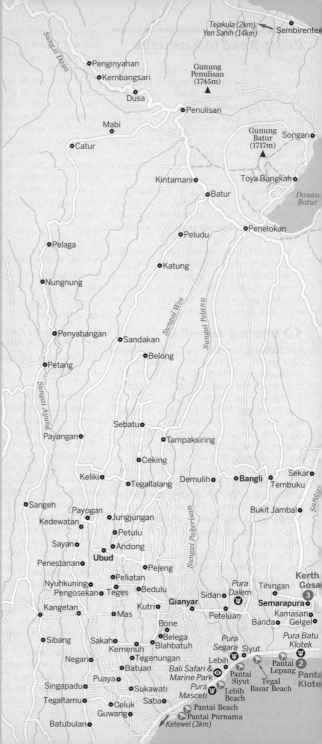

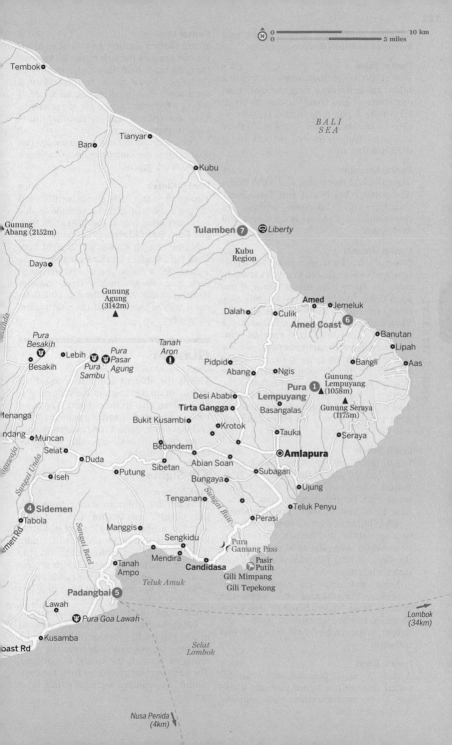

0 | 10 km
0 | 5 miles

Tembok

BALI SEA

Tianyar
Ban
Kubu

Gunung
Abang (2152m)

Tulamben **7** ◉ *Liberty*

Kubu
Region

Daya

Gunung
Agung
(3142m) ▲

Dalah   Culik   **Amed** Jemeluk
Amed Coast 6

Banutan
Lipah

*Pura
Besakih*   Lebih   *Pura
Pasar
Agung*

Tanah
Aron **!**

Pidpid   Ngis   Bangli   Aas
Abang
Gunung
Lempuyang
(1058m) ▲

Besakih   *Pura
Sambu*

Desi Ababi   **Pura
Lempuyang 1**

Tirta Gangga   Basangalas   Gunung Seraya
(1175m) ▲

Menanga   Bukit Kusambi   Krotok

dang   Muncan   Tauka   Seraya

Selat   Bebandem   Abian Soan   ◎ **Amlapura**

Duda   Sibetan   Subagan

Putung   Bungaya

Iseh   Tenganan   Ujung

4 Sidemen   Teluk Penyu

Tabola   Perasi

Manggis   *Pura
Gamang Pass*

Sengkidu   Pasir
Putih

Tanah
Ampo   Mendira   **Candidasa**   Gili Mimpang

Teluk Amuk   Gili Tepekong

Lombok
(34km) →

Padangbai 5

Lawah   **W** *Pura Goa Lawah*

*Selat
Lombok*

oast Rd   Kusamba

*Nusa Penida
(4km)* ↘

full-moon purification ceremonies are held here each month. Villas are appearing.

Pantai Saba
BEACH

(Map p176) Choose your access: a twisting 1.1km, junglelike drive from the coast road or a short and direct road just east; it's about 12km from Sanur. A few drinks vendors recline on the burnt-umber-hued sand; there is a small temple, covered shelters and a shady parking area.

Pantai Keramas
BEACH

(Map p176) Will this be the next Echo Beach (the popular beach and surf break near Canggu)? Villa and hotel projects are sprouting here. The surf is consistent and world-class.

Pantai Masceti
BEACH

(Map p176) 'What a strange place', our friend said. And indeed Masceti beach is a study in contrasts. Some 15km east of Sanur, it has a few drinks vendors and one of Bali's nine sacred directional temples, **Pura Masceti**. Right on the beach, the temple is built in the shape of a *garuda* (a large mythical bird) and enlivened with gaudy statuary.

There's a certain irony to the bird-shape as both the temple grounds and a huge building nearby are used for cockfights. The feathers of losing birds are everywhere. On days with no cockfights or ceremonies, the large pavilion is used for other gambling activities.

Lebih Beach
BEACH

Lebih Beach has glittering mica-infused sand. Just off the main road, the large Sungai Pakerisan (Pakerisan River), which starts near Tampaksiring, reaches the sea near here. Fishing boats line the shore, which is fitting as there's a strip of warungs with specialities that include fish sate and rich seafood soup. The air is redolent with the smell of BBQ fish; this is an excellent stop for lunch.

North, just across the coast road, the impressive **Pura Segara** looks across the strait to Nusa Penida, home of Jero Gede Macaling (see the boxed text, p133) – the temple helps protect Bali from his evil influence.

Pantai Siyut
BEACH

A mere 300m off the road, and often deserted, this beach is a good place for a parasol: there's no shade otherwise. It remains development-free.

Pantai Lepang
BEACH

Worth visiting just for the little slice of rural Bali you pass through on the 600m drive from the main road. Rice and corn grow in profusion. Down at the carbon-coloured sand you'll find small dunes, no shade, a couple of vendors and a lot of reasons to snap some pics. A sign explains that this is a sea turtle sanctuary.

Conversely, that huge development you see nearby is the Tamansari Jivva time-share condo development.

Pantai Klotek
BEACH

The lovely 800m drive along the hilly road off the coast road is but a prelude to this very interesting beach. The quiet at the temple, **Pura Batu Klotek**, belies its great significance: sacred statues are brought here from Pura Besakih for ritual cleansing.

Look for a *bakso ayam* (chicken soup) cart; the owner makes fresh noodles by hand all day. Admire the pale blue flowers – they're sacred – on the wild midori shrubs here.

Gianyar
☑ 0361

This is the affluent administrative capital and main market town of the Gianyar district, which also includes Ubud. The town has a number of factories producing batik and ikat fabrics, and a compact centre with some excellent food, especially at the famous night market.

⊙ Sights

Puri Gianyar
PALACE

(Jl Ngurah Rai) Although dating from 1771, Puri Gianyar was destroyed in a conflict with the neighbouring kingdom of Klungkung in the mid-1880s and rebuilt. Under threat from its aggressive neighbours, the Gianyar kingdom requested Dutch protection. A 1900 agreement let the ruling family retain its status and palace, though it lost all political power. The palace is an excellent example of traditional architecture.

While tourists are not usually allowed inside, you might convince the guard to let you have a quick look (otherwise the views are good through the wrought-iron gate). The huge banyan tree across from the compound is considered sacred and is a royal symbol.

GIANYAR'S TASTY NIGHT MARKET

The sound of hundreds of cooking pots and the glare of bright lights add a frenetic and festive clamour to Gianyar's delicious **Night Market** (Map p176; Jl Ngurah Rai; ⊘ 5-11pm), which any local will tell you has some of the best food in Bali.

Scores of stalls set up each night in the centre and cook up a mouth-watering and jaw-dropping range of dishes. Much of the fun is just strolling, browsing and choosing. There's everything from *babi guling* (spit-roasted pig, stuffed with chilli, tumeric. garlic and ginger) to succulent combinations of vegetables that defy description. The average cost of a dish is under 15,000Rp; with a group you can sample a lot, and be the happier for it. Peak time is the two hours after sunset.

Best of all, the night market is only a 20-minute drive from Ubud: a driver will bring you here for 120,000Rp, including waiting time (be sure to buy them something to enjoy as well).

✗ Eating

People come to Gianyar to sample the market food, like *babi guling* (spit-roast pig stuffed with chilli, turmeric, garlic and ginger – delicious), for which the town is noted. The descriptively named **Gianyar Babi Guleng** (Map p176; meals from 20,000Rp; ⊘ 7am-4pm) is favoured by locals among many competitors. It's in a tiny side street at the west end of the centre behind the bemo parking area.

Nearby are numerous stands selling fresh food, including delectable *piseng goreng* (fried banana). Also good for sampling is the **food market** (⊘ 11am-2pm), which lines both sides of the main section of Jl Ngurah Rai.

🔒 Shopping

At the western end of town on the main Ubud road are textile factories that are beloved by connoisseurs of handwoven fabrics. Two good stops are the large **Tenun Ikat Setia Cili** (Map p176; ☑ 0361-943409; Jl Astina Utara; ⊘ 9am-5pm) and **Cap Togog** (Map p176; ☑ 0361-943046; Jl Astina Utara 11; ⊘ 8am-5pm). Both are on the main road about 500m apart. The latter has a fascinating production area below; follow the sounds of dozens of clacking wooden looms. You'll see weavers at work and observe how the thread is dyed before being woven to produce the vibrantly patterned weft ikat, which is called *endek* in Bali.

You can buy material by the metre, or have it tailored. Prices are 50,000Rp to 100,000Rp per metre for handwoven ikat, depending on how fine the weaving is – costs will rise if it contains silk. You can get a top-quality batik sarong for about 600,000Rp (double that if you include gold accents for your wedding). The industry is struggling from competition with machine-made Javanese fabric, so your arrival will be welcomed.

ℹ Getting There & Away

Regular bemos run between Batubulan terminal near Denpasar and Gianyar's main terminal (15,000Rp), which is behind the main market. Bemo to/from Ubud (10,000Rp) use the bemo stop across the road from the main market.

Sidan

When driving east from Gianyar you come to the turn-off to Bangli about 2km out of Peteluan. Follow this road for about 1km until you reach a sharp bend, where you'll find Sidan's **Pura Dalem**. This good example of a temple of the dead has very fine carvings. Note the sculptures of Durga with children by the gate and the separate enclosure in one corner of the temple – this is dedicated to Merajapati, the guardian spirit of the dead.

Bangli

☑ 0366

Halfway up the slope to Penelokan, Bangli, once the capital of a kingdom, is a humble market town noteworthy for its sprawling temple, Pura Kehen, which is on a beautiful jungle road that runs east past rice terraces and connects at Sekar with roads to Rendang and Sidemen.

History

Bangli dates from the early 13th century. In the Majapahit era it broke away from Gelgel to become a separate kingdom, although it was landlocked, poor and involved in long-running conflicts with neighbouring states.

In 1849 Bangli made a treaty with the Dutch that gave it control over the defeated north-coast kingdom of Buleleng, but Buleleng then rebelled and the Dutch imposed direct rule there. In 1909 the rajah (lord or prince) of Bangli chose for it to become a Dutch protectorate rather than face suicidal *puputan* (a warrior's fight to the death) or complete conquest by the neighbouring kingdoms or the colonial power.

◉ Sights

★ Pura Kehen
HINDU TEMPLE

(adult/child 10,000/5000Rp; ⊘ 9am-5pm) The state temple of the Bangli kingdom, Pura Kehen, one of the finest temples in eastern Bali, is a miniature version of Pura Besakih. It is terraced up the hillside, with a flight of steps leading to the beautifully decorated entrance. The first courtyard has a huge banyan tree with a *kulkul* (hollow tree-trunk drum used to sound a warning) entwined in its branches.

The inner courtyard has an 11-roof *meru* (multitiered shrine), and there are other shrines with thrones for the Hindu trinity – Brahma, Shiva and Vishnu. The carvings are particularly intricate. See if you can count all 43 altars.

Pura Dalem Penunggekan
HINDU TEMPLE

(Jl Merdeka) The exterior wall of this fascinating temple of the dead features vivid relief carvings of evil-doers getting their just deserts in the afterlife. One panel addresses the lurid fate of adulterers (men in particular may find the viewing uncomfortable). Other panels portray sinners as monkeys, while another is a good representation of sinners begging to be spared the fires of hell. It's 3km south of the centre.

✕ Eating

The *pasar malam* (night market), on Jl Merdeka beside the bemo terminal, has some excellent traditional warungs, and you'll also find fresh and tasty food stalls in the shambolic market during the day. Temple-offering supplies are sold 24 hours a day.

❶ Getting There & Away

Bangli is located on the main road between Denpasar's Batubulan terminal (17,000Rp) and Gunung Batur, via Penelokan.

Semarapura (Klungkung)
📷 0366

A tidy regional capital, Semarapura should be on your itinerary for its fascinating Kertha Gosa complex, a relic of Bali from the time before the Dutch. Once the centre of Bali's most important kingdom, Semarapura is still commonly called by its old name, Klungkung.

It's a good place to stroll and get a feel for modern Balinese life. The markets are large, the shops many and the streets are reasonably calm.

History

Successors to the Majapahit conquerors of Bali established themselves at Gelgel (just south of modern Semarapura) around 1400, with the Gelgel dynasty strengthening the growing Majapahit presence on the island. During the 17th century the successors of the Gelgel line established separate kingdoms, and the dominance of the Gelgel court was lost. The court moved to Klungkung in 1710, but never regained a pre-eminent position.

In 1849 the rulers of Klungkung and Gianyar defeated a Dutch invasion force at Kusamba. Before the Dutch could launch a counter-attack, a force from Tabanan arrived and the trader Mads Lange was able to broker a peace settlement.

For the next 50 years, the south Bali kingdoms squabbled, until the rajah of Gianyar petitioned the Dutch for support. When the Dutch finally invaded the south, the king of Klungkung had a choice between a suicidal *puputan,* like the rajah of Denpasar, or an ignominious surrender, as Tabanan's rajah had done (or cutting a deal like the rajah did up the road in Bangli). He chose the first. In April 1908, as the Dutch surrounded his palace, the Dewa Agung and hundreds of his relatives and followers marched out to certain death from Dutch gunfire or the blades of their own kris (traditional daggers). It was the last Balinese kingdom to succumb and the sacrifice is commemorated in the towering **Puputan Monument**, just across Jl Serapati.

◉ Sights

★ Taman Kertha Gosa
HISTORIC BUILDING

(Jl Puputan; adult/child 12,000/6000Rp, parking 2000Rp; ⊘ 6am-6pm) When the Dewa Agung dynasty moved here in 1710, the Semara

Semarapura

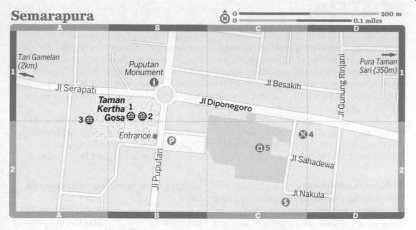

Pura was established. The palace was laid out as a large square, believed to be in the form of a mandala, with courtyards, gardens, pavilions and moats. The complex is sometimes referred to as Taman Gili (Island Garden). Most of the original palace and grounds were destroyed by the 1908 Dutch attacks – the **Pemedal Agung**, the gateway on the south side of the square, is all that remains of the palace itself (check out its carvings).

Two important buildings are preserved in a restored section of the grounds, and, with a museum, they comprise the Taman Kertha Gosa complex. Although vendors are persistent, parking is easy and it's easy to explore the town from here.

➡ Kertha Gosa

(Hall of Justice) In the northeastern corner of the complex, the Kertha Gosa was effectively the supreme court of the Klungkung kingdom, where disputes and cases that could not be settled at the village level were even-

tually brought. This open-sided pavilion is a superb example of Klungkung architecture. The ceiling is completely covered with fine paintings in the Klungkung style. The paintings, done on asbestos sheeting, were installed in the 1940s, replacing cloth paintings that had deteriorated.

The rows of ceiling panels depict several themes. The lowest level illustrates five tales from Bali's answer to the *Arabian Nights*, where a girl called Tantri spins a different yarn every night. The next two rows are scenes from Bima's travels in the afterlife, where he witnesses the torment of evil-doers. The gruesome tortures are shown clearly, but there are different interpretations of which punishment goes with what crime. (There's an authoritative explanation in *The Epic of Life – A Balinese Journey of the Soul* by Idanna Pucci, available for reference in the pavilion.) The fourth row of panels depicts the story of the search of the *garuda* (mythical man-bird) for the elixir of life, while the fifth row shows events on the Balinese astrological calendar. The next three rows return to the story of Bima, this time travelling in heaven, with doves and a lotus flower at the apex of the ceiling.

➡ Bale Kambang

The ceiling of the beautiful 'Floating Pavilion' is painted in Klungkung style. Again, the different rows of paintings deal with various subjects. The first row is based on the astrological calendar, the second on the folk tale of Pan and Men Brayut and their 18 children, and the upper rows on the adventures of the hero Sutasona.

EAST BALI SEMARAPURA (KLUNGKUNG)

DON'T MISS

EAST BALI'S BEST MARKET

Semarapura's sprawling **market** (Jl Diponegoro; ⊘ 6am-8pm) is one of the best in east Bali. It's a vibrant hub of commerce and a meeting place for people of the region. You can easily spend an hour wandering about the warren of stalls on three levels. It's grimy, yes, but also endlessly fascinating. Huge straw baskets of lemons, limes, tomatoes and other produce are islands of colour amid the chaos. A plethora of locally made snacks are offered in profusion; try several.

Glittering jewellery stalls crowd up against shops selling nothing but plastic buckets. Look for ikat vendors selling authentic fabric for a third of what you'd pay elsewhere. On breeze-ways out back, climb to the top for **views** of multicultural Semarapura, where mosque minarets crowd the sky along with Balinese temples. Mornings are the best time to visit.

➡ **Museum Semarajaya**

This diverting museum has an interesting collection of archaeological and other items. There are exhibits of *songket* (silver- or gold-threaded cloth) weaving and palm toddy (palm wine) and palm-sugar extraction. Don't miss the moving display about the 1908 *puputan*, along with some interesting old photos of the royal court. The exhibit on salt-making gives you a good idea of the hard work involved.

Pura Taman Sari   HINDU TEMPLE
(Jl Gunung Merapi) The quiet lawns and ponds around this temple, northeast of the Taman Kertha Gosa complex, make it a relaxing stop and live up to the translation of its name: Flower Garden Temple. The towering 11-roofed *meru* indicates that this was a temple built for royalty; today it seems built for the geese who wander the grounds.

✗ Eating

The best bet for food is browsing the myriad choices in and around the market. There's a small stall selling good coffee at the Taman Kertha Gosa parking lot.

Bali Indah   CHINESE, INDONESIAN $
(✆ 0366-21056; Jl Nakula 1; dishes 10,000-20,000Rp) A veteran and affable Chinese sit-down place with simple meals; you'll swear it's 1943. Sumber Rasa almost next door is similar.

ℹ Information

Jl Nakula and the main street, Jl Diponegoro, have several ATMs.

ℹ Getting There & Away

The best way to visit Semarapura is with your own transport and as part of a circuit taking in other sites up the mountains and along the coast.

Bemos from Denpasar (Batubulan terminal) pass through Semarapura (13,000Rp) on the way to points further east. They can be hailed from near the Puputan Monument.

Around Semarapura

East of Semarapura, the main road dramatically crosses Sungai Unda (Unda River), then swings south towards Kusamba and the sea. Lava from the 1963 eruption of Gunung Agung destroyed villages here, but the lava flows are now overgrown.

Tihingan

Several workshops in Tihingan are dedicated to producing **gamelan instruments**. Small foundries make the resonating bronze bars and bowl-shaped gongs, which are then carefully filed and polished until they produce the correct tone.

Workshops with signs out front are good for visits. Look for the welcoming **Tari Gamelan** (✆ 0366-22339) amid many along the main strip. The often hot work is usually done very early in the morning when it's cool, but at other times you'll still likely see something going on.

From Semarapura, head west along Jl Diponegoro and look for the signs.

◉ Sights

★ **Nyoman Gunarsa Museum**   MUSEUM
(✆ 0366-22256; Pertigaan Banda/Banda Intersection, Takmung; adult/child 50,000Rp/free; ⊘ 9am-4pm Mon-Sat) Dedicated to classical and contemporary Balinese painting, this slightly melancholy museum complex was established by Nyoman Gunarsa, one of the most respected and successful modern

artists in Indonesia. A vast three-storey building exhibits an impressive variety of older pieces, including stone carvings, woodcarvings, architectural antiques, masks, puppets and textiles.

Many of the classical paintings are on bark paper and are some of the oldest surviving examples. Check out the many old puppets, still seemingly animated even in retirement. The top floor is devoted to Gunarsa's own bold, expressionistic depictions of traditional life. Look for *Offering*.

The museum is about 4km west from Semarapura, near a bend on the Gianyar road – look for the dummy policemen at the base of a large statue nearby.

Gelgel

Situated about 2.5km south of Semarapura on the way to the coast road and 500m south of Kamasan, Gelgel was once the seat of Bali's most powerful dynasty. The town's decline started in 1710, when the court moved to present-day Semarapura, and finished when the Dutch bombarded the place in 1908.

Today the wide streets and the surviving temples are only faintly evocative of past grandeur. **Pura Dasar Bhuana** has huge banyan trees shading grassy grounds where you may feel the urge for a quiet contemplative stroll. The vast courtyards are a clue to its former importance, and festivals here attract large numbers of people from all over Bali.

About 500m to the east, the **Masjid Gelgel** is Bali's oldest mosque. Although modern-looking, it was established in the late 16th century for the benefit of Muslim missionaries from Java, who were unwilling to return home after failing to make any converts.

Sidemen Road

☑ 0366

Winding through one of Bali's most beautiful river valleys, the Sidemen road offers marvellous paddy-field scenery, a delightful rural character and extraordinary views of Gunung Agung (when the clouds permit). The region is getting more popular every year as a verdant escape, where a walk in any direction is a communion with nature.

German artist Walter Spies lived in Iseh for some time from 1932 in order to escape the perpetual party of his own making in Ubud. Later the Swiss painter Theo Meier, nearly as famous as Spies for his influence on Balinese art, lived in the same house.

The village of **Sidemen** has a spectacular location and is a centre for culture and arts, particularly *endek* cloth and *songket*. **Pelangi Weaving** (☑ 0366-23012; Jl Soka 67; ☉ 8am-6pm) has a couple of dozen employees busily creating downstairs, while upstairs you can relax with the Sidemen views from comfy chairs outside the showroom.

There are many **walks** through the rice and chilli fields and streams in the multi-hued green valley. One involves a spectacular three-hour round-trip climb up to **Pura Bukit Tageh**, a small temple with big views. No matter where you stay, you'll be able to arrange guides for in-depth trekking (about 80,000Rp per hour), or just set out on your own exploration.

🛏 Sleeping & Eating

Views throughout the area are sweeping, from terraced green hills to Gunung Agung, although the area's popularity means that new guesthouses have obstructed some views. Most inns have restaurants and there are simple warungs and cafes appearing along the roads. It can get cool and misty at night.

WORTH A TRIP

ROAD TO TEMBUKU

Travelling from the flatlands of the east up the slopes for Gunung Batur, Pura Besakih or even as part of a round-trip in combination with the Sidemen Road, you have several choices.

One of the best is the road that begins about 5km east of Gianyar on the main road to Semarapura. It runs north for about 12km to the village of Tembuku and is paved. It's narrow, which keeps the truck count down, and passes through a score of tiny, traditional villages. There are **rice terrace** and **river valley views** along its length.

You'll also see huge beams of yellow wood by the road. These are from jackfruit trees and are prized for their long-lasting qualities. They are used in temple construction.

Near the centre of Sidemen, a small road heads west for 500m to a fork and a signpost with the names of several places to stay. Meals can be arranged at all of these guesthouses, which are spread out.

★ Khrisna Home Stay HOMESTAY $
(☑ 0815 5832 1543; pinpinaryadi@yahoo.com; Jl Tebola; r 250,000-350,000Rp) Why go to a market for fruit when you can sleep with it? This wonderful seven-room homestay is surrounded by all-organic trees and plants with guava, bananas, passionfruit, papaya, oranges and more. Needless to say, breakfasts are excellent. The rooms are comfortable (with terraces) and the owners lovely. It's near the temple on the drive in.

Pondok Wisata Lihat Sawah GUESTHOUSE $
(☑ 0361-530 0516; www.lihatsawah.com; r 300,000-500,000Rp, mains 15,000-35,000Rp; 🛜🍽) Take the right fork in the road to this guesthouse. All 12 rooms have views of the valley and mountain (all have hot water – nice after a morning hike – and the best have lovely wooden verandahs). There are also three bungalows. Water courses through the surrounding rice fields. The cafe has wi-fi and serves Thai and Indo dishes.

★ Samanvaya INN $$
(☑ 0821 4710 3884; www.samanvaya-bali.com; r US$65-150; 🛜🍽) This attractive inn has sweeping views over the rice fields all the way south to the ocean. The Brit owners are steadily expanding the complex, it now has a new yoga and spa pavilion. The 11 units have thatched roofs and deep, wooden terraces. The infinity pool is a dream and the cafe serves Asian and Western dishes.

Darmada GUESTHOUSE $$
(☑ 0853 3803 2100; www.darmadabali.com; r from 500,000Rp; 🍽) Beautifully set in a small river valley on spacious, lush grounds, this seven-room guesthouse has a large pool lined with tiles in gentle shades of green. Rooms have hammocks on the patio near the babbling waters. The small warung has food made with vegetables grown on the grounds. It has cake and coffee for walkers in the afternoon (35,000Rp).

Kubu Tani GUESTHOUSE $$
(☑ 0366-530 0519, 0813 3858 8744; www.balikubutani.com; Jl Tebola; r from 500,000Rp) There are three apartments at this two-storey house. Open-plan living rooms have good views of the rice fields and mountains as well as large porches with loungers. Kitchens allow for cooking.

Nirarta HOTEL $$
(☑ 0366-530 0636; www.awareness-bali.com; r €30-50) Guests here partake in serious programs for personal and spiritual development, including meditation intensives and yoga. The motto: 'Centre for living awareness'. The 11 comfortable rooms are split among six bungalows, some right on the river.

Subak Tabola HOTEL $$$
(☑ 0811 386 6197; subak_tebolainn@indo.net.id; r from US$120; ❋🛜🍽) Set in an impossibly green amphitheatre of rice terraces, the 11 rooms are poshly upgraded and have open-air bathrooms; two very large bungalows are especially appealing. Verandahs have mesmerising views down the valley to the ocean. The grounds are spacious and there's a cool pool with frog fountains. It's nearly 2km from the hotel signpost.

ℹ Information

There is an excellent **website** (www.sidemen-bali.com) for the Sidemen area that details accommodation options and the many activities in the area.

ℹ Getting There & Away

The Sidemen road can be a beautiful part of any day trip from south Bali or Ubud. It connects in the north with the Rendang–Amlapura road just west of Duda. Unfortunately the road is busy due to huge trucks hauling rocks for Bali's incessant construction. (Note that all the places to stay listed here are far from the main Sidemen road.)

A less-travelled route to Pura Besakih goes northeast from Semarapura, via Sidemen and Iseh, to another scenic treat: the Rendang–Amlapura road.

Pura Besakih

Perched nearly 1000m up the side of Gunung Agung is Bali's most important temple, Pura Besakih. In fact, it is an extensive complex of 23 separate but related temples, with the largest and most important being Pura Penataran Agung. Unfortunately, many people find it a disappointing (and dispiriting) experience due to the avarice of various local characters.

The multitude of hassles aside, the complex comes alive during frequent ceremonies.

Pura Besakih Complex

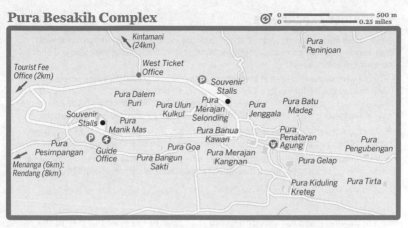

History

The precise origins of Pura Besakih are not totally clear, but it almost certainly dates from prehistoric times. The stone bases of Pura Penataran Agung and several other temples resemble megalithic stepped pyramids, and date back at least 2000 years. It was certainly used as a Hindu place of worship from 1284, when the first Javanese conquerors settled in Bali. By the 15th century, Besakih had become a state temple of the Gelgel dynasty.

Sights

The largest and most important temple is Pura Penataran Agung. The other Besakih temples – all with individual significance and often closed to visitors – are markedly less scenic. When it's mist-free, the view down to the coast is sublime.

Pura Penataran Agung HINDU TEMPLE

Pura Penataran Agung is built on six levels, terraced up the slope, with the entrance approached from below, up a flight of steps. This entrance is an imposing *candi bentar* (split gateway), and beyond it, the even more impressive *kori agung* is the gateway to the second courtyard.

You will find that it's most enjoyable during one of the frequent festivals, when hundreds or even thousands of gorgeously dressed devotees turn up with beautifully arranged offerings. Note that tourists are not allowed inside this temple.

Information

The temple's **main ticket office** is 2km south of the complex on the road from Menanga and the south. Admission is 15,000Rp per person plus 5000Rp per vehicle.

About 200m past the ticket office, there is a fork in the road with a sign indicating Besakih to the right and Kintamani to the left. Go left, because going to the right puts you in the **main parking area** at the bottom of a hill some 300m from the complex. Going past the road to Kintamani, where there is a **west ticket office**, puts you in the **north parking area** only 50m from the complex, and away from scammers at the main entrance.

Getting There & Away

The best way to visit is with your own transport, which allows you to explore the many gorgeous drives in the area.

Gunung Agung

Bali's highest and most revered mountain, Gunung Agung is an imposing peak seen from most of south and east Bali, although it's often obscured by cloud and mist. Many sources say it's 3142m high, but some say it lost its summit in the 1963 eruption. The summit is an oval crater, about 700m across, with its highest point on the western edge above Besakih.

As it's the spiritual centre of Bali, traditional houses are laid out on an axis in line with Agung and many locals always know where they are in relation to the peak, which is thought to house ancestral spirits. Climbing the mountain takes you through verdant

AN UNHOLY EXPERIENCE

So intrusive are the scams and irritations faced by visitors to Besakih that many wish they had skipped the complex altogether. What follows are some of the ploys you should be aware of before a visit.

➜ Near the main parking area at the bottom of the hill is a **'guide' building** where guides hang around looking for visitors. Guides here may emphatically tell you that you need their services and quote a ridiculously high price of US$25 for a short visit. You don't: you may always walk among the temples, and no 'guide' can get you into a closed temple.

➜ Other 'guides' may foist their services on you throughout your visit. There have been reports of people agreeing to a guide's services only to be hit with a huge fee at the end.

➜ Once inside the complex, you may receive offers to 'come pray with me'. Visitors who seize on this chance to get into a forbidden temple can face demands of 100,000Rp or more.

forest in the clouds and rewards with sweeping (dawn) views.

Climbing Gunung Agung

It's best to climb during the dry season (April to September); July to September are the most reliable months. At other times the paths can be slippery and dangerous and the views are clouded over (especially true in January and February). Climbing Gunung Agung is not permitted when major religious events are being held at Pura Besakih, which generally includes most of April.

Points to consider for a climb:

➜ Use a guide.

➜ Respect your guide's pauses at shrines for prayers on the sacred mountain.

➜ Get to the top before 8am – the clouds that often obscure the view of Agung also obscure the view *from* Agung.

➜ Take a strong torch (flashlight), extra batteries, plenty of water (2L per person), snack food, waterproof clothing and a warm jumper (sweater).

➜ Wear strong shoes or boots and have manicured toes – the trail is very steep and the descent is especially hard on your feet.

➜ This is a hard climb, don't fool yourself.

➜ Take frequent rests and don't be afraid to ask your guide to slow down.

GUIDES

Trips with guides on either of the routes up Gunung Agung generally include breakfast and other meals as well as a place to stay, but be sure to confirm all details in advance. Guides are also able to arrange transport.

Most of the places to stay in the region, including those at Selat, along the Sidemen road and at Tirta Gangga, will recommend guides for Gunung Agung climbs. Expect to pay a negotiable 900,000Rp to 1,000,000Rp for one to four people for your climb.

The following guides are recommended:

Gung Bawa Trekking   GUIDE
(✆ 0812 387 8168; www.gungbawatrekking.com) Experienced and reliable.

Wayan Tegteg   GUIDE
(✆ 0813 3852 5677; tegtegwayan@yahoo.co.id) Wins plaudits from hikers.

Yande   GUIDE
(✆ 0857 3988 5569, 0852 3025 3672) Affiliated with the Puri Agung Inn in Selat, which is a good place to stay for an early start.

ROUTES

It's possible to climb Agung from various directions. The two most popular routes are from the following places:

➜ Pura Pasar Agung (on the southern slopes; about eight hours) – this route involves the least walking, because Pura Pasar Agung (Agung Market Temple) is high on the southern slopes of the mountain (around 1500m) and can be reached by a good road north from Selat.

➜ Pura Besakih (on the southwest side of the mountain; about 12 hours) – this climb is much tougher than the already demanding southern approach and is only for the very physically fit; for the best chance of a clear view before the clouds close in you should start at midnight.

Either route can take you to the summit, although most people on the shorter route go to the crater rim (2866m).

Rendang to Amlapura

☑ 0366

A fascinating road goes around the southern slopes of Gunung Agung from Rendang almost to Amlapura. It runs through some superb countryside, descending more or less gradually as it goes east. Water flows everywhere and there are rice fields, orchards and carvers of stones for temples most of the way.

Cyclists enjoy the route and find going east to be a breezier ride.

You can get to the start of the road in Rendang from Bangli in the west on a very pretty road through rice terraces and thick jungle vegetation. Rendang itself is an attractive mountain village; the crossroads are dominated by a huge and historic banyan tree. After going east for about 3km, you'll come into a beautiful small valley of rice terraces. At the bottom is Sungai Telagawaja, a popular river for white-water rafting.

The old-fashioned village of Muncan has quaint shingle roofs. It's approximately 4km along the winding road. Note the statues at the west entrance to town showing two boys: one a scholar and one showing the naked stupidity of skipping class. Nearby are scores of open-air factories where the soft lava rock is carved into temple decorations.

The road then passes through some of the most attractive rice country in Bali before reaching Selat, where you turn north to get to Pura Pasar Agung, a starting point for climbing Gunung Agung. Puri Agung Inn (☑ 0366-530 0887; Jl Raya Selat; r 150,000-200,000Rp) has six clean and comfortable rooms; the inn has views of rice fields and stone carvers. You can arrange rice-field walks here or climbs up Gunung Agung with local guide Yande.

Just before Duda, the very scenic Sidemen road branches southwest via Sidemen to Semarapura. Further east, a side road (about 800m) leads to Putung. This area is superb for hiking: there's an easy-to-follow track from Putung to Manggis, about 8km down the hill.

Continuing east, Sibetan is famous for growing *salak*, the delicious fruit with a curious 'snakeskin' covering, which you can buy from roadside stalls. This is one of the villages you can visit on tours and homestays organised by JED (p196), the nonprofit group that promotes rural tourism.

Northeast of Sibetan, a poorly signposted road leads north to Jungutan, with its Tirta Telaga Tista – a decorative pool and garden complex built for the water-loving old rajah of Karangasem.

The scenic road finishes at Bebandem, which has a cattle market every three days, and plenty of other stuff for sale as well. Bebandem and several nearby villages are home to members of the traditional metal-worker caste, which includes silversmiths and blacksmiths.

Kusamba to Padangbai

The coast road from Sanur crosses the traditional route to the east at the fishing town of Kusamba before joining the road near Pura Goa Lawah.

Kusamba

A side road leaves the main road and goes south to the fishing and salt-making village of Kusamba, where you will see rows of colourful *prahu* (outrigger fishing boats) lined up all along the grey-sand beach. The fishing is usually done at night and the 'eyes' on the front of the boats help navigate through the darkness. The fish market in Kusamba displays the night's catch.

Small local boats travel to Nusa Penida and Nusa Lembongan, which are clearly visible from Kusamba (boats from Padangbai are faster and safer, the modern Kusamba car ferry being the exception). Both east and west of Kusamba are small salt-making huts lined up in rows along the beach.

East of Kusamba and west of Pura Goa Lawah, Merta Sari (Bingin; meals from 25,000Rp; ☺10am-3pm) is renowned for its *nasi campur* (steamed rice with assorted sides), which includes juicy, pounded fish sate; a slightly sour, fragrant fish broth; fish steamed in banana leaves; snake beans in a fragrant tomato-peanut sauce; and a fire-red sambal. The open-air pavilion is 300m north of the coast road in the village of Bingin. Look for the Merta Sari signs.

Also good is arch-rival Sari Baruna (Jl Raya Goa Lawa; meals 20,000Rp; ☺10am-6pm), which also grills fish with attitude and authority. It's in a substantial bamboo hut about 200m west of Pura Goa Lawah.

Pura Goa Lawah

One of nine directional temples in Bali, **Pura Goa Lawah** (Bat Cave Temple; Jl Raya Goa Lawa; adult/child 10,000/5000Rp; car park 2000Rp; ⊙8am-6pm), is 3km east of Kusamba. The cave in the cliff face is packed, crammed and jammed full of bats, and the complex is equally overcrowded with tour groups, foreign and local. You might exclaim 'Holy Bat Guano, Batman!' when you get a whiff of the odours emanating from the cave. Superficially, the temple is small and unimpressive, but it is very old and of great significance to the Balinese.

Legend says the cave leads all the way to Pura Besakih, some 19km away, but it's unlikely that you'd want to try this route. The bats provide sustenance for the legendary giant snake, the deity Naga Basuki, which is also believed to live in the cave.

Ignore touts offering guiding services and if someone asks your name, don't give it or when you exit the cave you'll be presented with a 'gift' with your name on it and told you have to buy it.

Padangbai

📞 0363

There's a real traveller vibe about this little beach town that is also the port for the public ferry connecting Bali with Lombok and many of the fast boats to the Gilis.

Padangbai is is an attractive stop: it sits on a small bay and has a nice little curve of beach. A compact seaside backpackers hub offers cheap places to stay and some fun cafes.

The pace is slow, but should ambition strike there's good snorkelling and diving plus some easy walks and a couple of great beaches. Meanwhile you can soak up the languid air punctuated by the occasional arrival and departure of a ferry.

◉ Sights

Padangbai is interesting for a stroll. At the west end of town near the post office there's a small **mosque** (Jl Penataran Agung) and a temple, **Pura Desa** (Jl Pelabuhan). Towards the middle of town are two more temples, **Pura Dalem** (Gang Segara II) and the **Pura Segara** (off Jl Silayukti).

On a headland at the northeast corner of the bay, a path leads uphill to three temples, including **Pura Silayukti**, where Empu Kuturan – who introduced the caste system

to Bali in the 11th century – is said to have lived. It is one of the four oldest in Bali.

🏖 Beaches

With its protected bay, Padangbai has clear waters and a good beach right in front. Others are nearby; about 500m up and over the headland in the east is the small, light-sand **Blue Lagoon Beach**, an idyllic place with a couple of cafes and gentle, family-friendly surf.

To the southwest, you can drive 1.3km on a curving route past the mosque and Pura Desa or you can do a shadeless 800m hike up and over a hill past a failed hotel project to the beige sand of **Bias Tugal**, on the exposed coast outside the bay. It rewards the effort with a pretty cove setting and a couple of warungs to sate your thirst. Note that the water here is subject to strong currents.

🏃 Activities

Diving

There is good diving on the coral reefs around Padangbai, but the water can be a bit cold and visibility is not always ideal. The most popular local dives are **Blue Lagoon** and **Teluk Jepun** (Jepun Bay), both in Teluk Amuk, the bay just east of Padangbai. There's a good range of soft and hard corals and varied marine life, including sharks, turtles and wrasse, and a 40m wall at Blue Lagoon.

Many local outfits offer diving trips in the area, including to Gili Tepekong and Gili Biaha, and on to Tulamben and Nusa Penida. All dive prices are competitive, costing from US$55 for dives in the area to US$110 for trips out to Nusa Penida.

Recommended operators include the following:

Geko Dive   DIVING
(📞0363-41516; www.gekodive.com; Jl Silayukti; 2-tank dives from 850,000Rp) This is the longest-established operator; it has a nice cafe across from the beach.

Water Worx   DIVING
(📞0363-41220; www.waterworxbali.com; Jl Silayukti; Blue Lagoon 2-tank dive US$55) A well-regarded dive operator.

Snorkelling

One of the best and most accessible walk-in snorkel sites is off **Blue Lagoon Beach**. Note that it is subject to strong currents when the tide is out. Other sites such as **Teluk Jepun** can be reached by local boat (or check with the dive operators to see if they have any room on their dive boats; the cost is around 350,000Rp). Snorkel sets cost about 30,000Rp per day.

Local *jukung* (boats) offer snorkelling trips (bring your own gear) around Padangbai (50,000Rp per person per hour) and as far away as Nusa Lembongan (500,000Rp for two passengers).

🛏 Sleeping

Accommodation in Padangbai – like the town itself – is pretty laid-back. Prices are fairly cheap and it's pleasant enough here that there's no need to hurry through to or from Lombok. It's easy to wander the town comparing rooms before choosing one.

🛏 Village

In the village there are several tiny places in the alleys, some with a choice of small, cheap downstairs rooms or bigger, brighter upstairs rooms.

Kembar Inn GUESTHOUSE $
(☎ 0363-41364; kembarinn@hotmail.com; near Gang Segara III; r with fan/air-con from 125,000/300,000Rp; ❋ 🛜) There are 11 rooms (the cheapest have cold water) at this inn linked by a steep and narrow staircase. The best awaits at the top and has a private terrace with views.

Darma Homestay HOMESTAY $
(☎ 0363-41394; pondokwisata_dharma@ yahoo.com; Gang Segara III; r with fan/air-con from 100,000/200,000Rp; ❋ @ 🛜) A classic Balinese family homestay. The more expensive of the 12 rooms have hot showers and air-con; go for the room on the top floor.

🛏 Jalan Silayukti

On this little strip at the east end of the village, places are close together and right across from the sand.

★ Topi Inn GUESTHOUSE $
(☎ 0363-41424; www.topiinn.nl; Jl Silayukti; r from 125,000Rp; @ 🛜) Sitting at the east end of the strip in a serene location, Topi has six pleasant rooms, some of which share bathrooms. The cafe is excellent for breakfast. Topi offers trekking and recommended crafts workshops; see the website for details.

★ Bamboo Paradise GUESTHOUSE $
(☎ 0822 6630 4330; www.bambooparadisebali. com; Jl Penataran Agung; dm 95,000Rp, r with fan/ air-con from 230,000/280,000Rp; ❋ 🛜) This spiffy newcomer has one of the cheapest crash in town (in four-bed dorms). Regular rooms are comfortable and it has a nice large lounging area with hammocks. It's about 200m up a gentle hill from the ferry port.

Lemon House GUESTHOUSE $
(☎ 0812 4637 1575; www.lemonhousebali.com; Gang Melanting 5; dm 90,000Rp, r 250,000-350,000Rp) This house on the hill beside town has two rooms with sweeping views. On a clear day you can see Lombok. Other rooms are good deals and share bathrooms. Of course, a good view means a good climb. It's about 300m and 70 steps up from the ferry port. They'll come down and help with your bags.

Padangbai Beach Inn GUESTHOUSE $
(☎ 0363-41439; Jl Silayukti; r with fan/air-con from 125,000/200,000Rp) The 20 tidy rooms in cute bungalows are the pick (the cheapest have cold water), but try to avoid the rice-barn-style two-storey cottages, which can get hot and stuffy.

Hotel Puri Rai HOTEL $$
(☎ 0363-41385; www.puriraihotel.com; Jl Silayukti 3; r from 500,000Rp; ❋ ❋ 🛜 ⛱) The Puri Rai has 34 rooms in a two-storey stone building pleasantly facing the good-sized pool. Other rooms enjoy harbour views or overlook a yucky parking area. Ask to see a couple. The cafe has a good view.

🛏 Blue Lagoon Beach

Bloo Lagoon Village HOTEL $$$
(☎ 0363-41211; www.bloolagoon.com; Jl Silayukti; r US$120-220; ❋ 🛜 ⛱) ✿ Perched above Blue Lagoon Beach, the 25 cottages and villas here are all designed in traditional thatched style and the compound is dedicated to sustainable practices. The stylish units come with one, two or three bedrooms. It offers good-value diving packages and has an 18m pool.

🍴 Eating & Drinking

Beach fare and backpacker staples are mostly what's on offer in Padangbai – lots of fresh seafood, Indonesian classics, pizza and, yes, banana pancakes. You can easily laze away a few hours soaking up the scene at the places along Jl Segara and Jl Silayukti, which have harbour views during the day and cool breezes in the evening.

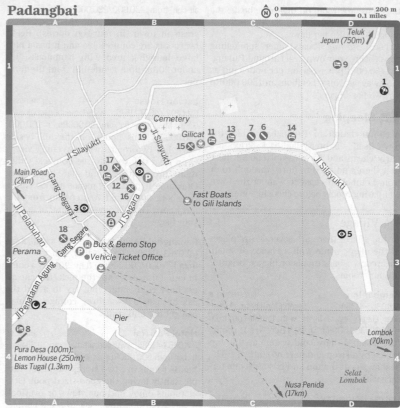

Colonial Restaurant
CAFE **$**

(📞 0811 385 8821; www.divingbali.cz; Jl Silayukti 6, OK Divers; mains from 40,000Rp; ⏱ 8am-11pm; 📶) This large cafe on the beach strip is the best place to while away time waiting for your boat. Lounge on beanbags, sofas or actual tables and enjoy the harbour view. Food spans the burger–Indo gamut. Diversions include shisha water pipes.

Topi Inn
CAFE **$**

(📞 0363-41424; Jl Silayukti; mains 20,000-40,000Rp; ⏱ 8am-10pm) 🍃 Juices, shakes and good coffees served up throughout the day. Breakfasts are big, and whatever is landed by the fishing boats outside the front door during the day is grilled by night. Refill your water bottle here for 2000Rp.

Depot Segara
SEAFOOD **$**

(📞 0363-41443; Jl Segara; dishes 10,000-30,000Rp; ⏱ 8am-10pm) Fresh seafood, such as barracuda, marlin and snapper, is pre-pared in a variety of ways at this slightly stylish cafe. Enjoy harbour views from the elevated terrace. In a town where casual is the byword, this is the slightly nicer option.

Ozone Café
INTERNATIONAL **$**

(📞 0363-41501; off Jl Silayukti; mains from 20,000Rp; ⏱ 8am-late) This popular travellers' gathering spot has low tables with pillows for lounging. It also has pizza and live music, sometimes by patrons.

Zen Inn
INTERNATIONAL **$**

(📞 0363-41418; Gang Segara; dishes 18,000-30,000Rp; ⏱ 8am-11pm; 📶) Burgers and BBQ mains are served in this airy cafe that goes late by local standards – often until 11pm. Lose yourself on the loungers amid vintage movie posters.

Babylon Bar
BAR

(Jl Silayukti; ⏱ 5pm-late) A tiny all-open-air bar in the market area back off the beach; a few

Padangbai

⊙ Sights
1	Blue Lagoon Beach	D1
2	Mosque	A3
3	Pura Dalem	A2
4	Pura Segara	B2
5	Pura Silayukti	D3

⊕ Activities, Courses & Tours
6	Geko Dive	C2
7	Water Worx	C2

⊟ Sleeping
8	Bamboo Paradise	A4
9	Bloo Lagoon Village	D1
10	Darma Homestay	B2
11	Hotel Puri Rai	C2

12	Kembar Inn	B2
13	Padangbai Beach Inn	C2
14	Topi Inn	C2

⊗ Eating
15	Colonial Restaurant	B2
16	Depot Segara	B2
17	Ozone Café	B2
	Topi Inn	(see 14)
18	Zen Inn	A3

⊙ Drinking & Nightlife
19	Babylon Bar	B2

⊞ Shopping
20	Ryan Shop	B3

chairs, tables and pillows scattered about are perfect for whiling away the evening with new friends.

🛍 Shopping

Ryan Shop MARKET
(☑ 0363-41215; Jl Segara 38; ☺ 8am-8pm) The perennial pleasures of the Ryan Shop can't be underestimated. It has good used paperbacks and sundries.

ⓘ Information

There are several ATMs around town. Ignore touts who meet all arriving boats.

ⓘ Getting There & Away

BEMO
Padangbai is 2km south of the main Semarapura–Amlapura road. Bemos leave from the car park in front of the port, some go east via Candidasa to Amlapura (10,000Rp); others go west to Semarapura (10,000Rp).

BOAT
Anyone who carries your luggage on or off the ferries or fast boats will expect to be paid, so agree to the price first or carry your own stuff. Also, watch out for scams where the porter may try to sell you a ticket you've already bought.

Lombok & Gili Islands
There are many ways to travel between Bali and Lombok and the Gilis. Be sure to consider important safety information (see p373).
➜ **Fast Boats** Several companies link Padangbai to the Gilis (p282). **Gilicat** (☑ 0363-41441; www.gilicat.com; Jl Silayukti, Made's Homestay) has an office at the waterfront.
➜ **Perama** (☑ 0878 6307 9153; Jl Pelabuhan; Senggigi & Gilis by fast boat 400,000Rp, Seng-

gigi by public ferry and shuttle 100,000Rp; ☺7am-8pm) Has a good-value option to Lombok.
➜ **Public Ferries** (child/adult/motorbike/car 27,000/40,000/112,000/773,000Rp, five to six hours) travel nonstop between Padangbai and Lembar on Lombok. Passenger tickets are sold near the pier. Boats supposedly run 24 hours and leave about every 90 minutes, but the service can be unreliable – boats have caught on fire and run aground.

BUS
To connect with Denpasar, catch a bemo out to the main road and hail a bus to the Batubulan terminal (18,000Rp).

TOURIST BUS
Perama has a stop here for its services around the east coast. Destinations include Kuta (60,000Rp, three hours), Sanur (60,000Rp, two hours) and Ubud (50,000Rp, 1¼ hours).

Padangbai to Candidasa
☑ 0363

It's 11km along the main road from the Padangbai turn-off to the tourist town of Candidasa. Between the two towns is an attractive stretch of coast, which has some tourist development and a large oil-storage depot in Teluk Amuk.

A short way beyond Padangbai, the new cruise-ship port at Tanah Ampo has proved a flop. Visions of mega-ships docking and spewing 5000 free-spending tourists into east Bali became fantasies after it was discovered that the new dock had been built in water too shallow for cruise ships. Blame is going around and around (Benoa Harbour is also too shallow for large cruise ships.)

Manggis

A pretty village inland from the coast, Manggis is the address used by luxury resorts hidden along the water off the main road.

🛏 Sleeping

★Amankila   RESORT $$$
(☑ 0363-41333; www.amankila.com; villas from US$800; ❈ ◉ ⓢ ☒) One of Bali's best resorts, the Amankila is perched along the jutting cliffs. About 5.6km beyond the Padangbai turn-off and 500m past the road to Manggis, a discreetly marked side road leads to the hotel. It features an isolated seaside location with views to Nusa Penida.

The renowned architecture includes three swimming pools that step down to the sea in matching shades. Of the restaurants here, the casual yet superb **Terrace** (lunch US$10-25; ◎ 8am-5pm) has a creative and varied menu with global and local influences. Service vies with the view for your plaudits.

Alila Manggis   RESORT $$$
(☑ 0363-41011; www.alilahotels.com; r from US$200; ❈ @ ⓢ ☒ ⊞) The Alila Manggis has elegant, white, thatch-roofed buildings in spacious lawn gardens facing a beautiful stretch of secluded beach. The 55 large rooms have minimalist interiors heavy on creams with muted wood accents; go for deluxe ones on the upper floor to enjoy the best views. Activities include a kids' camp, a spa and cooking courses.

Tenganan

Step back several centuries with a visit to Tenganan, home of the Bali Aga people – the descendants of the original Balinese who inhabited Bali before the Majapahit arrival in the 11th century.

The Bali Aga are reputed to be exceptionally conservative and resistant to change. Well, that's only partially true: TVs and other modern conveniences are hidden away in the traditional houses. But it is fair to say that the village has a much more traditional feel than most other villages in Bali. Cars and motorcycles are forbidden from entering. It should also be noted that this is a real village, not a creation for tourists.

The most striking feature of Tenganan is its postcardlike beauty, with the hills providing a photogenic backdrop to its setting. The compact 500m by 250m village is surrounded by a wall, and consists basically of two rows of identical houses stretching up the gentle slope of a hill. As you enter the village (10,000Rp donation) through one of only three gates, you'll likely be greeted by a guide who will take you on a tour – and generally lead you back to his family compound to look at textiles and *lontar* (specially prepared palm leaves) strips. However, there's no pressure to buy anything.

A peculiar, old-fashioned version of the gamelan known as the *gamelan selunding* is still played here, and girls dance an equally ancient dance known as the Rejang. There are other Bali Aga villages nearby, including **Tenganan Dauh Tenkad**, 1.5km west off the Tenganan road, with a charming old-fashioned ambience and several weaving workshops.

👉 Tours

JED   CULTURAL TOUR
(Village Ecotourism Network; ☑ 0361-366 9951; www.jed.or.id; day trips US$75, overnight stays US$125) Fully experience the ambience and culture of Tenganan on one of these highly regarded tours (some overnight) that feature local guides who explain the culture in detail and show how local goods are produced. Tours include transport from south Bali and Ubud.

🎎 Festivals

Tenganan has customs and festivals different from the Balinese norm.

Usaba Sambah Festival   CULTURAL
At the month-long Usaba Sambah Festival, which usually starts in May or June, men fight with sticks wrapped in thorny pandanus leaves. At this same festival, small, hand-powered Ferris wheels are brought out and the village girls are ceremonially twirled around.

🛍 Shopping

A magical cloth known as *kamben gringsing* is woven here – a person wearing it is said to be protected against black magic. Traditionally this is made using the 'double ikat' technique, in which both the warp and weft threads are 'resist dyed' before being woven. MBAs would be thrilled to study the integrated production of the cloth: everything, from growing the cotton to producing the dyes from local plants to the actual production, is accomplished here. It's very time-consuming, and the exquisite

THE MANGGIS–PUTUNG ROAD

Winding up a lush hillside scented with cloves, the little-used road linking Manggis on the coast with the mountain village of Putung is worth a detour no matter which way you are heading: east or west, up or down. Heading up you'll round curves to see east Bali and the islands unfolding before you. After stopping for photos, you'll feel good until you round another curve and the views are even better. At some scenic points families will appear offering beautiful handmade baskets for about 30,000Rp. It's hard not to exceed your basket-buying quota.

Coming from Manggis the road is in good shape for the first half but then deteriorates the rest of the way. It remains just OK for cars but you'll want to go slow for the views anyway; give it an hour.

pieces are costly (from 600,000Rp). You'll see cheaper cloth for sale but it usually comes from elsewhere in Bali or beyond.

Many baskets from across the region, made from *ata* palm, are on sale. Another local craft is traditional Balinese calligraphy, with the script inscribed onto *lontar* in the same way that the ancient *lontar* books were created. Most of these books are Balinese calendars or depictions of the Ramayana. They cost 150,000Rp to 300,000Rp, depending on quality. See p231 for more on *lontar* books.

Tenganan crafts are also sold in Ashitaba shops in Seminyak and Ubud.

ⓘ Getting There & Away

Tenganan is 3.2km up a side road just west of Candidasa. At the turn-off where bemos stop, motorcycle riders offer rides on *ojeks* (motorcycles that take passengers) to the village for about 15,000Rp. A nice option is to take an *ojek* up to Tenganan, and enjoy a shady downhill walk back to the main road, which has a Bali rarity: wide footpaths.

Mendira

Coming from the west, there are hotels and guesthouses well off the main road at Mendira, before you reach Candidasa. Although the beach has all but vanished and unsightly sea walls have been constructed, this area is a good choice for a quiet getaway if you have your own transport. Think views, breezes and a good book. A new footpath along the main road greatly improves the 2km walk east to Candidasa.

🛏 Sleeping & Eating

The following are on small tracks between the main road and the water; none are far from Candidasa but all have a sense of isola-

tion that makes them seem far from everywhere. They are reached via narrow roads from a single turn-off from the main road 1.5km west of Candidasa. Look for a large sign listing places to stay, a school and a huge banyan tree.

★ **Amarta Beach Cottages**   INN $
(☑ 0363-41230; www.amartabeachcottages.com; Jl Raya Mendira; r from 300,000Rp, villa from 700,000Rp; ✳@☎☀) In a panoramic and private seaside setting, the 16 rooms are right on the water and are good value. The more expensive ones have interesting open-air bathrooms; villas offer privacy. At low tide there is a tiny beach; at other times you can sit and enjoy the views out to Nusa Penida.

The **Sea Side Restaurant** (mains from 40,000Rp; ⊙8am-10pm) is a top choice for lunch whether you are staying here or not.

Candi Beach Resort   HOTEL $$
(☑ 0363-41234; www.candibeachbali.com; Jl Raya Mendira; r from US$90; ✳☎☀) The former Candi Beach Cottage has been given an upgrade to both its name and pool area. The latter has a nice beige stone look framed by the sea view and palm trees. The 64 rooms are comfortable, the individual bungalows cute. The much-lauded Bali Conservancy runs nature tours in conjunction with the hotel.

Anom Beach Inn   HOTEL $$
(☑ 0363-419024; www.anom-beach.com; Jl Raya Mendira; r US$40-60; ✳☎☀) This older resort from a simpler time has 24 rooms in a variety of configurations. The cheapest are fan-only – not a problem given the constant offshore breezes. The best are bungalow-style. Many loyal customers have been coming for years, ageing gracefully right along with the staff.

Candidasa

✓ 0363

Candidasa is a relaxed spot on the route east, with hotels and some decent restaurants. However, it also has problems stemming from decisions made three decades ago that should serve as cautionary notes to any previously undiscovered place that suddenly finds itself on the map.

Until the 1970s, Candidasa was just a quiet little fishing village, then beachside losmen (small Balinese hotels) and restaurants sprang up and suddenly it was *the* new beach sensation in Bali. As the facilities developed, the beach eroded – unthinkingly, offshore barrier-reef corals were harvested to produce lime for cement in the orgy of construction that took place – and by the late 1980s Candidasa was a beach resort with no beach.

Mining stopped in 1991, and concrete sea walls and breakwaters have limited the erosion and now provide some tiny pockets of sand. The relaxed seaside ambience and sweeping views from the hotels built right on the water appeal to a more mature crowd of visitors. Candidasa is a good base from which to explore the interior of east Bali on a walk; it's also a place to spend some quiet time.

◉ Sights

Pura Candidasa   HINDU TEMPLE
(Jl Raya Candidasa; admission by donation) Candidasa's temple is on the hillside across from the lagoon at the eastern end of the village strip. It has twin temples devoted to the male-female gods Shiva and Hariti.

🏃 Activities

Gili Tepekong, which has a series of coral heads at the top of a sheer drop-off, is perhaps the best local dive site. It offers the chance to see lots of fish, including some larger marine life, but it's recommended for experienced divers only.

Hotels rent snorkel sets for about 30,000Rp per day. For the best snorkelling, take a boat to offshore sites or to Gili Mimpang (a one-hour boat trip should cost about 100,000Rp for up to three people).

Dive Lite   DIVING
(✓ 0363-41660; www.divelite.com; Jl Raya Candidasa; dives from US$90) Dive Lite dives the local area plus the rest of the island. An 'intro to diving' course is an excellent deal: US$90 gets you a dive for basic instruction followed by a supervised fun dive. It's a great way to see if diving is for you. Snorkelling trips are US$30.

Alam Asmara Spa   SPA
(✓ 0363-41929; www.alamasmara.com; massage from 150,000Rp; ⊘ 9am-9pm) Candidasa's posh option is the Alam Asmara Spa at the hotel of the same name. Organic and natural products are used for a variety of traditional massages and treatments in a gently restful setting.

Ashram Gandhi Chandi   SPIRITUAL RETREAT
(✓ 0363-41108; www.ashramgandhi.com; Jl Raya Candidasa; s/d from 350,000/450,000Rp) This lagoon-side Hindu community follows the pacifist teachings of Mahatma Gandhi. Guests may stay for short or extended periods, but are expected to participate in community life. Simple guest cottages by the ocean are handy after a long day of yoga here.

👉 Tours

Apart from the Bali Aga village of Tenganan, there are several traditional villages inland from Candidasa and attractive countryside for walking.

★ Trekking Candidasa   WALKING TOUR
(✓ 0878 6145 2001; www.trekkingcandidasa.com; walks from 150,000Rp) The delightful Somat leads walks through the verdant hills behind Candidasa. One popular route takes 90 minutes and follows rice field paths to Tenganan.

Bali Conservancy   WALKING TOUR
(✓ 0822 3739 8415; www.bali-conservancy.com; walks from adult/child US$40/30) Offers good cultural and nature walks around east Bali, including the lush rice fields and the hills around beautiful Pasir Putih.

🛏 Sleeping

Candidasa's busy main drag is well supplied with seaside accommodation, as well as restaurants and other tourist facilities. Quieter places can be found east of the centre along Jl Pantai Indah. These are nicely relaxed and often have a sliver of beach. West of town also offers quiet lodging amid the flaccid lapping of the waves. Even quieter are the hotels 2km west in Mendira.

Candidasa

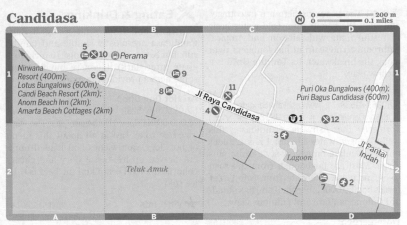

Candidasa

🛏 West of Candidasa

The following pair is a short walk from Candidasa.

Lotus Bungalows HOTEL $$
(☎ 0363-41104; www.lotusbungalows.com; off Jl Raya Candidasa; s/d from US$75/100; ❋@≋) Managed by earnest Europeans, the 20 rooms here (some with air-con) are in well-spaced, bungalow-style units. Four are right on the ocean. The decor is bright and airy, and there is a large and inviting pool area. It offers diving packages.

Nirwana Resort HOTEL $$
(☎ 0363-41136; www.thenirwana.com; off Jl Raya Candidasa; r US$90-200, villa from US$130; ❋@🛜≋) A dramatic walk across a lotus pond sets the tone at this intimate older resort that has been given a through update. The 18 units are near the infinity pool by the ocean. Go for one of six units right on the water.

🛏 Central Candidasa

Rama Shinta Hotel HOTEL $
(☎ 0363-41778; www.ramashintahotel.com; off Jl Raya Candidasa; r 400,000-600,000Rp; ❋🛜≋) On a little lane near the lagoon and ocean, the 15 rooms are split between a two-storey stone structure and bungalows. They've been nicely updated with outdoor bathrooms. Upstairs rooms have views of the lagoon and its birdlife.

Ari Home Stay GUESTHOUSE $
(☎ 0817 970 7339; garyv18@hotmail.com; Jl Raya Candidasa; r 150,000-300,000Rp; ❋🛜) Why go to Australia's Surfers Paradise when you can come here? The ebullient Gary and his family have created a place for a punter's holiday. Rooms ramble over the compound and range from cold-water with fans to air-con with hot water. Very cold beer is always available.

Seaside Cottages GUESTHOUSE $
(☎ 0363-41629; www.balibeachfront-cottages.com; Jl Raya Candidasa; cottages 150,000-470,000Rp;

✳ @ 🛜) The 15 rooms here are in cottages and span the gamut from cold-water basic to restful units with air-con and tropical bathrooms. The seafront has loungers right along the breakwater. Its **Temple Café** is a mellow place.

Bilik Bali   HOTEL **$$**
(📞 0363-41538;   www.ashyanacandidasa.com; Jl Raya Candidasa; r from US$80; ✳🛜❄) Formerly the Ashyana Candidasa, this well-managed waterside hotel has 12 older but immaculate bungalow-style units plus a spa. Most are far enough from the road to escape noise. The waterfront cafe **Lezat** (mains from 50,000Rp; ⊘ 8am-10pm) has standard Indonesian fare and fabulous views.

Watergarden   HOTEL **$$**
(📞 0363-41540; www.watergardenhotel.com; Jl Raya Candidasa; r from US$110; ✳🛜❄) The Watergarden boasts a swimming pool and fish-filled ponds that wind around the buildings. The gardens are lush and worth exploring. Each of the 13 rooms has a verandah projecting over the lily ponds, which are fresher than the somewhat dated interiors. Wi-fi is limited to the good **cafe**. Massages in the pretty **spa** are a mere 50,000Rp.

⌂ East of the Centre

A small road winds through banana trees passing several low-key lodgings that span the budget categories. This is the nicest area for lodging in Candidasa as you are less than 10 minutes by foot from the centre yet there is no traffic noise.

Puri Oka Beach Bungalows   GUESTHOUSE **$**
(📞 0363-41092; www.purioka.com; Jl Pantai Indah; r US$25-95; ✳🛜❄) Hidden by a banana grove east of town. The cheapest of the 17 rooms here are fan-cooled and small, while the better ones have water views. The beachside pool is small and is next to a cafe; at low tide there's a small beach out front. Two roomy bungalows are the pick here.

Puri Bagus Candidasa   HOTEL **$$$**
(📞 0363-41131; www.bagus-discovery.com; Jl Pantai Indah; r from US$130; ✳🛜❄) At the eastern end of the shore near an outcropping of outriggers, this mainstream resort is hidden away in the palm trees. The large pool and restaurant have good sea views; the beach is illusory. The 48 rooms have open-air bathrooms; look for deals.

✗ Eating & Drinking

The cafes and restaurants along Jl Raya Candidasa are mostly simple and family-run, but beware of traffic noise (which does abate after dark). If you're out of town, some places provide transport.

Ari Hot Dog Shop   FAST FOOD **$**
(📞 0817 975 5231; Jl Raya Candidasa; mains 25,000-50,000Rp; ⊘ 11am-8pm; 🛜) The sign 'rice-free zone' says it all about this menu of hot dogs, sandwiches and loaded burgers. Served up by Aussie Gary and cheery cohorts, the food is hot and the beer is cold, ice cold.

★ Vincent's   INTERNATIONAL **$$**
(📞 0363-41368; www.vincentsbali.com; Jl Raya Candidasa; meals 60,000-150,000Rp; ⊘ 8am-11pm; 🛜) One of east Bali's best restaurants has several distinct open-air rooms and a large and lovely rear garden with rattan furniture. The bar is an oasis of jazz. The menu combines excellent and inventive Balinese, fresh seafood and European dishes. The house selection of sambals is delicious.

Crazy Kangaroo   CAFE **$$**
(📞 0363-41996; Jl Raya Candidasa; mains 40,000-120,000Rp; ⊘ 8am-late) Wild by local standards, this cafe almost qualifies as a roadhouse (although a glass wall cuts down on traffic noise to the patio). The food from the open kitchen is good and mixes Western and local dishes with tasty seafood specials. There's a lively bar and blaring music.

ⓘ Information

Candidasa has many ATMs.

ⓘ Getting There & Away

Candidasa is on the main road between Amlapura and south Bali, but there's no terminal, so hail bemos as buses probably won't stop. You'll need to change in either Padangbai or Semarapura going west.

You can hire a ride to Amed in the far east for about 250,000Rp, and to Kuta and the airport for 300,000Rp. A driver, **I Nengah Suasih** (📞 0819 3310 5020; nengahsuasih@ yahoo.com), does day trips to Pasir Putih for 250,000Rp.

Ask at your accommodation about vehicle and bicycle rental.

Perama (📞 0363-41114; Jl Raya Candidasa; ⊘ 7am-7pm) is at the western end of the strip. Destinations include Kuta (60,000Rp, three hours), Sanur (60,000Rp, 2½ hours) and Ubud (50,000Rp, two hours).

Candidasa to Amlapura

The main road east of Candidasa curves up to **Pura Gamang Pass** (*gamang* means 'to get dizzy' – an overstatement), from where you'll find fine views down to the coast and lots of greedy-faced monkeys (who have become so prolific that they have stripped crops bare from here up the mountain to Tenganan). If you walk along the coastline from Candidasa towards Amlapura, a trail climbs up over the headland, with fine views over the rocky islets off the coast. Beyond this headland there's a long sweep of wide, exposed black-sand beach.

Pasir Putih

The most popular 'secret' beach on Bali, **Pasir Putih** (aka Dream Beach, aka Virgin Beach) is an idyllic white-sand beach whose name indeed means 'White Sand'. When we first visited in 2004, it was empty, save for a row of fishing boats at one end. Now it's an ongoing lab in seaside economic development.

A dozen thatched beach **warungs** and **cafes** now line the sand. You can get nasi goreng (fried rice) or grilled fish. Bintang is of course on ice and loungers await bikini-clad bottoms. The beach itself is truly lovely: a long crescent of white sand backed by coconut trees. At one end cliffs provide shade. The surf is often mellow; you can rent **snorkelling** gear to explore the waters.

The one thing saving Pasir Putih from being swamped is the difficult access. Look for crude signs with the various monikers near the village of Perasi. Turn off the main road (5.6km east of Candidasa) and follow a pretty paved track for about 1.5km to a temple, where locals will collect a fee (3000Rp per person). You can park here and walk the gentle hill down or drive a further 600m directly to the beach on a road that is barely passable (some say it's been kept rough so that people won't miss it too much when the inevitable resort gets built).

As for any qualms you might have about furthering the commercialisation of this beach, here's what the locals told us: 'The money you pay us for a ticket we spend on our school and medicine.'

Teluk Penyu

A little bend in the coast has earned the nickname Teluk Penyu, or Turtle Bay. The shelled critters do indeed come here to nest and there have been some efforts made to protect them. About 5km south of Amlapura, the area has attracted some expats and villas.

Turtle Bay Hideaway (✆0363-23611; www.turtlebayhideaway.com; Jl Raya Pura Mascime; cottages US$135-200; 🛜🏊) comprises a compound built from old wooden tribal houses brought over from Sulawesi. Three buildings together have five ocean-view rooms, near a large tiled pool. Interiors combine exotic details and modern comforts – there are fridges and organic food is served. There are enough shady verandahs, decks and loungers to keep you busy doing nothing for a week.

Amlapura

✆0363

Amlapura is the tidy capital of Karangasem district, and the main town and transport junction in eastern Bali. The smallest of Bali's district capitals, it's a multicultural place with Chinese shophouses, several mosques and confusing one-way streets. It's worth a stop to see the royal palaces.

◉ Sights

Amlapura's atmospheric palaces, on Jl Teuku Umar, are vintage reminders of Karangasem's period as a kingdom, at its most important when supported by Dutch colonial power in the late 19th and early 20th centuries.

Low-key guides offer helpful tours of both palaces for about 25,000Rp.

★**Puri Agung Karangasem**   PALACE
(Jl Teuku Umar; admission 10,000Rp; ⊙8am-5pm)
Outside the orderly Puri Agung Karangasem there are beautifully sculpted panels and an impressive multitiered **entry gate**. After you pass through the entry courtyard (all entrances point you towards the rising sun in the east), a left turn takes you to the main building, known as the **Maskerdam** (Amsterdam), because it was built as a gift by the Dutch as a reward for the Karangasem kingdom's acquiescence to Dutch rule. This allowed it to hang on long after the demise of other Balinese kingdoms.

Inside see several rooms, including the royal bedroom and a living room with furniture that was a gift from the Dutch royal family. The Maskerdam faces the ornately decorated Bale Pemandesan, which was used for royal tooth-filing ceremonies. Beyond this, surrounded by a pond, is the Bale Kambang, still used for family meetings and for dance practice.

Borrow one of the handy English-language info sheets and think about what this compound must have been like when the Karangasem dynasty was at its peak in the 19th century, having conquered Lombok. Don't miss the vintage photos.

Puri Gede PALACE
(Jl Teuku Umar; donation requested; ⊙8am-6pm) Across the street from Puri Agung Karangasem, Puri Gede is still used by the royal family. Surrounded by long walls, the palace grounds feature many brick buildings dating from the Dutch colonial period. Look for 19th-century stone carvings and woodcarvings. The **Rangki**, the main palace building, has been returned to its glory and is surrounded by fish ponds. Catch the stern portrait of the late king AA Gede Putu, while his descendents laughingly play soccer nearby.

✗ Eating & Shopping

Options are few in Amlapura; there is a good **night market** (⊙5pm-midnight). A vast **Hardy's Department Store** (☑0363-22363; Jl Diponegoro; ⊙8am-10pm) has groceries, sundries of all kinds, ATMs and a row of stalls cooking up good fresh Asian food fast. It has the best range of supplies, such as sunscreen, east of Semarapura and south of Singaraja.

❶ Getting There & Away

Amlapura is a major transport hub. Minibuses and bemos regularly ply the main road towards Denpasar's Batubulan terminal (25,000Rp, roughly three hours) via Candidasa, Padangbai and Gianyar. Plenty of minibuses also go around the north coast to Singaraja (about 20,000Rp) via Tirta Gangga, Amed and Tulamben.

Around Amlapura

Taman Ujung, 5km south of Amlapura, dates to 1921, when the last king of Karangasem completed the construction of a grand water palace here. Unfortunately it was mostly destroyed by a 1979 earthquake. The vast and bland replacement may leave you limp, as it somehow fails to impress despite its size.

However it is worth pushing on just a bit further past Taman Ujung to **Pantai Ujung** (Edge Beach), a rocky shoreline covered with boats from the nearby fishing village. Here you'll find one of the most exciting discoveries made in Bali recently: a 2m-long **penis-shaped rock** (*lingga*) that was exposed on the beach after a hard spell of storms. Locals attribute great power to the rock and it's now the scene of regular ceremonies. Experts have speculated that the stone is an ancient fertility symbol as there are signs of carving. And this has spawned additional speculation that a nearby large stone which somewhat resembles a *yoni* (the female counterpart of a *lingga*) may be a companion piece.

From Ujung, you can continue on the alternative road to Amed (see the boxed text, p208).

Tirta Gangga & Around
☑ 0363

Tirta Gangga (Water of the Ganges) is the site of a holy temple, some great water features and some of the best views of rice fields and the sea beyond in east Bali. Capping a sweep of green flowing down to the distant sea, it is a relaxing place to stop for an hour. With more time you can hike the surrounding terraced countryside, which ripples with coursing water and is dotted with temples. A small valley of rice terraces runs up the hill behind the parking area. It is a majestic vision of emerald steps receding into the distance.

◉ Sights

◉ Tirta Gangga

★**Taman Tirta Gangga** PALACE
(adult/child 10,000/5000Rp, parking 2000Rp; ⊙site 24hr, ticket office 6am-6pm) Amlapura's water-loving rajah, after completing his lost masterpiece at Ujung, had another go at building the water palace of his dreams in 1948. He succeeded at Taman Tirta Gangga, which has a stunning crescent of rice-terrace-lined hills for a backdrop.

This multilevel aquatic fantasy features two swimming ponds that are popular on weekends and ornamental water features filled with huge koi and lotus blossoms,

PURA LEMPUYANG

We swear, you'll thank us for this.

One of Bali's nine directional temples and the one responsible for the east, Pura Lempuyang is perched on a hilltop on the side of 1058m Gunung Lempuyang, a twin of neighbouring 1175m Gunung Seraya. Together, the pair form the distinctive double peaks of basalt that loom over Amlapura to the south and Amed to the north. The Lempuyang temple is part of a compact complex that looks across the mottled green patchwork that is east Bali. Its significance means there are always faithful Balinese in meditative contemplation and you may wish to join them as you recover from the one key detail of reaching the temple: the 1700-step climb up the side of the 768m hill.

Reaching the base of the stairs is about a 30-minute walk from Tirta Gangga. Take the turn south off the Amlapura–Tulamben road to Ngis (2km), a palm-sugar and coffee-growing area, and follow the signs another 2km to Kemuda (ask for directions if the signs confuse you). From Kemuda, climb those steps to Pura Lempuyang, allowing at least two hours, one way. If you want to continue to the peaks of Lempuyang or Seraya, you should take a guide.

---

which serve as a fascinating reminder of the old days of the Balinese rajahs. Look for the 11-tiered *meru* fountain and plop down under the huge old banyans and enjoy the views.

◉ Budakeling & Krotok

Budakeling, home to a Shiva-Buddhist community, dates back to at least the 15th century and is home to many artisans. From Tirta Gangga, Budakeling is a few kilometres southeast on the back road to Bebandem. It's a short drive or a pleasant three-hour walk through rice fields, via **Krotok**, home of traditional blacksmiths and silversmiths.

Tanah Aron, an imposing monument to the post-WWII resistance against the Dutch, is gloriously situated on the southeastern slopes of Gunung Agung. The road is quite good; you can also walk up and back in about six hours from Tirta Gangga.

🏃 Activities

Hiking in the surrounding hills transports you far from your memories of frenetic south Bali. This far east corner of Bali is alive with coursing streams through rice fields and tropical forests that suddenly open to reveal vistas taking in Lombok, Nusa Penida and the lush green surrounding lands stretching down to the sea. The rice terraces around Tirta Gangga are some of the most beautiful in Bali. Back roads and walking paths take you to many picturesque traditional villages.

Sights that make a perfect excuse for day treks are scattered in the surrounding hills. Or for the Full Bali, ascend the side of Gunung Agung. Among the possible treks is a six-hour loop to Tenganan village, plus shorter ones across the local hills, which include visits to remote temples and all the stunning vistas you can handle.

Guides for the more complex hikes are a good idea, as they help you plan routes and see things you simply would never find otherwise. Ask at any of the various accommodation options, especially Homestay Rijasa where the owner I Ketut Sarjana is one of several experienced guides. Another local who comes with good marks is **Komang Gede Sutama** (☑ 0813 3877 0893). Rates average about 75,000Rp per hour for one or two people.

★ **Bung Bung Adventure Biking** CYCLING (☑ 0363-21873, 0813 3840 2132; bungbung bikeadventure@gmail.com; Tirta Gangga; tours from 300,000Rp) Ride downhill through the simply gorgeous rice fields, terraces and river valleys around Tirta Gangga with this locally owned tour company. Itineraries last from two to four hours and include use of a mountain bike and helmet plus water. The office is close to Homestay Rijasa, across from the Tirta Gangga entrance. Book in advance.

🛏 Sleeping & Eating

You can overnight in luxury in old royal quarters overlooking the water palace or lodge in humble surrounds in anticipation of an early morning trek. Many places to stay have cafes with mains for about 20,000Rp; sedate fruit vendors surround the shady parking area.

🛏 Tirta Gangga

Homestay Rijasa HOMESTAY $
(📞0813 5300 5080, 0363-21873; JI Tirta Gangga;
r 100,000-300,000Rp; 🛜) With elaborately
planted grounds, this well-run nine-room
homestay is a recommended choice opposite the water palace entrance. Better rooms
have hot water, good for the large soaking
tubs. The owner, I Ketut Sarjana, is an experienced trekking guide. It has a warung
in front.

Good Karma HOMESTAY $
(📞0363-22445; goodkarma.tirtagangga@gmail.
com; JI Tirta Gangga; r 150,000-250,000Rp; 🛜) A
classic homestay, Good Karma has four very
clean and simple bungalows and a good vibe
derived from the surrounding pastoral rice
field. The recommended **cafe** (mains from
35,000Rp; ⊙8am-10pm) has gazebos that are
the setting for fine meals, including good
tempe sate.

Tirta Ayu Hotel HOTEL $$
(📞0363-22503; www.hoteltirtagangga.com; Pura
Tirta Gangga; villas US$125-200; ❄🛜🏊) Right
in the palace compound, this hotel has two
pleasant villas and three rooms that have a
vaguely royal decor. Enjoy the hotel's private
pool or use the vast palace facilities. The
restaurant (mains from 50,000Rp; ⊙7am-9pm)
is a tad upscale and serves creative takes on
local classics, which come with great water
palace views.

**Tirta Gangga
Villas** VILLA $$$
(📞0363-21383; www.tirtagangga-villas.com; Pura
Tirta Gangga; villas US$120-250; 🏊) Built on the
same terrace as the Tirta Ayu Hotel, the two
villas here are part of the old royal palace.
Thoroughly updated – but still possessing
that classic Bali-style motif – they look out
over the water palace from large shady
porches. You can rent the entire complex
and preside over your own court under a
500-year-old banyan tree.

Genta Bali INDONESIAN $
(📞0363-22436; JI Tirta Gangga; meals 15,000-
25,000Rp; ⊙8am-9pm) Across the road from
the parking area; you can find a fine homemade yoghurt lassi here, as well as pasta and
Indonesian food. Try out the house-made
black-rice wine.

🛏 Around Tirta Gangga

⭐**Side by Side Organic Farm** HOMESTAY $
(📞0812 3623 3427; http://sites.google.com/site/
sidebysidefarmorg/; Dausa; r from 150,000Rp) Set
amid lush rice fields near Tirta Gangga in
the tiny village of Dausa, Side by Side Organic Farm serves bounteous and delicious
buffet lunches (from 120,000Rp). Meals use
organic foods grown in the village farms.
Call at least one day before for directions
and to book lunch.

You can also arrange to stay in one of the
serene and traditional private Balinese *bale*
overlooking fish ponds. The farm is a unique
enterprise that works with the local community to raise crops with added value that will
increase incomes in what has always been
one of Bali's poorer areas.

ℹ Getting There & Away
Bemos and minibuses making the east-coast
haul between Amlapura (7000Rp) and Singaraja
stop at Tirta Gangga, which is 6km northwest of
Amlapura.

Tirta Gangga to Amed
The main road running from Amlapura
through Tirta Gangga and on to Amed and
the coast doesn't do the local attractions justice – although it is an attractive road. To appreciate things, you need to get off the main
road or go hiking.

Throughout the area the *rontal* palms all
look like new arrivals at army boot camp, as
they are shorn of their leaves as fast as they
grow them in order to meet the demand for
inscribed *lontar* books.

Amed & the Far East Coast
📞0363
Stretching from Amed to Bali's far eastern
tip, this semi-arid coast draws visitors with
its succession of small, scalloped, grey-sand
beaches (some more rocks than sand), relaxed atmosphere and excellent diving and
snorkelling.

The coast here is often called simply
'Amed' but this is a misnomer, as the coast
is a series of seaside *dusun* (small villages)
that starts with the actual Amed in the north
and then runs southeast to Aas. If you're
looking to get away from crowds, this is the

place to come and try some yoga. Everything is spread out, so you never feel like you're in the middle of anything much except maybe one of the small fishing villages.

Traditionally this area has been quite poor, with thin soils, low rainfall and very limited infrastructure. Salt production is still carried out on the beach at Amed. Villages further east rely on fishing, and colourful *jukung* (traditional boats) line up on every available piece of beach. Inland, the steep hillsides are generally too dry for rice – corn, peanuts and vegetables are the main crops.

🏃 Activities

Diving & Snorkelling

Snorkelling is excellent along the coast. Jemeluk is a protected area where you can admire live coral and plentiful fish within 100m of the beach. There are a few bits of wood remaining from a **sunken Japanese fishing boat** at Banyuning – just offshore from Eka Purnama bungalows – and coral gardens and colourful marine life at Selang. Snorkelling equipment rents for about 30,000Rp per day.

Diving is also good, with dive sites off Jemeluk, Lipah and Selang featuring coral slopes and drop-offs with soft and hard corals, and abundant fish. Some are accessible from the beach, while others require a short boat ride. The *Liberty* wreck at Tulamben is only a 20-minute drive away.

Several dive operators have shown a commitment to the communities by organising regular beach clean-ups and educating locals on the need for conservation. All have similar prices for a long list of offerings (eg local dives from about US$80 and open-water dive courses are about US$400).

Eco-Dive   DIVING
(☑0363-23482; www.ecodivebali.com; Jemeluk Beach; 🛜) 🍃 Full-service shop with simple,

cheap accommodation for clients. Has led the way on environmental issues.

Euro Dive   DIVING
(☑0363-23605; www.eurodivebali.com; Lipah; 🛜) 🍃 Has a large facility and offers packages with hotels. It wins praise for its guided trips. Offers shore diving to the sunken Japanese fishing boat for US$40.

Jukung Dive   DIVING
(☑0363-23469; www.jukungdivebali.com; Amed; 🛜) 🍃 Pushes its eco-credentials and has a dive pool. Also has bungalows for dive packages.

Trekking

Quite a few trails go inland from the coast, up the slopes of **Gunung Seraya** (1175m) and to some little-visited villages. The countryside is sparsely vegetated and most trails are well defined, so you won't need a guide for shorter walks – if you get lost, just follow a ridge-top back down to the coast road. Allow a good three hours to get to the top of Seraya, starting from the rocky ridge just east of Jemeluk Bay; ask for directions. Sunrise is spectacular and requires a climb in the dark; ask at your hotel about a guide.

Other

Apneista   YOGA, WATER SPORTS
(☑0812 3826 7356; www.apneista.com; Jemeluk; 90min yoga class 100,000Rp; ⊘8.30am-10pm) A one-stop shop for New Age enjoyment and adventure: this excellent cafe also has yoga classes, runs a freediving course, rents stand-up paddle boards and more.

🛏 Sleeping

The Amed region is very spread out, so take this into consideration when choosing accommodation. If you want to venture to restaurants beyond your hotel's own, you may have to find transport.

ⓘ DECODING AMED

The entire 10km stretch of far east coast is often called 'Amed' by both tourists and marketing-minded locals. Most development at first was around three bays with fishing villages: **Jemeluk**, which has a buzzy travellers strip; **Banutan**, with both a beach and headlands; and **Lipah**, which has a lively mix of cafes and commerce. Development has marched onwards through tiny **Lehan**, **Selang**, **Banyuning** and **Aas**, each a minor oasis at the base of the dry, brown hills. To appreciate the narrow band of the coast, stop at the **lookout** at Jemeluk, where you can see fishing boats lined up like a riot of multi-hued sardines on the beach.

Besides the main road via Tirta Gangga, you can also approach the Amed area from the Aas end in the south (see the boxed text, p208).

EAST BALI AMED & THE FAR EAST COAST

Amed & the Far East Coast

Amed & the Far East Coast

You will also need to choose between staying in the little beachside villages or on the sunny and dry headlands connecting the inlets. The former puts you right on the sand and offers a small amount of community life while the latter gives you broad, sweeping vistas and isolation.

Accommodation can be found in every price category; there's a crop of new simple budget places right in Amed village. Almost every place has a restaurant or cafe. Places with noteworthy dining are indicated in the listings.

🛏 Amed Village

Amed Stop Inn   HOMESTAY $

(📞 0817 473 8059; im.stop@yahoo.co.id; Amed Village; r from 200,000Rp) Right in Amed village, this homestay has two simple rooms that are close to the beach. There are numerous

walks in the surrounding rice fields and into the temple-dotted hills. The owners are charmers and are experienced guides. There are several other good choices nearby.

🛏 Jemeluk

You might say what's now called Amed started here.

Hoky Home Stay & Cafe   HOMESTAY $

(📞 0819 1646 3701; madejoro@yahoo.com; Jemeluk; r 200,000Rp; 🖾) Great cheap rooms (fan and hot water) at this place near the beach. The owner, Made, is tuned in to budget traveller needs. The **cafe** (mains 25,000Rp; ◷ 8am-10pm) has fresh and creative local foods, especially seafood.

Sama Sama Cafe & Bungalows   HOMESTAY $

(📞 0813 3738 2945; samasama_amed@yahoo.co.id; Jemeluk; r 300,000-400,000Rp; 🖫🖾)

Choose from a cold-water room with fan or something more posh (hot water and air-conditioning) in one of six bungalows here; there's also a good seafood **cafe** (mains from 50,000Rp; ⊘8am-9pm) across from the beach. The family here is often busy making offerings.

Galang Kangin Bungalows GUESTHOUSE **$**
(✓0363-23480; bali_amed_gk@yahoo.co.jp; Jemeluk; r 300,000Rp-600,000Rp; ❋ 🛜) Set on the hill side of the road amid a nice garden, the 10 rooms mix and match fans, cold water, hot water and air-con. The beach is right over the pavement, as is the cafe.

🛏 Banutan Beach

This is a classic little village with a swathe of sand and fishing boats between arid headlands.

Aiona Garden of Health GUESTHOUSE **$**
(✓0813 3816 1730; www.aionabali.com; Banutan Beach; s/d from €20/25) 🗲 This characterful place has enough signs outside that it qualifies as a roadside attraction. The simple bungalows are shaded by mango trees, which contribute to the uberhealthy menu. You can partake of organic potions and lotions, and classes in yoga, meditation, tarot reading etc. Your inner peace might improve with the high-fibre diet.

A small **shell museum** (⊘2pm-4pm) boasts that no bivalves died in its creation.

★Santai HOTEL **$$**
(✓0363-23487; www.santaibali.com; Banutan Beach; r US$80-150; ❋ 🛜⊠) This lovely option is on a slight hill down to the beach. The name means 'relax' and that's just what you'll do. A series of authentic traditional thatched bungalows gathered from around the archipelago hold 10 rooms with four-poster beds, open-air bathrooms and big balcony sofas. A swimming pool, fringed by purple bougainvillea, snakes through the property.

🛏 Banutan

These places are on a sun-drenched, arid stretch of highland. Most are on sloping hillsides and spill down to the water.

Wawa-Wewe II HOTEL **$$**
(✓0363-23522; www.bali-wawawewe.com; Banutan; s/d from 300,000/400,000Rp; ❋ 🛜⊠) From the headlands, this restful place has 10 bungalow-style rooms on lush grounds that shamble down to the water's edge. The natural-stone infinity pool is shaped like a Buddha and is near the water, as are two rooms with fine ocean views.

Anda Amed Resort HOTEL **$$**
(✓0363-23498; www.andaamedresort.com; villa US$90-150; ❋❋⊠) This whitewashed hillside hotel contrasts with its lushly green grounds. The infinity pool is an ahhh-inducing classic of the genre and has sweeping views of the sea from well above the road. There are nine rooms in four villas and lots of posh details such as deep soaking tubs, fridges and other niceties.

Puri Wirata HOTEL **$$**
(✓0363-23523; www.puriwirata.com; Banutan; r US$50-80, villa US$60-240; ❋🛜⊠) The most mainstream Amed choice, this 30-room resort with two pools has rooms ambling down the hill to the rocky ribbon at the waterline. Choices include rooms, bungalows and villas. Service is professional and there are many dive packages on offer.

🛏 Lipah

This village is just large enough for you to go wandering – briefly.

Double One Villas GUESTHOUSE **$**
(✓0363-22427; www.doubleonevillasamed.com; Lipah; r 300,000-600,000Rp; ❋🛜⊠) This charming guesthouse is split in two: cheaper rooms are on the hill side of the road, nicer ones are on the ocean side. There are six rooms running down a fairly steep hill to the pebbly shore where there's a small pool. The waterfront rooms are a good deal, although you'll get to know the stairs.

Coral View Villas HOTEL **$$**
(www.coralviewvillas.com; Lipah; r from US$90; ❋🛜⊠) Lush ground surrounding a naturalistic pool set this tidy property apart from other more arid places. The 19 rooms are in bungalow-style units and have nice terraces outside; inside, the rooms are large and there are stone-lined open-air bathrooms.

🛏 Lehan

Quiet, beachy Lehan has some of Amed's nicest boutique-style accommodation.

Life in Amed INN **$$**
(✓0363-23152, 0813 3850 1555; www.lifebali.com; Lehan; r US$70-90, villa US$120-140; ❋🛜⊠) Life

AMED, THE LONG WAY

Typically travellers bound for the coast of **Amed** travel the inland route through Tirta Gangga. However, there is a longer, twistier and more adventurous road much less travelled that runs from **Ujung** right around the coast to the Amed area. The road climbs up the side of the twin peaks of Seraya and Lempuyang, and the views out to sea are breathtaking. Along the way it passes through numerous small villages where people are carving fishing boats, bathing in streams or simply standing a bit slack-jawed at the appearance of *tamu* (visitors or foreigners). Don't be surprised to see a pig, goat or boulder on the road. After the lush east, it's noticeably drier here and the people's existence thinner; corn replaces rice as the staple.

About 10km east of Amalapura, you'll pass **Villa Arjuna** (☑ 0813 3897 7140; www.villa-bali.nl; s/d from €28/55; ☀), a large Dutch-owned seaside compound with eight very nice rooms and a pool right on the rocky shoreline.

Near **Seraya** (which has a cute market) look for weavers and cotton-fabric-makers. For long stretches, you'll drive through fruit-filled orchards and thick greenery. About 4km south of **Aas** there's a lighthouse.

The road is narrow but paved, and covering the 35km to Aas will take about one hour without stops. Combine this with the inland road through Tirta Gangga for a good circular visit to Amed from the west.

here is posh. Six bungalow-style units are in a compact compound around a sinuous pool; two villas are directly on the beach. Bathrooms are open-air works of art, created from beach stones.

★**Palm Garden** HOTEL **$$$**
(☑ 0828 9769 1850; www.palmgardenamed.com; Lehan; r US$110-250; ☀@☎) This oceanfront villa hotel verges on the elegant. Certainly it has the best beach in Amed, and the 10 units have large patios, the grounds are lined with palm trees, including one growing from its own island in the pool. There's a two-night minimum stay here.

Selang

Blue Moon Villas GUESTHOUSE **$$**
(☑ 0817 4738 100; www.bluemoonvilla.com; Selang; r from €65-145; ☀☎☀) On the hillside across the road from the cliffs, Blue Moon is a small and upmarket place, complete with three pools. The rooms are set in villa-style buildings and have open-air stone bathrooms. Rooms can be combined into larger multibedroom suites. The **restaurant** (mains from 50,000Rp; ⊘8am-10pm) serves good Balinese classics and grilled seafood.

Banyuning

By Banyuning you've left much of Amed's tourist hoopla behind.

Baliku HOTEL **$$**
(☑ 0828 372 2601; www.amedbaliresort.com; Banyuning; r from US$100; ☀☎☀) Large villa-style units are among the attractions at this hillside resort overlooking a pretty bit of Amed coast, where you often see fishing boats flying their brightly coloured sails. King-size beds and separate dressing areas and terraces primed for meals make for good retreats. There are Mediterranean accents throughout including on the restaurant's menu.

Aas

Once you've reached Aas, hole up for a spell and give your behind a rest.

★**Meditasi** GUESTHOUSE **$**
(☑ 0828 372 2738; www.meditasibungalows.blogspot.com; Aas; r 300,000-500,000Rp) Get off the grid and take a respite from the pressures of life at this chilled-out and charming hideaway. Meditation and yoga help you relax, and the eight rooms are close to good swimming and snorkelling. Open-air baths allow you to count the colours of the bougainvillea and frangipani that grow in profusion.

✖ Eating & Drinking

As noted, most places to stay have cafes. Ones worth seeking out are listed here.

★**Apneista Cafe** CAFE **$**
(☑ 0812 3826 7356; www.apneista.com; Jemeluk; mains from 35,000Rp; ⊘8.30am-10pm; ☑) After

you've chilled out, chill out some more. This excellent cafe has a good organic vegetarian menu, with many specials. There is a wide range of coffees, teas and juices. Sit at a table inside or on loungers outside. This is also a hub for yoga and other activities; evenings can features lectures and movies.

★ **Warung Enak**   BALINESE $
(✆0819 1567 9019; Jemeluk; mains from 20,000Rp; ◷8am-10pm) Black rice pudding and other less-common local treats are the specialties of this dead simple and super-tasty little eatery. The open-fronted dining area is nearly hidden by a tree, but diner's smiles seem to shine right through.

Cafe Garam   INDONESIAN $
(✆0363-23462; Hotel Uyah Amed, Amed; meals 20,000-50,000Rp; ◷8am-10pm) There's a re-laxed feel here, with pool tables and Balinese food plus the lyrical and haunting melodies of live *genjek* (traditional Balinese percussion music) at 8pm on Wednesday and Saturday. *Garam* means salt and the cafe honours the local salt-making industry. Try the *salada ayam,* an addictive mix of cabbage, grilled chicken, shallots and tiny peppers. The adjoining Hotel Uyah Amed is a good option.

Smiling Buddha Restaurant   ORGANIC $
(✆0828 372 2738; Aas; meals from 30,000Rp; ◷8am-10pm; ✎) The restaurant at this high-ly recommended guesthouse has excellent organic fare, much sourced from its own garden. Balinese and Western dishes are ex-cellent and there are good views out to sea. It even manages some full moon fun. Happy hour is 7pm to 8pm.

Wawa-Wewe I   BAR
(✆0363-23506; Lipah; ◷8am-late; ☏) You won't know your wawas from your wewes if you spend the evening here trying the lo-cal *arak* (fermented spirit) made with palm fronds. This is the coast's most raucous bar – which by local standards means that sometimes it gets sorta loud. Local bands jam on many nights. Meals are served (from 30,000Rp) and it also has budget rooms.

❶ Information

You may be charged a tourist tax to enter the area. Enforcement of a 5000Rp per-person fee at a tollbooth on the outskirts of Amed is spo-radic. ATMs remain thin on the ground. Wi-fi is nearly universal.

WORKING IN THE SALT BRINE

For a different day at the beach, try making some salt. You start by carrying, say, 500L of ocean water across the sand to bamboo and wood funnels, which filter the water after it is poured in. Next the water goes into a *palungan* (shallow trough), made of palm-tree trunks split in half and hollowed out, or cement canisters where it evaporates, leaving salt behind. And that's just the start, and just what you might see in Kusamba or on the beach in Amed.

In the volcanic areas around the east coast between Sanur and Yeh Sanih in the north, a range of salt-making methods is used. What is universal is that the work is hard, but is also an essential source of income for many families.

In some places the first step is drying sand that has been saturated with sea water. It's then taken inside a hut, where more sea water is strained through it to wash out the salt. This very salty water is then poured into a *palungan*. Hundreds of these troughs are lined up in rows along the beaches during salt-making season (the dry season), and as the sun evaporates the water, the almost-dry salt is scraped out and put in baskets. There are good exhibits on this method at the Museum Semarajaya (p186) in Semarapura.

Most salt produced on the coast of Bali is used for processing dried fish. And that's where Amed has an advantage: although its method of making salt results in a lower yield than that using sand, its salt is prized for its flavour. In fact, there is a fast-growing market for this 'artisan salt' worldwide.

Visitors to the Amed area can learn all about this fascinating process at Cafe Garam. Many of the staff here also work in salt production (ask about tours) and you can buy small bags of the precious stuff (10,000Rp) for a tiny fraction of what it costs once it reaches your local gourmet market.

❶ Getting There & Around

Most people drive here via the main highway from Amlapura and Culik. The spectacular road going all the way around the twin peaks from Aas to Ujung makes a good circle (see the boxed text, p208).

You can arrange for a driver and car to/from south Bali and the airport for about 500,000Rp.

Public transport is difficult. Minibuses and bemos between Singaraja and Amlapura pass through Culik, the turn-off for the coast. Infrequent bemos go from Culik to Amed (3.5km), and some continue to Seraya until 1pm. Fares average 7000Rp.

You can also charter transport from Culik for a negotiable 50,000Rp (by *ojek* is less than half). Specify which hotel you wish to go to – agree on 'Amed' and you could come up short in Amed village.

Amed Sea Express (☑ 0878 6306 4799; www.gili-sea-express.com; Jemeluk; per person from 300,000Rp) makes crossings to Gili Trawangan on an 80-person speedboat in under an hour.

Kubu Region

Driving along the main road you will pass through vast old lava flows from Gunung Agung down to the sea. The landscape is strewn with a moonscape of boulders, and is nothing like the lush rice paddies elsewhere.

Tulamben

☑ 0363
The big attraction here sunk over 60 years ago. The wreck of the US cargo ship *Liberty* is among the best and most popular dive sites in Bali and this has given rise to an entire town based on scuba diving. Even

---

THE WRECK OF THE LIBERTY

In January 1942 the small US Navy cargo ship USAT *Liberty* was torpedoed by a Japanese submarine near Lombok. Taken in tow, it was beached at Tulamben so that its cargo of rubber and railway parts could be saved. The Japanese invasion prevented this and the ship sat on the beach until the 1963 eruption of Gunung Agung broke it in two and left it just off the shoreline, much to the delight of scores of divers. (And just for the record, it was *not* a Liberty-class WWII freighter.)

---

snorkellers can easily swim out and enjoy the wreck and the coral.

But if you don't plan to explore the briny waves, don't expect to hang out on the beach either. The shore is made up of rather beautiful, large washed stones, the kind that cost a fortune at a DIY store.

For nonaquatic delights, check out the **morning market** in Tulamben village, 1.5km north of the dive site.

✹ Activities

Diving and **snorkelling** are the reason Tulamben exists.

The **shipwreck** *Liberty* is about 50m directly offshore from Puri Madha Bungalows (where you can park); look for the schools of black snorkels. Swim straight out and you'll see the stern rearing up from the depths, heavily encrusted with coral and swarming with dozens of species of colourful fish – and with scuba divers most of the day. The ship is more than 100m long, but the hull is broken into sections and it's easy for divers to get inside. The bow is in quite good shape, the midship's region is badly mangled and the stern is almost intact – the best parts are between 15m and 30m deep. You will want at least two dives to really explore the wreck.

Many divers commute to Tulamben from Candidasa or Lovina, and in busy times it can get quite crowded between 11am and 4pm, with 50 or more divers at a time around the wreck. Stay the night in Tulamben or in nearby Amed and get an early start.

Most hotels have their own diving centre, and some offer good-value packages if you dive with them as well.

Expect to pay from US$80 for two dives at Tulamben, and a little more for night dives around Amed. Snorkelling gear is rented everywhere for 30,000Rp.

Note that there is now a privately run parking area (10,000Rp) behind Tauch Terminal. There are gear-rental stands, vendors, porters and more here ready to get your attention. There are also pay-showers and toilets. You can still park for free by Puri Madha Beach Bungalows.

Tauch Terminal   DIVING
(☑ 0363-22911, 0363-774504; www.tauch-terminal.com; unlimited diving 24hr €120) Among the many dive operators, Tauch Terminal is one of the longest-established operators in Bali. A four-day PADI open-water certificate course costs from €325.

🛏 Sleeping & Eating

Tulamben is a quiet place, and is essentially built around the wreck – the hotels, all with cafes and many with dive shops, are spread along a 4km stretch either side of the main road. You have your choice of roadside (cheaper) or by the water (nicer). At high tide even the rocky shore vanishes.

Matahari Tulamben Resort HOTEL $
(📞 0859 3835 4762; www.divetulamben.com; r with fan/air-con from 185,000/250,000Rp; ❄️ 🛜 🏊) This modest 18-room hotel has a very loyal following of divers, many of whom stay for weeks at a time, only coming up for air to crash in one of the very clean rooms. It has a narrow section of waterfront south of the wreck. There's a spa and small cafe with ocean views.

Dive Concepts GUESTHOUSE $
(📞 0812 3684 5440; www.diveconcepts.com; dm 50,000Rp, r 100,000-350,000Rp; ❄️ 🛜) A great place to meet other divers, this busy shop has 12 rooms in a variety of flavours (from cold-water-fan to hot-water-air-con), including six-bed dorms. There are BBQ and film nights.

Deep Blue Studio GUESTHOUSE $
(📞 0363-22919; www.subaqua.cz; r US$28-45; 🛜 🏊) Owned by Czechs, this dive operation has 10 rooms in two-storey buildings on the hill side of the road. It's an attractive place and is well set up for dive classes and chilling out after a day in the depths. Rooms have fans and balconies. There is a variety of packages with the affiliated dive shop.

⭐ Puri Madha Beach Bungalows HOTEL $$
(📞 0363-22921; www.purimadhabeachhotel. weebly.com; r 500,000-600,000Rp; ❄️ 🛜 🏊) Re-styled bungalow-style units are directly opposite the *Liberty* site on shore. The best of the 21 rooms have air-con and hot water. The spacious grounds feel like a public park and there is a swish pool area overlooking the ocean. You can't beat getting out of bed and swimming right out to a famous shipwreck.

⭐ Liberty Dive Resort HOTEL $$
(📞 0363-23347; www.libertydiveresort.com; r US$45-75; ❄️ 🛜 🏊) Just 100m up the hill from the rocky shore in front of the wreck, this 20-room resort has a great open feel and a very nice pool. Rooms come in various levels of comfort but all are modern, clean and large. Some 2nd-floor rooms have sea views.

ℹ Information

There are ATMs and convenience stores.

ℹ Getting There & Away

Plenty of buses and bemos travel between Amlapura and Singaraja and will stop anywhere along the Tulamben road, but they're infrequent after 2pm. Expect to pay 12,000Rp to either town.

If you are driving to Lovina for the night, be sure to leave by about 3pm so you'll still have a little light when you get there.

If you're just going to snorkel the wreck and are day-tripping with a driver, don't let them park at a dive shop away from the wreck where you'll get a commission-paying sales pitch.

Tulamben to Yeh Sanih

North of Tulamben, the road continues to skirt the slopes of Gunung Agung, with frequent evidence of lava flows from the 1963 eruption. Further around, the outer crater of Gunung Batur slopes steeply down to the sea. The rainfall is low and you can generally count on sunny weather. The scenery is very stark in the dry season and it's a thinly populated area.

There are regular markets in **Kubu**, a roadside village about 5km northwest of Tulamben.

At **Les**, a road goes inland to the impressive **Air Terjun Yeh Mampeh** (Yeh Mampeh Waterfall; adult/child 20,000/10,000Rp), at 40m one of Bali's highest and least visited. Look for a large sign on the main road and then turn inland for about 2.5km over a road that is steadily being improved by the local communties in hopes of luring tourists. Walk the last 600m or so on a good path by the stream, shaded by rambutan and various other fruit trees. Guides – not needed for Yeh Mepeh – can take you to even more remote watefalls.

The next main town is **Tejakula**, famous for its stream-fed public bathing area, said to have been built for washing horses and often called the 'horse bath'. The renovated bathing areas (separate for men and women) are behind walls topped by rows of elaborately decorated arches, and are regarded as a sacred area. The baths are 100m inland on a narrow road with lots of small shops – it's a quaint village, with some finely carved *kulkul* towers. Take a stroll above the baths, past irrigation channels flowing in all directions.

HELPING BALI'S FORGOTTEN

Long the poorest region of Bali, the arid lands far up the northeast slopes of Gunung Agung were so poor for so long that as recently as the 1990s government bureaucrats wouldn't even admit that people lived there. Diseases from malnutrition were common, education was nil and incomes were under US$30 a year. It was poverty at its worst on an island that already 20 years ago was experiencing an economic boom from tourism.

Amazingly, this bleak scene no longer exists and although it sounds like a cliché, the efforts of one man, David Booth, are responsible. Irascible, idiosyncratic and relentless, the British-born Booth turned his engineering background on the region (which extends from the tiny village of Ban), starting in the 1990s. A tireless organiser, he rallied the locals, badgered the government, charmed donors and turned his **East Bali Poverty Project** (☑0361-410071; www.eastbalipovertyproject.org) into a powerful force of change.

There are schools, electricity, clinics and a sense of accomplishment that have liberated the people from their past. Now moving into a sustainable phase of development, the project has built the **Bamboo Centre** in the hamlet of Daya. It shows the possibilities for bamboo as a renewable resource. The now-supportive Balinese government has greatly improved a road running over the mountain from a point near Pura Besakih, all the way down to the coast at Tianyar, 20km northwest of Tulamben. If you're not worried about getting lost, exploring this area can make for a fascinating day's outing. There may not be anyone at the centre, but if there is, the welcome is warm.

At Pacung, about 10km before Yeh Sanih, you can turn inland 4km to **Sembiran**, a Bali Aga village, although it doesn't promote itself as such. The most striking thing about the place is its hillside location and brilliant coastal views.

🛏 Sleeping & Eating

Bali's remote northeast coast has a growing number of resorts where you can indeed get away from it all. These are places to settle in for a few days and revive your senses. Getting here from the airport or south Bali can take three hours or more via two routes: one up and over the mountains via Kintamani and then down a rustic, scenic road to the sea near Tejakula; the other going right round east Bali on the coast road via Candidasa and Tulamben.

Bali Sandat Guest House GUESTHOUSE $
(☑0813 3772 8680; www.bali-sandat.com; Bondalem; r from €30; 🛜) You'll feel like you're staying with friends at this low-key guesthouse located deep in a waterfront palm forest in a remote part of east Bali. The four rooms have open-air cold-water bathrooms and deep and shady verandahs. Balinese dinners are available. The village of Bondalem is a 1km walk away and has a simple morning market and a weaving workshop.

Segara Lestari Villa GUESTHOUSE $
(☑0815 5806 8811; Les; r from 310,000Rp; ❄) It doesn't get any simpler than this: four bungalows right on the ocean. There's hot water and air-con, though the shore breezes obviate the need to use the air-con. Use the kitchen or your hosts can cook you meals.

★**Alam Anda** HOTEL $$
(☑0812 465 6485; www.alamanda.de; Sambirenteng; r €45-110; ❄🛜) The striking tropical architecture at this oceanside resort, near Sambirenteng, is the creation of the German architect-owner. A reef just offshore keeps the dive shop busy. The 28 units come in various sizes, from losmen rooms to cottages with views. All have artful thatch and bamboo motifs. The resort is 1km north of Poinciana Resort, roughly between Kubu and Tejakula.

Spa Village Resort Tembok HOTEL $$$
(☑0362-32033; www.spavillage.com; Tembok; full board d from US$260; ❄@🛜❄) When you arrive at this 31-room oceanfront resort, you sign up for extensive spa treatments and daily activities geared to your inner rejuvination. Or course, improvements here are rather luxurious. Meals are healthful and focus on simple, local ingredients. It's northwest of Tembok.

Central Mountains

Best Places to Eat

➜ Pulu Mujung Warung (p217)
➜ Strawberry Hill (p220)
➜ Ada Babi Guleng (p225)
➜ Puri Lumbung Cottages (p224)

Best Places to Stay

➜ Puri Lumbung Cottages (p224)
➜ Sarinbuana Eco Lodge (p226)
➜ Lakeview Eco Lodge (p217)
➜ Bali Mountain Retreat (p227)
➜ Sanda Boutique Villas (p227)

Why Go?

Bali has a hot soul. The volcanoes stretching along the island's spine are seemingly cones of silence but their active spirits are just below the surface, eager for expression.

Gunung Batur (1717m) is constantly letting off steam; this place has an other-worldly beauty that may overwhelm the attendant hassles of a visit. At Danau Bratan there are sacred Hindu temples while the village of Candikuning has an engrossing botanic garden.

The old colonial village of Munduk, a hiking centre, has views down the hills to the coast of north Bali, which match the beauty of the many nearby waterfalls, and Danaus Tamblingan and Buyan. In the shadow of Gunung Batukau (2276m) you'll find one of Bali's most mystic temples. And, just south, the Unesco-listed ancient rice terraces around Jatiluwih dazzle.

Amid it all, little roads lead to untouched villages. Start driving north from Antosari for one surprise after another.

When to Go

➜ **Year-round** Bali's central mountains can be cool and misty throughout the year. They also get a lot of rain, and this is the starting point for the water that courses through rice terraces and fields all the way south. Temperatures show few seasonal variations but can drop to 10°C at night at high elevations.

➜ **Oct-Apr** It rains most in these months, but can pour any time throughout the year.

➜ **Jul-Aug** There's no peak tourist season, except for the hordes that hit the Kintamani area in these months.

GUNUNG BATUR AREA

🔊 0366

The Gunung Batur area is like a giant bowl, with its bottom half covered by water and a set of volcanic cones jutting out of the middle. Sound a bit spectacular? It is. On clear days – vital to appreciating the spectacle – the turquoise waters wrap around the newer volcanoes, which have old lava flows oozing down their sides.

In 2012 Unesco honoured the area by adding it to a list of more than 90 geological wonders worldwide and naming it the **Batur Caldera Geopark** (www.globalgeopark.org). So far this has meant little on the ground, although some interesting signs detailing the unique geology of the area have started to appear along roads in the region.

The road around the southwestern rim of the Gunung Batur crater is one of Bali's most important north–south routes and has one of its most stunning vistas.

Day trippers should bring some sort of wrap in case the mist closes in and the temperature drops (it can get to 16°C).

The villages around the Gunung Batur crater rim have grown into one continuous untidy strip. Kintamani is the main village, though the whole area is often referred to by that name. Coming from the south, the first village is Penelokan, where tour groups first stop to gasp at the view.

ℹ Information

Services are few in the Gunung Batur area. Bring anything you might need, including cash, from the lowlands.

The Gunung Batur area has a reputation as a place of greed and many visitors leave vowing never to return.

Be wary of touts on motorcycles, who will attempt to steer you to a tour or hotel of *their* choice as you descend into the Danau Batur area from the village of Penelokan. These young

Central Mountains Highlights

❶ Claiming your own waterfall while trekking around **Munduk** (p223).

❷ Identifying each ancient variety of rice grown at the magnificent Unesco-recognised ancient terraces of **Jatiluwih** (p225).

❸ Hearing the chant of priests at one of Bali's

holiest temples, **Pura Luhur Batukau** (p226).

❹ Taking a guided hike above and around the natural beauty and ancient temples of **Danau Tamblingan** (p222).

❺ Beholding the otherworldly, lava-strewn side of **Gunung Batur** (p215).

❻ Discovering one stunning feature after another on the beautifully scenic **road to Trunyan** (p218) via Buahan and Abang.

❼ Exploring the region's maze of back roads, such as the one north from **Antosari** (p227).

men offer no service of value and you should ignore them. Vendors in the area can be highly aggressive.

ⓘ Getting There & Around

From Batubulan terminal in Denpasar, bemo travel regularly to Kintamani (15,000Rp). Buses on the Denpasar–(Batubulan)–Singaraja route will stop in Penelokan and Kintamani (about 16,000Rp). Alternatively, you can just hire a car or use a driver, but be sure to rebuff buffet lunch entreaties.

Bemo shuttle between Penelokan and Kintamani (10,000Rp for tourists). Bemo from Penelokan down to the lakeside villages go in the morning (about 8000Rp to Toya Bungkah). Later in the day, you may have to hire transport (40,000Rp or more).

If you arrive by private vehicle, you will be stopped at Penelokan or Kubupenelokan to buy an entry ticket (11,000Rp per person, beware of scams demanding more) for the entire Gunung Batur area. You shouldn't be charged again – save your receipt.

Gunung Batur

Vulcanologists describe Gunung Batur as a 'double caldera', ie one crater inside another. The outer crater is an oval about 14km long, with its western rim about 1500m above sea level. The inner is a classic volcano-shaped peak that reaches 1717m. Geological activity occurs regularly, and activity over the last decade has spawned several smaller cones on its western flank. There were major eruptions in 1917, 1926 and 1963.

One look at this other-worldly spectacle and you'll understand why people want to go through the many hassles and expenses of taking a trek. Note that the odds of clouds obscuring your reason for coming are greater from July to December, but at any time of year you should check conditions before committing to a trip, or even coming up the mountain.

The cartel of local guides known as **HPPGB** has a monopoly on guided climbs up Gunung Batur. It requires that all trekking agencies that operate on the mountain hire at least one of its guides. In addition, the HPPGB has developed a reputation for tough tactics in requiring climbers to use its guides and in negotiations for its services.

That said, many people use the services of HPPGB guides without incident, and some of the guides win plaudits from visitors for their ideas for customising trips.

The following strategies should help you have a good climb:

➡ Be absolutely clear in your agreement with the HPPGB about the terms you're agreeing to, such as whether fees are per person or group, whether they include breakfast, and exactly where you will go.

➡ Deal with one of the trekking agencies. There will still be an HPPGB guide along, but all arrangements will be done through the agency.

HPPGB rates and times are posted at its offices along the **access road** (Mt Batur Tour Guides Association; ⊘ 3am-3pm) and in **Toya Bungkah** (Mt Batur Tour Guides Association; ✆ 0366-52362; Toya Bungkah; ⊘ 3am-3pm). Treks on offer include:

➡ Mt Batur Sunrise: A simple ascent and return, from 4am to 8am, 350,000Rp per person.

➡ Mt Batur Main Crater: Includes sunrise from the summit and time around the rim, from 4am to 9.30am, 500,000Rp per person.

➡ Mt Batur Exploration: Sunrise, caldera and some of the volcanic cones, from 4am to 10am, 600,000Rp per person.

Trekking Agencies

Even reputable and highly competent adventure-tour operators and trekking agencies cannot take their customers up Gunung Batur without paying to have one of the HPPGB guys tag along. However, they are useful for planning trips off well-trodden trails.

Most of the accommodation in the area can match you with guides and trekking agencies, which will add about 250,000Rp to 450,000Rp to the cost of a trek/climb.

Equipment

If you're climbing before sunrise, take a torch (flashlight) or be absolutely sure that your guide provides you with one. You'll need good strong footwear, a hat, a jumper (sweater) and drinking water.

Trekking Routes

The climb to see the sunrise from Gunung Batur is still the most popular trek. In high season 100 or more people will arrive at the top for dawn. Guides will provide breakfast on the summit for a fee (50,000Rp), which often includes the novelty of cooking an egg

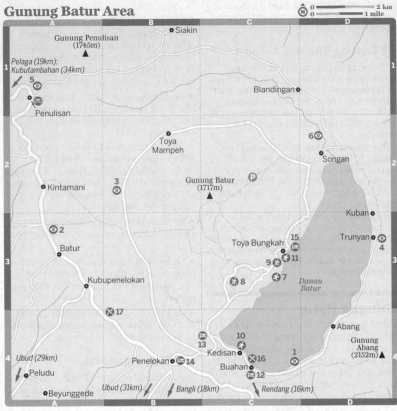

or banana in the steaming holes at the top of the volcano. There are pricey refreshment stops along the way.

Most travellers use one of two trails that start near Toya Bungkah. The shorter one is straight up (three to four hours' return), while a longer trek (five to six hours' return) links the summit climb with the other craters. Climbers have reported that they have easily made this journey without a HPPGB guide, although it shouldn't be tried while it's dark because people have fallen to their deaths. The major obstacle is actually avoiding any hassle from the guides.

There are a few separate paths at first, but they all rejoin sooner or later and after about 30 minutes you'll be on a ridge with quite a well-defined track. It gets pretty steep towards the top and it can be hard walking over the loose volcanic sand – you'll climb up three steps only to slide back two. Allow about two hours to get to the top.

There's also a track that enables you to use private transport to within about 45 minutes' walk of the top. From Toya Bungkah, take the road northeast towards Songan and take the left fork after about 3.5km at Serongga, just before Songan. Follow this inner-rim road for another 1.7km to a well-signposted track on the left, which climbs another 1km or so to a car park. From here, the walking track is easy to follow to the top.

Around Gunung Batur Crater

There are several villages on the ridge around Gunung Batur crater.

Penelokan

Appropriately, Penelokan means 'place to look' and you'll be stunned by the view

Gunung Batur Area

across to Gunung Batur and down to the lake at the bottom of the crater (check out the large lava flow on Gunung Batur). The area is often generically called Kintamani.

Although the huge tourist places on the road from Penelokan to Kintamani disappoint, there are some acceptable choices, including humble places where you can sit on a plastic chair and have a simple, freshly cooked meal while enjoying a priceless view. Look for *ikan mujair* signs, near which small sweet fish that are caught in the lake below are barbecued to a crisp with onion, garlic and bamboo sprouts.

★**Lakeview Eco Lodge** HOTEL $$
(☑ 0366-52525; www.lakeviewbali.com; dm/r from US$23/60; ☻restaurant 7.30am-3.30pm; ☎) ✦ This venerable hotel complex was recently revitalised by the family who've owned it for three generations. Twelve comfortable rooms have amazing views and access to a private lounge with snacks and meals until 10pm.

An annex, **Kintamani Backpackers** (www.kintamanibackpackers.com), offers dorms and rooms for budget travellers.

The restaurant serves a la carte and buffet meals that break with the low local standards by using organic ingredients sourced locally.

★**Pulu Mujung Warung** INDONESIAN $$
(☑ 0813 3864 4037; mains 35,000-60,000Rp; ☻9am-5pm) ✦ Easily the best option for a meal in the area, this small cafe has fabulous views and is affiliated with the much-loved Sari Organic restaurants in Ubud. Soups are good in the cool mountain air and you can also enjoy salads, pizzas, Indo specials, juices, smoothies and more. You can stay in one of four simple rooms (300,000Rp) but book ahead.

Kintamani & Batur

The villages of Kintamani and Batur now virtually run together. Kintamani is like a string bean: long, with pods of development. It is famed for its large and colourful **market**, which is held every three days. Activity starts early, and by 11am everything's all packed up. If you don't want to go on a trek, the sunrise view from the road here is good.

The original village of Batur was in the crater, but was wiped out by a violent eruption in 1917. It killed thousands of people before the lava flow stopped at the entrance to the village's main temple. Taking this as a good omen, the villagers rebuilt in the same location, but Gunung Batur erupted again in 1926. This time the lava flow covered everything except the loftiest temple shrine. Fortunately, few lives were lost.

The village was relocated up onto the crater rim, and the surviving shrine was also moved there and placed in the current temple, the ever-more-flamboyant **Pura Batur** (admission 10,000Rp, sarong & sash rental 3000Rp). Spiritually, Gunung Batur is the second-most important mountain in Bali (only Gunung Agung outranks it), so this temple is of considerable importance.

For lunch, look for some fine local warungs on the north end of Kintamani, past the market.

Penulisan

The road gradually climbs along the crater rim beyond Kintamani, and is often shrouded in clouds, mist or rain. Penulisan is where the road bends sharply and splits: the main branch runs down towards the north coast while the other leads to the remote scenic drive to Bedugul (p223). A **viewpoint** about 400m south of here offers an amazing panorama over three mountains: Gunung Batur, Gunung Abang and Gunung Agung.

TOUR BUS RESTAURANTS

Avoid the ugly monolithic restaurants lining the crater rim (many have closed anyway, their carcasses littering the view like the forgotten egg rolls inside). They offer lacklustre buffet lunches cost from 100,000Rp (your guide usually gets at least 25% of the bill as a commission) and offer uninspired food by the bucket. Drivers also get in on the action: the most crowded restaurants often have driver's lounges with gyms, TVs, beds and free food.

Near the road junction, several steep flights of steps lead to Bali's highest temple, **Pura Puncak Penulisan** (1745m). Inside the highest courtyard are rows of old statues and fragments of sculptures in the open *bale* (pavillion). Some of the sculptures date back to the 11th century. The temple views are superb: facing north you can see over the rice terraces clear to the Singaraja coast (weather permitting).

Around Danau Batur

The little villages around Danau Batur have a crisp lakeside setting and views up to the surrounding peaks. There's a lot of fish farming, and the air is pungent with the smell of onions from the myriad tiny vegetable farms. Don't miss the trip along the east coast to Trunyan.

A road hairpins its way down from Penelokan to the shore of Danau Batur. At the lakeside you can go left along the road that twists through lava fields to Toya Bungkah. Watch out for huge sand trucks battering the road into dust as they haul construction materials across Bali.

Kedisan & Buahan

Buahan is a pleasant 15-minute stroll from Kedisan, and has market gardens going right down to the lakeshore.

✈ Activities

★ **C.Bali**   ADVENTURE TOUR
(☑ info only 0813 5342 0541; www.c-bali.com; Hotel Segara; tours from 430,000Rp) Operated by an Australian-Dutch couple, C.Bali offers bike tours around the region and canoe tours on the lake. Prices include pick-up across south Bali. Packages also include multiday trips. A very important note: these tours often fill up in advance so book ahead through the website.

Lake Boats   BOAT
These boats leave from a jetty with gift shops. The price for a four-hour return trip (Kedisan–Trunyan–Kuban–Toya Bungkah–Kedisan) depends on the number of passengers, with a maximum of seven people (the boat costs 452,000Rp, although extra 'fees' may be added). Our advice: to spend time out on the lake, take one of the canoe trips with C.Bali.

🛏 Sleeping & Eating

Beware of the motorcycle touts who will follow you down the hill from Penelokan trying to nab a hotel commission. Local hotels ask that you call ahead and reserve so that they have your name on record and thus can avoid paying the touts.

The restaurants at the following two hotels are good places to sample the garlic-infused local fish.

Hotel Segara   GUESTHOUSE $
(☑ 0366-51136;   www.batur-segarahotel.com; Kedisan; r 250,000-500,000Rp; @🖤) The Segara has bungalows set around a cafe and courtyard. The cheapest of the 32 rooms have cold water, the best rooms have hot water and bathtubs – perfect for soaking away hypothermia from an early trek.

Kedisan Floating Hotel   CAFE $
(☑ 0366-51627, 0813 3775 5411; Kedisan; meals from 35,000Rp; 🖤) This hotel on the shores of the lake is hugely popular for its daily lunches. On weekends tourists vie with day trippers from Denpasar for tables out on the piers over the lake. The Balinese food, which features fresh lake fish, is excellent. You can also stay here: the best rooms are cottages at the water's edge (from 400,000Rp).

Buahan & Abang

These tiny lakeside villages have recently been busy building bicycle paths that make it easy to enjoy the incredible views across to Gunung Batur from along the lake's east side.

From the T-junction of the access road down from Penelokan near Kedisan it's 9km to Trunyan. Whether walking, cycling or riding a motorbike, this is a very rewarding adventure. Cyclists will need to dismount for a few short and steep stretches north of Abang. Besides the views, there is a magnificent **banyan tree** east of Buahan and some good Geopark-sponsored panels with information on the area's wild geology at the Abang pier.

Baruna Cottages GUESTHOUSE $
(☑ 0813 5322 2896; www.barunacottage.com; Buahan; r from 400,000Rp) The nine rooms at this small and tidy compound vary greatly in design and size; the middle grade have the best views. It's right across the Trunyan road from the lake, and there's a cute cafe.

Trunyan

The village of Trunyan is squeezed between the lake and the outer crater rim. It is inhabited by Bali Aga people and is the kind of place that can make you feel like you've left Bali altogether. Smiles are less common in this isolated corner of Danau Batur but the setting is beautiful. Stop and picnic on the road outside town.

Trunyan is known for the **Pura Pancering Jagat**, which is very impressive with its seven-roofed *meru* (shrine). Inside the temple is a 4m-high statue of the village's guardian spirit, although tourists are not usually allowed in. Ignore the touts and guides lurking about and know that 5000Rp is the absolute maximum you should pay to park here.

Kuban

About 500m beyond Trunyan, and accessible only by a hiking trail or boat, is the cemetery at Kuban (aka Kuburan). Locals don't cremate or bury their dead – they lay them out in bamboo cages to decompose. If you do decide to visit the cemetery you'll be met by characters demanding huge fees. Our advice is to enjoy the views on the road to Trunyan and skip this ghoulish spectacle.

You can get here on one of the lake boats from Kedisan or on a very short and expensive boat ride from Trunyan (about 450,000Rp plus 150,000Rp for a 'guide' who will insist on coming along).

Toya Bungkah

The main tourist centre is Toya Bungkah (also known as Tirta), which boasts hot springs (*tirta* and *toya* both mean water). It's a simple village where travellers stay so they can climb Gunung Batur early in the morning.

🏃 Activities

Hot springs bubble in a couple of spots, and have long been used for bathing pools.

Batur Natural Hot Spring HOT SPRINGS
(☑ 0813 3832 5552; admission from 150,000Rp; ⊙ 8am-6pm) This ever-expanding complex is on the edge of the lake. The three pools have different temperatures, so you can simmer yourself successively. The overall feel of the hot springs matches the slightly shabby feel of the entire region. Lockers and towels are included with admission, and the simple cafe has good views.

Toya Devasya HOT SPRINGS
(☑ 0366-51204; www.toyadevasya.com; admission 150,000Rp; ⊙ 8am-8pm) This glossy retreat is built around springs. One huge hot pool is 38°C while a comparatively brisk lake-fed pool is 20°C. Admission includes refreshments, and there is a cafe with delusions of grandeur as well as lodging options.

🛏 Sleeping

Avoid rooms near the noisy main road through town: opt instead for placid ones with lake views. A couple of local cafes have decent meals.

Under the Volcano III GUESTHOUSE $
(☑ 0813 3860 0081; r 250,000Rp) With a lovely, quiet lakeside location opposite chilli plots, this inn has six clean and simple rooms; go for room 1 right on the water. There are two other nearby inns in the Volcano empire, all run by the same lovely family (Under the Volcano II has wi-fi).

Songan

Around the lake, 2km from Toya Bungkah, Songan is a large and interesting village with market gardens extending to the water's edge. At the lakeside road end is **Pura Ulun Danu Batur**, under the edge of the crater rim.

A turn-off in Songan takes you on a rough but passable road around the crater floor. On the northwestern side of the volcano, the village of **Toya Mampeh** (Yeh Mampeh) is surrounded by a vast field of chunky black lava – a legacy of the 1974 eruption. Further on, **Pura Bukit Mentik** was completely surrounded by molten lava from this eruption, but the temple itself and its impressive banyan tree were quite untouched – it's called the 'Lucky Temple'.

DANAU BRATAN AREA

Approaching from south Bali, you gradually leave the rice terraces behind and ascend into the cool, often misty mountain country around Danau Bratan. Candikuning is the main village in the area, and has the important and picturesque temple Pura Ulun Danu Bratan. Munduk anchors the region with fine trekking to waterfalls and cloud-cloaked forests, and at nearby Danau Tamblingan.

The choice of accommodation near the lake is limited because much of the area is geared towards domestic, not foreign, tourists. On Sundays and public holidays the lakeside can be crowded with courting couples and Toyotas bursting with day-tripping families. But Munduk has many excellent inns.

Wherever you go, you are likely to see the tasty local strawberries on offer. Note that it is often misty and can get chilly up here.

Bedugul
☑ 0368

'Bedugul' is sometimes used to refer to the whole lakeside area but, strictly speaking, it's just the first place you reach at the top of the hill when coming from south Bali and, even then, you might not pause long because it's small.

🛏 Sleeping & Eating

Avoid the string of rundown places up at the ridge around Bedugul.

⭐ **Strawberry Hill**   GUESTHOUSE **$$**
(☑ 0368-21265; www.strawberryhillbali.com; Jl Raya Denpasar-Singaraja; r 450,000-600,000Rp; ☎) Seventeen conical little woodsy cottages are arrayed on a hill, each with a deep soaking tub and nice views down to south Bali (some have better views than others, so compare cottages on arrival if you can). The cafe's Indo menu (mains from 40,000Rp) includes soul-healing *soto ayam* (chicken soup) and *gudeg yogya* (jackfruit stew). You can pick your own strawberries for free from the hotel's patch.

Bali Ecovillage   BOUTIQUE HOTEL **$$**
(☑ 0819 9988 6035, reservations 0812 3646 3269; www.baliecovillage.com; Dinas Lawak; r/bungalow from US$50/100) 🍃 A vision in bamboo and set in a remote corner of Bali near coffee plantations, this idiosyncratic lodge is so green, about the only other colour you'll see is the blue sky. The restaurant serves organic local and Western fare and there are numerous cultural activities plus a spa and yoga.

It's located in a hidden valley near the village of Pelaga (p223), about 25km from Bedugul.

🛈 Getting There & Away

Any minibus or bemo between south Bali and Singaraja will stop at Bedugul on request.

Candikuning
☑ 0368

Often misty, Candikuning is home to a good botanic garden as well as one of Bali's most photographed temples.

◉ Sights & Activities

⭐ **Bali Botanic Garden**   GARDENS
(☑ 0368-2033211; www.balibotanicgarden.org; Kebun Raya Eka Karya Bali; domestic/foreign visitors 7,000/18,000Rp; parking 6000Rp; ☉7am-6pm) This garden is a showplace. Established in 1959 as a branch of the national botanic gardens at Bogor, near Jakarta, it covers more than 154 hectares on the lower slopes of Gunung Pohen. Don't miss the Panca Yadnya Garden (Garden of Five Offerings) which preserves plants used in ancient Hindu ceremonies.

Some plants are labelled with their botanical names, and a booklet of self-guided walks (20,000Rp) is helpful. The gorgeous orchid area is often locked to foil flower filchers; you can ask for it to be unlocked. Look for the 'roton' or rattan bush to see the unlikely source of so much furniture.

Within the park, you can cavort like an ape or a squirrel at the **Bali Treetop Adventure Park** (☑ 0361-852 0680; www.balitreetop.com; Kebun Raya Eka Karya Bali, Bali Botanic Garden; adult/child US$24/16; ☉9.30am-6pm). Winches, ropes, nets and the like let you explore the forest well above the ground. And it's not passive – you hoist, jump, balance and otherwise circumnavigate the park. Special programs are geared to different ages.

Danau Bratan Area

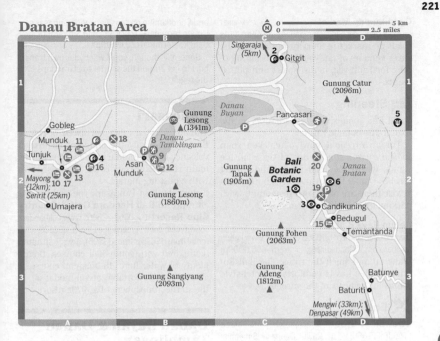

Danau Bratan Area

Pura Ulun Danu Bratan TEMPLE
(off Jl Raya Denpasar-Singaraja; adult/child 30,000/15,000Rp; parking 5000Rp; ⊙ tickets 7am-5pm, site 24hr) This important Hindu-Buddhist temple was founded in the 17th century. It is dedicated to Dewi Danu, the goddess of the waters, and is actually built on small islands. Pilgrimages and ceremonies are held here to ensure there is a supply of water for farmers all over Bali as part of the Unesco-recognised *subak* (irrigation) system.

The tableau includes classical Hindu thatch-roofed *meru* (multi-tiered shrines) reflected in the water and silhouetted against the often cloudy mountain backdrop. It's an iconic image of Bali.

Sadly, there's a bit of a sideshow atmosphere here: animals are squashed into small cages and punters stop to caress snakes or hold huge bats, while the parking lot is lined with souvenir stalls.

Candikuning Market

MARKET

(Jl Raya Denpasar-Singaraja; parking 2000Rp) This roadside market is touristy, but among the eager vendors of tat, you'll find locals shopping for fruit, veg, herbs, spices and potted plants.

🛏 Sleeping

You'll find some simple guesthouses on the road to the botanic garden.

For an excellent bowl of chicken soup (*bakso ayam*), stop at one of the roadside stands where the road from Candikuning reaches Danau Bratan and turns north. Otherwise there are numerous restaurants with parking lots suitable for tour buses.

Kebun Raya Bali

GUESTHOUSE $$

(Bali Botanic Garden; ☎ 0368-2033211; www.kebun rayabali.com; Candikuning; r from 450,000Rp) Wake up and smell the roses. The Bali Botanic Garden has 14 comfortable hotel-style rooms in the heart of the gardens.

🍴 Eating

Strawberry Stop

CAFE $

(☎ 0368-21060; Jl Raya Denpasar-Singaraja; snacks from 15,000Rp; ◷ 8am-7pm) Locally grown strawberries star in milkshakes, juices, pancakes and other treats. You can also get full meals. Bananas are used when berries are out of season.

Roti Bedugul

BAKERY $

(☎ 0368-21838; Jl Raya Denpasar-Singaraja; snacks 5000Rp; ◷ 8am-4pm) Just north of the market, this bakery produces fine versions of its namesake, as well as croissants and other treats.

❶ Getting There & Away

Danau Bratan is along the main north–south road between south Bali and Singaraja.

Although the main terminal is in Pancasari, minibuses will stop along the road in Bedugul

SUNRISE JOY

For an almost surreal experience, take a quiet paddle across Danau Bratan and see Pura Ulun Danu Bratan (p221) at sunrise – arrange it with a boatman at the temple the night before. The mobs see it by day, but you'll see something entirely different – and magical – in the mists of dawn.

and Candikuning on runs between Denpasar's Ubung terminal (20,000Rp) and Singaraja's Sangket terminal (20,000Rp).

Generally, though, you'll want your own transport to get around the scattered attractions of the region.

Pancasari

The broad green valley northwest of Danau Bratan is actually the crater of an extinct volcano. In the middle of the valley, on the main road, Pancasari is a nontourist town with a bustling market.

Just south of Pancasari, you will see the entrance to **Bali Handara Golf & Country Club Resort** (☎ 0362-22646; www.balihandara countryclub.com; greens fees from US$120, club rental from US$25; r from US$95), a well-situated (compared with south Bali courses, there's plenty of water here) 18-hole golf course. It also offers comfortable accommodation in the sterile atmosphere of a 1970s resort.

Danau Buyan & Danau Tamblingan

Northwest of Danau Bratan are two little-visited lakes, Danau Buyan and Danau Tamblingan, where some excellent new guided hikes are on offer. There are several tiny villages and old temples along the shores of both lakes.

◉ Sights & Activities

The Munduk road on the hill above the lakes has some **cafes** and good picnic spots with sweeping views.

Danau Buyan has parking right at the lake, a pretty 1.5km drive off the main road – when you park, an attendant will find you for the fees. The entire area is home to market gardens growing strawberries and other high-value crops, such as the orange and blue flowers used in offerings.

A 4km **hiking trail** goes around the southern side of Danau Buyan from the car park, then over the saddle to Danau Tamblingan, and on to Asan Munduk. It combines forest and lake views. If you have a driver, walk this path in one direction and get them to meet you at the other end.

Danau Tamblingan has parking at the end of the road from the village of Asan Munduk.

THE ROAD RARELY TRAVELLED

A series of narrow roads links the Danau Bratan area and the Gunung Batur region. Few locals outside of this area even know that the roads exist, and if you have a driver, they might need some convincing. Over a 30km route you not only step back to a simpler time, but also leave Bali altogether for something resembling less-developed islands such as Timor. The scenery is beautiful and may make you forget you had a destination.

South of Bedugul, turn east at Temantanda and take a small and winding road down the hillside into some lush ravines cut by rivers. After about 6km you'll come to a T-junction: turn north and travel about 5km to reach the pretty village of **Pelaga**. This area is known for its organic coffee and cinnamon plantations, which you'll both see and smell. Consider a tour and homestay in Pelaga organised by JED (p196), a nonprofit group that offers rural tourism experiences.

From Pelaga, ascend the mountain, following terrain that alternates between jungle and rice fields. Continue north to Catur, then veer east to the junction with the road down to north Bali and drive east again for 1km to Penulisan.

A fun detour on *this* detour is the **Tukad Bangkung Bridge** at Petang: at 71m it is reputed to be the tallest bridge in Asia. It is a local tourist attraction and the roads are lined with vendors on weekends.

★ **KT Kastana** HIKING GUIDES
(☑ 0857 3715 4849; guided hikes for 1-4 people from 350,000Rp; ⊘ 8am-5pm) Located in a hut along the road above Danau Tamblingan, this group of excellent guides offers several different trips down and around the lakes. A two-hour trip usually includes visits to ancient temples and a canoe trip on the lake.

★ **Organisasi Pramuwisata Bangkit Bersama** HIKING GUIDES
(Guides Organization Standing Together; ☑ 0852 3867 8092; Asan Munduk; guided hikes for 1-4 people from 300,000Rp; ⊘ 8.30am-4pm) This great group of guys is based in a hut near the parking lot for Danau Tamblingan. Like the guiding group located along the Munduk road, they offer a range of trips around the lakes, temples and mountains. You can ascend nearby Agung Lesong for 600,000Rp (they have walking sticks for you to use).

🛏 Sleeping & Eating

Pondok Kesuma Wisata GUESTHOUSE $
(☑ 0812 3791 5865; Asan Munduk; r from 350,000Rp) This nice 12-room guesthouse features clean rooms with hot water and a pleasant cafe (meals 15,000Rp to 30,000Rp). It's just up from the Danau Tamblingan parking lot.

Munduk & Around

☑ 0362
The simple village of Munduk is one of Bali's most appealing mountain retreats. It has a cool misty ambience set among lush hillsides covered with jungle, rice, fruit trees and pretty much anything else that grows on the island. **Waterfalls** tumble off precipices by the dozen. There are hikes and treks galore and a number of really nice places to stay, from old Dutch colonial summer homes, to retreats where you can plunge full-on into local culture. Many people come for a day and stay for a week.

Archaeological evidence suggests there was a developed community in the Munduk region between the 10th and 14th centuries. When the Dutch took control of north Bali in the 1890s, they experimented with commercial crops, establishing plantations for coffee, vanilla, cloves and cocoa.

⊙ Sights & Activities

Heading to Munduk from Pancasari, the main road climbs steeply up the rim of the old volcanic crater. It's worth stopping to enjoy the views back over the valley and lakes – show a banana and the swarms of monkeys will get so excited they'll start spanking themselves with joy. Turning right (east) at the top will take you on a scenic descent to Singaraja. Taking a sharp left turn (west), you follow a ridge-top road with

Danau Buyan on one side and a slope to the sea on the other.

At **Asan Munduk**, you'll find another T-junction. The left turn will take you down a road leading to Danau Tamblingan. Turning right takes you along beautiful winding roads to the main village of Munduk. Watch for superb panoramas of north Bali and the ocean. Consider a stop at **Ngiring Ngewedang** (☏ 0812 380 7010; snacks 15,000-40,000Rp; ☺ 10am-5pm), a coffeehouse 5km east of Munduk that grows its own beans on the surrounding slopes. This is real coffee and not the overhyped Luwak stuff.

Wherever you stay, staff will fill you in on **walking** and **hiking** options. There are numerous trails suitable for treks of two hours or much longer to coffee plantations, rice paddies, waterfalls, villages, or around both Danau Tamblingan and Danau Buyan. Most are easy to do on your own but guides will take you far off the beaten path to waterfalls and other delights that are hard to find.

🛏 Sleeping & Eating

Enjoy simple old Dutch houses in the village or more naturalistic places in the countryside. Most have cafes, usually serving good local fare. Besides several basic homestays, there are a couple of cute warungs in the village and a few stores with very basic supplies (including bug spray).

★ Villa Dua Bintang GUESTHOUSE $
(☏ 0812 3700 5593, 0361-401 1416; mrika30@yahoo.com; Jl Batu Galih; r from 400,000) This newcomer is 500m down a tree-shaded lane that's off the main road 1km east of Munduk. Four gorgeous rooms are elaborately built amid fruit trees and forest (two are family-size). Clove and nutmeg scents hang in the air from the porch, there's a cafe and the family who owns it is lovely.

Meme Surung GUESTHOUSE $
(☏ 0362-700 5378; www.memesurung.com; r 250,000-350,000Rp; ☎) Two atmospheric old Dutch houses adjoin each other in the village in a compound that has a total of 11 rooms. The decor is traditional and simple, which is just as well because the view from the long wooden verandah is both the focus and joy here.

Puri Alam Bali GUESTHOUSE $
(☏ 0812 465 9815; www.purialambali.com; r 250,000-500,000Rp; ☎ ≋) Perched on a precipice at the east end of the village, the 15 rooms (all with hot water and balconies) have better views the higher you go. The rooftop cafe is worth a visit for its huge views. Think of the long concrete stairs down from the road as trekking practice.

Guru Ratna GUESTHOUSE $
(☏ 0813 3719 4398; www.guru-ratna.com; r 175,000-350,000Rp; ☎) The cheapest place in the village has seven comfortable hot-water rooms (some share bathrooms). The best rooms have some style, carved wood details, nice porches and are in a colonial Dutch house.

★ Puri Lumbung Cottages GUESTHOUSE $$
(☏ 0362-701 2887, 0812 383 6891; www.purilumbung.com; cottages US$80-160; @ ☎) Founded by Nyoman Bagiarta to develop sustainable tourism, this lovely hotel has 43 bright two-storey cottages and rooms set among rice fields. Enjoy intoxicating views (units 32 to 35 have the best) down to the coast from the upstairs balconies. Dozens of trekking options and courses are offered.

MUNDUK'S WATERFALLS

Munduk's many waterfalls include the following three, which you can visit on a hike of four to six hours (note that the myriad local maps given out by guesthouses and hotels can be vague on details and it's easy to take a wrong turn). Fortunately, even unplanned detours are scenic. Clouds of mist from the water add to the already misty air; drips come off every leaf. There are a lot of often slippery and steep paths; rest up at tiny cafes perched above some of the falls.

Munduk Waterfall (Tanah Braak; admission 5000Rp) About 2km east of Munduk, look for signs for this waterfall (aka Tanah Braak) along the road. Though the signs say the trail is 700m, it feels longer than that. This is the easiest waterfall to access without a map or guide.

Golden Valley Waterfall Fairly short but wide falls, watched over by a cute coffee stand.

Melanting Waterfall Over 25m, these are about 500m from Munduk Waterfall.

DON'T MISS

JATILUWIH RICE FIELDS

At Jatiluwih, which means 'truly marvellous' (or 'real beautiful' depending on the translation), you will be rewarded with vistas of centuries-old rice terraces that exhaust your ability to describe green. Emerald ribbons curve around the hillsides, stepping back as they climb to the blue sky.

The terraces are part of Bali's emblematic – and Unesco-recognised – ancient rice-growing culture. You'll understand the nomination just viewing the panorama from the narrow, twisting 18km road, but getting out for a rice-field walk is even more rewarding, following the water as it runs through channels and bamboo pipes from one plot to the next. Much of the rice you'll see is traditional, rather than the hybrid versions grown elsewhere on the island. Look for heavy short husks of red rice.

Take some time, leave your driver behind and just find a place to sit and enjoy the views. It sounds like a cliché, but the longer you look the more you'll see. What at first seems like a vast palette of greens reveals itself to be rice at various stages of growth.

There are cafes for refreshments along the drive and one of the simplest is the best: **Ada Babi Guleng** (lunch 35,000Rp; ☉10am-4pm) serves an excellent version of Bali's signature dish, roast, marinated suckling pork. It has just a few tables but each has lush, emerald views and the fiery sambal is superb.

Because the road is sharply curved, vehicles are forced to drive slowly, which makes the Jatiluwih route a good one for bikes. There is a road toll for visitors (15,000Rp per person, plus 5000Rp per car) which does *not* seem to be going to road maintenance – it's rough. Still the drive won't take more than an hour.

You can access the road in the west off the road to Pura Luhur Batukau from Tabanan, and in the east off the main road to Bedugul near Pacung. Drivers all know this road well and locals offer directions.

The hotel's restaurant, Warung Kopi Bali (mains 45,000Rp to 85,000Rp), is sponsored by a Swiss cooking school. The hotel is on the right-hand side of the road coming from Bedugul, 700m before Munduk. Ask about the remote forest rooms.

Manah Liang Cottages   INN $$
(☎0362-700 5211; www.manahliang.com; r from 450,000Rp; ☎) About 800m east of Munduk, this country inn (whose name means 'feeling good') has traditional cottages overlooking the lush local terrain. The open-air bathrooms (with tubs) are as refreshing as the porches are relaxing. A short trail leads to a small waterfall. There are cooking classes and guided walks.

Don Biyu   CAFE $
(www.donbiyu.com; mains 25,000-50,000Rp; ☎) Catch up on your blog, enjoy good coffee, zone out to the sublime views and choose from a mix of Western and interesting Asian fare. It's all served in mellow open-air pavilions.

❶ Getting There & Away

Minibuses leave Ubung terminal in Denpasar for Munduk (22,000Rp) a few times a day. Driving to the north coast, the main road west of Munduk goes through a number of picturesque villages to Mayong (where you can head south to west Bali). The road then goes down to the sea at Seririt in north Bali.

GUNUNG BATUKAU AREA

☑0361

Gunung Batukau is Bali's second-highest mountain (2276m), the third of Bali's three major mountains and the holy peak of the island's western end. It's often overlooked, which is probably a good thing given what the vendor hordes have done to Gunung Agung.

You can climb its slippery slopes from one of the island's holiest and most underrated temples, Pura Luhur Batukau, or just revel in the ancient rice-terrace greenery around Jatiluwih.

There are two main approaches to the Gunung Batukau area. The easiest is via Tabanan: take the Pura Luhur Batukau road north 9km to a fork in the road, then take the left-hand turn (towards the temple) and go a further 5km to a junction near a school in Wangayagede village. Here you can continue straight to the temple or turn right (east) for the rice fields of Jatiluwih.

THE OTHER ROAD TO PUPUAN

You can reach the mountain village of Pupuan on the road from Antosari but there is another route, one that wanders the back roads of deepest mountain Bali. Start at Pulukan, which is on the Denpasar–Gilimanuk road in west Bali. A small road climbs steeply from the coast, providing fine views back down to west Bali and the sea. It runs through spice-growing country – you'll see (and smell) spices laid out to dry on mats by the road. After about 10km and just before Manggissari, the narrow and winding road actually runs right through **Bunut Bolong** – a tunnel formed by two enormous trees (the *bunut* is a type of ficus; *bolong* means 'hole').

Further on, the road spirals down to Pupuan through some of Bali's most beautiful rice terraces. It's worth stopping off for a walk to the magnificent **waterfalls** near Pujungan, a few kilometres south of Pupuan. Follow signs down a narrow rough road and then walk 1.5km to the first waterfall – it's nice, but before you say 'is that all there is?', follow your ears to a second one that's 50m high.

The other way is to approach from the east. On the main Denpasar–Singaraja road, look for a small road to the west, just south of the Pacung Indah hotel. Here you follow a series of small paved roads west until you reach the Jatiluwih rice fields. You'll get lost, but locals will quickly set you right and the scenery is superb anyway.

👁 Sights & Activities

⭐ **Pura Luhur Batukau**   HINDU TEMPLE
(donation 10,000Rp) On the slopes of Gunung Batukau, Pura Luhur Batukau was the state temple when Tabanan was an independent kingdom. It has a seven-roofed *meru* dedicated to Maha Dewa, the mountain's guardian spirit, as well as shrines for Bratan, Buyan and Tamblingan lakes. This is certainly the most spiritual temple you can easily visit in Bali.

The main *meru* in the inner courtyard have little doors shielding small ceremonial items. Outside the compound, the temple is surrounded by forest and the atmosphere is cool and misty; the chants of priests are backed by birds singing.

Facing the temple, take a short walk around to the left to see a small white-water stream where the air resonates with tumbling water. Note the unusual fertility shrine.

There's a general lack of touts and other characters here – including hordes of tourists. Respect traditions and act appropriately while visiting temples (see p317). Sarongs can be borrowed.

Gunung Batukau   VOLCANO
At Pura Luhur Batukau you are fairly well up the side of Gunung Batukau. For the trek to the top of the 2276m peak, you'll need a guide, which can be arranged at the temple ticket booth. Expect to pay 1,000,000Rp for a muddy and arduous journey that will take at least seven hours in one direction.

The rewards are amazing views alternating with thick dripping jungle, and the knowledge that you've taken a trail that is much less travelled than the ones on the eastern peaks. You can get a taste of the adventure on a two-hour mini-jaunt (200,000Rp for two).

Staying the night up the mountain might be possible but the assumption is that you will go up and back the same day. Talk to the guides ahead of time to see if you can make special arrangements to camp on the mountain.

🛏 Sleeping

Two remote lodges are hidden away on the slopes of Gunung Batukau. You reach both via a spectacular small and twisting road that makes a long inverted V far up the mountain from Bajera and Pucuk on the main Tabanan–Gilimanuk road in west Bali.

⭐ **Sarinbuana Eco Lodge**   LODGE $$
(☑ 0361-743 5198; www.baliecolodge.com; Sarinbuana; s/d from US$88/105; 📶) 🌿 These beautiful two-level bungalows are built on the side of a hill just a 10-minute walk from a protected rainforest preserve. Notable amenities include fridges, marble bathrooms and handmade soap. Think rustic luxe.

There are cultural workshops, yoga classes and guided treks. The lodge has top-notch green cred and the organic Balinese restaurant is excellent.

★ **Bali Mountain Retreat** LODGE **$$**
(☎ 082 8360 2645; www.balimountainretreat.com;
r 270,000-870,000Rp; 🛜) ⚘ Luxurious rooms
set in refined cottages are arrayed artisti-
cally at this hillside location. A pool and
gardens complement mannered architec-
ture that combines new and old influences.
Some rooms have large verandahs perfect
for contemplating the views. Budget options
include a bed in a vintage rice-storage barn.
There are excellent treks.

❶ Getting There & Away

The only realistic way to explore the Gunung
Batukau area is with your own transport (car hire
should be arranged in the more touristed areas
of Bali).

THE ANTOSARI ROAD

☎ 0361

Although most people cross the mountains
via Candikuning or Kintamani, there is a
very scenic third alternative that links Bali's
south and north coasts. From the Denpasar–
Gilimanuk road in west Bali, a road goes
north from **Antosari** through the village of
Pupuan and then drops to Seririt, west of
Lovina in north Bali.

Starting through rice paddies, after 8km
the road runs alongside a beautiful valley
of rice terraces. Another 2km brings you to
Sari Wisata (☎ 0812 398 8773; ⊘ 8am-6pm),
where a charming family has created what
should be the model for roadhouses every-
where. Gorgeous gardens line the bluff and
only enhance the already remarkable vistas.

Once you're deep in the foothills of
Gunung Batukau, 20km north of Antosari,
you'll smell the fragrant spice-growing vil-
lage of **Sanda** before you see it. Look for the
old wooden elevated rice barns that still fea-
ture in every house.

After another 8km north through coffee
plantations, you'll reach **Pupuan**. A further
6km and you'll reach a highlight of the trip:
the gorgeous **rice-growing valley** near Sub-
uk. From here it is 6km or so to Mayong,
where you can turn east to Munduk and on
to Danau Bratan or go straight to Seririt.

★ **Sanda Boutique Villas** LODGE **$$**
(☎ 0828 372 0055; www.sandavillas.com; bunga-
lows from US$85; ❊ ❄) This boutique hotel
offers a serene escape. Its large infinity pool
seems to disappear into the rice terraces,
while its seven bungalows are really quite
luxe. It's well run and the fusion cafe is excellent (dinner from US$5). The engaging
owners will recommend walks among the
coffee plantations and rice fields. It is just
north of the village of Sanda.

Kebun Villas LODGE **$$**
(☎ 0361-780 6068; www.kebunvilla.com; r US$60-
75; ❄) Eight antique-filled cottages scattered
down a hillside make the most of the sweep-
ing views over rice fields in the valley. Get-
ting to the pool area requires a hike down to
the valley floor but it's huge, and once there
you may just linger all day.

North Bali

Why Go?

The land on the other side, that's north Bali. Although one-sixth of the island's population lives here, the vast region is overlooked by many visitors who stay trapped in the southern Bali–Ubud axis.

The big draw here is the incredible diving and snorkelling at nearby Pulau Menjangan. Arcing around a nearby bay, Pemuteran may be Bali's best beach town. To the east is Lovina, a sleepy beach strip with cheap hotels and even cheaper sunset beer specials. All along the north coast are interesting little boutique hotels, while inland you'll find quiet treks to waterfalls.

Getting to north Bali for once lives up to the cliché: it's half the fun. Routes follow the thinly populated coastlines east and west, or you can go up and over the mountains by any number of routes, marvelling at crater lakes and maybe stopping for a misty trek on the way.

Best Places to Eat

→ Damai (p237)

→ Jasmine Kitchen (p237)

→ Buda Bakery (p237)

→ Global Village Kafe (p236)

When to Go

→ Most of north Bali doesn't have a high season in terms of visitors. The exception is Pemuteran, which is busy July, August and around Christmas and New Year.

→ Weather-wise it's always drier in the north compared to south Bali. Days of perpetual sun are the norm year-round (most visitors like air-con for sleeping). The only real variation will be found when you venture back into the hills; mornings will be cool.

Best Places to Stay

→ Taman Sari (p242)

→ Matahari Beach Resort (p242)

→ Damai (p236)

→ Taman Selini Beach Bungalows (p242)

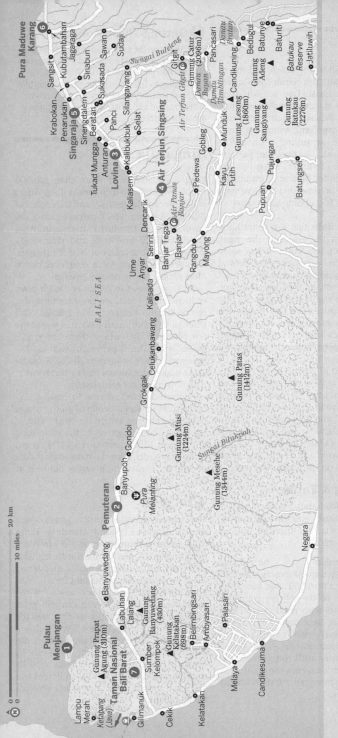

A | 0 | 10 miles
0 | 20 km

BALI SEA

Pulau Menjangan ❶

Taman Nasional Bali Barat ❼

Pemuteran ❷

Pura Madewe Karang ❻

Singaraja ❺

Lovina ❸

Air Terjun Singsing ❹

North Bali Highlights

❶ Plunging into the depths at **Pulau Menjangan** (p241) Bali's best dive spot, or enjoying the show while snorkelling.

❷ Exploring underwater marvels while staying at **Pemuteran** (p239), an idyllic beach town.

❸ Losing track of time, but not of your budget, at laid-back, beachside **Lovina** (p232).

❹ Hiking in the verdant hills that line north Bali, especially to waterfalls like refreshing **Air Terjun Singsing** (p238).

❺ Savouring Buleleng's rich culture at the museums of

Singaraja (p230), which has a long royal history.

❻ Communing at temples with elaborate art such as **Pura Madewe Karang** (p233).

❼ Discovering, by foot or

boat, Bali's national park, **Taman Nasional Bali Barat** (p244), and wildlife-spotting amidst mangroves, savannah and lush hillsides.

Yeh Sanih

📞 0362

On the coast road to the beach and diving towns of east Bali, Yeh Sanih (also called Air Sanih) is a hassle-free seaside spot. It's named for its fresh-water springs, **Air Sanih** (Jl Airsanih-Tejakula; adult/child 8000/5000Rp; ⊙8am-6pm), which are channelled into large swimming pools before flowing into the sea. The pools are particularly picturesque at sunset, when throngs of locals bathe under blooming frangipani trees – most of the time they're alive with frolicking kids. It's about 15km east of Singaraja.

Pura Ponjok Batu has a commanding location between the sea and the road, some 7km east of Yeh Sanih. It has some very fine limestone carvings in the central temple area. Legend holds that it was built to provide some spiritual balance for Bali, what with all the temples in the south.

Between the springs and the temple, the road is often close to the sea. It's probably Bali's best stretch of pure coast driving, with waves crashing onto the breakwater and great views out to sea.

Completely out of character for the area is a place run by quite a character: **Art Zoo** (www.symonstudios.com; Jl Airsanih-Tejakula; ⊙8am-6pm). Symon, the irrepressible American artist (who also has a gallery in Ubud), owns this gallery and studio, which are fairly bursting with a creativity that's at times vibrant, exotic and erotic. It's 5.7km east of Yeh Sanih on the Singaraja road.

🛏 Sleeping & Eating

A few warung (food stalls) hover near the entrance of Yeh Sanih and do a brisk business with the local trade. Otherwise, options are few and scattered.

Cilik's Beach Garden GUESTHOUSE $$
(📞0819 1570 0009; www.ciliksbeachgarden.com; Jl Airsanih-Tejakula; r from €60, villas from €100; @) Coming here is like visiting your rich friends, albeit ones with good taste. These custom-built villas, 3km east of Yeh Sanih, are large and have extensive private gardens. Other accommodation is in stylish *lumbung* (rice barns with round roofs) set in a delightful garden facing the ocean. The owners have even more remote villas further south on the coast.

ℹ Getting There & Away

Yeh Sanih is on the main road along the north coast. Frequent bemo and buses from Singaraja stop outside the springs (10,000Rp).

If heading to Tulamben or Amed, make certain you're on your way south from here by 4pm in order to arrive while there's still some light to avoid road hazards.

Singaraja

📞 0362

With a population of more than 120,000 people, Singaraja (which means 'Lion King') is Bali's second-largest city and the capital of Buleleng Regency, which covers much of the north. With its tree-lined streets, surviving Dutch colonial buildings and charmingly sleepy waterfront area north of Jl Erlangga, it's worth exploring for a couple of hours. Most people stay in nearby Lovina.

Singaraja was the centre of Dutch power in Bali and remained the administrative centre for the Lesser Sunda Islands (Bali through to Timor) until 1953. It is one of the few places in Bali where there are visible traces of the Dutch period, as well as Chinese and Islamic influences. Today, Singaraja is a major educational and cultural centre, with two university campuses.

A much-debated scheme to build a second airport on Bali is centered on the region of Kubutambahan, which lies to the east of Singaraja and is bisected by the main road down from Kintamani. Given Bali's record on large projects, even the mooted start date of 2018 for construction seems notional at best.

⊙ Sights

Old Harbour & Waterfront   NEIGHBOURHOOD
The conspicuous **Yudha Mandala Tama monument** commemorates a freedom fighter killed by gunfire from a Dutch warship early in the struggle for independence. Close by, there's the colourful Chinese temple, **Ling Gwan Kiong**. There are a few old canals here as well and you can still get a little feel of the colonial port that was the main entrance to Bali before WWII.

Check out the cinematically decrepit **old Dutch warehouses** opposite the water. A couple of warungs have been built on stilts over the water. Walk up Jl Imam Bonjol and you'll see the art deco lines of late-colonial Dutch buildings.

Gedong Kirtya Library
LIBRARY

(☑ 0362-22645; Jl Veteran; ⊙ 8am-4pm Mon-Thu, 8am-1pm Fri) This small historical library was established in 1928 by Dutch colonialists and named after the Sanskrit for 'to try'. It has a collection of *lontar* (dried palm leaves) books, as well as some even older written works in the form of inscribed copper plates called *prasasti*. Dutch publications, dating back to 1901, may interest students of the colonial period.

Museum Buleleng
MUSEUM

(Jl Veteran; ⊙ 9am-4pm Mon-Fri) **FREE** Museum Buleleng recalls the life of the last Radja (rajah; prince) of Buleleng, Pandji Tisna, who is credited with developing Lovina's tourism. Among the items here is the typewriter he used during his career as a travel writer before his death in 1978. It also traces the history of the region right back to when there was no history.

⚜ Festivals & Events

Bali Arts Festival
CULTURAL

(www.baliartsfestival.com) Held annually at some point between May and July, the Singaraja-based Bali Arts Festival is north Bali's big cultural event. Over one week dancers and musicians from some of the region's most renowned village troupes, such as those of Jagaraga, perform.

✕ Eating

Istana Cake & Bakery
BAKERY $

(☑ 0362-21983; Jl Jen Achmed Yani; snacks 3000Rp; ⊙ 8am-6pm) Fallen in love in Lovina? Get your wedding cake here. For lesser life moments like the munchies, choose from an array of tasty baked goods.

Ayam Pasir
INDONESIAN $

(☑ 0362-21635; Jl Ayani 144; mains from 13,000Rp; ⊙ 8am-10pm) Super-delicious chicken in all forms is the specialty at this bright and cheery storefront near the bus station. Dishes are fragrant and spicy, the juices blender-fresh.

Manalagi
BALINESE $

(Jl Sahadewa 8A; mains from 15,000Rp; ⊙ 8am-10pm) Down a pretty, tree-shaded street, this Balinese restaurant sits in its own compound and is very popular with locals looking for a special meal that includes fresh fish. The building, with its deep verandahs, has a colonial feel.

Dapur Ibu
INDONESIAN $

(☑ 0362-24474; Jl Jen Achmed Yani; mains 10,000-20,000Rp; ⊙ 8am-10pm) A nice local cafe with a small garden off the street. The *nasi goreng* (fried rice) is fresh and excellent; wash it down with a fresh juice or bubble tea.

ⓘ Information

Buleleng Tourism Office (Diparda; ☑ 0362-61141; Jl Veteran 23; ⊙ 8am-3.30pm Mon-Fri) Near the museum, the regional tourist office has some OK maps. Good information if you ask specifically about dance and other cultural events.

Singaraja Public Hospital (☑ 0362-22573, 0362-22046; Jl Ngurah Rai 30; ⊙ 24hr) Singaraja's hospital is the largest in northern Bali.

ⓘ Getting There & Away

Singaraja is the main transport hub for the northern coast, with three bemo/bus terminals. From the **Sangket terminal**, 6km south of town on the main road, minibuses go to Denpasar (Ubung terminal, 25,000Rp) via Bedugul/Pancasari sporadically.

The **Banyuasri terminal**, on the western side of town, has buses heading to Gilimanuk (25,000Rp, two hours) and plenty of bemos to Lovina (7000Rp). For Java, several companies have services, which include the ferry trip across the Bali Strait. Buses go as far as Yogyakarta (from 335,000Rp, 16 hours) and Jakarta (from 455,000Rp, 24 hours) – book at the Banyuasri terminal a day before.

The **Penarukan terminal**, 2km east of town, has bemos to Yeh Sanih (10,000Rp) and Amlapura (about 20,000Rp, three hours) via the coastal road; and also minibuses to Denpasar (Batubulan terminal, 25,000Rp, three hours) via Kintamani.

ⓘ Getting Around

Bemos link the three main bemo/bus terminals and cost about 7000Rp.

Around Singaraja

The interesting sites around Singaraja include some important temples.

Sangsit

About 8km northeast of Singaraja you can see an excellent example of the colourful architectural style of north Bali. Sangsit's **Pura Beji** (Jl Raya Sangsit) is a temple for the *subak* (village association of rice-growers), dedicated to the goddess Dewi Sri, who looks after irrigated rice fields. The over-the-top sculptured panels along the front wall set the tone with cartoonlike demons and amazing *naga* (mythical snakelike creatures). The inside also has a variety of sculptures covering every available space. It's 500m off the main road towards the coast.

OFF THE BEATEN TRACK

BACK-ROAD DISCOVERIES
....

The back roads around Singaraja offer interesting, seldom-visited discoveries.

Jagaraga The village's **Pura Dalem** is a small, interesting temple with delightful sculptured panels along its front wall. On the outer wall, look for a vintage car driving sedately past, a steamer at sea and even an aerial dogfight between early aircraft.

Sawan A centre for the manufacturing of gamelan gongs and instruments. You can see the gongs being cast and the intricately carved gamelan frames being fashioned. For a real jungle getaway, try **Villa Manuk** (☑0362-27080; www.villa-manuk.com; near Sawan; r from 460,000Rp; ﹡). This two-villa complex has a large natural-spring-fed pool. Guests enjoy rice field views, walks to waterfalls, village life and absolute peace and quiet.

The **Pura Dalem** (Temple of the Dead) shows scenes of punishment in the afterlife, and other humorous, sometimes erotic, pictures. You'll find it in the rice fields, about 500m northeast of Pura Beji.

Buses and bemo going east from Singaraja's Penarukan terminal will stop at Sangsit.

Gitgit

Around 11km south of Singaraja, a well-signposted path goes 800m west from the main road to the touristy waterfall, **Air Terjun Gitgit** (Map p221; adult/child 10,000/5000Rp). The path is lined with souvenir stalls and guides to nowhere. The 40m waterfalls pound away and the mists are more refreshing than any air-con.

About 2km further up the hill, there's a multi-tiered **waterfall** about 600m off the western side of the main road. The path crosses a narrow bridge and follows the river up past several small sets of waterfalls, through verdant jungle.

Regular minibuses between Denpasar and Singaraja stop at Gitgit. The falls are also a major stop on organised tours of central and north Bali.

Lovina
☑0362

'Relaxed' is how people most often describe Lovina and they are correct. This low-key, low-rise, low-priced beach resort is the polar opposite of Kuta. Days are slow and so are the nights. The waves are calm, the beach is thin and over-amped attractions nil. This is where you catch up on your journal, ponder a sunset, finish a book or simply let one day disappear into the next.

Lovina is sun-drenched, with patches of shade from palm trees. A highlight every afternoon at fishing villages like Anturan is watching *prahu* (traditional outrigger canoes) being prepared for the night's fishing; as sunset reddens the sky, the lights of the fishing boats appear as bright dots across the horizon.

The Lovina tourist area stretches over 8km, and consists of a string of coastal villages – Kaliasem, Kalibukbuk, Anturan, Tukad Mungga – collectively known as Lovina. The main focus is Kalibukbuk, 10.5km west of Singaraja and the heart of Lovina. Daytime traffic on the main road is loud and constant.

BALI'S FIRST CYCLIST

Pura Maduwe Karang (Temple of the Land Owner; Kubutambahan) is one of the most intriguing temples in north Bali and is particularly notable for its sculptured panels, including the famous stone-carved **bicycle relief** that depicts a gentleman riding a bicycle with a lotus flower serving as the back wheel. It's on the base of the main plinth in the inner enclosure. The cyclist may be WOJ Nieuwenkamp, a Dutch artist who, in 1904, brought what was probably the first bicycle to Bali.

Like Pura Beji at Sangsit, this temple of dark stone is dedicated to agricultural spirits, but this one looks after nonirrigated land. The temple is easy to find in the village of Kubutambahan – seek the 34 carved figures from the Ramayana outside the walls. Kubutambahan is on the road between Singaraja and Amlapura, about 1km east of the turn-off to Kintamani. Regular bemos and buses pass through.

◉ Sights & Activities

Beaches

The beaches are made up of washed-out grey and black volcanic sand, and while they're mostly clean near the hotel areas, they're not spectacular. Reefs protect the shore, calming the waves and keeping the water clear.

A paved **beach footpath** runs along the sand in Kalibukbuk and extends in a circuitous path along the seashore; it ranges from clean to grubby. Enjoy the postcard view to the east of the mountainous north Bali coast. Sunsets can be breathtaking.

The best beach areas include the main beach east of Kalibukbuk's elaborate **Dolphin Monument** (Jl Bina Ria), as well as the curving stretch a bit west. The cluster of cheap hotels in Anturan also enjoy fun on the sand. Or go upscale at the west end at the hipster Spice Beach Club (p237).

While moored near shore, the fishing boats can fascinate with their large, bare engines, menacing-looking props and individual paint schemes.

Dolphin Watching

Sunrise boat trips to see dolphins are Lovina's much-hyped tourist attraction, so much so that they have a monument in their honour.

Some days no dolphins are sighted, but most of the time at least a few surface.

Expect pressure from your hotel and touts selling dolphin trips. The price is fixed at 50,000Rp per person by the boat-owners' cartel. Trips start at a non-holiday-like 6am and last about two hours. Note that the ocean can get pretty crowded with loud, roaring powerboats.

There's great debate about what all this means to the dolphins. Do they like being chased by boats? If not, why do they keep coming back? Maybe it's the fish, of which there are plenty off Lovina.

Diving & Snorkelling

Diving on the local reef is better at lower depths and night diving is popular. Many people stay here and dive Pulau Menjangan, a two-hour drive west.

Generally, the water is clear and some parts of the reef are quite good for snorkelling, though the coral has been damaged by bleaching and, in places, by dynamite fishing. The best place is to the west, a few hundred metres offshore from Billibo Beach Cottages. A two-hour boat trip will cost about 200,000Rp, including equipment.

Spice Dive　　　　DIVING
(☑ 0362-41512; www.balispicedive.com; off Jl Raya Lovina; two-tank dive from €50; ⊙8am-9pm) Spice Dive is a large operation. It offers snorkelling trips and night dives (€60) plus popular Pulau Menjangan trips (snorkel/dive €35/65). It's based at the west end of the beach path with the Spice Beach Club.

Cycling

The roads south and west of Jl Raya Lovina are excellent for biking, with limited traffic and enjoyable rides amid the rice fields and into the hills for views.

It's easy to rent a bike from 20,000Rp per day; for a good selection, try **Sovina Shop** (☑ 0362-41 402; Jl Ketapang).

Other Activities

Araminth Spa　　　　SPA
(☑ 0362-41901; Jl Ketapang; massage from 150,000Rp; ⊙10am-9pm) Araminth Spa offers many types of therapies and massages, including Balinese and Ayurvedic, in a simple but soothing setting.

Lovina

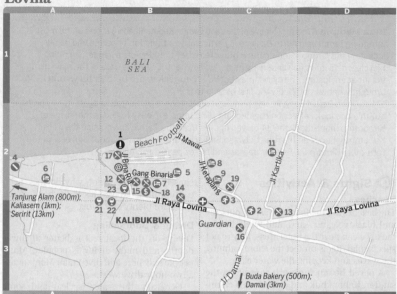

Lovina

Ciego Massage   MASSAGE
(☑0877 6256 1660; Jl Raya Lovina, Anturan; 1hr massage from 70,000Rp; ☺10am-7pm) Highly skilled blind massage therapists provide no-nonsense muscle relief in a simple setting.

🍲 Courses

★**Warung Bambu Pemaron**   COOKING
(☑0362-31455; Pemaron; classes for 1/2 people from 500,000/660,000Rp; ☺8am-1pm) Start with a trip to a large Singaraja food mar-

ket and then in a breezy setting amidst rice fields east of Lovina, learn to cook up to eight classic Balinese dishes. The staff are charmers and the fee includes transport within the area. And when you're done you get to feast on the fruits of your labours.

👉 Tours

★**Komang Dodik**   HIKING
(☑0877 6291 5128; lovina.tracking@gmail.com; hikes from 250,000Rp) Komang Dodik leads

from 200,000/250,000Rp; ✳🛜) This spiffy family-run guesthouse is right on a small strip of charcoal-sand beach. The 12 rooms are basic but tidy.

Gede Home Stay Bungalows   HOMESTAY $
(☎0362-41526; www.gede-homestay.com; Jl Kubu Gembong, Anturan; r 200,000-300,000Rp; ✳🛜) Don't forget to shake the sand off your feet as you enter this beachside eight-room homestay owned by a local fisherman. Cheap rooms have cold water while better ones have hot water and air-con.

🛏 Anturan to Kalibukbuk

Jl Pantai Banyualit has many modest hotels, although the beach is not very inspiring. There is a little park-like area by the water and the walk along the shore to Kalibukbuk is quick and scenic.

★ Villa Taman Ganesha   GUESTHOUSE $$
(☎0362-41272; www.taman-ganesha-lovina.com; Jl Kartika 45; r €30-60; ✳🛜🏊) This lovely guesthouse is down a quiet lane lined with Balinese family compounds. The grounds are lush and fragrant with frangipani from around the world that have been collected by the owner, a landscape architect from Germany. The four units are private and comfortable. The beach is 400m away and it's a 10-minute walk along the sand to Kalibukbuk.

Suma Hotel   GUESTHOUSE $$
(☎0362-41566; www.sumahotel.com; Jl Pantai Banyualit; r 300,000-750,000Rp; ✳@🛜🏊) Enjoy views of the sea from the upstairs rooms; the best of the 13 have air-con and hot water; large bungalows are quite nice as is the pool and cafe. An elaborate temple is nearby.

🛏 Kalibukbuk

The 'centre' of Lovina is the village of Kalibukbuk. Mellow Jl Mawar is quieter and more pleasant than Jl Bina Ria. Small *gang* (alleys) lined with cheap places to stay lead off both streets.

★ Harris Homestay   HOMESTAY $
(☎0362-41152; Gang Binaria, Kalibukbuk; r 120,000-200,000Rp; 🛜) Sprightly, tidy and white, Harris avoids the weary look of some neighbouring cheapies. The charming family live in the back; guests enjoy five bright, modern rooms up front.

hikes in the hills along the north coast. Trips can last from three to seven hours. The highlight of most is a series of waterfalls, over 20m high, in a jungle grotto. Routes can include coffee, clove and vanilla plantations.

🛏 Sleeping

Hotels are spread out along Jl Raya Lovina, and on the side roads going off to the beach. Overall, choices tend to be more budget-focused; don't come here for a luxe experience. Be wary of hotels right on the main road due to traffic noise.

During slow periods, all room prices are negotiable; beware of touts who will literally lead you astray and quote prices which include their large kickback.

🛏 Anturan

A few tiny side tracks and one proper sealed road, Jl Kubu Gembong, lead to this lively little fishing village that's a real travellers hang-out. But it's a long way from Lovina's nightlife – expect to pay around 20,000Rp for transport back to Anturan from Kalibukbuk.

Mandhara Chico   GUESTHOUSE $
(☎0812 360 3268; www.mandhara-chico-bali.com; off Jl Kubu Gembong, Anturan; r with fan/air-con

Sea Breeze Cabins GUESTHOUSE **$**
(☑ 0362-41138; off Jl Bina Ria, Kalibukbuk; r from 400,000Rp; ❄️ 🛜 🏊) One of the best choices in the heart of Kalibukbuk, the Sea Breeze has five bungalows and two rooms by the pool and beach, some with sensational views from their verandahs.

Puri Bali Hotel HOTEL **$**
(☑ 0362-41485; www.puribalilovina.com; Jl Mawar, Kalibukbuk; r with fan/air-con from 180,000/350,000Rp; ❄️ 🛜 🏊) The pool area is set deep in a lush garden – you could easily hang out here all day and let any cares wander off to the ether. The 25 rooms are simple but comfortable.

Padang Lovina GUESTHOUSE **$**
(☑ 0362-41302; padanglovina@yahoo.com; Gang Binaria, Kalibukbuk; r 200,000-350,000Rp; ❄️ 🛜 🏊) Down a narrow lane in the very heart of Kalibukbuk. There's no pretension at all around the 12 comfortable bungalow-style rooms set around spacious grounds teeming with flowers. The nicest rooms have air-con and bathtubs. There's wi-fi at the pool.

Homestay Purnama HOMESTAY **$**
(☑ 0362-41043; Jl Raya Lovina, Kalibukbuk; r from 100,000Rp; 🛜) One of the best deals on this stretch, Homestay Purnama has seven clean cold-water rooms, and the beach is only a two-minute walk away. This is a family compound, and a friendly one at that.

Rambutan Hotel HOTEL **$$**
(☑ 0362-41388; www.rambutan.org; Jl Mawar, Kalibukbuk; r US$30-80, villas US$95-190; ❄️ @ 🛜 🏊 🎮) The hotel, on one hectare of lush gardens, features two pools and a playground. The 28 rooms are decorated with Balinese style. The cheapest are fan-only. Villas are good deals; the largest are good for families and have kitchens.

🛏️ Around Lovina

★ **Damai** HOTEL **$$$**
(☑ 0362-41008; www.damai.com; Jl Damai; villas US$250-500; ❄️ 🛜 🏊) ✔️ Set on a hillside behind Lovina, Damai has sweeping views. Its 14 luxury villas mix antiques and a modern style accented by beautiful Balinese fabrics. The infinity pool seemingly spills onto a landscape of peanut fields, rice paddies and coconut palms.

Larger villas have private pools and multiple rooms that flow from one to another.

The restaurant is lauded for its organic fusion cuisine. Call for transport or, at the main junction in Kalibukbuk, go south on Jl Damai and follow the road for about 3km.

🍴 Eating

Just about every hotel has a cafe or restaurant. Walk along the beach footpath to choose from a selection of basic places with cold beer, standard food and sunsets.

🍴 Anturan to Kalibukbuk

Warung Dolphin SEAFOOD **$**
(☑ 0813 5327 6985; Jl Pantai Banyualit; mains from 30,000Rp) Near the beach, this simple cafe serves a fine grilled-seafood platter (which was probably caught by the guy next to you). There's live acoustic music many nights; a few other tasty cafes are nearby.

Bakery Lovina CAFE **$$**
(☑ 0362-42225; Jl Raya Lovina; breakfast 85,000Rp; ⏰ 7am-7pm; ❄️) Enjoy Lovina's best cup of coffee amid groceries at this upmarket deli that is a short walk from the centre. The croissants and German breads are baked fresh daily and there's a short selection of fresh meals including European-style breakfasts.

🍴 Kalibukbuk

This is ground zero for nightlife. There's a good range of restaurants, beachside cafes, bars where you can get a pizza and maybe hear some music, or fun places that defy description.

★ **Global Village Kafe** CAFE **$**
(☑ 0362-41928; Jl Raya Lovina, Kalibukbuk; mains from 15,000Rp; ⏰ 8am-10pm; 🛜) Che Guevara, Mikhail Gorbachev and Nelson Mandela are just some of the figures depicted in paintings lining the walls of this artsy cafe. The baked goods, fruit drinks, pizzas, breakfasts and much more are excellent. It has a welcoming, mellow vibe. There's free book and DVD exchanges plus a selection of local handicrafts. Watch for art-house movie nights.

Akar VEGETARIAN **$**
(☑ 0817 972 4717; Jl Bina Ria, Kalibukbuk; mains 40,000-50,000Rp; ⏰ 7am-10pm; 🛜 🍴) ✔️ The many shades of green at this cute-as-a-babyfrog cafe aren't just for show – they reflect the earth-friendly ethics of the owners. Enjoy organic smoothies, house-made gelato

and fresh and tasty noodle dishes. A tiny back porch overlooks the river.

Warung Barclona BALINESE $
(☑0362-41894; Jl Mawar, Kalibukbuk; mains from 40,000Rp; ☺8am-9pm) Despite the vaguely Catalan name, this family-run restaurant has an ambitious and good Balinese menu. Choose from but six tables on an open-air terrace. There are usually several seafood specials.

Night Market BALINESE $
(Jl Raya Lovina, Kalibukbuk; mains from 15,000Rp; ☺5-11pm) Lovina's night market is a good choice for fresh and cheap local food. Each year it adds a few more interesting stands. Try the *piseng goreng* (fried bananas).

★ Jasmine Kitchen THAI $$
(☑0362-41565; Gang Binaria, Kalibukbuk; mains 50,000-100,000Rp; ☺8am-10pm; 🛜) The Thai fare at this elegant two-level restaurant is excellent. The menu is long and authentic and the staff gracious. While soft jazz plays, try the homemade ice cream for dessert. You can refill water bottles here for 2000Rp. The ground-floor coffee bar is a fine stop.

Seyu JAPANESE $$
(www.seyulovina.com; Gang Binaria, Kalibukbuk; dishes from 50,000Rp; ☺10am-10pm; 🛜) This authentic Japanese place has a skilled sushi chef and a solid list of fresh nigiri and sashimi choices. The dining room is suitably spare and uncomplicated.

Sea Breeze Café INDONESIAN $$
(☑0362-41138; off Jl Bina Ria, Kalibukbuk; mains from 45,000Rp; ☺8am-10pm; 🛜) Right by the beach, this breezy cafe is the better – and more intimate – of the beachside choices. It has Indonesian and Western dishes and excellent breakfasts. The 'royal seafood platter' is like an entire fish market on a plate.

✖ Around Lovina

★ Buda Bakery BAKERY, CAFE $
(☑0812 469 1779; off Jl Damai; mains from 40,000Rp; ☺7am-10pm) North Bali's best bakery has an amazing array of breads, cakes and other treats produced fresh daily. However the real reason to make the 10-minute walk here from Jl Raya Lovina is for the upstairs cafe, which does simple yet superlative Indonesian and Western fare. Note that the baked goods often sell out fast.

Spice Beach Club INTERNATIONAL $$
(☑0362-701 2666; www.spicebeachclubbali.com; off Jl Raya Lovina; mains 70,000-150,000Rp; ☺kitchen 9am-11am, bar till 12:30am; 🛜) Mirrored shades are de rigueur at this stylish hang-out on a nice patch of beach. There's a whiff of Cannes about the rows of beach loungers backed by a pool. The menu ranges from burgers to seafood while the bar list is long. House music, lockers and showers are some of the amenities.

Tanjung Alam SEAFOOD $$
(☑0362-41223; Jl Raya Lovina; meals 30,000-80,000Rp; ☺11am-9pm) You'll see the fragrant column of smoke rising through the palms before you find this entirely open-air waterfront restaurant where grilled seafood is king. Settle back at one of the shady tables, let the gentle lapping of the nearby waves soothe you and enjoy an affordable feast. It's 1.2km west of the centre.

★ Damai FUSION, ORGANIC $$$
(☑0362-41008; www.damai.com; Jl Damai; lunch US$5-15, 5-course dinner from US$50; ☺noon-2pm & 5-9pm, from 11am Sun) 🖉 Enjoy the renowned organic restaurant at the boutique hotel in the hills behind Lovina. Tables enjoy views across the north coast. The changing menu draws its fresh ingredients from the hotel's organic farm and the local fishing fleet. Dishes are artful and the wine list one of the best in Bali. Sunday brunch is popular. Call for pick-up.

🍷 Drinking & Nightlife

Plenty of places to eat are also fine for a drink, especially those on the beach. There's a clutch of similar cafes good for a sunset Bintang at the end of Jl Mawar. Happy hours abound, with faux mixed drinks (aka ersatz 'gin') made with *arak*.

The following are some of the top picks from the fairly compact nightlife zone in Kalibukbuk.

Kantin 21 BAR
(☑0812 460 7791; Jl Raya Lovina, Kalibukbuk; ☺11pm-late; 🛜) Funky open-air place where you can watch traffic by day and groove to acoustic guitar or garage-band rock by night. There's a long drinks list, fresh juices and a few local snacks. On many nights, a local band plays after 9pm.

Poco Lounge BAR
(☑0362-41535; Jl Bina Ria, Kalibukbuk; ☺11am-1am; 🛜) Movies are shown at various times,

and cover bands perform at this popular bar-cafe. Classic travellers fare is served at tables open to street life in front and the river in back. Several other bars go past midnight here, including the neighbouring Zigiz.

Pashaa CLUB
(www.pashaabalinightclub.com; Jl Raya Lovina, Kalibukbuk; ⊘7pm-late) A small but high-concept club near the centre; DJs from around the island mix it up while bands play on and on.

ℹ Information
Kalibukbuk has ATMs, book stalls, internet places and pharmacies.

ℹ Getting There & Away

BUS & BEMO
To reach Lovina from south Bali by public transport, you'll need to change twice in Singaraja. Take a bus from Denpasar to the Sangket terminal, then a bemo to the Banyuasri terminal. Finally, get another bemo to the Lovina area. This will take much of a day.

Regular bemos go from Singaraja's Banyuasri terminal to Kalibukbuk (about 7000Rp) – you can flag them down anywhere along the main road.

If you're coming by long-distance bus from the west you can ask to be dropped off anywhere along the main road.

TOURIST SHUTTLE BUS
Perama (☑ 0362-41161; www.peramatour.com; Jl Raya Lovina) buses stop in Anturan. Passengers are then ferried to other points on the Lovina strip (10,000Rp). There's a daily bus to/from the south, including Kuta, Sanur and Ubud (all 100,000Rp).

ℹ Getting Around
The Lovina strip is *very* spread out, but you can easily travel back and forth on bemos (5000Rp).

West of Lovina
The main road west of Lovina passes temples, farms and towns while it follows the thinly developed coast. You'll see many vineyards, where the grapes work overtime producing the sugar used in Bali's very sweet local vintages. The road continues to Taman Nasional Bali Barat (West Bali National Park) and the port of Gilimanuk.

Air Terjun Singsing
About 5km west of Lovina, a sign points to Air Terjun Singsing (Daybreak Waterfall), and 1km from the main road, there's a warung on the left and a car park on the right. Walk past the warung and along the path for about 200m to the lower falls. The waterfall isn't huge, but the pool underneath is ideal for swimming, though not crystal-clear. The water, cooler than the sea, is very refreshing.

Clamber further up the hill to another, slightly bigger fall, **Singsing Dua**. It has a mud bath that is supposedly good for the skin (we'll let you decide about this). These falls also cascade into a deep swimming pool.

The area is thick with tropical forest and makes a nice day trip from Lovina. The falls are more spectacular in the wet season (October to March), and may be just a trickle other times.

Air Panas Banjar
These **hot springs** (adult/child 10,000/5000Rp; ⊘8am-6pm) percolate amid lush tropical plants. You can relax here for a few hours and have lunch at the restaurant, or even stay the night.

Eight fierce-faced carved stone *naga* (mythical snakelike creatures) pour water from a natural hot spring into the first bath, which then overflows (via the mouths of five more *naga*), into a second, larger pool. In a third pool, water pours from 3m-high spouts to give you a pummelling massage. The water is slightly sulphurous and pleasantly steamy (about 38°C). You must wear a swimsuit and you shouldn't use soap in the pools, but you can use an adjacent outdoor shower.

Overlooking the baths, there's a simple **cafe**.

From the bemo stop on the main road to the hot springs you can take an *ojek* (motorcycle that takes passengers); going back is a 2.4km downhill stroll.

Seririt & Around
Seririt is a junction for roads that run south through the central mountains to Munduk or to Papuan and west Bali via the beautiful Antosari road or an equally scenic road to Pulukan.

The **market** in the centre of town is renowned for its many stalls selling supplies for making offerings. It also has ATMs.

Some 10km west of Seririt at Celukanbawang you won't be able to miss a shockingly huge new power plant being built as a joint venture with China. Public details have been few, but it's designed to burn Chinese coal arriving on large ships at the new port.

🛏 Sleeping

Some 2km west of Seririt on the Singaraja–Gilimanuk Rd, a smaller road, Jl Ume Anyar, runs north towards the narrow beaches and passes several secluded small resorts.

Zen Resort Bali   BOUTIQUE HOTEL $$
(☑0362-93578; www.zenresortbali.com; Jl Ume Anyar; r from €95-115; 🏊) The name says it all, albeit very calmly. Yoga and a lavish spa figure prominently in the lifestyle at this resort devoted to your internal and mental well-being. Rooms in traditional bungalows have a minimalist look designed to not tax the synapses, gardens are dotted with water features and the beach is 200m away. It's 600m off the main road.

Villa Mayo Bali   RESORT $$
(☑0818 555 635; www.villamayobali.com; Jl Ume Anyar; r 650,000-1,100,000Rp; ❄🖨🏊) Rare for Bali, this small waterfront resort has a refreshing light-blue-and-white colour scheme. There are seven large units in a two-storey main building, each with a large terrace. And should you need it, a massage pavilion near the narrow beach. It is about 200m past Zen Resort Bali.

Kali Manik   LODGE $$
(☑0362-706 4888; www.bali-eco-resort.com; Kalisada; r US$55-150; 🖨) 🍃 An 'eco-resort' that's worthy of the name, the three units here are made from all native and natural materials; bamboo figures prominently and the design is free-form. The smallest sleeps two while the largest is family-sized. Don't expect aircon or a pool but there are hammocks and an organic cafe. It's down a small road 7km west of Seririt.

Pulaki

Pulaki is famous for its grape vines (Bali's Hattan Wines owns many), watermelons and for **Pura Pulaki**, a coastal temple that was completely rebuilt in the early 1980s,

and is home to a large troop of monkeys, as well as troops at a nearby army base. It's an easy walk from Pemuteran.

Pemuteran

This popular oasis in the northwest corner of Bali has a number of artful resorts set on a little dogbone-shaped bay that's alive with local life such as kids playing soccer until dark. Pemuteran offers a real beach getaway. Most people dive or snorkel the underwater wonders at nearby Pulau Menjangan while here.

The busy Singaraja–Gilimanuk road is the town's spine and ever-more businesses aimed at visitors can be found along it. Despite its popularity, Pemuteran's community and tourism businesses have forged a sustainable vision for development that should be a model for the rest of Bali.

◎ Sights

Strolling the beach is popular, especially at sunset, as you'd expect. The little fishing village is interesting, and if you walk around to the eastern end of the dogbone, you escape a lot of the development – although new projects are appearing. Look for various traditional-style boats being built on the shore.

Pemuteran is home to the nonprofit **Proyek Penyu** (Turtle Hatchery; ☑0362-93001; www.reefseenbali.com; ⊗8am-5pm), run by Reef Seen Divers' Resort. Turtle eggs and small turtles purchased from locals are looked after here until they're ready for ocean release. Thousands of turtles have been released since 1994. You can visit the small hatchery and make a donation to sponsor and release a tiny turtle. It's just off the main road, along the beach just east of Taman Selini Beach Bungalows.

🏃 Activities

Pemuteran Bay has a nice sandy **beach** that's good for swimming.

The extensive coral reefs are about 3km offshore. Coral closer in is being restored as part of the Bio Rocks project. **Diving** and **snorkelling** are universally popular and are offered by dive shops and hotels. Local dives cost from about US$50; snorkelling gear rents from 40,000Rp.

★ Reef Seen Divers' Resort   DIVING
(☑ 0362-93001; www.reefseenbali.com; night dive 520,000Rp, Pulau Menjangan from 920,000Rp) Right on the beach in a large compound, Reef Seen is active in local preservation efforts. It's a PADI dive centre and has a full complement of classes. It also offers one-hour sunset and sunrise **glass-bottomed boat** cruises (per person from 175,000Rp), and **pony rides** on the beach for kids (from 200,000Rp for 30 minutes).

Some dive packages include accommodation at the resort.

Easy Divers   DIVING
(☑ 0813 5319 8766; www.easy-divers.eu; Jl Singaraja–Gilimanuk; introductory dive from €50, snorkelling at Pulau Menjangan €35) The founder, Dusan Repic, has befriended many a diver new to Bali and this shop is well recommended. It's near the Taman Sari and Pondok Sari hotels.

Bali Diving Academy   DIVING
(☑ 0361-270252; www.scubali.com; Beachfront, Taman Sari hotel; Discover dive at Bio Rocks US$84, Pulau Menjangan dives from US$105) The well-respected Bali-wide dive company has

---

> ### ⓘ DIVING & SNORKELLING PULAU MENJANGAN
>
> With its great selection of lodgings, Pemuteran is the ideal base for diving and snorkelling Pulau Menjangan. Banyuwedang's harbour is just 7km west of town, so you have only a short ride before you're on a boat for the relaxing and pretty 30-minute journey to Menjangan. Dive shops and local hotels run snorkelling trips that cost US$35 to US$60; two-tank dive trips from US$80.

---

a shop right on the sand on the bay. It's near the Bio Rocs info booth. Ask about some of the lesser-known Menjangan dive sites.

🛏 Sleeping

Pemuteran has one of the nicest selections of beachside hotels in Bali, plus a growing number of budget guesthouses. Many have a sense of style and all are low-key and relaxed, with easy access to the beach.

Some of the hotels are accessed directly off the main road, while others are off small roads that run either to the bay or towards the mountains.

★ Double You Homestay   GUESTHOUSE $
(☑ 0813 3842 7000; www.doubleyoubali.com; off Jl Singaraja–Gilimanuk; r 300,000-600,000Rp; ❄️🛜) On a small lane south of the main road, this very attractive guesthouse is a good example of the many well-priced new places to stay that are springing up in Pemuteran. The four immaculate rooms are set on a flower-filled garden and have hot water and other comforts.

Jubawa Homestay   GUESTHOUSE $
(☑ 0362-94745; www.jubawa-pemuteran.com; r 300,000-600,000Rp; ❄️🛜🏊) Not far from the Matahari resort on the south (hill) side of the road, this is a rather plush budget choice. The 24 rooms are in expansive gardens around a pool. The popular cafe/bar serves Balinese and Thai food (mains from 40,000Rp).

Taruna   GUESTHOUSE $
(☑ 0813 3853 6318; www.tarunahomestaypemuteran.com; Jl Singaraja–Gilimanuk; r fan/air-con from 300,000/550,000Rp; ❄️🛜🏊) On the beach side of the main road and just a short walk from the sand, this professionally run place has nine well-designed rooms.

Bali Gecko Homestay   GUESTHOUSE $
(☑ 0852 5301 5928; bali.gecko@ymail.com; Desa Pemuteran; r 250,000-400,000Rp; ❄️🛜) About 500m west of Pemuteran's main strip and another 200m off the main road, this family-run guesthouse is isolated. You can walk to a quiet part of the beach along a short trail or ascend a nearby hill for great views. The four rooms (some with air-con) are very simple.

Rare Angon Homestay   HOMESTAY $
(☑ 0362-94747; Jl Singaraja–Gilimanuk; r 250,000-500,000Rp; ❄️) Four good basic rooms (some with air-con) in a homestay located on the

DIVING & SNORKELLING PULAU MENJANGAN

Bali's best-known underwater attraction, Pulau Menjangan is ringed by over a dozen superb dive sites. The experience is excellent – iconic tropical fish, soft corals, great visibility (usually), caves and spectacular drop-offs.

Lacy sea fans and various sponges provide both texture and myriad hiding spots for small fish that together form a colour chart for the sea. Few can resist the silly charms of parrotfish and clownfish. Among larger creatures, you may see whales, whale sharks and manta rays.

Of the named sites here, most are close to shore and suitable for snorkellers or diving novices. But you can also venture out to where the depths turn black as the shallows drop off in dramatic cliffs, a magnet for experienced divers looking for wall dives.

This uninhabited island boasts what is thought to be Bali's oldest temple, **Pura Gili Kencana**, dating from the 14th century and about 300m from the pier. You can walk around the island in about an hour and most people who take to the waters here take a break on the unfortunately not-entirely-unblemished beaches.

Practicalities

Divers have more scope to customise their experience, although it usually begins at an extraordinary 30m wall near the south side jetty. Snorkellers, however, may find themselves conveyed along the underwater beauty by guides who do this day-in and day-out and are just as happy to go home. This can happen with both top-end hotel-sponsored tours and the boats from Banyuwedang and Labuhan Lalang. Tips to maximise what will likely be a highlight of your Bali trip include:

➡ Boats usually tie up to the jetty at Palau Menjangan. The wall here – which rewards both divers and snorkellers – is directly out from the shore. Currents tend to flow gently southwest (the shore is on your right) so you can just literally go with the flow and enjoy the underwater spectacle.

➡ Your guide may try to get you to swim back to the boat at some point along the less-interesting bleached coral near the shore; this turns out to be for their break. Instead, suggest that the boat come down and pick you up when you're ready, thus avoiding the swim against the current followed by downtime at the pier.

➡ The wall extends far to the southwest and gets more pristine and spectacular as you go. If you're overcome with joy and can't stop, you could get to the end in one go or you can break up the experience by having the boat pick you up and then drop you off again.

➡ North of the jetty, you can snorkel from shore and cover the sites in a big circle.

➡ Although the jetty area on the south side of the island is spectacular, most boat operators will take you there simply as it's the closest to the harbours and lets them save gas. The north side is also spectacular and is the best place to go mid-day, while **Coral Gardens** to the west is another fine spot. The **Anker Wreck**, a mysterious sunken ship, challenges even experts.

➡ Try to hover over some divers along the wall. Watching their bubbles sinuously rise in all their multi-hued silvery glory from the inky depths is just plain spectacular.

➡ If your guide really adds to your experience, tip accordingly.

➡ **Friends of Menjangan** (www.friendsofmenjangan.blogspot.com) has info and updates.

Getting There & Away

The closest and most convenient dive operators are found at Pemuteran, where the hotels also arrange diving and snorkelling trips. Independent snorkellers can arrange trips from Banyuwedang and Labuhan Lalang. If you are coming from elsewhere on Bali on a daytrip, carefully find out how much time you'll be travelling each way. From Seminyak, traffic can make for seven or more total hours in a car.

BIO ROCKS: GROWING A NEW REEF

Pemuteran is set among a fairly arid part of Bali where people have always had a hard-scrabble existence. In the early 1990s tourist operators began to take advantage of the excellent diving in the area. Locals who'd previously been scrambling to grow or catch something to eat began getting training in language and other areas to welcome people to what would become a collection of resorts.

But there was one big problem: dynamite and cyanide fishing plus El Niño warming had bleached and damaged large parts of the reef.

A group of local hotels, dive-shop owners and community leaders hit upon a novel solution: grow a new reef using electricity. The idea had already been floated by scientists internationally, but Pemuteran was the first place to implement it on a wide – and hugely successful – scale.

Using local materials, the community built dozens of large metal cages that were placed out along the threatened reef. These were then hooked to *very* low-wattage generators on land (you can see the cables running ashore near the Taman Sari hotel). What had been a theory became a reality. The low current stimulated limestone formation on the cages which in turn quickly grew new coral. All told, Pemuteran's small bay is getting new coral (aka Bio Rocks) at five to six times the rate it would take to grow naturally.

The results are win-win all around. Locals and visitors are happy and so are the reefs; the project has gained international attention and awards. The collaborative local group, the **Pemuteran Foundation** (www.pemuteranfoundation.com), has an info booth with a sign reading 'Bio Rocks Reef Gardeners' on the beach by Pondok Sari. Info on their work is in most local resort lobbies. Note their list of rules for swimming in the bay, including not standing on coral, not taking coral and shells, and not feeding the fish.

mountain side of the main road. Patios overlook the gardens.

★ Taman Sari   HOTEL $$
(☑0362-93264; www.tamansaribali.com; bungalows US$85-200, villas from US$290; ❄@🖥🏊) Off a small lane, 31 rooms are set in gorgeous bungalows that feature intricate carvings and traditional artwork inside and out. The resort is located on a long stretch of quiet beach on the bay, and is part of the reef restoration project. A nearby compound holds large and lavish villas. The restaurant (mains from 50,000Rp) specialises in Thai cuisine.

★ Taman Selini
Beach Bungalows   BOUTIQUE HOTEL $$
(☑0362-94746; www.tamanselini.com; Jl Singaraja–Gilimanuk; r US$95-250; ❄🖥🏊) The 11 bungalows recall an older, refined Bali, from the quaint thatched roofs down to the antique carved doors and detailed stonework. Rooms, which open onto a large garden running to the beach, have four-poster beds and large outdoor bathrooms. The outdoor daybeds can be addictive. It's immediately east of Pondok Sari, on the beach and off the main road.

Pondok Sari   HOTEL $$
(☑0362-94738; www.pondoksari.com; Jl Singaraja–Gilimanuk; r €50-190; ❄🖥) There are 36 rooms here set in densely planted gardens that assure privacy. The pool is down by the beach; the cafe has sweet water views through the trees. Traditional Balinese details abound; bathrooms are open-air and a calling card for the stone-carvers. Deluxe units have elaborate stone tubs among other details. The resort is just off the main road.

Amertha Bali Villas   HOTEL $$
(☑0362-94831; www.amerthabalivillas.com; Jl Singaraja–Gilimanuk; r US$100-145, villas US$150-350; ❄🖥🏊) A slightly older resort with spacious grounds, the Amertha benefits from having large mature trees that give it that timeless tropical feel. The 15 villas vary from large to very large, with a lot of natural wood and spacious covered patios. All have plunge pools.

★ Matahari Beach Resort   RESORT $$$
(☑0362-92312; www.matahari-beach-resort.com; Jl Singaraja–Gilimanuk; r US$200-350; ❄🖥🏊) This lovely beachside resort, on the quieter east end of the bay, is set in spacious and verdant grounds. Widely spaced bungalows are works of traditional art. Common areas

include a library and other luxuries. The spa is elegant and the beachside bar a good place for a pause as you explore the bay.

Puri Ganesha Villas BOUTIQUE HOTEL $$$

(☑0362-94766; www.puriganeshabali.com; villas from US$550; ❄@❄) Four two-storey villas on sweeping grounds are the basics at Puri Ganesha. Each has a unique style that mixes antiques with silks and relaxed comfort. Outside the air-con bedrooms, life is in the open air, including time in your private pool. Dine in the small restaurant or in your villa. It's located on the western point of the bay.

🍴 Eating & Drinking

Cafes and restaurants are opening all along the main drag. Otherwise the beachside hotels and resorts have good midrange restaurants. You can wander along the beach debating which one to choose. Taman Sari is a good choice while Jubawa Homestay on the main road is also popular.

★ Balance Café & Bistro CAFE $

(☑0853 3745 5454; www.bali-balance.com; Jl Singaraja–Gilimanuk; mains from 30,000Rp; ⊙7.30am-8pm; 🛜) Excellent coffee, plus juices and tasty cakes, make this spotless cafe a good place for a pause anytime. There's a short menu of sandwiches and salads, which can be enjoyed in the leafy back garden. It's on the hill side, roughly in the middle of the main strip.

Bali Re BALINESE $

(Jl Singaraja–Gilimanuk; mains 33,000-85,000Rp; ⊙8am-10pm) The charming staff is as sweet as the meat is succulent at this open-air *babi guling* (suckling pig) cafe, set on the beach side of the main road. It also has tables in a small garden and seafood specials.

Joe's INDONESIAN $

(☑0852 3739 0151; Jl Singaraja–Gilimanuk; mains from 40,000Rp; ⊙11am-midnight) The closest thing Pemuteran has to a party bar, Joe's has a dash of vintage style. Enjoy a seafood meal sitting around an old boat in the open-air dining room. Later, listen to diving tales great and small at the genial bar. It's in the middle of the main strip.

ℹ️ Information

There are several ATMs on Pemuteran's main strip, which stretches along Jl Singaraja–Gilimanuk from the Matahari Beach Resort west to the lane down to the Taman Sari hotel.

ℹ️ Getting There & Away

Pemuteran is served by buses on the Gilimanuk–Lovina (30,000Rp)–Singaraja run. There's no stop, so just flag one down. It's a three- to four-hour drive from south Bali, either over the hills or around the west coast. A private car and driver costs 575,000Rp to either Ubud or Seminyak, among other destinations.

Banyuwedang

This mangrove-fringed cove just east of the national park is the main hub for journeys to Pulau Menjangan.

🏃 Activities

If you are visiting Menjangan to dive or snorkel as part of a group, it's highly likely that you'll catch your boat at this bustling little harbour, which is 1.2km off Jl Singaraja–Gilimanuk.

You can also arrange your own snorkelling trips here; they typically take three hours, with one hour of that transit time. You can leave from 8am to 2pm daily. Prices are fixed and reward groups: a boat (for one to 10 people) 450,000Rp; mandatory guide (for the group, many do little actual 'guiding') 150,000Rp; snorkel-set rental per person 40,000Rp; park-entrance fee per person 20,000Rp; and insurance per person 4000Rp.

🛏️ Sleeping

Mimpi Resort Menjangan RESORT $$

(☑0361-415020, 0362-94497; www.mimpi.com; Pejarakan; r US$100-150, villas US$180-400; ❄@🛜❄) Near the docks for boats to Menjangan, this 54-unit resort extends down to a small, mangrove-fringed, white-sand beach. The rooms have an unadorned monochromatic motif with open-air bathrooms. Hot springs feed communal pools and private tubs in the villas. The grand villas, with a private pool and lagoon views, are a great tropical fantasy escape.

Labuhan Lalang

To catch a boat to visit or snorkel Pulau Menjangan, head to the jetty at this small harbour inside Taman Nasional Bali Barat. Prices are the same as those at Banyuwedang. There are warung and a pleasant beach 200m to the east.

Taman Nasional Bali Barat

☑ 0365

Most visitors to Bali's only national park, Taman Nasional Bali Barat (West Bali National Park), are struck by the mellifluous sounds emanating from myriad birds darting amongst the rustling trees.

The park covers 190 sq km of the western tip of Bali. An additional 550 sq km is protected in the national park extension, as well as almost 70 sq km of coral reef and coastal waters. Together this represents a significant commitment to conservation on an island as densely populated as Bali.

It's a place where you can enjoy Bali's best diving at Pulau Menjangan, hike through forests and explore coastal mangroves.

Most of the natural vegetation in the park is not tropical rainforest, which requires year-round rain, but rather coastal savannah, with deciduous trees that become bare in the dry season. The southern slopes receive more-regular rainfall, and so have more tropical vegetation, while the coastal lowlands have extensive mangroves.

There are more than 200 species of plants growing in the park. Local fauna includes black monkeys, leaf monkeys and macaques (seen in the afternoon along the main road near Sumber Kelompok); rusa, barking, sambar, Java and *muncak* (mouse) deer; and some wild pigs, squirrels, buffalo, iguanas, pythons and green snakes. There were once tigers, but the last confirmed sighting was in 1937 – and that one was shot. The birdlife is prolific, with many of Bali's 300 species found here, including the very rare Bali starling.

Just getting off the road a bit on one of the many trails transports you into the heart of nature. One discordant note: hikes in fuel prices have seen lots of vendors along the road selling firewood taken from the forest.

🏃 Activities

By land, by boat or underwater, the park awaits exploration. However you'll need a guide and negotiating a fee can be confounding. Virtually all costs are variable. You can arrange things at the park offices in Cekik or Labuhan Lalang.

Boat Trips

The best way to explore the mangroves of Teluk Gilimanuk (Gilimanuk Bay) or the west side of Prapat Agung is by chartering a boat (maximum of 10 people) for about 450,000Rp per boat per three hours, plus a guide (150,000Rp) and entrance fees. This is

Taman Nasional Bali Barat

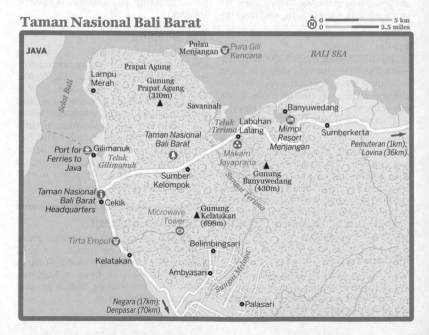

the ideal way to see bird life, including kingfishers, Javanese herons and more.

Trekking

All trekkers must be accompanied by an authorised guide. It's best to arrive the day before you want to trek and make arrangements at the park offices.

The set rates for guides in the park depend on the size of the group and the length of the trek – with one or two people it's 350,000Rp for one or two hours, with rates steadily increasing from there. Food (a small lunchbox) is included but transport is extra and all the prices are *very* negotiable. Early morning, say 6am, is the best time to start – it's cooler and you're more likely to see some wildlife.

If, once you're out, you have a good rapport with your guide, you might consider getting creative. Although you can try to customise your hike, the guides prefer to set itineraries, including some of the following sites.

From Sumber Kelompok, treks head up **Gunung Kelatakan** (Mt Kelatakan; 698m), then down to the main road near Kelatakan village (six to seven hours). You may be able to get permission from park headquarters to stay overnight in the forest – if you don't have a tent, your guide can make a shelter from branches and leaves, which will be an adventure in itself. Clear streams abound in the dense woods.

A three- to four-hour trek will allow you to explore the **Savannah** area along the coast northwest of Teluk Terima. You have a good chance of seeing monitor lizards, barking deer and black monkeys, and a very rare chance of spotting a Bali starling (p353). It includes a motorbike ride to the trailhead and a return trip by boat.

From a trail west of Labuhan Lalang, a three- to four-hour hike exploring **Teluk Terima** (Terima Bay) starts at the mangroves. You then partially follow Sungai Terima (Terima River) into the hills and walk back down to the road along the steps at Makam Jayaprana. You might see grey macaques, deer and black monkeys.

🛏 Sleeping

Park visitors will want to spend the night close to the park to get an early start the next day. Gilimanuk is closest and has a basic option. Much nicer are the many options going east to Pemuteran, 12km east of Labuhan Lalang.

❶ Information

The park headquarters (p254) at Cekik displays a topographic model of the park area, and has a little information about plants and wildlife. The **Labuhan Lalang Information Office** (Jl Singaraja–Gilimanuk; ⏰7.30am-4pm) is in a hut located in the parking area where boats leave for Pulau Menjangan. Park guides on hand usually include **Nyoman Kawit** (☑0852 3850 5291), who is knowledgeable.

You can arrange trekking guides and permits at either office; however, there are always a few characters hanging around, and determining who is an actual park official can be like spotting a Bali starling: difficult.

The main roads to Gilimanuk go through the national park, but you don't have to pay an entrance fee just to drive through. However, any activities in the park, such as hiking or diving Menjangan, require paying the 20,000Rp park fee.

❶ Getting There & Away

If you don't have your own transport, any Gilimanuk-bound bus or bemo from north or west Bali can drop you at park headquarters at Cekik (those from north Bali can also drop you at the Labuhan Lalang visitors centre).

West Bali

Best Beaches

➡ Balian Beach (p250)
➡ Yeh Gangga (p249)
➡ Pura Rambut Siwi (p252)

Best Places to Stay

➡ Bali Silent Retreat (p250)
➡ Alila Villas Soori (p250)
➡ Gajah Mina (p251)
➡ Taman Wana Villas & Spa (p254)
➡ Puri Dajuma Cottages (p252)

Why Go?

Even as development from south Bali, via hotspots like Canggu, creeps ever further west, Bali's true west, which is off the busy main road from Tabanan to Gilimanuk, remains mostly little-visited. It's easy to find serenity amid its wild beaches, jungle and rice fields.

On the coast, surfers hit the breaks at Balian and Medewi beaches. Some of Bali's most sacred sites are here, from the ever-thronged Pura Tanah Lot to the Pura Taman Ayun and on to the wonderful isolation of Pura Rambut Siwi.

The tidy town of Tabanan is at the hub of Bali's Unesco-listed *subak,* the system of irrigation that ensures everybody gets a fair share of the water. On narrow back roads you can cruise beside rushing streams with bamboo arching overhead and fruit piling up below.

When to Go

➡ **Apr–Sep** The best time to visit west Bali is during the dry season, although recent weather patterns have made the dry season wetter and the wet season drier. Hiking and trekking in Taman Nasional Bali Barat is much easier when it isn't muddy, and the waters of Pulau Menjangan are at their world-class best for diving on clear days.

➡ **May–Aug** Along the coast, the west has yet to develop a peak season – although surfing is best in months without an 'r'.

West Bali Highlights

1 Revelling in the cool beach vibe of **Balian Beach** (p250), where surfer hangouts and stylish digs rub shoulders.

2 Nailing the long left break at the low-key surfer haven at **Pantai Medewi** (p251).

3 Finding your own corner of serenity at **Pura Taman Ayun** (p248).

4 Enjoying the morning spirituality of **Pura Tanah Lot** (p248) before it gives way to the chaos of the afternoon.

5 Feeling the spiritual serenity of the important seaside temple at **Pura Rambut Siwi** (p252).

6 Witnessing the mud and fury of a bull race near **Negara** (p253).

7 Discovering your own back-road paradise of low-hanging fruit, arching bamboo and rushing water such as you'll find near **Kerambitan** (p249).

Pura Tanah Lot

📷 0361

An ever-popular day trip from south Bali, **Pura Tanah Lot** (adult/child 30,000/15,000Rp, parking cars/motorbikes 5000/2000Rp) is the most visited and photographed temple in Bali (receiving almost three million visitors a year), especially at sunset when crowds and traffic overwhelm the site. It has all the authenticity of a stage set – even the tower of rock that the temple sits upon is an artful reconstruction (the entire structure was crumbling). Over one-third of the rock you see is artificial.

For the Balinese, Pura Tanah Lot is one of the most important and venerated sea temples. Like Pura Luhur Ulu Watu, at the tip of the southern Bukit Peninsula, and Pura Rambut Siwi to the west, it is closely associated with the Majapahit priest Nirartha. It's said that each of the sea temples was intended to be within sight of the next, so they formed a chain along Bali's southwestern coast – from Pura Tanah Lot you can usually see the clifftop site of Pura Ulu Watu far to the south, and the long sweep of sea shore west to Perancak, near Negara.

But at Tanah Lot itself you may just see from one vendor to the next. To reach the temple, take the walkways that run from the vast parking lots through a mind-boggling sideshow of tatty souvenir shops down to the sea. Clamorous announcements screech from loudspeakers.

You can walk over to the temple itself at low tide, but non-Balinese people are not allowed to enter.

You won't be able to miss the looming Pan Pacific Nirwana Resort with its water-sucking golf course. It has been controversial since the day it was built, because many feel its greater height shows the temple disrespect.

ENJOYING TANAH LOT

Why shouldn't you just skip Tanah Lot? Because it is an important spiritual site and the temple itself does have an innate beauty. The secret is to arrive before noon: you'll beat the crowds and the vendors will still be asleep. You'll actually hear birds chirping rather than buses idling and people carping. Besides, you can enjoy the sunset from many other places – like a beachfront bar south towards Seminyak.

If coming from south Bali take the coastal road west from Kerobokan and follow the signs. From other parts of Bali, turn off the Denpasar–Gilimanuk road near Kediri and follow the signs. During the pre- and post-sunset rush, traffic is awful.

Kapal

About 10km north of Denpasar, Kapal is the garden-feature and temple-doodad centre of Bali. If you need a green tiger or other decorative critter rendered in colours not found in nature (we saw a pink beaver), then this is your place – although shipping might be a pain. Kapal is on the main road to the west, so it might be worth getting out of the traffic just to walk with the animals.

Pura Taman Ayun

The huge royal water temple of **Pura Taman Ayun** (adult/child 15,000/7500Rp; ⊘ 8am-6pm), surrounded by a wide, elegant moat, was the main temple of the Mengwi kingdom, which survived until 1891, when it was conquered by the neighbouring kingdoms of Tabanan and Badung. The large temple was built in 1634 and extensively renovated in 1937. It's a spacious place to wander around and you can get away from speed-obsessed group-tour mobs. The first courtyard is a large, open, grassy expanse and the inner courtyard has a multitude of *meru* (multi-tiered shrines). Lotus blossoms fill the pools; the temple forms part of the *subak* system (village association for rice-growers) of sites recognised by Unesco in 2012.

Pura Taman Ayun is an easy stop on a drive to/from Bedugal and the Jatiluwih rice fields (p225).

Marga

Between the walls of traditional family compounds in the village of Marga, there are some beautifully shaded roads – but this town wasn't always so peaceful. On 20 November 1946, a much larger and better-armed Dutch force, fighting to regain Bali as a colony after the departure of the Japanese, surrounded a force of 96 independence fighters. The outcome was similar to the *puputan* (warrior's fight to the death) of 40 years earlier – Ngurah Rai, who led the resistance against the Dutch (and later had the airport named after him), was killed, along with every one of his men. There was, however, one important difference – this time the Dutch suffered heavy casualties as well, and this may have helped weaken their resolve to hang on to the rebellious colony.

The independence struggle is commemorated at the **Margarana** (admission 5000Rp; ⊗8am-5pm, museum until noon), northwest of Marga village. Tourists seldom visit, but every Balinese schoolchild comes here at least once, and a ceremony is held annually on 20 November. In a large compound stands a 17m-high pillar, and nearby is a small **museum** with a few photos, homemade weapons and other artefacts from the conflict. Note the famous line from Ngurah Rai's last letter: 'Freedom or death!'.

Behind is a smaller compound with 1372 small stone memorials to those who gave their lives for the cause of independence – these are headstone markers in a military cemetery, though bodies are not actually buried here. Each memorial has a symbol indicating the hero's religion, mostly the Hindu swastika, but also Islamic crescent moons and even a few Christian crosses. Look for the memorials to 11 Japanese who stayed on after WWII and fought with the Balinese against the Dutch.

Even with your own transport it's easy to get lost finding Marga and the memorial so, as always, ask for directions. You can easily combine this trip with Pura Taman Ayun and the Jatiluwih rice terraces.

Tabanan

📋 0361

Tabanan, like most regional capitals in Bali, is a large, well-organised place. The verdant surrounding rice fields are emblematic of Bali's rice-growing traditions and are part of its Unesco recognition.

◎ Sights

Mandala Mathika Subak 　　　　MUSEUM
(Subak Museum; Jl Raya Kediri; adult/child 15,000/7500Rp; ⊗8am-4.30pm Mon-Fri, to 1pm Sat) Within a large complex devoted to Tabanan's *subak* organisations, you'll find this museum, which has displays about the irrigation and cultivation of rice and the intricate social systems that govern it. Staff will show you around; there is info on the Unesco designation, some placards in English and a good model showing the *subak* system in action.

Exhibits are housed in a large building with water streaming by right out front.

✖ Eating

There are plenty of warungs (food stalls) in the town centre and at the bustling regional market, where a tasty **night market** (Jl Gajah Mada; mains from 10,000Rp; ⊗5pm-midnight) sets up on the south side. Out on the main road is a **babi guling stall** (Jl Bypass; dishes 5000-15,000Rp; ⊗7am-7pm).

❶ Getting There & Away

All bemo (minibuses) and buses between Denpasar (Ubung terminal) and Gilimanuk stop at the terminal at the western end of Tabanan (10,000Rp).

The road to Pura Luhur Batukau and the beautiful rice terraces of Jatiluwih heads north from the centre of town.

South of Tabanan

Driving in the southern part of Tabanan district takes you through many charming villages and past a lot of vigorously growing rice. The fields are revered by many as the most productive in Bali.

About 10km south of Tabanan is **Pejaten**, a centre for the production of traditional pottery, including elaborate ornamental roof tiles. Porcelain clay objects, which are made purely for decorative use, can be seen in a few workshops in the village. Check out the small showroom of **Pejaten Ceramic Art** (📱0816 577 073; ⊗9am-4pm Mon-Sat), one of several local producers. The trademark pale-green pieces are lovely, and when you see the prices, you'll at least buy a toad. The shop is close to the interesting daily **village market**.

A little west of Tabanan, a road goes 8km south via Gubug to the secluded coast at **Yeh Gangga**, where activities include horse rides along the long flat beach and surrounding countryside – call **Island Horse** (📱0361-731 407; www.baliislandhorse.com; rides adult/child from US$70/65) for pick-up and bookings.

Further west of Tabanan on the main road, a road turns south to the coast via **Kerambitan**, a village noted for its dance troupe and musicians who perform across the south and in Ubud. *Waringin* (banyan) trees shade beautiful old buildings, including the 17th-century palace **Puri Anyar Kerambitan** (📱0361-812668; Jl Raya Kerambitan; donation requested). The current prince, Anak Agung, is enjoying his retirement here and

BALI'S UNESCO-RECOGNISED SUBAK

Playing a critical role in rural Bali life, the *subak* is a village association that deals with water, water rights and irrigation. With water passing through many, many scores of rice fields before it drains away for good, there is always the chance that growers near the source will be water-rich while those at the bottom could end up selling carved wooden critters at Tanah Lot. Regulating a system that apportions a fair share to everyone is a model of mutual cooperation and an insight into the Balinese character. (One of the strategies used is to put the last person on the water channel in control.)

This complex and vital social system was added to Unesco's World Heritage List in 2012. Specific sites singled out include much of the rice-growing region around Tabanan, Pura Taman Ayun, the Jatiluwih rice terraces and Danau Batur.

loves sharing stories of old Bali within the vast shambolic antique-filled compound. Stop by to see if he's around.

About 4km from southern Kerambitan is the small beachside village of **Tibubiyu**. For a lovely drive through huge bamboo, fruit trees, rice paddies and more, take the scenic road, Jl Meliling Kangin, northwest from Kerambitan to the main Tabanan–Gilimanuk road.

★ **Alila Villas Soori** VILLAS $$$
([phone] 0361-894 6388; www.alilahotels.com; Kelating; villas from US$500; ❋ 🛜 🗷) This luxury villa compound on a (still) remote stretch of Bali's west coast has 46 very private villas, each with their own plunge pool. The accommodation has a modern minimalism and the setting is very private. The nightlife of Canggu and Seminyak is 45 minutes to an hour away; the resort offers transport.

North of Tabanan

The area north of Tabanan is a good spot to travel around with your own transport. There are some B-grade attractions; the real appeal is just driving the fecund back roads where the bamboo arches, temple-like, over the road.

Bali Homestay Program HOMESTAY $
([phone] 0817 067 1788; www.bali-homestay.com; Jegu; r only per night from US$20) 🌿 You can sample village life as part of this innovative program that places travellers in the homes of residents of the rice-growing village of Jegu, 9km north of Tabanan. The recommended full package (US$175 per person) includes two nights' accommodation, activities such as making offerings and cultural tours plus all meals. Book at least two weeks in advance.

★ **Bali Silent Retreat** BOUTIQUE HOTEL $$
([phone] 0813 5348 6517; www.balisilentretreat.com; Penatahan; dm US$15, r US$40-120) Set amid gorgeous scenery, this place is just what the name says: somewhere to meditate, practice yoga, go on nature walks and more – all in total silence. Note that the minimalist ethos stops at the food, which is organic and fabulous (per day US$25). It's 18km northwest of Tabanan.

Antosari & Bajera

At Antosari, the main road takes a sharp turn south to the welcoming breezes of the ocean. Turn north and you'll enjoy a scenic drive to north Bali.

Balian Beach
[phone] 0361

Ever more popular, Balian Beach is a rolling area of dunes and knolls overlooking pounding surf. It attracts surfers and those looking to escape the bustle of south Bali.

You can wander between cafes and join other travellers for a beer, to watch the sunset and to talk surf. There are simple places to rent boards along the black-sand beach, while nonsurfers can simply enjoy bodysurfing the wild waves.

Balian Beach is right at the mouth of the wide Sungai Balian (Balian River). It is 800m south of the town of Lalang-Linggah, which is on the main road 10km west of Antosari.

🛏 Sleeping & Eating

All of the accommodation we review is fairly close together and near the beach. Warungs and simple cafes mean a bottle of Bintang is never more than a one-minute walk away.

★**Surya Homestay** GUESTHOUSE **$**
(📱0813 3868 5643; wayan.suratni@gmail.com;
r 150,000-200,000Rp) There are five rooms
in bungalow-style units at this sweet little
family-run place that is about 200m along a
small lane. It's spotless and rooms have cold
water and fans. Ask about long-term rates.

Ayu Balian HOMESTAY **$**
(📱0812 399 353; Jl Pantai Balian; r 100,000-
300,000Rp) The 15 rooms in this two-storey
cold-water block look down the road to the
surf. The small cafe serves crowd-pleasing
fare like Oreo-banana shakes.

Made's Homestay HOMESTAY **$**
(📱0812 396 3335; r 150,000-200,000Rp) Three
basic bungalow-style units are surrounded by
banana trees back from the beach. The rooms
are basic, clean, large enough to hold numerous surfboards, and have cold-water showers.

★**Gajah Mina** BOUTIQUE HOTEL **$$**
(📱081 2381 1630; www.gajahminaresort.com;
villas from US$120; ❋❂) Designed by the
French architect-owner, this eight-unit bou-
tique hotel is close to the ocean. The private
walled bungalows march out to a dramatic
outcrop of stone surrounded by surf. The
grounds are vast and there are little trails
for wandering and pavilions for relaxing.
The on-site seafood restaurant, **Naga** (mains
from 70,000Rp), overlooks its own little bowl
of rice terraces.

Pondok Pitaya: Hotel,
Surfing and Yoga GUESTHOUSE **$$**
(📱0819 9984 9054; www.pondokpitaya.com; Jl
Pantai Balian; r from 650,000Rp; ❂❂) With
a spray-scented location right on Balian
Beach, this complex combines vintage Indonesian buildings (including a 1950 Javanese
house and an 1860 Balinese alligator hunt-
er's shack) with more modest accommodation. The 19 rooms are like the surf: variable.
The cafe has juices, organic fare and pizzas
(mains 35,000Rp to 120,000Rp).

Pondok Pisces GUESTHOUSE **$$**
(📱0361-780 1735, 0813 3879 7722; www.pondok
piscesbali.com; Jl Pantai Balian; r 350,000-
800,000Rp; ❂) You can certainly hear the
sea at this tropical fantasy of thatched cot-
tages and flower-filled gardens. There are 10
rooms; those on the upper floor have large
terraces with surf views. In-house **Tom's
Garden Cafe** has grilled seafood and surf
views (mains 40,000Rp to 80,000Rp). Down
by the river and slightly upstream, there are

large villas and bungalows lushly set in a
teak forest.

Gubug Balian Beach GUESTHOUSE **$$**
(📱0812 3963 0605; gubugbalian@gmail.com; Jl
Pantai Balian; r 300,000-600,000Rp; ❋❂) On
a spacious site close to the beach are 10
rooms, some of which have views down the
lane to the surf. The cheapest rooms are fan
and cold-water only.

★**Mai Malu** INDONESIAN **$**
(📱0878 6284 6335; maimalu.medewi@yahoo.
com; off Jl Pantai Balian; mains from 30,000Rp;
⊙8am-10pm) Down a small lane 100m back
from the beach, this cute cafe has tables in
a quiet pavilion. The menu is broad, with all
the usual local and surfer favorites. The food
is excellent, especially the very popular big
Western-style breakfasts. There is accommodation, in two small cold-water/fan rooms
(200,000Rp).

🛈 Getting There & Away

Because the main west Bali road is usually
jammed with traffic, Balian Beach is often at
least a two-hour drive from Seminyak or the
airport (55km). A car and driver will cost about
500,000Rp for a day trip. You can also get a bus
(20,000Rp) going to Gilimanuk from Denpasar's
Ubung terminal and be dropped off at the road
entrance, which is 800m from the places to stay.

Jembrana Coast

About 34km west of Tabanan you cross
into Bali's most sparsely populated district,
Jembrana. The main road follows the south
coast most of the way to Negara. There's
some beautiful scenery and little tourist development, with the exception of the surfing
action at Medewi. At Pulukan you can turn
north and enjoy a remote and scenic drive
to north Bali.

Medewi

📱 0365

On the main road, a large sign points down
the short paved road (200m) to the surfing mecca of **Pantai Medewi** and its *long*
left-hand wave. Rides of 200m to 400m are
common.

The 'beach' is a stretch of huge, smooth
grey rocks interspersed among round black
pebbles. Think of it as free reflexology. Cattle graze by the shore, paying no heed to
the spectators watching the action out on

the water. There are a few guesthouses plus a couple of surf shops (board rental from 100,000Rp per day).

Medewi proper is a classic market town with shops selling all the essentials of west Bali life.

Sleeping & Eating

You'll find accommodation along the main lane to the surf break and down other lanes about 2km east of the main surf break. Some of the finest fare is freshly prepared and served up at a cart right by the beach/rocks.

Mai Malu GUESTHOUSE $
(📱0819 1617 1045; maimalu.medewi@yahoo; off Tabanan–Gilimanuk Rd; r from 150,000Rp; 🛜) Near the highway on the Medewi side road, Mai Malu is a popular (and almost the only) hang-out, serving crowd-pleasing pizza, burgers and Indonesian meals in its modern, breezy upstairs eating area (mains from 35,000Rp). Rooms have the basics plus fans.

Warung Gede & Homestay GUESTHOUSE $
(📱0812 397 6668; r from 100,000Rp) The absolute bargain leader of Medewi is right down by the rocky beach. From the simple open-air cafe (meals from 15,000Rp) you can watch the breaks and enjoy basic Indonesian fare as well as good Western breakfasts. Rooms are surfer-simple: cold water and fans.

Medewi Beach Cottages HOTEL $$
(📱0361-852 8521; www.medewibeachcottages.com; r from US$80; ❄🛜🏊) A large pool anchors 27 modern, comfortable rooms (with satellite TV) scattered about nice gardens right down by the surf break. The one 'off' note: security measures obstruct what should be a good view. It has a small annexe nearby for surfers with cold-water/fan rooms for 200,000Rp.

⭐**Puri Dajuma Cottages** HOTEL $$$
(📱0365-470 0118; www.dajuma.com; cottages from US$160; ❄@🛜🏊) Coming from the east on the main road, you won't be able to miss this seaside resort, thanks to its prolific signage. Happily, the 18 cottages actually live up to the billing. Each has a private garden, an ocean view and a walled outdoor bathroom. The Medewi surf break is 2km west.

ℹ Getting There & Away

Medewi Beach is 75km from the airport. A car and driver will cost about 600,000Rp for a day trip. You can also get a bus (25,000Rp) going to Gilimanuk from Denpasar's Ubung terminal and be dropped off at the road entrance.

Negara
📱0365

Set amid the broad and fertile flatlands between the mountains and ocean, Negara is a tidy, prosperous town and a useful pit stop. Although it's a district capital, there's not much to see, until the town springs to life for the region's famous **bull races**. On the main commercial road (south of the

---

PURA RAMBUT SIWI

Picturesquely situated on a clifftop overlooking a long, wide stretch of black-sand beach, this superb temple shaded by flowering frangipani trees is one of the important sea temples of west Bali. Like Pura Tanah Lot and Pura Luhur Ulu Watu, it was established in the 16th century by the priest Nirartha, who had a good eye for ocean scenery. Unlike Tanah Lot, it remains a peaceful and little-visited place: on non-ceremony days you'll just find a couple of lonely drink vendors.

Legend has it that when Nirartha first came here, he donated some of his hair to the local villagers. The hair is now kept in a box buried in a three-tiered *meru* (multi-tiered shrine), the name of which means 'Worship of the Hair'. Although the main *meru* is inaccessible, you can view it easily through the gate. The entire temple is reached by an imposing set of stone stairs from the parking area.

The caretaker rents sarongs for 2000Rp and is happy to show you around the temple and down to the beach. He will then open the guestbook and request a donation – a suitable sum is about 10,000Rp (regardless of the much higher amounts attributed to previous visitors). A path along the cliff leads to a staircase down to a small and even older temple, **Pura Penataran**.

The temple is located between Air Satang and Yeh Embang, 7km west of Medewi and 48km east of Gilimanuk. The 500m road to the site through lovely rice fields is well signposted; look for the turn-off near a cluster of warung on the Tabanan–Gilimanuk main road.

BULL RACES

The Negara region is famous for bull races, known as *mekepung,* which culminate in the **Bupati Cup** in Negara on the Sunday before 17 August, Indonesia's Independence Day.

The racing animals are actually the normally docile water buffalo, which charge down a 2km stretch of road or beach pulling tiny chariots. Gaily clad riders stand or kneel on top of the chariots forcing the bullocks on. The winner is not necessarily first past the post – style also plays a part and points are awarded for the most elegant runner. There is much wagering on the results.

Important races take place during the dry season on some Sundays from July to October. Races and practices are held at several sites around Perancak on the coast and elsewhere on Sunday mornings, including Delod Berawan and Mertasari. Actually finding these events can be somewhat like seeking the Holy Grail: if you're in Negara on a bull-race Sunday, people will gladly direct you, but trying to obtain info remotely is often frustrating. Try the **Jembrana Government Tourist Office** (☑ 0365-41060; Jl Dr Setia Budi 1, Negara; ⊘ 9am-3pm Mon-Fri) for details. Ask if there is an upcoming racing demonstration for visitors, which are held on some Thursday afternoons year-round.

Another good source of info is **Putu Surf Shop** (☑ 0817 973 5213; Medewi Beach; tours from 250,000Rp) in Medewi Beach, which takes groups to see the bull races on some Sunday mornings during the season (July to October). Given travel times, consider staying in Medewi Beach or Pemuteran the night before a race.

It must be noted, however, that Bali's bull races have been criticised by animal welfare experts as being inhumane. Chilli paste is reportedly rubbed into the anus of racing buffalo, and nail-studded wooden rods used as whips, to make them run faster.

Tabanan–Gilimanuk road), Jl Ngurah Rai, you will find ATMs, warungs, bakeries and a useful **Hardy's Department Store** (☑ 0365-40709; Jl Ngurah Rai; ⊘ 8am-10pm).

Around Negara

At the southern fringe of Negara, **Loloan Timur** is a largely Bugis community (originally from Sulawesi) that retains 300-year-old traditions. Look for distinctive houses on stilts, some decorated with wooden fretwork.

You can see bull-race practices Sunday mornings at a football field near Delod Berawan. To reach the area, turn off the main Gilimanuk–Denpasar road at Mendoyo and go south to the coast, which has a black-sand beach and irregular surf.

Perancak is the site of Nirartha's arrival in Bali in 1546, commemorated by a limestone temple, **Pura Gede Perancak**. Ignore the sad little zoo nearby and go for a walk along the fishing harbour.

Once capital of the region, **Jembrana** is the centre of the *gamelan jegog,* a gamelan (traditional orchestra) using huge bamboo instruments that produces a low-pitched, resonant sound. Performances often feature gamelan groups engaging in a musical contest. Your best bet to hear this music is at a local festival. Have your driver or other local ask around to see if one is on while you're there.

Belimbingsari & Palasari

Two fascinating religious towns north of the main road are reason enough for a detour.

Christian evangelism in Bali was discouraged by the secular Dutch, but sporadic missionary activity resulted in a number of converts, many of whom were rejected by their own communities. In 1939 they were encouraged to resettle in Christian communities in the wilds of west Bali.

Palasari is home to a Catholic community, which boasts a huge church largely made from white stone and set on a large town square. It is really rather peaceful, and with the gently waving palms it feels like old missionary Hawaii rather than Hindu Bali. The church does show Balinese touches in the spires, which resemble the *meru* in a Hindu temple, and features a facade with the same shape as a temple gate.

Nearby Belimbingsari was established as a Protestant community, and now has the largest Protestant church in Bali, although it doesn't reach for the heavens the way the church in Palasari does. Still, it's an amazing structure, with features rendered in a distinctly Balinese style – in place of a church bell there's a *kulkul* (hollow tree-trunk drum used to sound a warning) like those in a Hindu temple. The entrance is through an *aling aling*–style (guard wall) gate, and the attractive carved angels look very Balinese. Go on Sunday to see inside.

🛏 Sleeping

⭐ Taman Wana Villas & Spa
BOUTIQUE HOTEL $$

(☑ 0361-727770; www.bali-tamanwana-villas. com; Palasari; r US$80-300; ❄☎☂) For a near-religious experience you might consider staying at this remote boutique resort, a striking 2km drive through a jungle past the Palasari church. The architectural stunner has 27 rooms in unusual round structures, and 'posh' only begins to describe the luxuries available here. Views are panoramic; get a room overlooking the rice fields.

❶ Getting There & Away

The two villages are north of the main road, and the best way to see them is on a loop with your own transport. On the main road about 17km west from Negara, look for signs for the Taman Wana Villas. Follow these for 6.1km to Palasari. From the west, look for a turn for Belimbingsari, some 20km southeast of Cekik. A good road leads to the village. Between the two towns, only divine intervention will allow you to tackle the thicket of narrow but passable lanes unaided. Fortunately, directional help is readily at hand.

Cekik

At the Cekik junction one road continues west to Gilimanuk and another heads northeast towards north Bali. All buses and bemo to and from Gilimanuk pass through Cekik.

Archaeological excavations here during the 1960s yielded the oldest evidence of human life in Bali. Finds include burial mounds with funerary offerings, bronze jewellery, axes, adzes and earthenware vessels from around 1000 BC, give or take a few centuries. Look for some of this at the Museum Manusia Purbakala Gilimanuk in Gilimanuk.

On the southern side of the junction, the pagoda-like structure with a spiral stairway around the outside is a **war memorial**. It commemorates the landing of independence forces in Bali to oppose the Dutch, who were trying to reassert control of Indonesia after WWII.

Cekik is home to the **park headquarters** (☑ 0365-61060; www.tnbalibarat.com; Jl Raya Cekik; ☉ 7am-5pm) of the Taman Nasional Bali Barat (p245).

Gilimanuk

Gilimanuk is the terminus for ferries that shuttle back and forth across the narrow strait to Java. Most travellers to or from Java can get an onward ferry or bus straight away, and won't hang around.

◉ Sights

This part of Bali has been occupied for thousands of years. The **Museum Manusia Purbakala Gilimanuk** (Prehistoric People Museum; ☑ 0365-61328; suggested donation 10,000Rp; ☉ hours vary) is centred on a family of skeletons, thought to be 4000 years old, which were found locally in 2004. The museum is 500m east of the ferry port.

Stop anywhere along the north shore of town to see the huge, dramatic clash of waves and currents in the strait.

🛏 Sleeping & Eating

Good sleeping choices are thin on the ground. However, there are choices aplenty in Pemuteran.

Hotel Lestari
HOTEL $

(☑ 0365-61504; Jl Raya; r 110,000-250,000Rp; ❄) From fan-cooled singles to air-con suites, you have your choice of basic accommodation at this 21-room hotel, which feels strangely 1950s suburban. It's 1.7km east of the ferry terminal.

Asli Mentempeh
BALINESE $

(Terminal Lama; meals from 20,000Rp; ☉ 8am-10pm) An extended family runs several neighbouring iterations of this cafe, which serves a local dish Gilimanuk is known for: *betutu* chicken, a spicy form of steamed chicken that is redolent with herbs. They are located in the former bus terminal, about 500m east of the ferry port, 50m off the main road.

❶ Getting There & Away

Frequent buses run between Gilimanuk's large depot and Denpasar's Ubung terminal (30,000Rp, two to three hours), or along the north-coast road to Singaraja (25,000Rp). Smaller, slightly more comfortable minibuses serve both routes for 5000Rp more.

Car ferries to and from Ketapang on Java (30 minutes, adult/child 6500/5500Rp, car 124,000Rp) run around the clock.

Lombok

Best Beaches

➡ Sire (p266)

➡ Pantai Segar (p278)

➡ Pantai Dagong (p279)

➡ Mawi (p279)

➡ Selong Blanak (p279)

Best Places to Stay

➡ Pearl Beach (p261)

➡ Qunci Villas (p264)

➡ Rinjani Beach Eco Resort (p267)

➡ Tugu Lombok (p267)

➡ Coco Beach (p265)

Why Go?

Long overshadowed by its superstar neighbour across the Lombok Strait, there's a steady hum about Lombok that catches the ear of travellers looking for something different from Bali. Blessed with exquisite white-sand beaches, epic surf, a lush forested interior, and hiking trails through tobacco and rice fields, Lombok is fully loaded with equatorial allure. Oh, and you'll probably notice mighty Gunung Rinjani, Indonesia's second-highest volcano, its summit complete with hot springs and a dazzling crater lake.

And there's much more. Lombok's southern coastline is nature on a very grand scale: breathtaking turquoise bays, world-class surf breaks and massive headlands. They keep saying development on these splendid beaches is just around the corner, but until that moment comes, they are easy to explore over much-improved roads.

If you're going to the Gilis, a Lombok stopover is a must. Transport options are good and the mood could not be more laid back.

When to Go

➡ Lombok is hot, sticky and tropical throughout the year, with a marked rainy season (roughly between late October and April).

➡ The driest months coincide with the peak tourist period in July and August.

➡ The rainy season offers an excellent time to catch a local festival, such as the spectacular rice-throwing event called Perang Topat (held at Pura Lingsar in November or December), Peresean stick-fighting competitions (in December) or the Narmada buffalo races (in April).

Lombok Highlights

1 Surfing (or learning to surf) the ride of your life in **Gerupuk** (p278).

2 Scaling **Gunung Rinjani** (p271), Lombok's incomparable sacred peak.

3 Setting eyes on idyllic **Mawun beach** (p279) for the very first time.

4 Picking your own deserted-cove beach **north of Senggigi** (p265).

5 Catching a Sasak festival, such as Peresean near **Mataram** (p258).

6 Lounging in pure island bliss on **Gili Asahan** (p260).

7 Beholding the idyllic mountain splendour of the **Sembalun Valley** (p269).

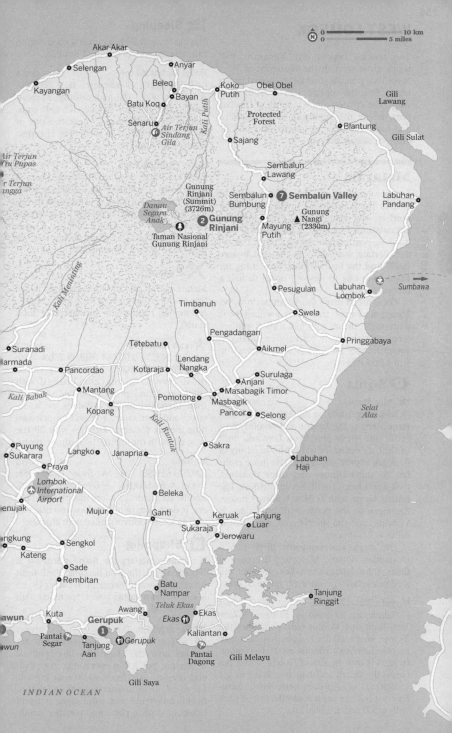

WEST LOMBOK

📱 0370

The region's biggest city, Mataram, just keeps growing with the economy of West Nusa Tenggara. Meanwhile the famed beach resort Senggigi continues in a 1990s time warp. The greatest allure is south of Lembar port, where the peninsula bends forward and back, the seas are placid, and bucolic offshore islands beckon.

Mataram

Lombok's capital is a blending sprawl of several (once separate) towns with fuzzy borders: Ampenan (the port); Mataram (the administrative centre); Cakranegara (the business centre, often called simply 'Cakra') and Bertais and Sweta to the east, where you'll find the bus terminal. Stretching for 12km from east to west it's home to half a million people.

There aren't many tourist attractions, yet Mataram's broad tree lined avenues buzz with traffic, thrum with motorbikes and are teeming with classic markets and malls. If you're hungry for a blast of Indo realism, you'll find it here.

👁 Sights

⭐**Pura Meru**   HINDU TEMPLE

(Jl Selaparang; admission 10,000Rp; ⏰8am-5pm) Pura Meru is the largest and second most important Hindu temple on Lombok. Built in 1720, it's dedicated to the Hindu trinity of Brahma, Vishnu and Shiva. The inner court has 33 small shrines and three thatched, teak-wood *meru* (multi-tiered shrines). The central *meru,* with 11 tiers, is Shiva's house; the *meru* to the north, with nine tiers, is Vishnu's; and the seven-tiered *meru* to the south is Brahma's.

The *meru* also represent three sacred mountains, Rinjani, Agung and Bromo, and the mythical Mount Meru. The caretaker will lend you a sash and sarong if you need one.

Mayura Water Palace   PARK

(Jl Selaparang; admission by donation; ⏰7am-7pm) Built in 1744, this palace includes the former king's family temple, a pilgrimage site for Lombok's Hindus on 24 December. In 1894 it was the site of bloody battles between the Dutch and Balinese. You can get a slight sense of history here, but unfortunately it has become a neglected public park with a polluted artificial lake.

🛏 Sleeping

Staying in central Mataram is a good way to fully engage with non-tourist local life.

Hotel Melati Viktor   GUESTHOUSE $

(📱0370-633830; Jl Abimanyu 1; r 100,000-200,000Rp; ❄🛜) The high ceilings, 37 clean rooms and Balinese-style courtyard, complete with Hindu statues, make this one of the best-value places in town. The cheapest rooms have fans.

Hotel Lombok Raya   HOTEL $$

(📱0370-632305; www.lombokrayahotel.com; Jl Panca Usaha 11; r 400,000-650,000Rp; ❄🛜🏊) Still a favourite of old-school business travellers, this well-located hotel has 134 spacious, comfortable rooms with balconies. It feels timeless in a good way, and recent renovations have given it some needed spunk.

🍴 Eating

Mataram Mall, and the streets around it, are lined with Western-style fast-food outlets, Indonesian noodle bars and warungs (food stalls).

⭐**Ikan Bakar 99**   SEAFOOD $

(📱0370-643335, 0370-664 2819; Jl Subak III 10; mains 20,000-55,000Rp; ⏰11am-10pm) Think: squid, prawns, fish and crab brushed with chilli sauce and perfectly grilled or fried, then drenched in spicy Padang or sticky sweet-and-sour sauce. You will munch and dine among Mataram families who fill the long tables in the arched, tiled dining room.

Mi Rasa   BAKERY $

(📱0370-633096; Jl AA Gede Ngurah 88; snacks from 5000Rp; ⏰6am-10pm) Cakra's middle-class families adore this modern bakery. It does doughnuts, cookies and cakes as well as local wontons stuffed with chicken.

🔒 Shopping

For handicrafts try the many stores on Jl Raya Senggigi, the road heading north from Ampenan towards Senggigi. Jl Panca Usaha is the main shopping street, sprinkled with interesting shops.

⭐**Pasar Mandalika**   MARKET

(⏰7am-5pm) There are no tourists at this market near the Mandalika bus terminal in Bertais, but it has everything else: fruit and veggies, fish (fresh and dried), baskets full of colourful, aromatic spices and grains, freshly butchered beef, palm sugar, pungent bricks of shrimp paste and cheaper handi-

Mataram

Mataram

crafts than you will find anywhere else in west Lombok.

It's a great place to get localised after you've overdosed on the *bule* (slang for foreigner) circuit.

Lombok Handicraft Centre   HANDICRAFTS
(Jl Hasanuddin; ◷9am-6pm) At Sayang Sayang (2km north of Cakra), there's a wide range of crafts, including masks, textiles and ceramics from across Nusa Tenggara.

Pasar Cakranegara   MARKET
(cnr Jl AA Gede Ngurah & Jl Selaparang; ◷9am-6pm) Collection of quirky stalls, some of which sell good-quality ikat (traditional cloth), as well as an interesting food market.

Mataram Mall   MALL
(Jl Selaparang; ◷7am-9pm) A multi-storey shopping mall with a supermarket, department stores, electronics and clothes stores, as well as some good restaurants.

ℹ Information

Rumah Sakit Harapan Keluarga (☎0370-670000; www.harapankeluarga.co.id; Jl Ahmad Yani 9; ◷24hr) The best private hospital on Lombok is just east of downtown Mataram and has English-speaking doctors and modern facilities.

ℹ Getting There & Around

Mataram's airport was closed after the new one near Praya opened in 2011.

BEMO

Mataram is *very* spread out. Yellow bemos (minibuses) shuttle between the Kebon Roek bemo terminal in Ampenan and the Mandalika terminal in Bertais (10km away) along the two main thoroughfares via the centre (4000Rp).

Outside the Pasar Cakranegara there is a handy bemo stop for services to Bertais, Ampenan, Sweta and Lembar. Kebon Roek has bemos to Bertais (3000Rp) and Senggigi (5000Rp).

BUS

The chaotic **Mandalika terminal** is 3km from the centre and is a bus and bemo hub. It's surrounded by the city's busy main market. Use the official ticket office to avoid touts. Yellow bemos shuttle to the centre (4000Rp).

Buses and bemos departing hourly from the Mandalika terminal include the following:

DESTINATION	FARE	DURATION
Kuta (via Praya & Sengkol)	15,000Rp	90min
Labuhan Lombok	15,000Rp	2hr
Lembar	15,000Rp	30min
Airport	15,000Rp	45min

TAXI

For a reliable metered taxi, call a Bluebird **Lombok Taksi** (☑ 627000).

Around Mataram

As well as Lombok's most important temple, sights around Mataram include the old port town of **Ampenan**. Although most people buzz through on their way to or from Senggigi, if you pause you'll discover a still-tangible sense of the Dutch colonial era in the tree-lined main street and the older buildings.

⊙ Sights

Pura Lingsar   HINDU TEMPLE
(admission by donation; ⊘ 7am-6pm) This large **temple compound** is the holiest in Lombok. Built in 1714 by King Anak Agung Ngurah, and nestled beautifully in lush rice fields, it's multi-denominational, with a temple for Balinese Hindus (Pura Gaduh) and one for followers of Lombok's mystical take on Islam, the Wektu Telu religion.

It's 8km northeast of Mataram in the village of Lingsar. Take a bemo from the Mandalika terminal to Narmada, and another to Lingsar. Ask to be dropped off near the entrance to the temple complex.

Pura Gaduh has four shrines: one orientated to Gunung Rinjani (seat of the gods on Lombok), one to Gunung Agung (seat of the gods in Bali) and a double shrine representing the union between the two islands.

The Wektu Telu temple is noted for its enclosed pond devoted to Lord Vishnu, and the holy eels, which can be enticed from their lair with hard-boiled eggs (available at stalls outside). It's considered good luck to feed them. You will be expected to rent a sash and/or sarong (or bring your own) to enter the temple.

Lembar

Lembar is Lombok's main port for ferries, tankers and Pelni liners coming in from Bali and beyond. Though the ferry port itself is scruffy, the setting – think azure inlets ringed by soaring green hills – is stunning. If you need cash there are ATMs near the harbour entrance.

Public ferries (child/adult/motorbike/car 27,000/40,000/112,000/773,000Rp, 5-6 hours) travel nonstop between Padangbai in Bali and Lembar. Passenger tickets are sold near the pier. Boats supposedly run 24 hours and leave about every 90 minutes, but the service can be unreliable – boats have caught on fire and run aground (see p373).

Bemo and bus connections are abundant and bemos run regularly to the Mandalika bus/bemo terminal (15,000Rp), so there's no reason to linger. Taxis cost about 80,000Rp to Mataram, and 150,000Rp to Senggigi.

Southwestern Peninsula

The sweeping coastline that stretches west of Lembar is blessed with boutique sleeps on deserted beaches and tranquil offshore islands. You can while away weeks here among the pearl farms, salty old mosques, friendly locals and relatively pristine islands.

Of the dozen islands off the coast here, **Gili Gede** is a favourite. Although popular with day-tripping snorkellers and divers from across Lombok, the island itself is utterly serene and has a couple of isolated places to stay and unwind.

Gili Asahan is another idyllic spot: soothing winds gust, birds flutter and gather in the grass just before sunset, muted calls to prayer rumble and the stars and moon light up the sky.

The only blot on the landscape is the gold-rush town of **Sekotong**, which you have to pass through on your way west, where crude goldmines riddle the rugged hills. Otherwise, you follow the narrow coastal road, along the contours of the peninsula, skirting white-sand beach after white-sand beach on your way to Bangko Bangko and one of Asia's legendary surf breaks, **Tanjung Desert** (Desert Point) which has one of the world's longest left-hand barrels.

🛏 Sleeping & Eating

There are a few hotels and resorts sprinkled along the northern coast of the peninsula, though the most atmospheric beaches and lodging are on the offshore islands. You'll eat where you sleep.

🛏 Mainland

Bola Bola Paradis INN $
(☑ 0817 578 7355; www.bolabolaparadis.com; Jl Raya Palangan Sekotong, Pelangan; r 350,000-465,000Rp; ❋) Just west of Pelangan, this 11-room place has clean octagonal bungalows on grassy palm-shaded grounds that bleed into the sand, and comfortable air-con rooms with tiled floors and private patios in the main lodge building.

Cocotino's RESORT $$$
(☑ 0819 0797 2401; www.cocotinos-sekotong.com; Jl Raya Palangan Sekotong, Tanjung Empat; r/villas from US$100/$275; ❋@🌐❄) This resort has an oceanfront location, private beach and 36 high-quality bungalows (some with lovely outdoor bathrooms), some with sea views. It offers deals via its website.

🛏 Islands

Madak Belo BUNGALOW $
(☑ 0818 0554 9637, 0878 6471 2981; www.madak-belo.com; Gili Gede; r 200,000-400,000Rp; ◉) Here's a sensational French hippie-chic paradise with three rooms upstairs in the main wooden and bamboo lodge. They share a bath and a bamboo lounge area strung with hammocks, and blessed with sea views. It also has two private bungalows with queen beds and private baths.

★ Pearl Beach BUNGALOW $$
(☑ 0819 0724 7696; www.pearlbeach-resort.com; Gili Asahan; cottages/bungalows from US$39/77; 🌐) A private-island resort; cottages are simple, bamboo affairs with outdoor baths and a hammock on the porch. The bungalows are chic, with polished concrete floors, soaring ceilings, gorgeous outdoor baths, and fabulous day-bed swings on the wooden porches. There's great diving, kayaks and more.

🛏 Tanjung Desert

An informal surf camp, there are several phone-free guesthouses scattered about the beaches here, as well as no-name warungs serving cheap Indo fare. If everywhere is full (which can happen during peak surfing season from May to October), backtrack about 6km to Labuhan Poh.

Desert Point Lodges BUNGALOW $
(www.desertpointlodges.com; Tanjung Desert; r from 250,000Rp) One of the more 'upscale' places at Tanjung Desert, with seven woven-bamboo and thatched bungalows with bamboo beds, hammocks on the porch and private baths attached. Surfing may be king here but you can also dive.

ℹ Getting There & Around

BEMO
Bemos run between Lembar and Pelangan (10,000Rp, 1½ hours) via Sekotong and Tembowong every 30 minutes until 5pm. West of Pelangan transport is less regular, but the route is still served by infrequent bemos until Selegang. Private wheels are your best transport option.

TAXI BOAT
Taxi boats (per person 20,000Rp) shuttle from Tembowong on the mainland to Gili Gede. You'll see them near the Pertamina gas station. Chartered boats also connect Tembowong with the islands of Gili Gede and Gili Asahan (from 300,000Rp return).

Senggigi

Lombok's traditional tourist resort, Senggigi enjoys a fine location along a series of sweeping bays, with light-sand beaches sitting pretty below a backdrop of jungle-clad mountains and coconut palms. In the late afternoon a setting blood-red sun sinks into the surf next to the giant triangular cone of Bali's Gunung Agung.

Tourist numbers are relatively modest here and you'll find some excellent-value hotels and restaurants. Still, the tacky main strip could be more appealing, the influx of bar girls is sleazy, and the resident beach hawkers can be over-persistent.

The Senggigi area spans 10km of coastal road; the upscale neighbourhood of Mangsit is 3km north of central Senggigi.

Senggigi

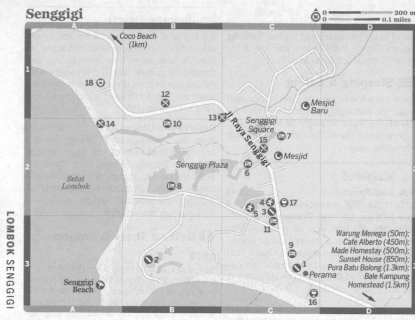

Coco Beach (1km)

Mesjid Baru

Senggigi Square

Jl Raya Senggigi

Mesjid

Senggigi Plaza

Selat Lombok

Senggigi Beach

Warung Menega (50m);
Cafe Alberto (450m);
Made Homestay (500m);
Sunset House (850m);
Pura Batu Bolong (1.3km);
Bale Kampung
Homestead (1.5km)

Perama

LOMBOK SENGGIGI

◉ Sights

Pura Batu Bolong HINDU TEMPLE

(off Jl Raya Senggigi; admission by donation; ⊙ 7am-7pm) It's not the grandest, but Pura Batu Bolong is Lombok's most-appealing Hindu temple, and particularly lovely at sunset. Join an ever-welcoming Balinese community as they leave offerings at the 14 altars and pagodas that tumble down a rocky volcanic outcropping into the foaming sea about 2km south of central Senggigi. The rock underneath the temple has a natural hole, hence the name (*batu bolong* literally means 'rock with hole').

🏃 Activities

Snorkelling, Diving & Surfing

There's reasonable snorkelling off the point in Senggigi, 3km north of the town. You can rent gear (per day 40,000Rp) from several spots on the beach. Diving trips from Senggigi usually visit the Gili Islands.

Blue Coral Diving DIVING

(☑ 0370-693441; www.bluecoraldive.com; Jl Raya Senggigi; 2-tank dive 800,000Rp) Senggigi's biggest dive shop hits the same sites as the shops in the Gilis.

Blue Marlin DIVING

(☑ 0370-693719; www.bluemarlindive.com; Holiday Resort Lombok, Jl Raya Senggigi; 2-tank dive 800,000Rp) The local branch of a well-regarded Gili Trawangan dive shop.

Dream Divers DIVING

(☑ 0370-693738; www.dreamdivers.com; Jl Raya Senggigi; 2-tank dive from 800,000Rp) The Senggigi office of the Gili original. It also organises activities such as Rinjani treks.

Hiking

Rinjani Trekking Club ADVENTURE SPORTS

(☑ 0370-693202; www.info2lombok.com; Jl Raya Senggigi; ⊙ 9am-8pm) Well informed about routes and trail conditions on Gunung Rinjani and has a wide choice of guided hikes. The best of the many places hawking Rinjani treks along the strip.

Massages, Spas & Salons

Very determined local masseurs, armed with mats, oils and attitude, hunt for business on Senggigi's beaches. Expect to pay about 60,000Rp for one hour after bargaining. Most hotels can arrange a masseur to visit your room; rates start at about 75,000Rp. Be warned, many of the streetside 'salons' you'll find are often fronts for more salacious services.

Senggigi

★ Qamboja Spa   SPA
(📞 0370-693800; www.quncivillas.com; Qunci Villas, Mangsit; massage from US$30; ⊘ 8am-10pm) Gorgeous hotel spa where you select your choice of oil (uplifting, harmony) depending on the effect and mood you require from your massage, which includes Thai, Balinese and shiatsu.

Royal Spa   SPA
(📞 0370-660 8777; off Jl Raya Senggigi, Senggigi Plaza; massage from 100,000Rp; ⊘ 10am-9pm) A professional yet inexpensive spa with a tempting range of scrubs, massages and treatments. The *lulur* massage is a real treat and includes a body mask.

🛏 Sleeping

Senggigi's accommodation is very spread out. But even if you're located a few kilometres away (say, in Mangsit) you're not isolated, as many restaurants offer free rides to diners and taxis are very inexpensive.

Heavy discounts of up to 50% are common in midrange and top-end places outside the July–August peak season.

🛏 Senggigi

★ Wira   GUESTHOUSE $
(📞 0370-692153; www.thewira.com; Jl Raya Senggigi; dm from 75,000Rp; r 250,000-350,000Rp; ❄ 🛜) This boutique losmen is on the beach side of the main Senggigi strip. It has 11 simple, tasteful, sizeable rooms with bamboo furnishings and private porches out back. There is also a 10-bed dorm room. Use the quiet entrance on the side street, away from Jl Raya Senggigi.

Hotel Elen   HOTEL $
(📞 0370-693077; Jl Raya Senggigi; r from 120,000Rp; ❄) Elen is the long-time backpackers' choice. Rooms are very basic, but those facing the waterfall fountain and koi pond come with spacious tiled patios that catch the ocean breeze.

Sonya Homestay   HOMESTAY $
(📞 0813 3989 9878; Jl Raya Senggigi; r 100,000-160,000Rp; ❄ 🛜) A family-run enclave of nine dead-simple rooms (the cheapest are fan-only) with nice patios. Nathan, the owner, offers driving tours of Mataram and the surrounding area. It's off the road amid a small, shady garden.

Sendok Hotel   INN $
(📞 0370-693176; www.sendokhotellombok.com; Jl Raya Senggigi; r from 350,000Rp; ❄ 🛜 🏊) This guesthouse is more attractive than the (friendly) pub it sits behind. The 28 rooms pair lovely Javanese antiques with garish tile, but they have high ceilings and decent bathrooms; all are bright and airy with their own private front porch. Some rooms have hot water.

Made Homestay   HOMESTAY $
(📞 0819 1704 1332; Jl Raya Senggigi; r 130,000-180,000Rp; ❄ 🛜) A good budget choice, the six rooms here have big bamboo beds and private front porches. The air-con rooms cost a bit more, but remain good value into high season. Cold-water showers only.

Bale Kampung Homestay   GUESTHOUSE $
(📞 0818 0360 0001, 0370-660 0001; Jl Raya Senggigi; r 150,000-250,000Rp; ❄ 🛜) Set 300m south of Pura Batu Bolong, this thatched brick compound is compact, but there's a range of 15 very-good-value rooms, the most

SASAK FESTIVALS & CEREMONIES

Although little is known about the origins of the Sasak people on Lombok, it is thought they are an offshoot of the Balinese. They began converting to Islam in the 17th century. Consequently, many ancient cultural rituals and celebrations based on animist and Hindu traditions have dwindled in practice, although some have endured.

Lebaran Topat Held during the seven days after the end of the fasting month (Idul Fitri; Ramadan) in the Islamic calendar, Lebaran Topat is a Sasak ceremony thought to be unique to west Lombok. Relatives gather in cemeteries to pour water over family graves, and add offerings of flowers, betel leaves and lime powder. Visitors can observe ceremonies at the **Bintaro cemetery** on the outskirts of Ampenan.

Malean Sampi Meaning 'cow chase' in Sasak, Malean Sampi are highly competitive buffalo races held over a 100m waterlogged field in **Narmada**, just east of Mataram. Two buffalo are yoked together and then driven along the course by a driver brandishing a whip. The event takes place in early April, and commemorates the beginning of the planting season.

Gendang Beleq These 'big drum' performances were originally performed before battles. Today, many villages in central Lombok have a *gendang* battery, some with up to 40 drummers, who perform at festivals and ceremonies. The drums themselves are colossal, up to a metre in length and not unlike an oil drum in shape or size. The drummers support the drums using a sash around their necks.

Peresean Martial-art 'stick fighting' performances by two young men stripped to the waist, armed with rattan sticks and square shields made of cowhide. The Sasaks believe that the more blood shed on the earth the better the rainfall will be in the forthcoming wet season. In late July, demonstrations can be seen in Senggigi, and in late December there's a championship in Mataram.

expensive of which have hot water and aircon. It's a little out of the way, but they offer free transport to and from Senggigi town.

Central Inn HOTEL $
(☑ 0370-692006; Jl Raya Senggigi; r from 300,000Rp; ❄ 🌐 ☒) The 54 rooms in motel-style blocks have high ceilings, fresh tiles and a bamboo seating area out front with views of the surrounding hills. It's on the beach side of the main drag and away from noise, although not on the sand. Service can be perfunctory.

Sunset House HOTEL $$
(☑ 0370-667 7196, 0370-692020; www.sunset house-lombok.com; Jl Raya Senggigi 66; r 350,000-700,000Rp; ❄ 🌐 ☒) Now with 35 rooms, all with a tasteful, well-equipped simplicity on this quiet oceanfront towards Pura Batu Bolong. Rooms on the upper floors have sweeping ocean views towards Bali. Wi-fi is only available in public areas.

Santosa Villas RESORT $$
(☑ 0370-693090; www.santosavillasresort.com; Jl Raya Senggigi; r from US$80; ❄ 🌐 ☒ 🐾) The Santosa resort has comfortable accommodation ranging from 187 standard hotel rooms

to high-end luxury villas set in large grounds on a nice beach, all smack in the centre of the Senggigi strip. It's the mainstream resort choice.

Chandi RESORT $$$
(☑ 0370-692198; www.the-chandi.com; Batu Balong; r from US$150; ❄ 🌐 ☒) This stylish boutique hotel that still manages a lot of thatch is about 1km south of the Pura Batu Balong. Each of the 15 rooms has an outdoor living room and hip modern interior with high ceilings and groovy outdoor baths. The ample oceanfront perch is likely to absorb your daylight hours.

Mangsit

★ **Qunci Villas** RESORT $$$
(☑ 0370-693800; www.quncivillas.com; Mangsit; r from US$140; ❄ 🌐 ☒) A spectacular, lovingly imagined property that comes close to a luxe experience. Everything from the food to the lovely pool area to the spa, and especially the sea views (160m of beachfront), are magical. It has 78 rooms that together with the rest of the diversions here will give you little reason to leave.

Jeeva Klui   RESORT $$$

(☑ 0370-693035; www.jeevaklui.com; Jl Raya Klui Beach; r from US$160, villas from US$330; ❄🛜⛱) One of the area's finest offerings, with a shimmering infinity pool and a lovely, almost private, beach sheltered by a rocky outcrop one bay north of Mangsit. The 35 rooms are stylishly thatched with bamboo columns and private porches. Villas are luxurious, private and have their own pools.

🍴 Eating & Drinking

Senggigi's dining scene ranges from tourist-friendly dining to simple warungs. Many places offer free transport for evening diners – phone for a ride.

Not long ago, Senggigi's bar scene was pretty vanilla, with most cafes and restaurants doing double duty. However, like something out of a Pattaya fever-dream, huge cinderblock buildings have now been built on the outskirts of the centre and feature arrays of 'karaoke' joints and massage parlors.

Few miss the chance to enjoy a sunset beverage at one of the many low-key places along the beach.

🍴 Senggigi

★ Cafe Tenda Cak Poer   INDONESIAN $

(Jl Raya Senggigi; mains 12,000-15,000Rp; ☺ 6pm-late) Barely enclosed, this roadside warung wows the stool-sitting masses with hot-outta-the-wok Indo classics. Get the nasi goreng (fried rice) made extra hot and with extra garlic and you'll be smiling through tears *and* sweating.

Asmara   INTERNATIONAL $

(☑ 0370-693619; www.asmara-group.com; Jl Raya Senggigi; mains 25,000-80,000Rp; ☺ 8am-11pm; 🛜👶) An ideal family choice, this place spans the culinary globe from tuna carpaccio to Wiener schnitzel to Lombok's own *sate pusut* (minced-meat or fish sate). It also has a playground and kids' menu.

Office   INTERNATIONAL $

(☑ 0370-693162; Jl Raya Senggigi, Pasar Seni; mains 25,000-65,000Rp; ☺ 9am-10pm) This pub near the euphemistic 'art market' offers typical Indonesian and Western choices along with pool tables, ball games and barflies. But it also has a popular Thai menu which is the choice of those in the know. Tables on the sand near fishing boats are among Senggigi's best places for a relaxed sunset drink.

Square   INTERNATIONAL $$

(☑ 0370-693688; Jl Raya Senggigi; mains 40,000-150,000Rp; ☺ 11am-11pm; 🛜) An upscale restaurant with beautifully crafted seating, and a menu that features Western and Indonesian fusion such as wok-fried king prawns with Worcestershire sauce. The cooking is a cut above the local norm in terms of ambition, the service is average. Get a table away from the road noise.

Warung Menega   SEAFOOD $$

(☑ 0370-663 4422; Jl Raya Senggigi, Batu Layar Beach; meals 80,000-250,000Rp; ☺ 11am-11pm) If you fled Bali before experiencing the Jimbaran fish grills, you can make up for it at this beachside seafood BBQ. Choose from a daily catch of barracuda, squid, snapper, grouper, lobster, tuna and prawns – all of which are grilled over smouldering coconut husks and served on candlelit tables in the sand.

Cafe Alberto   ITALIAN $$

(☑ 0370-693039; Jl Raya Senggigi; mains from 50,000Rp; ☺ 8am-11pm) A long-standing and well-loved beachside Italian kitchen, this place serves a variety of pasta dishes, but is known for its pizza. It offers free transport to and from your hotel.

Hotel Lina   BAR

(☑ 0370-693237; Jl Raya Senggigi; ☺ 8am-10pm) A small, aging hotel, Lina's seafront deck is a timeless spot for a sundowner. Happy hour starts at 4pm and ends an hour after dusk. You really can't get mellower than this.

Papaya Café   BAR

(☑ 0370-693136; Jl Raya Senggigi; ☺ 8am-11pm) The decor here is slick, with exposed stone walls, rattan furniture and evocative Asmat art from Papua. There's a wide selection of imported liquor. By day the road noise intrudes but it dies down at night.

🍴 North of Senggigi

★ Coco Beach   INDONESIAN $$

(☑ 0817 578 0055; Pantai Kerandangan; mains from 60,000Rp; ☺ noon-10pm; ⌖) ✏ About 2km north of central Senggigi, this wonderful beachside restaurant with tasteful, secluded seating features a healthy menu that includes lots of salads and choices for vegetarians (and uses organic produce wherever possible). The nasi goreng is locally renowned and the seafood is the best in the area. It has a full bar and blends its own authentic *jamu* tonics (herbal medicines).

Shopping

Shopping in Senggigi doesn't extend much further than the sale of dye-leaching sarongs. Much more interesting is a day trip to the big markets in Mataram.

Asmara Collection HANDICRAFTS
(☑ 0370-693619; Jl Raya Senggigi; ⊙ 8am-11pm) A cut above the rest, this store has well-selected tribal art, including wonderful carvings and textiles from Sumba and Flores.

ⓘ Information

The nearest hospitals are in Mataram. ATMs abound.
Tourist Police (☑ 0370-632733)

ⓘ Getting There & Away

Perama (☑ 0370-693007; www.peramatour. com; Jl Raya Senggigi; ⊙ 8am-8pm) Has an economical shuttle-bus service that connects with the public ferry in Lembar to Padangbai in Bali (125,000Rp) and onward shuttle-bus connections to Sanur, Kuta and Ubud (all 150,000Rp). These trips can take eight or more hours. It also offers a bus and boat connection to the Gilis for a reasonable 150,000Rp (two hours). It saves some of the Bangsal Harbour hassle.

Regular bemos travel between Senggigi and Ampenan's Kebon Roek terminal (3000Rp) where you can connect to Mataram. Wave them down on the main drag. A taxi to Lembar is 150,000Rp. Metered taxis to the airport in Praya cost about 150,000Rp and take an hour.

There's no public bemo service north to Bangsal harbour. A metered taxi costs about 90,000Rp.

ⓘ Getting Around

Senggigi's central area is easy to negotiate on foot. If you're staying further from the centre, many restaurants offer a free lift for diners.

Motorbikes rent from 60,000Rp per day. Vehicle rental is competitive and ranges from 150,000Rp to 300,000Rp per day. A car and driver costs from 600,000Rp per day.

Senggigi to Bangsal

As you head north along the scalloped coast from Senggigi, you catch glimpses of the white-sand-ringed Gili Islands glowing in the sun. The bays that make up the coast here are undeveloped, picture-perfect crescents backed by palm trees.

About 20km north of Senggigi is the wide bay of **Teluk Nare/Teluk Kade**. This is where several fast-boat companies stop as part of their service linking Bali and the Gilis. Private boats belonging to Gili Trawangan resorts use private docks here.

Another 5km brings you to the turn for **Bangsal harbour** and the busy public boats serving the Gilis (see p283).

NORTH & CENTRAL LOMBOK
☑ 0370

Lush and fertile, Lombok's scenic interior is stitched together with rice terraces, lush forest, undulating tobacco fields and fruit and nut orchards, and is crowned by sacred Gunung Rinjani. Entwined in all this big nature are traditional Sasak settlements, some of which are known for their handicrafts. Public transport is not frequent or consistent enough to rely on, but the main roads are in good condition. With your own wheels you can explore black-sand fishing beaches, inland villages and waterfalls.

Bangsal to Bayan

Public transport north from Bangsal is infrequent. Several minibuses a day go from the Mandalika terminal in Bertais (Mataram) to Bayan, but you'll have to get connections in Pemenang and/or Anyar, which can be difficult to navigate. Simplify things and get your own wheels.

Sire

A hidden upmarket enclave, the jutting Sire (or Sira) peninsula seems to be squirting the three Gilis out of its tip. It's blessed with gorgeous, broad white-sand **beaches** and good

WEKTU TELU

Wektu Telu is a complex mixture of Hindu, Islamic and animist beliefs, though it's now officially classified as a sect of Islam. At its forefront is a physical concept of the Holy Trinity. The sun, moon and stars represent heaven, earth and water, while the head, body and limbs represent creativity, sensitivity and control.

As recently as 1965, the vast majority of Sasaks in northern Lombok were Wektu Telu, but under Suharto's 'New Order' government, indigenous religious beliefs were discouraged, and enormous pressure was placed on Wektu Telu to become Wektu Lima (Muslims who pray five times a day). But in the Wektu Telu heartland around Bayan, locals have been able to maintain their unique beliefs by differentiating their cultural traditions (Wektu Telu) from religion (Islam). Most do not fast for the full month of Ramadan, only attend the mosque for special occasions, and there's widespread consumption of *brem* (alcoholic rice wine).

snorkelling offshore. Three opulent resorts are now established here, alongside a couple of fishing villages and some amazing private villas. There's one wonderful boutique mid-range property in the mix, too. Look out for the small **Hindu temple**, just beyond the Oberoi resort, which has shrines built into the coastal rocks and sublime ocean views.

🛏 Sleeping & Eating

⭐ **Rinjani Beach**
Eco Resort   BOUTIQUE HOTEL **$$**
(📱 0878 6515 2619, 0878 6450 9148; www.lombok-adventures.com; Karang Atas; bungalows 350,000-900,000Rp; ❄ ☀) This midrange gem has five large bamboo bungalows, each with its own theme, hammocks on private porches, and access to a pool on the black-sand beach. There is a dive shop and restaurant, plus sea kayaks and mountain bikes. There are also two cheaper, smaller cold-water bungalows for budget travellers.

⭐ **Tugu Lombok**   RESORT **$$$**
(📱 0370-612 0111; www.tuguhotels.com; bungalows from US$250, villas from US$280; ❄ 🛜 ☀) An astonishing fantasy of a hotel, this larger-than-life amalgamation of luxury accommodation, wacky design and spiritual Indonesian heritage sits on a wonderful white-sand beach. Room decor reflects Indonesian tradition, the exquisite spa is modelled on Java's Buddhist Borobudur temple and the main restaurant is like a rice barn on steroids.

Oberoi Lombok   RESORT **$$$**
(📱 0370-638444; www.oberoihotels.com; r from US$300, villas from US$450; ❄ 🛜 ☀) For sheer get-away-from-it-all bliss the Oberoi simply excels. The hotel's core is a triple-level

pool, which leads the eye to a lovely private beach. Indonesian rajah-style luxury is the look: sunken marble bathtubs, teak floors, antique furniture and oriental rugs. Service is flawless. It often has rooms for rates that are amazing value.

Gondang & Around

Just northeast of Gondang village, a 6km trail heads inland to **Air Terjun Tiu Pupas**, a 30m waterfall (per person 30,000Rp) that's only worth seeing in the wet season. Trails continue from here to other wet-season waterfalls, including **Air Terjun Gangga**, the most beautiful of all. A guide (about 80,000Rp) is useful to navigate the confusing trails in these parts.

Bayan

Wektu Telu, Lombok's animist-tinted form of Islam, was born in humble thatched mosques nestled in these Rinjani foothills. The best example is **Masjid Kuno Bayan Beleq**, next to the village of Beleq. Its low-slung roof, dirt floors and bamboo walls reportedly date from 1634, making this mosque the oldest on Lombok. Inside is a huge old drum which served as the call to prayer before PA systems. Ah, the good old days.

Senaru

The scenic villages that make up Senaru merge into one along a steep road with sweeping Rinjani and sea views. Most visitors here are volcano-bound but beautiful walking trails and spectacular waterfalls beckon to those who aren't.

Senaru derives its name from *sinaru* which means light. As you ascend the hill towards the sky and clouds, you'll understand why.

◉ Sights & Activities

Air Terjun Sindang Gila (10,000Rp) is a spectacular set of falls 20 minutes' walk from Senaru via a lovely forest and hillside trail. The hardy make for the creek, edge close and then get pounded by the hard, foaming cascade that explodes over black volcanic stone 40m above.

A further 50 minutes or so uphill is **Air Terjun Tiu Kelep**, another waterfall with a swimming hole. The track is steep and guides are compulsory (60,000Rp). Long-tailed macaques (locals call them *kera*) and the much rarer silvered leaf monkey sometimes appear.

In the traditional Sasak village of **Dusun Senaru**, at the top of the road, locals will invite you to chew betel nut (or tobacco) and show you around for a donation.

Guided walks and community tourism activities can be arranged at most guesthouses – they include a **rice-terrace and waterfalls walk** (per person 150,000Rp), which takes in Sindang Gila, rice paddies and an old bamboo mosque, and the **Senaru Panorama Walk** (per person 150,000Rp), which incorporates stunning views and insights into local traditions.

You do not need a guide to reach Air Terjun Sindang Gila, as it is on a well-marked path. A guide to the second waterfall is recommended. However, anyone lurking around the waterfall ticket office is most likely not an official guide. Avoid them. Legitimate guides are easy to find in town, especially in the small collection of shops by the entrance to Air Terjun Sindang Gila.

🛌 Sleeping & Eating

All of Senaru's places to stay and eat are strung along the 6.5km-long road that starts in Bayan and runs uphill via Batu Koq to the main Gunung Rinjani park office and Rinjani Trekking Centre.

Most of the dozen or so places here are simple mountain lodges; the cool altitude means you won't need air-con. The following are dotted along the road from Bayan to Senaru and listed in order from the top of the road down.

★Rinjani Lighthouse GUESTHOUSE $
(📞0818 0548 5480; www.rinjanilighthouse.mm.st; r 350,000-800,000Rp) Set on a wide plateau just 200m from the Rinjani park office, this impressive guesthouse has thatched-roof bungalows in sizes from double to family. The owners are founts of Rinjani info.

Gunung Baru Senaru COTTAGE $
(📞0819 0741 1211; rinjaniadventure@gmail.com; r 150,000Rp; 🛜) A small family-run property that has just five simple, tiled cottages with Western toilets and *mandis* (baths) in a blooming garden.

Pondok Senaru & Restaurant LODGE $
(📞0818 0362 4129; pondoksenaru@yahoo.com; r 250,000-600,000Rp, mains 20,000-50,000Rp; ⊗restaurant 7am-9pm; 🛜) This place has 14 lovely little cottages with terracotta-tiled roofs, and some well-equipped superior rooms with such niceties as hot water. The restaurant, with tables perched on the edge of a rice-terraced valley, is a sublime place for a meal. It's at the waterfall entrance.

Rinjani Lodge GUESTHOUSE $$
(📞0819 0738 4944; www.rinjanilodge.com; r 500,000-1,000,000Rp; ❄🛜🏊) A comfortable new option, the five bungalows here each have jaw-dropping views across north Lombok all the way to the ocean. Rooms are well furnished and both the restaurant and the pool enjoy the same vistas. In fact the local pack of grey monkeys enjoy them, too. The lodge is just down from the waterfall entrance.

Sinar Rinjani LODGE $
(📞0818 540 673; www.senarutrekking.com; r 150,000-350,000Rp; 🛜) The eight rooms here are huge with rain showers (some with hot water), king-sized beds, and the rooftop restaurant has outstanding views. It's 2.1km from the top of the road.

ⓘ Information

Rinjani Trek Centre (p270), at the top of the hill, is the local guiding and mountain authority. All Rinjani trips starting in Senaru are packaged with their guides and approval.

ⓘ Getting There & Away

From Mandalika terminal in Bertais (Mataram), catch a bus to Anyar (25,000-30,000Rp, 2½ hours). Bemos no longer run from Anyar to Senaru, so you'll have to charter an *ojek* (motorcycle that takes passengers; per person from 20,000Rp depending on your luggage).

Sembalun Valley

📞 0376

High on the eastern side of Gunung Rinjani is what could be the mythical Shangri-La: the beautiful Sembalun Valley. This high plateau is ringed by volcanoes and peaks. It's a rich farming region where the golden foothills turn vivid green in the wet season. When the high clouds part, Rinjani goes full frontal from all angles.

The valley has two main settlements, Sembalun Lawang and Sembalun Bumbung, tranquil bread baskets primarily concerned with growing cabbage, potatoes, strawberries and, above all, garlic – though trekking tourism brings in a little income, too.

🏃 Activities

Rinjani Information Centre HIKING
(RIC; 📞0818 0572 5754; Sembalun Lawang; ⊙6am-6pm) The Rinjani Information Centre is the place to enquire about Rinjani treks. They have well-informed English-speaking staff and lots of fascinating information panels about the area's flora, fauna, geology and history. They also offer a four-hour **Village Walk** (per person 150,000Rp, minimum two people) and a two-day rambling **Wildflower Walk** (per person including guide, porters, meals and camping gear 550,000Rp) past flowery grasslands. They have camping and trekking gear for hire.

The centre is right by a huge garlic statue on the main road.

🛏 Sleeping

Sembalun Lawang village is rustic; most guesthouses will heat *mandi* water for a fee. The Rinjani Information Centre (RIC) can direct you to small homestays where rooms cost between 150,000Rp and 500,000Rp.

Lembah Rinjani LODGE $
(📞0818 0365 2511, 0852 3954 3279; Sembalun Lawang; r 300,000-400,000Rp) This property has 15 basic but clean tiled rooms with private porches and breathtaking mountain and sunrise views.

Maria Guesthouse GUESTHOUSE $
(📞0852 3956 1340; Sembalun Lawang; r 250,000Rp) Choose from three large tin-roofed bungalows at the rear of a family compound. Digs are bright with garish tiled floors; the family vibe is fun and the garden location sweet.

SEMBALUN VALLEY DRIVES

Any road you take in and around the Sembalun Valley is going to be spectacular. The drive north to Koko Putih, for instance, passes through some rich cashew forests. For a real treat do the nearly 60km route between Aikmel and Sembalun Lawang. The higher slopes on this road are dense with tropical rainforest. Stop anywhere to see an array of flowers and both black and grey monkeys.

When you are on the south rim of the valley, the lookout views are sensational.

Rinjani Information Centre LODGE $
(RIC; 📞0817 571 3041; Sembalun Lawang; r from 200,000Rp) The staff at RIC offer five simple guest rooms with large beds, private baths and tiny decks, behind their office.

ℹ Getting There & Away

From Mandalika bus terminal in Bertais (Mataram), take a bus to Aikmel (20,000Rp) and change there for a bemo to Sembalun Lawang (15,000Rp).

There's no public transport between Sembalun Lawang and Senaru, so you'll have to charter an *ojek,* for a potentially uncomfortable ride costing about 200,000Rp.

Gunung Rinjani

Lording over the northern half of Lombok, Gunung Rinjani (3726m) is Indonesia's second-tallest volcano. It's an astonishing peak, and sacred to Hindus and Sasaks who make pilgrimages to the summit and lake to leave offerings for the gods and spirits. To the Balinese, Rinjani is one of three sacred mountains, along with Bali's Agung and Java's Bromo. Sasaks ascend Rinjani throughout the year, around the full moon.

The mountain also has climatic significance. Its peak attracts a steady stream of swirling rain clouds, while its ash emissions bring fertility to the island's rice fields and tobacco crops, feeding a tapestry of paddies, fields, and cashew and mango orchards.

Inside the immense caldera, sitting 600m below the rim, is a stunning, 6km-wide, turquoise crescent lake, **Danau Segara Anak** (Child of the Sea). The Balinese toss gold and jewellery into the lake in a ceremony called *pekelan,* before they slog their way towards the sacred summit.

Gunung Rinjani

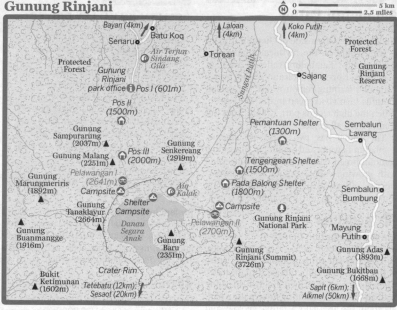

The mountain's newest cone, the minor peak of Gunung Baru (2351m), only emerged a couple of hundred years ago, its scarred, smouldering profile rising above the lake as an ominous reminder of the apocalyptic power of nature. This peak has been erupting fitfully for the last decade, periodically belching plumes of smoke and ash over the entire Rinjani caldera. Also in the crater are natural hot springs known as **Aiq Kalak**. Locals suffering from skin diseases trek here with a satchel of medicinal herbs to bathe and scrub in the bubbling mineral water.

Organised Treks

Treks to the rim, lake and peak should not be taken lightly, and guides are mandatory. Climbing Rinjani during the wet season (November to March) is usually completely forbidden due to the risk of landslide. June to August is the only time you are (almost) guaranteed minimal rain or clouds. Be prepared with layers and a fleece because it can get cold at the rim (and near-freezing at the summit) at any time of year.

The easiest way to organise a trip is to head to the **Rinjani Trek Centre** (RTC; ✆ 0817 572 4863, 0878 6432 3094; ☺ 6am-4pm) in Senaru or the **Rinjani Information Centre** (RIC; ✆ 0878 6334 4119; ☺ 6am-6pm) in Sembalun Lawang. These centres use a rotation system, and all local guides get a slice of the trekking purse.

Roughly the same trek packages and prices are offered by all operators (base guide and porter prices are set by RTC and RIC), though some outfitters have a 'luxury' option. Treks from Senaru to Sembalun Lawang via the lake summit are very popular, and the return hike from Sembalun Lawang to the summit is another well-trodden trail.

Trek prices get cheaper the larger the party. A three-day hike (including food, equipment, guide, porters, park fee and transport back to Senaru) to the summit and lake costs from US$300 per person based on a group of two to four. An overnight trek to the crater rim costs about US$150 to US$200.

OPERATORS

Agencies in Mataram, Senggigi and the Gili Islands can organise Rinjani treks too, with return transport from the point of origin.

John's Adventures TREKKING
(✆ 0817 578 8018; www.rinjanimaster.com; Senaru) John's Adventures is a very experienced outfitter that has toilet tents, thick sleeping mats and itineraries that start from either

CLIMBING GUNUNG RINJANI

The most popular way to climb Gunung Rinjani is the five-day trek that starts at Senaru and finishes at Sembalun Lawang. Other possibilities include a summit attempt from Sembalun, which sits higher on the slope and can be done as a gruelling two-day return hike.

Day One: Senaru Pos I to Pos III (Five to Six Hours)

At the southern end of Senaru is the **Rinjani Trek Centre** (Pos I, 601m), where you register, organise your guide and porters and pay the park fee. Just beyond the post, you'll head right when the trail forks. The trail climbs steadily through scrubby farmland for about half an hour to the entrance of **Gunung Rinjani National Park** (Taman Nasional Gunung Rinjani). The wide trail climbs for another 2½ hours until you reach Pos II (1500m), where there's a shelter. Another 1½ hours' steady walk uphill brings you to Pos III (2000m), where there are two shelters in disrepair. Pos III is usually the place to camp at the end of the first day.

Day Two: Pos III to Danau Segara Anak & Aiq Kalak (Four Hours)

From Pos III, it takes about 1½ hours to reach the rim, **Pelawangan I** (2641m). Setting off very early promises a stunning sunrise. It's possible to camp at Pelawangan I, but level sites are limited, there's no water and it can be very blustery.

It takes about two hours to descend to **Danau Segara Anak** and over to the hot springs, **Aiq Kalak**. The first hour is a very steep descent and involves a bit of bouldering. From the bottom of the crater wall it's an easy 30-minute walk across undulating terrain around the lake's edge. There are several places to camp, but most locals prefer to be near the hot springs to soak their weary bodies.

Day Three: Aiq Kalak to Pelawangan II (Three to Four Hours)

The trail starts beside the last shelter at the hot springs and heads away from the lake for about 100m before veering right. It then traverses the northern slope of the crater, and it's an easy one-hour walk along the grassy slopes before you hit a steep, unforgiving rise; from the lake it takes about three hours to reach the crater rim (2639m). At the rim, a sign points the way back to Danau Segara Anak. The trail forks here – straight on to Sembalun or along the rim to the campsite of **Pelawangan II** (2700m).

Day Four: Pelawangan II to Rinjani Summit (Five to Six Hours Return)

Gunung Rinjani's summit arcs above the campsite and looks deceptively close. You'll start the climb around 3am to reach it by sunrise. Depending on wind conditions, it may not be possible to attempt the summit at all, as the trail is along an exposed ridge.

It takes about 45 minutes to clamber up a steep, slippery and indistinct trail to the ridge that leads to Rinjani. Once on the ridge it's a relatively steady walk uphill. After about an hour heading towards a false peak, the real **summit of Rinjani** (3726m) looms. The trail then gets increasingly steeper. About 350m before the summit, the scree is composed of loose, fist-sized rocks. This section can take about an hour. The views from the top are truly magnificent. In total it takes around three hours to reach the summit, and two to return.

Day Four/Five: Pelawangan II to Sembalun Lawang (Six to Seven Hours)

After negotiating the peak, it's possible to reach Sembalun the same day. From the campsite, it's a steep descent to the village; you'll feel it in your knees. From the campsite, you head back along the crater rim. Shortly after the turn-off to Danau Segara Anak, there's a signposted right turn down to **Pada Balong** (also called Pos 3, 1800m). The trail is easy to follow; it takes around two hours to reach Pada Balong shelter.

The trail then undulates toward the **Sembalun Lawang** savannah, via Tengengean (or Pos 2, 1500m) shelter, beautifully situated in a river valley. It's another 30 minutes through long grass to lonely **Pemantuan** (or Pos 1, 1300m), and two more hours along a dirt track to Sembalun Lawang.

Senaru or Sembalun. The Senaru office is 2km below the park office.

Rudy Trekker   TREKKING
(☑0818 0365 2874; www.rudytrekker.com; Senaru) This conscientious organisation is based in Senaru. It has a variety of itineraries, though most trekkers prefer the three-day, two-night package starting from Sembalun Lawang. The office is near the entrance to Air Terjun Sindang Gila. It has a great list of what to pack displayed on the wall.

Guides & Porters

Hiking independently is simply not allowed, and deeply unwise. People have died on Rinjani, with or without guides, and only the most skilled climbers should consider themselves qualified to undertake such a journey. See p37 for safety guidelines.

Guides and porters operate on loosely fixed fees, which are included in whatever trekking package you purchase. Tips of 20,000Rp to 50,000Rp per day are sufficient and can be paid at the end of the trip.

Entrance Fee & Equipment

Entrance to Gunung Rinjani National Park is 150,000Rp *per day* – you register and pay at the RTC in Senaru or the RIC in Sembalun Lawang before your trek. Note that there are proposals to raise these fees even higher.

Sleeping bags and tents are essential and can be hired at either RTC or RIC. Decent footwear, warm clothing, wet-weather gear, gloves, cooking equipment and a torch are important (all can be hired if necessary). Expect to pay upwards of 100,000Rp a head per day for all your hired gear. Muscle balm (to ease aching legs) and a swimming costume (for the lake and hot springs) could also be packed. Discuss what to bring with your trekking orgnaisation or guide.

Take home your rubbish, including toilet tissue. Sadly several Rinjani camps are litter-strewn.

Food & Supplies

Trek organisers at RTC and RIC will arrange trekking food. Mataram is cheapest for supplies but many provisions are available in Senaru and Sembalun Lawang. Take more water than seems reasonable (dehydration can spur altitude sickness), extra batteries (as altitude can wreak havoc on those, as well) and a back-up lighter.

ⓘ Information

Rinjani National Park (Taman Nasional Gunung Rinjani; ☑0370-660 8874; www.rinjaninational park.com) The official website for the park has good maps, info and a very useful section on reported scams by dodgy trek operators.

Rinjani Trekking Club (☑0370-693202; www. info2lombok.com; Jl Raya Senggigi, Senggigi) This group sells treks on the mountain but it also has a very useful website and organises sustainable programs.

Tetebatu
☑0376

Laced with Rinjani spring-fed streams and blessed with rich volcanic soil, Tetebatu is a Sasak breadbasket. The surrounding countryside is quilted with tobacco and rice fields, fruit orchards and cow pastures that fade into remnant monkey forest gushing with waterfalls. Tetebatu's sweet climate is ideal for long country walks (at 400m it's high enough to mute that hot, sticky coastal mercury). Dark nights come saturated with sound courtesy of a frog orchestra accompanied by countless gurgling brooks. Even insomniacs snore here.

The town is spread out, with facilities on roads north and east (nicknamed 'waterfall road') of the central *ojek* stop, which happens to be the town's main intersection and a basis for all directions.

⊙ Sights & Activities

A shady 4km track leading from the main road, just north of the mosque, heads into the **Taman Wisata Tetebatu** (Monkey Forest) with black monkeys and waterfalls – you'll need a guide.

On the southern slopes of Rinjani, there are two **waterfalls**. Both are accessible by private transport or a spectacular two-hour walk (one way) through rice fields from Tetebatu. If walking, hire a guide (150,000Rp) through your guesthouse.

A steep 2km hike from the car park at the end of the access road to Gunung Rinjani National Park leads to beautiful **Air Terjun Jukut**, an impressive 20m drop to a deep pool surrounded by lush forest.

⌂ Sleeping & Eating

★**Tetebatu Mountain Resort**   LODGE $
(☑0812 372 4040, 0819 1771 6440; r 350,000-400,000Rp; ☎) These two-storey Sasak bungalows with 23 rooms are the best digs in town.

There are separate bedrooms on both floors (perfect for travelling buddies) and a top-floor balcony with magical rice-field views.

Cendrawasih Cottages
COTTAGE $

([✓]0878 6418 7063; r from 200,000Rp; mains 20,000-45,000Rp; ⊙restaurant 8am-9pm) Sweet little brick cottages, styled like *lumbung* (rice barns), with bamboo beds and private porches nestled in the rice fields. You'll sit on floor cushions in their stunning stilted restaurant, which has Sasak, Indonesian or Western fare and 360-degree rice-field views. It's about 500m east of the intersection.

Hakiki Inn
BUNGALOW $

([✓]0818 0373 7407; www.hakiki-inn.com; r 150,000-400,000Rp; [✿]) A collection of seven bungalows in a blooming garden at the edge of the rice fields.You'll find it perched over the family rice plot about 600m from the intersection.

Pondok Tetebatu
LODGE $

([✓]0370-632572, 0818 0576 7153; r 150,000-250,000Rp) Five hundred metres north of the intersection, these 12 detached, ranch-style rooms set around a flower garden are basic. They offer guided walks through farming villages to the falls.

ⓘ Getting There & Around

All cross-island buses pass Pomotong (15,000Rp from Mandalika terminal) on the main east–west highway. Get off here and you can hop an *ojek* (from 20,000Rp) to Tetebatu.

SOUTH LOMBOK

[✓]0370

Beaches just don't get much better: the water is warm, striped turquoise and curls into barrels, and the sand is silky and snow-white, framed by massive headlands and sheer cliffs that recall Bali's Bukit Peninsula 30 years ago. Village life is still vibrant in south Lombok as well, with unique festivals and an economy based on seaweed and to-bacco harvests. The south is noticeably drier than the rest of Lombok and more sparsely populated, with limited roads and public transport. But, with Lombok's international airport now located here, flights have in-creased and change will surely come. Soon.

Southern Lombok's incredible coastline of giant bite-shaped bays is startling, its beauty immediate, undeniable and arrest-ing. Yet this region has historically been the island's poorest, its sun-blasted soil parched and unproductive. These days those hills are also pocked with illegal, undocumented gold mines, which you'll see and hear grinding away as you head west to the surf beaches.

Praya

Sprawling Praya is the main town in the south, with tree-lined streets and the odd crumbling Dutch colonial relic. The bemo terminal is on the northwest side of town.

Lombok International Airport

Surrounded by rice fields and 5km south of Praya proper, the recently built **Lombok International Airport** (LOP; www.lombok-airport.co.id) has become an attraction in its own right: on weekends you'll see vast crowds of locals sitting around watching and snacking. They're not waiting on any-one, rather they are hanging out for the day enjoying the spectacle of people flying in and out.

The airport is not huge, but is very mod-ern and has a full range of services such as ATMs (and convenience stores with ludi-crous prices).

Thanks to new roads, the airport is only 30 minutes' drive from Mataram and Kuta and is well linked to the rest of the island.

Bus Damri operates tourist buses, buy tickets in the arrivals area. Destinations: Mataram's Mandalika terminal (20,000Rp) and Senggigi (30,000Rp).

Taxi The airport taxi cartel offers fixed-price rides to destinations that include: Kuta (84,000Rp, 30 minutes), Mataram (150,000Rp, 30 minutes), Senggigi (190,000Rp, one hour) and Bangsal (250,000Rp, 90 minutes), where you can access the Gili Islands.

Around Praya

Sukarara

The main street here is the domain of textile shops, where you can watch weavers work their old looms. **Dharma Setya** ([✓]0370-660 5204; ⊙8am-5pm) has an incredible array of hand-woven Sasak textiles, includ-ing ikat and *songket* (handwoven silver or gold-threaded cloth). To reach Sukarara from Praya, take a bemo to Puyung along the main road. From there, hire a *cidomo* (horse cart) or walk the 2km to Sukarara.

Penujak

Penujak is well known for its traditional *gerabah* pottery. Made from chocolatey terracotta-tinted local clay, it's hand-burnished and topped with braided bamboo. Huge floor vases cost US$6 or so, and there are also plates and cups on offer from the potters' humble home studios, most of which huddle around the eerie village cemetery. Any bemo from Praya to Kuta will drop you off here.

Rembitan & Sade

The area from Sengkol down to Kuta is a centre for Sasak culture – traditional villages full of towering *lumbung* (rice barn) and *bale tani* (family house), homes made from bamboo, mud, and cow and buffalo dung. Regular bemos cover this route.

Sade's **Sasak Village** has been extensively renovated and has some fascinating *bale tani*. Further south, **Rembitan** has more of an authentic feel to it, boasts a cluster of houses and *lumbung* and the 100-year-old **Masjid Kuno**, an ancient thatched-roof mosque that is a pilgrimage destination for Lombok's Muslims.

Both villages are worth a look but it's not possible to without a guide (around 40,000Rp).

Kuta

Imagine a crescent bay, turquoise in the shallows and deep blue further out. It licks a huge, white-sand beach, as wide as a football pitch and framed by headlands. It's deserted, save for a few fishermen, seaweed farmers and their children. Now imagine a coastline of nearly a dozen such bays, all backed by a rugged range of coastal hills spotted with lush patches of banana trees and tobacco fields, and you'll have a notion of Kuta's immediate appeal.

Kuta proper consists of no more than a few hundred houses, a likeable but scruffy-around-the-edges place with a ramshackle market area, and a seafront lined with a non-contiguous row of distinctly modest cafes and hotels.

Kuta's original attraction was the limitless world-class breaks within a short ride

of town. For now everyone seems to be sitting on their land, but the town's real-estate agents – who are already spearheading increasing villa development – are betting on change real soon. The big boom hasn't happened yet, but you can feel the tension.

Note that the main intersection in town, Jl Pantai Kuta and Jl ke Mawan, is commonly called 'the junction' and is a main point of reference for directions. Some 2km north of the beach on Jl Pantai Kuta is another important junction, where there is a big traffic circle with the optimistically planned four lanes of Jl Raya Bypass.

🏝 Beaches

Kuta's main beach can easily snare you and keep you from looking elsewhere. It's got ideal white sand and all those views. Plus the surf is just right for swimming. But even here change looms: the bamboo cafes that used to line the sand have been demolished and the local government talks vaguely of building a park. Even the goats, who once roamed freely, engaging in antics such as randomly eating your guidebook, have been largely moved on. What remains is a vast open area of rocky grass and parking areas.

🏃 Activities

There's a whole row of activity sales agents across the road from Lamancha Homestay. They can set you up on anything from surf tours to snorkelling in obscure locations. Bargain hard.

Surfing

For surfing, stellar lefts and rights break on the reefs off Kuta Bay (Telek Kuta) and east of Tanjung Aan. Boatmen will take you out for around 120,000Rp. Seven kilometres east of Kuta is the fishing village of **Gerupuk**, where there's a series of reef breaks, both close to the shore and further out, but they require a boat, at a negotiable 300,000Rp per day. Wise surfers buzz past Gerupuk, take the road to to **Ekas**, where crowds are thin and surf is plentiful. West of Kuta you'll find **Mawun (Mawan)**, a stunning swimming beach (the first left after Astari), and **Mawi**, a popular surf paradise with world-class swells and a strong riptide.

Kimen Surf   SURFING
(📞 0370-655064; www.kuta-lombok.net; Jl ke Mawan; board rental per day 100,000Rp, lessons per person from 500,000Rp; ⏰ 9am-8pm) Swell forecasts, tips, kitesurfing, board rental, re-

Kuta

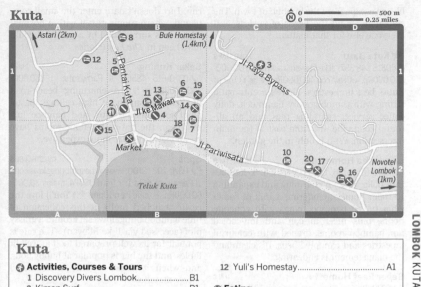

Astari (2km)
Bule Homestay (1.4km)
Jl Raya Bypass
Jl Pantai Kuta
Jl ke Mawan
Market
Jl Pariwisata
Teluk Kuta
Novotel Lombok (1km)

0 — 500 m
0 — 0.25 miles

pairs and lessons. It runs guided excursions to breaks such as Gerupuk (400,000Rp).

Diving
Scuba Froggy DIVING
(☏0877 6510 6945; www.scubafroggy.com; Jl ke Mawan; per dive from 400,000Rp; ☉9am-8pm) Runs local trips to a dozen sites, most above 18m. From June to November they also run trips to the spectacular and challenging ocean pinnacles in Blongas Bay, famous for schooling hammerheads and mobula rays. Snorkelling trips are 150,000Rp.

Discovery Divers Lombok DIVING
(☏0812 3629 4178; www.discoverydiverslombok.com; Jl ke Mawan; 2 local dives from 750,000Rp; ☉8am-9pm) A big and glossy operation, this dive shop has a very nice and welcoming cafe. Besides a full slate of courses, it runs tours through the region.

Horse Riding
Kuta Horses HORSE RIDING
(☏0819 1599 9436; www.horseridinglombok.com; Jl Raya Bypass; 1hr ride from 440,000Rp; ☉rides 8am & 4pm) Kuta Horses offers horseback riding through Sasak villages, on Kuta's country lanes, and on the beach at sunrise and sunset. They also have rather nice rental houses. It's back off the main road.

⊨ Sleeping

Prices increase markedly in the July–August high season. Beware of aging, rundown hotels along Jl Pariwisata.

★**Bombara Bungalows** GUESTHOUSE $
(☏0370-615 8056; bomborabungalows@yahoo.com; Jl Pantai Kuta; r from 350,000Rp; ☏☒) One of the best places for a low-cost stay in Kuta, these six fan-cooled bungalows are built around a lovely pool area. Coconut palms shade loungers and the entire place feels

like an escape from the hubbub of town. The staff understand the needs of surfers, and everyone else for that matter.

★ Kuta Baru
HOMESTAY $

(☑ 0818 548 357; Jl ke Mawan; r with fan 200,000-250,000Rp, with air-con 400,000Rp; ☎ ☀) One of Kuta's best homestays. There's a cute patio strung with the obligatory hammock, daily coffee service, sparkling tiles and an all-round good vibe. It's 110m east of the main intersection. Wi-fi is only in the garden.

Lamancha Homestay
HOMESTAY $

(☑ 0370-615 5186, 0819 3313 0156; r 150,000-250,000Rp; ☀ ☎) A charming and expanding 10-room homestay offering a mix of somewhat frayed bamboo rooms with concrete floors, plus nicer air-con and fan-cooled non-bamboo rooms, draped with colourful tapestries and canopied beds. It's clean and the management is endearing.

Seger Reef Homestay
INN $

(☑ 0370-655528; www.segerreef.com; Jl Pariwisata; r 150,000-200,000Rp; ☎) Twelve bright, spotless, family-owned bungalows across the street from the beach. Newest rooms are kitted out with wardrobes, and colourful headboards. Wi-fi only works in some rooms.

Bule Homestay
GUESTHOUSE $

(☑ 0819 1799 6256; www.bulehomestay.com; Jl Raya Bypass; r from 200,000Rp; ☎) Although it's about 2km back from the beach near the junction of Jl Pantai Kuta and Jl Raya Bypass, this eight-bungalow complex is worth consideration simply for the snappy way its

---

NYALE FESTIVAL

On the 19th day of the 10th month in the Sasak calendar (generally February or March), hundreds of Sasaks gather on the beach at Kuta, Lombok. When night falls, fires are built and teens sit around competing in a Sasak poetry slam, where they spit rhyming couplets called *pantun* back and forth. At dawn the next day, the first of millions of *nyale* (worm-like fish that appear here annually) are caught, then teenage girls and boys take to the sea separately in decorated boats, and chase one another with lots of noise and laughter. The *nyale* are eaten raw or grilled, and are considered to be an aphrodisiac. A good catch is a sign that a bumper crop of rice is coming.

---

run. Dirt doesn't dare enter the small compound, where rooms gleam with a hospital white. It is surrounded by a wall that could have been in *The Flintstones*.

Sekar Kuning
INN $

(☑ 0370-615 4856; Jl Pariwisata; r 150,000-200,000Rp; ☀ ☎) A charming beach-road inn. Tiled rooms have high ceilings, pastel paint jobs, ceiling fans, and bamboo furniture on the patio. Top-floor rooms have ocean views and are more expensive.

Spot
GUESTHOUSE $

(☑ 0370-702 2100; www.thespotbungalows.com; Jl Pariwisata Kuta 1; r from US$24, mains 30,000-60,000Rp; ⊘ cafe 7am-10pm; ☎) You'll love the rustic thatched motif at this collection of nine bamboo bungalows set around a grassy plot (accessed via Jl ke Mawan) . The cafe is popular for its well-prepared food at well-lit tables, and the bar is popular at happy hour, and when it shows notable international soccer matches.

Mimpi Manis
B&B $

(☑ 0818 369 950; www.mimpimanis.com; off Jl Pantai Kuta; r 200,000-350,000Rp; ☀) An inviting English-Balinese-owned B&B in a two-storey house with two spotless rooms, with ensuite shower and TV/DVD players. There's home-cooked food, plenty of good books to browse and DVDs to borrow. It's 1km inland from the beach, but the owners offer a free drop-off service to the beach and town and arrange bike and motorbike rental.

★ Yuli's Homestay
HOMESTAY $$

(☑ 0819 1710 0983; www.yulishomestay.com; off Jl Pantai Kuta; r from 400,000Rp; ☀ ☎ ☀) A very popular place, the 13 rooms here are immaculately clean, spacious and nicely furnished with huge beds and wardrobes (and have big front terraces, though cold-water bathrooms). There's a guest kitchen and a garden and pool to enjoy. Wi-fi is only in common areas.

Novotel Lombok Resort & Villas
RESORT $$$

(☑ 0370-615 3333; www.novotel.com; r from US$120, villas from US$250; ☀ ☎ ☀ ⌂) This appealing, Sasak-themed four-star resort spills onto a superb beach less than 3km east of the junction. The 102 rooms have high sloping roofs and modern interiors. There are two pools, a spa, resort-style restaurants, a swanky bar and a plethora of activities on offer including catamaran sailing, fishing and scuba diving. Surprisingly, the wi-fi doesn't work in the rooms.

✕ Eating & Drinking

Kuta's dining scene has improved with growth, but at most local joints the Indo nosh or fresh seafood are always the smart choices. The **market** (☺ Sun & Wed) sells an ever-changing variety of foodstuffs and basic necessities.

Cafe 7 · CAFE $

(Jl Pariswata Kuta; mains from 40,000Rp; ☺ 11am-1am; 🛜) The style here is lounge bar, there's frequent live music and the vibe is friendly. The cocktails are worth a splurge as they are made out of the real thing, not something else dressed up like gin etc. The food is mostly Western, with some delicious burgers. You'll find it on Jl ke Mawan.

DJ Coffee Corner · CAFE $

(Jl ke Mawan; treats from 15,000Rp; ☺ 8am-8pm; ❄) A switch from the thatch-and-bamboo look that dominates the local design palette: a sleek air-con coffee bar with a nice back garden. Get your real espresso fix here along with juices, light bites and baked goods.

Warung Jawa 1 · INDONESIAN $

(Jl ke Mawan; meals 15,000-20,000Rp; ☺ 11am-10pm) This big bamboo-and-tin open-air restaurant has a cheap-and-mean *nasi campur* (rice with a choice of side dishes). It does all the Indo standards, and the drinks list groans with juices and looks spry with Bintang for only 18,000Rp.

Warung Bamboo · INDONESIAN $

(Jl Pariwisata; mains 25,000-35,000Rp; ☺ 8am-10pm) Several of the former beach warungs have been revived in a little strip across the road from beach. This one – named after its principal building material – is dead simple but cooks up fine seafood specials and various rice and noodle staples. The secret here is ask for your food 'Lombok spicy'. They will very happily oblige.

Full Moon Cafe · CAFE $

(Jl Pariwisata; mains from 30,000Rp; ☺ 8am-late) Another former beach bar that hasn't missed a beat – literally – relocating back across the road. The second-floor cafe here is like a treehouse, but with killer ocean views. The menu has all the standards, from banana pancakes to various Indo rice creations. Come for the view and sunset, then hang out.

★ Warung Bule · SEAFOOD $$

(📋 0819 1799 6256; Jl Pariwisata; mains 40,000-250,000Rp; ☺ 8am-10pm; 🛜) The best restaurant in Kuta, founded by the long-time executive chef at the Novotel who delivers tropical seafood tastes at an affordable price. We like the tempura starter and his Tahitian take on *ceviche* (marinaded raw fish or seafood). His trio of lobster, prawns and mahi-mahi might have you cooing. It gets very busy in high season. so be prepared for a wait.

Ashtari · VEGETARIAN $$

(📋 0877 6549 7625; www.ashtarilombok.com; Jl ke Mawan; meals 20,000-80,000Rp; ☺ 7am-10pm; 🍴) Perched on a mountaintop 2km west of town on the road to Mawan, this breezy, Moroccan-themed lounge-restaurant has spectacular vistas of pristine bays and rocky peninsulas that take turns spilling further out to sea. Not quite the nouveau-hippy joint it was when it opened, it's now a slick yoga-luxe sort of place.

Dwiki's · PIZZA $$

(📋 0859 3503 4489; Jl ke Mawan; mains 35,000-70,000Rp; ☺ 8am-11pm; 🛜🍴) A choice, relaxcd spot for wood-fircd thin-crust pizza in tiki-bar surrounds. And they deliver! Has lots of Indo standards and an above-average list of veggie options.

★ Warung Rasta · CAFE

(📋 0882 1907 1744; Jl Pariwisata; ☺ 8am-late) There are Indo standards on the menu at this barely-there shack of a cafe, but what really puts it on the map are the young local owners who have created a laid-back party vibe that draws in crowds each night. Guitars get strummed and surfers compete in 'Stampedo' contests that involve beer-chugging with the strategic aid of straws.

❶ Information

ATMs are common, as is wi-fi.

DANGER & ANNOYANCES

If you decide to rent a bicycle or motorbike, take care with whom you deal – arrangements are informal and no rental contracts are exchanged. We have received occasional reports of some visitors having motorbikes stolen, and then having to pay substantial sums of money as compensation to the owner (who may or may not have arranged the 'theft' themselves). Renting a motorbike from your guesthouse is safest.

As you drive up the coastal road west and east of Kuta, watch your back – especially after dark. There have been reports of muggings in the area.

Throngs of vendors are relentless.

ⓘ Getting There & Away

You'll need at least three bemos to get here just from Mataram. Take one from Mataram's Mandalika terminal to Praya (10,000Rp), another to Sengkol (5000Rp) and a third to Kuta (5000Rp). Simpler are the daily tourist buses serving Mataram (125,000Rp) plus Senggigi and Lembar (both 150,000Rp).

A fixed-price taxi from the airport costs 85,000Rp. Shared-ride cars are widely advertised around town. Destinations include: Bangsal for Gili Islands public boats (160,000Rp), Seminyak on Bali via the public ferry (200,000Rp) and Senaru (400,000Rp).

ⓘ Getting Around

Irregular bemos go east of Kuta to Awang and Tanjung Aan (5000Rp), and west to Selong Blanak (10,000Rp), or can be chartered to nearby beaches. Guesthouses rent motorbikes for about 50,000Rp per day. *Ojek* congregate around the junction.

East of Kuta

A good paved road runs along the coast to the east and Ekas, passing a seemingly endless series of beautiful bays punctuated by headlands. It's a terrific motorbike ride.

Pantai Segar & Tanjung Aan

Pantai Segar, a lovely beach about 2km east of Kuta around the first headland, has unbelievably turquoise water, decent swimming (though no shade) and a break 200m offshore.

Continuing 3km east on an increasingly rough road, **Tanjung Aan** is a spectacular sight: a giant horseshoe bay with two sweeping arcs of fine sand with the ends punctuated by waves crashing on the rocks. Swimming is good here and there's a little shade under trees and shelters, plus safe parking (for a small charge). The huge international resort planned here may have finally begun. If construction follows through, this entire area will be significantly changed.

Gerupuk

Just 1.6km past Tanjung Aan, Gerupuk is a fascinating little ramshackle coastal village where the thousand or so local souls earn their keep from fishing, seaweed harvesting and lobster exports. Oh, and guiding and ferrying surfers to the five exceptional **surf breaks** in its huge bay.

To surf here you'll need to hire a boat to ferry you from the fishing harbour, skirting the netted lobster farms, to the break (200,000Rp). The boatman will help you find the right wave and wait patiently. There are four waves inside and a left break outside on the point. All can get head high or bigger when the swell hits.

🛏 Sleeping & Eating

There are a growing number of hotels and warungs popular with surfers in Gerupuk.

Surf Camp Lombok   GUESTHOUSE $
(☑0819 1608 6876; www.surfcampindonesia.com; Gerupuk; 1 week from €650) 🍴 At the eastern end of Gerupuk village, lodging here is in a bamboo Borneo-style longhouse, albeit with lots of high-tech diversions. The setting on the beach feels lush and remote. All meals are included plus surf lessons, yoga and more. Rooms sleep four, except for one double.

Edo Homestay   INN $
(☑0818 0371 0521; Gerupuk; r 150,000-600,000Rp; ❄🕸) Right in the village, this place offers 18 clean, simple rooms (some fan-cooled) with colourful drapes and double beds. They have a decent restaurant and a surf shop, too (boards per day 100,000Rp).

Spear Villa   GUESTHOUSE $
(☑0818 0371 0521; www.s-pear.com; r from 400,000Rp; ❄🗗) The nicest Gerupuk village digs, here you'll find clean, modern rooms (with air-con and satellite TV) that open onto a common plunge pool. It caters (not exclusively) to Japanese surfers.

⭐**Bumbangku**   BUNGALOW $$
(☑0370-620833, 0852 3717 6168; www.bumbangku-lombok.com; r 375,000-750,000Rp; ❄) Bumbangku is set across the bay from Gerupuk and is wonderfully remote – almost island-like. They have 28 rooms ranging from simple bamboo huts on stilts with outdoor baths to much nicer concrete rooms with queen beds, outdoor baths, plush linens and TV. Transfer from Gerupuk costs 100,000Rp, from the airport 250,000Rp. Warning: you and your gear will get wet en route.

Ekas & Around

Ekas is an uncrowded find, where the breaks and soaring cliffs recall Bali's Ulu Watu. It's easy to drive here from both the west and the north. From Kuta, it's under 90 minutes on a scooter.

Ekas itself is a sleepy little village but head south into the peninsula and you'll soon make the sorts of jaw-dropping discoveries that will have you tweeting like mad. Start by driving all the way south (6.5km from Ekas) over the rough but passable road to **Pantai Dagong**. Here, you'll find an utterly empty and seemingly endless white beach backed by azure breakers.

Ask directions to **Heaven Beach** for another bit of sandy wonder. It's a stunning little pocket of white sand and surf about 4km from Ekas. Despite the omnipresent resort, you're free to access the shore: all Indonesian beaches are public.

🛏 Sleeping & Eating

There are posh boutique resorts hidden on the beautiful coves south of Ekas. Also look out for new and simple guesthouses along the rural roads.

Ocean Heaven   BOUTIQUE RESORT **$$**
(📞 0812 375 1103; www.sanctuaryinlombok.com; r all-inclusive per person US$130-175; ❇ 🏃 ☃) Heaven Beach is not hyperbole. Occupying much of the land behind the beach is this resort, which shares owners with Heaven on the Planet up on the bluff. The six rooms are laid-back luxe and there's a new spa. Most guests arrive in transport arranged by the resort.

Heaven on the Planet   BOUTIQUE HOTEL **$$$**
(📞 0812 375 1103; www.sanctuaryinlombok.com; per person all-inclusive U$160-225; ❇ 🏃 ☃) The aptly named Heaven on the Planet has five units scattered along the cliff's edge, from where you'll have spectacular bird's-eye views of the sea and swell lines. Heaven is primarily a surf resort (you can even surf at night here thanks to ocean spotlights) but kitesurfing, scuba diving and snorkelling are also possible.

West of Kuta

West of Kuta is a series of awesome beaches and ideal surf breaks. Developers are nosing around here, and land has changed hands, but for now it remains almost pristine and the region has a raw beauty. In anticipation of future developments, the road has been much improved. It meanders inland, skirting tobacco, sweet potato and rice fields in between turn-offs to the sand and glimpses of the gorgeous coast.

Mawun (Mawan)

How's this for a vision of sandy paradise? Just 600m off the main road, this half-moon cove is framed by soaring headlands with azure water and a swathe of empty sand (save a fishing village of a dozen thatched homes). It's a terrific swimming **beach**. There's paved parking (car/motorbike 10,000/5000Rp) and some modest cafes.

Mawi

Some 16km west of Kuta, look for a small road down to Mawi. This is a surf paradise: a stunning scene, with legendary barrels and several beaches scattered around the great bay. Watch out for the strong riptide. There's parking (car/motorbike 10,000/5000Rp) and vendors.

Selong Blanak

Further west from Mawi, and just when you think you've seen the most beautiful beaches Kuta has to offer, you reach Selong Blanak. Behold the wide, sugar-white beach with water streaked a thousand shades of blue, ideal for swimming. You can rent surfboards (per day 100,000Rp) and arrange for a boat out to area breaks (three hours from 500,000Rp). The parking lot (car/motorbike 10,000/5000Rp) is just 400m off the main drag on a good road.

There is a fabulous boutique villa property tucked away on the cliffs, with a cafe inland from the beach. **Sempiak Villas** (📞 0821 4430 3337; www.sempiakvillas.com; Solong Blanak; villa from 1,100,000Rp; ❇ ☃) is one of the Kuta area's most upscale properties. The octagonal villas are built into the hillside above the beach. At sea level, **Laut Biru Cafe** (Solong Blanak; mains 40,000-80,000Rp; ☺8am-8pm; 🏃) is open to all comers. They keep it simple here with muesli and yoghurt, eggs and toast for breakfast and Indo classics for lunch and dinner. It's a thatched-roof construction, with remixed world music floating through the room and patio.

Blongas & Around

From **Pengantap**, the road climbs across a headland then descends to a superb bay; follow this around for 1km then look out for the turn-off west to **Blongas** – a steep and winding road with breathtaking scenery. Blongas is set on its secluded namesake

A GRIM CATCH

Every day fishing boats sail in and out of Tanjung Luar, a long-running fish market in southeast Lombok that has a bad reputation with environmental groups for the fishing of large species such as sharks, manta rays and dolphins.

On busy days as many as 100 sharks and mantas will get finned and gilled. Once in market, the meat is sold locally, but the shark fins and manta gills are auctioned to buyers who ship their bounty to Hong Kong, where the items are considered delicacies.

Shark-fin buyers in Tanjung Luar confirm that few sharks remain in the sea around Lombok. In the 1990s fishermen didn't have to go far to hunt their take but these days they travel all the way to the Sumba strait between Australia and Indonesia, an important shark-migration channel.

A recent survey by Project Aware (www.projectaware.org), a diving environmental group, found that mandatory government signs prohibiting dolphin catch as well as that of some shark species and sea turtles had been torn down.

What effect Indonesia's declaration in 2014 – of their waters being a protection zone for manta rays – remains to be seen.

bay that is positively breathtaking. Among a couple of worthy contenders, **Blongas Bay Lodge** (☑0370-645974; www.thelodge-lombok.com; bungalows 850,000-950,000Rp, meals 75,000Rp) offers spacious wooden bungalows with tiled roofs in a lovely coconut grove.

Dive Zone (☑0813 3954 4998; www.divezone-lombok.com; Blongas Bay; 2 dives from US$75) focuses on the famed nearby dive sites, **Magnet** and **Cathedrals**. Spotting conditions peak in mid-September when you may see schooling mobula rays in addition to hammerheads, which school around the pinnacle from June to November. It's not an easy dive, so you must be experienced and prepared for heavy current.

EAST LOMBOK

☑0376

All most travellers see of the east coast of Lombok is Labuhan Lombok, the port for ferries to Sumbawa. But the road around the northeast coast is pretty good, and can be traversed if you're hoping to complete a circumnavigation.

Labuhan Lombok

TRANSPORT HUB

Labuhan Lombok (also known as Labuhan Kayangan or Tanjung Kayangan) is the port for ferries and boats to Sumbawa. The town centre of Labuhan Lombok, 3km west of the ferry terminal, is a scruffy place but it does have great views of Gunung Rinjani.

🛈 Getting There & Away

BUS & BEMO

Very regular buses and bemos buzz between Mandalika terminal in Mataram and Labuhan Lombok; the journey takes two hours (25,000Rp). Some buses will only drop you off at the port entrance road from where you can catch another bemo to the ferry terminal. Don't walk – it's too far.

FERRY

There are ferry connections between Lombok and Sumbawa and bus connections between Mataram and Sumbawa.

South of Labuhan Lombok

Selong, the capital of the east Lombok administrative district, has some dusty Dutch colonial buildings. The transport junction for the region is just to the west of Selong at **Pancor**, where you can catch bemos to most points south.

Tanjung Luar is one of Lombok's main fishing ports (and home to one of Indonesia's most egregious shark finning operations) and has lots of Bugis-style houses on stilts. From here, the road swings west to **Keruak**, where wooden boats are built, and continues past the turn to **Sukaraja**, a traditional Sasak village where you can buy woodcarvings. Just west of Keruak a road leads south to **Jerowaru** and the spectacular southeastern peninsula. You'll need your own transport; be warned that it's easy to lose your way around here but the main roads are good.

Gili Islands

Best Places to Eat

→ Adeng Adeng (p296)

→ Scallywags (p300)

→ Kayu Café (p290)

→ Pasar Malam (p289)

Best Places to Stay

→ Kai's Beachouse (p299)

→ Adeng Adeng (p295)

→ Woodstock (p286)

→ Eden Cottages (p288)

→ Pondok Santi (p289)

Why Go?

Picture three minuscule desert islands, fringed by white-sand beaches and coconut palms, sitting in a turquoise sea: the Gilis are a vision of paradise. These islets have exploded in popularity, and are booming like nowhere else in Indonesia – speedboats now zip visitors direct from Bali and a hip new hotel opens practically every month.

It's not hard to understand the Gilis' unique appeal, for a serenity endures (no motorbikes or dogs!) and a green consciousness is growing. Development has been more tasteful than rapacious and there are few concrete eyesores.

Each island has its own special character. Trawangan (universally known as Gili T) is by far the most cosmopolitan, its bar and party scene vibrant, its accommodation and restaurants close to definitive tropical chic. Gili Air has the strongest local character, but also a perfect mix of buzz and languor. Meno is simply a desert-island getaway.

When to Go

→ The wet season is approximately late October until late March. But even in the height of the rainy season, when it's lashing it down in Mataram or Bali, the Gilis can be dry and sunny.

→ High season is between June and late August, when rooms are very hard to find and prices can double (though great weather is almost guaranteed).

→ The perfect months to visit are May and September.

→ There's no cyclone season to worry about.

ⓘ Getting There & Away

FROM BALI

Fast boats advertise swift connections (about two hours) between Bali and Gili Trawangan. They leave from several departure points in Bali, including Benoa Harbour, Sanur, Padangbai and Amed. Some go via Nusa Lembongan. Many dock at Teluk Nare/Teluk Kade on Lombok north of Senggigi before continuing onto Air and Trawangan (you'll have to transfer for Meno).

The website **Gili Bookings** (www.gilibookings.com) presents a range of boat operators and prices to your booking request. It's useful for getting an idea of the services offered, but it is not comprehensive and you may get a better price by buying direct from the operator.

Other considerations:

➡ Fares are not fixed, especially in quiet times, you should be able to get discounts on published fares.

➡ If you don't need transport to/from the boat, ask for a discount.

➡ The advertised times are illusionary. Boats are cancelled, unplanned stops are made or they simply run very late.

➡ Book ahead in July and August.

➡ The sea between Bali and Lombok can get very rough (particularly during rainy season).

➡ The fast boats are unregulated and operating and safety standards vary widely. There have been some major accidents and boats have been sunk (see p373).

Amed Sea Express (☎0878 6306 4799; www.gili-sea-express.com; per person from 300,000Rp) Makes 75-minute crossings to Amed on a large speedboat. This makes many interesting itineraries possible.

Blue Water Express (☎0361-895 1111; www.bluewater-express.com; one-way from 500,000Rp) From Serangan and Padangbai, Bali to Teluk Kade, Gili T and Gili Air.

Bali Brio (www.balibrio.com; adult/child 550,000/450,000Rp) Boats from Sanur to Nusa Lembongan and on to Bangsal and the Gilis.

Gili Cat (☎0361-271680; www.gilicat.com; adult/child 700,000/550,000Rp) A well-established company linking Padangbai, Gili T and Teluk Kade.

Perama (☎0361-750808; www.peramatour.com; per person 275,000Rp) Links Padangbai, the Gilis and Senggigi by a not-so-fast boat.

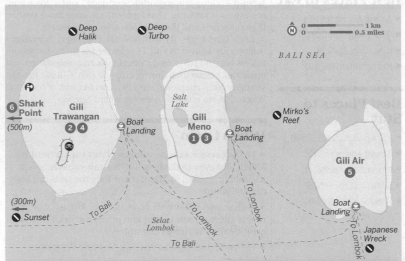

Gili Islands Highlights

❶ Snorkelling with hawksbill and green sea turtles off **Gili Meno** (p294).

❷ Dancing all night at one of **Gili Trawangan's** (in)famous parties (p291).

❸ Finding serenity on **Gili Meno's** west coast (p293).

❹ Learning to freedive on **Gili T** (p289).

❺ Spending a day walking around **Gili Air**, pausing frequently for swims and refreshments (p297).

❻ Diving with reef sharks at **Shark Point** (p287).

Scoot (Map p290; www.scootcruise.com; ⊙ 9am-9pm) Boats link Sanur, Padangbai, Nusa Lembongan and the Gilis.

Semaya One (☑ 0361-877 8166; www.semaya cruise.com; adult/child 650,000/550,000Rp) Network of services linking Sanur, Nusa Penida, Padangbai, Teluk Kade, Gili Air and Gili T.

FROM LOMBOK

Coming from Lombok, you can travel on one of the fast boats from Teluk Nare/Teluk Kade north of Senggigi. However, most people use the public boats that leave from **Bangsal Harbour**.

Boat tickets at Bangsal Harbour are sold at the port's large ticket office, which has posted prices, and which is where you can also charter a boat. Buy a ticket elsewhere and you're getting played.

Public boats run to all three islands before 11am, after that you may only find one to Gili T or Gili Air. Public boats in both directions leave when the boat is full – about 30 people. When no public boat is running to your Gili, you may have to charter a boat (280,000Rp to 375,000Rp, carries up to 20 people).

One-way fares are 10,000Rp to Gili Air, 12,000Rp to Gili Meno and 13,000Rp to Gili Trawangan. Boats often pull up on the beaches, prepare to wade ashore. Public fast boats also link Gili T and Bangsal; they run several times a day and cost 75,000Rp.

Although it had a bad reputation for years, Bangsal Harbour hassles are much reduced. Still, avoid touts and note that anyone who helps you with bags deserves a tip (10,000Rp per bag is appropriate). There are ATMs.

Coming by public transport via Mataram and Senggigi, catch a bus or bemo (minibus) to Pemenang, from where it's a 1.2km walk (5000Rp by *ojek*; motorcycle) to Bangsal Harbour. A metered taxi to the port will take you to the harbour. From Senggigi, Perama offers a bus and boat connection to the Gilis for a reasonable 150,000Rp (two hours).

Arriving in Bangsal, you'll be offered rides in shared vehicles at the port. To Senggigi, 100,000Rp is a fair price. Otherwise, walk down the access road to the Bluebird taxi stand for metered rides to Senggigi (90,000Rp), the airport (200,000Rp) and Kuta (300,000Rp).

ⓘ Getting Around

There's no motorised transport on the Gilis. In fact, the only motorbike in Gili T is on the Biorock reef, 5m deep in front of Cafe Gili.

CIDOMO

Cidomos (horse carts) operate as taxis; prices have soared in recent years. Even a short ride can cost 50,000Rp. For an hour-long clip-clop around an island expect to pay at least 100,000Rp. We cannot recommend using *cido-*

ⓘ HOTEL TRANSPORT

Most hotels and many guesthouses will be happy to help you sort out your transportation options to and from the Gilis as part of your reservation. If you use an online booking website, contact the hotel directly afterwards. Some high-end resorts have their own boats for transporting guests.

mos due to the significant questions about the treatment of the horses.

ISLAND-HOPPING

There's a twice-daily island-hopping boat service that loops between all three islands (20,000Rp to 25,000Rp), so you can sample another Gili's pleasures for the day – although you can't hit all three in one day by public boat. Check the latest timetable at the islands' docks. You can also charter boats between the islands (350,000Rp to 400,000Rp).

WALKING & CYCLING

The Gilis are flat and easy enough to get around by foot. Bicycles, available for hire on all three islands (per day 40,000Rp to 60,000Rp), can be a fun way to get around but sandy stretches of path mean that you will spend time pushing your bike in the hot sun.

Gili Trawangan

☑ 0370

Gili Trawangan is a paradise of global repute, ranking alongside Bali and Borobudur as one of Indonesia's top destinations. Trawangan's heaving main drag, busy with bikes, horse carts and mobs of scantily clad visitors can surprise those expecting some languid tropical retreat. Instead, a wall-to-wall roster of lounge bars, hip guesthouses, ambitious restaurants, mini-marts and dive schools clamour for attention.

And yet behind this glitzy facade, a bohemian character endures, with rickety warungs (food stalls) and reggae joints surviving between the cocktail tables, and quiet retreats dotting the much-less-busy north coast. Even as massive 200+ room hotels begin to colonise the still mostly wild and ragged west coast, you can head just inland to a village laced with sandy lanes roamed by free-range roosters, kibbitzing *ibu* (mothers) and wild-haired kids playing hopscotch. Here the call of the *muezzin* (the offical of a mosque), not happy hour, defines the time of day.

Gili Trawangan

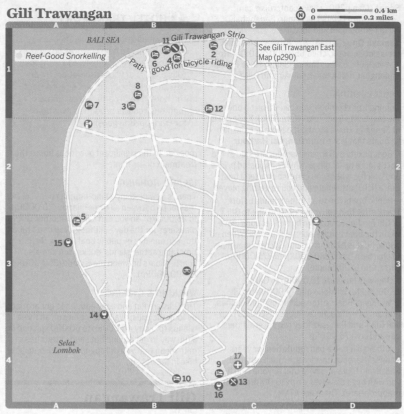

Settled just over 50 years ago (by Bugis fishermen from Sulawesi), travellers discovered Gili T in the 1980s, seduced by the white-sand beaches and coral reefs. By the 1990s Trawangan had mutated into a kind of tropical Ibiza, a stoney idyll where you could rave away from the eyes of the Indonesian police. And then the island began to grow up – resident Western hedonists morphed into entrepreneurs, diving rivalled partying in the economy, and outside money poured in to build resorts.

☂ Beaches

Gili T is ringed by the sort of powdery white sand people expect to find on Bali but don't. It can be crowded along the bar-lined main part of the strip but walk just a bit north or south and east and you'll find some of Gili T's nicest beaches for swimming and snorkelling. You can find even more solitude along the west and north coasts, where it will be

you and your towel on the sand – although water- and Bintang-vendors are never far.

Note that at low tide large portions of the west and north coasts have rocks and coral near the surface which makes trying to get off the shore deeply unpleasant. And the beach has eroded to oblivion on the northeast corner.

Many people simply enjoy the sensational views of Lombok and Gunung Rinjani as well as Bali and Gunung Agung.

🏃 Activities

Almost everything to do on Gili T will involve the water at some point.

Diving & Snorkelling

Trawangan is a diving mecca, with over a dozen professional scuba schools and one of Asia's only freediving schools. Most dive schools and shops have good accommodation for clients who want to book a package.

Gili Trawangan

There's fun snorkelling off the beach north of the boat landing – the coral isn't in the best shape here, but there are tons of fish. The reef is in much better shape off the northwest coast, but at low tide you'll have to scramble over some sharp, dead coral (bring rubber booties) to access it. Snorkel gear rental averages 40,000Rp per day.

★Lutwala Dive   DIVING
(Map p284; ☑0370-619 4835; www.lutwala.com; open-water course US$400) ✔ A nitrox and five-star PADI centre owned by Fern Perry, who held the women's world-record for deepest open-circuit dive (190m). A GIDA member, it also rents top-quality snorkelling gear.

Big Bubble   DIVING
(Map p290; ☑0370-612 5020; www.bigbubble diving.com; fun dives day/night US$35/45) ✔ The original engine behind the Gili Eco Trust, and a long-running dive school. It's a GIDA member (see p287).

Blue Marlin Dive Centre   DIVING
(Map p290; ☑0370-613 2424; www.bluemarlindive. com; 10-dive nitrox package US$395) ✔ Gili T's original dive shop, and one of the best tech diving schools in the world. It's a GIDA member *and* home to one of Gili T's classic bars.

Manta Dive   DIVING
(Map p290; ☑0370-614 3649; www.manta-dive. com; night diving courses from US$250) ✔ The biggest and still one of the best dive schools on the island. It has a large compound that spans the main road and recently enlarged pool. It offers freediving courses and is a GIDA member.

Trawangan Dive   DIVING
(Map p290; ☑0370-614 9220; www.trawangandive. com; 5 guided nitrox boat dives from US$225) ✔ A top, long-running dive shop and GIDA member with a fun (very large) pool-party vibe. Ask how you can join their regular beach clean-ups.

Boat Trips

South Sea Nomads   CRUISE
(Map p290; ☑0821 4778 9559; www.southse anomads.com; per person 300,000Rp; ⊙1-7pm Fri) Snorkelling, touring, beer-drinking and more, including sunset on this party boat. Buy tickets at Manta Dive.

Surfing

Trawangan has a fast right reef break that can be surfed year-round (though it is temperamental) and at times swells overhead. The Surf Bar (p293) rents boards (per hour/ day 30,000/100,000Rp) on the beach opposite the break.

Walking & Cycling

Trawangan is perfect for exploring on foot or by bike. You can walk around the whole island in a couple of hours – if you finish at the hill on the southwestern corner (which has the remains of an old Japanese gun placement c WWII), you'll have terrific sunset views of Bali's Gunung Agung.

Bikes (per day from 50,000Rp) are a great way to get around. You'll find loads of rental outlets on the main strip. Beware of the bike-unfriendly north coast and know that the paths across the interior of the island are usually in good shape for cycling.

Yoga

Gili Yoga   YOGA
(Map p290; ☑0370-614 0503; www.giliyoga.com; per person 100,000Rp; ⊙daily classes) Runs daily Vinyasa classes and is part of Freedive Gili.

Spas

Exqisit Spa   SPA
(Map p290; ☑0370-612 9405; www.exqisit.com; 1hr massage from 180,000Rp; ⊙10am-10pm) A day spa on the waterfront with curtained-off treatment rooms for massage, and leather

seats for mani-pedi or reflexology. Also has a coffee bar. The long list of services include shiatsu and a hangover-recovery massage treatment (220,000Rp) – talk about tapping in to market demand.

🎓 Courses

Gili Cooking Classes COOKING COURSE
(Map p290; ☑ 0877 6324 1215; www.gilicooking-classes.com; classes from 250,000Rp; ⊘ 11.30am, 4pm, 8pm) This slick operation has a large kitchen for classes right on the strip. You have a range of options of what you'll learn to cook – choose wisely as you'll be eating your work.

🛏 Sleeping

Gili T has over 5000 rooms and nearly 200 places to stay, ranging from thatched huts to sleek, air-conditioned villas with private pools. Yet, in peak season the entire island is often booked; reserve your room well ahead to arrive with a relaxed attitude. Many places are owned by local families with little or no experience of running hotels. Virtually all dive schools offer really good midrange accommodation, which may come with price breaks on diving packages. The cheapest digs are in the village, where the mosque is everyone's alarm clock. Head to the north or west coasts to escape the crowds.

All budget and most midrange places have brackish tap water. Pure water is available in some upmarket bungalows. The high-season rates quoted can drop up to 50% off-peak. Breakfast is included unless stated otherwise.

---

❶ CULTURAL RESPECT

As almost all locals are Muslim on the Gili Islands, visitors should keep these cultural considerations in mind:

➡ It's not at all acceptable to wander the lanes of the village in a bikini, no matter how many others you see doing so. Cover up away from the beach or hotel pool.

➡ Nude or topless sunbathing anywhere is offensive.

➡ During the month of Ramadan many locals fast during daylight hours and there are no all-night parties on Gili Trawangan.

🛏 Village

Oceane Paradise COTTAGE $
(Map p290; ☑ 0812 3779 3533; r from 300,000Rp; ❋ 🛜) A terrific compound of four wooden cottages with stylish outdoor bathrooms.

Pondok Gili Gecko GUESTHOUSE $
(Map p290; ☑ 0818 0573 2814; r from 350,000Rp; 🛜) An inviting guesthouse with a charming gecko motif. The four rooms are super clean, and have ceiling fans and private tiled patios overlooking the garden.

Rumah Hantu GUESTHOUSE $
(Map p290; ☑ 0819 1710 2444; r from 300,000Rp; 🛜) A well-tended if simple collection of five woven bamboo rooms with high ceilings and fresh paint, in a rootsy garden plot. Management is welcoming and conscientious.

★ **Woodstock** BUNGALOW $$
(Map p284; ☑ 0821 4765 5877; www.woodstockgili.com; r 350,000-700,000Rp; ❋🛜🏊) The hippest spot on Trawangan. Commune with the spirit of the Dead, Baez and Hendrix in 11 pristine rooms with tribal accents, private porches and outdoor baths, surrounding a laidback pool area. Wi-fi is only in reception.

Alexyane Paradise BUNGALOW $$
(Map p290; ☑ 0878 6599 9645; r 600,000-750,000Rp; ❋) Five great-quality dark-wood cottages with high ceilings, bamboo beds, and lovely light-flooded outdoor baths sprouting foliage.

Lumbung Cottages 2 BUNGALOW $$
(Map p290; ☑ 0878 6589 0233; www.lumbung cottage.com; bungalows from 600,000Rp; ❋🛜🏊) Eleven *lumbung* (rice barn)-style cottages, set deep in the village, tucked up against the hillside, surrounding a black-bottom pool.

Gili Joglo VILLA $$$
(Map p290; ☑ 0813 5678 4741; www.gilijoglo.com; villas from €160; ❋🛜) Three fabulous villas. One is crafted out of an antique Joglo with polished concrete floors, two bedrooms and a massive indoor-outdoor great room. Though slightly smaller, we prefer the one built from two 1950s *gladaks* (middle-class homes). Rooms come with butler service.

🛏 Main Strip

★ **Gili Hostel** HOSTEL $
(Map p290; ☑ 0877 6526 7037; www.gilihostel.com; dm from 155,000Rp; ❋🛜🏊) The island's only dedicated hostel is a co-ed dorm complex

SCUBA DIVING THE GILIS

The Gili Islands are a superb dive destination as the marine life is plentiful and varied. Turtles and black- and white-tip reef sharks are common, and there are also seahorses, pipefish and lots of crustaceans. Around the full moon, large schools of bumphead parrotfish appear to feast on coral spawn; at other times of year manta rays cruise past dive sites.

Though years of bomb fishing and an El Niño–induced bleaching damaged corals above 18m, the reefs are now well into a profound recovery and haven't looked this great in years. The Gilis also have their share of virgin coral.

Safety standards are reasonably high on the Gilis, but with the proliferation of new dive schools, several have formed the Gili Island Dive Association (GIDA), which comes together for monthly meetings on conservation and dive impact issues, and all mind a written list of standards that considers the safety of their divers, a limitation on number of divers per day, and preservation of the sites to be paramount concerns, which is why we highly recommend diving with GIDA-associated shops (identifiable by a logo). All GIDA shops carry oxygen on their boats and have working radios. They also have a price agreement for fun dives, training and certification. Sample prices include:

Introductory Dives US$65

Openwater Course US$370

Rescue Diver Course US$390

Some of the best dive sites include the following:

Deep Halik A canyon-like site ideally suited to drift diving. Black- and white-tip sharks are often seen at 28m to 30m.

Deep Turbo At around 30m, this site is ideally suited to nitrox diving. It has impressive sea fans and leopard sharks hidden in the crevasses.

Mirko's Reef Named for a beloved dive instructor who passed away, this canyon was never bombed and has vibrant, pristine soft and table coral formations.

Japanese Wreck For experienced divers only (it lies at 45m), this shipwreck of a Japanese patrol boat (c WWII) is another site ideal for tech divers.

Shark Point Perhaps the most exhilarating Gili dive: reef sharks and turtles are very regularly encountered, as well as schools of bumphead parrotfish and mantas.

Sunset (Manta Point) Some impressive table coral; sharks and large pelagics are frequently encountered.

with a shaggy Torajan-style roof. The seven rooms sleep seven, have concrete floors, high ceilings and a sleeping loft. There's a rooftop bar with bean bags, sun lounges and hammocks, and views of the treetops, the hills and the big new party pool.

Sama Sama Bungalows　　　　BUNGALOW **$$**
(Map p290; ☑0370-612 1106; r 400,000-700,000Rp; ❄☞) Just a few metres from where the fast boats drop you on the beach, the *lumbung*-style units here are perfect if you want to be right in the very heart of the action.

Kokomo　　　　LUXURY VILLAS **$$$**
(Map p284; ☑0370-613 4920; www.kokomogilit.com; villas US$225-600; ❄☞☎) Offering

beautifully finished and lavishly equipped modern accommodation, these 11 mini-villas are set in a small complex at the quieter southern end of the main strip. All have private pools, contemporary decor and lovely indoor-outdoor living quarters.

🛏 Beachside

Blu da Mare　　　　BUNGALOW **$$**
(Map p290; ☑0858 8866 2490; www.bludamare.it; r from 1,200,000Rp; ❄☞) Most notable for its exquisite kitchen, you can bed down in one of five lovely, antique Joglo from 1920s Java, with gorgeous old wood floors, queen beds, and fresh-water showers in a sunken bath.

DANGERS & ANNOYANCES ON THE GILIS

➡ Although it's rare, some foreign women have experienced sexual harassment and even assault while on the Gilis – it's best not to walk home alone to the quieter parts of the islands.

➡ As tranquil as these seas do appear, currents are strong in the channels between the islands. Do not try to swim between Gili islands as it can be deadly.

➡ The drug trade remains endemic to Trawangan. You'll get offers of mushrooms, meth and other drugs.

➡ Tourists have been injured and killed by adulterated *arak* (colourless, distilled palm wine) on the Gilis; skip it.

There are seldom **police** on any of the Gilis (though this is changing). Report thefts to the island *kepala desa* (village head) immediately, who will deal with the issue; staff at the dive schools will direct you to him. For trouble on Gili Trawangan, contact **Satgas**, the community organisation that runs island affairs, via your hotel or dive centre. Satgas tries to resolve problems and track down stolen property.

Balé Sampan
HOTEL $$

(Map p290; ☑ 0812 3702 4048; www.balesampan bungalows.com; r garden/pool view US$82/88; ❄🖥📶☕) Located on a nice wide-open stretch of beach. The 13 fine modern-edge rooms have stone baths and plush duvet covers. There's a freshwater pool and an on-site cafe that offers a proper English breakfast.

Tanah Qita
BUNGALOW $$

(Map p290; ☑ 0370-613 9159; bungalows 500,000-900,000Rp; ❄📶) Tanah Qita ('Homeland') has large, immaculate *lumbung* (with four-poster beds) and smaller fan-cooled versions. Cleanliness is taken very seriously. The garden is a bucolic delight.

Soundwaves
BUNGALOW $$

(Map p290; ☑ 0819 3673 2404; www.soundwaves resort.com; r 250,000-850,000Rp; 📶) The 12 rooms here are simple but clean with tiled floors. Some are set in wooden A-frames and others in a two-storey concrete building with staggered and recessed patios offering beach views from each room.

Trawangan Dive
HOSTEL $$

(Map p290; ☑ 0813 3770 2332, 0370-614 9220; www.trawangandive.com; dm US$12, r from US$88; ❄📶☕) Most notable for its dormitory with three beds that can sleep up to two people in each one. As on the rest of Gili Trawangan, upscale changes are in the offing: there are now 11 air-conditioned rooms, with another 28 planned. It's near the liveliest bars.

🛏 North, South & West Coasts

⭐ Eden Cottages
COTTAGE $$

(Map p284; ☑ 0819 1799 6151; www.edencottages. com; cottage 550,000Rp; ❄❄) Six clean, thatched concrete bungalows wrapped around a pool, fringed by a garden, and shaded by a coconut grove. Rooms have tasteful rattan furnishings, stone baths, TV-DVD and fresh-cold-water showers. The owner eschews wi-fi which only increases the serenity.

⭐ Wilson's Retreat
RESORT $$

(Map p284; ☑ 0370-612 0060; www.wilsons-retreat.com; r from US$120; ❄📶☕) A fine new addition to the north shore, Wilson's has 18 rooms plus four villas with private pools. Even though the setting is expansive and classy, it still manages some Gili languor. The excellent cafe overlooks a fine stretch of beach.

Coconut Garden
BUNGALOW $$

(Map p284; ☑ 0812 3782 6482; www.coconut gardenresort.com; r from 850,000Rp; ❄📶) An atmospheric spot with just four bright and airy glass-box Javanese Joglo with tiled roofs connected to outdoor terrazzo baths. Expect plush linens, queen beds and a rolling lawn dotted with coco palms. It's on its own in a quiet inland quarter of the island and can be hard to find. Call ahead.

Alam Gili
HOTEL $$

(Map p284; ☑ 0370-613 0466; www.alamgili.com; r US$65-95; 📶☕) A lush mature garden and a quiet beach location are the main draws here. The nine rooms and villas in a small compound boast elegant lashings of old-school Balinese style. There's a small pool and a cafe on the beach.

Danima GUESTHOUSE **$$**
(Map p290; ☎0878 6087 2506; www.giliresort danima.com; r 900,000-1,400,000Rp; ❋🛜❄) An intimate four-room boutique property. Nests are blessed with floating beds, vaulted ceilings, tasteful lighting, rattan deck seating and rain showers. It has a romantic pool and beach area, too.

Hotel Ombak Sunset RESORT **$$**
(Map p284; ☎0370-644333; www.ombaksunset. com; r US$100-250; ❋@🛜) This slick 100-room resort has a commanding position for sunsets on the previously very low-key west coast. Rooms come in many flavours, get one with a west-facing terrace for views across the water to Bali. This place even has its own ATM centre.

★Pondok Santi RESORT **$$$**
(Map p284; ☎0370-714 0711; www.pondoksanti. com; r from US$300; ❋🛜) Six gorgeous bungalows are widely spaced on this old coconut plantation. Lawns now cover the grounds and this is easily the classiest looking resort on Gili T. The units have outdoor showers and rich, traditional wood decor. It's on a great beach and *just* close enough to the strip.

Gili Eco Villas VILLA **$$$**
(Map p284; ☎0361-847 6419; www.giliecovillas. com; villas US$120-260; ❋🛜❄) ✐ Seven classy villas, made from recycled teak salvaged from old Javanese colonials, are set back from the beach on Trawangan's idyllic north coast. Comfort and style are combined with solid green principles (water is recycled, there's an organic vegetable garden, and solar and wind energy provide most of the power). Wi-fi is just in public areas.

Kelapa Villas VILLA **$$$**
(Map p284; ☎0812 3756 6003; www.kelapavillas. com; villas US$200-900; ❋🛜❄🔥) Luxury development in an inland location with a selection of 20 commodious villas, all with private pools, that offer style and space in abundance. There's a tennis court and a gym in the complex.

Five Elements VILLA **$$$**
(Map p284; ☎0828 9799 5545; www.gili.five elementsresorts.com; villa from US$250; ❋🛜❄) Widely spaced villas surround a 40m pool on a (still) lonely stretch of the west coast.

The units are very comfortable and you can really feel like you've gotten away from it all here. Like other places on the west coast, this one is a hike if you want to have dinner on the strip.

✖ Eating

In the evenings, numerous places on the main strip display and grill delicious fresh seafood. There's not much to distinguish them – pick by what looks good and how much chili and garlic you like in your marinade.

Elsewhere on the strip, you'll find timeless beach bars with lots of Indo standards you can enjoy with a cold Bintang and your feet in the sand. There's also a growing number of high-concept cafes.

★Pasar Malam MARKET **$**
(Map p290; mains 15,000-30,000Rp; ☉6pm-midnight) Blooming every evening in front of Gili T's market, this night market is the place to indulge in ample local eats, including tangy noodle soup, savoury fried treats, scrumptious *ayam goreng* (fried chicken) and grilled fresh catch. Just wandering around the stalls looking at all the dishes vying for your attention will get you drooling. Seating is at long tables.

Green Cafe INDONESIAN **$**
(Map p290; ☎0878 6335 4272; mains from 20,000Rp; ☉6-11pm) Our favourite stall at the Pasar Malam (night market) is towards the back, but you'll find it easily enough. Look for the crowds trying to decide between grilled mains, salads and an array of luscious desserts (which they cheerfully box to

GILI ISLANDS GILI TRAWANGAN

go). During the day they have a cafe at the very back of the square.

Ecco Cafe CAFE $
(Map p290; ☎0878 6027 0200; mains 33,000-60,000Rp; ⏲8am-10pm; 📶) Spanning the main drag, this excellent coffee bar has the currently mandatory distressed boat-wood look at its cute cafe on the beach. Across the road, it has a stylish clothing boutique.

Warung Kiki Novi INDONESIAN $
(Map p290; mains from 15,000Rp; ⏲8am-10pm) Long-time islanders will tell you that this is the best place for *nasi campur* (rice with a choice of side dishes) in the Gilis and they are right. This cheery dining room is the scene of budget-dining nirvana. Besides fine Indo mains there's a smattering of Western sandwiches and salads. Try the soups.

Cafe Gili INTERNATIONAL $$
(Map p290; mains 35,000-70,000Rp; ⏲8am-10pm; 📶) Think: cushioned beachside seating, candlelight, and Jack Johnson on repeat. The kitchen spills from a shabby chic whitewashed dining room and rambles across the street to the shore. The menu meanders from eggs Florentine and breakfast baguettes, to deli sandwiches and salads to decent pasta and seafood dishes.

★ **Kayu Café** CAFE $$
(Map p290; ☎0878 6239 1308; mains 40,000-80,000Rp; ⏲8am-10pm; ❄📶) There is a split option here: the main cafe on the inland side of the strip has a lovely array of healthy baked goods, salads, sandwiches and the island's best juices served in air-con comfort. Across the road, the beach cafe is all open-air and exposed wood. Service on the sand can be slow – head in with your order.

★ **Scallywags** INTERNATIONAL $$
(Map p290; ☎0370-614 5301; www.scallywagsresort.com; meals 40,000-180,000Rp; ⏲8am-10pm; 📶) Scallywags offers casual yet stylish beach decor, polished glassware, switched-on service and superb cocktails. The dinner menu features tasty seafood – fresh lobster, tuna steaks, snapper and swordfish – and a great salad bar. The seafood BBQ always looks best.

Kokomo INTERNATIONAL $$
(Map p284; ☎0370-613 4920; www.kokomogilit.com; mains 60,000-200,000Rp; ⏲8am-11pm; ❄📶) Kokomo is the only genuine fine-dining restaurant in town, using fresh local seafood and select imported meats.

Gili Trawangan East

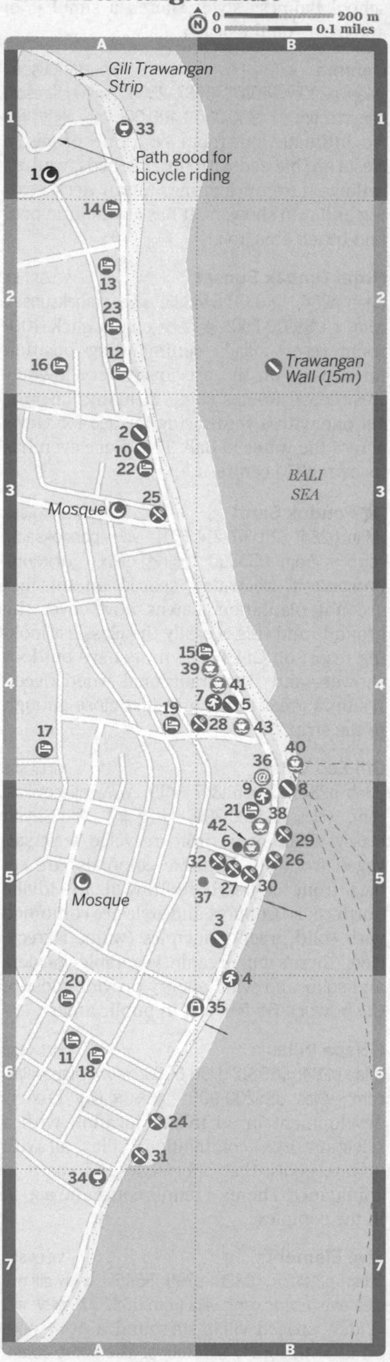

Gili Trawangan East

GILI ISLANDS GILI TRAWANGAN

Lots of healthy salads, wonderful steaks and pasta, but for the ultimate treat opt for a seafood or sashimi (with Atlantic salmon and yellowfin tuna) platter. It's got a superb waterfront location.

Il Pirata PIZZA $$
(Map p290; ☑ 0813 3842 0848; mains 70,000-100,000Rp; ⊙ 11am-11pm) The wood-fired oven rarely gets a break at this surprisingly good pizza-only joint, just inland. At busy times there's a long line for takeaway pizzas, but a better option is to find a table in the garden and have some cold ones with the fine thin-crust pies. The *Romana* is an authentic and tasty choice.

Pearl Beach Lounge INTERNATIONAL $$
(Map p284; ☑ 0370-613 7788; www.pearlbeachlounge.com; mains 60,000-180,000Rp; ⊙ 8am-11pm; 🔊) The bamboo flows only a little less fluidly than the beer at this high-concept beachside lounge and restaurant. During the day, spending 100,000Rp on food and

drink gets you access to a pool, comfy beach loungers and a burger-filled menu. At night the striking bamboo main pavilion comes alive, and more complex steak and seafood mains are on offer.

Beach House INTERNATIONAL $$
(Map p290; ☑ 0370-614 2352; www.beachhouse-gilit.com; mains 45,000-180,000Rp; ⊙ 11am-10pm; 🔊) Boasts an elegant marina terrace and wonderful nightly BBQ, salad bar, and fine wine. It's another contender for best barbecued seafood and is always popular. Book ahead.

🍷 Drinking & Nightlife

The island has oodles of great beachside drinking dens, ranging from sleek lounge bars to simple shacks. Parties are held several nights a week, shifting between mainstay bars like Tir na Nog and Rudy's Pub and other various upstarts. The strip south of Pasar Malam is the centre for raucous nightlife.

GREEN GILI

When you pay your hotel or diving bill on the Gilis you may be offered the chance to pay an 'Eco Tax' (50,000Rp per person). It's a voluntary donation, set up by the pioneering **Gili Eco Trust** (www.giliecotrust.com) to improve the island's environment.

It's a worthy cause. The environmental pressure on the Gilis as their popularity has grown is enormous. Intensive development and rubbish plus offshore reef damage from fishermen using cyanide and dynamite to harvest fish have been just some of the problems. 'In high season there are 5000 visitors on the Gilis and another 5000 workers, most of whom commute from Lombok by boat', notes Delphine Robbe, the Eco Trust coordinator.

More recently, Trawangan's once-wide white-sand beaches have eroded. In some places they've been swallowed whole, but several initiatives have tried to reclaim the reef and stem the rising tide.

Biorock, a coral regeneration project spearheaded by Gili Eco Trust and several dive shops, has been successful in mitigating beach erosion and nurturing marine life. Loose pieces of living coral (perhaps damaged by an anchor or a clumsy diving fin) are gathered and transplanted onto frames in the sea. Electrodes supplied with low-voltage currents cause electrolytic reactions, accelerating coral growth and ultimately creating an artificial reef, much like what has been done at Pemuteran on Bali. There are now well over 100 Biorock installations around the Gilis. You'll see them as you snorkel or dive; their shapes look quite startling in the water – flowers, an airplane, turtle, star, manta and even a heart – covered in fledgling coral and sponges.

Other Eco Trust initiatives include:

➡ Distributing free reusable shopping bags to cut down on plastic-bag use and encouraging restaurants to stop using plastic straws.

➡ An aggressive education campaign to get locals and business owners to recycle their trash. There are now over 1000 recycling bins on the islands.

➡ Care of the islands' horses. Vet clinics are offered and there are driver education programs, but as Robbe notes: 'many drivers work the horses hard for three years, then sell them for meat on Lombok and get another'.

There are many ways visitors to the Gilis can help, besides just paying the Eco Tax:

Clean up the beach Eco Trust and Trawangan Dive (p285) both organise weekly beach clean-ups and more hands are always needed. And, as you admire the white sand and azure waters, do your own freelance beach clean-up. Toss anything you find in a recycling bin.

Report horse mistreatment Anyone seeing a *cidomo* (horse cart) driver mistreating a horse can get the number of the cart and report it to Eco Trust (☑0370-625020 or ☑0813 3960 0553) who will follow up with the driver. Unfortunately, the many transport carts with their heavy loads of construction supplies and Bintang have no cart numbers for reporting.

Build a reef For US$600 you'll get two dives a day for two weeks and help build a Biorock installation. Eco Trust has details.

Most of the more casual beachside restaurants and cafes will cheerfully host you even if you just want a cocktail or two.

★ La Moomba
BAR

(Map p290; ⊙10am-midnight) If you wish to chill on a luscious white-sand beach, with bamboo lounges and reggae pumping from the tiki bar, head here, to Trawangan's best beach bar.

Tir na Nog
PUB

(Map p290; ☑0370-613 9463; ⊙7am-2am Thu-Tue, to 4am Wed; ☎) Known simply as 'The Irish', this barn-like place has a sports-bar interior with big screens ideal for international football matches and tasty pub grub (mains 35,000Rp to 80,000Rp). Its shoreside bar is probably the busiest meeting spot on the island. Jovial mayhem reigns on Wednesday nights when the DJ takes over.

Blue Marlin
BAR

(Map p290; ☉8am-very late) Of all the party bars, this upper-level venue has the largest dance floor and the meanest sound system – it pumps trance and tribal beats on Mondays.

Surf Bar
BAR

(Map p284; ☉8am-late) Opposite the break, this tiki bar has a sweet slab of beach, a rack of boards to rent, a pumping stereo and a young crowd. It does full- and dark-moon parties.

Sama Sama
BAR

(Map p290; ☉varies) An overly decorated reggae bar-slash-roadhouse with a top-end sound system, a killer live band (playing the same set list) at least six nights a week, and a beer garden on the beach.

Serene Sunset
BAR

(Map p284; ☉1-7pm) Mismatched loungers and a bamboo bar are the main features at this perfectly named little bar run by some very cheery young guys. It's there on a, yes, serene bit of the west coast for one reason: drinks at sunset.

Exile
BAR

(Map p284; ☑0819 0772 1858; ☉noon-late; @) This cool beach bar has a party vibe at all hours. It's Indonesian owned and 20 minutes from the main strip on foot, or an easy bike ride. There is also a compound of 10 woven bamboo bungalows with rooms from 450,000Rp here, in case home seems too far.

🛍 Shopping

Once the domain of cheap knick-knack stalls and not much else, a stream of refinement is rapidly taking root on Gili Trawangan. Look for smart boutiques on the strip south of the Pasar Malam.

★ Casa Vintage
CLOTHING

(Map p290; ☉9am-9pm) The best boutique on Gili T is tucked on a back street near II Pirata. It's a treasure trove of vintage fashion sourced internationally, and displayed with grace. Browse chunky earrings, superb leather hand- and shoulder bags, baby-doll dresses, and John Lennon shades.

Innuendo
FASHION

(Map p290; ☑0828 370 9648; ☉10am-9pm) A new boutique owned by a Bali-based French designer, there's real elegance here. All the dresses and shoes are the store's own brand, the handbags and accessories are sourced from other indie designers.

❶ Information

EMERGENCIES

There's a health **clinic** (Map p284; ☉9am-5pm) just south of Hotel Vila Ombak. For security issues contact **Satgas**, a community organisation, via your hotel or dive shop.

INTERNET & TELEPHONE

Wi-fi has proliferated on Trawangan and is common in hotels and cafes, but is not fast.
Flash Internet (Map p290; per hour 18,000Rp; ☉8am-11pm; ☎) offers speedy connections and printing on the strip.

MONEY

Gili T has abundant ATMs on the main strip and even on the west coast.

❶ Getting There & Away

You can buy tickets and catch public and island-hopping boats at the **boat landing** (Map p290). While you wait for your ship to sail, note the amazing amount of Bintang bottles arriving full and leaving empty. The following fast boat companies have offices on Gili T.

Bali Brio (Map p290; ☑0828 9710 2336; Sama Sama Bungalows; ☉9am-9pm)

Blue Water Express (Map p290; ☉9am-9pm)

Gili Cat (Map p290; ☑0361-271680; www.gilicat.com; ☉9am-9pm)

Perama (Map p290; ☑0370 638 514; www.peramatour.com; ☉9am-8pm)

Scoot (Map p290; www.scootcruise.com; ☉9am-9pm) Boats link Sanur, Padangbai, Nusa Lembongan and the Gilis.

Gili Meno
☑0370

Gili Meno is the smallest of the three islands and the perfect setting for your desert-island fantasy. Even in high season Meno still feels right off the grid. Most accommodation is strung out along the east coast, near the most picturesque beach. Inland you'll find scattered homesteads, coconut plantations and a salty lake. Some lonely stretches of the west coast can feel scrubby and even desolate, yet they evoke a mood all their own.

🏝 Beaches

Ringed by sand, Gili Meno has one of the best strips of beach in the Gilis at its south-east corner. The sand is wide and powdery white while the swimming is excellent. The west coast is rockier with crushed coral and a lot of rocks and coral near the surface at

Gili Meno

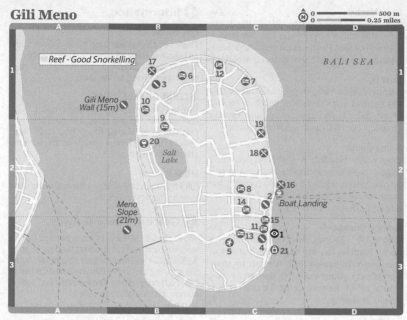

low tide. Meno's northeast also has nice sand, although erosion is a problem in parts.

◉ Sights

Unique to Gili Meno, the large inland Salt Lake is home to imposing white egrets, which make it an intriguing natural attraction.

Turtle Sanctuary   TURTLE HATCHERY
(www.gilimenoturtles.com; donations appreciated; ☺ office 9am-6pm; ◙) Meno's turtle sanctuary consists of an assortment of little pools and bathtubs on the beach, bubbling with filters and teeming with baby green and loggerhead turtles, where they're nurtured until they're around eight months old before being released. The impact of the hatchery on the turtle populations has been considerable. A simple snorkel and you're all but guaranteed a sighting.

🏃 Activities

Like the other Gilis, most of the fun here involves getting wet. **Walking** around the island is scenic and takes less than two hours.

Although you can rent **bikes** for 50,000Rp per day, you won't get far. The beach path from the southern tip right round up the west coast to the top of the salt lake is a shadeless dry sand path that will have you walking your wheels. You can go for a little jaunt to the northwest coast on the good path along the north side of the lake, but again soft sand along the very north will stymie riding further.

Diving & Snorkelling

It takes around two hours to circumnavigate Meno on foot. The best beach is the blonde beauty that unfurls south of the main harbour, just before the signed turn-off to Tao Kombo.

Snorkelling is good off the northeast coast; on the west coast towards the north; and also around the former jetty of the (abandoned) Bounty Resort. Gear is available from 40,000Rp per day.

Blue Marlin Dive Centre   DIVING
(☏ 0370-639980; www.bluemarlindive.com) The Meno shingle of the Trawangan original. It has rooms here, too.

Divine Divers   DIVING
(☏ 0852 4057 0777; www.divinedivers.com) On the west coast. This Meno-only dive shop also has a restaurant-bar on a sweet slice of beach.

Gili Meno Divers   DIVING
(☏ 0878 6536 7551; www.giliairdivers.com; Kontiki Cottages; ☺ 9am-5pm) French and Indonesian owned.

Gili Meno

GILI ISLANDS GILI MENO

Yoga

Mao Meno YOGA
(☑ 0819 9937 8359; www.mao-meno.com; class from US$9; ☉ daily classes) Offers classes in styles that include Ashtanga and Vinyasa. It has simple cottages on its inland compound that rent from US$45 per night.

🛏 Sleeping

Even Meno is not immune from Gili growth and new properties are appearing in the north – some rather posh. But it's still your best bet if you want a Robinson Crusoe-esque experience (minus the cannibals). Prices have also climbed sharply as visitor numbers have increased.

Tao Kombo BUNGALOW $
(☑ 0878 6033 1373; www.tao-kombo.com; r €30-40; ☎) ⟡ This innovatively designed place has seven *lumbung* cottages with thatched roofs, stone floors and outdoor bathrooms. It's home to the popular Jungle Bar, 200m inland from the main strip. The owners are heavily involved in community projects.

Diana Café BUNGALOW $
(☑ 0809 3317 1943; r 250,000-400,000Rp) This is a classic Meno desert-isle oasis. There are four hip, clean, thatched bungalows by the salt lake, a three-minute walk from the beach, where there are another four.

Tropicana Hideaway BUNGALOW $$
(☑ 0878 6431 3828; r 200,000-700,000Rp; ❄) A modest collection of five bungalows set in a sunny coconut-palm garden. Cottages are clean and basic; you'll find several similar places back here.

★ Adeng Adeng BUNGALOW $$
(☑ 0818 0534 1019; www.adeng-adeng.com; r €80-220; ❄ ☎) ⟡ A creative five-unit guesthouse set back in the trees from a fine stretch of sand. Its simple wooden bungalows have all the creature comforts and stylish outdoor terrazzo baths. The rambling property is sprinkled with artisanal accents.

Jepun Bungalows BUNGALOW $$
(☑ 0819 1739 4736; www.jepunbungalows.com; bungalow 250,000-500,000Rp; ❄ ☎) Just 100m from the main beach path and harbour, with charming accommodation dotted around a garden. Choose from lovely thatched *lumbung*, bungalows, or book the family house; all have bathrooms with fresh (hot) water and good-quality beds. Three have air-con.

Kebun Kupu Kupu GUESTHOUSE $$
(☑ 0819 0742 8165; www.facebook.com/kupukupu resort; r from 500,000Rp; ☎ ⛱) Situated 300m from the beach, this collection of six bungalows has a great pool, palm trees overhead and a quiet spot near the salt lake. The French owners honour their heritage by serving excellent food (try the crème brûlée).

Ana Bungalow BUNGALOW $$
(☑ 0878 6169 6315; www.anawarung.com; r 400,000-600,000Rp; ❄ ☎) Four sweet peaked-roof, thatch and bamboo bungalows with picture windows, and pebbled floors in the outdoor baths. This family-run place has a cute used-book exchange on the beach next to its four lovely dining *berugas* (open-sided pavilions) lit with paper lanterns. Seafood dinners are superb. Kudos for their honesty: 'the wi-fi is weak'.

Paul's Last Resort BUNGALOW $$
(☑ 0878 6569 2272; r from 500,000Rp; 🛜❄️)
Renovations have taken this former compound of three-walled bamboo shacks and turned it into a respectable collection of solid bungalows. It's comfortable and on a nice, white stretch of sand.

Mallias Bungalows INN $$
(☑ 0878 6413 0719; www.malliaschild.com; r 350,000-1,000,000Rp; ❄️🛜) This location right on Meno's best beach can't be beaten. The bungalows are very simple – although some have air-con – and are really just basic bamboo and thatch. As such they are a good deal at the lower end of the price range but not so much if staff quote prices at the upper end.

Villa Nautilus VILLA $$
(☑ 0370-642143; www.villanautilus.com; r from US$105; ❄️🛜❄️) A comfortable option, these five well-designed detached villas enjoy a grassy plot just off the beach. They're finished in contemporary style with natural wood, marble and limestone and the hip bathrooms have fresh water.

Mahamaya BOUTIQUE HOTEL $$$
(☑ 0888 715 5828; www.mahamaya.co; d from US$200; ❄️🛜❄️) A blindingly white-washed modern pearl with resort service and 14 rooms featuring attractive stone floors, rough-cut marble patios, and white-and-washed-wood furnishings. The restaurant is good; have dinner at the water's edge at your own private table.

🍴 Eating & Drinking

Almost all of Meno's restaurants have absorbing sea views, which is just as well as service can be slow everywhere.

Webe Café INDONESIAN $
(☑ 0821 4776 3187; mains from 20,000Rp; ⊗ 8am-10pm; 🛜) A wonderful location for a meal, Webe Café has low tables sunk in the sand, with the turquoise water just a metre away. It scores on Sasak and Indonesian food like *kelak kuning* (snapper in yellow spice); staff fire up a seafood BBQ most nights, too. There are three basic bungalows for rent as well (from 350,000Rp).

Zoraya Cafe CAFE $
(mains from 25,000Rp; ⊗ 8am-10pm) Little thatched platforms at the edge of the sea at this relaxed cafe allow you to enjoy a cheap Bintang and a simple meal while charter-boat skippers wander past and life drifts by around you.

Rust Warung INDONESIAN $
(☑ 0370-642324; mains 15,000-75,000Rp; ⊗ 8am-10pm) The most visible cog of the Rust empire (which includes Meno's one grocery) has a great position overlooking the harbour and the beach. It's renowned for its grilled fish (with garlic or sweet-and-sour sauce), but also serves pizza and makes a very fine banana pancake any time of the day or night. Ask for the homemade sambal.

Ya Ya Warung INDONESIAN $
(dishes 15,000-30,000Rp; ⊗ 8am-10pm) Ramshackle warung-on-the-beach that serves up Indonesian faves, curries, pancakes and plenty of pasta along with the views you came to Meno to enjoy.

★ Adeng Adeng THAI $$
(mains 30,000-80,000Rp; ⊗ 8am-10pm) For a fragrant change from Indo fare, try the Thai-inspired elegance of Adeng Adeng. Owned by Swedes, it does a few homeland favourites, and serves excellent dishes with just the right amount of fire. Cap the night with a fine cognac or whiskey.

Diana Café BAR
(⊗ 8am-9pm) If by any remote chance you find the pace of life on Meno too busy, head to this intoxicating little tiki bar par excellence. Diana couldn't be simpler: a wobbly-looking bamboo-and-thatch bar, a few tables on the sand, a hammock or two, reggae on the stereo and a chill-out zone that makes the most of the zillion-rupiah views.

🛍️ Shopping

Art Shop Botol HANDICRAFTS
(⊗ varies) Art Shop Botol is a large handicrafts stall just south of Kontiki Meno hotel with masks, Sasak water baskets, wood carvings and gourds. It's run by an elderly shopkeeper with 11 children and countless grandchildren.

ℹ️ Information

There are no ATMs on Meno and few places accept credit cards; bring cash.

ℹ️ Getting There & Away

The **boat landing** is a sleepy hub. Check the public boat schedules carefully as Meno's small size means that waiting for a boat to fill can take a long time. None of the fast boats directly serve

Meno, although some provide connections. Otherwise you can go to Trawangan or Air and take the late afternoon public island-hopping boat.

Gili Air

0370

Closest to Lombok, Gili Air falls between Gili T's sophistication and less-is-less Meno and is for many just right. The white-sand beaches here are arguably the best of the Gili bunch and there's just enough buzz to provide a dash of nightlife. Snorkelling is good right from the main strip – a lovely sandy lane dotted with bamboo bungalows and little restaurants where you can eat virtually on top of a turquoise sea.

Though tourism dominates Gili Air's economy, coconuts, fishing and creating the fake-distressed fishing-boat wood vital to any stylish Gili guesthouse are important income streams. A buzzy little strip has developed along the beach in the southeast, although the lane is still more sandy than paved.

🏖 Beaches

The entire east side of the island has great beaches with powdery white sand and a gentle slope into beautiful turquoise water with a foot-friendly sandy bottom. There are also good, private spots the rest of the way around Air, but low-tide rocks and coral are a problem.

🏃 Activities

Watersports

The entire east coast has an offshore reef teeming with colourful fish; there's a drop-off about 100m to 200m out. Snorkelling gear is easily hired for about 40,000Rp per day.

The island has an excellent collection of dive shops who charge the standard Gili rates.

Blue Marine Dive Centre   DIVING
(0812 377 0288; www.bluemarlindive.com) Has a nice location on the beautiful northeast corner of the island. Offers freediving courses.

Gili Air Divers   DIVING
(0878 6536 7551; www.giliairdivers.com; Sunrise Hotel; 8am-8pm) This French-Indo owned dive shop is long on charm and skill.

Oceans 5   DIVING
(0813 3877 7144; www.oceans5dive.com) Has a 25m training pool, an in-house marine biologist and nice hotel rooms.

GILI ISLANDS GILI AIR

SNORKELLING THE GILIS

Ringed by coral reefs, the Gilis offer superb snorkelling. Masks, snorkels and fins are widely available and can be hired for about 40,000Rp per day. It's important to check your mask fits properly: just press it gently to your face, let go and if it's a good fit the suction should hold it in place.

Snorkelling trips – many on glass-bottomed boats – are very popular. Typically, you'll pay about 150,000Rp per person or about 650,000Rp for the entire boat. Expect to leave about 10am and visit three or more sites, with possibly a stop for lunch on another island. On Gili T there are many places selling these trips along the main strip; prices are very negotiable.

On Trawangan and Meno turtles very regularly appear on the reefs right off the beach. You'll likely drift with the current, so be prepared to walk back to the starting line. Over on Air, the walls off the east coast are good, too.

It's not hard to escape the crowds. Each island has a less-developed side, usually where access to the water is obstructed by shallow patches of coral. Using rubber shoes makes it much easier to get into the water. Try not to stamp all over the coral but ease yourself in, and then swim, keeping your body as horizontal as possible.

Among the many reasons to snorkel in the Gilis are the high odds you'll encounter hawksbill and green sea turtles. Top overall snorkelling spots include:

➡ Gili Meno Wall

➡ The north end of Gili T's beach

➡ Gili Air Wall

Gili Air

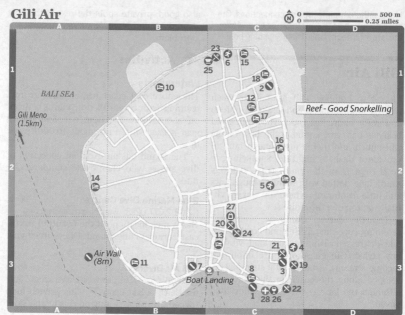

7 Seas DIVING
(☏0370-663 2150; www.7seas-international.com) 🏊 A vast dive shop with a range of accommodation and a good pool for training or just playing.

Gili Kite Surf KITESURFING
(☏0819 0746 6201; www.gilikitesurf.com; class 1,600,000Rp, rental per hour from 650,000Rp) This enthusiastic shop also rents stand-up paddle boards, wakeboards and kayaks. They are often set up on the southwest beach.

Cycling
Bikes can be rented for 50,000Rp a day but large sections of the coastal path in the north and west are annoying, as long slogs of deep sand swallow the trail at times. Inland lanes, however, are mostly concrete and very rideable. Some shops have bikes with huge tires which help with the slogs.

Spa & Yoga
H2O Yoga YOGA
(☏0877 6103 8836; www.h2oyogaandmeditation. com; per class from 100,000Rp; ⊘daily classes) This wonderful yoga and meditation retreat centre is set back from the beach on a well-signed path in the village. Top-quality classes are held in a lovely circular *beruga*. There's also massage available.

Harmony Spa SPA
(☏0812 386 5883; massage from 120,000Rp; ⊘10am-7pm) The beautiful north-coast location alone will make you feel renewed. Facials, body treatments and more are on offer. Call first.

🛏 Sleeping

Gili Air's 40 or so places to stay are mostly located on the east coast. You'll find more isolation in the west.

⭐**Bintang Beach 2** BUNGALOW **$**
(☏0877 6522 2554; r 200,000-350,000Rp; ❄) On Gili Air's quiet northwest coast, this sandy but tidy compound has 14 rooms and bunglows that range from budget-friendly fan-cooled to mildly snazzy. The bar area is a delight. The same enterprising clan also runs the nearby Bollata Bungalows and Nusa Indah, with similar rooms.

⭐**Gili Air Hostel** HOSTEL **$**
(www.giliairhostel.com; dms from 160,000Rp; ⊘reception 7.30am-7pm; ❄🛜) A great addition to the island, beds are in two- to seven-bed dorm rooms. The decor defines cheery, there's a cool bar, a huge frangipani tree and even a climbing wall.

Gili Air

Damai
GUESTHOUSE $

(☏ 0878 6142 0416; damaihomestay.giliair@gmail.com; r 350,000-450,000Rp; ☞) It's worth seeking out this thatched enclave. Rooms are basic yet tasteful and open onto a garden. The cosy dining patio has cushioned seating and is elegantly lit with paper lanterns.

Biba Beach Village
BUNGALOW $$

(☏ 0819 1727 4648; www.bibabeach.com; bungalows 600,000-1,000,000Rp; ☀☞) Biba offers nine lovely, spacious bungalows with large verandas and grotto-like bathrooms that have walls inlaid with shells and coral. The gorgeous garden has little chill-out zones. It's also home to a good Italian restaurant.

Sejuk Cottages
BUNGALOW $$

(☏ 0370-636461; www.sejukcottages.com; bungalows 380,000-900,000Rp; ☀☞☷❀) Eleven well-built, tastefully designed thatched *lumbung* cottages, and pretty two- and three-storey cottages (some have rooftop living rooms) scattered around a fine tropical garden with a salt-water pool.

Segar Village
BUNGALOW $$

(☏ 0818 0526 2218; www.segarvillages.blogspot.com; bungalows 500,000-1,200,000Rp; ☀☞) Eleven rather cute concrete rock and coral bungalows with quirky touches and more than a little grace. Wrap-around patios and soaring thatched ceilings are features and it's on the edge of a coconut grove just in front of a reef with resident sea turtles.

Pelangi Cottages
BUNGALOW $$

(☏ 0819 3316 8648; r from 600,000Rp; ☀) On the north end of the island with a coral reef out front, Pelangi has eight spacious but basic concrete and wood bungalows, friendly management and quality mountain bikes for rent.

7 Seas
HOSTEL $$

(☏ 0370-660 4485; www.7seas-cottages.com; dm from 80,000Rp, r from 800,000Rp; ☀☞☷) Part of the 7 Seas dive empire, this is an attractive bungalow compound in a great location. There are also fan-cooled bamboo loft-like hostel rooms. You can rent an entire one for 300,000Rp.

Youpy Bungalows
BUNGALOW $$

(☏ 0819 1706 8153; r 350,000-650,000Rp; ☀☞) Among the outcrop of driftwood-decorated beach cafes and guesthouses strung along the coast north of Blue Marine, Youpy has some of the best-quality bungalows. Bathrooms have colourful sand walls, the beds are big, and the ceilings high.

★ Kai's Beachouse
RENTAL HOUSE $$$

(☏ 0819 1723 2536; www.kaisbeachhouse.com; r US$105-265; ☀☞☷) There are just three airy rooms here, two in the main house and another in a Javanese *gladak* cottage out back. The common downstairs great room is comfortable and there's a massive kitchen. Lounges surround a tiny plunge pool, with a virginal beach just outside. Ideal for a group of friends.

Casa Mio
BUNGALOW $$$

(✆0370-646160; www.villacasamio.com; cottages 900,000-1,500,000Rp; ❄🛜🌊) Casa Mio has fine cottages that boast every conceivable mod con, as well as a riot of knick-knacks (from the artistic to the kitsch). It boasts a lovely beach area and good access via a paved portion of the beach lane from the boat landing. Several competitors have sprung up nearby.

✖ Eating

Most places on Gili Air are locally owned and offer an unbeatable setting for a meal, with tables right over the water.

★ Eazy Gili Waroeng
INDONESIAN $

(mains 25,000-40,000Rp; ☺8am-10pm) In the increasingly buzzy main village, this spotless corner cafe serves up local fare aimed at visitors. It's the slightly Westernised face of the beloved Warung Muslim immediately east. They also do breakfasts, sandwiches and a superb *pisang goreng* (banana fritter).

Warung Sasak II
INDONESIAN $

(mains from 15,000Rp; ☺8am-10pm) A fine find in the village, this dead simple warung has excellent versions of all the standards such as chicken sate and fish curry. It also has many variations on *parapek,* a Sasak specialty where foods are cooked in a spicy sauce. Jakarta soaps play on the TV.

★ Scallywags
INTERNATIONAL $$

(✆0370-645301; www.scallywagsresort.com; mains 45,000-120,000Rp; ☺8am-10pm; 🛜) Set on Gili Air's softest and widest beach, there's elegant decor, upscale comfort food, great grills, homemade gelati and superb cocktails here. But the best feature is the alluring beach dotted with loungers. Beware, the sambal is like a secret weapon.

★ Vista Mare
ITALIAN $$

(✆0812 386 5883; mains 30,000-90,000Rp; ☺8am-10pm) This whitewashed Italian cafe feels like it washed ashore from Naples. There are BBQ seafood specials each night (tuna, grouper etc) plus a range of pasta with a few Western and Asian dishes tossed in for variety. By day there are excellent juices and lighter meals. It's on a fine chunk of sand.

Biba
ITALIAN $$

(✆0819 1727 4648; www.bibabeach.com; mains 30,000-90,000Rp; ☺11.30am-10pm) Book a table on the sand for a memorable, romantic setting. Biba serves the best wood-oven piz-za and foccacia on the islands. It also does authentic ravioli, gnocchi and tagliatelle. The oven fires up at 7pm nightly.

Le Cirque
FRENCH, BAKERY $$

(✆0370-623432; www.lecirque-giliair.com; mains 35,000-110,000Rp; ☺7am-11pm; 🛜🍴) A clever French-accented place with a scrumptious bakery and tables along the shore. The dinner menu is ambitious and there are nightly seafood specials. Kids get their own menu with tasty treats like 'clown sausage'.

Chill Out
CAFE $$

(www.chilloutbungalows.com; mains 40,000-100,000Rp; ☺8am-11pm) Come for a swim and sip with stunning views, and stay for dinner at a table on the sand. They put on a full nightly seafood BBQ and cook up some good pizzas in the wood-fired oven.

🍷 Drinking & Nightlife

Gili Air is usually a mellow place, but there are full-moon parties and things can rev up on the strip in the southeast in high season. Still, where late-night Gili T is all about rave parties, Gili Air's hotspot is the waffle-cone stand.

Mirage
CAFE

(☺9am-late) Set on a sublime stretch of beach with technicolour sunsets nightly, there is no better place for a sundowner. The menu includes snacks and veggie options.

Zipp Bar
BAR

(☺9am-late) This large bar has an excellent booze selection (try the fresh-fruit cocktails) and tables dotted around a great beach. It hosts a beach party every full moon.

Legend Bar
BAR

(☺7am-late) Painted the requisite Rasta colours of red, green and gold, this raffish reggae bar has a large dance party every full moon.

ℹ Information

There are **ATMs** along the southeast strip. **Royal Medical** (✆0878 6442 1212; ☺phone answered 24hr) has a simple clinic. There's a good general store, **Siti Shop** (☺8am-8pm), in the village.

ℹ Getting There & Away

The **boat landing** is busy. Gili Air's commerce and popularity mean that public boats fill rather quickly for the 15-minute ride to Bangsal. The ticket office has a fine, shady waiting area.

Understand Bali & Lombok

Bali & Lombok Today

It's not just Bali's temperatures that are hot, it's the island itself. Deluged with record numbers of tourists (nearly four million foreigners, another eight million Indonesians), there are crowds of visitors everywhere you turn. In the media too, Bali is big news, with breathless coverage every time something sensational happens to a foreigner – especially an Australian. It has many locals and others who love Bali wishing the island could just take a big time out.

Best on Film

Act of Killing (director Joshua Oppenheimer, 2013) A searing documentary about the 1965 slaughter of accused Communist sympathisers in Indonesia (including tens of thousands on Bali).

Cowboys in Paradise (director Amit Virmani, 2011) Highly entertaining documentary about the scores of male gigolos working in south Bali.

Best in Print

Paradise Guest House (Ellen Sussman, 2013) A critically acclaimed novel about one woman's trip to Bali and her search for a place to call home.

Island of Bali (Miguel Covarrubias, 1937) The classic work about Bali and its civilisation remains stunningly relevant today.

Bali Daze: Freefall Off the Tourist Trail (Cat Wheeler, 2011) Accounts of daily life in Ubud make for a fun and illuminating read.

Secrets of Bali: Fresh Light on the Morning of the World (Jonathan Copeland and Ni Wayan Murni, 2010) One of the most readable books about Bali, its people and its traditions.

Eat, Pray, Love (Elizabeth Gilbert, 2007) This bestseller lures believers to Bali every year, hoping to capture something from the book.

Developments Beyond Control

Sidemen Rd in east Bali runs through one of the most beautiful parts of the island. It's a verdant, green paradise. What isn't nice is the road itself; where once it was smoothly paved, now it has been beaten into rubble in parts because of the constant stream of trucks hauling sand and rock to south Bali for construction projects. It's the same story across the island: convoys of trucks hauling materials needed for the booming south.

Yet what may be even more astonishing – beyond the pace of new construction – is that no one really knows what's being built. Bali's loose form of central government means that the individual regencies have more say in what goes on in their parts of the island. But there is little central planning or a permission process. One of the results has been an explosion in new midrange chain hotels. Seemingly overnight dozens of these places have opened across the south, many in areas far from beaches, restaurants and nightlife, and often on very busy roads. There has also been an explosion in the number of condotels, hotels where the rooms are sold like condominiums to investors who are promised a certain return. In 2014 Bali had 5000 condotel rooms (all in south Bali) and another 8000 new ones had been advertised.

Even the head of Bali's tourism board, Ngurah Wijaya, has been widely quoted saying 'we're loving Bali to death'. And the developments continue. In a truly cynical move, it was announced that 50% of the vast mangroves around Benoa Harbour and the airport were going to be preserved. That's because there are plans to cover the other 50% with landfill and build a vast complex of new hotels, tourist attractions and even a Formula One race car track. However, this proposal seems to have finally raised Balinese ire as large numbers of locals have joined with environmental groups to protest the destruction of the mangroves. Given the powerful interests behind the project, how this will play out remains to be seen.

Water Worries

The figures are staggering – and depressing: a series of reports and research papers have shown that 260 of Bali's 400 rivers now dry up at various times during the year, that brackish water is infiltrating the wells that the south depends on for water as demand sucks away the water table and new roads across the Bukit Peninsula are allowing even more development of the semi-arid region, which gets its water from other parts of Bali.

Ironically it was only in 2012 that Bali's unique system for irrigating rice fields received Unesco recognition as a World Heritage Site. But so severe have water shortages become as supplies are diverted to developments that now rice farmers face real problems. As one told us: 'Look at all the corn you see growing in rice fields. We only plant that when we can't get enough water as it doesn't need as much as rice. But corn is also much less profitable.' And while current figures are scarce, you see far more corn growing today amidst Bali's iconic rice fields than just five years ago.

Hope

He's been called the Indonesian Obama, and that may be the biggest hurdle that the new president, Joko Widodo, faces. The first democratically elected Indonesian president with no ties to the old Suharto dictatorship or the military, Jokowi, as he's commonly known, carries the dreams of every Indonesian who wants a brighter future for his or her country. It's a huge load of hope and one that will test the former mayor of Jakarta, whose supporters praise his common touch. Bali voted for him more than two to one over his opponent, the former general Prabowo Subianto. (On conservative Lombok, the results were reversed.) For Balinese Hindus who have been nervously watching the rise of hardline Muslim rhetoric in Jakarta, the hope is that Jokowi will be a uniter and not a divider.

POPULATION: **BALI 4.2 MILLION; LOMBOK 3.3 MILLION**

AREA: **BALI 5620 SQ KM; LOMBOK 5435 SQ KM**

PERCENTAGE OF BALI'S LAND USED FOR RICE PRODUCTION: **28%**

AVERAGE MONTHLY TOURISM WORKER WAGE: **US$100–200**

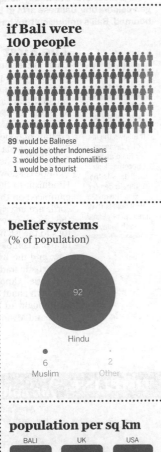

if Bali were 100 people

89 would be Balinese
7 would be other Indonesians
3 would be other nationalities
1 would be a tourist

belief systems
(% of population)

92 Hindu

6 Muslim

2 Other

population per sq km

BALI   UK   USA

♟ ≈ 30 people

History

When Islam swept through Java in the 12th century, the kings of the Hindu Majapahit kingdom moved to Bali while the priest Nirartha established temples, including Rambut Siwi, Tanah Lot and Ulu Watu. In the 19th century, the Dutch formed alliances with local princes and eventually conquered the island (along with Lombok). Westerners began celebrating Balinese arts in the 1930s; surfers arrived in the 1960s. As tourism has boomed, Bali's unique culture has proved to be remarkably resilient.

The First Balinese

The 14th-century epic poem *Sutasoma* has been given a sparkling new translation by Kate O'Brien. It follows the life of a Javanese prince as he becomes king and defeats the ultimate demon using the mystical beliefs that underpin Balinese faith today.

There are few traces of Stone Age people in Bali, although it's certain that the island was populated very early in prehistoric times – fossilised humanoid remains from neighbouring Java have been dated to as early as 250,000 years ago. The earliest human artefacts found in Bali are stone tools and earthenware vessels dug up near Cekik in west Bali, which are estimated to be 3000 years old. Discoveries continue, and you can see exhibits of bones that are estimated to be 4000 years old at the Museum Situs Purbakala Gilimanuk (p254). Artefacts indicate that the Bronze Age began in Bali before 300 BC.

Little is known of Bali during the period when Indian traders brought Hinduism to the Indonesian archipelago, although it is thought it was embraced on the island by the 7th century AD. The earliest written records are inscriptions on a stone pillar near Sanur, dating from around the 9th century; by that time, Bali had already developed many similarities to the island you find today. Rice, for example, was grown with the help of a complex irrigation system, probably very like the one employed now, and the Balinese had already begun to develop their rich cultural and artistic traditions.

If little is known about the earliest inhabitants of Bali, then even less is known about Lombok until about the 17th century. Early inhabitants are thought to have been Sasaks from a region encompassing today's India and Myanmar.

TIMELINE

50 million BC	2000 BC	7th century
A permanent gap in the Earth's crust forms between Asia and Australia. The Wallace Line keeps Australian species from crossing to Bali until the invention of cheap Bintang specials.	A Balinese gentleman passes away. One of the first known inhabitants of the island, he rests peacefully until his bones are found and placed on display in Gilimanuk.	Indian traders bring Hinduism to Bali. Little is known about what was traded, although some speculate that they left with lots of wooden carvings of penises and bootleg *lontar* books.

Hindu Influence

Java began to spread its influence into Bali during the reign of King Airlangga (1019–42), or perhaps even earlier. At the age of 16, when his uncle lost the throne, Airlangga fled into the forests of western Java. He gradually gained support, won back the kingdom once ruled by his uncle and went on to become one of Java's greatest kings. Airlangga's mother had moved to Bali and remarried shortly after his birth, so when he gained the throne, there was an immediate link between Java and Bali. It was at this time that the courtly Javanese language known as Kawi came into use among the royalty of Bali, and the rock-cut memorials seen at Gunung Kawi (p172), near Tampaksiring, provide a clear architectural link between Bali and 11th-century Java.

After Airlangga's death, Bali remained semi-independent until Kertanagara became king of the Singasari dynasty in Java two centuries later. Kertanagara conquered Bali in 1284, but the period of his greatest power lasted a mere eight years, until he was murdered and his kingdom collapsed. However, the great Majapahit dynasty was founded by his son, Vijaya (or Wijaya). With Java in turmoil, Bali regained its autonomy, and the Pejeng dynasty rose to great power. Temples and relics of this period can still be found in Pejeng, near Ubud.

Exit Pejeng

In 1343 the legendary Majapahit prime minister, Gajah Mada, defeated the Pejeng king Dalem Bedaulu, and Bali was brought back under Javanese influence.

Although Gajah Mada brought much of the Indonesian archipelago under Majapahit control, this was the furthest extent of their power. The 'capital' of the dynasty was moved to Gelgel, in Bali, near modern Semarapura, around the late 14th century, and this was the base for the 'king of Bali', the Dewa Agung, for the next two centuries. The Gelgel dynasty in Bali, under Dalem Batur Enggong, extended its power eastwards to the neighbouring island of Lombok and westwards across the strait to Java.

The collapse of the Majapahit dynasty into weak, decadent, petty kingdoms opened the door for the spread of Islam from the trading states of the north coast into the heartland of Java. As the Hindu states fell, many of the intelligentsia fled to Bali. Notable among these was the priest Nirartha, who is credited with introducing many of the complexities of Balinese religion to the island, as well as establishing the chain of 'sea temples', which includes Pura Luhur Ulu Watu and Pura Tanah Lot. Court-supported artisans, artists, dancers, musicians and actors also fled to Bali at this time and the island experienced an explosion of cultural activity that has not stopped to this day.

Oldest Sites

Goa Gajah

Gunung Kawi

Tirta Empul

Stone Pillar

HISTORY HINDU INFLUENCE

A Short History of Bali: Indonesia's Hindu Realm, by Robert Pringle, is a thoughtful analysis of Bali's history from the Bronze Age to the present, with excellent sections on the 2002 bombings and ongoing environmental woes caused by tourism and development.

9th century	1019	12th century	1292
A stone carver creates an account in Sanskrit of now long-forgotten military victories. Bali's oldest dated artefact proves early Hindu influence and ends up hidden in Sanur.	A future king, Airlangga, is born in Bali. He lives in the jungles of Java until he gains political power and becomes king of the two islands, unifying both cultures.	Ten incredible 7m-high statues are carved from stone cliffs at Gunung Kawi, north of Ubud. Further monuments are created in nearby valleys.	Bail gains complete independence from Java with the death of Kertanagara, a powerful king who had ruled the two islands for eight years. Power shifts frequently between the islands.

ARTISTS IN CHARGE

The lasting wholesale change to Balinese life because of the mass exodus of Hindu elite from Javanese kingdoms in the 16th century cannot be overstated. It's as if all the subscribers to the opera were put in charge of a town – suddenly there would be a lot more opera. The Balinese had already shown a bent for creativity but once the formerly Javanese intelligentsia exerted control, music, dance, art and more flowered like the lotus blossoms in village ponds. High status was accorded to villages with the most creative talent, a tradition that continues today.

This flair for the liberal arts found a perfect match in the Hinduism that took full hold then. The complex and rich legends of good and evil spirits found ample opportunity to flourish, such as the legend of Jero Gede Macaling, the evil spirit of Nusa Penida.

Dutch Dealings

In 1597, Dutch seamen were among the first Europeans to appear in Bali. Setting a tradition that has prevailed to the present day, they fell in love with the island and when Cornelius de Houtman, the ship's captain, prepared to set sail from the island, two of his crew refused to come with him. At that time, Balinese prosperity and artistic activity, at least among the royalty, was at a peak, and the king who befriended de Houtman had 200 wives and a chariot pulled by two white buffalo, not to mention a retinue of 50 dwarfs, whose bodies had been bent to resemble the handle of a kris (traditional dagger). By the early 1600s, the Dutch had established trade treaties with Javanese princes and controlled much of the spice trade, but they were interested in profit, not culture, and barely gave Bali a second glance.

In 1710, the 'capital' of the Gelgel kingdom was shifted to nearby Klungkung (now called Semarapura), but local discontent was growing; lesser rulers were breaking away, and the Dutch began to move in, using the old strategy of divide and conquer. In 1846, the Dutch used Balinese salvage claims over shipwrecks as a pretext to land military forces in northern Bali, bringing the kingdoms of Buleleng and Jembrana under their control. Their cause was also aided by the various Balinese princes who had gained ruling interests on Lombok and were distracted from matters at home, and also unaware that the wily Dutch would use Lombok against Bali.

In 1894, the Dutch, the Balinese and the people of Lombok collided in battles that would set the course of history for the next several decades.

With the north of Bali long under Dutch control and the conquest of Lombok successful, the south was never going to last long. Once again, it was disputes over the ransacking of wrecked ships that gave the Dutch

Locks of hair from Nirartha, the great priest who shaped Balinese Hinduism in the 16th century, are said to be buried at Pura Rambit Siwi, an evocative seaside temple in west Bali.

1343	1520	1546	1579
The legendary Majapahit prime minister, Gajah Mada, brings Bali back under Javanese control. For the next two centuries, the royal court is just south of today's Semarapura (Klungkung).	Java fully converts to Islam, leaving Bali in isolation as a Hindu island. Priests and artists move to Bali, concentrating and strengthening the island's culture against conversion.	The Hindu priest Nirartha arrives in Bali. He transforms religion and builds temples by the dozen including Pura Rambut Siwi, Pura Tanah Lot and Pura Luhur Ulu Watu.	Sir Francis Drake, while looking for spice, is thought to be Bali's first European visitor.

an excuse to move in. In 1904, after a Chinese ship was wrecked off Sanur, Dutch demands that the rajah of Badung pay 3000 silver dollars in damages were rejected and in 1906 Dutch warships appeared at Sanur.

Balinese Suicide

The Dutch forces landed despite Balinese opposition and, four days later, had marched 5km to the outskirts of Denpasar. On 20 September 1906, the Dutch mounted a naval bombardment of Denpasar and began their final assault. The three princes of Badung realised that they were completely outnumbered and outgunned, and that defeat was inevitable. Surrender and exile, however, would have been the worst imaginable outcome, so they decided to take the honourable path of a suicidal *puputan* (a warrior's fight to the death). First the princes burned their palaces, and then, dressed in their finest jewellery and waving ceremonial golden kris, the rajah led the royalty, priests and courtiers out to face the modern weapons of the Dutch.

The Dutch implored the Balinese to surrender rather than make their hopeless stand, but their pleas went unheeded and wave after wave of the Balinese nobility marched forward to their death, or turned their kris on themselves. In all, nearly 4000 Balinese died. The Dutch then marched northwest towards Tabanan and took the rajah of Tabanan prisoner – he also committed suicide rather than face the disgrace of exile.

The kingdoms of Karangasem (the royal family still lives in the palaces of Amlapura) and Gianyar had already capitulated to the Dutch and were allowed to retain some of their powers, but other kingdoms were defeated and their rulers exiled. Finally, in 1908, the rajah of Semarapura followed the lead of Badung, and once more the Dutch faced a *puputan*. As had happened at Cakranegara on Lombok, the beautiful palace at Semarapura, Taman Kertha Gosa, was largely destroyed.

With this last obstacle disposed of, all of Bali was under Dutch control and became part of the Dutch East Indies. There was little development of an exploitative plantation economy in Bali, and the common people noticed little difference between Dutch rule and the rule of the rajahs. On Lombok, conditions were harder, as new Dutch taxes took a toll on the populace.

WWII

In 1942, the Japanese landed unopposed in Bali at Sanur (most Indonesians saw the Japanese, at first, as anticolonial liberators). The Japanese established headquarters in Denpasar and Singaraja, and their occupation became increasingly harsh for the Balinese. When the Japanese left in August 1945 after their defeat in WWII, the island was suffering from extreme poverty. The occupation had fostered several paramilitary,

OPIUM

For much of the 19th century, the Dutch earned enormous amounts of money from the Balinese opium trade. Most of the colonial administrative budget went to promoting the opium industry, which was legal until the 1930s.

1580	1597	1795–1815	1830
The Portuguese also come looking for spice but in a foreshadowing of today's surfers, they wipe out on rocks at Ulu Watu and give up.	A Dutch expedition arrives off Kuta. A contemporary describes the skipper, Cornelius de Houtman, as a braggart and a scoundrel.	European wars mean that control of Indonesia nominally shifts from the Dutch to the French to the British and back to the Dutch.	The Balinese slave trade ends. For over two centuries, squabbling Balinese royal houses helped finance their wars by selling some of their most comely subjects.

Bali's airport is named for I Gusti Ngurah Rai, the national hero who died leading the resistance against the Dutch at Marga in 1946. The text of a letter he wrote in response to Dutch demands to surrender ends with 'Freedom or death!'.

nationalist and anticolonial groups that were ready to fight the returning Dutch.

Independence

In August 1945, just days after the Japanese surrender, Sukarno, the most prominent member of the coterie of nationalist activists, proclaimed the nation's independence. It took four years to convince the Dutch that they were not going to get their great colony back. In a virtual repeat of the *puputan* nearly 50 years earlier, Balinese freedom fighters led by the charismatic Gusti Ngurah Rai (namesake of the Bali airport) were wiped out by the Dutch in the battle of Marga in western Bali on 20 November 1946. The Dutch finally recognised Indonesia's independence in 1949 – though Indonesians celebrate 17 August 1945 as their Independence Day.

At first, Bali, Lombok and the rest of Indonesia's eastern islands were grouped together in the unwieldy province of Nusa Tenggara. In 1958 the central government recognised this folly and created three new governmental regions from the one, with Bali getting its own and Lombok becoming part of Nusa Tenggara Barat.

THE BATTLE FOR LOMBOK

In 1894, the Dutch sent an army to back the Sasak people of eastern Lombok in a rebellion against the Balinese rajah who controlled Lombok with the support of the western Sasak. The rajah quickly capitulated, but the Balinese crown prince decided to fight on.

The Dutch camp at the Mayura Water Palace was attacked late at night by a combined force of Balinese and western Sasak, forcing the Dutch to take shelter in a temple compound. The Balinese also attacked another Dutch camp further east at Mataram, and soon, the entire Dutch army on Lombok was forced back to Ampenan where, according to one eyewitness, the soldiers 'were so nervous that they fired madly if so much as a leaf fell off a tree'. These battles resulted in enormous losses of men and arms for the Dutch.

Although the Balinese had won the first battles, they had begun to lose the war. They faced a continuing threat from the eastern Sasak, while the Dutch were soon supported with reinforcements from Java.

The Dutch attacked Mataram a month later, fighting street-to-street against Balinese and western Sasak soldiers and civilians. Rather than surrender, Balinese men, women and children opted for the suicidal *puputan* (a warrior's fight to the death) and were cut down by rifle and artillery fire.

In late November 1894, the Dutch attacked Sasari and, again, a large number of Balinese chose the *puputan*. With the downfall of the dynasty, the local population abandoned its struggle against the Dutch.

1856	1891-1894	1908	1912
Mads Lange, a Danish trader, dies mysteriously in Kuta after earning a fortune selling goods to ships anchored off the beach. His death is blamed on poisoning by jealous rivals.	Years of failed Sasak rebellions in eastern Lombok finally take hold after a palace burning. With Dutch assistance the Balinese rulers are chased from the islands within three years.	The Balinese royalty commit suicide. Wearing their best dress and armed with 'show' daggers, they march into Dutch gunfire in a suicidal *puputan* (warrior's fight to the death) in Klungkung.	A German, Gregor Krause, photographs beautiful Balinese women topless. WWI intervenes, but in 1920 an 'art book' of photos appears and Dutch steamers docking in Singaraja now bring tourists.

Coup & Backlash

Independence was not an easy path for Indonesia to follow. When Sukarno assumed more direct control in 1959 after several violent rebellions, he proved to be as inept as a peacetime administrator as he was inspirational as a revolutionary leader. In the early 1960s, as Sukarno faltered, the army, communists, and other groups struggled for supremacy. On 30 September 1965, an attempted coup – blamed on the Partai Komunis Indonesia (PKI, or Communist Party) – led to Sukarno's downfall. General Suharto emerged as the leading figure in the armed forces, displaying great military and political skill in suppressing the coup. The PKI was outlawed and a wave of anticommunist massacres followed throughout Indonesia.

In Bali, the events had an added local significance as the main national political organisations, the Partai Nasional Indonesia (PNI, Nationalist Party) and the PKI, crystallised existing differences between traditionalists, who wanted to maintain the old caste system, and radicals, who saw the caste system as repressive and were urging land reform. After the failed coup, religious traditionalists in Bali led the witch-hunt for the 'godless communists'. Eventually, the military stepped in to control the anticommunist purge, but no one in Bali was untouched by the killings, estimated at between 50,000 and 100,000 out of a population of about two million, a percentage many times higher than on Java. Many tens of thousands more died on Lombok.

The 1963 Eruption

Amid the political turmoil, the most disastrous volcanic eruption in Bali in 100 years occurred in 1963. Gunung Agung blew its top in no uncertain manner, at a time of considerable prophetic and political importance.

Eka Dasa Rudra, the greatest of all Balinese sacrifices and an event that takes place only every 100 years on the Balinese calendar, was to culminate on 8 March 1963. It had been well over 100 Balinese years since the last Eka Dasa Rudra, but there was dispute among the priests as to the correct and most favourable date.

Naturally, Pura Besakih was a focal point for the festival, but Gunung Agung was acting strangely as final preparations were made in late February. Despite some qualms, political pressures forced the ceremonies forward, even as ominous rumblings continued.

On 17 March, Gunung Agung exploded. The catastrophic eruption killed more than 1000 people (some estimate 2000) and destroyed entire villages – 100,000 people lost their homes. Streams of lava and hot volcanic mud poured right down to the sea at several places, completely

Kuta was never a part of mainstream Bali. During royal times, the region was a place of exile for malcontents and troublemakers. It was too arid for rice fields, the fishing was barely sustainable and the shore was covered with kilometres of useless sand...

A woman of many aliases, K'tut Tantri breezed into Bali from Hollywood in 1932. After the war, she joined the Indonesian Republicans in their postwar struggle against the Dutch. As Surabaya Sue, she broadcast from Surabaya in support of their cause. Her book, *Revolt in Paradise*, was published in 1960.

1925	1936	1945	1946
The greatest modern Balinese dancer, Mario, first performs the Kebyar Duduk, his enduring creation. From a stooped position, he moves as if in a trance to the haunting melody of gamelan.	Americans Robert and Louise Koke build a hotel of thatched bungalows on then-deserted Kuta Beach. Gone is stuffy, starched tourism, replacing it is fun in the sun followed by a drink.	Following the Japanese surrender at the end of WWII, nationalists, Sukarno among them, proclaim independence from the Netherlands. It sets off an intense period of revolution.	Freedom fighter Ngurah Rai dies with the rest of his men at Marga. But this *puputan* slays the Dutch colonial spirit, and soon Indonesia is independent.

covering roads and isolating the eastern end of Bali for some time. Driving the main road near Tulamben you can still see some lava flows.

Suharto Comes & Goes

Following the failed coup in 1965 and its aftermath, Suharto established himself as president and took control of the government. Under his 'New Order' government, Indonesia looked to the West for its foreign and economic policies.

Politically, Suharto ensured that his political party, Golkar, with strong support from the army, became the dominant political force. Other political parties were banned or crippled. Regular elections maintained the appearance of a national democracy, but until 1999, Golkar won every

THE TOURIST CLASS

Beginning in the 1920s, the Dutch government realised that Bali's unique culture could be marketed internationally to the growing tourism industry. Relying heavily on images that emphasised the topless habits of Bali's women, Dutch marketing drew wealthy Western adventurers, who landed in the north at today's Singaraja and were whisked about the island on rigid three-day itineraries that featured canned cultural shows at a government-run tourist hotel in Denpasar. Accounts from the time are ripe with imagery of supposedly culture-seeking Europeans who really just wanted to see a boob or two. Such desires were often thwarted by Balinese women who covered up when they heard the Dutch jalopies approaching.

But some intrepid travellers arrived independently, often at the behest of members of the small colony of Western artists, such as Walter Spies in Ubud. Two of these visitors were Robert Koke and Louise Garret, an unmarried American couple who had worked in Hollywood before landing in Bali in 1936 as part of a global adventure. Horrified at the stuffy strictures imposed by the Dutch tourism authorities, the pair (who were later married) built a couple of bungalows out of palm leaves and other local materials on the otherwise deserted beach at Kuta, which at that point was home to only a few impoverished fishing families.

Word soon spread, and the Kokes were booked solid. Guests came for days, stayed for weeks and told their friends. At first, the Dutch dismissed the Kokes' Kuta Beach Hotel as 'dirty native huts', but soon realised that increased numbers of tourists were good for everyone. Other Westerners built their own thatched hotels, complete with the bungalows that were to become a Balinese cliché in the decades ahead.

WWII wiped out both tourism and the hotels (the Kokes barely escaped ahead of the Japanese), but once people began travelling again after the war, Bali's inherent appeal made its popularity a foregone conclusion.

In 1987, Louise Koke's long-forgotten story of the Kuta Beach Hotel was published as *Our Hotel in Bali,* illustrated with her incisive sketches and her husband's photographs.

1949	1960s	1963	1965
South Pacific, the musical, opens on Broadway and the song 'Bali Hai' fixes a tropical cliché of Bali in the minds of millions (even though it's based on Fiji).	The lengthening of the airport runway for jets, reasonably affordable tickets and the opening of the Bali Beach Hotel in Sanur mark the start of mass tourism.	The sacred volcano Gunung Agung erupts, destroying a fair bit of east Bali, killing a thousand or more, leaving 100,000 homeless and sending out large lava flows.	Indonesia's long-running rivalry between communists and conservatives erupts after a supposed coup attempt by the former. The latter triumph and in the ensuing purges, tens of thousands are killed in Bali.

THE BALI BOMBINGS

On Saturday, 12 October 2002, two bombs exploded on Kuta's bustling Jl Legian. The first blew out the front of Paddy's Bar. A few seconds later, a far more powerful bomb obliterated the Sari Club.

The number of dead, including those unaccounted for, exceeded 200, although the exact number will probably never be known. Many injured Balinese made their way back to their villages, where, for lack of adequate medical treatment, they died.

Indonesian authorities eventually laid the blame for the blasts on Jemaah Islamiyah, an Islamic terrorist group. Dozens were arrested and many were sentenced to jail, including three who received the death penalty. But most received relatively light terms, including Abu Bakar Bashir, a radical cleric who many thought was behind the explosions. His convictions on charges relating to the bombings were overturned by the Indonesian supreme court in 2006, enraging many in Bali and Australia. (In 2011 he was sent back to prison for 15 years after a new conviction on terrorism charges.)

On 1 October 2005, three suicide bombers blew themselves up: one in a restaurant on Kuta Sq and two more at beachfront cafes in Jimbaran. It was again the work of Jemaah Islamiyah, and although documents found later stated that the attacks were targeted at tourists, 15 of the 20 who died were Balinese and Javanese employees of the places bombed.

There was also justice as Umar Patek was convicted in 2012 of helping to assemble the 2002 Bali bombs and sentenced to 20 years in jail. But threats continue: in 2012 police on Bali shot dead five suspected terrorists.

election hands down. This period was also marked by great economic development in Bali and later on Lombok as social stability and maintenance of a favourable investment climate took precedence over democracy. Huge resorts – often with investors in government – appeared in Sanur, Kuta and Nusa Dua during this time.

In early 1997, the good times ended as Southeast Asia suffered a severe economic crisis, and within the year, the Indonesian currency (the rupiah) had all but collapsed and the economy was on the brink of bankruptcy.

Unable to cope with the escalating crisis, Suharto resigned in 1998, after 32 years in power. His protégé, Dr Bacharuddin Jusuf Habibie, became president. Though initially dismissed as a Suharto crony, he made the first notable steps towards opening the door to real democracy, such as freeing the press from government supervision.

Bali's history is reduced to miniature dramas with stilted dolls at the delightfully unhip Bajra Sandhi Monument in Denpasar. Meaning the 'Struggle of the People,' the museum brings cartoon-like 3D veracity to important moments in the island's history.

1970	1972	1979	1998
A girl ekes out a living selling candy in Kuta. Surfers offer advice, she posts a menu, then she builds a hut and calls it Made's Warung. She prospers.	Filmmaker Alby Falzon brings a band of Australians to Bali for his surfing documentary *Morning on Earth*, which proves seminal for a generation of Australians who head to Kuta.	Australian Kim Bradley, impressed by the gnarly surfing style of locals, encourages them to start a club. Sixty do just that (good on an island where people fear the water).	Suharto, who always had close ties to Bali, resigns as president after 32 years. His family retains control of several Bali resorts, including the thirsty Pecatu Indah resort.

BOOKS

Peace Shattered & Democracy Dawns

In 1999, Indonesia's parliament met to elect a new president. The front-runner was Megawati Sukarnoputri, who was enormously popular in Bali, partly because of family connections (her paternal grandmother was Balinese) and partly because her party was essentially secular (the mostly Hindu Balinese are very concerned about any growth in Muslim fundamentalism). However, Abdurrahman Wahid, the moderate, intellectual head of Indonesia's largest Muslim organisation, emerged as president.

On Lombok, however, religious and political tensions spilled over in early 2000 when a sudden wave of attacks starting in Mataram burned Chinese and Christian businesses and homes across the island. The impact on tourism was immediate and severe, and the island took a decade to emerge from the violence and its legacies.

After 21 months of growing ethnic, religious and regional conflicts, parliament had enough ammunition to recall Wahid's mandate and hand the presidency to Megawati in 2001. In 2004 she was replaced by Indonesia's first democratically elected president, Susilo Bambang Yudhoyono. He had gained international recognition after he led the hunt for the 2002 Bali bombers.

In recent years, visitors have been big news on Bali (and the Gilis). As fears sparked by the bombings faded, international arrivals have increased by 10% to 15% a year on average. Where a short time ago two million visitors was a big deal, now that number looks set to hit around four million. Tourism is literally taking over many aspects of Balinese life, especially economic ones.

With staff reviews, hard-to-find titles and stellar recommendations, *the* place for books about Bali is Ganesha Books in Ubud. The website (www.ganeshabooksbali.com) offers a vast selection and the shop does mail orders.

2000	2002	2005	2013
Indonesian rioting spreads to Lombok and hundreds of Chinese, Christian and Balinese homes and businesses are looted and burned, particularly after a Muslim-sponsored rally to decry violence turns ugly.	Bombs in Kuta kill more than 200, many at the Sari Club. Bali's economy is crushed as tourists stay away and there is economic devastation across the island.	Three suicide bombers blow themselves up in Kuta and Jimbaran, killing 20 mostly Balinese and Javanese.	Bali tops 3 million foreign tourists for the year, a new record that continues several years of growth that averaged more than 15% a year.

Local Life & Religion

Everyone seems so relaxed on Bali and Lombok. There is a gentleness to people that easily obscures their deep cultural heritage and belief systems. Balinese Hindus and Lombok Muslims – with plenty of geographic cross-over between the two – live lives deeply entwined in their belief systems. And on Bali in particular, religion plays a role in so much of what makes the island appealing to visitors: the art, the music, the offerings, the architecture, the temples and more.

Bali

Ask any traveller what they love about Bali and, most times, 'the people' will top their list. Since the 1920s, when the Dutch used images of bare-breasted Balinese women to lure tourists, Bali has embodied the mystique and glamour of an exotic paradise.

For all the romanticism, there is a harsher reality. For many Balinese, life remains a near hand-to-mouth existence, even as the island prospers due to tourism and the middle class grows. And the idea of culture can sometimes seem misplaced as overzealous touts test your patience in their efforts to make a living.

But there's also some truth to this idea of paradise. There is no other place in the world like Bali, not even in Indonesia. Being the only surviving Hindu island in the world's largest Muslim country, its distinctive culture is worn like a badge of honour by a fiercely proud people. After all, it's only in the last century that 4000 Balinese royalty, dressed in their finest, walked into the gunfire of the Dutch army rather than surrender and become colonial subjects.

True, development has changed the landscape and prompted endless debate about the displacement of an agricultural society by a tourism-services industry. And the upmarket spas, clubs, boutiques and restaurants in Seminyak and Kerobokan might have you mistaking hedonism, not Hinduism, for the local religion. But scratch the surface and you'll find that Bali's soul remains unchanged.

A great resource on Balinese culture and life is www.murnis.com, the website for one of Ubud's original restaurants. Find explanations on everything from kids' names to what one wears to a ceremony, to how garments are woven; see the 'culture' section.

SMALL TALK

'Where do you stay?', 'Where do you come from?', 'Where are you going?'... You'll hear these questions over and over from your super-friendly Balinese hosts. While Westerners can find it intrusive, it's just Balinese small talk and a reflection of Bali's communal culture; they want to see where you fit in and change your status from stranger to friend.

Saying you're staying 'over there' or in a general area is fine, but expect follow-ups to get increasingly personal. 'Are you married?' Even if you're not, it's easiest to say you are. Next will be: 'Do you have children?' The best answer is affirmative: never say you don't want any. 'Belum' (not yet) is also an appropriate response, which will likely spark a giggle and an, 'Ah, still trying!'.

On Lombok, Sasak language does not have greetings such as 'good morning' or 'good afternoon.' Instead, they often greet each other with 'How's your family?'. Don't be surprised if a complete stranger asks about yours!

The island's creative heritage is everywhere you look, and the harmonious dedication to religion permeates every aspect of society, underpinning the strong sense of community. There are temples in every house, office and village, on mountains and beaches, in rice fields, trees, caves, cemeteries, lakes and rivers. Yet religious activity is not limited to places of worship. It can occur anywhere, sometimes smack-bang in the middle of peak-hour traffic.

Balinese Tolerance

The Balinese are famously tolerant of and hospitable towards other cultures, though they rarely travel themselves, such is the importance of their village and family ties, not to mention the financial cost. If anything, they're bemused by all the attention, which reinforces their pride; the general sense is, whatever we're doing, it must be right to entice millions of people to leave their homes for ours.

The Balinese are unfailingly friendly, love a chat and can get quite personal. English is widely spoken but they love to hear tourists attempt Bahasa Indonesia or, better still, throw in a Balinese phrase such as *sing*

WHAT'S IN A NAME?

Far from being straightforward, Balinese names are as fluid as the tides. Everyone has a traditional name, but their other names often reflect events in each individual's life. They also help distinguish between people of the same name, which is perhaps nowhere more necessary than in Bali.

Traditional naming customs seem straightforward, with a predictable gender non-specific pattern to names. The order of names, with variations for regions and caste, is:

➡ **First-born** Wayan (Gede, Putu)

➡ **Second-born** Made (Kadek, Nengah, Ngurah)

➡ **Third-born** Nyoman (Komang)

➡ **Fourth-born** Ketut (or just Tut, as in toot)

Subsequent children reuse the same set, but as many families now settle for just two children, you'll meet many Wayans and Mades.

Castes also play an important role in naming and have naming conventions that clearly denote status when added to the birth order name. Bali's system is much less complicated than India's.

➡ **Sudra** Some 90% of Balinese are part of this, the peasant caste. Names are preceded by the title 'I' for a boy and 'Ni' for a girl.

➡ **Wesya** The caste of bureaucrats and merchants. Gusti Bagus (male) and Gusti Ayu (female).

➡ **Ksatria** A top caste, denoting royalty or warriors. I Gusti Ngurah (male) and I Gusti Ayu (female), with additional titles including Anak Agung, and Dewa.

➡ **Brahman** The top of the heap: teachers and priests. Ida Bagus (male) and Ida Ayu (female).

Traditional names are followed by another given name – this is where parents can get creative. Some names reflect hopes for their child, as in I Nyoman Darma Putra, who's supposed to be 'dutiful' or 'good' (dharma). Others reflect modern influences, such as I Wayan Radio who was born in the 1970s, and Ni Made Atom who said her parents just liked the sound of this scientific term that also had a bomb named after it.

Many are tagged for their appearance. Nyoman Darma is often called Nyoman Kopi (coffee) for the darkness of his skin compared with that of his siblings. I Wayan Rama, named after the *Ramayana* epic, is called Wayan Gemuk (fat) to differentiate his physique from his slighter friend Wayan Kecil (small).

ken ken (no worries); do this and you'll make a friend for life. They have a fantastic sense of humour and their easygoing nature is hard to ruffle. They generally find displays of temper distasteful and laugh at 'emotional' foreigners who are quick to anger.

Lombok

While Lombok's culture and language is often likened to that of Bali, this does neither island justice. True, Lombok's language, animist rituals and music and dance are reminiscent of the Hindu and Buddhist kingdoms that once ruled Indonesia, and of its time under Balinese rule in the 18th century. But the majority of Lombok's Sasak tribes are Muslim – they have very distinct traditions, dress, food and architecture, and have fought hard to keep them. While the Sasak peasants in western Lombok lived in relative harmony under Balinese feudal control, the aristocracy in the east remained hostile and led the rebellion with the Dutch that finally ousted their Balinese lords in the late 1800s. To this day, the Sasaks take great joy in competing in heroic trials of strength, such as the stick-fighting matches held every August near Tetebatu.

Lombok remains poorer and less developed than Bali, and is generally more conservative. Its Sasak culture is not as prominently displayed as Bali's Hinduism, but you'll see evidence of it, not the least of which in the proud mosques that stand in every town.

Family Ties

Through their family temple, Balinese have an intense spiritual connection to their home. As many as five generations share a Balinese home, in-laws and all. Grandparents, cousins, aunties, uncles and various distant relatives all live together. When the sons marry, they don't move out – their wives move in. Similarly, when daughters marry, they live with their in-laws, assuming household and child-bearing duties. Because of this, Balinese consider a son more valuable than a daughter. Not only will his family look after them in their old age, but he will inherit the home and perform the necessary rites after they die to free their souls for reincarnation, so they do not become wandering ghosts.

A Woman's Work Is Work

Men play a big role in village affairs and helping to care for children, and only men plant and tend to the rice fields. But women are the real workhorses in Bali, doing everything from manual labour jobs (you'll see them carrying baskets of wet cement or bricks on their heads) to running market stalls and almost every job in tourism. In fact, their traditional role of caring for people and preparing food means that women have established many successful shops and cafes.

In between all of these tasks, women also prepare daily offerings for the family temple and house, and often extra offerings for upcoming ceremonies; their hands are never idle. You can observe all of this and more when you stay at a classic Balinese homestay, where your room is in the family compound and everyday life goes on about you. Ubud has many homestays.

Religion

Hinduism

Bali's official religion is Hindu, but it's far too animistic to be considered in the same vein as Indian Hinduism. The Balinese worship the trinity of Brahma, Shiva and Vishnu, three aspects of the one (invisible) god, Sanghyang Widi, as well as the *dewa* (ancestral gods) and village founders. They also worship gods of the earth, fire, water and mountains; gods of

---

LOCAL LIFE & RELIGION LOMBOK

Balinese culture keeps intimacy behind doors. Holding hands is not customary for couples in Bali, and is generally reserved for small children; however, linking arms for adults is the norm.

Motorbikes are an invaluable part of daily life. They carry everything from towers of bananas and rice sacks headed to the market, to whole families in full ceremonial dress on their way to the temple, to young hotel clerks riding primly in their uniforms.

fertility, rice, technology and books; and demons who inhabit the world underneath the ocean. They share the Indian belief in karma and reincarnation, but much less emphasis is attached to other Indian customs. There is no 'untouchable caste,' arranged marriages are very rare, and there are no child marriages.

Bali's unusual version of Hinduism was formed after the great Majapahit Hindu kingdom that once ruled Indonesia evacuated to Bali as Islam spread across the archipelago. While the Bali Aga (the 'original' Balinese) retreated to the hills in places such as east Bali's Tenganan to escape this new influence, the rest of the population simply adapted it for themselves, overlaying the Majapahit faith on their animist beliefs incorporated with Buddhist influences. A Balinese Hindu community can be found in west Lombok, a legacy of Bali's domination of its neighbour in the 19th century.

The most sacred site on the island is Gunung Agung, home to Pura Besakih and frequent ceremonies involving anywhere from hundreds to sometimes thousands of people. Smaller ceremonies are held across the island every day to appease the gods, placate the demons and ensure balance between dharma (good) and adharma (evil) forces.

Don't be surprised if on your very first day on Bali you witness or get caught up in a ceremony of some kind.

The ancient Hindu swastika seen all over Bali is a symbol of harmony with the universe. The German Nazis used a version where the arms were always bent in a clockwise direction.

Islam

Islam is a minority religion in Bali; most followers are Javanese immigrants or descendants of seafaring people from Sulawesi.

The majority of Lombok's Sasak people practise a moderate version of Islam, as in other parts of Indonesia. It was brought to the island by Gujarati merchants via the island of Celebes (now Sulawesi) and Java in the 13th century. The Sasaks follow the Five Pillars of Islam; the pillars decree that there is no god but Allah and Muhammad is His prophet, and that believers should pray five times a day, give alms to the poor, fast during the month of Ramadan and make the pilgrimage to Mecca at least once in their lifetime. However, in contrast to other Islamic countries, Muslim women are not segregated, head coverings are not compulsory, and polygamy is rare. In addition, many Sasaks still practise ancestor and spirit worship. A stricter version of Islam is beginning to emerge in east Lombok.

Wektu Telu

Believed to have originated in Bayan, north Lombok, Wektu Telu is an indigenous religion unique to Lombok. Now followed by a minority of Sasaks, it was the majority religion in northern Lombok until as recently as 1965, when Indonesia's incoming president Suharto decreed that all Indonesians must follow an official religion. Indigenous beliefs such as Wektu Telu were not recognised. Many followers thus state their official religion as Muslim, while practising Wektu traditions and rituals. Bayan remains a stronghold of Wektu Telu; you can spot believers by their *sapu puteq* (white headbands) and white flowing robes.

Wektu means 'result' in Sasak and *telu* means 'three,' and it probably signifies the complex mix of Balinese Hinduism, Islam and animism that the religion is. The tenet is that all important aspects of life are underpinned by a trinity. Like orthodox Muslims, they believe in Allah and that Muhammad is Allah's prophet; however, they pray only three times a day and honour just three days of fasting for Ramadan. Followers of Wektu Telu bury their dead with their heads facing Mecca and all public buildings have a prayer corner facing Mecca, but they do not make pilgrimages there. Similar to Balinese Hinduism, they believe the spiritual world is firmly linked to the natural; Gunung Rinjani is the most revered site.

BLACK MAGIC

Black magic is still a potent force and spiritual healers known as *balian* are consulted in times of illness and strife. There are plenty of stories floating around about the power of this magic. Disputes between relatives or neighbours are often blamed on curses, as are tragic deaths.

Ceremonies & Rituals

Between the family temple, village temple and district temple, a Balinese person takes part in dozens of ceremonies every year, on top of their daily rituals. Most employers allow staff to return to their villages for these obligations, which consume a vast chunk of income and time (and although many bosses moan about this, they have little choice unless they wish for a staff revolt). For tourists, this means there are ample opportunities to witness ceremonial traditions.

Ceremonies are the unifying centre of a Balinese person's life and a source of much entertainment, socialisation and festivity. Each ceremony is carried out on an auspicious date determined by a priest and often involves banquets, dance, drama and musical performances to entice the gods to continue their protection against evil forces. The most important ceremonies are Nyepi, which includes a rare day of complete rest, and Galungan, a 10-day reunion with ancestral spirits to celebrate the victory of good over evil.

Under their karmic beliefs, the Balinese hold themselves responsible for any misfortune, which is attributed to an overload of *adharma* (evil).

SHOWING RESPECT

Bali has a well-deserved reputation for being mellow, which is all the more reason to respect your hosts, who are enormously forgiving of faux pas if you're making a sincere effort. Be aware and respectful of local sensibilities, and dress and act appropriately, especially in rural villages and at religious sites. When in doubt, let the words 'modest' and 'humble' guide you.

Dos & Don'ts

➡ You'll see shorts and short skirts everywhere on locals but overly revealing clothing is still frowned upon, as is wandering down the street shirtless quaffing a beer.

➡ Many women go topless on Bali's beaches, offending locals who are embarrassed by foreigners' gratuitous nudity.

➡ On Lombok, nude or topless bathing is considered very offensive anywhere.

➡ Don't touch anyone on the head; it's regarded as the abode of the soul and is therefore sacred.

➡ Do pass things with your right hand. Even better, use both hands. Just don't use only your left hand, it's considered unclean.

➡ Beware of talking with hands on hips – a sign of contempt, anger or aggression (as displayed in traditional dance and opera).

➡ Beckon someone with the hand extended and using a downward waving motion. The Western method of beckoning is considered very rude.

➡ Don't make promises of gifts, books and photographs that are soon forgotten. Pity the poor local checking their mailbox or email inbox every day.

Religious Etiquette

➡ Cover shoulders and knees if visiting a temple or mosque; in Bali, a *selandong* (traditional scarf) or sash plus a sarong is usually provided for a small donation or as part of the entrance fee.

➡ Women are asked not to enter temples if they're menstruating, pregnant or have recently given birth. At these times women are thought to be *sebel* (ritually unclean).

➡ Don't put yourself higher than a priest, particularly at festivals (eg by scaling a wall to take photos).

➡ Take off your shoes before entering a mosque.

This calls for a *ngulapin* (cleansing) ritual to seek forgiveness and recover spiritual protection. A *ngulapin* requires an animal sacrifice and often involves a cockfight, satisfying the demons' thirst for blood.

Ceremonies are also held to overcome black magic and to cleanse a *sebel* (ritually unclean) spirit after childbirth or bereavement, or during menstruation or illness.

On top of all these ceremonies, there are 13 major rites of passage throughout every person's life. The most extravagant and expensive is the last – cremation.

Birth & Childhood

The Balinese believe babies are the reincarnation of ancestors, and they honour them as such. Offerings are made during pregnancy to ensure the mini-deity's well-being, and after birth, the placenta, umbilical cord, blood and afterbirth water – representing the child's four 'spirit' guardian brothers – are buried in the family compound.

Newborns are literally carried everywhere for the first three months, as they're not allowed to touch the 'impure' ground until after a purification ceremony. At 210 days (the first Balinese year), the baby is blessed in

---

BALI PLAYS DEAD

Nyepi

This is Bali's biggest purification festival, designed to clean out all the bad spirits and begin the year anew. It falls around March or April according to the Hindu caka calendar, a lunar cycle similar to the Western calendar in terms of the length of the year. Starting at sunrise, the whole island literally shuts down for 24 hours. No planes may land or take off, no vehicles of any description may be operated, and no power sources may be used. Everyone, including tourists, must stay off the streets. The cultural reasoning behind Nyepi is to fool evil spirits into thinking Bali has been abandoned so they will go elsewhere.

For the Balinese, it's a day for meditation and introspection. For foreigners, the rules are more relaxed, so long as you respect the 'Day of Silence' by not leaving your residence or hotel. If you do sneak out, you will quickly be escorted back to your hotel by a stern *pecalang* (village police officer).

As daunting as it sounds, Nyepi is actually a fantastic time to be in Bali. Firstly, there's the inspired concept of being forced to do nothing. Catch up on some sleep, or if you must, read, sunbathe, write postcards, play board games... just don't do anything to tempt the demons! Secondly, there are colourful festivals the night before Nyepi.

I Go, You Go, Ogoh-Ogoh!

In the weeks prior to Nyepi, huge and elaborate papier-mâché monsters called *ogoh-ogoh* are built in villages across the island. Involving everybody in the community, construction sites buzz with fevered activity around the clock. If you see a site where *ogoh-ogoh* are being constructed, there'll be a sign-up sheet for financial support. Contribute, say, 50,000Rp and you'll be a fully fledged sponsor and receive much street cred.

On Nyepi eve, large ceremonies all over Bali lure out the demons. Their rendezvous point is believed to be the main crossroads of each village, and this is where the priests perform exorcisms. Then the whole island erupts in mock 'anarchy,' with people banging on *kulkuls* (hollow tree-trunk drums), drums and tins, letting off firecrackers and yelling '*megedi megedi!*' (get out!) to expel the demons. The truly grand finale is when the *ogoh-ogoh* all go up in flames. Any demons that survive this wild partying are believed to evacuate the village when confronted with the boring silence on the morrow.

Christians find unique parallels to Easter in all this, especially Ash Wednesday and Shrove Tuesday, with its wild Mardi Gras–like celebrations the world over.

In coming years, dates for Nyepi are 9 March 2016, 28 March 2017 and 17 March 2018.

the ancestral temple and there is a huge feast. Later in life, birthdays lose their significance and many Balinese couldn't tell you their age.

A rite of passage to adulthood – and a prerequisite to marriage – is the tooth-filing ceremony at around 16 to 18 years. This is when a priest files a small part of the upper canines and upper incisors to flatten the teeth. Pointy fangs are, after all, distinguishing features of dogs and demons. Balinese claim the procedure doesn't hurt, likening the sensation to eating very cold ice: it's slightly uncomfortable, but not painful. Most tooth-filings happen in July and August.

Another important occasion for girls is their first menstrual period, which calls for a purification ceremony.

Marriage

Marriage defines a person's social status in Bali, making men automatic members of the *banjar* (local neighbourhood organisation). Balinese believe that when they come of age, it's their duty to marry and have children, including at least one son. Divorce is rare, as a divorced woman is cut off from her children.

The respectable way to marry, known as *mapadik*, is when the man's family visits the woman's family and proposes. But the Balinese like their fun and some prefer marriage by *ngrorod* (elopement or 'kidnapping'). After the couple returns to their village, the marriage is officially recognised and everybody has a grand celebration.

Marriage ceremonies include elaborate symbolism drawn from the island's rice-growing culture. The groom will carry food on his shoulders like a farmer while the bride will pretend to peddle produce, thus showing the couple's economic independence. Other actions need little explanation: the male digs a hole and the female places a seed inside for fertility, which comes after the male unsheathes his kris (knife) and pierces the female's unblemished woven mat of coconut leaves.

Death & Cremation

The body is considered little more than a shell for the soul, and upon death it is cremated in an elaborate ceremony befitting the ancestral spirit. It usually involves the whole community, and for important people, such as royalty, it can be a spectacular event involving thousands of people.

Because of the burdensome cost of even a modest cremation (estimated at around 7,000,000Rp), as well as the need to wait for an auspicious date, the deceased is often buried, sometimes for years, and disinterred for a mass cremation.

The body is carried in a tall, incredibly artistic, multi-tiered pyre on the shoulders of a group of men. The tower's size depends on the deceased's importance. A rajah's or high priest's funeral may require hundreds of men to tote the 11-tiered structure.

Along the way, the group sets out to confuse the corpse so it cannot find its way back home; the corpse is considered an unclean link to the material world, and the soul must be liberated for its evolution to a higher state. The men shake the tower, run it around in circles, simulate war battles, hurl water at it and generally rough-handle it, making the trip anything but a stately funeral crawl.

At the cremation ground, the body is transferred to a funeral sarcophagus reflecting the deceased's caste. Finally, it all goes up in flames and the ashes are scattered in the ocean. The soul is then free to ascend to heaven and wait for the next incarnation, usually in the form of a grandchild.

LOCAL LIFE & RELIGION RELIGION

The Balinese tooth-filing ceremony closes with the recipient being given a delicious *jamu* (herbal tonic), made from freshly pressed turmeric, betel-leaf juice, lime juice and honey.

BALINESE CEREMONIES

The Ubud tourist office is an excellent source for news of cremations and other Balinese ceremonies that occur at erratic intervals. Another good source is the website www.ubudnowandthen.com.

In classic Balinese fashion, respectful visitors are welcome at cremations. It's always worth asking around or at your hotel to see if anyone knows of one going on. The Ubud tourist office is a good source, too.

Although illegal because it involves gambling, cock-fighting is the top sport on Bali. It's easy to spot one when you know the main clue: lots of cars and motorbikes parked by the side of the road but no real sign of people. Or, just go to Pantai Masceti in east Bali where there is a huge cockfight arena.

Offerings

No matter where you stay, you'll witness women making daily offerings around their family temple and home, and in hotels, shops and other public places. You're also sure to see vibrant ceremonies, where whole villages turn out in ceremonial dress, and police close the roads for a spectacular procession that can stretch for hundreds of metres. Men play the gamelan while women elegantly balance magnificent tall offerings of fruit and cakes on their heads.

There's nothing manufactured about what you see. Dance and musical performances at hotels are among the few events 'staged' for tourists, but they do actually mirror the way Balinese traditionally welcome visitors, whom they refer to as *tamu* (guests). Otherwise, it's just the Balinese going about their daily life as they would without spectators.

Lombok

On Lombok, *adat* (tradition, customs and manners) underpins all aspects of daily life, especially regarding courtship, marriage and circumcision. Friday afternoon is the official time for worship, and government offices and many businesses close. Many, but not all, women wear headscarves, very few wear the veil, and large numbers work in tourism. Middle-class Muslim girls are often able to choose their own partners. Circumcision of Sasak boys normally occurs between the ages of six and 11 and calls for much celebration following a parade through their village.

The significant Balinese population on Lombok means you can often glimpse a Hindu ceremony while there; the minority Wektu Telu, Chinese and Buginese communities add to the diversity.

KEEPING TRACK OF TIME

Wondering what day of the week it is? You may have to consult a priest. The Balinese calendar is such a complex, intricate document that it only became publicly available some 60 years ago. Even today, most Balinese need a priest or *adat* leader to interpret it in order to determine the most auspicious day for any undertaking.

The calendar defines daily life. Whether it's building a new house, planting rice, having your teeth filed or getting married or cremated, no event has any chance of success if it does not occur on the proper date.

Three seemingly incompatible systems comprise the calendar (but this being Bali, that's a mere quibble): the 365-day Gregorian calendar, the 210-day *wuku* (or Pawukon) calendar, and the 12-month *caka* lunar calendar, which begins with Nyepi every March or April. In addition, certain weeks are dedicated to humans, others to animals and bamboo, and the calendar also lists forbidden activities for each week, such as getting married or cutting wood or bamboo.

Besides the date, each box on a calendar page contains the lunar month, the names of each of the 10 week 'days', attributes of a person born on that day according to Balinese astrology, and a symbol of either a full or new moon. Along the bottom of each month is a list of propitious days for specific activities, as well as the dates of *odalan* temple anniversaries – colourful festivals that visitors are welcome to attend.

In the old days, a priest consulted a *tika* – a piece of painted cloth or carved wood displaying the *wuku* cycle – which shows auspicious days represented by tiny geometric symbols. Today, many people have their own calendars, but it's no wonder the priests are still in business!

Village Life

Village life doesn't just take place in rural villages. Virtually every place on Bali is a village in its own way. Under its neon flash, chaos and other-worldly pleasures, even Kuta is a village; the locals meet, organise, celebrate, plan and make decisions, as is done across the island. Central to this is the *banjar* (local neighbourhood organisation).

Local Rule Bali-Style

Within Bali's government, the more than 3500 *banjar* wield enormous power. Comprising the married men of a given area (somewhere between 50 and 500), a *banjar* controls most community activities, whether it's planning for a temple ceremony or making important land-use decisions. These decisions are reached by consensus, and woe to a member who shirks his duties. The penalty can be fines or worse: banishment from the *banjar*. (In Bali's highly socialised society where your community is your life and identity – which is why a standard greeting is 'Where do you come from?' – banishment is the equivalent of the death penalty.)

Although women and even children can belong to the *banjar*, only men attend the meetings where important decisions are made. Women, who often own the businesses in tourist areas, have to communicate through their husbands to exert their influence. One thing that outsiders in a neighbourhood quickly learn is that one does not cross the *banjar*. Entire streets of restaurants and bars have been closed by order of the *banjar* after it was determined that neighbourhood concerns over matters such as noise were not being addressed.

Rice Farming

Rice cultivation remains the backbone of rural Bali's strict communal society. Traditionally, each family makes just enough to satisfy their own needs and offerings to the gods, and perhaps a little to sell at market. The island's most popular deity is Dewi Sri, goddess of agriculture, fertility and success, and every stage of cultivation encompasses rituals to express gratitude and to prevent a poor crop, bad weather, pollution or theft by mice and birds.

Subak: Watering Bali

The complexities of tilling and irrigating terraces in mountainous terrain require that all villagers share the work and responsibility. Under a centuries-old system, the four mountain lakes and criss-crossing rivers irrigate fields via a network of canals, dams, bamboo pipes and tunnels bored through rock. More than 1200 *subak* (village associations) oversee this democratic supply of water, and every farmer must belong to his local *subak*, which in turn is the foundation of each village's powerful *banjar*.

Subak is a fascinating and democratic system and in 2012 was placed on Unesco's World Heritage List.

Although Bali's civil make-up has changed with tourism, from a mostly homogenous island of farmers to a heterogeneous population with diverse activities and lifestyles, the collective responsibility rooted in rice farming continues to dictate the moral code behind daily life, even in the urban centres.

BAMBOO POLES

Huge decorated *penjor* (bamboo poles) appear in front of homes and line streets for ceremonies such as Galungan. Designs are as diverse as the artists who create them, but always feature the signature drooping top – in honour of the Barong's tail and the shape of Gunung Agung. The decorated tips, *sampian*, are exquisite.

1. Ogoh-Ogoh 2. Collection of offerings
3. *Subak* system, Jatiluwih (p225) 4. Cremation procession

FARLEY BARICUATRO (WWW.COLLOIDFARL.BLOGSPOT.COM) / GETTY IMAGES ©

Top 5 Local Encounters

It's not the beaches, diving or even the nightlife that make Bali a destination like no other, it's the deep and rich culture that pervades every aspect of daily life. And even Lombok gets in on the action with its huge volcano.

Cremation

Balinese cremations (p319) are elaborate ceremonies that are memorable for anyone attending. When someone dies, their body may be temporarily buried while the relatives raise money for a proper – and fiery – send-off in a decorated tower.

Famous Subak

A key to the Balinese psyche is the *subak* system of rice-field irrigation (p321). Through collaborative arrangements, water that starts high in the mountains flows from one farmer's field to the next, with the last plot of land assured it won't be left dry.

Offerings

Throughout the day women leave offerings (p320) at the 10,000-plus temples on Bali, which, like the offerings, also come in many sizes. Offerings may be tiny, such as a few flower petals on a banana leaf, or large and elaborate creations.

Ogoh-Ogoh!

Huge monsters appear all over Bali in the weeks before Nyepi, the Day of Silence (p318). Built from papier-mâché, the elaborate figures stand up to 10m tall and take weeks to create. On Nyepi these 'evil spirits' are torched in ceremonies island-wide.

Sacred Mountain

Just as the Balinese have their sacred volcanos, the Sasak people of Lombok have Gunung Rinjani (p269). This volcano, the second-tallest mountain in Indonesia, occupies a vital part of their belief system, which also has elements of Islam.

Food & Drink

Bali is a splendid destination for food. The local cuisine, whether truly Balinese or influenced by the rest of Indonesia and Asia, draws from the bounty of fresh local foods and is rich with spices and flavours. Savour this fare at roadside warungs (food stalls) or top-end restaurants, and for tastes further afield, you can choose from restaurants offering some of the best dining in the region.

Balinese Cuisine

Cooking courses are increasingly popular and are great ways to learn about Balinese food and markets. Many are taught by chefs with reputations well beyond Bali. Recommended are Sate Bali, in Seminyak; Bumbu Bali Cooking School, in Tanjung Benoa; and Casa Luna Cooking School, in Ubud.

Food, glorious food – or should that be food, laborious food? Balinese cooking is a time-consuming activity, but no effort at all is required to enjoy the results. That part is one of the best things about travelling around Bali: the sheer variety and quality of the local cuisine will have your taste buds dancing all the way to the next warung.

The fragrant aromas of Balinese cooking will taunt you wherever you go. Even in your average village compound, the finest food is prepared fresh every day. Women go to their local marketplace first thing in the morning to buy whatever produce has been brought in from the farms overnight. They cook enough to last all day, diligently roasting the coconut until the smoky sweetness kisses your nose, painstakingly grinding the spices to form the perfect *base* (paste) and perhaps even making fresh fragrant coconut oil for frying. The dishes are covered on a table or stored in a glass cabinet for family members to serve themselves throughout the day.

Six Flavours

Compared with that of other Indonesian islands, Balinese food is more pungent and lively, with a multitude of layers making up a complete dish. A meal will contain the six flavours (sweet, sour, spicy, salty, bitter and astringent), which promote health and vitality and stimulate the senses.

There's a predominance of ginger, chilli and coconut, as well as the beloved candlenut, often mistaken for the macadamia which is native to Australia. The biting combination of fresh galangal and turmeric is matched by the heat of raw chillies, the complex sweetness of palm sugar, tamarind and shrimp paste, and the clean fresh flavours of lemon grass, musk lime, kaffir lime leaves and coriander seeds.

There are shades of south Indian, Malaysian and Chinese flavours, stemming from centuries of migration and trading with seafaring pioneers. Many ingredients were introduced in these times: the humble chilli was brought by the fearless Portuguese, the ubiquitous snake bean and bok choy by the Chinese, and the rice substitute cassava by the Dutch. In true Balinese style, village chefs selected the finest and most durable new ingredients and adapted them to local tastes and cooking styles.

Revered Rice

Rice is the staple dish in Bali and Lombok and is revered as a gift of life from god. It is served generously with every meal – anything not served with rice is considered a *jaja* (snack). Rice acts as the medium for the various fragrant, spiced foods that accompany it, almost like condiments, with many dishes chopped finely to complement the dry, fluffy grains and for ease of eating with the hand. In Bali, a dish of steamed rice with mixed goodies is known as *nasi campur*. It's the island's undisputed 'signature' dish, eaten for breakfast, lunch and dinner.

There are as many variations of *nasi campur* as there are warungs. Just like a sandwich in the West can combine any number of fillings, each warung serves its own version according to budget, taste and whatever ingredients are fresh at the market. There are typically four or five dishes that make up a single serving, including a small portion of pork or chicken (small because meat is expensive), fish, tofu and/or tempeh (fermented soy-bean cake), egg, various vegetable dishes and crunchy *krupuk* (flavoured rice crackers). Beef seldom features because the Balinese believe cows are sacred. The 'side dishes' are arrayed around the centrepiece of rice and accompanied by the warung's signature sambal (paste made from chillies, garlic or shallots, and salt). The food is not usually served hot, because it would have been prepared during the morning.

Every town of any size in Bali and Lombok will have a *pasar malam* (night market), at which you can sample a vast range of fresh offerings from warungs and carts after dark. Gianyar has a great one.

A Taste of Asia

Bali's multicultural population means many warungs serve pan-Indonesian and Asian cuisine, offering a taste of different foods from across the archipelago. Common menu items are often confused with being Balinese, such as *nasi goreng* (fried rice), *mie goreng* (fried noodles), the ever-popular gado gado (vegetables and peanut sauce), which is actually from Java, and *rendang sapi* (beef curry), which is from Sumatra. There are many restaurants serving Padang fare (which originates from Sumatra) in Bali and Lombok, and Chinese food is especially common on Lombok.

MARKET LIFE

There's no better place to get acquainted with Balinese cuisine than the local market. But it's not for late sleepers. The best time to go is around 6am to 7am. If you're any later than 10am, the prime selections would have been snapped up and what's left would have begun to rot in the tropical climate.

Markets offer a glimpse of the variety and freshness of Balinese produce, often brought from the mountains within a day or two of being harvested, sometimes sooner. The atmosphere is lively and colourful with baskets loaded with fresh fruits, vegetables, flowers, spices, and varieties of red, black and white rice. There are trays of live chickens, dead chickens, freshly slaughtered pigs, sardines, eggs, colourful cakes, ready-made offerings and *base* (paste), and stalls selling es *cendol* (colourful iced coconut drink), *bubur* (rice porridge) or *nasi campur* (rice with side dishes) for breakfast. There's no refrigeration, so things come in small packages and what you see is for immediate sale. Bargaining is expected.

Markets ideal for visits include the following:

➡ Denpasar's huge Pasar Badung (p123) has every kind of food grown on Bali.

➡ Jimbaran's morning market (p96) of fruit and vegetables, and its legendary fish market (p96).

➡ Semarapura's market (p186) with its all-day bounty.

➡ Ubud's high quality produce market (p159) hidden behind reams of tourist tat, and its twice weekly organic market (p159) where some of Bali's most creative vendors sell their goods.

➡ Sukawati's market (p175) with its selection of foods, temple offerings and snacks.

➡ Kerobokan's **fruit market** (Map p72; cnr Jl Raya Kerobokan & Jl Gunung Tangkuban Perahu; ⊙7am-10pm), which has all the goodness of local markets close to the heart of tourist land.

Breakfast

Many Balinese save their appetite for lunch. They might kick-start the day with a cup of rich, sweet black coffee and a few sweet *jaja* at the market: colourful temple cakes, glutinous rice cakes, boiled bananas in their peels, fried banana fritters and *kelopon* (sweet-centred rice balls). Popular fresh fruits include snake fruit, named after its scaly skin, and jackfruit, which is also delicious stewed with vegetables.

The famous *bubuh injin* (black-rice pudding with palm sugar, grated coconut and coconut milk), which most tourists find on restaurant dessert menus, is actually a breakfast dish and a fine way to start the day. A variation available at the morning market is the nutty *bubur kacang hijau* (green mung-bean pudding), fragrantly enriched with ginger and *pandanus* leaf and served warm with coconut milk.

Lunch & Dinner

The household or warung cook usually finishes preparing the day's dishes mid-morning, so lunchtime happens around 11am when the food is freshest. This is the main meal of the day. Leftovers are eaten for dinner, or by tourists who awake late and do not get around to lunch until well and truly after everyone else has had their fill. Dessert is a rarity; for special occasions, it consists of fresh fruit or gelato-style coconut ice cream.

The secret to a good *nasi campur* is often in the cook's own *base*, which flavours the pork, chicken or fish, and the sambal, which may add just the right amount of heat to the meal at one place, or set your mouth ablaze at another. The range of dishes is endless. Some local favourites include *babi kecap* (pork stewed in sweet soy sauce), *ayam goreng* (fried chicken), *urap* (steamed vegetables with coconut), *lawar* (salad of chopped coconut, garlic and chilli with pork or chicken meat and blood), fried tofu or tempeh in a sweet soy or chilli sauce, fried peanuts, salty fish

> *The Food of Bali*, by Heinz von Holzen and Lother Arsana, brings to life everything from *cram cam* (clear chicken soup with shallots) to *bubuh injin* (black-rice pudding). Von Holzen also has a forthcoming book on Balinese markets.

SAMBAL JOY

Heinz von Holzen, the chef-owner of Tanjung Benoa's landmark Bumbu Bali restaurant and the author of numerous books on Balinese cuisine, says many people mistakenly believe Balinese food is spicy. 'The food itself is not normally spicy, the sambal is', Heinz says. That said, the Balinese certainly like some heat, and relish a dollop of fiery sambal with every meal; you may want to taste it to gauge the temperature before ploughing in. If you're averse to spicy food, request *tanpa* sambal (without chilli paste); better for most, though, is *tamba* (more) sambal!

One other note on sambal: if your request results in a bottle of the generically sweet commercial gloop, ask for 'Balinese sambal'. This latter request can open many more doors to eating joy because every Balinese (and Lombok) cook has their own favourite way of creating sambal. If you add the many sambals adopted from other parts of Indonesia, you could get one of many variations, including:

Sambal bajak A Javanese sambal, this is a creamy tomato-based sauce that is redolent with crushed chillies, yet gets smoothed out with palm sugar and shallots and then fried. Very common.

Sambal balado Chillis, shallots, garlic and tomatoes are sauteed in oil for a literally hot sambal. Often fried up fresh on the spot.

Sambal matah A raw Balinese sambal made from thinly sliced shallots, tiny chilies, shrimp paste and lemongrass. Divine.

Sambal plecing Another Lombok sambal, this one takes hot chillies and puts them in a tomato base, letting the heat sneak up on you.

Sambal taliwang A Lombok sambal made with special peppers, garlic and shrimp paste. One of the few true culinary highlights of Bali's neighbour.

LOMBOK'S SPICY SASAKS

Lombok's Sasak people are predominantly Muslim, so Bali's porky plethora does not feature in their diet of fish, chicken, vegetables and rice. The fact that *lombok* means chilli in Bahasa Indonesia makes sense, because Sasaks like their food spicy; *ayam Taliwang* (whole split chicken roasted over coconut husks served with tomato-chilli-lime dip) is one example.

Ares is a dish made with chilli, coconut juice and banana-palm pith; sometimes it's mixed with chicken or meat. *Sate pusut* is a delicious combination of minced fish, chicken or beef flavoured with coconut milk, garlic, chilli and other spices; this mixture is wrapped around a lemon-grass stick or sugar-cane skewer and grilled.

or eggs, *perkedel* (fried corn cakes) and various sate made from chunks of goat meat, chicken and pork.

If you visit a homestay, like the many in Ubud, you'll see family members busily preparing food throughout the day.

Reason to Celebrate

Food is not just about enjoyment and sustenance. Like everything in Balinese life, it is an intrinsic part of the daily rituals and a major part of ceremonies to honour the gods. The menu varies according to the importance of the occasion. By far the most revered dish is *babi guling* (suckling pig), presented during rites-of-passage ceremonies such as a baby's three-month blessing, an adolescent's tooth filing, or a wedding.

Babi guling is the quintessential Bali experience. A whole pig is stuffed with chilli, turmeric, ginger, galangal, shallots, garlic, coriander seeds and aromatic leaves, basted in turmeric and coconut oil and skewered on a wooden spit over an open fire. Turned for hours, the meat takes on the flavour of the spices and the fire-pit, giving a rustic smoky flavour to the crispy crackling.

Short of being invited to a ceremonial feast, you can enjoy *babi guling* at stands, warungs and cafes across Bali. Some good ones include the following:

➡ Warung Ibu Oka (p160) Ubud's touristy temple of tender pork.

➡ Warung Babi Guling Sanur (p115) The beachside city's roadside sensation.

➡ Bali Re (p243) Just the meal needed after a hard day diving off Pemuteran.

➡ Sari Kembar (p85) A much-lauded place for *babi* midway between Kerobokan and Denpasar.

➡ Gianyar Babi Guleng (p183) If you can't wait for Gianyar's great night market, stop in here.

Bebek or *ayam betutu* (smoked duck or chicken) is another ceremonial favourite. The bird is stuffed with spices, wrapped in coconut bark and banana leaves, and cooked all day over smouldering rice husks and coconut husks. Ubud is the best place to enjoy smoked duck – head to Bebek Bengil (p162) (it's actually the source for the many restaurants that offer *bebek betutu* if ordered in advance).

Often served at marriage ceremonies, *jukut ares* is a light, fragrant broth made from banana stem and usually containing chopped chicken or pork. The sate for special occasions, *sate lilit*, is a fragrant combination of good-quality minced fish, chicken or pork with lemon grass, galangal, shallots, chilli, palm sugar, kaffir lime and coconut milk. This is wrapped onto skewers and grilled.

Cradle of Flavor is a mouth-watering treatise on Indonesian foods and cooking by James Oseland, the editor of *Saveur* magazine.

Despite its name, mangosteen is not related to the mango. It is, however, a popular tropical fruit for the peach-like flavour and texture of its white centre, and is often called 'queen of fruit'.

Warungs

The most common place for dining out in Bali and Lombok is a warung, the traditional roadside eatery. There's one every few metres in major towns, and several even in small villages. They are cheap, no-frills hangouts with a relaxed atmosphere; you may find yourself sharing a table with strangers as you watch the world go by. The food is fresh and different at each, and is usually displayed in a glass cabinet at the entrance where you can create your own *nasi campur* or just order the house standard.

Both Seminyak and Kerobokan in particular are blessed with numerous warungs that are visitor-friendly.

The following list of our top warungs only scratches the surface. Many more are on offer – find your own favourite.

➡ Warung Satria (p122) A Denpasar classic serving wonderful fare.

➡ Nasi Ayam Kedewatan (p164) The place for *sate lilit* (minced fish, chicken or pork sate) in a simple open-front dining room on the edge of Ubud.

➡ Warung Kolega (p85) Excellent Balinese dishes by the dozen.

➡ Warung Sulawesi (p85) Delicious dishes from across the archipelago, served in a shady family courtyard.

➡ Warung Teges (p162) Great Balinese fare loved by locals, just south of Ubud.

Dining – or Not – Balinese Style

Eating is a solitary exercise in Bali and conversation is limited. Families rarely eat together; everyone makes up their own plate whenever they're hungry.

The Balinese eat with their right hand, which is used to give and receive all good things. The left hand deals with unpleasant sinister elements (such as ablutions). It's customary to wash your hands before eating, even if you use a spoon and fork; local restaurants always have a sink outside the restrooms. If you choose to eat the local way, use the bowl of water provided at the table to wash your hands after the meal, as licking your fingers is not appreciated.

Balinese are formal about behaviour and clothing, and it isn't polite to enter a restaurant or eat a meal half-naked, no matter how many sit-ups you've been doing or how many new piercings and tattoos you've acquired.

If you wish to eat in front of a Balinese, it's polite to invite them to join you, even if you know they will say 'no', or even if you don't have anything to offer. If you're invited to a Balinese home for a meal, your hosts will no doubt insist you eat more, but you may always politely pass on second helpings or refuse food you don't find appealing.

BALI EATS

For an exhaustive run-down of eating options in Bali, check out www.balieats.com. The listings are encyclopedic, continually updated and many have enthusiastic reviews.

FAST FOOD BALI STYLE

Usually the most authentic Balinese food is found street-side (although Denpasar has some sit-down places that are excellent). Locals of all stripes gather around simple food stalls in markets and on village streets, wave down *pedagang* (mobile traders) who ferry sweet and savoury snacks around by bicycle or motorcycle, and queue for sate or *bakso* (Chinese meatballs in a light soup) at the *kaki-lima* carts. *Kaki-lima* translates as something five-legged and refers to the three legs of the cart and the two of the vendor, who is usually Javanese.

One note on health: food cooked fresh from carts and stalls is usually fine but that which has been sitting around for a while can be dodgy at best or riddled with dubious preservatives.

VEGETARIAN DREAMS

Bali is a dream come true for vegetarians. Tofu and tempeh are part of the staple diet, and many tasty local favourites just happen to be vegetarian. Try *nasi sayur* (rice flavoured with toasted coconut and accompanied by tofu, tempeh, vegetables and sometimes egg), *urap* (a delightful blend of steamed vegetables mixed with grated coconut and spices), gado gado (tofu and tempeh mixed with steamed vegetables, boiled egg and peanut sauce), and *sayur hijau* (leafy green vegetables, usually *kangkung* – water spinach – flavoured with a tomato-chilli sauce).

In addition, the way *nasi campur* is served means it's easy to request no meat, instead enjoying an array of stir-fries, salads, tofu and tempeh. When ordering curries and stir-fries such as *cap cay* in Bali and Lombok, diners can usually choose meat, seafood or vegetarian.

Western-style vegetarian pasta and salads abound in most restaurants and many purely vegetarian eateries cater for vegans. Seminyak is good for meat-free fare while Ubud excels thanks to its yoga and healthy lifestyle ethos.

Drinks

Beer

Beer drinkers are well catered for in Bali thanks to Indonesia's crisp, clean national lager, Bintang. Bali Hai beer sounds promising but isn't.

Wine

Wine connoisseurs had better have a fat wallet. The abundance of high-end eateries and hotels has made fine vino from the world's best regions widely available but it is whacked with hefty taxes. Medium-grade bottles from Australia go for US$50.

Of the local producers of wine, the least objectionable is Artisan Estate, which overcomes the import duties by bringing in crushed grapes from Western Australia. Hatten Wine, based in north Bali, has gained quite a following among those who like its very sweet pink rosé. Two Islands also has a following.

Local Booze

At large social gatherings, Balinese men might indulge in *arak* (fermented wine made from rice or palms or...other materials) but generally they are not big drinkers. Watch out for adulterated *arak* (see p379), which is rare but can be poisonous. Lombok's majority Muslim population frowns upon alcohol consumption.

Fresh Juice

Local nonalcoholic refreshments available from markets, street vendors, some warungs and many cafes are tasty and even a little psychedelic (in colour) – and without the hangover! One of Bali's most popular is *cendol,* an interesting mix of palm sugar, fresh coconut milk, crushed ice and various other random flavourings and floaties.

Coffee & Tea

Many Western eateries sell imported coffees and teas alongside local brands, some of which are very good.

The most expensive – and over-hyped – is Indonesia's *kopi luwak*. About 200,000Rp a cup, this coffee is named after the cat-like civet *(luwak)* indigenous to Sulawesi, Sumatra and Java that feasts on ripe coffee cherries. Entrepreneurs initially collected the intact beans found in the civet's droppings and processed them to produce a supposedly extra-piquant brew. But now that interest in coffee *luwak* has exceeded all reason, trouble abounds, from fraudulent claims to documented animal mistreatment (see p173).

Admired Local Producers

Big Tree Farms – *chocolate, palm sugar*

FREAK Coffee – *coffee*

Kopi Bali – *coffee*

Sari Organik – *juices, teas*

If you happen to be drinking coffee with a Balinese person, don't be surprised if they tip the top layer of their coffee on the ground. This is an age-old protection against evil spirits.

M. GEBICKI / GETTY IMAGES ©

1. Bintang beer **2.** *Nasi campur* **3.** *Babi guling* at Warung Ibu Oka (p160), Ubud **4.** *Sate* with various sambals

CARLINA TETERIS / GETTY IMAGES ©

Top 5 Balinese Treats

Colourful, aromatic and fabulously flavourful, Bali's food (and drink) will have you coming back for more.

Babi Guling

What was once a dish reserved for special occasions is now one of Bali's favourite foods: *babi guling* (p327), a suckling pig filled with spices and roasted, is sold at scores of outlets.

Nasi Campur

Bali's equivalent of a national dish, this lunchtime staple (p325) defies description. At hundreds of warungs (food stalls) across the island you start with a plate and then select some rice (yellow? white? red?) and then the fun begins. Choose from an array of tempting meat, seafood and veggie dishes.

Sambal

There are as many variations on this staple condiment (p326) as there are versions of *nasi campur* and that's only fitting as it's the source of spicy heat in most Balinese foods. Chefs jealously guard their sambal recipes which are myriad.

Night Markets

Pasar malam (night markets) are popular sources for after-dark eats on Bali and Lombok. The best will have dozens of stalls and stands with staff cooking away like mad and offering a range of locally favourite dishes. Wander, browse and snack your way to joy.

Bintang

It's a marketer's dream: you don't say 'beer' on Bali, you say 'Bintang'. The beer that launched the branded singlet empire is a crisp, clean lager that refreshes on a hot day. Whether it's cooling off a fiery feast or making the sunset seem that much rosier, it goes down smoothly.

The Arts

Bali's vibrant arts scene makes the island so much more than just a tropical beach destination. In the paintings, sculpture, dance and music, you will see the natural artistic talent inherent in all Balinese, a legacy of their Majapahit heritage. The artistry displayed here will stay with you long after you've moved on from the island.

An Island of Artists

Colin McPhee's iconic book about Balinese dance and culture, *A House in Bali*, has been made into an opera of the same name. It's the creation of Evan Ziporyn, a composer who spends much time in Ubud.

It is telling that there is no Balinese equivalent for the words 'art' or 'artist'. Until the tourist invasion, artistic expression was exclusively for religious and ritual purposes, and was almost exclusively done by men. Paintings and carvings were purely to decorate temples and shrines, while music, dance and theatrical performances were put on to entertain the gods who returned to Bali for important ceremonies. Artists did not strive to be different or individual as many do in the West; their work reflected a traditional style or a new idea, but not their own personality.

That changed in the late 1920s when foreign artists began to settle in Ubud; they went to learn from the Balinese and to share their knowledge, and helped to establish art as a commercial enterprise. Today, it's big business. Ubud remains the undisputed artistic centre of the island, and artists come from near and far to draw on its inspiration, from Japanese glass-blowers to European photographers and Javanese painters.

Galleries and craft shops are all over the island; the paintings, stone-carvings and woodcarvings are stacked up on floors and will trip you up if you're not careful. Much of it is churned out quickly, and some is comically vulgar – put that 3m vision of a penis as Godzilla in your entryway, will you? – but there is also a great deal of extraordinary work.

There are some excellent crafts available on Lombok as well, including pottery in villages such as Banyumulek.

Dance
Bali

There are more than a dozen different dances in Bali, each with rigid choreography, each requiring high levels of discipline. Most performers have learned through painstaking practice with an expert. No visit is complete without enjoying this purely Balinese art form; you will be delighted by the many styles, from the formal artistry of the Legong to crowd-pleasing antics in the Barong. One thing Balinese dance is *not* is static. The best troupes, like Semara Ratih in Ubud, are continually innovating.

You can catch a quality dance performance at any place where there's a festival or celebration, and you'll find exceptional performances in and around Ubud. Performances are typically at night and last about 90 minutes; tickets are about 80,000Rp and you'll have a choice of eight or more performances a night.

With a little bit of research and some good timing, you can attend performances that are part of temple ceremonies. Here you'll see the full beauty of Bali's dance and music heritage as it was meant to be seen. Performances can last several hours. Absorb the hypnotic music and the alluring moves of the performers, as well as the rapt attention of the crowd. Music, theatre and dance courses are also available in Ubud.

With the short attention spans of tourists in mind, many hotels offer a smorgasbord of dances – a little Kecak, a taste of Barong and some Legong to round it off. These can be pretty abbreviated, with just a few musicians and a couple of dancers.

Kecak

Probably the best-known dance, for its spellbinding, hair-raising atmosphere, the Kecak features a 'choir' of men and boys who sit in concentric circles and slip into a trance as they chant and sing 'chak-a-chak-a-chak', imitating a troupe of monkeys. Sometimes called the 'vocal gamelan', this is the only music to accompany the dance re-enactment from the Hindu epic *Ramayana*, the familiar love story about Prince Rama and his Princess Sita.

The tourist version of Kecak was developed in the 1960s. This performance is easily found in Ubud (look for Krama Desa Ubud Kaja with its 80 shirtless men chanting hypnotically) and also at the Pura Luhur Ulu Watu.

Legong

Characterised by flashing eyes and quivering hands, this most graceful of Balinese dances is performed by young girls. Their talent is so revered that in old age, a classic dancer will be remembered as a 'great Legong'.

Peliatan's famous dance troupe, Gunung Sari, often seen in Ubud, is particularly noted for its Legong Keraton (Legong of the Palace). The very stylised and symbolic story involves two Legong dancing in mirror image. They are elaborately made up and dressed in gold brocade, relating a story about a king who takes a maiden captive and consequently starts a war, in which he dies.

Balinese Dance, Drama and Music: A Guide to the Performing Arts of Bali, by I Wayan Dibia and Rucina Ballinger, is a lavishly illustrated and highly recommended in-depth guide to Bali's cultural performances.

THE ARTS DANCE

MONKEYS & MONSTERS

The Barong and Rangda dance rivals the Kecak as Bali's most popular performance for tourists. Again, it's a battle between good (the Barong) and evil (the Rangda).

The Barong is a good but mischievous and fun-loving shaggy dog–lion, with huge eyes and a mouth that clacks away to much dramatic effect. Because this character is the good protector of a village, the actors playing the Barong (who are utterly lost under layers of fur-clad costume) will emote a variety of winsome antics. But as is typical of Balinese dance, it is not all light-hearted – the Barong is a very sacred character indeed and you'll often see one in processions and rituals.

There's nothing sacred about the Barong's buddies. One or more monkeys attend to him and these characters often steal the show. Actors are given free rein to range wildly. The best aim a lot of high-jinks at the audience, especially audience members who seem to be taking things a tad too seriously.

Meanwhile, the widow-witch Rangda is bad through and through. The Queen of Black Magic, the character's monstrous persona can include flames shooting out her ears, a tongue dripping fire, a mane of wild hair and large breasts.

The story features a duel between the Rangda and the Barong, whose supporters draw their kris (traditional dagger) and rush in to help. The long-tongued, sharp-fanged Rangda throws them into a trance, making them stab themselves. It's quite a spectacle. Thankfully, the Barong casts a spell that neutralises the kris power so it cannot harm them.

Playing around with all that powerful magic, good and bad, requires the presence of a pemangku (priest for temple rituals), who must end the dancers' trance and make a blood sacrifice using a chicken to propitiate the evil spirits.

In Ubud, Barong and Rangda dance troupes have many interpretations of the dance, everything from eerie performances that will give you the shivers (until the monkeys appear) to jokey versions that could be a variety show or Brit pantomime.

Barong masks are valued objects; you can find artful examples in Mas, south of Ubud.

Sanghyang & Kekac Fire Dance

Women often bring offerings to a temple while dancing the Pendet, their eyes, heads and hands moving in spectacularly controlled and coordinated movements. Every flick of the wrist, hand and fingers is charged with meaning.

These dances were developed to drive out evil spirits from a village – Sanghyang is a divine spirit who temporarily inhabits an entranced dancer. The Sanghyang Dedari is performed by two young girls who dance a dreamlike version of the Legong in perfect symmetry while their eyes are firmly shut. Male and female choirs provide a background chant until the dancers slump to the ground. A *pemangku* (priest for temple rituals) blesses them with holy water and brings them out of the trance.

In the Sanghyang Jaran, a boy in a trance dances around and through a fire of coconut husks, riding a coconut palm 'hobby horse'. Variations of this are called the Kecak Fire Dance and are performed in Ubud almost daily.

Other Dances

The warrior dance, the Baris, is a male equivalent of the Legong – grace and femininity give way to an energetic and warlike spirit. The highly skilled Baris dancer must convey the thoughts and emotions of a warrior first preparing for action, and then meeting the enemy: chivalry, pride, anger, prowess and, finally, regret are illustrated.

In the Topeng, which means 'pressed against the face', as with a mask, the dancers imitate the character represented by the mask. This requires great expertise because the dancer cannot convey thoughts and meanings through facial expressions – the dance must tell all.

Lombok

Lombok has its own unique dances, but they are not widely marketed. Performances are staged in some top-end hotels and in Lenek village, known for its dance traditions. If you're in Senggigi in July, you might catch dance and *gendang beleq* (big drum) performances. The *gendang beleq*, a dramatic war dance also called the Oncer, is performed by men and boys who play a variety of unusual musical instruments for *adat* (traditional customs) festivals in central and eastern Lombok.

Music

Bali

Balinese music is based around an ensemble known as a gamelan, also called a *gong*. A *gong gede* (large orchestra) is the traditional form, with 35 to 40 musicians. The more ancient gamelan *selunding* is still occasionally played in Bali Aga villages such as Tenganan.

The popular modern form of a *gong gede* is *gong kebyar*, with up to 25 instruments. This melodic, sometimes upbeat and sometimes haunting percussion that often accompanies traditional dance is one of the most lasting impressions for tourists to Bali.

Preserving and performing rare and ancient Balinese dance and gamelan music is the mission of Mekar Bhuana (www.balimusicanddance.com), a Denpasar-based cultural group. They sponsor performances and offer lessons.

The prevalent voice in Balinese music is from the xylophone-like *gangsa,* which the player hits with a hammer, dampening the sound just after it's struck. The tempo and nature of the music is controlled by two *kendang* (drums), one male and one female. Other instruments are the deep *trompong* drums, small *kempli* gong and *cengceng* (cymbals) used in faster pieces. Not all instruments require great skill and making music is a common village activity.

Many shops in south Bali and Ubud sell the distinctive gongs, flutes, bamboo xylophones and bamboo chimes, and CDs are everywhere.

Lombok

The *genggong*, a performance seen on Lombok, uses a simple set of instruments, including a bamboo flute, a *rebab* (two-stringed bowed lute) and knockers. Seven musicians accompany their music with dance movements and stylised hand gestures.

Wayang Kulit

Much more than sheer entertainment, *wayang kulit* has been Bali's candle-lit cinema for centuries, embodying the sacred seriousness of classical Greek drama. (The word drama comes from the Greek *dromenon,* a religious ritual.) The performances are long and intense – lasting six hours or more and often not finishing before sunrise.

Originally used to bring ancestors back to this world, the shows feature painted buffalo-hide puppets believed to have great spiritual power, and the *dalang* (puppet master and storyteller) is an almost mystical figure. A person of considerable skill and even greater endurance, the *dalang* sits behind a screen and manipulates the puppets while telling the story, often in many dialects.

Stories are chiefly derived from the great Hindu epics, the *Ramayana* and, to a lesser extent, the *Mahabharata.*

You can find performances in Ubud, which are attenuated to a manageable two hours or less.

An *arja* drama is not unlike *wayang kulit* puppet shows in its melodramatic plots, its offstage sound effects and its cast of easily identifiable goodies (the refined *alus*) and baddies (the unrefined *kras*). It's performed outside and a small house is sometimes built on stage and set on fire at the show's climax!

Painting

Balinese painting is probably the art form most influenced by Western ideas and demand. Traditional paintings, faithfully depicting religious and mythological subjects, were for temple and palace decoration, and the set colours were made from soot, clay and pigs' bones. In the 1930s, Western artists introduced the concept of paintings as artistic creations that could also be sold for money. To target the tourist market, they encouraged deviance to scenes from everyday life and the use of the full palette of modern paints and tools. The range of themes, techniques, styles and materials expanded enormously, and women painters emerged for the first time.

A loose classification of styles is classical, or Kamasan, named for the village of Kamasan near Semarapura; Ubud style, developed in the 1930s under the influence of the Pita Maha; Batuan, which started at the same time in a nearby village; Young Artists, begun post-war in the 1960s, and influenced by Dutch artist Arie Smit; and finally, modern or academic, free in its creative topics, yet strongly and distinctively Balinese.

INFLUENTIAL WESTERN ARTISTS

Besides Arie Smit, several other Western artists had a profound effect on Balinese art in the early and middle parts of the 20th century. In addition to honouring Balinese art, they provided a critical boost to its vitality at a time when it might have died out.

Walter Spies (1895–1942) A German artist, Spies first visited Bali in 1925 and moved to Ubud in 1927, establishing the image of Bali for Westerners that prevails today.

Rudolf Bonnet (1895–1978) Bonnet was a Dutch artist whose work concentrated on the human form and everyday Balinese life. Many classical Balinese paintings with themes of markets and cockfights are indebted to Bonnet.

Miguel Covarrubias (1904–57) *Island of Bali,* written by this Mexican artist, is still the classic introduction to the island and its culture.

Colin McPhee (1900–65) A Canadian musician, McPhee wrote *A House in Bali.* It remains one of the best written accounts of Bali, and his tales of music and house building are often highly amusing. His patronage of traditional dance and music cannot be overstated.

Adrien Jean Le Mayeur de Merpres (1880–1958) This Belgian artist arrived on Bali in 1932 and did much to establish the notions of sensual Balinese beauty, often based on his wife, the dancer Ni Polok. Their home is now an under-appreciated museum in Sanur.

Where to See & Buy Paintings

There is a relatively small number of creative original painters in Bali, and an enormous number of imitators. Shops, especially in south Bali, are packed full of paintings in whatever style is popular at the time – some are quite good and a few are really excellent (and in many you'll swear you see the numbers used to guide the artists under the paint).

Top museums in Ubud, such as the Neka Art Museum, Agung Rai Museum of Art and the Museum Puri Lukisan, showcase the best of Balinese art and some of the European influences that have shaped it. Look for the innovative work of women artists at Ubud's Seniwati Gallery.

Commercial galleries such as Ubud's Neka Gallery and Agung Rai Gallery offer high-quality works. Exploring the dizzying melange of galleries – high and low – makes for a fun afternoon or longer.

Classical Painting

There are three basic types of classical painting – *langse, iders-iders* and calendars. *Langse* are large decorative hangings for palaces or temples that display *wayang* figures (which have an appearance similar to the figures used in shadow puppetry), rich floral designs and flame-and-mountain motifs. *Iders-iders* are scroll paintings hung along temple eaves. Calendars are used to set dates for rituals and predict the future.

Langse paintings helped impart *adat* (traditional customs) to ordinary people in the same way that traditional dance and *wayang kulit* puppetry do. The stylised human figures depicted good and evil, with romantic heroes like Ramayana and Arjuna always painted with small, narrow eyes and fine features, while devils and warriors were prescribed round eyes, coarse features and facial hair. The paintings tell a story in a series of panels, rather like a comic strip, and often depict scenes from the *Ramayana* and *Mahabharata*. Other themes are the Kakawins poems, and demonic spirits from indigenous Balinese folklore – see the ceilings of the Kertha Gosa (Hall of Justice) in Semarapura for an example.

A good place to see classical painting in a modern context is at the Nyoman Gunarsa Museum near Semarapura, which was established to preserve and promote classical techniques.

The Pita Maha

In the 1930s, with few commissions from temples, painting was virtually dying out. European artists Rudolf Bonnet and Walter Spies, with their patron Cokorda Gede Agung Surapati, formed the Pita Maha (literally, Great Vitality) to take painting from a ritual-based activity to a commercial one. The cooperative had more than 100 members at its peak in the 1930s and led to the establishment of Museum Puri Lukisan in Ubud, the first museum dedicated to Balinese art.

The changes Bonnet and Spies inspired were revolutionary. Balinese artists such as the late I Gusti Nyoman Lempad started exploring their own styles. Narrative tales were replaced by single scenes, and romantic legends by daily life: the harvest, markets, cockfights, offerings at a temple or a cremation. These paintings were known as Ubud style.

Meanwhile, painters from Batuan retained many features of classical painting. They depicted daily life, but across many scenes – a market, dance and rice harvest would all appear in a single work. This Batuan style is also noted for its inclusion of some very modern elements, such as sea scenes with the odd windsurfer.

The painting techniques also changed. Modern paint and materials were used and stiff formal poses gave way to realistic 3-D representations. More importantly, pictures were not just painted to fit a space in a palace or a temple.

TREASURES OF BALI

Treasures of Bali, by Richard Mann, is a beautifully illustrated guide to Bali's museums, big and small. It highlights the gems often overlooked by group tours.

In one way, the style remained unchanged – Balinese paintings are packed with detail. A painted Balinese forest, for example, has branches, leaves and a whole zoo of creatures reaching out to fill every tiny space.

This new artistic enthusiasm was interrupted by WWII and Indonesia's independence struggle, and stayed that way until the development of the young artists' style.

The Young Artists

Arie Smit was in Penestanan, just outside Ubud, in 1956, when he noticed an 11-year-old boy drawing in the dirt. Smit wondered what the boy could produce if he had the proper equipment. As the legend goes, the boy's father would not allow him to take up painting until Smit offered to pay somebody else to watch the family's ducks.

Other 'young artists' soon joined that first pupil, I Nyoman Cakra, but Smit did not actively teach them. He simply provided the equipment and encouragement, unleashing what was clearly a strong natural talent. Today, this style of rural scenes painted in brilliant Technicolor is a staple of Balinese tourist art.

I Nyoman Cakra still lives in Penestanan, still paints, and cheerfully admits that he owes it all to Smit. Other 'young artists' include I Ketut Tagen, I Nyoman Tjarka and I Nyoman Mujung.

Other Styles

There are some other variants to the main Ubud and young artists' painting styles. The depiction of forests, flowers, butterflies, birds and other naturalistic themes, for example, sometimes called Pengosekan style, became popular in the 1960s. It can probably be traced back to Henri Rousseau, who was a significant influence on Walter Spies. An interesting development in this particular style is the depiction of underwater scenes, with colourful fish, coral gardens and sea creatures. Somewhere between the Pengosekan and Ubud styles sit the miniature landscape paintings that are popular commercially.

A carefully selected list of books about art, culture and Balinese writers, dancers and musicians can be found at www. ganeshabooks bali.com, the website for the excellent Ubud bookstore (with branches in Kerobokan and Sanur).

TODAY'S BALINESE PAINTERS

Numerous Balinese artists are receiving international recognition for their work, which often has a strong theme of social justice and a questioning of modern values. Still, being Balinese and all, the works have a sly wit and even a wink to the viewer. Some names to watch for:

Nyoman Masriadi Born in Gianyar, Masriadi is easily the superstar of Bali's current crop of painters, and his works sell for upwards of a million dollars. He is renowned for his sharp-eyed observations of Indonesian society today and his thoroughly modern techniques and motifs.

Made Djirna Hailing from the comparatively wealthy tourist town of Ubud, Djirna has the perfect background for his works, which criticise the relationship between ostentatious money and modern Balinese religious ceremonies.

Agung Mangu Putra This painter from the deeply green hills west of Ubud finds inspiration in the Balinese people being bypassed by the island's uneven economic boom. He decries the impact on his natural world.

Wayan Sudarna Putra Uses satire and parody in his works, which cross media to question the absurdities of current Indonesian life and values. An Ubud native.

Gede Suanda Sayur His works are often dark as he questions the pillaging of Bali's environment. He joined Putra to create an installation in a rice field near Ubud that featured huge white poles spelling out 'Not for sale'.

The new techniques also resulted in radically new versions of Rangda, Barong, Hanuman and other figures from Balinese and Hindu mythology. Scenes from folk tales and stories appeared, featuring dancers, nymphs and love stories, with an understated erotic appeal.

Crafts

Bali is a showroom for crafts from around Indonesia. The nicer tourist shops will sell puppets and batiks from Java, ikat garments from Sumba, Sumbawa and Flores, and textiles and woodcarvings from Bali, Lombok and Kalimantan. The kris, so important to a Balinese family, will often have been made in Java.

On Lombok, where there's never been much money, traditional handicrafts are practical items, but they are still skilfully made and beautifully finished. The finer examples of Lombok weaving, basketware and pottery are highly valued by collectors.

Textiles & Weaving

Bali

Textiles in Bali and Lombok are woven by women for daily wear and ceremonies, as well as for gifts. They are often part of marriage dowries and cremations, where they join the deceased's soul as it passes to the afterlife.

The most common material in Bali is the sarong, which can be used as an article of clothing, a sheet or a towel, among other things. The cheap cottons, either plain or printed, are for everyday use, and are popular with tourists for beachwear.

For special occasions such as a temple ceremony, Balinese men and women use a *kamben* (a length of *songket* wrapped around the chest). The *songket* is silver- or gold-threaded cloth, hand woven using a floating weft technique, while another variety is the *endek* (like *songket,* but with pre-dyed weft threads).

The men pair the *kamben* with a shirt and the women pair it with a *kebaya* (long-sleeved lace blouse). A separate slim strip of cloth known as a *kain* (or known as *prada* when decorated with a gold leaf pattern) is wound tightly around the hips and over the sarong like a belt to complete the outfit.

Where to Buy

Any market, especially in Denpasar, will have a good range of textiles. Oftentimes groups of textiles stores will cluster on one street, such as Jl Sulawesi across from the main market in Denpasar and Jl Arjuna in Legian. Threads of Life in Ubud is a Fair Trade–certified textiles gallery that preserves traditional Balinese and Indonesian hand-weaving skills. Factories around Gianyar in east Bali and Blahbatuh southeast of Ubud have large showrooms.

For exquisite work, seek out Gusti Ayu Made Mardiani's home and workshop Jepun Bali (p123) in southern Denpasar.

Batik

Traditional batik sarongs, which fall somewhere between a cotton sarong and *kamben* for formality, are handmade in central Java. The dyeing process has been adapted by the Balinese to produce brightly coloured and patterned fabrics. Watch out for 'batik' that has been screenprinted: the colours will be washed out and the pattern is often only on one side (the dye in proper batik should colour both sides to reflect the belief that the body should feel what the eye sees).

COMICAL INSIGHTS

The magazine/ comic *Bog Bog*, by Balinese cartoonists, is a satirical and humorous insight into the contrast between modern and traditional worlds in Bali. It's available in warungs, bookshops and supermarkets or online at www. bogbogcartoon. com.

Ikat

Ikat involves dyeing either the warp threads (those stretched on the loom) or weft threads (those woven across the warp) before the material is woven. The resulting pattern is geometric and slightly wavy. The colouring typically follows a similar tone – blues and greens; reds and browns; or yellows, reds and oranges. Gianyar, in east Bali, has a few factories where you can watch ikat sarongs being woven on a hand-and-foot-powered loom. A complete sarong takes about six hours to make.

Lombok

Lombok is renowned for traditional weaving on backstrap looms, the techniques handed down from mother to daughter. Abstract flower and animal motifs such as buffalo, dragons, crocodiles and snakes sometimes decorate this exquisite cloth. Several villages specialise in weaving cloth, while others concentrate on fine baskets and mats woven from *rotan* (hardy, pliable vine) or grass. You can visit factories around Cakranegara and Mataram that produce weft ikat on old hand-and-foot-operated looms.

Sukarara and Pringgasela are centres for traditional ikat and *songket* weaving. Sarongs, Sasak belts and clothing edged with brightly coloured embroidery are sold in small shops.

Woodcarving

Woodcarving in Bali has evolved from its traditional use for doors and columns, religious figures and theatrical masks to modern forms encompassing a wide range of styles. While Tegallalang and Jati, on the road north from Ubud, are noted woodcarving centres, along with the route

---

OFFERINGS: FLEETING BEAUTY

Traditionally, many of Bali's most elaborate crafts have been ceremonial offerings not intended to last: *baten tegeh* (decorated pyramids of fruit, rice cakes and flowers); rice-flour cookies modelled into entire scenes with a deep symbolic significance and tiny sculptures; *lamak* (long, woven palm-leaf strips used as decorations in festivals and celebrations); stylised female figures known as *cili*, which are representations of Dewi Sri (the rice goddess); and intricately carved coconut-shell wall hangings.

Tourists in Bali may be welcomed as honoured guests, but the real VIPs are the gods, ancestors, spirits and demons. They are presented with these offerings throughout each day to show respect and gratitude, or perhaps to bribe a demon into being less mischievous. Marvel at the care and energy that goes into constructing huge funeral towers and exotic sarcophagi, all of which will go up in flames.

A gift to a higher being must look attractive, so each offering is a work of art. The most common is a palm-leaf tray little bigger than a saucer, artfully topped with flowers, food (especially rice, and modern touches such as Ritz crackers or individually wrapped lollies) and small change, crowned with a *saiban* (temple or shrine offering). More important shrines and occasions call for more elaborate offerings, which can include the colourful towers of fruits and cakes called *baten tegeh*, and even entire animals cooked and ready to eat, as in Bali's famous *babi guling* (suckling pig).

Once presented to the gods an offering cannot be used again, so new ones are made each day, usually by women. You'll see easy-to-assemble offerings for sale in markets, much as you'd find quick dinner items in Western supermarkets.

Offerings to the gods are placed on high levels, and those to the demons on the ground. Don't worry about stepping on these; given their ubiquity, it's almost impossible not to (just don't try to). In fact, at Bemo Corner in Kuta offerings are left at the shrine in the middle of the road and are quickly flattened by cars. Across the island, dogs with a taste for crackers hover around fresh offerings. Given the belief that gods or demons instantly derive the essence of an offering, the critters are really just getting leftovers.

KRIS: SACRED BLADES

Usually adorned with an ornate, jewel-studded handle and a sinister-looking wavy blade, the kris is Bali's traditional, ceremonial dagger, dating back to the Majapahit era. A kris is often the most important of family heirlooms, a symbol of prestige and honour and a work of high-end art. Made by a master craftsperson, it's believed to have great spiritual power, sending out magical energy waves and thus requiring great care in its handling and use. Many owners will only clean the blade with waters from Sungai Pakerisan (Pakerisan River) in east Bali, because it is thought to be the magical 'River of Kris'.

Balinese men literally will judge each other in a variation of 'show me your kris'. The size of the blade, the number owned, the quality, the artistry of the handles and much more will go into forming a judgement of a man and his kris. Handles are considered separately from a kris (the blade). As a man's fortunes allow, he will upgrade the handles in his collection. But the kris itself remains sacred – often you will see offerings beside ones on display. The undulations in the blade (called *lok*) have many meanings and there's always an odd number – three, for instance, means passion.

The Museum Negeri Propinsi Bali in Denpasar has a rich kris collection.

from Mas through Peliatan, you can find pieces in any souvenir store. See beautiful work and possibly try your hand at creating some of your own at the workshop of Ida Bagus Anom Suryawan (p148) in Mas.

The common style of a slender, elongated figure reportedly first appeared after Walter Spies gave a woodcarver a long piece of wood and commissioned him to carve two sculptures from it. The carver couldn't bring himself to cut it in half, instead making a single figure of a tall, slim dancer.

Other typical works include classical religious figures, animal caricatures, life-size human skeletons, picture frames, and whole tree trunks carved into ghostly 'totem poles'. In Kuta there are various objects targeting beer drinkers: penis bottle openers (which are claimed to be Bali's bestselling souvenir) and signs to sit above your bar bearing made-to-order slogans.

Almost all carving is of local woods including *belalu* (quick-growing light wood) and the stronger fruit timbers such as jackfruit wood. Ebony from Sulawesi is also used. Sandalwood, with its delightful fragrance, is expensive and soft and is used for some small, very detailed pieces, but beware of widespread fakery.

On Lombok, carving usually decorates functional items such as containers for tobacco and spices, and the handles of betel-nut crushers and knives. Materials include wood, horn and bone, and you'll see these used in the recent trend: primitive-style elongated masks. Cakranegara, Sindu, Labuapi and Senanti are centres for carving on the island.

Wooden articles lose moisture when moved to a drier environment. Avoid possible shrinkage – especially of your penis bottle opener – by placing the carving in a plastic bag at home, and letting some air in for about one week every month for four months.

Masks used in theatre and dance performances such as the Topeng require a specialised form of woodcarving. The mask master – always a man – must know the movements each performer uses so the character can be accurately depicted in the mask. These masks are believed to possess magical qualities and can even have the ability to stare down bad spirits.

Other masks, such as the Barong and Rangda, are brightly painted and decorated with real hair, enormous teeth and bulging eyes.

Puaya near Sukawati, south of Ubud, is a centre of mask carving. You can visit workshops there and see all manner of ceremonial art being created. The Museum Negeri Propinsi Bali in Denpasar has an extensive mask collection, so you can get acquainted with different styles before buying.

Stone Carving

Traditionally for temple adornment, stone sculptures now make popular souvenirs ranging from frangipani reliefs to quirky ornaments that display the Balinese sense of humour: a frog clutching a leaf as an umbrella, or a weird demon on the side of a bell clasping his hands over his ears in mock offence.

At temples, you will see stone carving in set places. Door guardians are usually a protective personality such as Arjuna. Kala's monstrous face often peers out above the main entrance, his hands reaching to catch evil spirits. The side walls of a *pura dalem* (temple of the dead) might feature sculpted panels showing the horrors awaiting evildoers in the afterlife.

Among Bali's most ancient stone carvings are the scenes of people fleeing a great monster at Goa Gajah, the so-called 'Elephant Cave', believed to date to the 11th century. Inside the cave, a statue of Ganesha, the elephant-like god, gives the rock its name. Along the road through Muncan in east Bali you'll see roadside factories where huge temple decorations are carved in the open.

Much of the local work is made in Batubulan from grey volcanic stone called *paras,* so soft it can be scratched with a fingernail (which, according to legend, is how the giant Kebo Iwa created the Elephant Cave).

Pottery

Pejaten, near Tabanan, has a number of pottery workshops producing ceramic figures and glazed ornamental roof tiles. Stunning collections of designer, contemporary glazed ceramics are produced at Jenggala Keramik in Jimbaran, which also hosts exhibitions of various Indonesian art and antiques.

Earthenware pots have been produced on Lombok for centuries. They're shaped by hand, coated with a slurry of clay or ash to enhance the finish, and fired in a simple kiln filled with burning rice stalks. Pots are often finished with a covering of woven cane for decoration and extra strength. Newer designs feature bright colours and elaborate decorations. You can see these *gerabah* works being created today at the village of Penujak in south Lombok near the airport.

Jewellery

Silversmiths and goldsmiths are traditionally members of the *pande* caste, which also incudes blacksmiths and other metalworkers. Bali is a major producer of fashion jewellery and produces variations on currently fashionable designs.

Very fine filigree work is a Balinese speciality, as is the use of tiny spots of silver to form a pattern or decorative texture – this is considered a very skilled technique, because the heat must be perfectly controlled to weld the delicate wire or silver spots to the underlying silver without damaging it. Balinese work is nearly always handmade, rarely involving casting techniques.

Expat John Hardy built an empire worth hundreds of millions of dollars by adapting old Balinese silver designs along with his own beautiful innovations before he sold his company and started building bamboo buildings. Meanwhile Ubud, especially upper Jl Hanoman, has numerous creative silver jewellery shops.

The nonprofit Lontar Foundation (www.lontar. org) works to get Indonesian books translated into English so that universities around the world can offer courses in Indonesian literature.

YUNAIDI JOEPOET / GETTY IMAGES ©

1. Double ikat weaving 2. Stone dragon 3. Kecak performance
4. Barong mask, Garuda Wisnu Kencana Cultural Park (p99)

Top 5 Arts Experiences

For such a little island, there's a lot of art on Bali. From works created by hand to performances using hands, Balinese art is all-encompassing.

Ikat

At an ikat factory you may find the frenetic clacking of dozens of ancient wooden looms hypnotic or cacophonous, but you'll likely find the results beautiful. Traditionally dyed threads are woven together to form beautiful and distinctly handmade patterns (p339).

Legong Dancing

The movements of the best Legong dancers (p333) seem impossibly robotic and rigidly controlled. Young girls and women dressed in tight-embroidered and gold-highlighted finery perform rigorous dances with precise movements of their eyes and virtually every muscle. Watch their hands as they create the flights of butterflies.

Kecak Chanting

You'll be haunted for hours after you see a Kecak performance (p333). The sounds of dozens of men chanting and singing for more than an hour is bewitching and you may find you're slipping into a trance not unlike the performers. The sounds are rhythmic, the effect mesmerising.

Barong & Rangda

With a brightly coloured mask, Barongs (p333) are hard to miss in performance – and that's before you take in the rest of their huge shaggy costume. Representing good, Barongs clack their wooden mouths and generally do their best to steal the spotlight from their evil counterpart, Rangda.

Stone Carving

If Indiana Jones hired an artist it would be a Balinese carver. Using the island's soft volcanic stone, these craftspeople create elaborate designs that quickly age, so that a new temple soon looks like an ancient wonder (p341).

Architecture

Design is part of Bali's spiritual heritage and gives the look of traditional homes, temples and even modern buildings, such as resorts. Bali style is timeless, whether it is centuries old or embodied in a new hip villa. And it's not static; Bali is the site of world renowned architecture made with renewable materials like bamboo.

Architecture & Life

Architecture brings together the living and the dead, pays homage to the gods and wards off evil spirits, not to mention the torrential rain. As spiritual as it is functional, as mystical as it is beautiful, Balinese architecture has a life force of its own.

On an island bound by deep-rooted religious and cultural rituals, the priority of any design is appeasing the ancestral and village gods. This means reserving the holiest (northeast) location in every land space for the village temple, the same corner in every home for the family temple, and providing a comfortable, pleasing atmosphere to entice the gods back to Bali for ceremonies.

So while it exudes beauty, balance, age-old wisdom and functionality, a Balinese home is not a commodity designed with capital appreciation in mind; even while an increasing number of rice farmers sell their ancestral land to foreigners for villa developments, they're keeping the parcel on which their home stands.

The various open-air *bale* (pavilions) in family compounds are where visitors are received. Typically, drinks and small cakes will be served and friendly conversations will ensue for possibly an hour or more before the purpose of a visit is discussed.

Preserving the Cosmic Order

A village, a temple, a family compound, an individual structure – and even a single part of the structure – must all conform to the Balinese concept of cosmic order. It consists of three parts that represent the three worlds of the cosmos – *swah* (the world of gods), *bhwah* (world of humans) and *bhur* (world of demons). The concept also represents a three-part division of a person: *utama* (the head), *madia* (the body) and *nista* (the legs). The units of measurement used in traditional buildings are directly based on the anatomical dimensions of the head of the household, ensuring harmony between the dwelling and those who live in it.

The design is traditionally done by an *undagi* (a combination architect-priest); it must maintain harmony between god, man and nature under the concept of Tri Hita Karana. If it's not quite right, the universe may fall off balance and no end of misfortune and ill health will visit the community involved.

Building on the Bale

The basic element of Balinese architecture is the *bale*, a rectangular, open-sided pavilion with a steeply pitched roof of thatch. Both a family compound and a temple will comprise of a number of separate *bale* for specific functions, all surrounded by a high wall. The size and proportions of the *bale*, the number of columns and the position within the compound are all determined according to tradition and the owner's caste status.

The focus of a community is a large pavilion, called the *bale banjar,* used for meetings, debates and gamelan practice, among many other activities. You'll find that large modern buildings such as restaurants and the lobby areas of resorts are often modelled on the larger *bale,* and they can be airy, spacious and very handsomely proportioned.

The Family Compound

The Balinese house looks inward – the outside is simply a high wall. Inside there is a garden and a separate small building or *bale* for each activity – one for cooking, one for washing and the toilet, and separate buildings for each 'bedroom'. In Bali's mild tropical climate people live outside, so the 'living room' and 'dining room' will be open verandah areas, looking out into the garden. The whole complex is oriented on the *kaja–kelod* (towards the mountains–towards the sea) axis.

TYPICAL FAMILY COMPOUND

The following are elements commonly found in family compounds. Although there are variations, the designs are surprisingly similar, especially given they occur thousands of times across Bali.

Sanggah or Merajan Family temple, which is always at the *kaja–kangin* (sunrise in the direction of the mountains) corner of the courtyard. There will be shrines to the Hindu 'trinity' of Brahma, Shiva and Vishnu, and to *taksu,* the divine intermediary.

Umah Meten Sleeping pavilion for the family head.

Tugu Shrine to god of evil spirits in the compound but at the far *kaja–kuah* (sunset in the direction of the mountains) corner; by employing the chief evil spirit as a guard, others will stay away.

Pengijeng Small shrine amid the compound's open space, dedicated to the spirit who is the guardian of the property.

Bale Tiang Sanga Guest pavilion, also known as the *bale duah.* Literally the family room, it's used as a gathering place, offering workplace or temporary quarters of lesser sons and their families before they establish their own home.

Natah Courtyard with frangipani or hibiscus shade trees, with a few chickens pecking about.

Bale Sakenam or Bale Dangin Working and sleeping pavilion; may be used for important family ceremonies.

Fruit trees & coconut palms Serve both practical and decorative purposes. Fruit trees are often mixed with flowering trees such as hibiscus, and caged song birds hang from the branches.

Vegetable garden Small; usually just for a few spices not grown on larger plots.

Bale Sakepat Sleeping pavilion for children; highly optional.

Paon Kitchen; always in the south, as that direction is associated with Brahma, god of fire.

Lumbung Rice barn – the domain of both the precious grain and the Dewi Sri, the rice goddess. It's elevated to discourage rice-eating pests.

Rice-threshing area Important for farmers to prepare rice for cooking or storage.

Aling Aling Screen wall requiring visitors to turn a sharp left or right. This ensures both privacy from passers-by and protection from demons, which the Balinese believe cannot turn corners.

Candi Kurung Gate with a roof, resembling a mountain or tower split in half.

Apit Lawang or Pelinggah Gate shrines, which continually receive offerings to recharge the gate's ability to repel evil spirits.

Pigsty or garbage pit Always in the *kangin–kelod* (sunrise in the direction away from the mountains) corner, the compound's waste goes here.

Homes from Head to...

Analogous to the human body, compounds have a head (the family temple with its ancestral shrine), arms (the sleeping and living areas), legs and feet (the kitchen and rice storage building), and even an anus (the garbage pit or pigsty). There may be an area outside the house compound where fruit trees are grown or a pig is kept.

There are several variations on the typical family compound. For example, the entrance is commonly on the *kuah* (sunset side), rather than the *kelod* (away from the mountains and towards the sea) side, but *never* on the *kangin* (sunrise) or *kaja* (in the direction of the mountains) side.

Traditional Balinese homes are found in every region of the island; Ubud remains an excellent place to see them simply because of the concentration of homes there. Many accept guests. South of Ubud, you can enjoy an in-depth tour of the Nyoman Suaka Home (p176) in Singapadu.

Temples

Every village in Bali has several temples, and every home has at least a simple house-temple. The Balinese word for temple is *pura,* from a Sanskrit word literally meaning 'a space surrounded by a wall'. Similar to a traditional Balinese home, a temple is walled in – so the shrines you see in rice fields or at 'magical' spots such as old trees are not real temples. Simple shrines or thrones often overlook crossroads, to protect passers-by.

All temples are built on a mountains–sea orientation, not north–south. The direction towards the mountains, *kaja,* is the end of the temple, where the holiest shrines are found. The temple's entrance is at the *kelod. Kangin* is more holy than the *kuah,* so many secondary shrines are on the *kangin* side. *Kaja* may be towards a particular mountain – Pura Besakih in east Bali is pointed directly towards Gunung Agung – or towards the mountains in general, which run east–west along the length of Bali.

Temple Types

There are three basic temple types found in most villages. The most important is the *pura puseh* (temple of origin), dedicated to the village founders and at the *kaja* end of the village. In the middle of the village is the *pura desa,* for the many spirits that protect the village community in daily life. At the *kelod* end of the village is the *pura dalem* (temple of the dead). The graveyard is also here, and the temple may include representations of Durga, the terrible side of Shiva's wife Parvati. Both Shiva and Parvati have a creative and destructive side; their destructive powers are honoured in the *pura dalem.*

Other temples include those dedicated to the spirits of irrigated agriculture. Because rice growing is so important in Bali, and the division of water for irrigation is handled with the utmost care, these *pura subak* or *pura ulun suwi* (temple of the rice-growers association) can be of considerable importance. Other temples may also honour dry-field agriculture, as well as the flooded rice paddies.

In addition to these 'local' temples, there are a lesser number of great temples. Often a kingdom would have three of these temples that sit at the very top of the temple pecking order: a main state temple in the heartland of the state (such as Pura Taman Ayun, p248) in Mengwi, western Bali); a mountain temple (such as Pura Besakih, p188, eastern Bali); and a sea temple (such as Pura Luhur Ulu Watu, p103), southern Bali).

Every house in Bali has its house temple, which is at the *kaja–kangin* corner of the courtyard and has at least five shrines.

Temple Decoration

Temples and their decoration are closely linked on Bali. A temple gateway is not just erected; every square centimetre of it is carved in sculptural relief and a diminishing series of demon faces is placed above it as protection. Even then, it's not complete without several stone statues to act as guardians.

The level of decoration inside varies. Sometimes a temple is built with minimal decoration in the hope that sculpture can be added when more funds are available. The sculpture can also deteriorate after a few years

---

TYPICAL TEMPLE ELEMENTS

No two temples on Bali are identical. Variations in style, size, importance, wealth, purpose and much more result in near infinite variety. But there are common themes and elements. Use this as a guide and see how many design elements you can find in each Balinese temple you visit.

Candi Bentar The intricately sculpted temple gateway, like a tower split down the middle and moved apart, symbolises that you are entering a sanctum. It can be quite grand, with auxiliary entrances on either side for daily use.

Kulkul Tower The warning-drum tower, from which a wooden split drum (kulkul) is sounded to announce events at the temple or warn of danger.

Bale A pavilion, usually open-sided, for temporary use or storage. It may include a bale gong, where the gamelan orchestra plays at festivals; a paon, or temporary kitchen, to prepare offerings; or a wantilan, a stage for dances or cockfights.

Kori Agung or Paduraksa The gateway to the inner courtyard is an intricately sculpted stone tower. Entry is through a doorway reached by steps in the middle of the tower and left open during festivals.

Raksa or Dwarapala Statues of fierce guardian figures who protect the doorway and deter evil spirits. Above the door will be the equally fierce face of a Bhoma, with hands outstretched against unwanted spirits.

Aling Aling If an evil spirit does get in, this low wall behind the entrance will keep it at bay, as evil spirits find it difficult to make sharp turns. (Also found in family compounds.)

Side Gate (Betelan) Most of the time (except during ceremonies), entry to the inner courtyard is through this side gate, which is always open.

Small Shrines (Gedong) These usually include shrines to Ngrurah Alit and Ngrurah Gede, who organise things and ensure the correct offerings are made.

Padma Stone Throne for the sun god Surya, placed in the most auspicious kaja-kangin (sunrise in the direction of the mountains) corner. It rests on the badawang (world turtle), which is held by two naga (mythical snakelike creatures).

Meru A multiroofed shrine. Usually there is an 11-roofed meru to Sanghyang Widi, the supreme Balinese deity, and a three-roofed meru (10B) to the holy mountain Gunung Agung. However, meru can take any odd number of steps in between, depending on where the intended god falls in the pecking order. The black thatching is made from sugar palm fronds and is very expensive.

Small Shrines (Gedong) At the kaja end of the courtyard, these may include a shrine to the sacred mountain Gunung Batur; a Maospahit shrine to honour Bali's original Hindu settlers (Majapahit); and a shrine to the taksu, who acts as an interpreter for the gods. (Trance dancers or mediums may be used to convey the gods' wishes.)

Bale Piasan Open pavilions used to display temple offerings.

Gedong Pesimpangan A stone building dedicated to the village founder or a local deity.

Paruman or Pepelik Open pavilion in the inner courtyard, where the gods are supposed to assemble to watch the ceremonies of a temple festival.

because much of the stone used is soft and the tropical climate ages it very rapidly (that centuries-old temple you're looking at may in fact be less than 10 years old!). Sculptures are restored or replaced as resources permit – it's not uncommon to see a temple with old carvings, which are barely discernible, next to newly finished work.

Sculpture often appears in set places in Bali's temples. Door guardians – representations of legendary figures such as Arjuna or other protective personalities – flank the steps to the gateway. Above the main entrance to a temple, Kala's monstrous face often peers out, sometimes a number of times, and his hands reach out beside his head to catch any evil spirits foolish enough to try and sneak in.

Temple Design

Although overall temple architecture is similar in both northern and southern Bali, there are some important differences. The inner court-yards of southern temples usually house a number of *meru* (multi-

TOP TEMPLE VISITS

Over 10,000 temples are found everywhere on Bali – from cliff tops and beaches to volcanoes – and are often beautiful places to experience. Visitors will find the following especially rewarding.

Directional Temples

Some temples are so important they are deemed to belong to the whole island rather than particular communities. There are nine *kahyangan jagat* (directional temples) including the following:

Pura Luhur Batukau (p226) One of Bali's most important temples is situated magically up the misty slopes of Gunung Batukau.

Pura Luhur Ulu Watu (p103) As important as it is popular, this temple has sweeping Indian Ocean views, sunset dance performances and monkeys.

Pura Goa Lawah (p192) See Bali's own Bat Cave at this cliffside temple filled with the winged critters.

Sea Temples

The legendary 16th-century priest Nirartha founded a chain of temples to honour the sea gods. Each was intended to be within sight of the next, and several have dramatic locations on the south coast. They include the following:

Pura Rambut Siwi (p252) On a wild stretch of the west coast and not far from where Nirartha arrived in the 16th century. Locks of his hair are said to be buried in a shrine.

Pura Tanah Lot (p248) Sacred as the day begins, it becomes a temple of mass tourism at sunset.

Other Important Temples

Some temples have particular importance because of their location, spiritual function or architecture. The following reward visitors:

Pura Maduwe Karang (p233) An agricultural temple on the north coast, this is famous for its spirited bas-reliefs, including one of possibly Bali's first bicycle rider.

Pura Pusering Jagat (p170) One of the famous temples at Pejeng, near Ubud, which dates to the 14th-century empire that flourished here. It has an enormous bronze drum from that era.

Pura Taman Ayun (p248) This vast and imposing state temple was a centrepiece of the Mengwi empire and has been nominated for Unesco recognition.

Pura Tirta Empul (p173) The beautiful temple at Tampaksiring, with holy springs discovered in AD 962 and bathing pools at the source of Sungai Pakerisan (Pakerisan River).

tiered shrines), together with other structures, whereas in the north, everything is grouped on a single pedestal. On the pedestal you'll find 'houses' for the deities to use on their earthly visits; they're also used to store religious relics.

While Balinese sculpture and painting were once exclusively used as architectural decoration for temples, you'll soon see that sculpture and painting have developed as separate art forms influencing the look of every aspect of the island. And the art of temple and shrine construction is as vibrant as ever: more than 500 new ones in all sizes are built every month.

The Birth of Bali Style

Tourism has given Balinese architecture unprecedented exposure and it seems that every visitor wants to take a slice of this island back home with them.

Shops along Ngurah Rai Bypass (the main road in south Bali, running from the airport around to Sanur) churn out prefabricated, knock-down *bale* for shipment to far-flung destinations: the Caribbean, London, Perth and Hong Kong. Furniture workshops in Denpasar and handicraft villages near Ubud are flat out making ornaments for domestic and export markets.

The craze stems back to the early 1970s, when Australian artist Donald Friend formed a partnership with Manado-born Wija Waworuntu, who had built the Tandjung Sari on Sanur beach a decade earlier. With a directive to design traditional, village-style alternatives to the Western multi-storeyed hotels, they brought two architects to Bali: Australian Peter Muller and the late Sri Lankan Geoffrey Bawa who took traditional architecture and adapted it to Western standards of luxury.

Before long, the design sensation known as 'Bali Style' was born. Then, the term reflected Muller and Bawa's sensitive, low-key approach, giving precedence to culture over style, and respect for traditional principles and craftspeople, local renewable materials and age-old techniques. Today, the development of a mass market has inevitably produced a much looser definition.

Contemporary Hotel Design

For centuries, foreign interlopers, such as the priest Nirartha, have played an intrinsic part in the island's myths and legends. These days, tourists are making an impact on the serenity of Balinese cosmology and its seamless translation into the island's traditional architecture. And while these visitors with large credit limits aren't changing the island's belief system – much – they are changing its look.

Most hotel designs on Bali and Lombok are purely functional or pastiches of traditional designs, but some of the finest hotels on the islands aspire to something greater. The following are notable examples in rough order of completion:

Tandjung Sari (p113) Located in Sanur, it is Wija Waworuntu's classic prototype for the Balinese boutique beach hotel.

Amandari (p159) The crowning achievement of architect Peter Muller, who also designed the two Oberois. Located near Ubud, the inclusion of traditional Balinese materials, crafts and construction techniques, as well as Balinese design principles, respects the island's approach to the world.

Oberoi (p76) The very first luxury hotel, located in Seminyak, remains Muller's relaxed vision of a Balinese village. The *bale agung* (village assembly hall) and *bale banjar* form the basis for common areas.

Oberoi Lombok (p267) Both the most luxurious and the most traditionally styled hotel on Lombok.

Look for carved wooden *garuda*, the winged bird that bears the god Wisnu, in the most surprising places – high up in pavilion rafters, at the base of columns, pretty much anywhere.

HEIGHT RULES

The rule that no building shall exceed the height of a coconut palm dates back to the 1960s when the 10-storey Bali Beach Hotel caused much consternation. However, soaring land prices in the south and ineffectual enforcement of building codes mean that this 'rule' is being increasingly challenged.

THE POWER OF BAMBOO

Bali has always had natural cathedrals of bamboo. In the dense tropical forests of the east and west, soaring stalks arch together in ways that lift the soul. Now bamboo, one of the world's great renewable resources, is being used to create soaring and inspirational buildings whose sinuous designs are simply awe-inspiring.

Much credit for the current bamboo revolution goes to famed jeweller John Hardy, who had bamboo used for the revolutionary structures that formed the landmark Green School (p175) southwest of Ubud in 2007. People took one look at the fabulous fantasy of its bridge and came away inspired. Since then bamboo's use in buildings has taken off across Bali and there are some beautiful examples of its use that go far beyond the old bamboo hut cliché of *Gilligan's Island*. These include the following:

Fivelements (p175) A new health resort, not far from the Green School.

Power of Now Oasis (p112) A striking beachside yoga studio in Sanur.

Hai Bar & Grill (p131) A beachside bar on Nusa Lembongan.

Sardine (p85) The lauded restaurant on its own rice field in Kerobokan.

Pearl Beach Lounge (p291) A luxe beachside erection on Gili Trawangan.

Big Tree Farms (p174) A huge temple to chocolate that's also near the Green School.

Amankila (p196) In east Bali, Amankila adopts a garden strategy, with a carefully structured landscape of lotus ponds and floating pavilions that steps down an impossibly steep site.

Hotel Tugu Bali (p91) In Canggu, exemplifies the notion of instant age, the ability of materials in Bali to weather quickly and provide 'pleasing decay'.

Four Seasons Resort (p159) A striking piece of aerial sculpture near Ubud, with a huge elliptical lotus pond sitting above a base structure that appears like an eroded and romantic ruin set within a spectacular river valley.

Alila Villas Uluwatu (p104) In far south Bali, Alila employs an artful contemporary style that's light and airy, conveying a sense of great luxury. Set amid hotel-tended rice fields, it embodies advanced green building principles.

Lombok Architecture

Traditional laws and practices govern Lombok's architecture. Construction must begin on a propitious day, always with an odd-numbered date, and the building's frame must be completed on that day. It would be bad luck to leave any of the important structural work until the following day.

A traditional Sasak village layout is a walled enclosure. There are three types of buildings: the *beruga* (open-sided pavilion), the *bale tani* (family house) and the *lumbung* (rice barn). The *beruga* and *bale tani* are both rectangular, with low walls and a steeply pitched thatched roof, although, of course, the *beruga* is much larger. A *bale tani* is made of bamboo on a base of compacted mud. It usually has no windows and the arrangement of rooms is very standardised. There is a *serambi* (open verandah) at the front and two rooms on two different levels inside – one for cooking and entertaining guests, the other for sleeping and storage. There are some picturesque traditional Sasak villages in Rembitan and Sade, near Kuta.

RICE BARNS

When you stay in a hotel featuring *lumbung* (rice barn) design, you are really staying in a place derived from rice storage barns – the 2nd floor is meant to be airless and hot!

Environment

Bali and Lombok have rich and varied natural environments which belie their relative small sizes. Volcanoes, beaches and reefs are just some of the prominent features. Along with this are an array of creatures, from ducks in the rice fields to one of the world's rarest birds. Still, with record tourism, the threats to these unique environments are many but there's much each visitor can do to lessen their impact.

The Landscape

Bali is a small island, midway along the string of islands that makes up the Indonesian archipelago. It's adjacent to the most heavily populated island of Java, and immediately west of the chain of smaller islands comprising Nusa Tenggara, which includes Lombok.

The island is visually dramatic – a mountainous chain with a string of active volcanoes, it includes several peaks around 2000m. The agricultural lands in Bali are south and north of the central mountains. The southern region is a wide, gently sloping area, where most of the country's abundant rice crop is grown. The northern coastal strip is narrower, rising rapidly into the foothills of the central range. It receives less rain, but coffee, copra, rice and cattle are farmed there.

Bali also has some arid, less-populated regions. These include the western mountain region, and the eastern and northeastern slopes of Gunung Agung. The Nusa Penida islands are dry, and cannot support intensive rice agriculture. The Bukit Peninsula is similarly dry, but with the growth of tourism, it's becoming quite populous.

The Indonesian Ecotourism Centre (www.indecon.or.id) is devoted to highlighting responsible tourism; Bali Fokus (http://balifokus.asia) promotes sustainable community programs on Bali for recycling and reuse.

Volcanoes

Bali is volcanically active and extremely fertile. The two go hand-in-hand as eruptions contribute to the land's exceptional fertility, and high mountains provide the dependable rainfall that irrigates Bali's complex and amazingly beautiful patchwork of rice terraces. Of course, the volcanoes are a hazard as well – Bali has endured disastrous eruptions in the past, such as in 1963, and no doubt will again in the future. Gunung Agung, the 'Mother Mountain', is 3142m high and thickly wooded on its south side. You can climb it or its steam-spewing neighbour, the comparatively diminutive 1717m Gunung Batur. The latter is a geographic spectacle: a soaring, active volcano rising from a lake that itself is set in a vast crater.

On Lombok, the 3726m Gunung Rinjani is Indonesia's second-tallest volcano. Within the huge caldera is an aquamarine lake, Danau Segara Anak, which astounds those who spy it for the first – or even second – time.

Beaches

Bali has beaches in all shapes, characters and colours. From hidden coves to dramatic sweeps, from lonely strands to party scenes, from pearly white to sparkling black. See p59 for more about Bali's beaches.

Animals & Plants

Bali is geologically young, most of its living things have migrated from elsewhere and true native wild animals are rare. This is not hard to imagine in the heavily populated and extravagantly fertile south of Bali, where the orderly rice terraces are so intensively cultivated they look more like a work of sculpture than a natural landscape.

In fact, rice fields cover only about 20% of the island's surface area, and there is a great variety of other environmental zones: the dry scrub of the northwest, the extreme northeast and the southern peninsula; patches of dense jungle in the river valleys; forests of bamboo; and harsh volcanic regions that are barren rock and volcanic tuff at higher altitudes. Lombok is similar in all these respects.

Balinese Flora & Fauna, published by Periplus, is a concise and beautifully illustrated guide to the animals and plants you'll see in your travels.

RESPONSIBLE TRAVEL

The best way to responsibly visit Bali and Lombok is to try to be as minimally invasive as possible. This is, of course, easier than it sounds, but consider the following tips:

Watch your use of water Travel into the rice-growing regions of Bali and you'll think the island is coursing with water, but demand outstrips supply. Take up your hotel on its offer to save water, by not washing your sheets and towels every day. At the high end you can also forgo your own private plunge pool, or a pool altogether – although this is almost impossible at any price level.

Don't hit the bottle Those bottles of Aqua (the top local brand of bottled water, owned by Danone) are convenient but they add up. The zillions of such bottles tossed away each year are a major blight. Still, you're wise not to refill from the tap, so what to do? Ask your hotel if you can refill from their huge containers of drinking water. And if your hotel doesn't give you in-room drinking water in reusable glass containers, tell them you noticed.

In Ubud, stop by the Pondok Pekak Library & Learning Centre (p167) – staff will refill your water bottle and tell you which other businesses offer this service. Elsewhere, simply ask; the service is slowly spreading. In restaurants, ask for '*air putih*', which will get you a glass of water from the Aqua jug out back, saving yet more plastic bottles.

Don't play golf Having two golf courses on the arid Bukit Peninsula is environmentally unsustainable.

Support environmentally aware businesses The number of businesses committed to good environmental practices is growing fast in Bali and Lombok. Keep an eye out within this guide for the sustainable icon (✔), which identifies environmentally savvy businesses.

Conserve power Sure you want to save your own energy on a sweltering afternoon, but using air-con strains an already overloaded system. Much of the electricity in Bali comes from Java and the rest is produced at the roaring, smoking plant near Benoa Harbour. Open the windows at night in Ubud for cool mountain breezes and the symphony of sounds off the rice fields.

Don't drive yourself crazy The traffic is already bad – why add another vehicle to it? Can you take a tourist bus instead of a chartered or rental car? Would a walk, trek or hike be more enjoyable than a road journey to an over-visited tourist spot? The beach is a fast and fun way to get around Kuta and Seminyak (often faster than a taxi in traffic). Cycling is more popular than ever, and you can hire a bike for US$3.

Bag the bags Bali's governor is trying to get plastic bags banned. Help him out by refusing them (and say no to plastic straws, too). Note that many Circle K convenience stores now ask if you want a bag.

Leave the animals be Skip swimming with captive dolphins, elephant rides, and attractions where wild animals such as dolphins or elephants are made to perform for crowds. Animal welfare groups decry these spectacles.

BALI STARLING

Also known as the Bali myna, Rothschild's mynah, or locally as *jalak putih*, the Bali starling is perhaps Bali's only endemic bird (opinions differ – as other places are so close, who can tell?). It is striking white in colour, with black tips to the wings and tail, and a distinctive bright-blue mask. These natural good looks have caused the bird to be poached into virtual extinction. The wild population is thought to number under 100. In captivity, however, there are hundreds if not thousands.

Near Ubud, the Bali Bird Park (p176) has large aviaries where you can see Bali starlings. The park was one of the major supporters of efforts to reintroduce the birds into the wild. Efforts to reintroduce the species include a breeding program run by the NGO Friends of the National Parks Foundation (p134) on Nusa Penida as well as another program west of Ubud.

Animals

Wild Animals

Bali has lots and lots of lizards, and they come in all shapes and sizes. The small ones (onomatopoeically called *cecak*) that hang around light fittings in the evening, waiting for an unwary insect, are a familiar sight. Geckos are lizards often heard but less often seen. The loud and regularly repeated two-part cry 'geck-oh' is a nightly background noise that many visitors soon enjoy.

Bali has more than 300 species of birds, but the one that is truly native to the island is the Bali starling. Much more common are colourful birds such as the orange-banded thrush, numerous species of egrets, kingfishers, parrots, owls and many more.

Bali's only wilderness area, Taman Nasional Bali Barat (West Bali National Park), has a number of wild species, including grey and black monkeys (which you will also see in the mountains, Ubud and east Bali), *muncak* (barking deer), squirrels, bats and iguanas.

Domestic Animals

Bali is thick with domestic animals, including ones that wake you up in the morning and others that bark at night. Chickens and roosters are kept as food and as domestic pets.

Cockfighting A popular but male activity – a man's fighting bird is his prized possession. If you see a thicket of cars and motorbikes by the side of the road in rural Bali but don't see any people, they may all be at a cockfight 'hidden' behind a building. Cockfighting is banned in Bali for its cruelty; religious ceremonies excepted.

Dogs When not pampered pets, dogs have hard lives – they're far down the social ladder, bedeviled by the rabies epidemic and thought by some to be friendly with evil spirits (thus the constant barking). Bali has one native breed, the medium-sized Kintamani, that is growing in international popularity.

Ducks Another everyday Balinese domestic animal and a regular dish at feasts. Ducks are kept in the family compound, and are put out to a convenient pond or flooded rice field to feed during the day. They follow a stick with a small flag tied to the end, and the stick is left planted in the field. As sunset approaches, the ducks gather around the stick and wait to be led home again. With tourism booming and duck-based dishes like *bebek betutu* (smoked, stuffed duck) more popular than ever, rice farmers can now charge duck farmers for access to their fields.

Marine Animals

For information about the myriad aquatic creatures around Bali and Lombok, see p66.

BALI'S DOGS

The plight of Bali's dogs and the irony of the important role they play in island life is captured by filmmakers Lawrence Blair and Dean Allan Tolhurst in *Bali: Island of the Dogs*.

SEA TURTLES

Both green sea and hawksbill turtles inhabit the waters around Bali and Lombok, and both species are supposedly protected by international laws that prohibit trade in anything made from sea turtles.

In Bali, however, green sea turtle meat *(penyu)* is a traditional and very popular delicacy, particularly for Balinese feasts. Bali is the site of the most intensive slaughter of green sea turtles in the world – no reliable figures are available, although in 1999 it was estimated that more than 30,000 are killed annually. It's easy to find the trade on the backstreets of waterside towns such as Benoa.

Still, some progress is being made, especially by groups like ProFauna (p367), which has made great progress in raising awareness on Bali about sea turtles and other animals across Indonesia.

A broad coalition of divers and journalists supports the **SOS Sea Turtles campaign** (www.sos-seaturtles.ch), which spotlights turtle abuse in Bali. It has been instrumental in exposing the illegal poaching of turtles at Wakatobi National Park in Sulawesi for sale in Bali. This illegal trade is widespread and, like the drug trade, hard to prevent. Bali's Hindu Dharma, the body overseeing religious practice, has decreed that turtle meat is essential in only very vital ceremonies.

Turtle hatcheries open to the public do a good job of educating locals about the need to protect turtles and think of them as living creatures (as opposed to sate), but many environmentalists are still opposed to them because they keep captive turtles.

On Nusa Penida, volunteers can join the efforts of Green Lion Bali (p134), which runs a turtle hatchery.

Plants

Trees

Much of the island is cultivated. As with most things in Bali, trees have a spiritual and religious significance, and you'll often see them decorated with scarves and black-and-white chequered cloths (*kain poleng,* a cloth signifying spiritual energy) signifying their sacred status. The *waringin* (banyan tree) is the holiest Balinese tree and no important temple is complete without a stately one growing within its precincts. The *waringin* is an extensive, shady tree with an exotic feature: creepers that drop from its branches take root to propagate a new tree. *Jepun* (frangipani or plumeria trees), with their beautiful and sweet-smelling white flowers, are found everywhere.

Bali's forests cover 127,000 hectares, ranging from virgin land to tree farms to densely forested mountain villages. The total is constantly under threat from wood poaching for carved souvenirs and cooking fuel, and from development.

Bali has monsoonal rather than tropical rainforests, so it lacks the valuable rainforest hardwoods that require rain year-round. Nearly all the hardwood used for carving furniture and high end artwork is imported from Sumatra and Kalimantan.

A number of plants have great practical and economic significance. *Tiing* (bamboo) is grown in several varieties and is used for everything from sate sticks to building hip and stylish resorts.

One hawksbill sea turtle that visited Bali was tracked for the following year. His destinations: Java, Kalimantan, Australia (Perth and much of Queensland) and then back to Bali.

Flowers & Gardens

Balinese gardens are a delight. The soil and climate can support a huge range of plants, and the Balinese love of beauty and the abundance of cheap labour means that every space can be landscaped. The style is generally informal, with curved paths, a rich variety of plants and usually a water feature.

You can find almost every type of flower in Bali, but some are seasonal and others are restricted to the cooler mountain areas. Many of the flowers will be familiar to visitors – hibiscus, bougainvillea, poinsettia, oleander, jasmine, water lily and aster are commonly seen in the southern tourist areas.

Less-familiar flowers include Javanese *ixora (soka, angsoka),* with round clusters of red-orange flowers; *champak (cempaka),* a fragrant member of the magnolia family; flamboyant, the flower of the royal poinciana flame tree; *manori (maduri),* which has several traditional uses; and water convolvulus *(kangkung),* whose leaves are commonly used as a green vegetable. There are thousands of species of orchid.

Bali's climate means that gardens planted today look mature – complete with soaring shade trees – in just a couple of years. Good places to see Bali's plant bounty include Bali Botanic Garden (p220), Bali Orchid Garden (p110) and the many plant nurseries (north from Sanur and along the road to Denpasar).

Despite villa construction and other loss of rice fields, Bali's rice production hit a record in 2013 to 822,115 tons. With island consumption at 455,000 tons, that keeps Bali as a rice exporter. The top producing regency is Tabanan (27%) followed by Gianyar (21%).

Environmental Issues

Fast-growing populations, limited resources, pressure from the increasing number of visitors and lax and/or nonexistent environmental regulations mean that Bali and Lombok are under great threat.

Bali

Some of Bali's environmental worries are larger than the island: climate change is causing increased water levels that are damaging the coast and beaches.

GROWING RICE

Rice cultivation has shaped the social landscape in Bali – the intricate organisation necessary for growing rice is a large factor in the strength of community life. Rice cultivation has also changed the environmental landscape – terraced rice fields trip down hillsides like steps for a giant, in shades of gold, brown and green, green and more green. Some date back 1000 years or more.

Subak, the village assocation that deals with water rights and irrigation, makes careful use of all the surface water. The fields are a complete ecological system, home for much more than just rice. In the early morning you'll often see the duck herders leading their flocks out for a day's paddle around a flooded rice field; the ducks eat various pests and leave fertiliser in their wake.

A harvested field with its leftover burnt rice stalks is soaked with water and repeatedly ploughed, often by two bullocks pulling a wooden plough. Once the field is muddy enough, a small corner is walled off and seedling rice is planted there. When it is a reasonable size, it's replanted, shoot by shoot, in the larger field. While the rice matures, there is time to practise the gamelan (instruments used to play traditional Balinese orchestral music), watch the dancers or do a little woodcarving. Finally, the whole village turns out for the harvest – a period of solid hard work. While it's only men who plant the rice, everybody takes part in harvesting it.

In 1969, new high-yield rice varieties were introduced. These can be harvested a month sooner than the traditional variety and are resistant to many diseases. However, the new varieties also require more fertiliser and irrigation water, which strains the imperilled water supplies. More pesticides are also needed, causing the depletion of the frog and eel populations that depend on the insects for survival.

Although everyone agrees that the new rice doesn't taste as good as the traditional rice, the new strains now account for more than 90% of the rice grown in Bali. Small areas of traditional rice are still planted and harvested in traditional ways to placate the rice goddess, Dewi Sri. Temples and offerings to her dot every rice field.

THE WALLACE LINE

The 19th-century naturalist Sir Alfred Wallace (1822–1913) observed great differences in fauna between Bali and Lombok – as great as the differences between Africa and South America. In particular, there were no large mammals (elephants, rhinos, tigers etc) east of Bali, and very few carnivores. He postulated that during the ice ages, when sea levels were lower, animals could have moved by land from what is now mainland Asia all the way to Bali, but the deep Lombok Strait would always have been a barrier. He drew a line between Bali and Lombok, which he believed marked the biological division between Asia and Australia.

Plant life does not display such a sharp division, but there is a gradual transition from predominantly Asian rainforest species to mostly Australian plants, such as eucalypts and acacias, which are better suited to long, dry periods. This is associated with the lower rainfall as one moves east of Java. Environmental differences – including those in the natural vegetation – are now thought to provide a better explanation of the distribution of animal species than Wallace's theory about limits to their original migrations.

Meanwhile, a fast-growing population in Bali has put pressure on limited resources. The tourist industry has attracted new residents, and there is a rapid growth in urban areas and of resorts and villas that encroach onto agricultural land. Concerns include:

Water Usage is a major concern. Typical top-end hotels uses 1000 to 1500 litres of water a day per room, and the growing number of golf courses – the ones on the arid Bukit Peninsula in the Pecatu Indah development and at Nusa Dua, for example – put further pressure on an already stressed resource.

Water pollution A major problem, both from deforestation brought on by firewood collecting in the mountains, and lack of proper treatment for the waste produced by the local population. Streams that run into the ocean at popular spots like Double Six Beach in Legian are very polluted, often with waste water from hotels. The vast mangroves along the south coast near Benoa Harbour are losing their ability to filter the water that drains here from much of the island and are themselves threatened with development.

Air pollution As anyone stuck behind a smoke-belching truck or bus on one of the main roads knows, south Bali's air is often smoggy. The view of south Bali from a hillside shows a brown blanket hanging in the air that could be LA in the 1960s.

Waste The problem is not just all the plastic bags and water bottles but the sheer volume of waste produced by the growing population – what to do with it? The Balinese look with sadness at the enormous amounts of waste – especially plastic – that have accumulated in their once pristine rivers. 'I used to swim there,' said one driver to us, looking at a plastic-bag-choked stream near his boyhood home.

WATER USE

A recent study showed that the average occupied hotel room in south Bali accounted for 1000 to 1500 litres of water a day for use by its occupants and to service their needs. In contrast, the average local requires less than 120 litres a day for all needs.

On the upside, there is a nascent effort to grow rice and other foods organically. A sewage treatment program in the south is finally operating in some areas but businesses are objecting to the costs and refusing to connect.

In Pemuteran and Gili Trawangan, artificial reef-growing programs have won universal praise. This is important as a study by the World Wide Fund for Nature found that less than 5% of Bali's reefs were fully healthy.

Lombok

On Lombok, environmental disaster in the gold rush town of Sekotong is ongoing. Gold mining using mercury in huge open-cast pits is causing enormous damage to once-pristine areas such as Kuta.

Coastal erosion is a problem as it is on Bali. The Gilis are naturally concerned. On the plus side, the reefs around the Gilis have been quick to recover as tourism has spurred intense preservation efforts.

Survival Guide

Directory A–Z

Accommodation

Bali has a huge range of accommodation: approximately 30,000 hotel rooms and tens of thousands more in guesthouses, villas etc. It has great value lodging no matter what your budget. The touristy areas of Lombok and the Gili Islands have the same range of options as Bali; elsewhere on Lombok accommodation is simpler and more limited.

Accommodation attracts a combined tax and service charge (called 'plus plus') of 21%. In budget places, this is generally included in the price, but check first. Many midrange and top-end places will add it on, which can add substantially to your bill.

The rates quoted in this book include tax and are those that travellers are likely to pay during the high season. Nailing down rates is difficult, as some establishments publish the rates they actually plan to charge, while others publish rates that are pure fantasy, fully expecting to discount by 50%.

Rates are almost always negotiable, especially outside the main peak season. In the low season, discounts between 30% and 50% aren't uncommon at midrange and top-end hotels. With Bali enjoying record visitor numbers, prices are climbing sharply.

Hotels

Pretty much every place to stay on Bali and Lombok can arrange tours, car rental and other services. Laundry service is universally available, often cheap and sometimes free.

BUDGET HOTELS

The cheapest accommodation on Bali and Lombok is in small places that are simple but clean and comfortable. Names usually include the word 'losmen,' 'homestay,' 'inn' or '*pondok*.' Many are built in the style of a traditional Balinese home.

There are budget hotels all over Bali (less so on Lombok), and they vary widely in standards and price. Expect the following:

➡ Maybe air-con

➡ Maybe hot water

➡ Private bathroom with shower and Western-style toilet

➡ Often a pool

➡ Simple breakfast

➡ Carefree and cheery staff

International budget chains are making a splashy entry into south Bali, but note that a tiny US$9 room quickly hits US$40 when you add various extras such as taxes and fees for items included elsewhere like internet and towels.

MIDRANGE HOTELS

Midrange hotels are often constructed in Balinese bungalow style or in two-storey blocks and are set on spacious grounds with a pool. Many have a sense of style that is beguiling and may help postpone your departure. In addition to what you'll get at a budget hotel, expect:

➡ Balcony/porch/patio

➡ Satellite TV

➡ Small fridge

➡ Often wi-fi

TOP-END HOTELS

Top-end hotels in Bali are world-class. Service is refined and you can expect decor plucked from the

---

SLEEPING PRICE RANGES

The following price ranges refer to a double room with a bathroom. Unless otherwise stated taxes are included in the price.

$ less than 500,000Rp (under US$50)

$$ 500,000Rp–1,500,000Rp (US$50 to $150)

$$$ more than 1,500,000Rp (over US$150)

HOTELS TOO FAR

When booking a south Bali hotel room, be careful where you book.

As tourist numbers on Bali have exploded, so have the number of chain hotels. In fact in 2013 alone, Bali's hotel room count went from 24,000 to 30,000. The boom in building large hotels in Kuta, Legian, Seminyak and now Kerobokan are changing the area's character in fundamental ways, especially as the many family-run, cheap and cheerful small inns are pushed out.

While some of these large new hotels are appearing in traditionally appealing areas of south Bali, not far from the beaches and nightlife, scores more are opening far from the areas visitors consider desirable. Many chains have properties in both good and unappealing areas and it is easy to get misled about a hotel's actual location, especially on booking websites. In the tradition of real estate agents everywhere, 'Seminyak' is now the address used for hotels far into Denpasar.

So when you see that great web bargain of a midrange room for US$30, carefully consider the following:

➡ Anything west of the Jl Legian–Jl Seminyak–Jl Kerobokan spine will be close to both beaches and nightlife.

➡ East of the spine and things begin to get inconvenient fast. There will be less to walk to, beaches can be far and cruising cabs hard to come by.

➡ Jl Ngurah Rai Bypass and Jl Sunset are both noisy major streets that lack charm and are hard to cross. Many new chain hotels are located right on these traffic-choked thoroughfares.

➡ East of Jl Ngurah Rai Bypass and Jl Sunset and you are deep into suburban Denpasar, where you will be loath to find cabs or much else you'll be interested in.

➡ In Sanur, which is also getting an influx of chain hotels, Jl Ngurah Rai Bypass should be your absolute western border in your room hunt.

➡ With careful shopping, you can usually find great room deals in the most appealing parts of south Bali, and often you can end up at a small or family-run guesthouse with oodles more charm and character than a generic cheap hotel.

---

pages of a glossy magazine, along with the following:

➡ Superb service

➡ Views – ocean, lush valleys and rice fields or private gardens

➡ Spa

➡ Maybe a private pool

➡ Not wanting to leave

Villas

Villas are scattered around south Bali and Ubud and are now appearing in the east. They're often built in the middle of rice paddies, seemingly overnight. The villa boom has been quite controversial for environmental, aesthetic and economic reasons. Many skip collecting government taxes from guests, which has raised the ire of their luxury hotel

competitors and brought threats of crack-downs.

Large villas can be bacchanal retreats for groups of friends, such as those found in the Canggu area. Others are smaller, more intimate and part of larger developments – common in Seminyak and Kerobokan – or top-end hotels. Expect the following:

➡ Private garden

➡ Private pool

➡ Kitchen

➡ Air-con bedroom(s)

➡ Open-air common space

Villas will also potentially include:

➡ Your own staff (cook, driver, cleaner)

➡ Lush grounds

➡ Private beachfront

➡ Isolation (which can be good or bad)

Rates range from under US$200 per night for a modest villa to US$2000 per week and beyond for your own tropical estate. There are often deals, especially in the low season, and several couples sharing can make something grand affordable.

You can sometimes save quite a bit by waiting until the last minute, but during the high season the best villas book up far in advance.

HOLIDAY VILLA AGENTS

Websites such as homeaway.com and airbnb.com are useful, however many listed properties are not licensed which makes for an unregulated market with all the associated pros and cons. Local agents include:

Bali Discovery (☑0361-286 283; www.balidiscovery.com) Has villa and hotel deals.

Bali Private Villas (☑0361-316 6455; www.baliprivatevillas.com)

Bali Tropical Villas (☑0361-732083; www.bali-tropical-villas.com)

VILLA RENTAL QUESTIONS

It's the Wild West out there. There are myriad agents, some excellent, others not. It is essential to be as clear as possible about what you want when arranging a rental. Some things to keep in mind and ask about when renting a villa:

➡ How far is the villa from the beach and stores?

➡ Is a driver or car service included?

➡ If there is a cook, is food included?

➡ Is there an electricity surcharge?

➡ Are there extra cleaning fees?

➡ Is laundry included?

➡ What refunds apply on a standard 50% deposit?

➡ Is there wi-fi?

Long-Term Accommodation

For longer stays, you can find flats for US$300 to US$1200 a month and much more. Sources include:

➡ Facebook groups. There are scores with rentals on Bali; Bali Rooms for Rent is one large board. You can also try looking for groups with names like '[name of town] Housing'.

➡ Bali Advertiser (www.baliadvertiser.biz)

➡ The local website www.banjartamu.org

➡ Notice boards in popular cafes such as Bali Buda in Ubud and Umalas, plus the many Cafe Moka locations. Bintang supermarkets in Seminyak and Ubud are also good.

➡ Word of mouth. Tell your new Bali friends you're looking as everybody seems to know someone with a place for rent.

Village Accommodation

A good way to arrange a village stay is through the **JED** (Village Ecotourism Network; ☑0361-366 9951; www.jed.or.id; tours from US$75) Village Ecotourism Network. Another good option is the **Bali Homestay Program** (☑0817 067 1788; www.bali-homestay.com; Jegu; r only per night from US$20) 🍃, north of Tabanan.

Customs Regulations

Indonesia's list of prohibited imports includes drugs, weapons, fresh fruit and anything remotely pornographic. Items allowed include:

➡ 200 cigarettes (or 50 cigars or 100g of tobacco)

➡ a 'reasonable amount' of perfume

➡ 1L of alcohol

Surfers with more than two or three boards may be charged a fee, and this can apply to other items if the officials suspect that you intend to sell them in Indonesia.

There is no restriction on foreign currency, but the import or export of rupiah is limited to 5,000,000Rp. Greater amounts must be declared.

Electricity

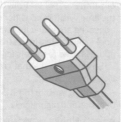

220v/50hz

220v/50hz

Climate

Denpasar

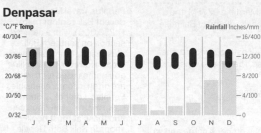

°C/°F Temp

40/104 —
30/86 —
20/68 —
10/50 —
0/32 —

J F M A M J J A S O N D

Rainfall Inches/mm

— 16/400
— 12/300
— 8/200
— 4/100
— 0

Embassies & Consulates

Foreign embassies are in Jakarta, the national capital. Most of the foreign representatives in Bali are consular agents (or honorary consuls) who cannot offer the same services as a full consulate or embassy. As such, a lost passport may mean a trip to an embassy in Jakarta.

The US, Australia and Japan have formal consulates in Bali (citizens from these countries make up half of all visitors).

Indonesian embassies and consulates abroad are listed on the website of Indonesia's **Ministry of Foreign Affairs** (www.kemlu.go.id). There is a handy search function under the 'Mission' menu item.

Australian Consulate (Map p120; ☎0361-241118; www.bali.indonesia.embassy.gov.au; Jl Tantular 32, Denpasar; ☉8am-4pm Mon-Fri) The Australian consulate has a consular sharing agreement with Canada.

Japanese Consulate (Map p120; ☎0361-227628; konjpdps@indo.net.id; Jl Raya Puputan 170, Denpasar; ☉10am-3pm Mon-Fri)

US Consulate (☎0361-233 605; BaliConsularAgency@ state.gov; Jl Hayam Wuruk 310, Renon, Denpasar; ☉9am-noon & 1-3.30pm Mon-Fri)

Food

For an overview of Balinese cuisine, see p324.

Eating Price Ranges

The following price ranges refer to a typical meal. Taxes and tips are included in the price.

$ less than 60,000Rp (under US$5)

$$ 60,000Rp–250,000Rp (US$5 to US$25)

$$$ more than 250,000Rp (over US$25)

Insurance

Unless you are definitely sure that your health coverage at home will cover you in Bali and Lombok, you should take out travel insurance; bring along a copy of the policy as evidence that you are covered. It's a good idea to get a policy that will pay for medical evacuation if necessary.

Some policies specifically exclude 'dangerous activities,' which can include scuba diving, renting a local motorcycle and even trekking. Be aware that a locally acquired motorcycle licence is not valid under some policies.

Worldwide travel insurance is available at www.lonelyplanet.com/bookings. You can buy, extend and claim online anytime – even if you're already on the road.

Internet Access

Internet centres are uncommon although you'll still find a few in Kuta and Gili Trawangan.

Hotel wi-fi access in rooms is common except in remote areas. Many cafes and restaurants have free wi-fi. Connection speeds outside of south Bali and Ubud can be slow across Bali and Lombok.

Large portions of Bali and some parts of Lombok have 3G networks.

Indonesia requires internet providers to censor access to websites deemed pornographic, but in practice this is inconsistently enforced. A few providers don't censor sites; others block any pages with words like gay or breast. Avoid this by using VPN for connections.

Language Courses

Many visitors to Bali like to learn at least the basics of Bahasa Indonesia. South Bali and Ubud have many tutors who advertise in the same places you'll find rental listings.

Indonesia Australia Language Foundation (IALF; ☎0361-225243; www.ialf.edu; Jl Raya Sesetan 190, Denpasar) The best place for courses in Bahasa Indonesia.

Seminyak Language School (Map p72; ☎0361-733342; www.learnindonesianinbali.com; Jl Raya Seminyak 7, Seminyak) Popular with visitors, it is conveniently located down a lane near the Bintang Supermarket.

Legal Matters

The Indonesian government takes the smuggling, using and selling of drugs very seriously and the drug laws are unambiguous. If caught with drugs, you may have to wait for up to six months in

PRACTICALITIES

➡ Radio in Bali includes Gema Merdeka 97.7FM, the most popular station among locals; plenty of Balinese music.

➡ Indonesia uses the PAL broadcasting standard, the same as Australia, New Zealand, the UK and most of Europe.

➡ Indonesia uses the metric system.

jail before trial. As seen in high-profile cases involving foreigners, multi-year prison terms are common for people caught with illegal drugs, including marijuana. Those found guilty of dealing can be subject to the death penalty.

Gambling is illegal (although it's common, especially at cockfights), as is pornography.

Generally, you are unlikely to have any encounters with the police unless you are driving a rented car or motorcycle.

In both Bali and Lombok, there are police stations in all district capitals. If you have to report a crime or have other business at a police station, expect a lengthy and bureaucratic encounter. You should dress respectably, bring someone to help with translation, arrive early and be polite. You can also call the **Bali Tourist Police** (☏0361-224111) for advice.

Some police officers may expect to receive bribes, either to overlook some crime, misdemeanour or traffic infringement (whether actual or not), or to provide a service that they should provide anyway. Generally, it's easiest to pay up – and the sooner this happens, the less it will cost. Travellers may be told there's a 'fine' to pay on the spot, or some travellers offer to pay a 'fine' to clear things up. How much? Generally, 50,000Rp can work wonders and the officers are not proud. If things seem unreasonable, however, ask for the officer's name and write it down.

Bali instituted a smoking ban in 2014 that covers most tourist facilities, markets, shops, restaurants, hotels, taxis and more. In practice, adoption has been uneven.

LGBT Travellers

Gay travellers in Bali will experience few problems, and many of the island's most influential expat artists have been more-or-less openly gay. Physical contact between same-sex couples is acceptable and friends of the same sex often hold hands, though this does not indicate homosexuality.

There are many venues where gay men congregate, especially in Seminyak. There's nowhere that's exclusively gay, and nowhere that's even inconspicuously a lesbian scene. Gay men in Indonesia are referred to as *homo* or *gay* and are quite distinct from the female impersonators called *waria*.

Many gays from other parts of the country come to live in Bali, as it is more tolerant, and also because it offers opportunities to meet foreign partners.

On Lombok, gay and lesbian travellers should refrain from public displays of affection (advice that also applies to straight couples).

Gaya Dewata (www.gayadewata.com) Bali's gay organisation.

Maps

Periplus Travel Maps has a decent Bali contour map (1:250,000), with a detailed section on southern Bali, plus maps of the main town areas. However, the labelling and names used for towns are often incomprehensible. Periplus' Lombok & Sumbawa map is useful. You can find these at most bookshops in Bali. Both Google and Apple maps are generally accurate, although labels can be lacking.

Money

Indonesia's unit of currency is the rupiah (Rp). There are coins worth 50Rp, 100Rp, 500Rp and 1000Rp. Notes come in denominations of 2000Rp, 5000Rp, 10,000Rp, 20,000Rp, 50,000Rp and 100,000Rp.

Always carry a good supply of rupiah in small denominations. Individuals will struggle to make change for a 50,000Rp note or larger.

ATMs

There are ATMs all over Bali and in non-rural areas of Lombok. Notable exceptions include Nusa Lembongan and Gili Meno. Most accept nonlocal ATM cards and major credit cards for cash advances.

➡ The exchange rates for ATM withdrawals are usually quite good, but check to see if your home bank will hit you with outrageous fees.

➡ Most ATMs allow a maximum withdrawal of one million rupiah.

➡ ATMs have stickers indicating whether they issue 50,000Rp or 100,000Rp notes (the former are easier to use for small transactions).

➡ Most ATMs return your card last instead of before dispensing cash, so it's easy to forget your card.

Credit Cards

Visa, MasterCard and Amex are accepted by larger businesses that cater to tourists. Be sure to confirm that a business accepts credit cards before you show up cashless.

Moneychangers

US dollars are by far the easiest currency to exchange. Try to have new US$100 bills.

Follow these steps to avoid getting ripped off exchanging money:

➡ Find out the going exchange rate online. Know that anyone offering a better rate will need to make a profit through other means.

➡ Stick to banks, airport exchange counters or large and reputable operations such as the Central Kuta Money Exchange (www.centralkutabali.com) which has locations across south Bali and Ubud.

➡ Skip any place offering too-good exchange rates and claiming to charge no fees or commissions.

➡ Avoid exchange stalls down alleys or in otherwise dubious locations (that sounds obvious but scores of tourists are ripped off daily).

➡ Common exchange scams include rigged calculators, sleight of hand schemes, 'mistakes' on the posted rates and demands that you hand over your money before you have counted the money on offer.

➡ Use an ATM to obtain rupiah.

Tipping

➡ Tipping a set percentage is not expected in Bali, but if the service is good, it's appropriate to leave at least 5000Rp or 10% or more.

➡ Most midrange hotels and restaurants and all top-end hotels and restaurants add 21% to the bill for tax and service (known as 'plus plus'). This service component is distributed among hotel staff (one hopes).

➡ Hand cash directly to individuals if you think they deserve recognition for their service.

➡ Tip good taxi drivers, guides, people giving you a massage or fetching you a beer on the beach etc; 5000Rp to 10,000Rp or 10% to 20% of the total fee is generous.

Travellers Cheques

Travellers cheques are not used.

Opening Hours

Typical opening hours are as follows:

➡ **Banks** 8am to 2pm Monday to Thursday, 8am to noon Friday, 8am to 11am Saturday

➡ **Government offices** 8am to 3pm Monday to Thursday, 8am to noon Friday (although these are not standardised)

➡ **Post offices** 8am to 2pm Monday to Friday, longer in tourist centres

➡ **Restaurants and cafes** 8am to 10pm daily

➡ **Shops and services catering to visitors** 9am to 8pm daily

Post

Every substantial town has a *kantor pos* (post office). In tourist centres, there are also postal agencies, which are often open long hours and provide postal services. Sending postcards and normal-sized letters (ie under 20g) by airmail is cheap, but not really fast.

RUPIAH REDENOMINATION

Indonesia has plans to redenominate the rupiah by removing three digits from the currency, although the timing of this has been debated for years. For example, the 20,000Rp note would become the 20Rp note. The exchange value of the new notes would remain the same. Changing the national currency is likely to be a very complex process, with many implications for travellers. These include:

➡ New notes will be introduced that are identical to the current ones, with the exception of the final three zeros missing. Long-term plans call for all-new designs.

➡ The government stresses that current banknotes will retain their value (eg the 100,000Rp note will be the same as the new 100Rp note), however, how this will play out is anyone's guess. In other nations, such as Russia, there has been widespread refusal to accept old notes, even after government guarantees of their value.

➡ It will likely take years for price lists and computer systems to be fully updated, so it will be up to customers to make certain that they are being charged – and paying – appropriately.

➡ Introduction of the new denominations is likely to occur with little notice to avoid financial upheavals.

➡ Old notes will remain good for at least six years after introduction, the Bank of Indonesia said in 2014.

Mail delivery times from Bali:

➡ **Australia** Two weeks

➡ **UK & rest of Europe** Three weeks

➡ **USA** Two weeks

Most post offices will properly wrap your parcels over 20g for shipping for a small fee. Don't use the post for anything you'd miss.

International express companies like DHL, Fedex and UPS operate on Bali and offer reliable, fast and expensive service.

Public Holidays

The following holidays are celebrated throughout Indonesia. Many of the dates change according to the phase of the moon (not by month) or by religious calendar, so the following are estimates only.

Tahun Baru Masehi (New Year's Day) 1 January

Idul Adha (Muslim festival of sacrifice) February

Muharram (Islamic New Year) February/March

Nyepi (Hindu New Year) March/April

Hari Paskah (Good Friday) April

Ascension of Christ April/May

Hari Waisak (Buddha's birth, enlightenment and death) April/May

Maulud Nabi Mohammed/Hari Natal (Prophet Mohammed's birthday) May

Hari Proklamasi Kemerdekaan (Indonesian Independence Day) 17 August

Isra Miraj Nabi Mohammed (Ascension of the Prophet Mohammed) September

Hari Natal (Christmas Day) 25 December

The Muslim population in Bali observes Islamic festivals and holidays, including Ramadan. Religious and other holidays on Lombok are as follows:

Anniversary of West Lombok (Government holiday) 17 April

Ramadan June 18 in 2015; 10 to 11 days earlier each year

Idul Fitri (End of Ramadan) Thirty days after the start of Ramadan

Founding of West Nusa Tenggara (Public holiday) 17 December

Safe Travel

It's important to note that compared to many places in the world, Bali and Lombok are fairly safe. There are some hassles from the avaricious, but most visitors face many more dangers at home. There have been some high-profile cases of visitors being injured or killed on Bali but in many cases these tragedies have been inflamed by media sensationalism.

Boat travel carries risks (see p373).

Alcohol Poisoning

There are ongoing reports of injuries and deaths among tourists and locals due to *arak* (local booze that should be distilled from palm or cane sugar) being adulterated with methanol, a poisonous form of alcohol. *Arak* is usually legitimate and is a popular drink. The safest approach is to avoid *arak*; never accept any outside of legitimate, established cafes and restaurants.

Drugs

Numerous high-profile drug cases on Bali and Lombok should be enough to dissuade anyone from having anything to do with illicit drugs. As little as two ecstasy tabs or a bit of pot have resulted in huge fines and multi-year jail sentences in Bali's notorious jail in Kerobokan. Try smuggling and you may pay with your life. Kuta is filled with cops posing as dealers.

THE ART OF BARGAINING

Many everyday purchases in Bali and Lombok require bargaining. Accommodation has a set price, but this is usually negotiable in the low season, or if you are staying at the hotel for several days. Items for sale at department stores, supermarkets and convenience stores will have a fixed price; elsewhere, be prepared to bargain.

Bargaining can be an enjoyable part of shopping, so maintain your sense of humour and keep things in perspective. Try following these steps:

➡ Have some idea of what the item is worth.

➡ Establish a starting price – ask the seller for their price rather than making an initial offer.

➡ Your first price can be from one-third to two-thirds of the asking price – assuming that the asking price is not outrageous.

➡ With offers and counter-offers, move closer to an acceptable price.

➡ If you don't get to an acceptable price, you're entitled to walk – the vendor may call you back with a lower price.

➡ When you name a price, you're committed – you must buy if your offer is accepted.

Hawkers & Touts

Many visitors regard hawkers and touts as *the* number one annoyance in Bali (and in tourist areas of Lombok). Visitors are frequently, and often constantly, hassled to buy things. The worst places for this are Jl Legian in Kuta, Kuta Beach, the Gunung Batur area and the temples at Besakih and Tanah Lot. And the cry of 'Transport?!?' – that's everywhere. Many touts employ fake, irritating Australian accents ('Oi! Mate!').

Use the following tips to deflect attention:

➡ Completely ignore touts/hawkers.

➡ Don't make any eye contact.

➡ A polite *tidak* (no) actually encourages them.

➡ Never ask the price or comment on the quality of their goods unless you're interested in buying. Keep in mind, though, that ultimately they're just people trying to make a living, and if you don't want to buy anything, you are wasting their time trying to be polite.

Orphanages

Bali has a number of 'fake' orphanages designed to extract money from well-meaning tourists. If you are considering donating anything to an orphanage, carefully research its reputation online. Orphanages using cab drivers as hawkers are especially suspect.

Swimming

Kuta Beach and those to the north and south are subject to heavy surf and strong currents – always swim between the flags. Trained lifeguards are on duty, but only at Kuta, Legian, Seminyak, Nusa Dua, Sanur and (sometimes) Senggigi. Other beaches can have strong currents, even when protected by reefs.

Be careful when swimming over coral, and never

walk on it. It can be very sharp and coral cuts are easily infected. In addition, you are damaging a fragile environment.

Water pollution is a problem, especially after rain. Swim far away from any open streams you see flowing into the surf, including the often foul and smelly ones at Double Six Beach and Seminyak Beach. The seawater around Kuta is commonly contaminated by run-off from built-up areas.

Theft

Violent crime is uncommon, but bag-snatching from motorbikes, pickpocketing and theft from rooms and parked cars occurs. Take the same precautions you would in any urban area. Other common sense tips:

➡ Secure money before leaving an ATM (and don't forget your card!)

➡ Don't leave valuables on a beach while swimming

➡ Use front desk/in-room safes

Traffic & Footpaths

Apart from the dangers of driving in Bali, the traffic in most tourist areas is often annoying and frequently dangerous to pedestrians. Footpaths can be rough, even unusable; gaps in the pavement are a top cause of injury. Carry a torch (flashlight) at night.

Telephone
Internet Calling

Most hotel wi-fi service in south Bali and Ubud will allow Skype to work. Internet centres may add a surcharge for the call to your connection time.

Mobile Phones

➡ SIM cards for mobile phones cost only 5000Rp. They come with cheap rates for calling other countries, starting at US$0.20 per minute.

➡ SIM cards are widely available and easily refilled with credit.

➡ Watch out for vendors who sell SIM cards to visitors for 50,000Rp or more. If they don't come with at least 45,000Rp in credit you are being ripped off. Go elsewhere.

➡ Data plans average about 200,000Rp for 3.5GB of data.

➡ Telkomsel, a major carrier, often has reps selling SIM cards in the airport arrivals area just before the 'duty-free' shop. They cost 50,000Rp, and come with credit, plus they offer good data deals. This is an easy way to get set up, but make sure you're not dealing with a faux vendor charging outlandish rates.

➡ Mobile numbers start with a four-digit prefix that begins

with 08 and has a total of 10 to 12 digits.

Phone Codes

Phone numbers beginning with 08 belong to mobile phones. Useful numbers include:

Directory Assistance	☏108
Indonesia Country Code	☏62
International Call Prefix	☏001/☏017
International Operator	☏102

Time

Bali and Lombok are on Waktu Indonesian Tengah or WIT (Central Indonesian Standard Time), which is eight hours ahead of Greenwich Mean Time/Universal Time or two hours behind Australian Eastern Standard Time. Java is another hour behind Bali and Lombok.

Not allowing for daylight-saving time elsewhere, when it's noon in Bali and Lombok, it's 11pm the previous day in New York, 8pm in Los Angeles, 4am in London and 2pm in Sydney and Melbourne.

Toilets

Western-style toilets are almost universally common in tourist areas.

During the day, look for a cafe or hotel and smile (public toilets only exist at some major sights).

Tourist Information

The tourist office in Ubud is an excellent source of information on cultural events. Otherwise, the tourist offices in Bali are not useful.

Some of the best information is found in the many free publications and websites aimed at tourists and expats. There are also numerous Facebook groups, although some are simply forums for the intolerant.

➡ **Bali Advertiser** (www.baliadvertiser.biz) Has excellent columns with info for visitors including Greenspeak by journalist Cat Wheeler and Bali Explorer by legendary travel writer Bill Dalton.

➡ **Bali Discovery** (www.balidiscovery.com) The weekly online news report by Jack Daniels is a must-read of events in Bali.

➡ **Hello Bali** (www.hellobalimagazine.com) An engrossing glossy magazine with features about the island and its culture.

➡ **The Beat** (www.beatmag.com) Useful website and bi-weekly with extensive entertainment and cultural listings.

➡ **The Yak** (www.theyakmag.com) Glossy, cheeky mag celebrating the expat swells of Seminyak and Ubud.

Travellers with Disabilities

Bali is a difficult destination for those with limited mobility.

Public transport is not accessible; ditto for the minibuses used by shuttle bus and tour companies. Ramps and other disabled facilities at hotels and inns are uncommon. Your best bet are the international chains, but even then you should confirm your needs with the property. Out on the street, the footpaths, where they exist at all, tend to be narrow, uneven, potholed and frequently obstructed.

Visas

The visa situation in Indonesia seems to be constantly in flux. It is essential that you confirm current formalities before you arrive in Bali or Lombok. Failure to meet all the entrance requirements can see you on the first flight out.

No matter what type of visa you are going to use, your passport *must* be valid for at least six months from the date of your arrival.

The main visa options for visitors to Indonesia are:

➡ **Visa in Advance** Visitors can apply for a visa before they arrive in Indonesia. Typically this is a visitor's visa, which comes in two flavours: 30 or 60 days. Details vary by country; contact your nearest Indonesian embassy or consulate to determine processing fees and times. Note: this is the only way to obtain a 60-day visitor visa, even if you qualify for Visa on Arrival.

➡ **Visa on Arrival** Citizens of over 60 countries may apply for a 30-day visa when they arrive at the airports in Bali and Lombok. The cost is US$35; be sure to have the exact amount in US

WRONG NUMBER?

Bali's landline phone numbers (those with area codes that include 0361, across the south and Ubud) are being changed on an ongoing basis. To accommodate more lines, a digit is being added to the start of the existing six- or seven-digit phone number. So 0361-761 xxxx might become 0361-4761 xxxx. You'll hear a recording first in Bahasa Indonesia and then in English, telling you what digit to add to the changed number.

currency. Eligible countries include Australia, Canada, much – but not all – of the EU including France, Germany, Ireland, the Netherlands and the UK, plus New Zealand and the USA. VOA renewals for 30 days are possible. If you don't qualify for VOA, you must get a visa in advance.

➡ **Visa Free** Citizens of Singapore and a smattering of other countries can receive a nonextendable 30-day visa for free upon arrival.

Whichever type of visa you use to enter Bali or Lombok, you'll be issued with a tourist card for your stay (if you have obtained one of the coveted 60-day visas in advance, be sure the immigration official at the airport gives you a 60-day card). Keep the tourist card with your passport, as you'll have to hand it back when you leave the country.

Fines for overstaying your visa expiration date are 300,000Rp per day and include additional hassles.

Volunteering

There's a plethora of opportunities to lend a hand in Bali and Lombok. Many people have found that they can show their love for these places by helping others. Information sources include:

➡ **Bali Advertiser** (www.baliadvertiser.biz) Look under Community Groups.

➡ **Bali Spirit** (www.balispirit.com/ngos)

There are also Ubud organisations helping Bali's dogs (see p166).

Local Organisations

The following organisations need donations, supplies and often volunteers. Check their websites to see their current status.

Bali Children's Project (www.balichildrensproject.org) Funds education, offers English and computer training.

East Bali Poverty Project (☎0361-410071; www.eastbalipovertyproject.org) Works to help children in the impover-

---

ished mountain villages of east Bali (see p212). Uses English teachers.

Friends of the National Parks Foundation (☎0361-977978; www.fnpf.org; Jl Bisma, Ubud) Main office in Ubud. Has volunteer programs on Nusa Penida.

Gus Bali (www.gus-bali.org) Works to raise environmental awareness on Bali, runs beach clean-ups anyone can join.

IDEP (Indonesian Development of Education & Permaculture; ☎0361-294993; www.idepfoundation.org) Has projects across Indonesia; works on environmental projects, disaster planning and community improvement.

JED (Village Ecotourism Network; ☎0361-366 9951; www.jed.or.id; tours from US$75) Organises highly regarded tours of small villages, some overnight. Often needs volunteers to improve its services and work with the villagers.

ProFauna (www.profauna.net) A large nonprofit animal-protection organisation operating across Indonesia; the Bali office has been aggressive in protecting sea turtles. Volunteers needed to help with hatchery releases and editing publications.

ROLE Foundation (www.rolefoundation.org) Works to improve well-being and self-reliance in under-privileged Bali communities; has environmental projects.

Smile Foundation of Bali (Yayasan Senyum; ☎0361-233758; www.senyumbali.org) Organises surgery to correct facial deformities; operates the **Smile Shop** (Map p144; ☎0361-233758; www.senyumbali.org; Jl Sriwedari; ☺10am-8pm) in Ubud to raise money.

Yayasan Rama Sesana (☎0361-247363; www.yrsbali.org) Dedicated to improving reproductive health for women across Bali.

Yayasan Bumi Sehat (☎0361-970002; www.bumisehatbali.org) Operates an internationally recognised clinic

---

RENEWING YOUR VISA

You can renew a 30-day Visa on Arrival once. However, the procedures are complex:

➡ At least seven days before your visa expires, go to the **Kuta Immigration Office** (Map p57; Jl Ngurah Rai Bypass, Tuban; ☺8am-4pm Mon-Fri), which is just off the bypass in Tuban (not actually Kuta), near the Pertimina gas station on the west side.

➡ Bring your passport, a photocopy of your passport and a copy of your ticket out of Indonesia (which should be for a date during the renewal period).

➡ Pay a fee of 250,000Rp.

➡ List an address in Kuta (saying 'I'm staying in the Gilis,' for instance, will get you sent to Lombok; Ubud will get you sent to Denpasar).

➡ You may have to return to the office twice.

One way to avoid the renewal hassle is to use a visa agent such as **ChannelOne** (Map p72; ☎0361-780 4047; www.channel1.biz; Jl Sunset Road 100X, Kerobokan) who for a fee will do the bureaucratic work for you.

STOPPING CHILD-SEX TOURISM

Strong laws exist in Indonesia to prosecute people seeking to sexually exploit local children, and many countries also have extraterritorial legislation which allows nationals to be prosecuted in their own country for these crimes.

Travellers can help stop child-sex tourism by reporting suspicious behaviour. Reports can be made to the **Anti Human Trafficking Unit** (☑021-721 8098) of the Indonesian police. If you know the nationality of the individual, you can contact their embassy directly.

Humantrafficking.org (www.humantrafficking.org) is an international group that has numerous links to groups working to prevent human exploitation in Indonesia.

and gives reproductive services to disadvantaged women in Ubud; accepts donated time from medical professionals. The founder, Robin Lim, has had international recognition.

YKIP (Humanitarian Foundation of Mother Earth; ☑0361-761208; www.ykip. org) Established after the 2002 bombings, it organises and funds health and education projects for Bali's children.

Women Travellers
Bali

Women travelling solo in Bali will get attention from Balinese men, but they are, on the whole, fairly benign. Generally, Bali is safer for women than many areas of the world, and with the usual care and common sense, women should feel secure travelling alone.

Lombok

Traditionally, women on Lombok are treated with respect, but in the touristy areas, harassment of single foreign women may occur. Would-be guides/boyfriends/gigolos are often persistent in their approaches, and can be aggressive when ignored or rejected. Clothes that aren't too revealing are a good idea – beachwear should be reserved for the beach. Two or more women together are less likely to experience problems, and women accompanied by a man are unlikely to be harassed.

Transport

GETTING THERE & AWAY

Most visitors to Bali will arrive by air. Island-hoppers can catch frequent ferries between eastern Java and Bali, between Bali and Lombok, and between Lombok and Sumbawa. Most people visit Lombok via Bali.

Flights, tours and rail tickets can be booked online at www.lonelyplanet.com/bookings.

Entering the Region

Arrival procedures at Bali's Ngurah Rai International Airport are straightforward, although it can take some time for planeloads of visitors to clear immigration; afternoons are typically worst.

At baggage claim, porters are keen to help get your luggage to the customs ta-

bles and beyond, and they've been known to ask up to US$20 for their services – if you want help with your bags, agree on a price beforehand. The formal price is 10,000Rp per piece. Luggage carts are always free.

Once through customs, you're out with the tour operators, touts and taxi drivers. Ignore the touts as they offer no service of value, except to themselves.

Your passport *must* be valid for six months after your date of arrival in Indonesia. Visas are the most troublesome detail (see p366).

Air

Although Jakarta, the national capital, is the gateway airport to Indonesia, there are also many direct international flights to Bali and a few to Lombok.

Airports & Airlines

BALI AIRPORT

The only airport in Bali, **Ngurah Rai International Airport** (DPS) is just south of Kuta. It is sometimes referred to internationally as Denpasar or on some internet flight-booking sites as Bali.

Bali's new airport terminal opened in 2013 but was still under construction over a year later. Unfortunately, it has problems:

➡ Outrageous food and drink prices, even by airport standards.

➡ It is often filthy.

➡ Long lines at immigration and customs. Immigration officials will offer passengers a chance to cut the queue for an unsanctioned fee of 750,000Rp.

➡ Non-operating escalators.

➡ Touts offering dubious accommodation and transport services in the arrivals area.

CLIMATE CHANGE & TRAVEL

Every form of transport that relies on carbon-based fuel generates CO_2, the main cause of human-induced climate change. Modern travel is dependent on aeroplanes, which might use less fuel per kilometre per person than most cars but travel much greater distances. The altitude at which aircraft emit gases (including CO_2) and particles also contributes to their climate change impact. Many websites offer 'carbon calculators' that allow people to estimate the carbon emissions generated by their journey and, for those who wish to do so, to offset the impact of the greenhouse gases emitted with contributions to portfolios of climate-friendly initiatives throughout the world. Lonely Planet offsets the carbon footprint of all staff and author travel.

International airlines flying to and from Bali have myriad flights to Australia and Asian capitals. The present runway is too short for planes flying direct to/from Europe.

Domestic airlines serving Bali from other parts of Indonesia change frequently. All have ticket offices at the domestic terminal, which you may need to use, because internet sales are often difficult.

Air Asia (www.airasia.com) Serves Jakarta as well as Bangkok, Kuala Lumpur, Singapore and Australian cities.

Cathay Pacific Airways (www.cathaypacific.com) Serves Hong Kong.

China Airlines (www.china-airlines.com) Serves Taipei.

Eva Air (www.evaair.com) Serves Taipei.

Garuda Indonesia (www.garuda-indonesia.com) Serves Australia, Japan, Korea and Singapore direct plus cities across Indonesia.

Jetstar (www.jetstar.com) Serves Australia.

KLM (www.klm.com) Serves Amsterdam via Singapore.

Korean Air (www.koreanair.com) Serves Seoul.

Lion Air (www.lionair.co.id) Serves cities across Indonesia and Kuala Lumpur.

Malaysia Airlines (www.mas.com.my) Serves Kuala Lumpur.

Qatar Airways (www.qatarairways.com) Serves Doha non-stop with good connections to Europe.

Singapore Airlines (www.singaporeair.com) Several Singapore flights daily.

Thai Airways International (www.thaiair.com) Serves Bangkok.

Virgin Australia (www.virginaustralia.com) Serves Australia.

LOMBOK AIRPORT

Lombok International Airport (Bandara Internasional Lombok; LOP) is in the south of the island near Praya. It has flights to a few major Indonesian cities but limited international service.

Air Asia (www.airasia.com) Serves Kuala Lumpur.

Garuda Indonesia (Map p259;☎0804 180 7807; www.garuda-indonesia.com; Jl Pejanggik 42, Mataram) Serves Bali and Jakarta.

Lion Air/Wings Air (www.lionair.co.id) Serves Bali, Jakarta and Surabaya.

Silk Air (www.silkair.com) Serves Singapore.

Trans Nusa (☎0361-847 7395; www.transnusa.co.id) Nusa Tenggara destinations, plus Bali.

Tickets

From Europe and North America, the least expensive way to Bali may be a cheap ticket to Jakarta, Kuala Lumpur or Singapore and a connection to Bali on a budget carrier such as Air Asia or Lion Air.

Asia

Bali is well connected to major Asian hubs. Lombok is linked to Kuala Lumpur and Singapore.

Australia

Service to Australia is at record levels.

Europe

Fly KLM on the one-stop from Amsterdam or change to a Bali flight at Bangkok, Kuala Lumpur or Singapore.

New Zealand

Air New Zealand may have non-stop service.

North America

The best connections are through any of the major Asian hubs with non-stop service to Bali. No US airline serves Bali.

Other Indonesian Islands

From Bali, you can get flights to major Indonesian cities, often for under US$50 – buy tickets at local travel agents or the airport. Deals to Jakarta put the price of a plane ticket in the same class as the bus, and with a saving of about 22 hours.

From Lombok, direct service is mostly limited to Bali, Surabaya and Jakarta.

Land

Bus

The ferry crossing from Bali is included in the services offered by numerous bus companies, many of which travel overnight to Java. It's advisable to buy your ticket at least one day in advance from a travel agent or at the terminals in Denpasar (Ubang) or Mengwi. Note that flying can be as cheap as the bus.

Fares vary between operators; it's worth paying extra for a decent seat (all have air-con). Typical fares/travel times include Yogyakarta 350,000Rp/16 hours and Jakarta 470,000Rp/24 hours. You can also get buses from Singaraja in north Bali.

On Lombok, public buses go daily from the Mandalika terminal in Mataram via Bali to major cities on Java.

Train

Bali doesn't have trains but the **State Railway Company** (Kerata API; Map p120; ☎0361-227131; www.kereta-api.co.id; Jl Diponegoro 150/B4; ☺8am-3pm Mon-Fri, 9am-2pm Sat & Sun) does have an office in Denpasar. From here buses leave for eastern Java where they link with trains at Banyuwangi for

Surabaya, Yogyakarta and Jakarta, among other destinations. Fares and times are comparable to the bus, but the air-conditioned trains are more comfortable, even in economy class. Note: Google Translate works well on the website.

Sea

Java

You can reach Java, just west of Bali, via the ferries that run between Gilimanuk in west Bali and Ketapang (Java), and can take a bus all the way to Jakarta. Sumbawa, just east of Lombok, is also connected by ferry.

Sumbawa

Ferries travel between Labuhan Lombok in Lombok and Poto Tano on Sumbawa frequently throughout the day.

Other Indonesian Islands

Pelni (www.pelni.co.id), the national shipping line, operates large boats on long-distance runs throughout Indonesia.

For Bali, Pelni ships stop at the harbour in Benoa. Schedules and fares are found on the website. You can inquire and book at the **Pelni ticket office** (Map p57; ☎0361-763 963; www.pelni.co.id; Jl Raya Kuta 299; ☺8am-noon & 1-4pm Mon-Fri, 8am-1pm Sat) in Tuban.

Pelni ships link Lembar on Lombok with other parts of Indonesia. Check schedules

and buy tickets at Mataram's **Pelni office** (☎0370-637212; Jl Industri 1; ☺8am-noon & 1-3.30pm Mon-Thu & Sat, 8-11am Fri).

GETTING AROUND

The best way to get around is with your own transport, whether you drive, hire a driver or ride a bike. This gives you the flexibility to explore at will and allows you to reach many places that are otherwise inaccessible.

Public transport is cheap but can be cause for long journeys if you're not sticking to a major route. In addition, some places are just impossible to reach.

There are also tourist shuttle buses, which combine economy with convenience.

Air

Several airlines fly daily between Bali and Lombok. The route is competitive.

Bali's **Ngurah Rai International Airport** is immediately south of Tuban and Kuta. There is a fixed-price taxi monopoly inside the terminal. You prepay (more than you would for a metered taxi) and go. To catch a metered taxi you'll have to exit the airport.

If you have a surfboard, you'll be charged extra, depending on its size. Ignore any touts that aren't part of the official scheme.

Many hotels will offer to pick you up at the airport but there's no need to use these services if they cost more than the official rates.

Those who are really travelling light might be able to walk the less than 30 minutes north to Kuta Beach.

Bemo

Bemos are normally a minibus or van with a row of low seats down each side. They usually hold about 12 people in very cramped conditions.

Bemos were once the dominant form of public transport in Bali. But widespread motorbike ownership (which can be cheaper than daily bemo use) has caused the system to wither. Expect to find that getting to many places is both time-consuming and inconvenient. It's uncommon to see visitors on bemos in Bali but on Lombok they are an important means of transport for visitors and locals.

Fares

Bemos operate on a standard route for a set (but unwritten) fare. The minimum is about 5000Rp. If you get into an empty bemo, always make it clear that you do not want to charter it.

Terminals & Routes

Every town has at least one terminal (terminal bis) for all forms of public transport. There are often several terminals in larger towns. Terminals can be confusing, but most bemos and buses have signs, and if you're in doubt, people will usually help you.

To travel from one part of Bali to another, it is often necessary to go via one or more terminals. For example, to get from Sanur to Ubud by bemo, you go to the Kereneng terminal in Denpasar, transfer to the Batubulan terminal, and then take a third bemo to Ubud. This is circuitous and time-consuming, two of the reasons so few visitors take bemos in Bali.

Bicycle

More and more people are touring the island by *sepeda* (bike). Many visitors are using bikes around towns and for day trips in Bali and on Lombok.

There are plenty of bicycles for rent in the tourist areas, but many are in poor condition. On Lombok, you can find good bikes in Senggigi.

Ask at your accommodation about renting a bike. Prices are about 30,000Rp per day.

Boat

Taking the boat is simpler than the hassle of flying between Bali and Lombok, and fast boats make it competitive time-wise, but there are some important safety considerations that need to be taken into account.

Public ferries travel slowly between Padangbai and Lembar on Lombok.

There are many fast boats operating between Bali and Lombok's Gilis.

Bus

Public Bus

BALI

Larger minibuses and full-size buses ply the longer routes, particularly on routes linking Denpasar, Singaraja and Gilimanuk. They operate out of the same terminals as bemos. However, with everybody riding motorbikes, there are long delays waiting for buses to fill up at terminals before departing.

LOMBOK

Buses and bemos of various sizes are the cheapest and most common way of getting around Lombok. Mandalika in Bertais is the main bus terminal for all of Lombok. There are also regional terminals at Praya and Pancor (near Selong). You may have to go via one or more of these transport hubs to get from one part of Lombok to another.

Public transport fares are fixed by the provincial government. You may have to pay more if you have a large bag or surfboard.

Tourist Bus

Tourist buses are economical and convenient ways to get around. You'll see signs offering services in major tourist areas. Typically, a tourist bus is an eight- to 20-passenger vehicle. Service is not as quick as with your own car and driver but is far easier than trying for public bemos and buses.

A common route uses shuttle buses to link Kuta and Senggigi on Lombok with Kuta and south Bali via the public ferry. These trips cost 100,000Rp and take upwards of 10 hours.

Perama (☑0361-751170; www.peramatour.com) is the major tourist bus operator. It has offices or agents in Kuta, Sanur, Ubud, Lovina, Padangbai and Candidasa as well as Gili Trawangan and Senggigi on Lombok.

Advantages of tourist buses:

➡ Fares are reasonable (eg Kuta to Lovina is 100,000Rp).

➡ They have air-con.

➡ You can meet other travellers.

Disadvantages of tourist buses:

➡ Stops are often outside the centre, requiring another shuttle/taxi.

➡ Buses may not provide a direct service – stopping, say, at Ubud between Kuta and Padangbai.

➡ Popular spots like Bingen and Seminyak are not served.

➡ Three or more people can hire a car and driver for less.

Car & Motorcycle

Renting a car or motorbike can open up Bali and Lombok for exploration – and can also leave you counting the minutes until you return it; there can be harrowing driving conditions on the islands at certain times and south Bali traffic is often awful. But it gives you the freedom to explore myriad back roads and lets you set your own schedule.

Most people don't rent a car for their entire visit but rather get one for a few days of meandering.

Driving Licences

CAR LICENCES

If you plan to drive a car, you're supposed to have an International Driving Permit (IDP). You can obtain one from your national motoring organisation if you have a normal driving licence. Bring your home license as well. Without an IDP, add 50,000Rp to any fine you'll have to pay if stopped by the

---

TRANS-SARBAGITA BUS

Trans-Sarbagita runs large, air-con commuter buses like you find in major cities the world over. Each ride costs 3500Rp. The highly visible roadside bus stops have maps, showing the routes, which include from Batubulan and along the bypass linking Sanur to Nusa Dua, and from Denpasar to Jimbaran. These routes converge at a stop just east of Kuta in the large parking lot south of the Istana Kuta Galleria shopping centre.

TRAVELLING SAFELY BY BOAT

Fast boats linking Bali, Nusa Lembongan, Lombok and the Gili Islands have proliferated, especially as the latter places have become more popular. But safety regulations are non-existent and accidents continue to happen.

Crews on these boats may have little or no training: in one accident, the skipper freely admitted that he panicked and had no recollection of what happened to his passengers. And rescue is far from assured: a volunteer rescue group in east Bali reported that they had no radio.

Conditions are often rough in the waters off Bali. Although the islands are in close proximity and are easily seen from each other, the ocean between can get more turbulent than is safe for the small speedboats zipping across it.

With these facts in mind, it is essential that you take responsibility for your own safety because no one else will. Consider the following points:

Bigger is better It may add 30 minutes or more to your journey, but a larger boat will simply deal with the open ocean better than the over-powered small speedboats. Also, trips on small boats can be unpleasant because of the ceaseless pounding through the waves and the fumes coming from the screaming outboard motors.

Check for safety equipment Make certain your boat has life preservers and that you know how to locate and use them. In an emergency, don't expect a panicked crew to hand them out. Also, check for lifeboats. Some promotional materials show boats with automatically inflating lifeboats that have later been removed to make room for more passengers.

Avoid overcrowding Some boats leave with more people than seats and with aisles jammed with stacked luggage. Passengers are forced to sit on cabin roofs in unsafe conditions. If this happens, don't use the boat.

Look for exits Cabins may have only one narrow entrance, making them death traps in an accident. Sitting at the open back may seem safer but in a 2013 fuel explosion the passengers in that area were badly burned.

Avoid fly-by-nighters Taking a fishing boat and jamming too many engines on the rear in order to cash in on booming tourism is a recipe for disaster.

Don't ride on the roof It looks like care-free fun but travellers are regularly bounced off when boats hit swells and crews may be inept at rescue. Rough seas can drench passengers and ruin their belongings.

The ferry isn't safer One of the big Padangbai–Bangsal car ferries caught fire and sank in 2014.

Use common sense There are good operators on the waters around Bali but the line-up changes constantly. If a service seems sketchy before you board, go with a different operator. Try to get a refund but don't risk your safety for the cost of a ticket.

---

police (although you'll have to pay this fine several times to exceed the cost and hassle of getting the mostly useless IDP).

MOTORCYCLE LICENCES

If you have a motorcycle license at home, get your IDP endorsed for motorcycles too; with this you will have no problems. Otherwise, you have to get a local license – something of an adventure.

Officially, there's a 2,000,000Rp fine for riding without a proper licence, and your motorcycle can be impounded. Unofficially, you may be hit with a substantial 'on-the-spot' payment (50,000Rp seems average) and be allowed to continue on your way. Also, if you have an accident without a licence your insurance company might refuse coverage.

To get a local motorcycle licence in Bali (valid for a

year), go to the **Poltabes Denpasar** (Map p176; ☏0361-142 7352; Jl Gunung Sanhyang; ⏰8am-1pm Mon-Sat), which is northwest of Kerobokan on the way to Denpasar. Bring your passport, a photocopy of your passport (just the page with your photo on it) and a passport-size photo. Then follow these steps:

➜ Ignore the mobbed hall filled with jostling permit seekers.

→ Look helpless and ask uniformed officials 'motorcycle license?'.

→ Be directed to cheery English-speaking officials and pay 250,000Rp.

→ Take the required written test (in English, with the answers provided on a sample test).

→ Get your permit. Sure it costs more than in the hall of chaos, but who can argue with the service?

Fuel

Bensin (petrol) is sold by the government-owned Pertamina company, and costs a cheap 6500Rp per litre (it's subsidised). Bali has scads of petrol stations. On Lombok there are stations in major towns. Motorbike fuel is often sold from roadside stands out of Absolut vodka bottles.

Hire

Very few agencies in Bali will allow you to take their rental cars or motorcycles to Lombok.

CAR

The most popular rental vehicle is a small 4WD – they're compact and are well suited to exploring back roads. Automatic transmissions are unheard of.

Rental and travel agencies in tourist centres rent vehicles quite cheaply. A small jeep costs a negotiable 50,000Rp per day, with unlimited kilometres and very limited insurance. Extra days often cost much less than the first day.

There's no reason to book rental cars in advance or with a tour package; doing so will almost certainly cost more than arranging it locally. Any place you stay can set you up with a car, as can the ever-present touts in the street.

MOTORCYCLE

Motorbikes are a popular way of getting around Bali and Lombok – locals ride pillion almost from birth. A family of five will ride cheerfully along on one motorbike is called a Bali minivan.

Rentals cost 50,000Rp a day, less by the week. This should include minimal insurance for the motorcycle but not for any other person or property. Many have racks for surfboards.

Think carefully before renting a motorbike. It is dangerous and every year visitors go home with lasting damage – this is no place to learn to ride. Helmet use is mandatory.

Insurance

Rental agencies and owners usually insist that the vehicle itself is insured, and minimal insurance should be included in the basic rental deal – often with an excess of as much as US$100 for a motorcycle and US$500 for a car (ie the customer pays the first US$100/500 of any claim).

Check to see what your own vehicle, health and travel insurance covers, especially if you are renting a motorbike.

Road Conditions

Bali traffic can be horrendous in the south, up to Ubud, and as far as Padangbai to the east and Tabanan to the west. Finding your way around the main tourist sites can be a challenge because roads are only sometimes signposted and maps are unreliable. Off the main routes, roads can be rough but they are usually surfaced.

Roads on Lombok can be rough but traffic is lighter than on Bali.

Avoid driving at night or at dusk. Many bicycles, carts and vehicles do not have proper lights, and street lighting is limited.

Road Rules

Visiting drivers commonly complain about crazy Balinese drivers, but often it's because the visitors don't understand the local conventions of road use. For instance, the constant use of horns doesn't mean 'Get the @£*&% out of my way!'; rather it is a very Balinese way of saying 'Hi, I'm here.'

→ Watch your front – it's your responsibility to avoid anything that gets in front of your vehicle. In effect, a car, motorcycle or anything else pulling out in front of you has right of way.

→ Often drivers won't even look to see what's coming when they turn left at a junction – they listen for the horn.

→ Use your horn to warn anything in front that you're there, especially if you're about to overtake.

→ Drive on the left side of the road.

Hitching

Hitchhiking is almost unseen on Bali and Lombok. Instead, consider *ojek*.

BALI'S TOLL ROAD

The Bali Madara Toll Road avoids the worst of the traffic in and around Kuta. Some 12.7km in length, it runs from the bypass near Denpasar over the mangroves to a point near Nusa Dua with a branch to Ngurah Rai International Airport. It has good views of the threatened mangroves and Benoa Harbour as you sail along.

The toll is 10,000Rp. It definitely saves time going south, especially to Nusa Dua. But going north you will get in the traffic-clogged intersection with the Jl Ngurah Rai Bypass.

HIRING A VEHICLE & DRIVER

An excellent way to travel anywhere around Bali is by hired vehicle, allowing you to leave the driving and inherent frustrations to others. If you're part of a group, it can make sound economic sense as well. This is also possible on Lombok but less common.

It's easy to arrange a charter: just listen for one of the frequent offers of 'transport?' in the streets around the tourist centres. Approach a driver yourself or ask at your hotel, which is often a good method because it increases accountability. Also consider the following:

➡ Although great drivers are everywhere, it helps to talk with a few.

➡ Get recommendations from other travellers.

➡ You should like the driver and their English should be sufficient for you to communicate your wishes.

➡ Costs for a full day should average 400,000Rp to 600,000Rp.

➡ The vehicle, usually a late-model Toyota Kijang seating up to seven, should be clean.

➡ Agree on a route beforehand.

➡ Make it clear if you want to avoid tourist-trap restaurants and shops (smart drivers understand that tips depend on following your wishes).

➡ On the road, buy the driver lunch (they'll want to eat elsewhere, so give them 20,000Rp) and offer snacks and drinks.

➡ Many drivers find ways to make your day delightful in unexpected ways. Tip accordingly.

Local Transport

Dokar & Cidomo

Small *dokar* (horse carts) are still seen in parts of Denpasar and Kuta, but they're uncommon. Treatment of the horses is a major concern and there is no good reason to go for an expensive tourist ride.

The horse cart used on Lombok is known as a *cidomo* – a contraction of *cika* (a traditional handcart), *dokar* and *mobil* (because car wheels and tyres are used). A typical *cidomo* has a narrow bench seat on either side. Treatment of the horses is a concern, especially on the vehicle-free Gili Islands where they are the main means of transport. We do not recommend using *cidomos*.

Ojek

Around towns and along roads, you can always get a lift by *ojek* (a motorcycle or motorbike that takes a paying passenger). Formal *ojek*

are less common now that anyone with a motorbike can be a freelance *ojek* (stand by the side of the road, look like you need a ride and people will stop and offer). They're OK on quiet country roads, but a risky option in the big towns. *Ojek* are more common on Lombok.

Fares are negotiable, but about 20,000Rp for 5km is fairly standard.

Taxi

BALI

Metered taxis are common in south Bali and Denpasar (but not Ubud). They are essential for getting around and you can usually flag one down in busy areas. They're often a lot less hassle than haggling with drivers offering 'transport!'.

➡ Taxis are fairly cheap: Kuta to Seminyak can be only 50,000Rp.

➡ The best taxi company by far is **Blue Bird Taxi** (☏701 111), which uses blue vehicles with a light on the roof

bearing a stylised bluebird. Watch out for fakes – there are many. Look for 'Blue Bird' over the windscreen and the phone number. Drivers speak reasonable English and use the meter at all times. Many expats will use no other firm. Blue Bird has a slick phone app that summons a taxi to your location.

➡ Avoid any taxis where the driver won't use a meter, even after dark when they claim that only fixed fares apply.

➡ Other taxi scams include: lack of change, 'broken' meter, fare-raising detours, and offers for tours, massages, prostitutes etc.

LOMBOK

There are plenty of bemos and taxis around Mataram and Senggigi. Drivers for **Lombok Taksi** (☏627 000), owned by the Blue Bird Group, always use the meter without you having to ask; this is the best choice.

Tours

Standardised organised tours are a convenient and popular way to visit a few places in Bali. There are dozens and dozens of operators who provide a similar product and service. Much more interesting are specialised tour companies that can take you far off the beaten track, offer memorable experiences and otherwise provide you with a different side of Bali and Lombok. You can also easily arrange your own custom tour.

Tours originating on Lombok are based in Senggigi. You can usually book market visits in Mataram, a jaunt out to the Gilis or a more complex trip up Gunung Rinjani.

Standard Day Tours

Tours are typically in white minibuses with air-con, which pick you up from and drop you off at your hotel. Prices range from 100,000Rp to 500,000Rp for what are essentially similar tours, so it pays to shop around. Consider the following:

➡ Will lunch be at a huge tourist buffet or somewhere more interesting?

➡ How much time will be spent at tourist shops?

➡ Will there be a qualified English-speaking guide?

➡ Are early morning pick-ups for the convenience of the company, which will then dump you at a central point to wait for another bus?

Specialist Tours

Many Bali tour operators offer experiences that vary from the norm. These can include cultural experiences hard for the casual visitor to find, such as cremations or trips to remote villages where life has hardly changed in decades. Often you'll avoid the clichéd tourist minibus and travel in unusual vehicles or in high comfort.

Bali Discovery Tours (☎0361-286283; www.bali discovery.com) Personalised and customisable tours across Bali.

JED (Village Ecotourism Network;☎0361-366 9951; www. jed.or.id; tours from US$75) Organises highly regarded tours of small villages, some overnight.

Suta Tours (☎0361-741 6665, 0361-788 8865; www. sutatour.com) Arranges the standard tours and also trips to cremation ceremonies and special temple festivals, market tours and other custom plans.

Health

Treatment for minor injuries and common traveller's health problems is easily accessed in Bali and to a lesser degree on Lombok. For serious conditions, you will need to leave the islands.

Travellers tend to worry about contracting infectious diseases when in the tropics, but infections are a rare cause of serious illness or death in travellers. Pre-existing medical conditions, such as heart disease, and accidental injury (especially traffic accidents) account for most life-threatening problems. Becoming ill in some way is relatively common, however; ailments you may suffer from include gastro, overexposure to the sun and other typical traveller woes.

It's important to note certain precautions you should take on Bali and Lombok, especially in regard to rabies, mosquito bites and the tropical sun.

The following advice is a general guide only and does not replace the advice of a doctor trained in travel medicine.

BEFORE YOU GO

Make sure all medications are packed in their original, clearly labelled containers. A signed and dated letter from your physician describing your medical conditions and medications (including generic names) is also a good idea. If you are carrying syringes or needles, be sure to have a physician's letter documenting their medical necessity. If you have a heart condition ensure you bring a copy of a electrocardiogram taken just prior to travelling.

If you take any regular medication bring double your needs in case of loss or theft. You can buy many medications over the counter without a doctor's prescription, but it can be difficult to find some of the newer drugs, particularly the latest antidepressant drugs, blood-pressure medications and contraceptive pills.

Insurance

Even if you are fit and healthy, don't travel without sufficient health insurance – accidents do happen. If you're uninsured, emergency evacuation is expensive – bills of more than US$100,000 are not uncommon.

Find out in advance if your insurance plan will make payments directly to providers or reimburse you later for overseas health expenditures.

Recommended Vaccinations

Specialised travel-medicine clinics are your best source of information; they stock all available vaccines and will be able to give specific recommendations for you and your trip.

Most vaccines don't produce immunity until at least two weeks after they're given. Ask your doctor for an International Certificate of Vaccination (otherwise known as the yellow booklet), which will list all the vaccinations you've received.

The World Health Organization recommendations for Southeast Asia include the following:

Hepatitis A Provides almost 100% protection for up to a year; a booster after 12 months provides at least another 20 years' protection. Mild side effects such as headache and sore arm occur in 5% to 10% of people.

Hepatitis B Now considered routine for most travellers. Given as three shots over six months.

HEALTH ADVISORIES

It's usually a good idea to consult your government's travel-health website before departure, if one is available:

➜ Australia: www.smarttraveller.gov.au

➜ UK: www.gov.uk/foreign-travel-advice

➜ USA: www.travel.state.gov

Lifetime protection occurs in 95% of people.

Measles, mumps and rubella
Two doses of MMR are required unless you have had the diseases. Many young adults require a booster.

Typhoid Recommended unless your trip is less than a week and only to developed cities. The vaccine offers around 70% protection, lasts for two to three years and comes as a single shot.

Required Vaccinations

The only vaccine required by international regulations is yellow fever. Proof of vaccination will only be required if you have visited a country in the yellow-fever zone (primarily some parts of Africa and South America) within the six days prior to entering Southeast Asia.

Medical Checklist

Recommended items for a convenient personal medical kit (other items can be easily obtained on Bali if needed):

➡ antibacterial cream (eg muciprocin)

➡ antihistamine – there are many options (eg cetirizine for daytime and promethazine for night time)

➡ antiseptic (eg Betadine)

➡ contraceptives

➡ DEET-based insect repellent

➡ first-aid items such as scissors, bandages, thermometer (but not a mercury one) and tweezers

➡ ibuprofen or another anti-inflammatory

➡ steroid cream for allergic/itchy rashes (eg 1% to 2% hydrocortisone)

➡ sunscreen and hat

➡ throat lozenges

➡ thrush (vaginal yeast infection) treatment (eg clotrimazole pessaries or diflucan tablet)

IN BALI & LOMBOK

Availability & Cost of Health Care

In south Bali and Ubud there are clinics catering to tourists, and just about any hotel can put you in touch with an English-speaking doctor.

International Medical Clinic

For serious conditions, foreigners are best served in the costly private clinic, BIMC, that caters mainly to tourists and expats. Confirm that your health and/or travel insurance will cover you. In cases where your medical condition is considered serious you may be evacuated by air ambulance to Singapore or beyond; this is where proper insurance is vital because these flights can cost more than US$20,000.

BIMC (Map p50;☑0361-761263; www.bimcbali.com; Jl Ngurah Rai 100X; ☑24hr) On the bypass road just east of Kuta near the Bali Galleria. It's a modern Australian-run clinic that can do tests, hotel visits and arrange medical evacuation. Visits can cost US$100 or more. It has a branch in Nusa Dua.

Hospitals

There are two facilities in Denpasar that offer a good standard of care. Both are more affordable than the international clinics.

BaliMed Hospital (☑0361-484748; www.balimedhospital.co.id; Jl Mahendradatta 57) On the Kerobokan side of Denpasar, this private hospital has a range of medical services. A basic consultation is 220,000Rp.

Rumah Sakit Umum Propinsi Sanglah (Sanglah Hospital; Map p120;☑227 911; Denpasar; ☑24hr) The city's general hospital has English-speaking staff and an ER. It's the best hospital on the island, although standards are not the same as at those in first-world countries. It has a special wing for well-insured foreigners, **Paviliun Amerta Wing International** (☑257 477, 740 5474).

Remote Care

In more remote areas facilities are basic – generally a small public hospital, doctor's surgery or *puskesmas* (community health centre). In government-run clinics and hospitals, services such as meals, washing and clean clothing are normally provided by the patient's family.

The best hospital on Lombok is **Rumah Sakit Harapan Keluarga** (☑0370-670000; www.harapankeluarga.co.id; Jl Ahmad Yani 9; ☑24hr), in Mataram.

Pharmacies

Many drugs requiring a prescription in the West are available over the counter in Indonesia, including powerful antibiotics.

The **Kimia Farma** chain is recommended. It has many locations, charges fair prices and has helpful staff. The **Guardian** chain of pharmacies has appeared in tourist areas, but the selection is small and prices can be shocking even to visitors from high-priced countries. Elsewhere you need to be more careful as fake medications and poorly stored or out-of-date drugs are common.

Infectious Diseases

Bird Flu

Otherwise known as avian influenza, the H5N1 virus has claimed more than 100 victims in Indonesia. Most of the cases have been in Java.

Dengue Fever

This mosquito-borne disease is a major problem. As

there is no vaccine available it can only be prevented by avoiding mosquito bites. The mosquito that carries dengue bites day and night, so use insect avoidance measures at all times. Symptoms include high fever, severe headache and body ache (dengue was previously known as 'breakbone fever'). Some people develop a rash and experience diarrhoea. It's vital to see a doctor to be diagnosed and monitored.

Hepatitis A

A problem throughout the region, this food- and water-borne virus infects the liver, causing jaundice (yellow skin and eyes), nausea and lethargy. There is no specific treatment for hepatitis A; you just need to allow time for the liver to heal. All travellers to Southeast Asia should be vaccinated against hepatitis A.

Hepatitis B

The only sexually transmitted disease that can be prevented by vaccination, hepatitis B is spread by body fluids.

HIV

HIV is a major problem in many Asian countries, and Bali has one of the highest rates of HIV infection in Indonesia. The main risk for most travellers is sexual contact with locals, prostitutes and other travellers.

The risk of sexual transmission of the HIV virus can be dramatically reduced by the use of a *kondom* (condom). These are available from supermarkets, street stalls and drugstores in tourist areas, and from the *apotik* (pharmacy) in almost any town. Don't buy a cheap brand.

Malaria

The risk of contracting malaria is greatest in rural areas of Indonesia. Generally, malaria is not a concern on Bali or in the main touristed areas of Lombok. Consider pre-

cautions if you are going into remote areas or on side trips beyond the two islands.

Two strategies should be combined to prevent malaria: mosquito avoidance and antimalarial medications. Most people who catch malaria are taking inadequate or no antimalarial medication.

Travellers are advised to prevent mosquito bites by taking these steps:

➡ Use a DEET-containing insect repellent on exposed skin. Wash this off at night, as long as you are sleeping under a mosquito net. Natural repellents such as citronella can be effective, but must be applied more frequently than products containing DEET.

➡ Sleep under a mosquito net impregnated with permethrin.

➡ Choose accommodation with screens and fans (if not air-conditioned).

➡ Impregnate clothing with permethrin in high-risk areas.

➡ Wear long sleeves and trousers in light colours.

➡ Use mosquito coils.

➡ Spray your room with insect repellent before going out for your evening meal. If you are going to an area of Indonesia where there is a malaria problem, consult with a clinic about the various prescription drugs you can use to reduce the odds you'll get it.

Rabies

Rabies is a disease spread by the bite or lick of an infected animal, most commonly a dog or monkey. Once you are exposed, it is uniformly fatal if you don't get the vaccine very promptly. Bali has had a major outbreak dating to 2008 and people continue to die each year.

To minimise your risk, consider getting the rabies vaccine, which consists of three injections. A booster after one year will then provide

10 years' protection. This may be worth considering given Bali's rabies outbreak. The vaccines are often unavailable on Bali, so get them before you go.

Also, be careful to avoid animal bites. Especially watch children closely.

Having the pre-travel vaccination means the post-bite treatment is greatly simplified. If you are bitten or scratched, gently wash the wound with soap and water, and apply an iodine-based antiseptic. It is a good idea to also consult a doctor.

Those not vaccinated will need to receive rabies immunoglobulin as soon as possible. Clean the wound immediately and do not delay seeking medical attention. Note that Bali is known to run out of rabies immunoglobulin, so be prepared to go to Singapore immediately for medical treatment.

Typhoid

This serious bacterial infection is spread via food and water. Its symptoms are a high and slowly progressive fever, headache and possibly a dry cough and stomach pain. It is diagnosed by blood tests and treated with antibiotics. Vaccinations are 80% effective and should be given one month before travelling to an infected area.

ALCOHOL POISONING

There are ongoing reports of injuries and deaths among tourists and locals due to *arak* (the local booze that should be distilled from palm or cane sugar) being adulterated with methanol, a poisonous form of alcohol. Although *arak* is a popular drink, it should be avoided outside established restaurants and cafes.

Traveller's Diarrhoea

Traveller's diarrhoea (aka 'Bali belly') is by far the most common problem affecting travellers – between 30% and 50% of people will suffer from it within two weeks of starting their trip. In over 80% of cases, traveller's diarrhoea is caused by bacteria (there are numerous potential culprits), and therefore responds promptly to treatment with antibiotics.

Traveller's diarrhoea is defined as the passage of more than three watery bowel actions within 24 hours, plus at least one other symptom such as fever, cramps, nausea, vomiting or feeling generally unwell.

Treatment

Loperamide is just a 'stopper' and doesn't get to the cause of the problem. However, it can be helpful, for example, if you have to go on a long bus ride. Don't take Loperamide if you have a fever or blood in your stools. Seek medical attention quickly if you do not respond to an appropriate antibiotic.

➡ Stay well hydrated; rehydration solutions such as Gastrolyte are the best for this.

➡ Antibiotics such as Norfloxacin, Ciprofloxacin or Azithromycin will kill the bacteria quickly.

Giardiasis

Giardia lamblia is a parasite that is relatively common in travellers. Symptoms include nausea, bloating, excess gas, fatigue and intermittent diarrhoea. The parasite will eventually go away if left untreated but this can take months. The treatment of choice is Tinidazole, with Metronidazole being a second-line option.

Environmental Hazards

Diving

Divers and surfers should seek specialised advice before they travel to ensure their medical kit contains treatment for coral cuts and tropical ear infections, as well as the standard problems. Divers should ensure their insurance covers them for decompression illness – get specialised dive insurance if necessary.

Divers should note that there is a **decompression chamber** in Sanur, which is a fast-boat ride from Nusa Lembongan. Getting here from north Bali can take three to four hours.

Heat

Most parts of Indonesia are hot and humid throughout the year. It takes most people at least two weeks to adapt to the hot climate. Swelling of the feet and ankles is common, as are muscle cramps caused by excessive sweating. Prevent these by avoiding dehydration and excessive activity in the heat. Be careful to avoid the following conditions:

Heat exhaustion Symptoms include weakness, headache, irritability, nausea or vomiting, sweaty skin, a fast, weak pulse and a normal or slightly elevated body temperature. Treatment involves getting out of the heat and/or sun, fanning the victim and applying cool wet cloths to the skin, laying the victim flat with their legs raised, and rehydrating with water containing one-quarter of a teaspoon of salt per litre. Recovery is usually rapid and it is common to feel weak for some days afterwards.

Heatstroke A serious medical emergency. Symptoms come on suddenly and include weakness, nausea, a hot dry body with a body temperature of over 41°C, dizziness, confusion, loss of coordination, fits and eventually collapse and loss of consciousness. Seek urgent medical help and commence cooling by getting the person out of the heat, removing their clothes, fanning them and applying cool wet cloths or ice to their body, especially to hot spots such as the groin and armpits.

Prickly heat A common skin rash in the tropics, caused by sweat being trapped under the skin. The result is an itchy rash of tiny lumps. Treat by moving out of the heat into an air-conditioned area for a few hours and by having cool showers.

Bites & Stings

During your time in Indonesia, you may make some unwanted friends.

Bedbugs These don't carry disease but their bites are very itchy. They live in the cracks of furniture and walls and then migrate to the bed at night to feed on you as you sleep. You can treat the itch with an antihistamine.

DRINKING WATER

Never drink tap water in Indonesia.

Widely available and cheap, bottled water is generally safe but check the seal is intact when purchasing. Look for places that allow you to refill containers, thus cutting down on landfill.

Most ice in restaurants is fine if it is uniform in size and made at a central plant (standard for large cities and tourist areas). Avoid ice that is chipped off larger blocks (more common in rural areas).

Avoid fresh juices outside of tourist restaurants and cafes.

Jellyfish Most are not dangerous, just irritating. Stings can be extremely painful but rarely fatal. First aid for jellyfish stings involves pouring vinegar onto the affected area to neutralise the poison. Do not rub sand or water onto the stings. Take painkillers, and anyone who feels ill in any way after being stung should seek medical advice.

Ticks Contracted after walking in rural areas, ticks are commonly found behind the ears, on the belly and in armpits. If you have had a tick bite and experience symptoms such as a rash at the site of the bite or elsewhere, fever or muscle aches, you should see a doctor.

Skin Problems

Fungal rashes There are two common fungal rashes that affect travellers. The first occurs in moist areas that get less air such as the groin, armpits and between the toes. It starts as a red patch that slowly spreads and is usually itchy. Treatment involves keeping the skin dry, avoiding chafing and using an antifungal cream such as Clotrimazole or Lamisil. *Tinea versicolor* is also common – this fungus causes small, light-coloured patches, most commonly on the back, chest and shoulders. Consult a doctor.

Cuts and scratches These can easily get infected in tropical climates so take meticulous care of any cuts and scratches. Immediately wash all wounds in clean water and apply antiseptic. If you develop signs of infection see a doctor. Divers and surfers should be careful with coral cuts because they become easily infected.

Sunburn

Even on a cloudy day sunburn can occur rapidly, especially near the equator. Don't end up like the dopey tourists you see roasted pink on Kuta Beach. Instead:

➡ Use a strong sunscreen (at least factor 30).

➡ Reapply sunscreen after a swim.

➡ Wear a wide-brimmed hat and sunglasses.

➡ Avoid baking in the sun during the hottest part of the day (10am to 2pm).

Women's Health

In the tourist areas and large cities, sanitary napkins and tampons are easily found. This becomes more difficult the more rural you go.

Birth-control options may be limited so bring adequate supplies of your own form of contraception.

Language

Indonesian, or Bahasa Indonesia as it's known to the locals, is the official language of Indonesia. It has approximately 220 million speakers, although it's the mother tongue for only about 20 million. Most people in Bali and on Lombok also speak their own indigenous languages, Balinese and Sasak respectively. The average traveller needn't worry about learning Balinese or Sasak, but it can be fun to learn a few words, which is why we've included a few in this chapter. For practical purposes, it probably makes better sense to concentrate your efforts on learning Bahasa Indonesia.

Indonesian pronunciation is easy to master. Each letter always represents the same sound and most letters are pronounced the same as their English counterparts, with c pronounced as the 'ch' in 'chat'. Note also that kh is a throaty sound (like the 'ch' in Scottish loch), and that the ng combination, which is found in English at the end or in the middle of words such as 'ringing', also appears at the beginning of words in Indonesian.

Syllables generally carry equal emphasis – the main exception is the unstressed e in words such as besar (big) – but the rule of thumb is to stress the second-last syllable.

In written Indonesian there are some inconsistent spellings of place names. Compound names are written as one word or two, eg Airsanih or Air Sanih, Padangbai or Padang Bai. Words starting with 'Ker' sometimes lose the e, eg Kerobokan/Krobokan. Some Dutch variant spellings also remain in use, with tj instead of the modern c (eg Tjampuhan/Campuan), and oe instead of u (eg Soekarno/Sukarno).

Pronouns, particularly 'you', are rarely used in Indonesian. Anda is the egalitarian form used to overcome the plethora of words for 'you'.

WANT MORE?

For in-depth language information and handy phrases, check out Lonely Planet's *Indonesian Phrasebook*. You'll find it at **shop.lonelyplanet.com**.

BASICS

Hello.	Salam.
Goodbye. (if leaving)	Selamat tinggal.
Goodbye. (if staying)	Selamat jalan.
How are you?	Apa kabar?
I'm fine, and you?	Kabar baik, Anda bagaimana?
Excuse me.	Permisi.
Sorry.	Maaf.
Please.	Silahkan.
Thank you.	Terima kasih.
You're welcome.	Kembali.
Yes./No.	Ya./Tidak.
Mr/Sir	Bapak
Ms/Mrs/Madam	Ibu
Miss	Nona
What's your name?	Siapa nama Anda?
My name is ...	Nama saya ...
Do you speak English?	Bisa berbicara Bahasa Inggris?
I don't understand.	Saya tidak mengerti.

ACCOMMODATION

Do you have any rooms available?	Ada kamar kosong?
How much is it per night/person?	Berapa satu malam/orang?
Is breakfast included?	Apakah harganya termasuk makan pagi?
I'd like to share a dorm.	Saya mau satu tempat tidur di asrama.
campsite	tempat kemah
guesthouse	losmen
hotel	hotel
youth hostel	pemuda
a ... room	kamar ...
single	untuk satu orang
double	untuk dua orang

air-conditioned	dengan AC
bathroom	kamar mandi
cot	velbet
window	jendela

DIRECTIONS

Where is ...?	Di mana ...?
What's the address?	Alamatnya di mana?
Could you write it down, please?	Anda bisa tolong tuliskan?
Can you show me (on the map)?	Anda bisa tolong tunjukkan pada saya (di peta)?

at the corner	di sudut
at the traffic lights	di lampu merah
behind	di belakang
in front of	di depan
far (from)	jauh (dari)
left	kiri
near (to)	dekat (dengan)
next to	di samping
opposite	di seberang
right	kanan
straight ahead	lurus

EATING & DRINKING

What would you recommend?	Apa yang Anda rekomendasikan?
What's in that dish?	Hidangan ituisinya apa?
That was delicious.	Ini enak sekali.
Cheers!	Bersulang!
Bring the bill/check, please.	Tolong bawa kuitansi.

I don't eat ...	Saya tidak mau makan ...
dairy products	susu dan keju
fish	ikan
(red) meat	daging (merah)
peanuts	kacang tanah
seafood	makanan laut

a table ...	meja ...
at (eight) o'clock	pada jam (delapan)
for (two) people	untuk (dua) orang

KEY PATTERNS

To get by in Indonesian, mix and match these simple patterns with words of your choice:

When's (the next bus)?
Jam berapa (bis yang berikutnya)?

Where's (the station)?
Di mana (stasiun)?

How much is it (per night)?
Berapa (satu malam)?

I'm looking for (a hotel).
Saya cari (hotel).

Do you have (a local map)?
Ada (peta daerah)?

Is there (a toilet)?
Ada (kamar kecil)?

Can I (enter)?
Boleh saya (masuk)?

Do I need (a visa)?
Saya harus pakai (visa)?

I have (a reservation).
Saya (sudah punya booking).

I need (assistance).
Saya perlu (dibantu).

I'd like (the menu).
Saya minta (daftar makanan).

I'd like (to hire a car).
Saya mau (sewa mobil).

Could you (help me)?
Bisa Anda (bantu) saya?

Key Words

baby food (formula)	susu kaleng
bar	bar
bottle	botol
bowl	mangkuk
breakfast	sarapan
cafe	kafe
children's menu	menu untuk anak-anak
cold	dingin
dinner	makan malam
dish	piring
drink list	daftar minuman
food	makanan
food stall	warung
fork	garpu
glass	gelas
highchair	kursi tinggi
hot (warm)	panas
knife	pisau

SIGNS

Buka	Open
Dilarang	Prohibited
Kamar Kecil	Toilets
Keluar	Exit
Masuk	Entrance
Pria	Men
Tutup	Closed
Wanitai	Women

lunch	makan siang
menu	daftar makanan
market	pasar
napkin	tisu
plate	piring
restaurant	rumah makan
salad	selada
soup	sop
spicy	pedas
spoon	sendok
vegetarian food	makanan tanpa daging
with	dengan
without	tanpa

Meat & Fish

beef	daging sapi
carp	ikan mas
chicken	ayam
duck	bebek
fish	ikan
lamb	daging anak domba
mackerel	tenggiri
meat	daging
pork	daging babi
shrimp/prawn	udang
tuna	cakalang
turkey	kalkun

Fruit & Vegetables

apple	apel
banana	pisang
beans	kacang
cabbage	kol
carrot	wortel
cauliflower	blumkol
cucumber	timun
dates	kurma
eggplant	terung
fruit	buah
grapes	buah anggur
lemon	jeruk asam
orange	jeruk manis
pineapple	nenas
potato	kentang
raisins	kismis
spinach	bayam
vegetable	sayur-mayur
watermelon	semangka

Other

bread	roti
butter	mentega
cheese	keju
chilli	cabai
chilli sauce	sambal
egg	telur
honey	madu
jam	selai
noodles	mie
oil	minyak
pepper	lada
rice	nasi
salt	garam
soy sauce	kecap
sugar	gula
vinegar	cuka

Drinks

beer	bir
coconut milk	santan
coffee	kopi
juice	jus
milk	susu
palm sap wine	tuak
red wine	anggur merah
soft drink	minuman ringan
tea	teh
water	air
white wine	anggur putih
yogurt	susu masam kental

EMERGENCIES

Help!	Tolong saya!
I'm lost.	Saya tersesat.
Leave me alone!	Jangan ganggu saya!
There's been an accident.	Ada kecelakaan.
Can I use your phone?	Boleh saya pakai telpon genggamnya?
Call a doctor!	Panggil dokter!
Call the police!	Panggil polisi!
I'm ill.	Saya sakit.
It hurts here.	Sakitnya di sini.
I'm allergic to (antibiotics).	Saya alergi (antibiotik).

SHOPPING & SERVICES

I'd like to buy ...	Saya mau beli ...
I'm just looking.	Saya lihat-lihat saja.
May I look at it?	Boleh saya lihat?
I don't like it.	Saya tidak suka.
How much is it?	Berapa harganya?
It's too expensive.	Itu terlalu mahal.
Can you lower the price?	Boleh kurang?
There's a mistake in the bill.	Ada kesalahan dalam kuitansi ini.
credit card	kartu kredit
foreign exchange office	kantor penukaran mata uang asing
internet cafe	warnet
mobile/cell phone	hanpon
post office	kantor pos
signature	tanda tangan
tourist office	kantor pariwisata

TIME & DATES

What time is it?	Jam berapa sekarang?
It's (10) o'clock.	Jam (sepuluh).
It's half past (six).	Setengah (tujuh).

QUESTION WORDS

How?	Bagaimana?
What?	Apa?
When?	Kapan?
Where?	Di mana?
Which	Yang mana?
Who?	Siapa?
Why?	Kenapa?

in the morning	pagi
in the afternoon	siang
in the evening	malam
today	hari ini
tomorrow	besok
yesterday	kemarin
Monday	hari Senin
Tuesday	hari Selasa
Wednesday	hari Rabu
Thursday	hari Kamis
Friday	hari Jumat
Saturday	hari Sabtu
Sunday	hari Minggu
January	Januari
February	Februari
March	Maret
April	April
May	Mei
June	Juni
July	Juli
August	Agustus
September	September
October	Oktober
November	Nopember
December	Desember

TRANSPORT

Public Transport

bicycle-rickshaw	becak
boat (general)	kapal
boat (local)	perahu
bus	bis
minibus	bemo
motorcycle-rickshaw	bajaj
motorcycle-taxi	ojek
plane	pesawat
taxi	taksi
train	kereta api
I want to go to ...	Saya mau ke ...
How much to ...?	Ongkos ke ... berapa?
At what time does it leave?	Jam berapa berangkat?
At what time does it arrive at ...?	Jam berapa sampai di ...?
Does it stop at ...?	Di ... berhenti?

NUMBERS

1	satu
2	dua
3	tiga
4	empat
5	lima
6	enam
7	tujuh
8	delapan
9	sembilan
10	sepuluh
20	duapuluh
30	tigapuluh
40	empatpuluh
50	limapuluh
60	enampuluh
70	tujuhpuluh
80	delapanpuluh
90	sembilanpuluh
100	seratus
1000	seribu

What's the next stop?	Apa nama halte berikutnya?
Please tell me when we get to ...	Tolong, beritahu waktu kita sampai di ...
Please stop here.	Tolong, berhenti di sini.
the first	pertama
the last	terakhir
the next	yang berikutnya
a ... ticket	tiket ...
1st-class	kelas satu
2nd-class	kelas dua
one-way	sekali jalan
return	pulang pergi
aisle seat	tempat duduk dekat gang
cancelled	dibatalkan
delayed	terlambat
platform	peron
ticket office	loket tiket
timetable	jadwal
train station	stasiun kereta api
window seat	tempat duduk dekat jendela

Driving & Cycling

I'd like to hire a ...	Saya mau sewa ...
4WD	gardan ganda
bicycle	sepeda
car	mobil
motorcycle	sepeda motor
child seat	kursi anak untuk di mobil
diesel	solar
helmet	helem
mechanic	montir
petrol/gas	bensin
pump (bicycle)	pompa sepeda
service station	pompa bensin
Is this the road to ...?	Apakah jalan ini ke ...?
(How long) Can I park here?	(Berapa lama) Saya boleh parkir di sini?
The car/motocycle has broken down.	Mobil/Motor mogok.
I have a flat tyre.	Ban saya kempes.
I've run out of petrol.	Saya kehabisan bensin.

LOCAL LANGUAGES

Balinese

How are you?	Kenken kabare?
What's your name?	Sire wastene?
My name is ...	Adan tiange ...
I don't understand.	Tiang sing ngerti.
How much is this?	Ji kude niki?
Thank you.	Matur suksma.
What do you call this in Balinese?	Ne ape adane di Bali?
Which is the way to ...?	Kije jalan lakar kel ...?

Sasak

What's your name?	Saik aranm side?
My name is ...	Arankah aku ...
I don't understand.	Endek ngerti.
How much is this?	Pire ajin sak iyak?
Thank you.	Tampak asih.
What do you call this in Sasak?	Ape aran sak iyak elek bahase Sasek?
Which is the way to ...?	Lamun lek ..., embe eak langantah?

*(m) indicates masculine gender,
(f) feminine gender and (pl)
plural*

adat – tradition, customs and manners

adharma – evil

aling aling – gateway backed by a small wall

alus – identifiable 'goodies' in an *arja* drama

anak-anak – children

angker – evil power

apotik – pharmacy

arja – refined operatic form of Balinese theatre; also a dance-drama, comparable to Western opera

Arjuna – a hero of the *Mahabharata* epic and a popular temple gate guardian image

bahasa – language; Bahasa Indonesia is the national language of Indonesia

bale – an open-sided pavilion with a steeply pitched thatched roof

bale banjar – communal meeting place of a *banjar;* a house for meetings and *gamelan* practice

bale tani – family house in Lombok; see also *serambi*

balian – faith healer and herbal doctor

banjar – local division of a village consisting of all the married adult males

banyan – a type of ficus tree, often considered holy; see also *waringin*

bapak – father; also a polite form of address to any older man; also *pak*

Barong – mythical lion-dog creature

baten tegeh – decorated pyramids of fruit, rice cakes and flowers

batik – process of colouring fabric by coating part of the cloth with wax, dyeing it and melting the wax out; the waxed part is not coloured, and repeated waxing and dyeing builds up a pattern

batu bolong – rock with a hole

belalu – quick-growing, light wood

bemo – popular local transport in Bali and on Lombok; usually a small minibus but can be a small pick-up in rural areas

bensin – petrol (gasoline)

beruga – communal meeting hall in Bali; open-sided pavilion on Lombok

bhur – world of demons

bhwah – world of humans

Brahma – the creator; one of the trinity of Hindu gods

Brahmana – the caste of priests and the highest of the Balinese castes; all priests are Brahmanas, but not all Brahmanas are priests

bu – mother; shortened form of *ibu*

bukit – hill; also the name of Bali's southern peninsula

bulau – month

candi – shrine, originally of Javanese design; also known as *prasada*

candi bentar – entrance gates to a temple

cendrawasih – birds of paradise

cengceng – cymbals

cidomo – horse cart with car wheels (Lombok)

cili – representations of Dewi Sri, the rice goddess

dalang – puppet master and storyteller in a *wayang kulit* performance

Dalem Bedaulu – legendary last ruler of the Pejeng dynasty

danau – lake

desa – village

dewa – deity or supernatural spirit

dewi – goddess

Dewi Sri – goddess of rice

dharma – good

dokar – horse cart; known as a *cidomo* on Lombok

Durga – goddess of death

and destruction, and consort of Shiva

dusun –small village

endek – elegant fabric, like *songket,* with pre-dyed weft threads

Gajah Mada – famous *Majapahit* prime minister who defeated the last great king of Bali and extended *Majapahit* power over the island

Galungan – great Balinese festival; an annual event in the 210-day Balinese *wuku* calendar

gamelan – traditional Balinese orchestra, with mostly percussion instruments like large xylophones and gongs; may have one to more than two dozen musicians; also used to refer to individual instruments such as drums; also called a *gong*

Ganesha – Shiva's elephant-headed son

gang – alley or footpath

Garuda – mythical man-bird creature, vehicle of Vishnu; modern symbol of Indonesia and the national airline

gedong – shrine

genggong – musical performance seen in Lombok

gili – small island (Lombok)

goa – cave; also spelt *gua*

gong – see *gamelan*

gong gede – large orchestra; traditional form of the *gamelan* with 35 to 40 musicians

gong kebyar – modern, popular form of a *gong gede,* with up to 25 instruments

gua – cave; also spelt *goa*

gunung – mountain

gunung api – volcano

gusti – polite title for members of the *Wesia* caste

Hanuman – monkey god who plays a major part in the *Ramayana*

homestay – small, family-run accommodation; see also *losmen*

ibu – mother; also a polite form of address to any older woman

Ida Bagus – honourable title for a male Brahmana

ikat – cloth where a pattern is produced by dyeing the individual threads before weaving

jalak putih – local name for Bali starling

jalan – road or street; abbreviated to Jl

jepun – frangipani or plumeria trees

Jl – *jalan;* road or street

kahyangan jagat – directional temples

kain – a length of material wrapped tightly around the hips and waist, over a sarong

kain poleng – black-and-white chequered cloth

kaja – in the direction of the mountains; see also *kelod*

kaja-kangin – corner of the courtyard

kaki lima – mobile food carts

kala – demonic face often seen over temple gateways

kamben – a length of *songket* wrapped around the chest for formal occasions

kampung – village or neighbourhood

kangin – sunrise

kantor – office

kantor imigrasi – immigration office

kantor pos – post office

Kawi – classical Javanese; the language of poetry

kebyar – a type of dance

Kecak – traditional Balinese dance; tells a tale from the *Ramayana* about Prince Rama and Princess Sita

kelod – in the direction away from the mountains and towards the sea; see also *kaja*

kempli – gong

kendang – drums

kepala desa – village head

kori agung – gateway to the second courtyard in a temple

kras – identifiable 'baddies' in an *arja* drama

kris – traditional dagger

kuah – sunset side

kulkul – hollow tree-trunk drum used to sound a warning or call meetings

labuhan – harbour; also called *pelabuhan*

laki-laki – boy

lamak – long, woven palm-leaf strips used as decorations in festivals and celebrations

langse – rectangular decorative hangings used in palaces or temples

Legong – classic Balinese dance

legong – young girls who perform the *Legong*

lontar – specially prepared palm leaves

losmen – small Balinese hotel, often family-run

lulur – body mask

lumbung – rice barn with a round roof; an architectural symbol of Lombok

Mahabharata – one of the great Hindu holy books, the epic poem tells of the battle between the Pandavas and the Kauravas

Majapahit – last great Hindu dynasty on Java

mekepung – traditional water buffalo races

meru – multi-tiered shrines in temples; the name comes from the Hindu holy mountain Mahameru

mobil – car

moksa – freedom from earthly desires

muncak – barking deer

naga – mythical snake-like creature

nusa – island; also called *pulau*

Nusa Tenggara Barat (NTB) – West Nusa Tenggara; a province of Indonesia comprising the islands of Lombok and Sumbawa

nyale – worm-like fish caught off Kuta, Lombok

Nyepi – major annual festival in the Hindu *saka* calendar,

this is a day of complete stillness after a night of chasing out evil spirits

ogoh-ogoh – huge monster dolls used in the *Nyepi* festival

ojek – motorcycle that carries paying passengers

open – tall red-brick buildings

padi – growing rice plant

padmasana – temple shrine resembling a vacant chair

pak – father; shortened form of *bapak*

pantai – beach

paras – a soft, grey volcanic stone used in stone carving

pasar – market

pasar malam – night market

pecalang – village or *banjar* police

pedagang – mobile traders

pemangku – temple guardians and priests for temple rituals

perempuan – girl

plus plus – a combined tax and service charge of 21% added by midrange and top-end accommodation and restaurants

pondok – simple lodging or hut

prada – cloth highlighted with gold leaf, or gold or silver paint and thread

prahu – traditional Indonesian boat with outriggers

prasasti – inscribed copper plates

propinsi – province; Indonesia has 27 *propinsi* – Bali is a *propinsi,* Lombok and its neighbouring island of Sumbawa comprise propinsi Nusa Tenggara Barat (NTB)

pulau – island; also called *nusa*

puputan – warrior's fight to the death; an honourable but suicidal option when faced with an unbeatable enemy

pura – temple

pura dalem – temple of the dead

pura desa – village temple for everyday functions

pura puseh – temple of the

village founders or fathers, honouring the village's origins

pura subak – temple of the rice growers' association

puri – palace

pusit kota – used on road signs to indicate the centre of town

rajah – lord or prince

Ramadan – Muslim month of fasting

Ramayana – one of the great Hindu holy books; these stories form the keystone of many Balinese dances and tales

Rangda – widow-witch who represents evil in Balinese theatre and dance

raya – main road, eg Jl Raya Ubud means 'the main road of Ubud'

RRI – Radio Republik Indonesia; Indonesia's national radio broadcaster

rumah makan – restaurant; literally 'eating place'

saiban – temple or shrine offering

Sasak – native of Lombok; also the language

sate – satay

sawah – rice field; see also *subak*

selat – strait

sepeda – bicycle

Shiva – the creator and destroyer; one of the three great Hindu gods

songket – silver- or gold-threaded cloth, handwoven using a floating weft technique

stupas – domes for housing Buddha relics

subak – village association that organises rice terraces and shares out water for irrigation

Sudra – common caste to which the majority of Balinese belong

sungai – river

swah – world of gods

tahun – year

taksu – divine interpreter for the gods

tanjung – cape or point

teluk – gulf or bay

tika – piece of printed cloth or carved wood displaying the Pawukon cycle

tirta – water

toya – water

undagi – designer of a building, usually an architect-priest

Vishnu – the preserver; one of the three great Hindu gods

wantilan – large *bale* pavilion used for meetings, performances and cockfights; community hall

waria – female impersonator, transvestite or transgendered person; combination of the words *wanita* and *pria*

waringin – large shady tree with drooping branches which root to produce new trees; see banyan

wartel – public telephone office; contraction of *warung telekomunikasi*

warung – food stall

wayang kulit – leather puppet used in shadow puppet plays; see also *dalang*

Wektu Telu – religion peculiar to Lombok; originated in Bayan and combines many tenets of Islam and aspects of other faiths

wuku – Balinese calendar made up of 10 different weeks, between one and 10 days long, all running concurrently; see also *saka*

yeh – water; also river

yoni – female symbol of the Hindu god Shiva

Behind the Scenes

SEND US YOUR FEEDBACK

We love to hear from travellers – your comments keep us on our toes and help make our books better. Our well-travelled team reads every word on what you loved or loathed about this book. Although we cannot reply individually to postal submissions, we always guarantee that your feedback goes straight to the appropriate authors, in time for the next edition. Each person who sends us information is thanked in the next edition – the most useful submissions are rewarded with a selection of digital PDF chapters.

Visit **lonelyplanet.com/contact** to submit your updates and suggestions or to ask for help. Our award-winning website also features inspirational travel stories, news and discussions.

Note: We may edit, reproduce and incorporate your comments in Lonely Planet products such as guidebooks, websites and digital products, so let us know if you don't want your comments reproduced or your name acknowledged. For a copy of our privacy policy visit lonelyplanet.com/privacy.

OUR READERS

Many thanks to the travellers who used the last edition and wrote to us with helpful hints, useful advice and interesting anecdotes:

Francesca Accornero, Josephine Anderson, Sophie Baldwin, Maarten Baltussen, Alex Boladeras, Matt Burgess, Roxanne Capaldi, Sung Choi, Claudio Cuccu, Alix Degrez, Douglas Ferris, Catherine Georgarakis, Shaline Geske, Aly Hendriks, Adloff Hortense, Michelle Jansen, Wayan Karja, Dika Kartika, Chris Keithley, Hiroshi Kubo, Nicolas Kuster, Jessica Laan, Jing Bo Li, Adrian Gonzalez Lopez, Wendy Mackay, Johanny Mascunan, Alan Matis, Julie McLennan, Eline Morsch, Maja Olip, Simon Pridmore, Michelle Read, Rinjani Trek Club, Tari Ritchie, Bradey Rykers, Lisette Sørensen, Putu Sridiniari, Martin Stanek, Richard Teunissen, Gerard Vissers, Jan Wijbenga, John Young, Bahri Zul

AUTHOR THANKS

Ryan Ver Berkmoes

For this, my 100th guidebook for Lonely Planet, many thanks to friends like Patticakes, Ibu Cat, Hanafi, Stuart, Suzanne, the indefatigable Ketut, Rucina, Nicoline, Eliot Cohen, Jamie James, Kerry and Milt Turner, Pascal & Pika and many more including Samuel L Bronkowitz. At Lonely Planet, thanks first to some of those whose passion for the book over the years helped build this edition: Marg Toohey, Virginia Maxwell, Tashi Wheeler, Ilaria Walker and others. The talents of these creative people cannot be dismissed. Thanks to Sarah Reid whose hand guided this edition. Love to Alexis Averbuck; we'll always have Bali, whether the swans are singing or not.

ACKNOWLEDGMENTS

Climate map data adapted from Peel MC, Finlayson BL & McMahon TA (2007) 'Updated World Map of the Köppen-Geiger Climate Classification', Hydrology and Earth System Sciences, 11, 1633–44.

Cover photograph: Pura Ulun Danu Bratan Temple, Candikuning, Martin Puddy/Getty

THIS BOOK

This 15th edition of Lonely Planet's *Bali & Lombok* guidebook was researched and written by Ryan Ver Berkmoes. The previous two editions were written by Ryan Ver Berkmoes, Adam Skolnick and Iain Stewart. This guidebook was produced by the following:

Destination Editor Sarah Reid

Commissioning Editor Glenn van der Knijff

Product Editor Luna Soo

Senior Cartographer Julie Sheridan

Cartographer Gabriel Lindquist

Book Designer Wibowo Rusli

Assisting Editors Nigel Chin, Katie Connolly, Kate Evans, Justin Flynn, Carly Hall, Jodie Martire, Jenna Myers, Rosie Nicholson, Kirsten Rawlings, Sally Schafer, Amanda Williamson

Cover Researcher Naomi Parker

Thanks to Sasha Baskett, Ryan Evans, Larissa Frost, Jouve India, Andi Jones, Claire Naylor, Karyn Noble, Jessica Rose, Saralinda Turner, Samantha Tyson, Lauren Wellicome, Tracy Whitmey

Index

Map Pages **000**
Photo Pages **000**

Map Legend

Sights

- Beach
- Bird Sanctuary
- Buddhist
- Castle/Palace
- Christian
- Confucian
- Hindu
- Islamic
- Jain
- Jewish
- Monument
- Museum/Gallery/Historic Building
- Ruin
- Shinto
- Sikh
- Taoist
- Winery/Vineyard
- Zoo/Wildlife Sanctuary
- Other Sight

Activities, Courses & Tours

- Bodysurfing
- Diving
- Canoeing/Kayaking
- Course/Tour
- Sento Hot Baths/Onsen
- Skiing
- Snorkelling
- Surfing
- Swimming/Pool
- Walking
- Windsurfing
- Other Activity

Sleeping

- Sleeping
- Camping

Eating

- Eating

Drinking & Nightlife

- Drinking & Nightlife
- Cafe

Entertainment

- Entertainment

Shopping

- Shopping

Information

- Bank
- Embassy/Consulate
- Hospital/Medical
- Internet
- Police
- Post Office
- Telephone
- Toilet
- Tourist Information
- Other Information

Geographic

- Beach
- Hut/Shelter
- Lighthouse
- Lookout
- Mountain/Volcano
- Oasis
- Park
- Pass
- Picnic Area
- Waterfall

Population

- Capital (National)
- Capital (State/Province)
- City/Large Town
- Town/Village

Transport

- Airport
- Border crossing
- Bus
- Cable car/Funicular
- Cycling
- Ferry
- Metro station
- Monorail
- Parking
- Petrol station
- Subway station
- Taxi
- Train station/Railway
- Tram
- Underground station
- Other Transport

Note: Not all symbols displayed above appear on the maps in this book

Routes

- Tollway
- Freeway
- Primary
- Secondary
- Tertiary
- Lane
- Unsealed road
- Road under construction
- Plaza/Mall
- Steps
- Tunnel
- Pedestrian overpass
- Walking Tour
- Walking Tour detour
- Path/Walking Trail

Boundaries

- International
- State/Province
- Disputed
- Regional/Suburb
- Marine Park
- Cliff
- Wall

Hydrography

- River, Creek
- Intermittent River
- Canal
- Water
- Dry/Salt/Intermittent Lake
- Reef

Areas

- Airport/Runway
- Beach/Desert
- Cemetery (Christian)
- Cemetery (Other)
- Glacier
- Mudflat
- Park/Forest
- Sight (Building)
- Sportsground
- Swamp/Mangrove

OUR STORY

A beat-up old car, a few dollars in the pocket and a sense of adventure. In 1972 that's all Tony and Maureen Wheeler needed for the trip of a lifetime – across Europe and Asia overland to Australia. It took several months, and at the end – broke but inspired – they sat at their kitchen table writing and stapling together their first travel guide, *Across Asia on the Cheap*. Within a week they'd sold 1500 copies. Lonely Planet was born.

Today, Lonely Planet has offices in Franklin, London, Melbourne, Oakland, Beijing and Delhi, with more than 600 staff and writers. We share Tony's belief that 'a great guidebook should do three things: inform, educate and amuse'.

OUR WRITER

Ryan Ver Berkmoes

Ryan Ver Berkmoes was first entranced by the echoing beat of a Balinese gamelan in 1993. On his visits since he has explored almost every corner of the island – along with Nusas Lembongan and Penida, the Gilis and Lombok. Just when he thinks Bali holds no more surprises, he finds, for example, a new seaside temple on nobody's map. Ryan never tires of Bali; sometimes his island social calendar is busier than anywhere else. Away from the gamelans, Ryan writes about travel and more at ryanverberkmoes.com and on Twitter @ryanvb.

Published by Lonely Planet Publications Pty Ltd
ABN 36 005 607 983
15th edition – Apr 2015
ISBN 978 1 74321 389 6
© Lonely Planet 2015   Photographs © as indicated 2015
10 9 8 7 6 5 4 3 2 1
Printed in China